"Levine's 10th edition of *Urban Politics* remains a handbook for the practitioner concerned with using public policy to support sustainable cities with a 'development triangle' of environmental, economic, and social goals. It supports a progressive urban agenda with practical examples and extensive research. In the current age, Levine's unifying theme of power as 'the ability to get things done' brings idealistic goals from blue skies down to the streets of America's cities."

Minchin Lewis, Syracuse University, USA

"Thoroughly revised and rewritten, the new edition of *Urban Politics* provides a comprehensive view of urban development, contemporary urban politics, and urban issues. Its ample illustrations and boxed case material provide course instructors with substantial material for classroom discussion and student analysis."

Heywood Saunders, University of Texas at San Antonio, USA

Urban Politics

Urban Politics blends the most insightful classic and contemporary political science and related literature with current issues in urban affairs. The book's integrative theme is "power," demonstrating that the study of urban politics requires an analysist to look beyond the formal institutions and procedures of local government. The book also develops important subthemes: the impact of globalization; the dominance of economic development over competing local policy concerns; the continuing importance of race in the urban arena; local government activism versus the "limits" imposed on local action by the American constitutional system and economic competition; and the impact of national and state government action on cities. *Urban Politics* engages students with pragmatic case studies and boxed material that use classic and current urban films and TV shows to illustrate particular aspects of urban politics. The book's substantial concluding discussion of local policies for environmental sustainability and green cities also appeals to today's students. Each chapter has been thoroughly rewritten to clearly relate the content to current events and academic literature, including the following:

- the importance of the intergovernmental city
- the role of local governments as active policy actors and vital policy makers even in areas outside traditional municipal policy concerns
- the prospects for urban policy and change in and beyond the Trump administration, including the ways in which urban politics is affected by, but not determined by, Washington.

Mixing classic theory and research on urban politics with the most recent developments and data in urban and metropolitan affairs, *Urban Politics, 10e* is an ideal introductory textbook for students of regional politics and policy. The book's material on citizen participation, urban bureaucracy, policy analysis, and intergovernmental relations also makes the volume an appropriate choice for Urban Administration courses.

Myron A. Levine is a Professor in the Urban Affairs and Public Administration programs in the School of Public and International Affairs at Wright State University in Dayton, Ohio. His writings have appeared in the *Journal of Urban Affairs*, *Urban Affairs Review*, and various other urban studies and political science journals. In addition to authoring *Urban Politics*, he is the editor of *Taking Sides: Urban Affairs* and of a number of the volumes in the *Annual Editions: Urban Society* series. His research focuses on national urban policy, the politics of local economic development and gentrification, and the prospects for effective urban political leadership. He has received various Fulbright Foundation fellowships to study and teach in the Netherlands, Germany, the Slovak Republic, and Latvia, as well as an NEH award to study in France.

Urban Politics

Cities and Suburbs in a Global Age

Tenth Edition

Myron A. Levine

Routledge
Taylor & Francis Group
NEW YORK AND LONDON

First published 2020
by Routledge
605 Third Avenue, New York, NY 10017

and by Routledge
2 Park Square, Milton Park, Abingdon, Oxon, OX14 4RN

Routledge is an imprint of the Taylor & Francis Group, an informa business

Library of Congress Cataloging-in-Publication Data
Names: Levine, Myron A., author.
Title: Urban politics : cities and suburbs in a Golden Age / Myron Levine.
Description: Tenth Edition. | New York : Routledge, 2019. | Previous edition: 2015.
Identifiers: LCCN 2019003602 | ISBN 9781138604339 (Hardback : alk. paper) | ISBN 9781138604346 (Paperback : alk. paper) | ISBN 9780429468544 (E-book)
Subjects: LCSH: Municipal government—United States. | Metropolitan government—United States.
Classification: LCC JS323 .R67 2019 | DDC 320.8/50973—dc23
LC record available at https://lccn.loc.gov/2019003602

Typeset in Times
by Apex CoVantage, LLC

ISBN 13: 978-1-138-60433-9 (hbk)
ISBN 13: 978-1-138-60434-6 (pbk)
ISBN 13: 978-0-429-46854-4 (ebk)

DOI: 10.4324/9780429468544

To Nancy, for her endless patience, wisdom, and love.

To Alex, Marisa, Evie, and Rick, for reminding me of the vitality of the American city and for keeping me in touch with life in New York, Chicago, Minneapolis, and the San Francisco Bay area.

"Did you really love the city
Or did you just pretend?"
L. Cohen, *Samson in New Orleans* (2014)

Contents

Preface

Urban Politics focuses on the issues facing cities and suburbs in the United States in a postindustrial, global age. *Urban Politics* pays special attention to contemporary issues and controversies. The book draws on the extensive literature from political science and other urban-related disciplines to provide the reader with an in-depth understanding of the challenges and choices facing America's communities. *Urban Politics* underscores how the interplay of public and private power helps to determine "who gets what" in the urban political arena.

The 10th edition's opening case study—the lead poisoning of the children of Flint, Michigan—underscores that all is not well with the American city. In more recent years, journalistic commentary has told the story of the "comeback" of America's cities, that after decades of decline, American cities were experiencing a rebirth. This rebirth is evident in the construction of soaring commercial towers, the renaissance of once-faded downtowns, and new investment and residential development in inner-city neighborhoods that had been overlooked for decades. Yet, as depressed conditions in Flint, Detroit, and other former industrial centers underscore, local population growth and economic prosperity are quite uneven. While a number of cities and suburbs have exhibited significant growth, other communities, by contrast, continue their long-term decline and their desperate search for a strategy that will produce a local economic revival. Even in cities and suburbs that appear to be prospering, too many communities remain centers of poverty, family dissolution, opioid addiction, crime, unaffordable housing, property abandonment, homelessness, and underperforming schools. As U.S. Census Bureau data makes quite clear, poverty in the United States is now a suburban as well as a central-city problem. Racial and ethnic segregation has not disappeared; instead, new patterns of segregation—which may be more properly referred to as *resegregation*—are emerging. Urban inequality is the hallmark characteristics of the contemporary American city, suburban, and metropolis.

The importance of "race" and social class in the urban arena have not diminished. In Flint, a white-controlled state government essentially stripped the governing elected officials of a poor, minority-majority city of much of their governing authority. The state intervened to force the fiscally strapped city to find ways of saving money. State officials essentially ordered the city to switch the source of its drinking water, a change that precipitated the lead poisoning of city tap water. In cities across the nation, issues of race continue to emerge in other policy areas, most notably in the controversies surrounding the shooting of unarmed minority youth by law enforcement officials.

The integrative theme of *Urban Politics* relates to "power." The study of urban politics requires an informed citizen to look at the exercise of power in the urban arena and not merely focus on the actions of public officials. An understanding of the formal institutions, procedures, and decisions of municipal government does not by itself provide a full understanding of the politics of United States cities and suburbs. Of course, the formal rules of local government are important. The formal structure of local governments and the rules governing local elections help to determine just which groups enjoy—and which groups are denied—effective representation and political "clout" in city hall. The formal rules of local government also help to define just what cities can and cannot do in response to local problems. Compared to the national government and the states, local governments possess rather limited taxing authority and problem-solving powers. However, as we shall see, cities are beginning to test those restraints, as local officials seek to undertake new initiatives to combat the problems faced by their communities.

Private interests often possess considerable power in the local arena. When it comes to major decisions, local elected officials are seldom in a position to do whatever they want. Instead, mayors and other city leaders are constrained by the need to work with top corporate executives and other private actors whose investment decisions can have a great impact on a city's economic and fiscal health. Local elected leaders often discover the benefits that come from working collaboratively with the leaders of businesses and nonprofit organizations who control resources critical to the success of a local project. Private interests are major players in the local arena, even if they occupy no formal position in a municipality's organizational charts.

The 10th edition of *Urban Politics*, as has previous editions, continues to develop a number of subthemes, including: the impact that globalization (including a "new immigration" from Latin America and Asia) has had on cities and suburbs; the dominance of economic development concerns in the urban area (often, to the neglect of other local policy concerns); and, the continuing importance of questions of race and ethnicity in the politics of American cities and suburbs. Cities in the United States also exist in an intergovernmental system where the actions of the national and state government actions have a great—albeit often unintended—impact on cities, suburbs, and their neighborhoods. The study of urban politics requires that we look beyond local borders to the actions taken by the national government and the states as well as to the actions taken by private actors.

CHANGES IN THE TENTH EDITION OF *URBAN POLITICS*

Each chapter of the new edition of *Urban Politics* has been thoroughly rewritten to incorporate recent events as well as the voluminous new research on cities and suburbs that has surfaced in recent years. While there are many constants in the study of urban politics, there are also a number of trends and patterns that have begun to emerge. These new trends receive special attention in the 10th edition of *Urban Politics*.

The American intergovernmental system is in a state of flux. In an era of extreme partisanship and divided government, President Barack Obama sought to forge new relationships with willing states and cities to achieve domestic policy goals that were otherwise blocked by an obstructionist Congress. President Donald Trump has arguably had an even greater impact on American intergovernmental relations. The 10th edition of *Urban Politics* details the changes that the Trump Administration initiated in its budgetary, spending, taxing, and regulatory policies. The volume reviews the Trump administration's attempts to curb immigration as well as its efforts to reduce state and local actions intended to protect the natural environment and reduce global warming. Particularly noteworthy are the changes that Trump and a Republican Congress effected by rewriting of the nation's tax code in the Tax Cuts and Jobs Act of 2017. All of this is discussed in detail in the various chapters of *Urban Politics*, especially in a thoroughly revised Chapter 11, "The Intergovernmental City."

The 10th edition of *Urban Politics* pays increased attention to the new political activism of mayors and of cities. The beginnings of the new local activism predate Trump's arrival in Washington and was already evident in a number of policy areas, including local efforts to promote sustainable growth, to recognize gay and lesbian marriages, to assure the protection of LGBT persons against acts of discrimination, to welcome immigrants who could contribute to local economic growth and neighborhood renewal, to curtail tobacco usage, and to limit the potential harm resulting from gun violence. Local activism increased markedly in response to what local leaders saw as Trump's lack of concern for cities, as evident in: the Trump administration's efforts to relax clean air and vehicle emission standards; the President's decisions to withdraw the United States national government from international accords to reduce greenhouse gas emissions (GHGs) and fight global warming; and the Trump administration's attempts to punish cities that refused to have local law enforcement agencies cooperate with national immigration officers in their efforts to detain and expel undocumented immigrants.

The 10th edition also gives renewed emphasis to a theme that was introduced in the previous edition: Cities and suburbs have come to see the importance of enacting policies to protect the natural environment and to promote "green" construction, "smart growth," and sustainable development. *Urban Politics* highlights such efforts throughout its various chapters. Chapter 12, the concluding chapter on the future of urban America, devotes substantial attention to describing the prominent place that questions of sustainability have gained on local policy agendas. As not all instructors have the time to devote to an extensive discussion to such matters, the material on sustainable development is presented in a separate section after the book's other concluding observations on the future of American cities and suburbs have already been presented. This formatting allows instructors maximum flexibility; a professor who lacks class time for a discussion of the politics of urban sustainability can "lop off" this portion of the chapter and not assign it to students.

Users of the previous editions of *Urban Politics* will also note one other major change in the book's 10th edition. The chapter "A Suburban Nation" has been moved toward the front of the volume and now appears as Chapter 3. This change in chapter placement had been considered for a long time. The book's material on the changing shape of contemporary suburbia now directly follows the more historical account of suburban development that appears in Chapter 2. Just as important, material on suburban politics merits a prominent position in the study of urban affairs, a prominence that was not effectively communicated when material devoted to suburban policies was situated much later in the book.

Indeed, *Urban Politics* argues that, in terms of population, economic activity, and political power, the United States is a suburban nation. Google's corporate headquarters complex, for instance, is not situated in San Francisco but instead is located nearly 40 miles south in the suburb of Mountain View. By moving the "Suburban Nation" material toward the front of the volume, the structure of *Urban Politics* now more accurately reflects one of book's most important substantive messages: The suburbs are no longer "sub" in terms of their economic and political importance. Substantial political power resides in the suburbs. In recent national elections, the suburbs have been a crucial battleground, a swing area that to a great extent has decided just which political party holds the reins of power in Washington and just what urban programs and policies will ensue. Suburban constituencies similarly dominate many state governments. In a suburban United States, the study of urban politics and policy cannot focus narrowly on central cities but must also address the needs and concerns of the residents of a still-growing and increasingly diverse suburbia.

Urban Politics is pragmatic in tone. It notes injustices and inequalities. It seeks to identify ameliorative policy solutions—policies that have a realistic chance of being adopted and strategies that can be used to build winning coalitions—in an age where population, problems, and political power have shifted to the suburbs.

HELPING STUDENTS: PEDAGOGICAL FEATURES IN THIS BOOK

An in-depth overview of urban politics risks overwhelming students. The book contains a number of features that are intended to help guide and assist student learning. Clear **message-oriented section titles and subtitles** serve as signposts that help readers understand the material that immediately follows. The book highlights a number of **boldfaced terms** to focus students on new concepts and major points, so that important material is not overlooked when a student reads (or even skims) each chapter. A list of **Key Terms** at the end of each chapter refers to the boldfaced terms in the chapter and provides a useful study guide. Finally, the book includes **numerous photographs** as "every picture tells a story." Such photos and the visual messages they contain are a welcome supplement to what otherwise might seem to be endless words of text.

The 10th edition also attempts to engage students with **boxed case studies** and even with **boxed references to classic and current urban films and TV shows** that help illustrate particular aspects of urban politics. Instructors who value a multimedia approach in the classroom may decide, on occasion, to show in class a clip from the film or TV program described in the book. In an age of cell phones, PCs, satellite television, and narrowcasting, it is likely that many students in a class will not be familiar with the movies, TV shows, and other "pop culture" references.

WORDS OF THANKS

There are a number of people, over the years, who have helped to provide me with a better understanding of the workings of cities and communities. I will mention only a few. Bill Peterman and Janet Smith, geographers and housing and community activists, have shown me the extensive changes taking place in postindustrial Chicago. Jack Dustin, my friend and colleague at Wright State University, helped tutor me as to the possibilities inherent in regional partnerships and collaborative action, as well as the importance of performance measurement and management. The late Bernard M. Ross has my eternal gratitude for asking me to coauthor the book's earlier editions. Bernie was an advocate of citizen participation, a lover of cities, a true gentleman, and a good friend.

Special thanks go to colleagues who provided detailed assessment of the proposal for the book's 10th edition, including Adriana Allen, David L. Imbroscio, and Cathy Yang Liu. Their suggestions are reflected in the new emphases, themes, and structure of the 10th edition. Minchin "Minch" Lewis also provided valuable feedback, having used draft chapters in his Public Administration graduate classes.

A number of people at Routledge and Taylor & Francis have extended their enthusiastic support and offered their skills and assistance in helping to prepare this volume. At Routledge, special thanks go to Laura Stearns for her faith in this volume's continuing contribution to the study of urban politics, and to Emma Harder and Katie Horsfall for taking charge of the book's production. Misha Kydd handled some of the more arduous detailed work. Marie Louise Roberts at Apex CoVantage did extensive work on guiding the book through copyediting. All of these people and the many members of the profession who over the years shared their insights with me have my gratitude.

Myron A. Levine
Wright State University
Dayton, Ohio
April 2019

1 | The Urban Situation

Global City, Tourist City, Bankrupt City

Urban refers to cities and suburbs—to central cities and their surroundings as distinct from less-densely populated rural areas. This book examines the politics of cities and suburbs. It focuses on how "power" is exercised in the urban arena.

An insightful study of urban politics must do more than describe the formal structures and procedures of local government. A focus solely on the actions of local officeholders would miss much of what is truly important in the urban political arena. Many of the more important decisions that affect a community's well-being are not made by *municipal* (that is, local government) officials but by actors who hold no formal governmental position in a city's or suburb's government. Corporate CEOs (chief executive officers) make decisions as to where will they will build a firm's headquarters, back offices, and production facilities. These decisions have a great influence on a locality's economic growth or decline.

The state and national governments, too, are outside actors whose decisions affect local well-being. The states, in particular, have an ability to reach deep into city affairs. Numerous states, for instance, have named state-appointed managers to oversee a city's fiscal affairs or to run a city or a local school system, taking authority away from local elected officials. Municipal government (that is, local government) officials have only a limited ability to respond to local problems. Acting on their own, municipal officials lack the ability to combat local population decline, a loss of jobs, increases in local poverty, property abandonment, and even the racial imbalance of public-school populations. An effective response to such problems requires that local officials enter into effective partnerships with other actors: the heads of corporations, national and state officials, and even the leaders of nonprofit and community organizations.

Cities and suburbs are not in total control of their fate. The precarious position of localities is most dramatically illustration by a brief examination of fairly recent events in Flint, Michigan. Flint has suffered long-term decline as a result of corporate rationalization decisions that downsized Flint's industrial base. Flint also saw its population dwindle as residents moved to the suburbs and to communities in the Sunbelt (the American South and Southwest). Flint gained national headlines when studies revealed

1

that thousands of Flint children were the victims of lead poisoning, that they were suffering very dangerous levels of lead in their blood. This disastrous problem was largely
the result of the State of Michigan's power to intrude in local affairs. State-appointed
managers forced Flint to switch the source of its water, a decision that was supposed to
save money but was not well researched. The nonelected outside-appointed managers
essentially ignored the outcries of local residents who protested the smell and color of
their tap water.

The Flint case study reminds us that not all cities and neighborhoods in the United
States are faring well, even in an age where popular commentators have celebrated the
renaissance or revival of so many cities—as seen in the comeback of central business
districts and the revival of neighborhoods located in close proximity to a city's downtown.
However, as we shall see, there is no simple and uniform story to be told regarding the
contemporary urban condition. While many communities are doing well, others have
not been able to reverse decades-old patterns of decline. Even the nation's suburbs have
become a new site of American poverty.

The metaphors that are often used to describe the urban condition denote complexity,
a mix of progress and continued decline. As this chapter will detail, there are glaring
differences between the *Global City* (communities that have adapted and prospered in
a postindustrial and global age), the *Tourist City* (where local economic policies have
revived certain areas of the local economy but not others), and the *Bankrupt City* (cities
like Flint that continue to face severe economic, fiscal, and social problems as a result
of the U.S. transition to a postindustrial economy). In suburbia, too, dynamic "edge
city" growth and "edgeless" strip-mall development contrast with communities that are
increasingly home to unemployment, poverty, and recently arrived immigrants. A growing
suburbia in the United States has become increasingly diverse and politically powerful.

We begin by reviewing the dramatic story of the lead poisoning of drinking water
in Flint and just what that unfortunate situation reveals about the nature of politics and
political power in urban America.

THE LEAD POISONING OF FLINT'S CHILDREN

A 2015 health study of Flint, Michigan, children below the age of five revealed that
lead blood levels had doubled—and in some cases tripled. No similar increases were
observed in young children residing in the city's suburbs.[1]

Lead is a neurotoxin. The introduction of high lead levels in young children has
serious health consequences that are "believed to be irreversible."[2] High levels of lead
adversely affect a child's brain development, reducing IQ levels, shortening attention
spans, lowering educational achievement, and increasing antisocial behavior over the
course of a person's life. High lead levels are also associated with a number of health
problems, including anemia, hypertension, seizures, and immunotoxicity. In Flint, lead
poisoning appears to help account for the sudden and precipitous drop in third-grade
achievement scores. Before the crisis, 42 percent of the city's third-graders scored as
proficient on state reading exams; after the lead poisoning that resulted from a switch in
the city's water supply, only 11 percent of the third graders—that is, only one of every
nine students—scored as proficient in reading.[3]

How could something as horrendous as the lead poisoning of children occur in the modern United States? Of course, the poisoning was not intentional—although state officials (and at times federal and city officials as well) sadly were slow to acknowledge the crisis and attempt to correct the problem. Flint parents had protested that a state-forced change in Flint's water provision had produced tap water that was odorous, cloudy, and discolored, indications that rust and chemicals had leached from city water pipes. General Motors factories in Flint even stopped using city water which it saw as corroding automobile parts. But state officials were largely unmoved by the complaints of Flint residents, and the befouled water was piped into residents's homes.

The lead poisoning of Flint was no natural disaster; it was neither a natural nor an unavoidable problem. As Flint's newly elected mayor (who came to office in the middle of the crisis) correctly observed, lead poisoning in Flint was a man-made disaster, the result of decisions made by officials and forces from beyond Flint's borders.

The water crisis in Flint had its roots in the Michigan state government's concern that Flint's political leaders were unwilling to enact business-like practices that would produce greater efficiencies and reduce costs. Flint was a postindustrial city in deep financial trouble. Over the decades, the city had witnessed the shutdown of much of its manufacturing base. Residents watched as population and commercial activity migrated to the city's suburbs. Contemporary Flint is predominantly poor (nearly half of Flint residents fall below the poverty line) and has a population that is mostly African American.

At the time, a state government audit showed that unless new cost-saving steps were initiated, the city was facing projected deficits that would add $25 million a year to the city's outstanding debt.[4] Frustrated by the city's inaction, as no easy solutions were readily available, Republican Governor Rick Snyder and a Republican-controlled state legislature took matters more directly into their own hands. The Michigan state legislature had previously enacted a law that enabled state officials to place problem cities under the control of a state-appointed emergency manager. Governor Snyder utilized the law to force changes in Flint's operations.

The state's emergency manager for Flint argued that the city could realize millions of dollars in cost savings—at estimated $5 million or more over two years, with some estimates even pointing to the possibility of $100 million in savings over the long term— by providing its own water. The state-appointed manager pushed the city to discontinue the contract that the city had with the Detroit Water Department to supply Flint with water from Lake Huron, the fifth largest fresh water lake on the planet. Critics of the change argued that the projected estimates of costs savings were highly exaggerated. Still, the emergency manager, backed by efficiency-minded political forces in the state government, continued to insist that Flint terminate its contract with Detroit and, instead, begin to draw its water from the city's older and disused source, the Flint River.

The emergency manager was neither elected by Flint's residents nor appointed by the city's elected officials. Instead, the emergency manager reported to the Michigan Department of Treasury, a body committed to budget savings, an agency that had no particular expertise in water quality and public health.[5] Under pressure from the state, Flint's city council followed the emergency manager's lead.

Residents of the overwhelmingly poor, African-American, and Democratic city began immediately to complain about the appearance, taste, and odor of the water drawn from their taps. Parents reported that their children suffered a sudden breakout of body rashes. But the complaints were largely ignored by state and local officials intent on cutting costs and unwilling to admit that their own participation in the decision to switch may have been a mistake.[6] Reflecting the distaste of state Republicans for strong regulation, the state regulatory agency in charge of water safety took a "minimalist approach" to its job. The agency's members insisted that the water posed no hazard to health; members of the agency even sought to "discredit" citizens who raised complaints.[7]

Within a year, pediatricians, university scientists, and even the U.S. Environmental Protection Agency all reported that the city's drinking water contained dangerously high levels of lead; in some instances, lead levels were seven times higher than the EPA standard.[8] A later study further reported that the switch in the city's drinking water produced a "horrifyingly large" increase in miscarriages and fetal deaths.[9] Why did that happen? Simply put, water from the Flint River was not properly treated to prevent corrosion in the system's aging and long-disused iron water pipes. The old pipes leached unsafe levels of lead into city drinking water.

At last, in the face of mounting evidence and citizen outrage, public officials finally determined that the city's drinking water was unsafe. A state of emergency was declared. The Michigan National Guard helped to distribute bottled water to affected residents (Figure 1.1).

Figure 1.1   **The National Guard Distributes Bottled Water in Flint, Michigan, January 2016.**

Source: Photo by Linda Parton/Shutterstock.com.

In the wake of the crisis, the Governor Snyder and the State of Michigan ultimately decided to spend approximately a hundred million dollars to reconnect Flint to the Detroit water system and to replace the iron and galvanized steel pipes that were the source of contamination. But at the height of the city's dire health emergency, even such a common-sense (but expensive) course of action was not readily forthcoming. Flint's city council voted seven to one to reconnect the city to Detroit Water. But the state-appointed fiscal manager warned of skyrocketing costs and overruled the initial vote! The Michigan Department of Treasury expressed similar concerns about the high costs of reconnecting Flint to Detroit water.

When it came to water decisions and the health of the city's children, the most important actions in Flint were made by state officials and state appointees, not the people of Flint and their elected city officers. Flint, a Bankrupt City, had lost its autonomy. City residents and local officials were denied the ability to control their own affairs, as the state's Republican leaders pursued a policy agenda of deregulation and cost reduction. Decision makers from outside the community had no direct accountability to city residents.[10]

The Michigan Civil Rights Commission accused the state of "systemic racism." The Commission asked if state officials would have been as detached and irresponsive had the poisoning crisis occurred in Birmingham, an affluent and white suburb, or even Ann Arbor instead of minority-majority Flint.[11]

After seven years, the state decided to bring to an end its direct control over Flint. The Michigan Department of Treasury returned control over daily policy and spending decisions to the city's elected officials.

POSTINDUSTRIAL AMERICA AND THE URBAN SITUATION

The Flint story provides a tale of a once-vital industrial city confronting long-term decline. The American city of the twenty-first century is a vastly different entity than the industrial or manufacturing city that had dominated the United States for much of the nation's history. During the industrial age, cities like New York, Pittsburgh, Buffalo, Detroit, Chicago, Cincinnati, San Francisco, and Flint all enjoyed preeminence as centers of industry: steel and automobile manufacturing, meat packing, garment manufacturing, and a large variety of other heavy and light industry. Cities were also vital transportation hubs and the site of bustling warehousing, distribution, and port-related activities that were essential to a growing American economy.

But as the decline of Flint underscores, cities in the twenty-first century are not guaranteed continued prosperity as centers of manufacturing. A great many cities, especially former industrial centers in the Northeast and Midwest, lost their economic edge as automation, advances in transportation, and competition from low-wage production sites in the South and Southwest and overseas all diminished the city's manufacturing base. Cities in the United States lost political power as well as economic preeminence as residents and commercial activity migrated to the suburbs.

The ability of cities to cope with the forces of deindustrialization and globalization (as manufacturing operations also were shifted overseas) has been uneven. Some cities adapted and found a new niche in a postindustrial, global economy. Other cities, like

Flint, found no such niche and continued to decline, with some facing great economic distress and even the risk of bankruptcy.

Suburban America, too, was transformed, with innovations in transportation and information technology leading to a geographical decentralization of economic activities once found only in central cities. Still, while numerous suburban cities grew and prospered, others were bypassed in the new economy; these latter suburbs suffered a growth of poverty and other city-like problems. The dynamic and diverse suburbia of the early twenty-first century is a much different animal as compared to the string of serene bedroom communities that dominated images of suburbia at the height of the industrial age.

GLOBAL CITY

Former industrial center like Flint have been unable to find their "fit" in a changed economy. Other cities, however, were able to build on various advantages that they possessed; these cities transformed themselves and found a new role to play in a postindustrial and an increasingly globalized economy. The evolution of New York City illustrates the transformation.

At the beginning of the 1950s, New York City was still, to a very great extent, a city of numerous small factories, warehouses, and shipping, with "finger piers" jutting into the Hudson River from Manhattan. But the manufacturing jobs in the city soon began to disappear, as manufacturers took advantage of lower-cost production sites in the suburbs, the South, and, later, overseas. Manufacturing businesses closed and port activity slowed. The city's famed finger piers were abandoned and rotted away. Smaller manufacturing operations located along the city's narrow streets were no longer competitive. In the 1970s, faced with continued economic decline, New York even confronted the prospects of defaulting on its debts and possible bankruptcy.

But New York transformed, and a new postindustrial and even more globally oriented city emerged. The city's finger piers were removed, a visual indication that manufacturing, warehousing, and shipping no longer play a dominant role in the New York economy as they once did. Once-gritty industrial and working-class sections of New York seemingly disappeared, giving way to a new city of globally connected corporate headquarters, soaring office towers, and high-rise condominiums. Restaurants, nightlife and entertainment centers, and luxury residential high-rises sprouted on sites where warehouses and manufacturing operations once stood. New York is no longer the industrial city of old. Contemporary New York City is a hub of global corporate headquarters, international banks, financial services firms, and start-ups and expanding businesses in the information technology and the digital and "new media" fields. The city is also a host to major cultural institutions and entertainment activities that continue to add to the city's lure as a major tourist destination.

Other former industrial centers underwent a similar transformation. Contemporary Pittsburgh looks quite different from the industrial Pittsburgh of old. For much of the twentieth century, Pittsburgh rose to prominence as Steel Town USA; its landscape was dotted by blast furnaces, slag heaps, and other heavy manufacturing. Toward the end of the twentieth century, however, many of city's industrial plants lay idle. Steel manufacturing had migrated elsewhere, and the city lost both jobs and population. Pittsburgh found its path to rebirth only when its civic leaders decided to tear down much of city's industrial infrastructure as part of an effort to seek new economic activity in such areas as higher education, entertainment, and health care. Pittsburgh demolished the rusting hulks of the city's obsolescent steel mills and removed the industry's slag heaps in order to build a very different and new postindustrial infrastructure: riverfront bike paths and green parks, office campuses, shopping complexes, and modern professional sports stadiums (Figure 1.2a,b).

In Pittsburgh, New York, and in cities across the country, central business districts, which had suffered a steep decline beginning in the 1950s, enjoyed a revival, as did numerous nearby inner-city residential areas. By the beginning of the twenty-first century, cities became the preferred location of corporate headquarters. Once overlooked, core-city neighborhoods blossomed as the site of new upscale residences, sidewalk cafés, and fashionable bistros and boutiques. City leaders made substantial investments in their

Figure 1.2(a) **The Industrial City: Steel Mills and the South Slopes Neighborhood of Pittsburgh, 1940**.

Source: From Wikimedia Commons, User PerryPlanet, June 28, 2009, https://commons.wikimedia.org/wiki/File: Pittsburgh_northshorepark.jpg.

Figure 1.2(b) **Pittsburgh's Postindustrial Transformation.** Pittsburgh redeveloped its riverfront, once the site of idle steel mills and slag heaps, into a place of commerce and recreation. The river banks are now lined with parkland, bike paths, walkways, restaurants, pubs, new office developments, shopping centers, and stadiums for the city's professional baseball and football teams.

Source: Photo by Jack Delano, January 1940/Library of Congress Prints and Photographs Division, Washington, DC, courtesy of Wikimedia.

telecommunications infrastructure and other upgrades to make their cities attractive to firms in health care, education, telecommunications, and the leisure industry—growth fields of the new economy.

In a neighborhood transformation process that was soon labeled as **gentrification**, young professionals and the well-paid workers of the major corporations took up residence in areas near the downtown, sometimes in lofts converted from vacant warehouses. Developers built luxury apartments and condominiums for more affluent home seekers. Singles, newly married, and young professionals sought to live in close proximity to the job opportunities and the cultural and nightlife opportunities of an active city.

Globalization, too, provided a basis for this urban comeback. Young professionals enjoyed good-paying jobs in the offices of multinational corporations that coordinated the operations of their subsidiaries located in a multitude of countries. Globalization had been a cause of the decline of the Industrial City, as manufacturing centers in the United State lost jobs to production facilities located overseas. But globalization also offered strategically well-positioned cities in the United States a chance to offset those losses by attracting the headquarters, back offices, and research and development facilities of international corporations. In a **globalized economy**, political borders decrease in importance as the organization of production and a corporation's activities transcend the boundaries of a single nation.

New York City of the 1970s, badly hurt by the decline of its manufacturing base and the exodus of population and commercial activity to the suburbs, teetered on the edge of fiscal default. The city could not find the revenues necessary to pay off its creditors as municipal loans came due. The intervention of the state and federal governments helped New York gain access to the funds (that is, to borrow money through the municipal bond market) that the city required in order to maintain operations while implementing various fiscal reforms. But state and federal intervention provides only part of the story of New York City's rebirth from the depth of fiscal despair. New York City, even during the era of its immense fiscal problems, enjoyed important advantages as a critical national and global economic center. The city was able to escape the specter of default, and reemerge as a top-tier **Global City**, by building on its position as a hub of corporate headquarters, banking, and financial services firms essential to the world economy.

New York City's decline and rebound point to the significance of *globalization* and the "fit" of a city in the world economy. **Globalization**, as previously observed, denotes the eroding significance of national and local borders. Contemporary cities exist in a system of interconnected relationships that transcend national borders. As we have seen, economic competition from overseas helps to explain New York City's mid-twentieth-century fiscal descent. But globalization also provides the international economic connections that soon provided a basis for the city's renaissance. As this book shall discuss in much greater detail, globalization also denotes the mobility of people—that is, the increased prominence of immigration—as well as the mobility of capital.

Of course, certain cities occupy critical roles in the new global economy. New York, London, and Tokyo are generally regarded as the world's three top-tier cities, cities that have a large concentration of business firms (especially corporate headquarters and banking and financial firms) that are critical to the operation of businesses located around the globe. Global cities gain vitality as centers of commerce, corporate control, knowledge, creativity, communications, and entrepreneurship.[12]

New York City, as does other global giants, benefits from the economics of **agglomeration**; major multinational and national firms find considerable advantages in locating key facilities in close proximity to other corporations doing similar work in their field. Cities offer industries the possibility of **cluster development**: By locating in the same geographical area as similar firms, a corporation can tap a large pool of qualified workers and draw on the specialized support services provided by the financial, accounting, legal, and managerial assistance firms that work in their field.[13] New York provides one of the world's premier clusters of banking, finance, and corporate activities.

The 9/11 terrorists targeted New York City because of the prominent role the city plays as a global center of finance and communications. Somewhat ironically, New York City was able to rebound from the destruction of the World Trade Center, as the disaster did not eliminate many of the advantages that the city enjoys as a critical headquarters and fiscal services center in the global economy.[14] Massive new headquarters facilities—the soaring Freedom Tower (Figure 1.3) and other nearby office towers—were erected on the site of the demolished Twin Towers. The World Trade Center area is an important site for

Figure 1.3 **The Freedom Tower and the Rebuilding of Lower Manhattan.** The soaring 1776-foot Freedom Tower is actually taller than the Twin Towers that fell during the 9/11 attacks. Construction of the Freedom Tower proceeded despite concerns for the building's safety and objections that developers were commercializing a site that should be treated as sacred ground. The office space provided by the Freedom Tower and other nearby World Trade Center towers helped to reinforce the position of Lower Manhattan as a top-tier financial center of the global economy.

Source: Photo by Hakilon, December 2013/Wikimedia Commons, http://commons.wikimedia.org/wiki/File: One_World_Trade_Center_im_Dezember_2013.jpg.

offices in the global economy, given the area's location only blocks away from the dense concentration of headquarters and financial firms of Wall Street. The construction of new office towers at the 9/11 site had the backing of city, state, and national officials, as well as that of major corporations.

As we shall discuss in Chapter 4, there exists a hierarchy of global cities based on a city's importance to the functioning of the global economy. Los Angeles ranks a rung or so below New York on the Global City ladder. Los Angeles is an important center of communications (especially the film industry) and Pacific Rim banking. Los Angeles is increasingly the beneficiary of investments made by firms and individuals from overseas. L.A. quite obviously is also a very diverse, multicultural, and multilinguistic city. Still, the city lacks the concentration of world-class firms found in New York.

Chicago, Houston, Denver, Miami, and San Francisco are other U.S. cities that have built on their global connections and are important national and regional commercial centers. Compared to New York and even to Los Angeles, however, these cities are less critical command-and-control centers of the global economy.

New Orleans's relatively low position in the global hierarchy even helps to explain why there was no similar sense of urgency to rebuild New Orleans after the devastation and flooding of Hurricane Katrina as there was to reconstruct a vital economic hub in New York City after 9/11.

Globalization also denotes the permeability of national borders to population flows, not just to the movement of capital. In the United States, a **new immigration**, primarily from Latin America and Asia, has provided the investment funds, the creative talent, and the physical labor that has helped to fuel the rebound of numerous troubled urban communities, including smaller industrial cities and suburbs in the Northeast and the Midwest. The physical rebuilding of New Orleans after Hurricane Katrina was achieved with the labor provided by a record increase in the city's Mexican population. Thousands of Hispanics came to New Orleans seeking work in the rebuilding of the flood-ravaged city.[15]

The new urban diversity is especially apparent in cities located near the nation's southern border. In the 1950s, Anglos comprised nearly 75 percent of Houston's population. By 2010, the number had fallen to only 33 percent, with the city's Latino population (41 percent) surpassing the Anglo population. Asians, an insignificant part of Houston's population in 1950, had grown to 8 percent in 2010. Nearly all Houston's population growth in more recent decades has been due to immigration. While the people of greater Houston tend to view immigration and population diversity as "good things," older Anglo residents retain a nostalgia for an Anglo Houston that no longer exists.[16]

A brief look back at a list of the persons who died as a result of the 9/11 attacks on New York's World Trade Center (WTC) underscores the importance of immigration to the Global City. The homelands of the victims when the Twin Towers fell ranged from the Dominican Republic to Canada to Poland.[17] The victims of 9/11 included both legal and undocumented immigrants, including a large number of immigrants from Mexico who worked as window washers, custodial staff, and food-service personnel in the WTC's below-ground eateries and its top-floor world-renowned Windows on the World restaurant. Mexicans are New York's fastest-growing minority and an important source of labor in the city's service industries.

TOURIST CITY

Postindustrial cities have had little choice but to diversify their development efforts. The **Tourist City** seeks to generate new jobs by attracting visitors in the areas of sports and entertainment. The Tourist City promotes the construction of sports stadiums, convention centers, and casinos, as well as the development of distinctive tourist and shopping districts (see Box 1.1).

Economist Richard Florida argues that a city's investment in lifestyle amenities does more than merely increase tourism. Cities that provide interesting living spaces, a variety of arts and leisure activities, and a high quality of life are able to attract computer programmers, Web designers, media specialists, and other knowledge-based workers. Members of the **creative class** comprise a pool of entrepreneurial talent likely to take a risk in "start-up" enterprises. Such a pool of talent also make a community attractive to firms seeking highly skilled and creative workers.[18]

For much of its history, Chicago was the prototypical Industrial City (the "City of the Big Shoulders" in the words of poet Carl Sandburg). Over the years, however, Chicago's economic position slipped as manufacturing declined and residents and industry moved to the suburbs and the Sunbelt. In a postindustrial era, the city had to look beyond manufacturing in its search for jobs.

Mayor Richard M. Daley (whose long tenure in office ran from 1989 to 2011) sought to refashion Chicago as a center of globally and nationally oriented corporate offices. Nearby neighborhoods were cleared (the city even demolished high-rise public housing structures) and improved to make surrounding areas ripe for new investment and gentrification—upscale residential areas attractive to the professionals who would work in Chicago's new tech-oriented industries and corporate offices. Heightened police protection in the tourist center and the city's near-north residential

Box 1.1
Baltimore's Harborplace: The Rotting Ruins of the Industrial City Are Converted Into a Fun Postindustrial Center

Like other industrial cities, Baltimore suffered decades of factory and warehouse closings. The shallow shipping channel of the Inner Harbor could not handle big ships, and port-related activity moved elsewhere. The Inner Harbor area, located next to the city's troubled central business district, was marred by extensive abandonment, including empty warehouses and shuttered factories.

Baltimore's civic leaders sought to alter the city's image and revive the city by transforming the Inner Harbor area. Harborplace (Figure 1.4), a pier-side entertainment/shopping/dining complex, was built at the heart of the redevelopment effort. Harborplace was designed as a fun place; visitors walk along the harbor, watch jugglers and street entertainers, board historic ships, and eat and drink in the project's crab houses and Irish-themed bars. The State of Maryland and the city invested heavily in efforts to transform the derelict waterfront area

Figure 1.4 **The Tourist/Entertainment City: Baltimore's Harborplace, With the USS Constellation**.

Source: Photo by Cszmurlo/Wikimedia Commons, March 6, 2007, http://commons.wikimedia. org/wiki/File:USS-Constellation-Szmurlo.jpg.

into a dynamic tourist zone. Baltimore opened the Maryland Science Center and planetarium (1976), a new convention center (1979), which the city in subsequent years later expanded), and the "National Aquarium" (1981). Baltimore also helped build a retro-style Camden Yards ballpark for the American League Orioles (1992) and a 71,000-seat football stadium for the NFL Ravens (1998), along with extensive parking facilities. A new light-rail line served the football stadium, ballpark, convention center, nearby hotels—and parts of the old downtown as well. New townhomes and condominiums began to sprout up on the sites of abandoned warehouses. More upscale residential developments soon began to appear in nearby historic neighborhoods.

Critics ask just "who benefits?" and "who loses?" from such extensive government investment in the city's tourist bubble. The upgraded Inner Harbor area has been successful in attracting tourists and conventions to the city. But the massive investment in the Inner Harbor brought little improvement in the lives of persons living in Baltimore's more poverty-stricken neighborhoods. *The Wire*, the 2002 Home Box Office (HBO) television sensation that ran for five years, took viewers to some of the poorest neighborhoods of Baltimore, showing viewers the dilapidated housing and the drug and gang activity in sections of the city that are seemingly on a different planet from the festive entertainment activities of the Inner Harbor. The revival of the Inner Harbor also led to an increase in land prices and rents in adjacent residential neighborhoods, with gentrifying pressures leading to the displacement of working class and poorer families.

Mayor Kurt Schmoke (1991–1997) attempted to break the public-private alliance that had focused such great attention and resources on the redevelopment on the Inner Harbor and the city's downtown. Schmoke sought economic development efforts that would improve the opportunities available to schoolchildren and turn around condition in the city's more distressed neighborhoods. His effort to redirect investment had only the most limited success. Neighborhood associations and residents were largely unable to convince public and private officials to give greater attention to community revitalization. In 2018, Mayor Catherine Pugh supported the expansion of the convention center and the continued updating and modernization of Harborplace as part of the Baltimore's overall economic development strategy.

neighborhoods contributed to a sense of safety that attracted both tourists and young professionals. The new emphasis on policing, however, did not offer the same sense of security to African-American south- and west-siders or to young black males who suffered fatal encounters with the police.

To rebrand the city, Richard M. Daley removed a large antiquated railroad yard located in the midst of the downtown near the city's lakefront and built a transformative project, Millennium Park. This was no ordinary park. With its concert venues, interactive public art, skating rink, active water feature, festival places, and acres of underground parking, Millennial Park helped to make Chicago a fun city.

The city's efforts at transformation did not stop there. In up-and-coming residential neighborhoods, the city planted trees, introduced wrought-iron fences, upgraded softball fields and lakefront beaches, and provided trails for jogging, cycling, and rollerblading. The city introduced clearly marked bicycle lanes on thoroughfares to connect the Chicago's newly "hip" neighborhoods with its downtown. Where necessary, the city even removed a lane of automobile traffic in order to make way for bike paths. The Chicago River, long the site of vacant and obsolescent warehouses, became the location of pricey new waterfront condominiums and even leisure activities such as kayaking. Mayor Daley "wanted the Chicago River to become as lively as the Seine in Paris." By the time Daley left office in 2011, entertainment had become Chicago's Number One industrial sector.[19] Mayor Rahm Emanuel, Daley's successor, continued the focus on amenities, dedicating additional bicycle lanes on city streets and supporting development along the "606," the three-mile elevated Bloomingdale Trail bicycle path built on a disused rail spur just north of the downtown.

Critics argue that such Tourist City and Global City growth strategies do little to help a city's poorer residents and the residents of more distressed neighborhoods. Too often, growth projects construct a **tourist bubble**, an island of privilege for visitors, young professionals, and major corporations that flourishes in an urban landscape characterized by extensive class and racial inequality and ghettoization.[20] Global City and Tourist City policies result in what economist Richard Florida labels a **winner-take-all urbanism** where the benefits of growth are concentrated in "superstar" cities and high-priced neighborhoods.

BANKRUPT CITY

Numerous communities still suffer a postindustrial hangover and have not enjoyed the economic resurgence evident in such global centers as a New York or Chicago. New York's 2016 poverty rate of 19 percent was considerably lower than the poverty rate of other cities: Detroit (36 percent in poverty); Cleveland and Youngstown (35 percent); Buffalo (31 percent); Camden (31 percent); Newark (28 percent); Milwaukee (27 percent); Cincinnati, Toledo, and Philadelphia (26 percent each); and St. Louis (24 percent). In Flint, the poverty rate stood at a stunningly high 46 percent. In Benton Harbor, Michigan, a community often referred to as a "disaster city," the poverty rate (49 percent) was higher still. In the South, Shreveport, Louisiana, had a 31 percent poverty rate. On the west coast, San Bernardino, California, suffered a poverty rate that was nearly as high.

As these poverty rates indicate, a fairly large number of United States communities are not prospering. The nation's much-touted urban renaissance has not extended to all cities and neighborhoods. The contemporary urban situation is characterized by a heightened inequality between winner cities and struggling cities that have difficulty in finding the funds for basic municipal services. The new urban inequality is also apparent in suburbia, where numerous inner-ting suburbs have found it difficult to replace lost industrial jobs and to cope with the rise of poverty inside their borders. Fashionable "main-line" suburbs that were once the most desirable communities in a metropolis are now dotted by vacant storefronts, closed shopping malls, and "For Rent" signs posted in front of single-family homes.

Detroit illustrates the immense difficulties faced by the Bankrupt City. In 2013, Detroit became the largest city in United States history to file for bankruptcy. Once the nation's most significant center of automobile manufacturing, Detroit was buffeted by the nation's transition to a postindustrial, globalized, and suburban age. In a relatively short period of time, Detroit lost half its population. The city's population, which stood at 1.2 million in 1980, fell to just 660,000 in 2016. Acres of vacant properties, razed homes and factories, and closed storefronts testified to Detroit's steep descent.

Detroit's ability to provide its residents with basic municipal service was undermined by the **erosion of the city tax base**. Extensive property abandonment and declining property values meant the loss of property tax revenues (Figure 1.5). Detroit assumed responsibility for maintaining over 46,000 abandoned properties where property owners were no longer paying property taxes. The city's revenue coffers suffered additional blows as a result of the property tax exemptions and reductions granted by both the state and the city in an effort to spur new development. As is typical of other U.S. cities, Detroit was also prohibited from levying property taxes on churches, private schools, and hospitals.[21]

Figure 1.5   **Thousands of Abandoned Houses in Detroit.** Detroit has hemorrhaged population and has no hope of regaining its former size. The photograph reveals not only a vacant structure but also vacant lots where housing once stood. Detroit no longer needs the extensive housing stock that once provided shelter for the city's peak population. As a result, Detroit, like other "shrinking cities," initiated extensive efforts to raze abandoned houses and properties suffering advanced disrepair.

Source: Photo by Notorious4life, May 20, 2010/Wikimedia Commons, http://commons.wikimedia.org/ wiki/File: AbandonedHouseDelray.jpg.

Detroit could not simply tax its way to improved municipal services. The State of Michigan sharply limited the type of taxes and the maximum tax rates that Detroit could levy. Detroit imposed tax rates that were near the maximum permitted by state law; yet, the city still suffered from devastating revenue shortfalls. In a last-ditch effort to attract business and improve its deteriorating fiscal position, the city reduced municipal spending, even though the cuts reduced neighborhood services. The city also had to set aside revenues to help meet its obligations to municipal retirees. The city, however, did reach a court-approved settlement that reduced its obligation to creditors by $7 billion.[22]

As the details of Detroit's circumstances underscore, the Bankrupt City is not even allowed the autonomy to decide just what courses of action it will take in its attempts to emerge from bankruptcy while also providing for the basic needs of its citizens. Federal rules for bankruptcy establish municipal bondholders as "superior claimants"[23] who stand first in line to get paid. A city must repay creditors, even at the cost of having to make further reductions in the municipal services provided city residents.

Detroit's plan to emerge from bankruptcy entailed an extensive reduction in municipal services and in the health and pensions benefits provided municipal workers—all actions demanded by more conservative business elites and the city's creditors. Yet, in some instances, the leaders of a Bankrupt City have been successful in fighting for somewhat more equitable plans in the effort to escape bankruptcy. Detroit's leaders fought to have the city's creditors share in the pain, that creditors accept only a partial repayment of some outstanding obligations. Detroit's legal team skillfully argued that major financial institutions were partially at fault for the city's fiscal situation, that the Bank of America, UBS, and other financial institutions had provided the city with bad investment advice that eroded the city's ability to meet its pension obligations. Armed with such information, Detroit's fiscal manager offered the holders of certain types of bonds only 20 cents on the dollar. Stockton, California, a city that was also in municipal bankruptcy, offered a major creditor only a penny on a dollar to settle outstanding debts.[24] Even in the Bankrupt City, despite the severe constraints imposed on municipal action, local politics and leadership skill still matter.

In 2018, Detroit emerged from bankruptcy; the state terminated its active oversight of major city fiscal decisions and returned governing authority to local elected officials. But the return of power to the city was not complete. The state retained a "passive monitoring" role over Detroit; the city was required to submit to the state a monthly financial statement, copies of the city's adopted budgets, and a longer-term financial plan. The State of Michigan's financial review commission retained the authority to decide each year if local control in Detroit would be permitted to continue.[25]

Declarations of municipal bankruptcy in the United States have historically been rare events. In more recent years, however, the number of municipalities filing for "Chapter 9" bankruptcy protection jumped. The Detroit bankruptcy followed in the wake of bankruptcy filings by two California cities: Stockton (with a population of 296,300) and San Bernardino (population 212,600). Vallejo and Orange County are other large California municipalities that previously filed for bankruptcy after cutting back municipal services and failing to get the municipality's creditors to accept partial debt forgiveness.[26] Jefferson County, Alabama, home to the City of Birmingham, filed for bankruptcy in 2011.

Harrisburg, Pennsylvania, similarly began the steps necessary to file for bankruptcy, only to face the intrusion of the state government, which enacted a new law to bar the filing. Bankruptcy was no longer an option for Harrisburg. Instead, the city limped by: reducing municipal services, receiving additional assistance from the state, and working out a deal with the city's creditors.[27]

In each of the cases described above, the municipal economy had been severely deteriorated by long-term trends, including deindustrialization and the exodus of the local jobs and tax base to the suburbs. In Detroit, Stockton, and Harrisburg, past labor agreements had further undermined municipal financial stability by saddling the city with the costs of providing municipal workers with generous pensions and health benefits. Stockton permitted police officers to retire and draw benefits at age 50.[28] Chicago, Philadelphia, New Orleans, Omaha, and Portland are among the more seemingly prosperous cities to have discovered that they, too, were facing a looming **municipal pension crisis**, and that they are likely to have great difficulty in finding the monies to cover the unfunded pension liabilities owed municipal workers.[29]

Why did cities agree to such generous pension provisions? The roots can be found in politics. When negotiating contracts with municipal labor unions, city officials find it relatively easy to commit to generous pension provisions that will be paid out in future years rather than increase taxes to cover the pay increases and benefits given for city workers and public-school teachers. Such deferrals in spending cannot be sustained indefinitely. Over the years, as more and more workers retired, cities and school systems discovered that they had failed to contribute sufficient monies to municipal pension funds. The necessity to commit funds to cover the pension benefits owed municipal workers crowds out the money that a city has for other important urban services. The need to fund contractually agreed-upon pensions reduces the money available for such basic services as policing, fire protection, the operation of local public schools, libraries, and the repair of crumbling infrastructure.

The judicial system tends to enforce public pension obligations, viewing them as contractual obligations to which a city freely agreed. However, this legal doctrine is undergoing reexamination. Federal judges supervising the Detroit, Stockton, and Central Falls (Rhode Island) bankruptcies ruled that a city can impose pension reductions upon unwilling workers as part of its efforts to put its fiscal house in order. Federal law is supreme and takes precedence over state law. Federal bankruptcy law even takes preeminence over the provisions of a state's constitution that seemingly protect the integrity of municipal pension benefits.[30]

The long-term impact of such bankruptcy rulings remains to be seen. The rulings may help set a precedent that public pension benefits are not sacrosanct, that retirees, like other constituencies, must accept a share of the pain of when a fiscally strapped municipality must decide on cutbacks. Such judicial rulings would ease some of the immense burden that outstanding pension obligations impose on numerous big- and medium-sized cities and school systems. Municipal workers and retirees, however, respond that a forced reduction in previously agreed-upon benefits is unfair, the city is denying them compensation for work they have already performed.

Not all cities experienced a downhill slide as extreme as that of Detroit and Flint, cities that suffered from a lack of economic diversification. Detroit and Flint were reliant on an automobile industry. When the industry underwent restructuring, when manufacturers in the United States began to assemble automobiles from parts produced overseas, Detroit and Flint bled. Detroit and Flint also suffered an exodus of wealth and population to the suburbs beyond that experienced by other major cities in the Northeast and the Midwest.[31]

As seen in Detroit as well as in Flint, race too played a prominent role in urban problems. Detroit is arguably the nation's most divided metropolis by race, with white flight to the suburbs leaving behind a central city with an overwhelmingly nonwhite population.

Critics of Detroit blame for the city's downfall on the incompetence and shenanigans of Detroit's political leaders.[32] These critics tend to overlook the impacts of deindustrialization, suburbanization, and metropolitan segregation, the root causes of Detroit's precipitous decline. The 50-year "downward economic trajectory" of Detroit suggests that "no single policy regime"[33]—no single political administration or set of policies—bears the full responsibility for the city's downfall. As Chapter 2 describes in greater detail, a vast range of government policies and the self-interested actions of private-sector actors created the problem conditions found in Detroit and other cities.

A TRANSFORMED SUBURBIA

As Chapter 3 underscores, the United States is a suburban nation. More Americans live in suburbs than in central cities. **Suburbanization**—the move of population, commerce, and wealth to the suburbs—has been occurring for well over half a century and continues today.

For a brief few years at the beginning of the twenty-first century, census data seemed to indicate a reversal of the normal trend toward suburbanization. A "back to the city" movement was undergirding the comeback of central-city downtowns and nearby neighborhoods. According to numerous social commentators, Millennials were transforming the metropolitan landscape as they were less interested than their parents in the automobile- and home-centered lifestyle of suburbia. Millennials preferred the active life of cities—dining with friends, attending music concerts, and using smart phone apps to hails rides via Uber and Lyft.[34]

Millennials did indeed help to bring a new vitality to core urban areas. Yet, Millennials are unlikely to alter shape of metropolitan America: the movement of population and affluence to the suburbs continues. In important ways, Millennials may not be as different from preceding generations as popular commentators assumed. Survey data seem to reveal that Millennials as a whole have no animosity toward suburban living. Millennials also aspire to homeownership. Survey responses indicate that Millennials still view homeownership as part of the "good life." Many eventually envision moving to the suburbs.[35] As they grow older and have children, Millennials increasingly seek a home in the suburbs, just as preceding generations have done.[36] Millennials value city life, but they also value suburban communities that offer affordable homes, population diversity, walkability, public transportation, and interesting bars, restaurants, and leisure activities.[37]

Since 2012, the overall movement of population in metropolitan areas is once again clearly to the suburbs, even to more far-off *exurbs*.[38] For a brief moment at the beginning of the century, the movement to the suburbs appeared to have slowed. In part, the suburban slow-down was the result of the national economic recession and the meltdown of the mortgage-finance industry, problems that made it difficult to buy a home. When the banking crisis ended and the economy rebounded, the great American migration to the suburbs commenced anew.

Today's "infinite suburbia" is considerably more varied and dynamic than the 1950s stereotype of America's suburbs as a string of leafy, affluent, single-home communities.[39] At mid-century, at a time when many Americans families still did not own an automobile or had only one car, suburban development was in its relative infancy. Over the decades that followed, advances in transportation and telecommunication led to the emergence of a new suburbia that became home to corporate office parks, research-and-technology firms, various retail and entertainment activities, and a new population diversity.

Economic activities once sited only in central cities are now commonly found along highways and around airports, in **edge cities** (where the concentration of office parks, technology-related firms, restaurants, shopping, and entertainment centers form "suburban downtowns"), in big-box retail outlets, and in the **edgeless city** of "strip malls" of offices, specialty stores, and restaurants located along less prominent suburban roadways.[40]

A rising number of immigrants and ethnic and racial minorities now reside in the suburbs. The number of immigrants and minorities who live in the suburbs actually surpasses the number who reside in central cities![41] The geographical changes are even reflected in food and dining; in Los Angeles as in other metropolitan areas, the most interesting ethnic restaurants and cafés can be found in the suburbs.

Contrary to the 1950s suburban stereotype, contemporary suburbia is not uniformly affluent. By the twenty-first century, the number of poor families living in suburbs surpassed the number living in central cities—even though poverty rates (which indicate the chance that a person will be poor) remain higher in central cities.[42]

PUBLIC AND PRIVATE POWER IN URBAN AMERICA

Patterns of urban growth, decline, and inequality are not inevitable. Urban change is not simply the unalterable result of natural forces. As Flint's and Detroit's deindustrialization and long-term decline serve to demonstrate, urban problems are also the result of decisions made by governmental officials and by private-sector actors pursuing corporate investment decisions and practices that have great impacts on local communities.

As we have already seen, the Flint water crisis offers a clear glimpse of the immense impact that the state and national governments have on local well-being. The State of Michigan exercised its formal prerogative to put the City of Flint into virtual receivership. The state government and state-appointed officials essentially forced the city to switch its water source, the action that precipitated the lead poisoning crisis. State and federal regulatory officials failed to adequately monitor the water quality of the Flint River and the purity of the water supplied to Flint's taps. State officials were particularly irresponsive when Flint parents expressed their concerns over the appearance of the water and the health problems their children were suffering. State officials even objected to plans to reconnect Flint to Detroit Water. Chapter 2 presents an overview of the numerous state and national government spending, taxing, and regulatory policies that have had an impact—often an inadvertent impact—on local well-being.

Chapter 3 details the long-term shift of population and power to America's suburbs. But a second great power shift in the United States is the result of a much different demographic change, the shift of population and power from the **Frostbelt** (the Northeast and Central United States) to the **Sunbelt** (the South and Southwest). The long-term movement of population and power to the Sunbelt has decreased Congress's interest in enacting strong programs of assistance designed to combat the ills faced by cities like Flint and Detroit.

The 2010 United States Census led to further a reapportionment of congressional representatives that reinforced the political power of the Sunbelt: Sunbelt states gained an additional 12 seats in the United States House of Representative. Texas, alone, picked up four additional seats; Florida gained two new members of Congress. In contrast, the Northeast and the Midwest saw their representation in Congress continue to fall. New York and Ohio each lost two congressional seats; Illinois, Massachusetts, Michigan, and Pennsylvania lost one apiece. A majority of the seats in the U.S. House of Representatives—263 of 435—are in the South and the West.[43]

Private actors, too, possess significant power in the urban arena. The renaissance of central business districts and core-city reflects the power and actions of a city's **growth coalition**, the global corporations, locally rooted business enterprises, property developers, real-estate firms, construction unions, and other interests that benefit from a city's promotion and continued subsidization of specific growth projects. As Chapters 4 and 5 describe, cities invest heavily in new sports stadiums, convention centers, gaming casinos, and historic-themed entertainment districts as demanded by private actors who gain financially from the development of the Tourist City. State governments, like their municipal counterparts, similarly invest heavily to build the Global City, "wiring" the city and providing the "smart grids" and cutting-edge telecommunications infrastructure demanded by multinational corporations and technology-oriented firms.

Private interests act to take advantage of municipal fiscal emergencies. In fiscally strapped Detroit, Flint, and Vallejo and Stockton (California), private interests and their conservative political allies used the prospect of impending municipal bankruptcy to force unwilling local governments to adopt a more business-like model of municipal operations, lowering the taxes imposed on business, downsizing government, reducing public services, and dismissing public workers from their jobs. Elite interests used the threat of an impending local fiscal crises to make past labor contracts "rewritable."[44] These interests sought to force municipal labor unions to accept reductions in the level of health care and pension benefits provided municipal workers.

POWER: THE ABILITY TO GET THINGS DONE

The particular focus of this book is on power and how it is exercised in the urban arena. The study of cities and suburbs requires that we look not only at the structure and formal powers of local government and the decisions made by local public officials. A more complete understanding of urban politics requires that we examine the important impact that intergovernmental actors—state and national officials—exert on urban affairs. We must also examine the ability of corporations and other private actors to influence what gets done (and what courses of action and whose needs are ignored) in the urban arena.

Power is often viewed as **social control**; a political actor possesses power when he or she can force others to comply with his or her wishes. Under this rudimentary definition of power, an actor has "power over" others who fear sanctions or punishments should they fail to behave as expected.

In the study of urban politics, however, the exercise of power does not refer only to situations of social control where a person or group has "power over" someone else. Rather, power also exercised in **social production** or the "power to" get important things done. An actor has power when he or she has the ability to organize action that will get important projects accomplished. A person whose involvement is essential to the construction of a new office project or sports arena or who can bring about a major change in programs that a city offers its homeless population has power. Power is exercised when a person or group successfully arranges coordination—joint action—in the pursuit of goals.[45]

Joint action denotes that power can be exercised positively as part of collaborative actions. The exercise of power does not always entail conflict and a resort to overt or even hidden threats. When a person or private entity refuses to commit to a joint venture and the project folds, his or her power is readily revealed.

Local elected officials in Detroit and Flint simply lacked the ability to organize much in the way of meaningful social production. They lacked the power to get meaningful things done. Local officials lacked the means to attract new investments to the city, investments that would provide the basis for local economic growth and reduce joblessness. Local officials lacked the ability to provide quality public services to the residents of poorer neighborhoods. Local officials in these cities possessed no power to constrain suburbanization, reduce racial segregation in city schools, provide quality housing to families in need, upgrade the city's deteriorating physical infrastructure, and otherwise reverse the effects of their city's decades-long decline. Locally elected officials in Detroit and Flint further lacked the authority to impose forms of taxation that could raise the funds necessary to sustain neighborhood service provision and to avert municipal bankruptcy.

In Detroit and Flint, state-appointed fiscal managers—not local elected officials—possessed the ability to force municipal service cutbacks and even the abrogation of key elements in past contracts with municipal workers. In Flint, only the state-appointed emergency manager had power to arrange a key decision of social production; he had the power to force other actors to switch the source of the city's drinking water. The state and its appointed emergency managers exercised power. But, in this case, the exercise of power without the safeguards of citizen participation (the subject of Chapter 8) and democratic accountability to local voters proved disastrous.

POWER VERSUS POWERS

The concept of *power*—the ability to get things done—needs to be distinguished from the related concept of *powers* or the formal bits of authority that are granted to a city and to municipal officials. The term "powers" denotes a city's "formal authority to engage in particular activities," a definition that urban law expert Richard Schragger utilizes in his analysis of the paucity of formal powers typically granted cities, a paucity that limits the ability of local governments and regional bodies to respond effectively to urban problems. Each state government determines just what exact powers will be granted to its various units of local government. In general, the states have allowed localities only limited governing powers, denying them the more extensive taxing, borrowing, spending, and regulatory powers that would enable municipalities to take strong and effective action to alleviate urban ills. Cities in the United States are severely hobbled in their efforts to combat urban problems as they are seldom given the formal powers—the legal grants of authority—necessary to get important things done.[46]

Chapter 6 of *Urban Politics* details the degree to which the states delegate to municipal governments only limited taxing, spending, and problem-solving powers. States also establish local political boundaries and require forms of local government—such as the weak-mayor structure of city government and the creation independent narrow-purpose special service districts—that wind up dispersing political power at the local level.

Effective urban problem solving is further constrained by an anti-government element in the American culture known as *privatism*. In the United States a prevailing culture of **privatism** serves to keep public planning and governmental authority to a minimum so as to keep governments from intruding on the liberty of individual citizens and other private-sector actors. The privatist American culture tends to view the appropriate functions of local government rather narrowly; cities are seen primarily as places where private actors pursue homeownership, make investment decisions, and freely engage in business activities. In the American "private city,"[47] homeowners and business enterprises enjoy great leeway to utilize their property as they see fit. Privatism views governmental powers as a threat to individual freedoms and property rights.

A privatist nation limits the formal authority of local and regional governments. As a result, many of the most consequential decisions that affect a city's economic health and well-being are made not by public officials but by private actors: business leaders, real-estate developers, bankers, mortgage lenders, the directors of nonprofit organizations, and even individual home seekers. City officials cannot dictate "good" urban development. Instead, public officials in the United States must seek to persuade private actors to undertake actions that are important to a city. In the United States, urban problem solving requires effective coalition building, partnerships that entail joint action by various government entities and private-sector actors.

Americans as a whole resist the enactment of strong urban planning requirements and land-use restrictions that are so commonplace in European cities. Local and regional officials in Europe often have a variety of land-use and policy tools that American mayors and regional planners can only look upon with envy. In Europe, government officials can enact strong regulations on land use, even regulating building facades and storefronts in order to protect the architectural integrity and attractiveness of historic core-city areas. Local and regional governments in Europe also rely on public investment, with municipalities buying up available land in order to guide urban development, to preserve natural areas from the encroachment of new construction and development. In the United States, cities are only just beginning to engage in "land banking" (a tool that is described in Chapter 11).

Compared to the United States, local and regional governments in Europe possess stronger policy tools to curb urban sprawl, to preserve historic areas and the city streetscape, to construct effective mass transit systems, and to build affordable housing. Indeed, "social housing" developments in Europe typically serve a broader range of citizenry, with public housing projects providing homes to working-class as well as low-income families who lack the money to secure suitable apartments in the private market. In the United States, the provision of public housing is much more limited.[48]

To discourage automobile usage, protect the natural environment, and promote city livability, European governments invest heavily in mass transit systems, establish pedestrian-free zones in the center of cities, limit parking in the downtown, and even set the timing of stoplights to slow the movement of traffic.[49] A number of American communities, as we shall see in Chapter 12, are beginning to follow the Europe example by promoting bicycling and other public actions to reduce pollution and promote sustainable development. U.S. cities have been increasingly innovative in their actions to protect the natural environment; but compared to Europe, U.S. cities are playing catch-up.

In more recent years, cities in the United States have demonstrated their willingness to act in a number of relatively new local policy areas. Cities have legislated an increase in the local minimum wage, protected the rights of gays and lesbians, and adopted a series of steps to curb global warming. As Richard Schragger points out, "political localism" or the actions that a city decides to initiate can actually exceed "legal localism, or the powers that a state formally grants a local jurisdiction."[50] *Urban Politics* will pay special attention to this relatively new wrinkle in the political development of cities—the rise of more activist American cities willing to undertake actions in a broad range of policy areas, including areas not traditionally seen as falling under the domain of local government.

THE THEMES OF THE BOOK

As already noted, the major focus of this book is on power, especially the interrelationship of public authority and private power in urban affairs. Six additional themes (or subthemes) further guide this book's study of the politics of U.S. cities and suburbs.

GLOBALIZATION: A POWERFUL INFLUENCE IN THE LOCAL ARENA

Globalization—the cross-border flow of investment, the outsourcing of production to sites located in other countries, the rise of internationally based as opposed to locally rooted businesses, and heightened immigration—has had a great influence on the contemporary urban situation. The competition for business no longer takes place only among the cities and suburbs of a single metropolitan region; instead, economic competition has become national and global in its scope. The actions of private managers have always had an impact on a locality's affairs. But in a global age, managers who move from city to city may lack the sense of civic loyalty and engagement in a locality's affairs that an earlier generation of locally rooted downtown business leaders once displayed.

Globalization also entails the cross-border flow of population. Modern transportation enables large numbers of people from abroad to travel to the United States. The relaxation of the nation's immigration laws in the decades preceding the Trump presidency, too, served to alter the demography and the politics of U.S. cities. In 2016, 22 of the nation's 30 largest cities had a population that was more than one-fifth foreign born. Over half the residents of the City of Miami (52 percent) were born outside the United States; in Santa Ana, nearly half (46 percent) came from other countries. Other cities with large foreign-born populations included San Jose (39 percent foreign born), Los Angeles (38 percent), Anaheim (37 percent), New York City (37 percent) San Francisco (35 percent), Houston (29 percent), and Boston (27 percent).[51]

In a global age, both legal and undocumented immigrants represent an infusion of capital and labor into the local economy. Immigrants can provide the initiative, labor, and capital for new business start-ups. New arrivals, however, can add to the costs of public service provision. But the burden on the taxpayer varies considerably from jurisdiction to jurisdiction. The burden largely represents the costs of educating the children of new arrivals, as immigrants tend to have families with children. In terms of non-school services, immigrants are similar to the native population in their public cost profile.[52]

The new immigration is not only reshaping the politics of big cities; it is also altering politics in suburbs and smaller cities. As Chapters 3 and 4 discuss in further detail, newcomers to the United States now reside in a more widely dispersed set of communities than did the waves of immigrants who came to America during earlier eras in the nation's history. Foreign-born families are no longer found solely in port-of-entry cities; today, recent arrivals can also be found in heartland cities like Denver, Indianapolis, Minneapolis, and St. Paul. Today, immigrants look to smaller cities and the suburbs for affordable housing and job opportunism. By 2010, over half of the immigrant population of the United States was living in suburbs.[53]

THE CONTINUING IMPORTANCE OF THE FORMAL RULES AND STRUCTURES OF URBAN GOVERNMENT

This book stresses the critical role played by private power in the urban arena. Nongovernmental institutions and players are key participants in urban decision making even though they have no formal position of authority in city government. Yet the formal rules and structures of local government remain important. The formal structures and processes of local government help determine just whose interests are heard and represented in city hall. This book examines the extent to which different interests in the city have sought to change the structures and formal rules of local politics, including present-day voter identification and registration requirements and other rules for the conduct of local elections. This book also examines the extent to which different forms of local government (for instance, the council-manager plan as opposed to the strong-mayor form of government) privilege different interests and policy actions in the local political arena.

The formal position of local government in the American federal system is largely set by the U.S. Constitution. To be more precise, the U.S. Constitution makes no explicit mention of cities and lists no constitutionally protected powers for cities. Each of the 50 states decides just what units of local government it will create and just what exact authority or formal powers each unit may—and may not—possess. While the powers that are decentralized to the various types of local government (i.e. cities, counties, townships, special districts) vary considerably from state to state, in general, state-imposed rules have tended to fragment local authority. The states have created numerous and relatively autonomous general-purpose governments (cities, counties, townships, etc.), specialized local political bodies (including school districts, water conservation districts, and library districts), and multiservice entities such as the bi-state Port Authority of New York and New Jersey that are active in a broad range of regional transportation and economic development projects.

Constitutionally speaking, municipalities are mere administrative subdivisions of a state's government. Each state determines the exact powers of its various local governments. State laws tend to limit the taxing and borrowing capacities of local governments. Even the question of whether or not a fiscally distressed city or county may file for federal bankruptcy protection is a matter that is left up to each state. Nearly half (23) of the states prohibit municipal filings for bankruptcy protection.[54] State constitutions and laws generally serve to constrain, but on occasion may facilitate, local action.

THE INTERGOVERNMENTAL CITY: THE IMPACT OF THE STATES AND THE FEDERAL GOVERNMENT IN URBAN AFFAIRS

Cities and suburbs exist in an intergovernmental setting where the actions of national and state decision makers have a profound impact on the resources and problem-solving capabilities of local governments. The *intergovernmental city* is highly dependent on decisions made by the state and national governments.

The concept of the **Intergovernmental City** underscores the significant impact that state and national government decision making has on local affairs. State and national financial assistance accounts for 36 percent of local general revenues, a figure that surpasses the revenues that local governments collect from their own property tax levies.[55] Financially distressed communities are even more greatly dependent on intergovernmental assistance for the continued provision of basic municipal and social services. Limited by state laws as to what taxes and tax rates they can levy, many cities cannot easily cover the costs of service provision to compensate for cutbacks in national social and urban programs.[56]

The states and the national government influence cities in other ways that go beyond the provision of fiscal assistance. State and national tax laws have a great impact on local affairs. Changes in the federal tax laws, for instance, can alter the willingness of private investors to buy municipal bonds, affecting the interest rates that municipalities ultimately pay when borrowing funds to finance new schools, roads, and other infrastructure projects. The tax provisions of federal law affect the willingness of house seekers to purchase new home. The federal tax code also can affect the willingness of private investors to participate in joint actions to help construct affordable housing.

The regulations that accompany state and federal aid programs often serve to constrain local government. Federal and state **mandates** can be particularly burdensome as they require local governments to provide specific services but without providing the accompanying funds to cover the full costs of those services. A state can impose expensive service costs on local governments that other states do not. Less than half of the states (that is, only 18 states) require counties to contribute to the state share of providing Medicaid, the nation's $500 billion program that helps to pay for health care for the poor and working poor. New York State mandates that its counties, including multicounty New York City, cover approximately half the state share (the non-federal share) of the Medicaid services provided to needy residents. This is the largest Medicaid burden that any of the 50 states imposes on local government. The state mandate means that each year New York City must find $5 billion in revenues to help provide Medicaid,[57] a requirement that effectively diverts city resources from other local service areas.

Chapter 11 details the rather tenuous position of local government in the American intergovernmental system. The chapter also traces the evolving Democratic and Republican approaches to urban policy. Special attention is given to how the actions of President Donald Trump (and, during his first two years in office, those of a Republican-controlled Congress) have added to the precarious position of the Intergovernmental City.

THE DOMINANCE OF ECONOMIC DEVELOPMENT CONCERNS IN THE LOCAL ARENA

By the early twenty-first century, local economic development was clearly the Number One issue on the agenda of most cities, crowding out more traditional local government concerns. Cities and suburbs employ a variety of strategies as they seek to win the interlocal competition for the location of businesses, a competition that at times will occur on a national and global scale. Postindustrial dislocation, advances in telecommunications, and the globalization of corporate structures have all served to increase capital mobility, adding to the sense of economic insecurity of local communities.

Local economic development concerns did not always occupy such a dominant place in urban politics. In the 1960s, battles over school busing, community control, big-city riots, civilian-police review boards, and antipoverty programs defined urban politics. A half century later, however, these competing issue concerns have largely fallen to the wayside as local officials give priority to efforts aimed at attracting new industries.

Of course, even today, economic development is not the only matter before cities. Crime remains a salient issue in many communities (even though crime data reveal a drop in recent years). The Black Lives Matter movement is attempting to force the issue of police violence—especially the police shooting of unarmed black youth—onto the big-city political agenda. Younger and more upscale voters also exhibit a concern for **ecological sustainability**, for having the city take actions that will conserve energy resources and protect the natural environment. Communities in the arid Southwest and West seek creative ways to respond to the limited availability of water, as shortages of this critical resource can impose severe constraints on local industrial and residential growth. By the early 2010s, the debate over immigration and the status of undocumented workers was also clearly on the local as well as the national agenda.

Still, despite the attention that these other issues can at times command, economic development remains the single dominant issue in the urban arena. Cities and suburbs have responded to the fragility of their economic position with a large variety of programs aimed at promoting local economic growth and job creation. Cities provide considerable financial subsidies in their efforts to attract and retain businesses. Cities even provide massive subsidies for the construction of new sports arenas. This is money that cities could have spent to improve public health and safety or to increase workforce training and the quality of education in troubled neighborhoods. The undue emphasis on economic development represents a distorted sense of just what urban politics is about, as cities prioritize economic growth over initiatives aimed at improving troubled neighborhoods and mitigating urban inequality.[58]

THE NEW ACTIVISM OF CITIES

As we have already observed, the constitutional position of cities generally serves to limit a city's formal powers and the power of a city to get important things done. Yet, as a wave of contemporary local policy activism reveals, the limited constitutional position of cities does *not* put local governments in a policy straitjacket where movement is impossible. Instead, modern city governments are active problem solvers that initiate their own courses of action in response to urban problems.

U.S. cities have taken a number of actions aimed at protecting residents who have committed no crime other than their residential status, actions that cities ramped up when confronted by President Trump's decision to round up and deport illegal immigrants. New York's Bill de Blasio and Los Angeles's Eric Garcetti were among the mayors who boycotted a White House meeting when the President Trump threatened to reduce federal law enforcement assistance funds to cities that refused to assist federal officials in the round-up of undocumented immigrants. Cities responded to the Trump directive by suing the federal government in court. The cities argued that the president possessed no legal authority to add new program requirements to a law enforcement assistance program that had already been authorized by Congress. The cities argued that the national administration lacked the legal authority to alter the contractual terms of programs to which communities had previously agreed.

As Chapters 11 and 12 will describe in further detail, the American federal system gives subnational government a considerable degree of autonomy. The national government cannot simply commandeer local government personnel in an effort to accomplish its own policy ends. Austin, Texas, not only fought the restrictive immigration policies of Trump administration; the city also sought to thwart a new anti-sanctuary-city law enacted by the State of Texas. Austin, declared itself a "freedom city" where local police officers were not permitted to ask persons about their immigration status. Faced with the new Texas law, a unanimous vote of the city council simply added a new instruction, that Austin officers inform suspects that they had the right not to answer any queries about their immigration status.[59]

Mayors Garcetti, De Blasio, and Chicago's Rahm Emanuel were among the local officials who attacked President Trump for threatening to deport the so-called Dreamers, the 800,000 persons who as children had been brought illegally to the United States. The Obama administration's Deferred Action for Childhood Arrivals (DACA) program gave these children a reprieve from deportation, offering them a path to citizenship, a status that President Trump allowed to expire. The DACA children completed high school and, as they grew older, gained employment, paid taxes, and contributed tens of billions of dollars to the nation's economy. The mayors not only objected that Trump was punishing younger persons who knew no home other than the United States. The mayors also argued that the expulsion of the Dreamers would hurt the local economy.

Mayor Emanuel declared Chicago a "Trump-free zone," observing that the city would continue to welcome the Dreamers who would not have to worry about expulsion.[60] Emanuel announced that the city would continue to offer free tuition at the City Universities of Chicago to undocumented children who graduated from the city's public schools with a grade average of "B" or better. San Diego's Kevin Faulconer, a Republican who in the past had observed that San Diego was not a "sanctuary city," took to Twitter to declare his support for the Dreamers and to urge DACA's renewal.

When Trump ordered the separation of families who had no documented status—a move that at the border separated children from their parents—Garcetti, de Blasio, Miami's Francis Suarez, and Austin's Steve Adler were among the mayors who visited a Texas detention center—a tent city for the children taken into custody—in order to cast a spotlight on the lack of human compassion of Trump's actions.

Atlanta Mayor Keisha Lance Bottoms went further and issued an executive order that prohibited the city jail from accepting new detainees from Immigration and Customs Enforcement (ICE) officials until the national government ended its "despicable immigration policy" of separating families at the border. Sacramento and Contra Costa Counties in northern California announced that they would not renew their contracts to house ICE detainees in county jails, despite the loss of revenues the counties would suffer as a result of the contract terminations.[61]

In their actions to protect immigrants, cities were claiming policy authority. New York Mayor Bill de Blasio defiantly observed, "There is not a national police force." Instead, New York City would continue to "stand up for" and protect its people. New York would not let its police officer comply with federal actions that discriminated against immigrants and tore families apart. Community theorist Benjamin Barber characterized de Blasio's proclamation as "fighting words" in defense of cities.[62]

A second important policy area further underscores the increased policy activism of cities: Cities have undertaken a new range of actions in response to climate change. After President Trump withdrew the United States from the 2015 Paris climate accord, more than 30 mayors publicly pledged that their cities would continue programs to meet greenhouse gas (GHG) emission targets.[63] New York City had previously pledged to reduce its GHG emissions by 80% by 2050. In the wake of Trump's withdrawal, New York Mayor de Blasio signed an executive order committing the city to the goals of the Paris accord. New York also became the first U.S. city to voluntarily give the United Nations a progress report showing the steps that the city was implementing to meet sustainable development goals.[64]

Why have cities continued to seek participation in global councils on climate change? City leaders are aware of the costs that a rise in global temperatures will impose on their people and their communities. New York, Miami, Ft. Lauderdale, Tampa, Charleston, Atlantic City, and Boston are among the more vulnerable coastal cities that would suffer increases in flooding and a loss of real estate with a rise in sea levels.[65] As cities are "heat islands" where concrete, asphalt, and paved surfaces concentrate heat, spikes in temperatures would likely result in spikes in urban mortality. Utility costs in cities would rise with the greater need for air conditioning.

Higher temperatures may also impair labor productivity, making cities less attractive locations for businesses.[66]

Former New York City Mayor Michael Bloomberg explained how the structure of federalism gives cities the constitutional power to join in global efforts to counter global warming: "While the executive branch of the U.S. government speaks on behalf of our nation in matters of foreign affairs, it does not determine many aspects of whether and how the United States takes action on climate change."[67] Cities stepped onto a global stage when President Trump withdrew.[68]

Chapter 12 looks at the future of urban politics and concludes with an overview of the wide variety of "green" actions that U.S. cities have adopted to reduce energy consumption, to stem GHG emissions, to curtail pollution, and to promote sustainable development. In the fight against global warming, as in efforts to protect immigrant families, mayors find that to truly govern they must move beyond limited conceptualizations of a city's powers and authority.[69]

RACE AND ETHNICITY: THEIR CONTINUING IMPORTANCE IN URBAN AFFAIRS

In the United States, urban politics is intertwined with the politics of race and ethnicity. The new immigration has further added to the complexity of intergroup relations in the American city.

In recent decades, there has been much good news when it comes to race and ethnicity in the American metropolis. Statistical trends reveal an increase in residential integration in most metropolitan areas. The all-white suburb has virtually disappeared from the metropolitan landscape. Important progress toward residential desegregation has occurred.

Yet, despite these very important gains, the data also point to the persistence of ghettoization and to continued racial disparities and discrimination in housing markets. The federal government's fair housing laws have helped to eradicate the most blatant forms of housing discrimination. But more subtle discriminations still mar the search for housing.[70]

Despite the gains in residential integration, the **hypersegregation** of African Americans continues as African Americans continue to be concentrated in core areas of the city, areas of poverty and spatial disadvantage. One-third of African Americans live in hypersegregated portions of the city. Baltimore, Birmingham, Chicago, Cleveland, Detroit, Flint, Milwaukee, and St. Louis are all cities that have particularly high levels of racial isolation and hypersegregation.[71]

Local zoning and land-use ordinances have an impact that serves to physically divide Americans. Land-use and zoning regulations help to assure that richer and poorer families, and families of different races and ethnicities, will reside in different communities and that their children attend different school systems. Numerous suburbs use their powers to control land uses to bar or limit low-income housing projects. Other communities limit the development of multifamily housing, implementing zoning and land-use restrictions that reinforce the class and racial segregation of the contemporary metropolis.

Statistical evidence reveals troubling trends when it comes to the racial makeup of public-school populations in an era when judicial decisions have given localities new latitude to terminate desegregation efforts.[72] The United States is no longer making progress toward school integration. In fact, the United States has moved in the opposite direction, toward an increasing **resegregation** of public schools, with an increasing number of African-American and Latino students learning in racially isolated school environments.[73] Many suburban schools have only a quite minimal African-American enrollment.

Figure 1.6   **Race Still Shapes the Metropolis: "Thank You" Sign to the Local Sheriff in Gretna, Louisiana**. After Hurricane Katrina, the 2005 storm that devastated New Orleans, residents of the white working-class suburb of Gretna placed "Thank You" signs in their front yards to express their support for the controversial actions of local sheriff. Sheriff Arthur Lawson. Lawson had gained national notoriety when he had local officers barricade his side of the bridge across the Mississippi River, blocking entry by poor African Americans who were attempting to cross the bridge to Gretna in order to flee death-ravaged New Orleans. CNN broadcasts at the time even revealed dead bodies floating down city streets amid the extensive flooding of the Crescent City. When buses did not arrive to evacuate the poor, and water and supplies ran out, and when toilets and air conditioning stopped at the Superdome (the city's evacuation point), a number of New Orleans residents attempted to flee to safety—only to be stopped by Lawson's police. Was race a factor in the lack of humanity extended to people, including the elderly and children, in the midst of such a dire emergency?

The famous 1954 U.S. Supreme Court decision ***Brown v. Board of Education*** began the prolonged process of bringing an end to ***de jure* segregation**, that is, an end to state- or government-ordered school segregation. But *Brown* did not end ***de facto* segregation**, the extensive segregation of public-school classrooms that exists "in fact" but is not required by state or local law. The racial imbalances that exist today in public schools are largely a reflection of residential patterns, the differences in the racial and ethnic composition of various city neighborhoods, and the difference in the demographics of city and suburban school districts. While Americans continue to decry the evil of *de jure* segregation, there is no equivalent willingness to combat *de facto* segregation.

The racial divisions that characterize contemporary metropolitan American are sometimes revealed in moments of crisis. In the midst of the misery wrought by Hurricane Karina, the 2005 storm that devastated New Orleans, the police department of suburban Gretna barricaded the bridge across the Mississippi, turning back black New Orleans residents who were attempting to flee the death and destruction in their flood-ravaged city (see Figure 1.6 for more details). In Flint, Michigan, where state officials were slow to respond to the urgent concerns of parents for the health of their children, some observers wondered if the state would have been equally insensitive to complaints from more affluent and largely white communities. Across the nation, the state takeover of

Source: Photo by Infrogman, November 25, 2005/Wikimedia Commons, http://commons.wikimedia.org/wiki/File: Gretna 23NovThankChiefLarson1.jpg.

cities and school systems has largely affected poor minority communities. Would the states be as willing to exert their powers to deny white suburbs their political autonomy?

The continuing significance of race in urban affairs is also apparent in the controversies over the police shootings of African-American youth, who often were unarmed. In 2014 in Ferguson, Missouri, a suburb outside of St. Louis, riots erupted as protestors vented their anger over the shooting of an unarmed black youth by a white officer. Protestors complained about the city's militaristic approach to policing and the irresponsiveness of the municipal government to African-American voices. Although two-thirds of Ferguson's population is African American, the suburban municipality had a white-dominated government: the mayor, the police chief, and five of the six city council members were white.

The Black Lives Matter movement protested what residents saw as the too-quick willingness of police officers to resort to lethal force in situations that could have been resolved by less deadly means. A number of deadly encounters gained national attention and continued to drive the national debate.

In Baltimore in 2015, Freddie Gray died from spinal injuries sustained as a result of the "rough ride" he was given, as he was left unbuckled and bounced around the back of a police van. In the preceding year on New York City's Staten Island, Eric Garner died as the result of a chokehold, firmly applied by a plainclothes officer while two other officers held Garner down and compressed his chest despite Garner's last words: "I can't breathe" (Figure 1.7). The crime that led to the deadly encounter? Garner had sold individual cigarettes without having paid the required tax.

Figure 1.7   **"I Can't Breathe."** Protesters hold a sign repeating the last words of Eric Garner, as they march against the resort to lethal force by police. Photo taken at a rally in Washington, DC, December 13, 2014.

Source: Photo by Rena Schild/Shutterstock.com.

In 2018, an independent autopsy showed that the Sacramento police had fired eight bullets into unarmed Stephon Clark, age 22, while he was in his grandparents's backyard. The officers, looking for a person who was reported to be wearing a hoodie and breaking car windows, tracked Clark by helicopter. Officers pursued him into the backyard, yelled "Gun!" as they entered, and opened fire, having mistaken Clark's cell phone for a handgun.[74]

In Chicago, a police officer shot 17-year-old Laquan McDonald 16 times, with most of the shots fired as McDonald fell and was lying on the ground. Three years later, prompted by continuing protests and the unrelenting glare of media coverage given the killing, the white officer who fired the shots was charged with first-degree murder. Such attempts at punishment and accountability are rare. Even when an incident gains substantial national attention, law enforcement officers are rarely punished as the use of lethal force is viewed as justified.[75] Police officers are seldom seriously penalized for filing false reports that attempt to put an officer's use of lethal force in a more favorable light (a matter that will be discussed further in Chapter 9).

CONCLUSION: THE URBAN SITUATION

There is no single urban situation. The contemporary urban situation is certainly one of great metropolitan inequalities. A number of American cities and suburbs have "come back" and are doing quite well; but others have not. While numerous inner-city communities across the nation have gentrified, other neighborhoods in the urban core continue to suffer disinvestment and descent. The nation's most distressed cities, especially former industrial centers, have lost such substantial population and economic activity that they may lack the ability to come back on their own. Cleveland, Youngstown, and other hard-hit cities, particularly in the Frostbelt, have turned to a **shrinking cities strategy**, repurposing large tracts of the city for use as community gardens, urban farms, and green space. Detroit's shrinking cities strategy (or a "right-sizing" strategy, as its advocates euphemistically call it), seeks to save money by taking certain depopulated neighborhoods "off line," reducing the level of municipal services provided to depopulated neighborhoods.

New York, San Francisco, San Jose, San Diego, and Boston are among the cities where economic transformation has led to soaring housing prices, with housing often priced beyond the reach of workers, not just the poor. In the postindustrial city, pricey areas of privilege are found in close proximity to areas suffering continued decline. Suburbia, too, shows evidence of a new diversity and inequality. Affluent residential communities and dynamic technoburbs and edge cities are areas of economic prosperity and privilege that are clearly different from older and inner-ring suburban communities that have had to cope with poverty, vacant housing and storefronts, and the arrival of new immigrants.

One political fact is quite clear: The United States is a suburban nation. Despite the much acclaimed downtown revival and the comeback of numerous core-city neighborhoods, the march of population and voting power to the suburbs continues. "Urban politics" is about suburbs as much as about cities. The shift of population and voting power to the suburbs will continue to have a lasting impact on urban politics and policy.

The next chapter tells the story of how the great cities of the United States grew but then saw population and power shift to the suburbs. The demographic shifts and economic dislocations that buffeted cities and suburbs were not entirely "natural" or foreordained. Exercises of public and private power shaped the urban situation, helping to determine which communities grew and which declined.

KEY TERMS

agglomeration, cities and the advantages of economic (*p. 9*)
Brown v. Board of Education (*p. 30*)
cluster development (*p. 9*)
creative class (*p. 11*)
de facto segregation (*p. 30*)
de jure segregation (*p. 30*)
ecological sustainability (*p. 26*)
edge cities (*p. 19*)
edgeless city (*p. 19*)
erosion of the city tax base (*p. 15*)
Frostbelt (*p. 20*)
gentrification (*p. 8*)
Global City (*p. 9*)
globalization (*p. 9*)
globalized economy (*p. 8*)
growth coalition, a city's (*p. 20*)

hypersegregation (*p. 29*)
Intergovernmental City (*p. 25*)
mandates, state and federal (*p. 25*)
municipal pension crisis (*p. 17*)
new immigration (*p. 10*)
power as social control (*p. 21*)
power as social production (*p. 21*)
privatism (*p. 22*)
resegregation of public schools (*p. 30*)
shrinking cities strategy (*p. 32*)
social control (*p. 21*)
social production (*p. 21*)
suburbanization (*p. 18*)
Sunbelt (*p. 20*)
tourist bubble, a city's (*p. 14*)
Tourist City (*p. 11*)
winner-take-all urbanism (*p. 14*)

NOTES

1. Hurley Medical Center, "Pediatric Lead Exposure in Flint, MI: Concerns from the Medical Community," September 2015, http://flintwaterstudy.org/2015/09/pediatric-lead-exposure-presentation-from-hurley-medical-center-doctors-concerning-flint-mi/.
2. World Health Organization, "Lead Poisoning and Health," *Fact Sheet*, February 9, 2018, www.who.int/en/news-room/fact-sheets/detail/lead-poisoning-and-health; Yanan Wang, "In Flint, Mich., There's So Much Lead in Children's Blood That a State of Emergency Is Declared," *Washington Post*, December 15, 2015.
3. Rochelle Riley, "Sh-h-h. Snyder State Update Left Out 75% Drop in Reading Proficiency in Flint," *Detroit Free Press*, February 6, 2018.
4. For details of Flint's mounting debt problem, see the State of Michigan Department of Treasury, "Report of the Flint Financial Review Team," *Letter to the Governor*, November 7, 2011, www.michigan.gov/documents/treasury/Flint-ReviewTeamReport-11-7-11_417437_7.pdf.
5. John Counts, "Flint Water Crisis Got Its Start as a Money-Saving Move in Department of Treasury," *MLive*, May 3, 2016, www.mlive.com/news/index.ssf/2016/05/flint_water_crisis_got_its_sta.html. Counts traces the very complex story of the shifting positions of Governor Snyder and other state officials on whether Flint should be permitted to withdraw from its arrangement for Detroit water.

6. Siddhartha Roy, "Commentary: MDEQ Mistakes and Deception Created the Flint Water Crisis," *Flint Water Studies Update Blog Post*, September 30, 2015, http://flintwaterstudy.org/2015/09/commentary-mdeq-mistakes-deception-flint-water-crisis/.

7. Flint Water Advisory Task Force, letter to Governor Snyder, December 29, 2015, http://flintwaterstudy.org/wp-content/uploads/2015/12/FWATF-Snyder-Letter-12-29-15.pdf.

8. Mona Hanna-Attisha, Jenny LaChance, Richard Casey Sadler, and Allison Champney Schnepp, "Elevated Blood Lead Levels in Children Associated with the Flint Drinking Water Crisis: A Spatial Analysis of Risk and Public Health Response," *American Journal of Public Health* 106, no. 2 (February 2016): 283–290.

9. Christopher Ingraham, "Flint's Lead-Poisoned Water Had a 'Horrifyingly Large' Effect on Fetal Deaths, Study Says," *Washington Post*, September 21, 2017.

10. For an account of the crisis that emphasizes the narrow concerns of state officials and their lack of accountability to the citizens of Flint, see Anna Clark, *The Poisoned City: Flint's Water and the American Urban Tragedy* (New York: Metropolitan Books and Henry Holt & Co., 2018).

11. Michigan Civil Rights Commission, *The Flint Water Crisis: Systemic Racism through the Lens of Flint*, February 17, 2017, www.michigan.gov/documents/mdcr/VFlintCrisisRep-F-Edited3-13-17_554317_7.pdf. The Ann Arbor remark appears on p. 4.

12. Edward Glaeser, *Triumph of the City: How Our Greatest Invention Makes Us Richer, Smarter, Greener, Healthier, and Happier* (New York: Penguin, 2011).

13. Glaeser, *Triumph of the City*; Saskia Sassen, *Cities in a World Economy*, 4th ed. (Los Angeles: Pine Forge Press and Sage Publications, 2011). For classic works on the importance of clustering to economic development, see the writings of economist Michael Porter.

14. Of course, there was no unified vision of just how New York's position in the global economy would be restored and just what should be built on the site of the fallen Twin Tower. In a city as diverse as New York, there are contending interests and competing perspectives on almost every major program. Sagalyn Lynne B, *Power at Ground Zero: Politics, Money, and the Remaking of Lower Manhattan* (Oxford: Oxford University Press, 2016), details the competing interests, perspectives, ambitions, manipulations, and power games—in short, the politics and the exercises of power—that ultimately shaped the post-9/11 reconstruction of Lower Manhattan.

15. Zach Patton, "New Orleans' Latino Population Boom," *Governing*, February 29, 2012, www.governing.com/topics/health-human-services/gov-new-orleans-latino-population-boom.html.

16. See, for instance, Stephen L. Klineberg, "Prophetic City: Houston on the Cusp of a Changing America" (paper presented at the annual meeting of the Urban Affairs Association, Minneapolis, April 20–22, 2017). For slides of polling data on how the residents of Harris County (metropolitan Houston) view immigration, go to http://cmsny.org/wp-content/uploads/2017/04/Stephen-Klineberg.pdf.

17. Steven Greenhouse and Mireya Navarro, "The Hidden Victims," *New York Times*, September 17, 2001.

18. See the following writings by Richard Florida: *The Rise of the Creative Class* (New York: Routledge, 2004); *Cities and the Creative Class* (New York: Routledge, 2004); *Who's Your City: How the Creative Economy Is Making Where to Live the Most Important Decision of Your Life* (New York: HarperCollins, 2009); and *The Rise of the Creative Class: Revisited* (New York: Basic Books, 2012).

19. Terry Nichols Clark with Richard Lloyd, Kenneth K. Wong, and Pushpam Jain, "Amenities Drive Urban Growth: A New Paradigm and Policy Linkages," in *The City as an Entertainment Machine*, ed. Terry Nichols Clark (Lanham, MD: Rowman and Littlefield, 2011), 209–239. The "Seine" quotation appears on p. 221. Also see Timothy J. Guilfoyle, *Millennium Park: Creating a Chicago Landmark* (Chicago: University of Chicago Press, 2006).

20. Dennis R. Judd, "Constructing the Tourist Bubble," in *The Tourist City*, ed. Dennis R. Judd and Susan S. Fainstein (New Haven, CT: Yale University Press, 1999), 35–53; Richard Florida, *The New Urban Crisis: How Our Cities Are Increasing Inequality, Deepening Segregation, and Failing the Middle Class: And What We Can Do About It* (New York: Basic Books, 2017).

21. Gary Sands and Mark Skidmore, "Making Ends Meet: Options for Property Tax Reform in Detroit," *Journal of Urban Affairs* 36, no. 4 (2014): 682–700, esp. 697.
22. Pete Saunders, "Detroit After Bankruptcy," *Forbes Magazine*, April 24, 2016.
23. John L. Mikesell, *Fiscal Administration: Analysis and Applications for the Public Sector*, 8th ed. (Boston, MA: Cengage, 2011), 648–649.
24. Mary Williams Walsh, "Detroit Turns Bankruptcy into Challenge of Banks," *New York Times*, February 4, 2014; Walsh, "Cracks Starting to Appear in Public Pensions' Armor," *New York Times*, February 25, 2015.
25. Nicquel Terry, "Detroit in Full Control of Itself for the 1st Time in Decades," *The Detroit News*, April 30, 2018.
26. The figures for Stockton and San Bernardino are from the California Departments of Finance, "Population Estimates for Cities, Counties, and the State—January 1, 2012 and 2013," (2013). The story of Orange County's 2004 bankruptcy is rather unique, as the county, one of most affluent areas of the nation, should have had no problem in paying its bills. But county voters defeated one proposed tax after another. The county treasurer turned to a high-risk strategy of borrowing funds to invest in the stock market, with the expectation that the investment would yield a return that could help pay for high-level community services. But when the stock market unexpectedly turned sour, the county could not even repay its creditors the money it had borrowed, and the county filed for bankruptcy. See Marc Baldassare, *When Government Fails: The Orange County Bankruptcy* (Berkeley, CA: University of California Press, 1998).
27. Mary Williams Walsh and Jon Hurdle, "Harrisburg Sees Path to Restructuring Debts without Bankruptcy Filing," *New York Times*, July 24, 2013.
28. Jim Christie (Reuters), "Stockton Bankruptcy the Result of 15-Year Spending Binge," *The Huffington Post*, July 4, 2012, www.huffingtonpost.com/2012/07/04/stockton-bankruptcy_n_1648634.html; Mary Williams Walsh, "Creditors of Stockton Fight City Over Pension Funding While in Bankruptcy," *New York Times*, August 24, 2012; Robert C. Pozen, "The Retirement Surprise in Detroit's Bankruptcy," *Brookings Institution*, July 25, 2013, www.brookings.edu/opinions/the-retirement-surprise-in-detroits-bankruptcy/; Jess Bidgood, "Plan to End Bankruptcy in Rhode Island City Gains Approval," *New York Times*, September 7, 2012.
29. Matt Bevilacqua, "Five Major Cities with Pension Troubles Worse Than Detroit," *Next City*, July 19, 2013, http://nextcity.org/daily/entry/five-major-cities-with-pension-troubles-worse-than-indetroit; Melanie Hicken, "Moody's Downgrades Chicago Amid Pension Crisis," *CNN Money*, March 4, 2014, http://money.cnn.com/2014/03/04/news/chicago-credit-rating/.
30. Chuck Reed, "Think Public Pensions Can't Be Cut? Think Again," *Governing Magazine*, April 26, 2017, www.governing.com/gov-institute/voices/col-public-pension-cuts-unsustainable-retirement-systems.html; Monica Davey, Bill Vlasic, and Mary Williams Walsh, "Detroit Ruling on Bankruptcy Lifts Pension Protections," *New York Times*, December 3, 2013; Liz Farmer, "Stockton Bankruptcy Judge Rules against Pensions," *Governing*, October 2, 2014, www.governing.com/news/headlines/gov-stockton-bankruptcy.html.
31. John F. McDonald, "What Happened to and in Detroit?" *Urban Studies* 51, no. 16 (December 2014): 3309–3329.
32. The city suffered from numerous incidents of corruption and mismanagement. Detroit Mayor Kwame Kilpatrick was found guilty in U.S. District Court of bid-rigging in the issuance of city contracts in order to enrich himself, family members, and friends. At one time, the city's misguided pension managers handed municipal retirees a "13th check" or bonus check in a year, resulting in a loss of nearly $2 billion that could have helped shore up the shortfalls in pension accounts.
33. Brent D. Ryan, *Design after Decline: How America Rebuilds Shrinking Cities* (Philadelphia: University of Pennsylvania Press, 2012), xii.
34. See, for instance, Robert Cervero, Erick Guerra, and Stefan Al, *Beyond Mobility: Planning Cities for People and Places* (Washington, DC: Island Press, 2017), 215–216.

35. Morley Winograd and Michael D. Hais, "Millennials' Hearts Are in the Suburbs," in *Infinite Suburbia*, ed. Alan M. Berger and Joel Kotkin (Hudson, NY: Princeton Architectural Press, 2017), 66–77.

36. For different interpretations as to what these trends mean for the future of cities, see two articles by David Johnson, "The 25 Suburbs Where Millennials Are Moving," *Time Magazine*, May 3, 2017, and "These Cities Have Already Reached 'Peak Millennial' as Young People Begin to Leave," *Time Magazine*, December 14, 2017; and Joe Cortright, "No, Young People Aren't Fleeing Cities," *CityLab Web Posting*, December 20, 2017, www.citylab.com/life/2017/12/are-young-people-really-leaving-cities/548864/.

37. Dowell Myers, "Peak Millennials: Three Reinforcing Cycles That Amplify the Rise and Fall of Urban Concentration by Millennials," *Housing Policy Debate* (April 2016), DOI: 10.1080/10511482.2016.1165722, http://popdynamics.usc.edu/pdf/2016_Myers_Peak-Millennials.pdf

38. William H. Frey, "US Population Disperses to the Suburbs, Exurbs, Rural Areas, and to 'Middle of the Country' Metros," *The Avenue*, a newsletter of the Brookings Institution, Washington, DC, March 26, 2018, www.brookings.edu/blog/the-avenue/2018/03/26/us-population-disperses-to-suburbs-exurbs-rural-areas-and-middle-of-the-country-metros/.

39. Jon C. Teaford, "The Myth of Homogeneous Suburbia," in *Infinite Suburbia*, 126–133, argues that there is no "one" suburbia. He describes the class, ethnic and racial heterogeneity of suburbs in the United States and around the globe.

40. Joel Garreau, *Edge City: Life on the New Frontier* (New York: Doubleday, 1991); Robert Lang, *Edgeless Cities: Exploring the Elusive Metropolis* (Washington, DC: Brookings Institution, 2003).

41. Alan M. Berger and Joel Kotkin, "Introduction," in *Infinite Suburbia*, 13.

42. Elizabeth Kneebone and Emily Garr, *The Suburbanization of Poverty: Trends in Metropolitan America, 2000 to 2008* (Washington, DC: Brookings Institution, 2010), www.brookings.edu/~/media/Files/rc/papers/2010/0120_poverty_kneebone/0120_poverty_paper.pdf; Scott W. Allard and Benjamin Roth, *Strained Suburbs: The Social Service Challenges of Rising Suburban Poverty* (Washington, DC: Brookings Institution, 2010), www.brookings.edu/research/reports/2010/10/07 suburban-poverty-allard-roth; and U.S. Department of Housing and Urban Development, "Meeting the Challenges of Suburban Poverty," *Evidence Matters* (Winter 2012): 16–23, www.huduser.org/portal/periodicals/em/EM_Newsletter_winter_2012_FNL.pdf.

43. U.S. Census Bureau, "Total Population and Population in Incorporated Places by Region: 2000 to 2013," *Current Population Reports: Population Trends in Incorporated Places, 2000–2013* (March 2015), p. 3, Table 1, www.census.gov/content/dam/Census/library/publications/2015/demo/p25-1142.pdf

44. Mary Williams Walsh and Jonathan Glater, "Contracts Now Seen as Being Rewritable," *New York Times*, March 31, 2009. Also see Melody Petersen, "Cities May Use Bankruptcy to Cut Worker Pensions," *Los Angeles Times*, October 2, 2014.

45. For the distinction between power as "social production" as opposed to power as "social control," see Clarence N. Stone, *Regime Politics: Governing Atlanta, 1946–88* (Lawrence: University Press of Kansas, 1989), 8–9, 222–226, and 289.

46. Richard C. Schragger, *City Power: Urban Governance in a Global Age* (New York: Oxford University Press, 2016), 1.

47. For the classic statement that identifies privatism as imposing a severe limit on the actions of U.S. local governments, see Sam Bass Warner, Jr., *The Private City* (Philadelphia: University of Pennsylvania Press, 1968).

48. Lawrence J. Vale and Yonah Freemark, "From Public Housing to Public-Private Housing: 75 Years of American Social Experimentation," *Journal of the American Planning Association* 78, no. 4 (2012): 379–402.

49. Elisabeth Rosenthal, "Across Europe, Irking Drivers Is Urban Policy," *New York Times*, June 26, 2011.

50. Schragger, *City Power*, 83.

51. The 2016 estimates of a city's foreign-born population were obtained from the U.S. Census Bureau's *Quick Facts* report and from the Census Bureau's interactive web portal, www.census.gov/quickfacts/.

52. National Academies of Sciences, Engineering, and Medicine, *The Economic and Fiscal Consequences of Immigration* (Washington, DC: National Academies Press, 2017), www.nap.edu/catalog/23550/the-economic-and-fiscal-consequences-of-immigration. For a somewhat different perspective, see Congressional Budget Office, *The Impact of Unauthorized Immigrants on the Budgets of State and Local Governments* (Washington, DC: CBO, 2007). The CBO report emphasizes the costs that illegal immigration imposes on certain states and communities, especially those located near the United States' southern border.

53. U.S. Census Bureau, *2010 American Community Survey*. See Jill H. Wilson and Audrey Singer, "Immigrants in 2010 Metropolitan America: A Decade of Change," a report of the Metropolitan Policy Program of The Brookings Institution, Washington, DC, October 2011.

54. De Angelis and Tian, "United States: Chapter 9 Municipal Bankruptcy—Utilization, Avoidance, and Impact," 317.

55. The figures is for 2014. See "State (and Local) Taxes" in Tax Policy Center, *The Tax Policy Briefing Book* (Washington, DC: The Urban Institute and The Brookings Institution, 2016), www.taxpolicycenter.org/briefing-book/what-are-sources-revenue-local-governments.

56. Michael A. Pagano and Christopher Hoene, *City Budgets in an Era of Increased Uncertainty: Understanding the Fiscal Policy Space of Cities* (Washington, DC: Brookings Institution, 2018).

57. "County Medicaid Costs," 2015–2016, table cited by U.S. Representative John Faso of New York, https://faso.house.gov/uploadedfiles/nyscountymedicaidcosts.pdf. Also see: Gerald Benjamin and Thomas Gals, "Paying for Medicaid: A Good Idea Whose Time Has Not Yet Come," *The Benjamin Center at SUNY-New Paltz, Blog Post*, September 26, 2017, https://hawksites.newpaltz.edu/currents/2017/09/26/paying-for-medicaid-a-good-idea-whose-time-has-not-yet-come/#_ftnref2; Citizens Budget Commission, *A Poor Way to Pay for Medicaid: Why New York Should Eliminate Local Funding for Medicaid* (New York: December 2011), 12.

58. Schragger, *City Power*.

59. Jaweed Kaleem, "'Freedom City'? Going Beyond 'Sanctuary,' Austin, Texas, Vows to Curb Arrests," *Los Angeles Times*, June 19, 2018.

60. United State Conference of Mayors, "US Mayors to Protect Dreamers," *Web Posting*, September 6, 2017, www.citymayors.com/society/usa-daca-dreamers.html.

61. Jacqueline Thomsen, "Atlanta Mayor Signs Order Blocking City Jail from Accepting New ICE Detainees," *The Hill*, June 20, 2018, http://thehill.com/homenews/state-watch/393340-atlanta-mayor-signs-order-blocking-city-jail-from-accepting-new-ice; Hamed Aleaziz and Rachel Swan, "Amid Immigration Protests, Another California County Cancels Its ICE Contract," *Governing Online Magazine*, July 12, 2018, www.governing.com/topics/public-justice-safety/tns-contra-costa-jail-ice.html.

62. The quotations in this paragraph are from Benjamin R. Barber, *Cool Cities: Urban Sovereignty and the Fix for Global Warming* (New Haven, CT: Yale University Press, 2017), 20–22.

63. Hiroko Tabuchi and Henry Fountain, "Bucking Trump, These Cities, States and Companies Commit to Paris Accord," *New York Times*, June 1, 2017.

64. Nicole Javorsky, "Why New York City Is Reporting Its Sustainability Progress to the UN," *CityLab Web Posting*, July 13, 2018, www.citylab.com/environment/2018/07/why-new-york-city-is-reporting-its-sustainability-progress-to-the-un/564953/.

65. "These U.S. Cities Are Most Vulnerable to Major Coastal Flooding and Sea Level Rises," a *Research Report of Climate Central*, October 25, 2017, www.climatecentral.org/news/us-cities-most-vulnerable-major-coastal-flooding-sea-level-rise-21748.

66. Natalie Delgadillo, "MAP: How Much Climate Change Will Cost Each U.S. County," *Governing Magazine*, August 23, 2017, www.governing.com/topics/transportation-infrastructure/gov-counties-climate-change-damages-economic-effects-map.html.

67. Tabuchi and Fountain, "Bucking Trump, These Cities, States and Companies Commit to Paris Accord."

68. Barber, *Cool Cities: Urban Sovereignty and the Fix for Global Warming*.

69. Alaina Harkness, Bruce Katz, Caroline Conroy, and Ross Tilchin, *Leading Beyond Limits: Mayoral Powers in the Age of New Localism* (Washington, DC: Brookings Institution, 2017).

70. Margery Austin Turner, Rob Santos, Diane K. Levy, Doug Wissoker, Claudia Aranda, and Rob Pitingolo, *Housing Discrimination against Racial and Ethnic Minorities 2012* (Washington, DC: U.S. Department of Housing and Urban Development, 2013). The full report runs over a hundred pages. An executive summary is available at www.huduser.org/portal/Publications/pdf/HUD-514_ HDS2012_execsumm.pdf.

71. Douglas S. Massey and Jonathan Tannen, "A Research Note on Trends in Black Hypersegregation," *Demography* 52, no. 3 (June 2015): 1025–1034.

72. Sean F. Reardon and Demetra Kalogrides, "Brown Fades: The End of Court-Ordered School Deseg-regation and the Resegregation of American Public Schools," *Journal of Policy Analysis and Man-agement* 31, no. 4 (Fall 2012): 876–890; Gary Orfield, Jongyeon Ee, Erica Frankenberg, and Gen-evieve Siegel-Hawley, "*Brown* at 62: School Segregation by Race, Poverty, and State," a paper of the UCLA Civil Rights Project/Projecto Derechos Civiles, May 2016, https://files.eric.ed.gov/fulltext/ ED565900.pdf.

73. Erica Frankenberg and Gary Orfield, eds., *The Resegregation of Suburban Schools: A Hidden Crisis in American Education* (Cambridge: Harvard Education Press, 2012).

74. Richard Winter, Sarah Parvini, and Monte Morin, "Stephon Clark Shooting: How Police Opened Fire on an Unarmed Black Man Holding a Cellphone," *Los Angeles Times*, March 23, 2018.

75. Jasmine C. Lee and Haeyoun Park, "In 15 High-Profile Cases Involving Deaths of Blacks, One Offi-cer Faces Prison Time," *New York Times*, December7, 2017.

2 | The Evolution of Cities and Suburbs

Are urban problems "natural," that is, the unavoidable result of the choices made by citizens in a free society? That's what many Americans think. This point of view was also reflected in the opinion of United States Supreme Court Chief Justice John Roberts who argued that present-day school segregation is largely natural, that it is the result of private residential choices. Justice Roberts does not fully recognize the role that various governments have had in supporting and reinforcing segregation. Government actions that support segregation violate the "equal protection of the laws" clause of the United States Constitution (see Box 2.1).

This book recognizes that individual choices and free-market forces have indeed had a large influence in determining the shape of urban development. But this book also recognizes the important role played by less visible forces that have shaped—and continue to shape—patterns of urban growth and decline. The "natural forces" explanation of urban problems and inequalities is quite incomplete. More than is commonly recognized, governmental policies have exacerbated urban inequality and numerous urban problems, including: the decline of industrial "Rustbelt" communities; racial segregation in the **metropolis** (a term that refers to a central city and its surrounding suburbs); and the sprawled nature of urban development that eats up green space and exacerbates problems of pollution.

Urban problems also result from the exercise of private power. Self-interested private actors act to protect their privileges and, in doing so, have limited the housing and school choices available to others. Such actions helped to produce contemporary metropolitan areas that look quite different from the ones that an unobstructed free market would have produced.

Box 2.1
A *"Willful Blindness"*: Failing to Recognize Government's
Role in Promoting Racial Imbalances in the Metropolis

In 2007, the United States Supreme Court struck down moderate school integration programs in Denver and Seattle. Denver and Seattle established high-quality
"magnet schools" in an attempt to promote voluntary school integration. No one
would be forced to attend the special schools. But public officials hoped that the
schools would attract families of all races who were interested in schools of excellence. The admissions program took an applicant's racial and ethnic background
into account in order to ensure that school enrollments would be well integrated.
The parents of some white students, however, objected that their children were
suffering discrimination as a consequence of the school systems's effort to shape
classroom diversity.

The Supreme Court struck down the voluntary integration plans. In his plurality
opinion, Chief Justice John Roberts stated that the school districts had given
unallowable consideration to race in their admissions decisions. According to
Roberts, a district could consider a student's race in determining a school's
enrollment only if the district, an agency of government, had previously engaged
in actions that produced school segregation. As Denver and Seattle had no
proven history of past actions intended to segregate local schools, it was impermissible for school officials to take a student's race into account when making
school assignments.

Chief Justice Roberts argued that contemporary racial imbalances in school
enrollments are largely a reflection of "societal discrimination," a reflection of the
fact that families of different races and ethnic groups tend to reside in different
communities. The United States Constitution, Roberts observed, does not require
the government to correct all racial patterns that exist in society but only those that
are the result of government action. The wording of the Equal Protection Clause
of the 14th Amendment explicitly bars discriminatory action by the "State," that
is, by government: "No State shall . . . deny to any person within its jurisdiction
the equal protection of the laws." As Chief Justice Roberts and Justice Clarence
Thomas both underscored in their written opinions, the Equal Protection Clause
prohibits only **state action**: The clause prohibits governments from engaging in
acts of racial discrimination and does not require the government to step in and
correct the effects of the residential choices made by millions of American families
as they conduct their daily lives and private affairs.

Essentially, Roberts rejected the contention that government programs had
helped to create and maintain local levels of segregation. Are patterns of community and school segregation largely natural, that is, a reflection of societal
patterns, as Justices Roberts and Thomas saw it? Or are racial imbalances in
the schools also the result of state action, that is, of the discriminatory programs
of government?

Richard Rothstein, in *The Color of Law: The Forgotten History of How Our Government Segregated America*, rebuts the Chief Justice. Rothstein details the great many actions taken by all levels of government—by national, state, and local governments including public-school districts—that have perpetuated and exacerbated racial segregation: "This misrepresentation of our racial history, indeed out willful blindness, became the consensus view of American jurisprudence."

As we shall see throughout this book, government programs—especially local zoning and land-use plans—have served to produce patterns of both residential and school segregation. Residential and school segregation are the result of state action—that is, government action—and cannot be attributed solely to the differences in housing preferences and incomes of individuals operating in a free market.

Sources: Richard Rothstein, *The Color of Law: A Forgotten History of How Our Government Segregated America* (New York: Liveright Publishing, 2017), esp. xiii-xv and 215. Justice Roberts's statements are from his plurality opinion in *Parents Involved in Community Schools v. Seattle School District No. 1*, 551 U.S. 701 (2007). Also see Jake Blumgart, "Housing is Shamefully Segregated. Who Segregated It?" *Slate*, June 2, 2017, www.slate.com/articles/business/metropolis/2017/06/an_interview_with_richard_rothstein_on_the_color_of_law.html.

Urban Politics recognizes the important role that natural forces and free choice have played in shaping urban growth and decline. But *Urban Politics* also points to the important role that government programs and private power have also played in shaping urban America.

This chapter details three quite different sets of factors that each help to explain a local community's growth and decline. The chapter first describes such factors as population pressures and technological change that can indeed be viewed as "natural" forces that have determined the shape and health of America's communities. The chapter then describes a second and quite different set influences, how the various programs of the national, state, and local governments have shaped local communities, at times compounding urban problems. The phrase **hidden urban policy** refers to the various government programs intended for nonurban purposes—such as completing the interstate highway system, rewarding veterans, or promoting homeownership—that have had a major, albeit often unintended, impact on America's communities.

The chapter then shifts its focus to a third set of factors, the exercise of private power, as quite distinct from the exercise of free-market choices. The chapter reveals how the self-interested and discriminatory actions of private actors have helped to determine patterns of investment, homeownership, and segregation that cannot be viewed simply as the result of free individual choice. The theme of private power will be further elaborated in the chapters that follow, for instance, in describing how business officials have distorted the information presented to public officials to justify the award of extensive federal, state, and local subsides for the construction of sports stadiums, conventions centers, casinos, and other growth projects. Such manipulations are a violation of free-market theory which assumes that decisions are made in response to perfect information, not distorted information.[1]

THE NATURAL FACTORS THAT SHAPE THE GROWTH AND DECLINE OF CITIES AND SUBURBS

Political conservatives tend to argue that little can be done to remediate urban problems as patterns of urban development are largely dictated by societal forces beyond the control of government. Government has only a quite limited capacity to ameliorate urban and social problems. Especially in a society that values individual freedom, government is largely powerless to reverse the residential, business, and investment choices made by its citizens.

Political scientist Edward C. Banfield eloquently elaborated the conservative point of view in a classic essay that he wrote in the middle of the twentieth century. Banfield pointed to three sets of natural forces that had such a strong influence on cities that he referred to them as "imperatives" that essentially determine urban growth and decline.[2] The first imperative is **demographic**: Increases in population put pressures on housing and commercial activities to grow. As a result, the footprint of the city expands outward, resulting in the growth of suburbs. This decentralization of population and economic activity serves to weaken central cities. Families with the financial means leave the congested and crime-ridden city core for better communities. Business firms, too, soon follow the exodus to the suburbs.

The second imperative is **technological**: Transportation and communications technology determines just how far from the city center residents and businesses can conveniently locate. More recent advances in telecommunications have continued to alter development patterns, with new telecommunications technology enabling businesses to locate at increasing distances from cities that traditionally served as the central hubs of the nation's economy.

The third factor Banfield calls **economic**, but we can more easily understand it if we refer to it as *wealth* or *affluence*: Just who lives where in the Americas? More affluent families have the ability to seek housing in the "best" communities in a metropolitan area. Middle-class families similarly seek the "good life" in suburban communities located far away from the congestion, grit, cramped housing, and crime of inner-city areas. Working-class and poorer families, possessing much less buying power, have little alternative but to live in the parts of the central city and the declining suburbs that more affluent home seekers have abandoned.

NATURAL FACTORS AND THE EVOLUTION OF THE AMERICAN METROPOLIS

Population pressure, changes in transportation and communication technology, and patterns of affluence clearly have had a large influence on the evolving shape of American communities. The oldest parts of cites are usually found by a major locus of transportation—a harbor, river, canal, or a railroad or trail junction that provided early American communities with commercial connections essential to the economic viability of the early American city.[3] The primitive nature of transportation also meant that the American city in the 1800s was relatively small and compact in terms of its geographical expanse. A person could traverse a good portion of the city by foot, leading urban historian Kenneth Jackson refers to America's early preindustrial communities as **walking cities**.[4]

The rudimentary nature of transportation in the early American city also meant that workshops, warehouses, and residential spaces had to be located in close proximity to one another. Wealthy merchants, shippers, manual workers, and the poor all lived inside the city, close to work. During this early era, cities had not yet lost population and wealth to suburbs, as the hamlets and farm villages outside the city's borders were difficult to reach. The residents of the countryside had little interaction with the city. It would take advances in transportation to transform these rural villages into suburbs where residents have more extensive interaction with the central city.

Cities grew as a result of **urbanization**: Migrants left the poverty and economic vagaries of life in the countryside for the promise of jobs, education, and opportunity offered by the city. In the industrial age, job seekers from the countryside and immigrants from overseas both came to the city in search of work. The population pressures forced the city to expand.

But the movement of population away from the center city had to await progress in transportation technology (Figure 2.1). In the early and mid-1800s, workers could move

Figure 2.1 **Center-Focused Transportation: Steam Trains, Electric Trams, and Even Horse-Pulled Wagons on "The Bowery" in New York City, 1896.** In the pre-automobile age, cities were the central hubs of industry and commerce, with trains and electric streetcars providing essential transportation lifelines.

Source: Originally published in 1896 in *The New York Times,* http://commons.wikimedia.org/wiki/File:
The_Bowery,_New_York_Times,_1896.JPG.

only as far out as a horse-pulled streetcar could take them. Successive transportation innovations—the electric trolley, the steam railroad, electric commuter trains, and the automobile—each enabled new waves of residents to move farther and farther away from the city center.

But even during the age of the electric trolley or streetcar, urban areas were relatively compact, quite unlike the sprawling megalopolises of today. At first, innovations in technology, especially the introduction of the elevator, reinforced the urban core, with the first skyscrapers appearing in the late 1880s. The American city expanded upward before new transportation technology allowed it to spread greatly outward.

For a long while, permissive laws in many states enabled a city to extend its political boundaries to reflect the outward movement of population. Cities possessed the power of **annexation** to adjoin neighboring areas to the city; the city swallowed up an abutting community that then became part of the larger city. The residents of underdeveloped outlying communities, where streets were barely paved and service provision was quite inadequate, often looked to the larger city for road paving, street lighting, and the provision of municipal water and gas. During this early stage of city expansion, there was no massive suburban resistance to annexation.

A turning point came in 1893 in a **political revolt by Brookline, Massachusetts**, a growing suburb surrounded on three sides by the City of Boston. Brookline spurned annexation by Boston. Brookline residents saw their community as a "refuge" from the dirt and corruption of the industrial city. They feared that joining the city would lead to higher taxes. Ethnocentrism, that is, the distrust of foreigners, also played a role in the suburb's rejection of the city. Brookline residents opposed to annexation "frankly stated that independent suburban towns could maintain native American life free from Boston's waves of incoming poor immigrants."[5] After the Brookline revolt, suburbs across the United States increasingly fought to maintain their independence from the city.

As suburban populations grew, changes in state laws began to favor the suburbs by making it increasingly difficult for cities to extend their political boundary lines outwards. **Streetcar suburbs** sprouted along the path of the electric trolley tracks; their residents were beyond the political reach of the central city. As historian Sam Bass Warner, Jr., summarized, "the metropolitan middle-class abandoned their central city."[6]

The middle class began to shift to the suburbs. But poorer migrants from rural areas continued to pour into cities in search of economic opportunity. In the **Great Migration** (roughly from 1910 through the 1940s), millions of poor African Americans—and whites—left the rural South to go to Chicago, Detroit, Pittsburgh, and other big cities in the North. The mechanization of agriculture and the end of the sharecropper system in the South pushed the rural poor off the land. To meet their production needs during both World Wars I and II, city factories sent their agents to the South to recruit workers. African Americans migrated to the cities of the North, searching for economic security, social and political freedoms, and a reprieve from oppression. Appalachian and rural whites moved northward, searching for economic opportunity.[7]

The automobile revolutionized urban form; new residential and commercial development no longer needed to be located in close proximity to streetcar stops and railway stations. The automobile enabled home seekers to fill in the spaces between the "fingers" of development that already existed along streetcar and rail lines. The automobile also enabled commuters to reside at a considerable distance from the city center.

Manufacturers, seeking the space necessary for assembly line production, were attracted by the relatively low price of undeveloped land located on the rim of urban areas. By the middle of the twentieth century, the rise of the trucking industry enabled warehousing and distribution firms to leave their older facilities situated along the rail spurs in the central city. Older manufacturing and warehousing sections of the core city, areas such as New York's SoHo and Lower East Side, suffered a steep decline. By 1970s, advances in cargo containerization further accelerated the suburbanization of warehousing and distribution activities; narrow and congested city streets and the small loading docks of old central-city warehouses could not accommodate the new shipping technologies.

Retail and entertainment establishments followed the middle class to the suburbs. Suburbanites did not want to be bothered with long drives for shopping, city traffic jams, and the difficulties in finding parking downtown. Commercial developers responded by constructing open-air, plaza-type shopping centers and, later, enclosed shopping malls in the suburbs. In the 1950s and 1960s, retail sales in the central city plummeted. In 1983, Hudson's department store, long associated with Detroit, closed the doors of its downtown flagship store, having opened new stores in the region's various suburban shopping malls. Detroit gained the dubious distinction of being the largest city in the country not to have a major department store within the city's borders. Baltimore, Cleveland, Toledo, Dayton, Davenport, Charlotte, Fort Worth, and a large number of other cities soon saw long-established department stores close, signaling the decline of the downtown core.

The development of airports, too, served as an impetus to the decentralization of warehousing, distribution, and other commercial activities. The increase in the volume of high-valued freight shipped by air led to the construction of warehouses and distribution facilities convenient to airports. Increased business travel by air similarly promoted office development in the suburbs.

Central cities were in trouble, having lost population and commercial activity and a good portion of their tax base to the suburbs. Rival commercial centers, virtual mini-cities, sprouted in the suburbs. Orange County, south of Los Angeles, enjoyed a dynamic office boom. Northwest of Chicago, the office towers of Schaumburg constituted a virtual second downtown in Chicagoland. Also in Chicagoland, the arrival of Bell Labs, helped suburban Naperville mushroom as yet another dynamic concentration of office and retail, Naperville became the fifth largest city in Illinois.[8]

Edge cities—concentrations of offices, shopping centers, and hotels—sprang up on the rim of virtually every major metropolitan area: Route 128 outside of Boston; White Plains (New York) and the New Jersey suburbs of New York City; King of Prussia (outside of Philadelphia); Rosslyn, Crystal City, and Tyson's Corner (in the northern Virginia section of the Washington, DC, metropolitan area); Troy and Southfield (just north of Detroit); the Houston Galleria; the Perimeter Center north of Atlanta's beltway; and various communities in Silicon Valley lying on the peninsula between San Francisco and San Jose, to name only a few. **Technoburbs**, high-technology-oriented suburbs, mushroomed as the sites of globally oriented and foreign-owned firms.[9] The **multicentered metropolis** became the new urban reality. The old central city and its downtown business district no longer dominated the urban region.

In the 1950s and 1960s, when the movement of America to the suburbs was still in its relative infancy, suburbia was stereotyped as a land of tranquil **bedroom communities** from where husbands commuted to the central city for work. Industrial and factory suburbs also existed, but did little to mar the overall portrayal of suburbia as a series of serene, middle- and upper-class, and predominantly white communities.

Over the decades that followed, suburbia would evolve and mature. Today, suburbia is much more diverse and dynamic than the early stereotype. Suburbs are now the sites of high-tech industry, office campuses, entertainment venues, cultural centers, universities, and fine dining. For the residents of suburbia, their communities do not at all seem "sub" to central cities.

The population of contemporary suburbia has also become increasingly diverse. The all-white suburb, a community which had no African-American residents, has largely disappeared from the urban landscape. Nor is contemporary suburbia uniformly white and affluent. A diverse racial and ethnic population, immigrants, and families in poverty are increasingly found in the suburbs.[10] Conditions in the most nation's troubled inner-ring suburbs, including East Cleveland, Trenton (New Jersey, just across the river from Philadelphia), East St. Louis (Illinois), and East Palo Alto (California), are in many ways indistinguishable from those of the urban core.

NATURAL FACTORS AND THE SHIFT TO THE SUNBELT

Suburbanization is not the only population and economic shift to reshape urban America. The latter half of the twentieth century and the beginning of the twenty-first century saw a major demographic shift, the movement of population and economic activity from the older **Frostbelt** cities and suburbs of the Northeast and the Midwest to the growing **Sunbelt** communities of the South and West. The nation's most dynamically growing areas are in the Sunbelt, while communities in the Northeast and North Central regions continue to lose population. As census data from 2016 reveals, all of the nation's 25 fastest-growing metropolitan areas (including metropolitan Las Vegas, Austin, Raleigh, Sarasota-Bradenton, and Orlando) are to be found in the Sunbelt![11] The nation's top ten counties in terms of population increase likewise were in the South and the West

Table 2.1

10 Largest-Gaining Counties (by Numeric Population Gain): July 1, 2015 to July 1, 2016

County	Population	Net Population Gain	Percent Change	Domestic Migration
Maricopa County, Arizona	4,242,997	81,360	1.95	43,189
Harris County, Texas	4,589,928	56,587	1.25	−16,225
Clark County, Nevada	2,155,664	46,375	2.20	27,735
King County, Washington	2,149,970	35,714	1.69	8,511
Tarrant County, Texas	2,016,872	35,462	1.79	13,411
Riverside County, California	2,387,741	34,849	1.48	16,961
Bexar County, Texas	1,928,680	33,198	1.75	13,077
Orange County, Florida	1,314,367	29,503	2.30	10,083
Dallas County, Texas	2,574,984	29,209	1.15	−6,193
Hillsborough County, Florida	1,376,238	29,161	2.16	14,806

Source: Adapted from United States Census Bureau, "Maricopa County Added Over 222 People Per Day in 2016, More Than Any Other County," release CB17–44, March 23, 2017, www.census.gov/newsroom/press-releases/2017/cb17-44.html.

(see Table 2.1). Two southwestern communities—Maricopa County (Phoenix) and Harris County (Houston)—had the greatest population gains, followed closely by Las Vegas. In contrast, the counties in 2016 that suffered the most severe population loss—including Cook County (Chicago), Wayne County (Detroit), Baltimore, and Cuyahoga (Cleveland)—were almost all in the Frostbelt, that is, in the Northeast and the Midwest (see Table 2.2).

Natural factors help explain the regional shift. The introduction of jet travel and innovations in computers and telecommunications enabled citizens and corporations to move to Sunbelt communities and enjoy their warm weather, sunny skies, good beaches, and the promise of escape from the congestion and social ills of northern communities. Businesses were further attracted to the Sunbelt's relatively cheap land. The introduction of air conditioning was essential for the growth of cities in the torridly hot South. With the marvel of machine-cooled air, northerners could even retire in Miami Beach, a city built on a mangrove swamp!

Table 2.2
**10 Largest-Declining Counties or County Equivalents (by Numeric Population Loss):
July 1, 2015 to July 1, 2016**

County	Population	Net Population Loss	Percent Change	Domestic Migration
Cook County, Illinois	5,203,499	−21,324	−0.41	−66,244
Wayne County, Michigan	1,749,366	−7,696	−0.44	−17,346
Baltimore city, Maryland	614,664	−6,738	−1.08	−11,008
Cuyahoga County, Ohio	1,249,352	−5,673	−0.45	−10,122
Suffolk County, New York	1,492,583	−5,320	−0.36	−11,278
Milwaukee County, Wisconsin	951,448	−4,866	−0.51	−13,186
Allegheny County, Pennsylvania	1,225,365	−3,933	−0.32	−5,821
San Juan County, New Mexico	115,079	−3,622	−3.05	−4,341
St. Louis City, Missouri	311,404	−3,471	−1.10	−6,189
Jefferson County, New York	114,006	−3,254	−2.78	−4,674

Source: Adapted from United States Census Bureau, "Maricopa County Added over 222 People Per Day in 2016, More Than Any Other County," release CB17–44, March 23, 2017, www.census.gov/newsroom/press-releases/2017/cb17-44.html.

NATURAL FACTORS AND POSTINDUSTRIAL ADAPTATION AND DECLINE

After a prolonged period of decline, a number of former manufacturing cities reemerged as postindustrial **global cities**, the corporate and financial centers of the knowledge-based world economy. (Chapter 4 will describe the impact of globalization on cities in more extensive detail.) New York, Los Angeles, Chicago, and San Francisco have lost much of their former manufacturing character. Today, however, these former port cities and factory centers have blossomed as the dynamic centers of corporate headquarters, banking and finance activities, conventions and tradeshows, and tourism.

But not all cities had the extensive cross-border economic ties that enabled them to emerge as centers of global economic activity. Many smaller and more peripheral manufacturing communities, and a number of larger industrial cities as well, could not break their downward trajectory. Such communities faced long-term decline as they lacked the sort of highly educated, technologically skilled, and professional workers that global firms and entrepreneurial ventures valued. These cities lost population, with their neighborhoods increasingly marred by extensive abandoned housing, shuttered storefronts, and vacant lots. Cleveland lost over half of its population, plummeting from 915,000 in 1950 to a mere 385,800 in 2016.

Cleveland and other **shrinking cities** like Detroit, Flint, Dayton, Youngstown, Buffalo, Rochester, Syracuse, and New Orleans have come to realize that they cannot recover their lost population and former economic significance. Such cities have begun to initiate creative responses in the face of decline. Shrinking cities often emphasize **greening strategies**: demolishing dilapidated buildings; turning vacant properties into side lots and gardens for neighboring homeowners; expanding parks; using newfound green space to abet storm water retention; and promoting urban farms in parts of the city where agricultural activities were once prohibited.[12]

HIDDEN URBAN POLICY: HOW THE GOVERNMENT SHAPES URBAN GROWTH, DECLINE, AND INEQUALITY

As already noted, natural factors—population pressures, technology, and affluence—have a great impact on determining just where people live and just which communities thrive while others decline. But contrary to Edward Banfield's assertion, such natural forces are not "imperatives" that dictate exact patterns of urban growth and decline. Other factors, too, shape urban development. Government policies and the actions taken by powerful private actors—including banks and lending institutions, real-estate firms, and land developers—help to determine which communities prosper while others decline. In this section, we describe the numerous government programs that have served to accelerate disinvestment in, and the decline of, core-city neighborhoods. Government programs have also served to catalyze the shift of population and economic activity to the suburbs and the Sunbelt.[13]

The federal programs with the greatest impact on America's communities do not always have an explicit urban orientation. Instead, many of these programs have quite laudable objectives: helping Americans to buy homes of their own; rewarding veterans for their service; building the interstate highway system; promoting the construction of much-needed hospitals and sewage plants; and incentivizing business expansion. These programs constitute a hidden urban policy as they also have a tremendous, albeit often unstated and unintended, influence on the growth and decline of America's communities.

THE FHA AND THE VA: THE URBAN BIAS OF FEDERAL ASSISTANCE TO HOMEOWNERS

Federal assistance helped millions of working-class and middle-class families to buy homes of their own. The **Federal Housing Administration (FHA)** sought to make America a nation of homeowners by incentivizing banks and other mortgage-lending institutions to extend loans to home seekers whom the financial institutions would not normally extend credit.

FHA loan insurance typically provides protection for up to 80 percent of the value of an approved property. The FHA essentially guarantees that a credit institution will be repaid 80 percent of a loan if an FHA-certified homeowner defaults on scheduled payments. By removing most of the risk that a lender faces in issuing a home loan, FHA insurance spurred financial institutions to give mortgages to millions of Americans who would not, in the program's absence, have received a home loan. Facing less risk with FHA-backed loans, lenders could also reduce down payment requirements and interest rates, putting homeownership within the reach of the working and middle classes.

The **GI Bill of Rights of 1944** extended similar assistance through the **Veterans Administration (VA)** to millions of soldiers returning home from World War II. As "the VA very largely followed FHA procedures and attitudes . . . the two programs can be considered as a single effort."[14] Together, the FHA and VA programs offered prospective homebuyers a very attractive package of low or no down payment, easy credit, and a 25- to 30-year period of very manageable monthly payments.[15]

These federal programs accelerated suburban development and central-city decline. While the programs backed the purchase of new homes, the programs did not offer similar insurance for the purchase of apartments or for the renovation of older housing in the central city. The FHA was guilty of **redlining** large portions of central cities, refusing to approve loans in inner-city areas even when they received credit applications from otherwise qualified homebuyers.

The anti-city bias of the FHA were codified in the agency's 1939 *Underwriting Manual*. These government rules instructed FHA underwriters to minimize homeowner defaults by looking for "economic stability" when making neighborhood evaluations. As the *Manual* explicitly declared, "crowded neighborhoods lessen desirability."[16] The FHA chose not to aid homeownership in the "graying" areas of the inner city and instead chose to finance suburban development.

The suburban bias of the FHA is clearly evident in greater St. Louis. From 1934 to 1960, home seekers in the suburban portions of St. Louis County received five times as many FHA-backed loans as did applicants in the city of St. Louis. Some cities suffered from even more extensive bias as the FHA redlined entire cities it saw as risky. In New Jersey, the FHA approved no loans for homes in Camden and Paterson.[17] By shutting off mortgage funds, the FHA guaranteed the precipitous decline of already-fragile communities.

A second FHA bias was even more pernicious, as agency policies mandated racial segregation.[18] The FHA, a government agency, explicitly endorsed racial segregation as a means of protecting the value of government-insured homes. The agency's *Underwriting Manual* stated, "If a neighborhood is to retain stability, it is necessary that properties shall continue to be occupied by the same social and racial classes."[19] The *Manual* instructed federal underwriters to give a low rating to mortgage applications that would lead to the "infiltration of inharmonious racial or nationality groups" into a neighborhood.[20] In other words, the government would approve a home loan only in cases where homeownership continued patterns of residential racial segregation! The FHA even endorsed the use of **restrictive covenants**, legally binding agreements that prohibited a buyer from reselling a home to someone of a different race.[21]

Levittown and other major new suburban developments of the post–World War II era had to follow VA- and FHA-endorsed practices of racial exclusion; otherwise the developer risked losing VA and FHA certification essential to the sale of a home.[22] This was government-enforced racial segregation; government policies intruded and preempted the free-market move of racial minorities to the suburbs.

The FHA further promoted segregation through its policy of **racial steering**, using its power over of loan approvals to ensure that black and white home seekers would reside in different neighborhoods. The FHA did not approve loans to minority applicants who sought to buy homes in all-white suburbs. In fact, very few African Americans received FHA approval. Only a paltry 2 percent of FHA-backed mortgage in the post–World War II era went to minorities, and half of those were for homes in all-minority subdivisions.[23] In the 1940s, the FHA even required the developer of a suburban all-white subdivision to build a six-foot-high, half-mile-long concrete wall along the border with Detroit in order to seal off the new housing from a nearby black neighborhood (Figure 2.2).[24]

Why did the FHA and VA, important federal agencies that helped millions of Americans to become homeowners, practice segregation? FHA administrators feared that racial integration would jeopardize real-estate values, that white families fleeing neighborhoods undergoing racial change would default on their loans. The FHA reflected a point of view that, at the time, was prevalent in the real-estate industry. Both the FHA and the real-estate industry viewed "racial homogeneity" as "essential" for residential areas to retain their "stability and desirability."[25] The National Association of Real Estate Boards in its code of ethics even encouraged practices to preserve the racial homogeneity of a neighborhood!

Figure 2.2   **"The Wall," Detroit, 1941.** A half-mile long concrete wall was constructed along Detroit's outer boundary. The wall was built in an effort to keep African Americans from Detroit out of a suburban area where new housing for whites was being developed just outside the city border. Interestingly, government housing finance agencies, and not just private investors, insisted on the construction of the wall to promote the marketability and stability of the new housing.

Source: From the Library of Congress Prints & Photographs Division, Washington, DC 20540, www. loc.gov/pictures/item/fsa2000044373/pp/.

Outcries from civil rights groups eventually led the FHA to end its blatantly discriminatory practices. By 1949, the agency deleted from its manual the references to "racial groups" and "infiltration." But the harm that the FHA had done in distorting racial patterns in the American metropolis could not be undone. The FHA had helped to underwrite the growth of racially homogeneous suburban communities as well as the decline of minority-dominated central-city neighborhoods.

The agency's actions also promoted sprawled development into the urban periphery. In Los Angeles, FHA examiners approved home loans for "leap-frog" housing projects built in previously undeveloped natural areas on the edges of the metropolis.[26]

To its credit, the FHA in the 1960s reversed course and began to aggressively approve home loans in the inner-city areas that the agency had previously ignored. Unfortunately, even this U-turn in FHA policy wound up, albeit unintentionally, hastening the decline of numerous inner-city neighborhoods. In its rush to make up for its racist past, the FHA approved loans to applicants who lacked strong work and credit histories. Properties in the inner city deteriorated as the new owners lacked the financial means and readiness to assume the responsibilities of homeownership.[27] As a review of FHA activity in the late 1960s further explains, "the well-intentioned program turned into a scam for unethical real-estate speculators who bought decaying inner-city dwellings, slapped on coats of paint, and haphazardly made other superficial improvements before selling the houses at grossly inflated prices to unsuspecting buyers."[28] Dissatisfied homeowners walked away from "unfit" dwellings that had severe structural problems. As a result, FHA-backed properties too often wound up in default, boarded up and abandoned, accelerating the decline of inner-city neighborhoods.

Critics charge that the FHA was exceedingly lax in its standards for mortgage approval, a process that put families into homes they could not afford, leading to crisis in foreclosure and abandonment that plagued the banking and housing sectors in the early 2000s. Yet, an examination of the data reveals that this indictment of the FHA is overly harsh. The great bulk of home foreclosures did not involve FHA-insured properties. In fact, in the midst of the crisis, FHA-approved loans actually had a better record of repayment than did home loans issued by the newer private mortgage firms.[29]

It was not the FHA but a much different federal policy—**Republican-era deregulation** of the credit industry—that led to the wave of loan foreclosures and property abandonment that plagued inner-city neighborhoods.[30] FHA review actually served to avert loan defaults. In contrast, default rates were much higher among borrowers who obtained a "subprime" loan without FHA approval from a private lender who deceptively advertised unrealistically low monthly payments and easy repayment terms. By relaxing government rules on the issuance of home loans, deregulation enabled more unscrupulous private lenders to engage in **predatory lending**, offering homebuyers seemingly advantageous lending terms without safeguards against "high-cost, abusive, and often fraudulent transactions."[31] Deregulation was a hidden urban policy that marred inner-city neighborhoods with a flood of home foreclosures.

THE FEDERAL TAX CODE: A VERY IMPORTANT HIDDEN URBAN POLICY

The federal tax code provides subsidies for homeownership, allowing homeowners who itemize to deduct mortgage interest and property taxes from their taxable gross income. In 2016 alone, homeowners received an estimated $95.5 billion in assistance through the tax code.[32]

The subsidies provided to homeowners through the tax code can be viewed as **tax expenditures**, as the federal treasury loses a considerable sum of money each year as a result of the various deductions and credits claimed by homeowners. The tax expenditures given each year to homeowners surpasses by far the total sums that the federal government spends annually to assist low- and moderate-income families in need of affordable housing.[33]

Such generous federal tax expenditures for homeowners has had significant urban impacts, providing subsidies that fueled suburban development while enabling middle-class families to flee the central city. As the tax advantages are awarded only to home-buyers, the programs do little to assist the urban poor or to promote the construction of rental housing in poor inner-city neighborhoods. As lower-income persons seldom itemize tax deductions, the mortgage interest deduction is of no real value to them.

The tax expenditures for homeowners can also be seen as inequitable, as the provisions give the greatest subsidies to the most affluent homeowners, not to families most in need of housing assistance.[34] Tax benefits for homeowners are often criticized as being **Robin Hood in reverse**; unlike the legendary Robin Hood who stole from the rich to give to the poor, the homeowner provisions of the tax code "give to the rich" while providing little to the poor. Critics deride such tax provisions as a **mansion subsidy** and **welfare for the rich**. Wealthier families buy the most expensive houses, pay the biggest mortgages, and hence receive the biggest subsidies under the tax code.

The tax deductions for homeownership also serve to stimulate **condominium and cooperative apartment conversions** in the city. As a tenant receives a subsidy only for buying—not for renting—a dwelling unit, the program serves to generate market forces that lead landlords to convert apartment buildings into condominiums and cooperatives. Tenants who lack the funds to purchase their dwelling units in a building that is "going condo" are displaced. Such tax subsidies incentivize gentrification, the upscaling of poorer neighborhood located in good proximity to a city's thriving central business district.

In 2017, the Republican Congress and President Trump enacted the **Tax Cuts and Jobs Act (TCJA)**, making major changes in the nation's tax code. How exactly the changes, especially the Act's expansion of the standard deduction allowed taxpayers, will affect homebuyers's use of the code's mortgage incentives remains to be seen. The TCJA is part of America's "hidden urban policy" where the urban impacts of non-urban actions are not readily discerned or understood.

The TCJA, for instance, may ultimately diminish the revenues that municipalities collect in property taxes. Why is this so? The TCJA set $10,000 as the maximum amount that a tax filer can claim in federal deductions for the taxes, including property taxes, paid to state and local governments. The TCJA also roughly doubled the standard

Box 2.2
**Hidden Urban Policy: How Reducing the Corporate Tax Rate
Can Impair the Production of Affordable Housing**

The stated goal of the Tax Cuts and Jobs Act (TCJA) of 2017 was to reduce tax rates in order to promote economic expansion. But by lowering the corporate tax rate from 35 percent to 21 percent, the legislation also acts as a "hidden" urban policy that may diminish the willingness of banks and other corporations to invest in the construction of affordable housing. Previously, banks and other institutions sought out partners in affordable housing production in order to obtain the substantial tax credits offered through the Low Income Housing Tax Credit (LIHTC) program. Investors earn LIHTC credits by making investments that help nonprofit community groups piece together the financing for a low-income housing development. By reducing corporate tax rates so dramatically, the TCJA wound up reducing the impetus of businesses to find such tax credits. As a result of the TCJA, fewer corporations will be facing the need to reduce high corporate tax obligations by investing in in affordable housing construction. While the exact impact of the TCJA remains to be seen, a number of experts in housing policy expect that the TCJA will slow the production of affordable housing, reducing by tens of thousands the number of affordable housing units that will be built in the United States.

Source: For further reading, see Kery Murakami, "Tax Reform's Impact on Affordable Housing, Local Nonprofits," *Crosscut*, December 20, 2017, http://crosscut.com/2017/12/tax-reform-affordable-housing-washington-state-seattle-charitable-giving-nonprofits/; Kriston Capps, "Uncertainty over Tax Reform is Already Hurting Affordable Housing," *CityLab*, January 10, 2017, www.citylab.com/equity/2017/01/uncertainty-over-tax-reform-is-already-hurting-affordable-housing/514235/.

deduction, a change that will likely lead large numbers of homeowners to claim the standard deduction rather than itemize their mortgage interest, property taxes, and other homeowners expenses. Such change in the law may mean that many homebuyers will no longer gain substantial tax benefits when buying a home. Without such tax expenditures fueling the demand for homes, sellers may find that they have no choice but to lower the asking price for homes they have on the market, actions that in turn serve to reduce the assessed value of property in the immediate area. Such actions reduce the taxable value of homes, lowering the amount of money that schools and cities can gain from a property tax levy. The TCJA may have the hidden effect of exacerbating the fiscal squeeze on municipal governments.[35]

The federal tax code contains numerous impacts that are not easily understood or even seen. One little-known provisions of the Tax Cuts and Jobs Act may even have the effect of undermining the production of affordable housing (see Box 2.2).

EXAMINING THE URBAN IMPACTS OF A NEW FEDERAL TAX INITIATIVE: OPPORTUNITY ZONES

One provision inserted at the last minute into the Tax Cuts and Jobs Act actually promises to promote new investment in poorer urban and rural communities. The provision, which was created with both Democratic and Republican support, allows each state to designate a limited number of high-poverty census tracts as **Opportunity Zones**. Corporations and individuals earn tax advantages by putting money into "qualified opportunity funds" that will invest in entrepreneurial projects, such as infrastructure upgrades and new housing and commercial development, in the designated zones. Investors will be allowed to defer capital gains taxes, thereby reducing their tax bill. The creation of Opportunity Zones is expected to cost the federal government an estimated $7.7 billion in lost tax revenues in just five years.

Opportunity Zone funds are primarily intended to promote entrepreneurship. As critics observe, there is no guaranty that the investments that result will improve the lives of the residents of distressed communities. The managers of opportunity funds could decide to bypass a region's most distressed communities and simply choose to make investments in less troubled areas that received zone designation. Speculators could even claim tax advantages by buying land which is allowed to lie idle, as the investor does not intend to make improvements but simply seeks to sell at a profit when land prices eventually rise.[36] Opportunity Zone incentives can also wind up supporting the construction of new upscale housing, construction that will likely inflate rents in the immediate area, a process that will displace some of the most vulnerable residents from the community.

Still, despite these concerns, cities rushed to have the state designate qualified areas as Opportunity Zones. They hoped to use the new tax incentives as part of their strategic efforts to recruit anchor tenants and to stimulate market activity in medical districts, university areas, and in communities located near a city's downtown.[37]

THE ANTI-CITY IMPACTS OF THE FEDERAL HIGHWAY PROGRAM

In the middle of the twentieth century, in the midst of the Cold War with the Soviet Union, the U.S. government committed itself to completing a national highway network for the quick and efficient transport of military personnel and materiel. The National Defense Highway Act of 1956 increased the federal share of funding for highway construction projects from 50 percent to 90 percent.

The new highways did more than facilitate military and interstate automobile travel. The roadways also opened outlying areas in a metropolis to new development. Federally funded highways became the "main streets" of a growing suburbia. For investors, the intersections of major highways with the "beltway" road that encircled the city became the obvious choice for shopping centers, enclosed malls, power stores, and office parks. The construction of such highway-oriented facilities enabled people to move still further away from the central city.

In numerous cities, federal highway construction undermined the vitality of inner-city neighborhoods.[38] The new highways divided communities, displacing tenants and erecting physical barriers that made it difficult for residents who lived on one side of a highway to reach schools and neighborhood stores located on the other side. The stores closed, the neighborhoods declined.

In city after city, local decision makers used highway construction as a tool to remove a city's black population from areas located near the city center. In Florida in the mid-1960s, highway planners built a leg of the I-95 expressway that "tore through the center of Overtown," Miami's large African-American community. The construction displaced more than ten thousand residents and razed Overtown's business district, destroying an inner-city community that was once renowned as the "Harlem of the South." In Nashville, Tennessee, highway planners put a "kink" in the route of I-40, destroying hundreds of homes and putting a divider through black North Nashville.[39]

African Americans were not the only victims of highway construction. In order to build new highway capacity for suburban commuters, highway planners demolished working- and middle-class communities. The construction of the Cross Bronx Expressway in New York City in the 1950s tore the heart out of blue-collar Jewish, Italian, and Irish neighborhoods. Forced from their homes, many residents left the city, never to return. The construction led to the social descent of the South Bronx.

Since the 1960s urban planners have begun to question the desirability of government programs that promote highway construction and suburban sprawl at the cost of accelerating the decline of inner-city neighborhoods and inner-ring suburbs. Federal regulations were changed to call for increased citizen participation and greater respect for environmental protection, and historic preservation.[40] Environmentalists have called for **transit-oriented development (TOD)**, with housing and commercial activates sited along rail and light-rail stops.[41]

Cities have also torn down overhead expressways, removed ground-level urban freeways, or otherwise halted urban highway projects in order to improve city livability by making core-city areas more attractive to revitalization. New York City's West Side Drive, San Francisco's Embarcadero Freeway, Boston's Central Artery, Rochester's Inner Loop, Milwaukee's Park East Freeway, and Portland's Harbor Drive are among the more notable urban freeways that have been demolished.

Urban highway projects are no longer judged solely on their ability to increase traffic speeds and improve traffic flow. Yet, despite new concerns for urban "livability" and mass transit, on the whole, federal highway monies and other economic development policies continue to promote edge city development and "highway-driven economies."[42]

MILITARY AND AEROSPACE SPENDING: ANOTHER HIDDEN URBAN POLICY

Defense-related spending, too, served to promote the growth of both the suburbs and the Sunbelt. During World War II, decision makers sought spread-out production sites that could not easily be bombed by the enemy. Rather than expand production in Detroit, the war planners built new plants outside the city. After the war's end, the U.S. Defense Department continued its preference for dispersed production sites, providing the employment base for continued suburban development.[43]

World War II production catalyzed the economic dynamism of Sunbelt cities, including Los Angeles, San Diego, Phoenix, Fort Worth, San Antonio, Oklahoma City,

New Orleans, and Atlanta.[44] Warm-weather locations provided ideal locations for port activities, troop training, and airplane testing. The corporate executives who served on the War Production Board also preferred cheap-labor Sunbelt locations that lacked the strong labor unions found in the manufacturing centers of the North.

In the Cold War years that ensued, military and aerospace spending continued to fuel Sunbelt economies. From 1951 to 1981, Defense Department spending for prime contracts (that is, the money spent by the government to have private firms help construct military facilities, develop weapons systems, and provide other services) increased by 810 percent in the South and 402 percent in the West, but fell by 1.5 percent in the Midwest.[45] The Defense Department closed the New York and Philadelphia naval yards, deciding to retrofit the Navy's Atlantic and Pacific fleets in lower-cost nonunion Norfolk (Virginia) and San Diego. Massive governmental expenditures for space exploration led to an economic boom in Florida (the Cape Canaveral launch site) and Texas (especially in areas around the NASA Johnson Space Center in Houston).

Government contracts for missile-guidance systems and other high-tech computerized and electronic components propelled the growth of communities in California's Silicon Valley and the Pacific Northwest. Defense-related contracts even paid engineers to relocate to Silicon Valley.[46] Contracts to Boeing fueled the economy of greater Seattle. Federal spending for high-tech projects favored suburbs in the South and West that had the space for modern research parks and that offered a quality of life that could appeal to a talented and super-educated workforce.[47]

THE URBAN IMPACTS OF OTHER FEDERAL PROGRAMS

Generous **federal grant programs for hospitals and sewage processing facilities** helped pay for the infrastructure costs of new development in the suburbs and the Sunbelt. Federal **tax incentives to businesses** to increase private investment in modern machinery and physical plants likewise served to spur commercial development in the suburbs and the Sunbelt. The government did not offer a similar array of tax benefits to firms to rehabilitate and remain in the aging manufacturing plants of the Northeast and Midwest. Critics derisively referred to the federal investment tax credit to as an **urban disinvestment tax credit**, as the incentive led businesses to abandon older central-city plants.

Federal tax incentives for the oil and gas industries catalyzed economic development in the South and West. Houston's dynamic growth is at least partly due to the quite favorable tax treatment accorded the petrochemical industry. Federal grants for port development and highway construction, too, helped to pay for the infrastructure improvements essential to Houston's economic takeoff.[48]

The stated intent of the federal **urban renewal** program in the 1950s and 1960s was to revitalize troubled cities. But in clearing large parcels of land for expanded business districts and new university campuses, urban renewal displaced low-income and minority residents and destroyed existing neighborhoods. Urban renewal tore down more housing than it built. In numerous cities, federal urban renewal funds were used to reinforce racial segregation.[49]

Urban renewal has often been referred to as **Negro removal**: Local governments used federal renewal assistance to tear down the homes of African Americans who resided too close to a city's central business district or to privileged white neighborhoods. In Pittsburgh, city planners relocated African-American families from urban renewal areas to low-income housing projects built in black sections of the city. City planners also created a racial "buffer zone" of open space to separate Pittsburgh's central business district from nearby African-American neighborhoods.[50]

Cities have also used urban renewal programs to remove Latino populations from strategic areas of the city. San Antonio cleared neighborhoods in the Central West project, nearly 70 acres of land abutting the downtown and HemisFair '68, the World's-Fair-style exhibition intended to attract new investment to the city. Public officials showed little concern for relocating the displaces. Very little of the new housing that was built could be considered affordable.[51]

Suburbs, too, have at times resorted to urban renewal efforts in an attempt to alter local racial and ethnic patterns. The Chicago suburb of Addison in 1997 agreed to pay $1.8 million to Hispanic families whom the local redevelopment agency had pushed out of their homes in the name of urban renewal. "It was Mexican removal in the guise of urban renewal," said the lead attorney representing the Leadership Council for Metropolitan Open Communities.[52]

A CITY'S "SECOND GHETTO": HOW PROGRAMS BY LOCAL GOVERNMENT BUILT AN EXPANDED GHETTO

As the Pittsburgh, San Antonio, and Addison stories reveal, local governments have often acted to reinforce residential segregation. Among the most well-known cases is Chicago which, during the decades that followed World War II, the city council and various public agencies undertook a series of actions to reinforce local racial boundaries. To maintain neighborhood segregation, the Chicago Housing Authority (CHA) discriminated in tenant assignments on the basis of race. The CHA did not simply award a vacant public housing unit to the next family on a waiting list. Instead, the CHA looked to the applicant's race in order to ensure that the occupants of public housing would be compatible with the racial profile of the surrounding neighborhood. Whites were admitted to housing projects in white areas; African Americans were sent to housing projects in black areas. Each individual alderman (Chicago's name for a member of its city council) also possessed the power to reinforce segregation. Each member of the city council had the ability to veto the placement of a new public housing project in his or her ward. White council members barred the construction of public housing projects that would introduce racial minorities into their neighborhoods.

Chicago, Miami, and a sizeable number of other cities can be seen to have chosen the construction of a **second ghetto**.[53] Of course, every major city has an area of dilapidated housing that becomes a slum or ghetto when better-off families move away. But a city's "second ghetto" is quite different; it is less a natural phenomenon and more a government creation. Local governments have undertaken actions that created a new or expanded ghetto area with boundaries quite different from those of the city's naturally occurring ghetto. In Chicago, civic leaders sought to prevent blacks, displaced by urban renewal projects, from moving into neighboring white areas. The city relocated African Americans in immense high-rise public housing projects built in isolated industrial areas

Figure 2.3   **"We Want White Tenants in Our White Community,"** sign opposite the Sojourner
Truth Housing Project, Detroit, 1942. Racism and segregated housing were
found in northern cities, not just in the South. In Detroit, a riot by white neighbors
prevented African Americans from moving into a federally funded housing project.

Source: Photo by Arthur S. Siegel/Library of Congress Prints and Photographs Division, Washington,
DC www.loc.gov/pictures/item/owi2001018484/pp/.

or on the edges of the city's existing black neighborhoods. A half century later, living
conditions in the segregated high-rises proved so awful that Chicago, with financial
assistance from the federal government, at long last decided to tear down much of the
high-rise ghetto that public officials had previously constructed.

Numerous cities have a hidden history of government decisions that have reinforced
and extended residential segregation. Such actions were not confined to the South. Detroit
reversed a decision on just who would occupy the Sojourner Truth Housing Project in
response to the protests of white who objected to racial integration (Figure 2.3). New
York City violated the federal Fair Housing Act by setting racial quotas for certain public
housing projects and steering African-American and Hispanic applicants away from
projects that had a white population of tenants. The city also gave preferential treatment
to applicants who lived in the area surrounding a housing project, a policy that helped to
block black families from gaining entrance to public housing in white neighborhoods.[54]

ZONING AND LAND-USE POWERS: HOW LOCAL GOVERNMENTS "KEEP OUT" UNWANTED ACTIVITIES AND POPULATIONS

In 1916, New York became the first city in the United States to adopt a *zoning* ordinance,
a move so revolutionary that it was hailed as opening "a new era of civilization."[55] The
New York ordinance regulated new construction, setting different standards for the use,
height, and bulk of what could be built in different areas or the city. The regulations were
meant to protect residential neighborhoods against the intrusion of new skyscrapers.

Zoning helps to assure orderly land development by preventing incompatible land
uses. No homeowner, for instance, wants to see a factory or an automobile repair
shop built next to his or her home. Zoning prevents such incongruous development by

designating different sections or zones of a community for different uses. Certain land parcels are designated for industrial and commercial uses; other parcels are reserved for residential development. Light industry can be kept separate from heavy industry. Apartment buildings may be allowed in certain areas, while other sections of a community are zoned only for more luxurious single-family homes.

Suburbs have traditionally relied on their zoning and land-use powers to keep out both "nuisance" activities and to keep heavy industry apart from residential areas. The modern suburb, however, also uses these powers for a much different purpose: to keep out lower-income people.

More affluent communities use **land-use and zoning regulations** in an effort to restrict entry by lower-income and working-class families. More affluent suburbs maintain their exclusivity by failing to designate land on which apartment buildings and townhomes can be built, housing units that would be more affordable than detached single-family homes. Suburban ordinances typically require that new homes be built on large lots with large-size rooms and other expensive construction features. Such local ordinances can put the price of residence in the community beyond the reach of middle- and working-class families as well as the poor. A great many suburbs simply zone out multifamily housing and subsidized housing for the poor. Other communities refuse to apply for federal funds for subsidized housing projects.

Exclusionary zoning and land-use practices are a root cause of the racial and income imbalances of communities in the contemporary metropolis. Such practices confer economic advantages on more privileged groups by serving to help concentrate poorer and minority residents in the central city and a region's older and more troubled "first suburbs."[56]

Suburban officials use zoning to prevent levels of overdevelopment and overcrowding that can diminish the quality of local life. Yet, suburbs also use zoning as a potent weapon of exclusion, a tool that restricts the construction of more affordable housing and that keeps out less-well-off persons.[57] In the United States, local control of zoning virtually assures that single-family homes dominate the suburbs and that the development of alternative housing types will be quite limited. In Europe, where there is no similar local control of zoning, suburban housing types are more varied.[58] The United States system of local zoning exacerbates class and racial segregation, virtually assuring that working-class and minority children will have less access to quality schooling.[59]

Suburbs are not alone when it comes to the use of zoning and land-use regulations to reinforce patterns of inequality and segregation. Central cities, too, often have strict zoning regulations and procedural rules that thwart the development of more affordable forms of housing in upper-income neighborhoods.[60]

In New York City in more recent years, rezoning enabled developers to build housing at greater densities than was previously allowed. The relaxation of zoning restrictions can facilitate the production of housing, easing the housing affordability crunch, especially on a city's middle-class families. But rezoning does not always produce such positive effects. In some cities, rezoning led to new high-end developments that only served to drive up land values, home prices and rents, displacing the working-class and the poor. The rezoning (or "upzoning") of a neighborhood can even lead to new residential and commercial projects that entail a demolition of existing affordable housing units.

New York Mayor Bill de Blasio has emphasized upzoning and the construction of new affordable housing units in his policy efforts to expand the supply of housing in the city. Still, housing activists question the degree to which many of the new "affordable" units are truly within the financial reach of working-class and lower-middle-income families. Housing activists argue that the set-aside of a relatively small number of affordable units does little to offset the exclusionary pressures generated when "upzoning" allows new luxury housing developments to dominate a neighborhood.[61]

STATE AND LOCAL PROGRAMS THAT PROMOTED SUNBELT GROWTH

The growth of Sunbelt communities is not simply the result of such natural factors as the region's sunny climate and innovations in transportation and communications that made the South and the West accessible. Government actions—including those undertaken by states and localities—served to catalyze the interregional population and economic shift.

States and municipalities in the South offered a pro-business climate. Taxes on business were kept low as welfare benefits and social service spending were kept to a minimum. Compared to the industrial north, business owners in the South faced fewer regulations for worker benefits and environmental protection.

Right-to-work laws in southern states served to undermine labor organizing, making the South an attractive location for business. In a right-to-work state, a worker cannot be forced to join a union. Employers can undermine union organizing efforts by choosing to hire only nonunion workers.

Cities in the Sunbelt undertook expensive public programs to attract growth. Los Angeles, Houston, San Antonio, and San Jose are among the Sunbelt cities that incurred huge public debts in order to provide the sewer, street, highway, and other infrastructure improvements demanded by businesses.

In the Sunbelt, local government devoted considerable public monies to building the infrastructure that business leaders demanded. In the years that followed World War II, Houston boosted its debt eightfold in order to pay for a municipal construction boom. In Houston, the "public sector actively fueled and sustained the urban development process with public dollars."[62] Similarly, business leaders and local officials in Phoenix demanded continued public investment, especially in the city's airport, as key to local economic growth.[63] In Los Angeles, the "local state" invested heavily in the region's shipping port, airport and rail facilities, enabling the region to emerge as a center of global trade.[64] This was no unfettered free market at work. Instead, extensive government investment by cities, a sort of business-oriented municipal socialism, paved the way for the economic expansion of the Sunbelt!

SUMMING UP: THE GOVERNMENT'S ROLE ASSESSED

In his review of American urban development, historian Kenneth Jackson asks, "Has the American government been as benevolent—or at least as neutral—as its defenders claim?"[65] The answer is a resounding "No!" Urban problems are not purely the result of natural ecological evolution. Urban problems are also the consequence—often unintended—of various government policies and programs.

Government policies—especially its hidden urban policies—have played a great role in shaping the metropolis. An advocate of cities may reasonably argue that the government has an obligation to remedy the urban ills it helped to create.

THE INFLUENCE OF CORPORATE AND PRIVATE POWER

Private actors, oftentimes working hand in hand with public officials, make decisions that help dictate patterns of urban growth and decline. Urban trends that at first glance seem "natural" may, under closer examination, reveal the manipulations and intrusions of private-sector actors.

PRIVATE POWER AND THE SELLING OF THE SUBURBAN IDEAL

The "natural forces" theory of urban development observes the important role play by the automobile in shaping and reshaping the American metropolis. The automobile enabled citizens to achieve the American ideal: to own a home of their own in the suburbs. Urban areas in the Northeast and Midwest are relatively compact as cities in these regions were largely shaped by mass transit; their spatial forms were determined before the age of the automobile. By contrast, Los Angeles and cities in the West grew rapidly during the age of the automobile, producing a more spread or sprawled pattern of development.

But a closer look at Los Angeles reveals a more complex history, that suburban development is not solely the result of such natural factors as the desire for homeownership and the introduction of the automobile. Development in greater Los Angeles actually took on much of its fabled "spread city" character in an era *before* the automobile gained popularity, that is, *before* the region's famed freeways were built.

How could suburban development commence in an age when there were relatively few automobiles and little highway development? The machinations of powerful private-sector actors dictated such development. Fringe development outside Los Angeles began in the early years of the twentieth century. Local real-estate developers, including Henry Huntington who also owned a private streetcar company, the Pacific Electric Railway, sought to make their fortunes in real estate. Huntington built his system of electric interurban streetcars as a means to bring potential buyers to his suburban home sites. The finest mass transit system of its day, Huntington's Red Cars (featured in the cartoon movie *Who Framed Roger Rabbit?*) traveled at speeds of 45 to 55 miles per hour. Huntington's streetcars operated at a loss, but the monetary losses did not matter. The streetcars were there to help him sell homes; the streetcar losses were the subsidy that Huntington was willing to pay in order to generate a demand for the homes that he was building on the outer edges of Los Angles. Suburban development in Los Angeles was not a purely natural phenomenon. It took the action of Huntington and his advertising to help create it.[66]

Private real-estate interests in California and across the nation vigorously promote the ideal of suburban living. The Irvine Company touted the rural tranquility of its new community, Irvine, California, 40 miles south of Los Angeles: "Come to Irvine and hear the asparagus grow." The company sold the public on a highly exaggerated and idealized picture of the tranquil life of suburbia. The reality, of course, was vastly different from the suburban ideal that the company advertised to the public. As one company executive admitted, "When you live between two highways, it's hard to hear the asparagus grow."[67]

PRIVATE INSTITUTIONS AND THE RACIAL STRATIFICATION OF U.S. CITIES AND SUBURBS

Contrary to the "natural factors" view of urban development, residential patterns do not simply reflect differences in group income and buying power. Nor is racial and ethnic stratification a mere reflection of the preference of people "to live with their own kind." Instead, private financial institutions undertook actions that produced levels of segregation and racial imbalance that are beyond what can be considered "natural." Private institutions have even interfered with the workings of the free market, with discriminatory actions that impeded the ability of minority families with the financial means from being able to move to a region's better-off communities. The actions of private institutions helped to segregate the American metropolis.

This chapter has already described the actions of a government agency, the Federal Housing Administration which, for a good portion of its history, pursued an explicit policy of housing segregation, even endorsing such discriminatory practices as *restrictive covenants* and *racial steering*. Why did the FHA practice discrimination? In part, the FHA's discriminatory actions reflected the practices that, at the time, were prevalent in private real estate, banking, and mortgage-finance firms. FHA agents came to the government with experience in a private industry that practiced racial restrictions.

As previously observed, restrictive covenants are binding deed restrictions that prohibited a property owner from selling or renting a housing unit to the members of specified ethnic and racial groups. Depending on the part of the country, restrictive covenants barred home sales to African Americans, Hispanics, Asians, and Jews. Local real-estate boards often insisted that racial restrictions be included in sales contracts. The Chicago Real Estate Board even formulated a model restrictive covenant for its members to include in property contracts.[68]

In many cities, restrictive covenants effectively barred ethnic and racial minorities from moving into vast areas of the city. As a consequence, the population of racial ghettos and local Chinatowns swelled. In Austin, Texas, deed restrictions similarly specified "white" or "Caucasian only." Such wording served to keep out Latinos (who, in Texas at the time, were largely viewed as nonwhite) as well as African Americans. The property restrictions helped keep parts of the city exclusive and white while concentrating racial minorities in East Austin.[69]

Restrictive racial covenants produced patterns of urban segregation that continued well after the Supreme Court's **Shelley v. Kraemer** (1948) decision. The Court ruled that restrictive covenants were no longer legally enforceable as such enforcement would violate the Equal Protection Clause of the Fourteenth Amendment of the U.S. Constitution.[70] *Shelley v. Kraemer* effectively put an end to the active use of restrictive covenants as a tool of housing segregation. The Court's ruling, however, did *not* bring an end to the various other mechanisms that private entities used to maintain residential segregation.

Many real-estate agencies practiced racial steering, refusing to show homes in a white neighborhood to a minority buyer. Instead, white and minority home seekers were shown homes in different parts of the city. Banks and home finance institutions also engaged in racial steering and would not approve loans or home insurance to a minority homebuyer seeking to move into a white neighborhood. Instead, real-estate agents, loan officers, and other private financial officials "steered" or directed minority home seekers to neighborhoods that already had a racial minority presence.

In Pittsburgh, white brokerage boards blocked membership by black brokers, denying African-American real-estate agents access to property listings that would have enabled the agents to show properties in white neighborhoods to prospective African-American buyers and renters. In Mt. Lebanon, a suburb of Pittsburgh, real-estate agents refused to show properties to blacks and Jews. The city's white-owned newspapers were complicit in racial steering; their classified ads indicated if a home or rental unit was "for Colored," that is, open to African Americans. The absence of the "for Colored" designation in ads for homes in outlying areas indicated suburbs that were "closed" to minorities.[71]

As the previous paragraphs indicate, private actions to constrain free-market choice and enforce residential segregation were found in the North as well as the South. Suburban developers, too, practiced racial exclusion.

Outside New York City and Philadelphia, developer William Levitt in the 1950s built new communities of mass-produced tract housing that put a three-bedroom home within the financial reach of the working class. At the time, the building of the so-called **Levittowns** represented quite an achievement. The Levittowns were viewed as a suburban working-class paradise, places where ordinary citizens could live the American dream (Figure 2.4). However, "by William Levitt's orders, not a single resident was black."

The racial homogeneity of Levittown's population was "not the result of a shortage of potential black buyers." African Americans who worked the region's factories could afford a home in Levittown. But they were not allowed entry. Levitt refused to sell to blacks, as he feared that whites would be reluctant to buy a home in a mixed-race community. Levitt's sales agents even refused to offer homes to African-American war veterans. When the Supreme Court's *Shelley v. Kraemer* decision barred communities from enforcing racially restrictive covenants, Levitt's agents enforced racial homogeneity by evicting a black family for being an "undesirable" tenant. In the Pennsylvania Levittown, white residents turned to mob action—a grassroots, community white riot—in their efforts to oust the first African-American family who moved to the community, having purchased a Levittown home from a willing white reseller.[72] The story eventually became the basis for the 2017 movie *Suburbicon* (see Box 2.3).

Figure 2.4 **Racial Exclusion in a Working-Class Suburban Paradise: Aerial View of Levittown, Pennsylvania, 1950s.** In the era following World War II, FHA- and VA-insured loans enabled the lower-middle class and the working class to flee the cities for the suburbs. The mass-produced tract housing of Levittown put the suburban dream within the reach of the working class. Levittown would grow over the years.

Levittown was racially restricted, a decision the developer made at the time in order to maintain the community's attractiveness to white buyers. The threat of community violence—that is, a threat of violence by the community's white residents—further helped to enforce racial exclusion in Levittown.

Source: User Shani/Wikicommons, https://commons.wikimedia.org/wiki/File: LevittownPA.jpg.

The **1968 Fair Housing Act** made racial steering and other forms of housing discrimination illegal. Over the years, the law succeeded in eliminating the most blatant forms of housing discrimination.

Yet, discrimination against minority home seekers has not entirely disappeared. Racial steering remains a potent form of housing discrimination, but is conducted more subtly than in the past. In an estimated 20 percent of cases, African Americans and Hispanics are denied information regarding the availability of home loans, information that is more freely provided to comparable white home seekers. The selective withholding of information serves to deny minority buyers the ability to arrange the financing that would allow them to purchase a home in a region's more desirable communities.[73]

Box 2.3
Film Images of the City: *Suburbicon* and the Story of Racial Exclusion in America's Suburbs

Suburbicon (2017), directed by and starring George Clooney, tells the story of a family whose dream-like suburban existence is interrupted by an explosion of violence as their neighbors seek to oust the first black family who has gained entrance into their community. In its primary plot, *Suburbicon* presents a somewhat comedic and ever-twisting tale of crime, murder, and revenge. The film's secondary plot or backstory, however, alludes to real-world events: a community riot that occurred in the 1950s in Levittown, a suburb in Bucks County outside of Philadelphia.

William and Daisy Myers, both college educated, and their infant daughter had become the first African Americans to move into the planned suburb. The residents of Levittown drew up a petition demanding the eviction of the Myers. When that failed, angry whites turned to rock-throwing and mob violence, burning a cross outside the Myers's home. Despite continuing harassment and threats, the Myers would not leave.

Source: For further discussion, see: David Kushner, *Levittown: Two Families, One Tycoon, and the Fight for Civil Rights in America's Legendary Suburb* (New York: Walker Books, 2009); and Stephen Galloway, "The Real-Life Battle That Inspired George Clooney's 'Suburbicon,'" *Hollywood Reporter*, September 1, 2017, www.hollywoodreporter.com/news/suburbicon-real-life-racial-battle-inspired-george-clooneys-film-1034430.

Dramatic documentation of modern-day racial steering was produced in 2015 when a civil rights group secretly recorded videotapes showing that M&T Bank, one of the largest in the nation, discriminated against black, Latino, and Asian home seekers. The bank offered minority mortgage applicants lower loan amounts than those the bank offered to lesser qualified white buyers. By making different amounts of money available to white and nonwhite buyers, the bank's loan approval process served to steer home seekers from different races and ethnic groups to different-priced neighborhoods.[74]

How does such discrimination continue despite the provisions of the Fair Housing Act? Quite simply, racial steering often takes place in forms that are difficult to document and prove. Home seekers who feel that they are the victims of racial steering have a very difficult time proving in court that racial discrimination did indeed occur. No home seeker knows for sure exactly which houses an agent has shown other buyers and exactly what loan amounts, financial terms and other information a real-estate agency or bank has provided other buyers. Nor can a buyer easily prove that differences in treatment were the result of racial prejudice, that the agent or banker was not responding to the differences in family size, income, savings, and credit rating of different home seekers.

BLOCKBUSTING, REDLINING, AND REVERSE REDLINING: HOW BANKS, REAL-ESTATE AGENTS, AND INSURANCE COMPANIES ACCELERATED INNER-CITY DECLINE

In the mid-1900s, numerous big-city real-estate agencies sought the quick profits that could be realized from stirring up racial tensions in residential areas. The manipulative of racial fears could prompt whites to sell their homes, with real-estate agents and agencies earning considerable profits from the racial transformation, and ultimately the resegregation, of inner-city neighborhoods.

In a process commonly referred to as **blockbusting** or **panic selling**, real-estate agents publicized the fact that a black family had moved into an all-white neighborhood. Real-estate agents would go door to door, preying on the fears of white homeowners and the elderly, warning that the value of their homes would soon plummet as the neighborhood underwent further racial change. The frightened owners, worried about the diminished value of their primary financial asset, would agree to list their homes for sale. The unscrupulous real-estate dealer would then use that listing to scare their neighbors to sell, before it was "too late." The real-estate agents profited from the sales fees they earned as property in the neighborhood turned over. Their fear tactics had a great cost, accelerating "white flight" to the suburbs and undermining the stability of inner-city neighborhoods.

Blockbusting "broke" all-white neighborhoods but did not produce neighborhoods that remained racially integrated over the years. Rather, each home sale to a black family only increased the sense of urgency among remaining white owners to sell and flee the area. Panic selling ultimately resulted in a neighborhood's **resegregation**; in some cases it took just a little more than a decade for an all-white area to quickly become an all-minority area as panicked whites fled.

As the whites left, speculators profited by buying properties at low prices and **subdividing single-family homes** into small, shabby apartments that were rented at inflated prices to black families who had few other neighborhoods open to them. Subdividing single-family homes into multifamily apartments increased the wear and tear on the structures. As the rental conversions were often built with plywood walls and other cheap materials, the physical condition of the rental units soon deteriorated, becoming one more factor in a neighborhood's downslide.

Redlining by financial institutions was another major factor in the decline of core-city neighborhood. Redlining occurs when a bank, insurance company, and other financial institutions simply refuses to approve of loans in neighborhoods that credit officers view as posing greater-than-usual financial risks. The practice gets its name from the early years of redlining when numerous banks and insurance companies drew a red line on a map to indicate the areas of a city in which they would not approve or insure a property loan. The redlining of geographical areas is the result of gross racial stereotyping where individuals are discriminated against because of their skin color and the skin color of their neighbors. Even workers with excellent job histories and credit histories found that they could not get a loan to rehabilitate or buy a home in a neighborhood that had been redlined. The cutoff of credit resulted in **disinvestment** in a neighborhood and its certain decline. The redlining practices of private institutions cut off the economic lifeblood necessary for major structural repairs, new home construction, and a community's rejuvenation.

The Fight Against Redlining: The Community Reinvestment Act (CRA)

Four decades ago, the federal government enacted legislation to put an end to redlining. The **Community Reinvestment Act (CRA) of 1977** banned redlining. A bank can no longer choose to overlook entire sections of a city. The CRA requires banks to meet the credit needs of homeowners, homebuyers and small businesses throughout the entire region that the bank is chartered to serve, with special emphasis given to low- and moderate-income communities.

The CRA also requires regulated mortgage-finance institutions to disclose the geographical area of each loan. Activist community groups have used this information to document just which banks ignore minority areas of the city, with bad publicity serving to put pressure on banks to extend credit to applicants in disadvantaged communities. The CRA gives community organizations the right to challenge bank mergers if they could prove that a bank has failed to meet its lending obligations under the Act

Over its four-decades history, the CRA has had a tremendous impact on inner-city economies, leveraging an infusion of hundreds of billions dollar of investment capital, including loans to persons in underserved neighborhood seeking to buy or rehabilitate a home or expand a small business. The statistical evidence underscores the success of the CRA in prompting banks to advance credit and increase homeownership in low- and moderate-income communities.[75]

Yet despite the CRA's overall success, discriminatory lending practices persist, albeit often in forms that are less stark than classic redlining. Given the requirements of the CRA, few financial institutions are foolish enough to simply draw a red line on a map or otherwise prohibit the issuance of loans in an entire neighborhood; such broad-brush neighborhood disinvestment can easily be detected in the data that banks must file under the CRA. Nonetheless, race continues to be an unacknowledged factor in lending decisions. A lending institution may offer financing for condominium and cooperative conversions in a core-city area while denying loan applications to minority residents and community-based organizations that seek to renovate older structures for affordable housing.

A bank can discourage the flow of credit applications from low- and moderate-income households and from minority neighborhoods simply by failing to open branches in inner-city neighborhoods. Hudson City Savings Bank, the largest savings bank in New Jersey, "steered clear of black and Hispanic neighborhoods as they opened new branches," a strategy that effectively diminished loan requests from minority-dominated portions of the city. In 2014, Hudson issued 1,886 mortgages in New Jersey and in nearby New York and Connecticut, but only a paltry 25 mortgages went to black borrowers! The bank was reluctant to assume the risks and community entanglements that can accompany an effort to promote lending in poorer communities.[76]

Redlining occurs in home insurance. A Richmond, Virginia, jury in 1998 ordered Nationwide Insurance to pay more than $100 million in damages as a result of the company's reluctance to insure homes in black neighborhoods. Nationwide had instructed its agents to avoid "black urbanite households with many children."[77]

Evans Bank, a relatively small New York lending institution, was not at all subtle in its discriminatory actions. The bank excluded the predominantly black East Side of Buffalo from a map of the bank's "trade area," the area where the bank would concentrate its lending efforts. Between 2009 and 2012, the bank received over 1,100 loan applications; but only four came from African Americans! Even African Americans in Buffalo with good credit scores had virtually no chance of securing a loan from the bank. In its agreement to settle the lawsuit, Evans Bank committed itself to increased advertising and marketing efforts on Buffalo's East Side (Figure 2.5).[78]

Figure 2.5 **Redlining Still Exists: Evans Bank Draws a "Trade Area" That Excludes Buffalo's Predominantly Black East Side**.

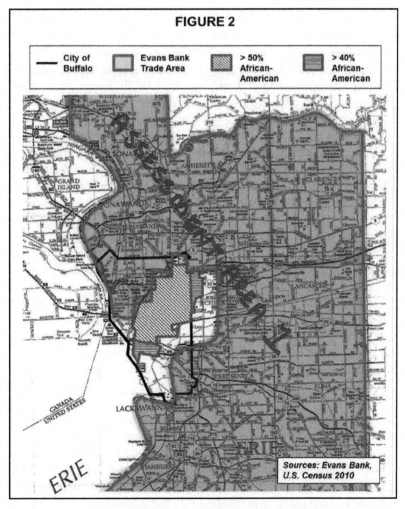

Source: The People of the State of New York by ERIC T. SCHNEIDERMAN, Attorney General of the State of New York against Evans Bancorp, Inc. and Evans Bank, complaint filed in United States District Court, Western District, Case 1:14-cv-00726 Document 1 Filed 09/02/14, www.scribd.com/document/238424223/Evans-Bank-Complaint-As-Filed-By-A-G-Schneiderman.

More unscrupulous private lenders have sought the profits that can be obtained from **predatory lending practices**, saddling minority borrowers with higher interest rates and extra fees as compared to those charged white homebuyers, and targeting communities of color for insurance and other loan products that are more expensive than necessary. Wells Fargo Bank, one of the nation's most important home finance institutions, had its agents instruct minorities to apply for adjustable rate mortgages, without informing loan seekers of the availability of fixed-rate low-interest mortgages. The bank's agents touted the initial low-interest rates and monthly mortgage payments of adjustable rate mortgages without warning novice homebuyers of the risks they were assuming and the difficulty they would face in meeting their monthly mortgage payments should interest rates rise. Fragile communities are harmed when homeowners "walk away" from a loan when they cannot meet their monthly mortgage obligations and where the resale of a house will not even cover the amount owed.

Wells Fargo also organized so-called wealth building seminars that targeted African Americans in order to have them sign up for high-cost loans that the bank's agents deceptively praised as "alternative" financing instruments. The bank's mortgage agents, talking among themselves, derisively referred to such profitable but high-cost subprime lending instruments as "ghetto loans."[79] Wells Fargo eventually agreed to pay $175 million to settle a lawsuit that charged the bank with deceptive practices and illegally targeting higher-cost loans to minority communities.

As previously observed, the record of the CRA is one of overwhelming success. The CRA has increased the willingness of banks to make loans to minority-owned businesses.[80] In Cleveland, Chicago, Pittsburgh, and a great many other cities, the CRA led banks to "'rediscover' the inner city as a viable and profitable market."[81]

Still, the CRA has powerful critics who argue that the Act imposes costly and unnecessary regulations on banks that pressures them to make unwise high-risk loans. Banking lobbyists and Republican legislators even attempted to blame the CRA for the wave of home defaults and the banking crisis of the early 2000s. But the CRA does not deserve such blame. A review of the data shows that home loans subject to CRA supervision actually suffered lower rates of default than did comparable loans made in other parts of the metropolis.[82] The highest default rates and the most abusive predatory lending practices—loans with outrageously high placement fees and loans that initially offered a buyer super-low monthly payments but within just a few years required the borrower to pay a super-high final **balloon payment** (the entire amount still owed, including the outstanding principle and accumulated unpaid interest)—were pushed by lending institutions that were not subject to the CRA's provisions.[83]

Nothing in the CRA requires a bank to issue loans to applicants with low credit scores. Lenders have a variety of options in deciding how to increase their activity and the awareness of banking services in low- and moderate-income communities.[84] To meet CRA requirements, a bank can locate branches in low- and moderate-income communities or, alternatively, increase the advertising and marketing of its loan products in disadvantaged neighborhoods. A number of banks work with community groups to help identify potential homebuyers and increase their "fiscal literacy" when it comes to budgeting funds for home repairs and taking other steps that will enable first-time buyers to anticipate the demands of homeownership. Overall, banks have had little difficulty in meeting the CRA's requirements. Each year, from 2006 through 2014, only 2 or 3 percent of the banks examined received less than a satisfactory grade from regulators.[85]

Nonetheless, Donald Trump sided with political conservatives and business interests who argued the virtues of **deregulation**, that government regulations on business, including those of the CRA, should be relaxed. The Office of the Controller of the Currency, the part of the Treasury Department that oversees the nation's biggest banks, revised its agency manual in order to diminish the ability of activist community groups to thwart a bank merger or expansion in instances where the bank had failed to live up to its lending obligations under the CRA. The new agency manual explicitly declared that a low CRA rating "is not a bar to approval of application" for bank expansion or merger.[86]

Of potentially greater significance, the Department of Treasury under Trump called for a new system of "metrics" to update the CRA to the age of online banking (as banks no longer confine their business activities to precisely defined geographical areas). The new metrics would also simplify the process that a bank has to endure in order to demonstrate that it has met the requirements of the CRA. The new metrics-based system would enable bank to readily report that have met the target set for its offering of credit to an underserved community.

Civil rights advocates were outraged, charging the new system of metrics would diminish the ability of the CRA to counter discriminatory lending patterns. A bank that had a poor record of approving loans to inner-minority residents (even to persons with good credit scores) and to community-based organization seeking to build affordable housing would still be able to meet the "metrics" target set for the bank by counting the dollar value of the loans that the bank had extended to developers constructing luxury apartments and condominiums in the neighborhood.[87]

HOW THE ACTIONS OF GOVERNMENT AND THE PRIVATE SECTOR ADDED TO HOMELESSNESS

There are numerous reasons why people are homeless. Some individuals are drug and alcohol abusers who cannot hold steady employment. Others have developmental disabilities or suffer mental illness. Young people may leave home in order to escape abusive homes. Families with children may wind up homeless because they can no longer pay the monthly rent due to a loss of employment.

Yet personal failings are not the sole cause of homelessness. Homelessness is also a result of government programs that deinstitutionalize psychiatric patients at a time when government offers limited funding for halfway houses, assisted living arrangements, and counseling to help people who have difficulty in functioning on their own and may find themselves living on the street.

Of course, governments in the United States offer numerous programs to assist the homeless and to aid persons who are at risk of being homeless. Yet, homelessness is also the result of the shrinking of the supply of low-cost housing units in the city. Local governments and private businesses share culpability for the virtual disappearance of the **single room occupancy (SRO) hotel** from the urban landscape, the cheap by-the-night or by-the-week housing that offered a city's most marginal residents a last-chance refuge from the streets. An SRO, with its tiny rooms and toilets down the hall, is not what any tourist would deem an acceptable hotel. SROs tend to be rather run-down facilities located in the less desirable parts of town. Still, an SRO offers a poor person with a few dollars a place to sleep for the night or the week.

Today, the supply of SRO housing has dropped dramatically as private developers and public redevelopment officials implemented plans to revitalize stagnant downtowns and their nearby neighborhoods. Denver razed SRO housing in response to pressures on the housing market generated by new downtown construction and newly expanded central retail and entertainment districts.[88] Private developers and public officials constantly seek to convert properties to higher land uses. In doing so, they have destroyed some of the city's lowest-rent housing units, leaving vulnerable residents little alternative to municipal and nonprofit-run shelters.

CONCLUSION: PUBLIC AND PRIVATE POWER AND THE URBAN SITUATION

Population pressures, technological advances, and citizen affluence have all had a great influence on the shape of urban development in the United States. Yet such forces do not dictate the exact urban patterns and problems found today. Government programs—including those that make up the "hidden" urban policy of government—and the manipulations by private-sector actors, too, have a great influence on urban development. Urban sprawl, the decline of core-city neighborhoods, patterns of racial segregation, the shift of economic activity and population to the Sunbelt, and the rise of homelessness are all problems and patterns that are *not* purely natural occurrences that lie beyond the reach of government.

Residential segregation is not simply a reflection of the differences among groups in terms of their buying power, levels of education, and housing preferences. Increased income and education do not enable African Americans to move to better neighborhoods to the same extent that similar gains enhance the residential choices available to whites and even to Latinos.[89] Racial biases and institutional discriminations continue to mar the workings of local housing markets.

Even the extent of **dual migration**, where the poor move into cities while the better-off middle class seeks the comforts of suburban living, is not simply the result of population pressures, technological changes, and citizens's desires. Instead, numerous government programs and policies, including the extensive tax breaks provided to homeowners, have subsidized the outflow of middle-class and better-off families to the suburbs. Local control of zoning further allows more privileged suburbs to maintain their exclusiveness, limiting the construction of affordable housing that could enable a much broader range of people to move into the community.

Various private-sector manipulations, including racial steering, blockbusting, and discriminatory disinvestment, have also contributed to the inequality of American communities. In an earlier era, real estate and financial institutions maximized profits by promoting property turnover and neighborhood churn, not residential stability. Today, corporate-backed redevelopment projects serve to make city neighborhoods attractive to well-off condominium buyers, tourists, and global businesses and other corporate investors. These projects generate pressures that displace some of the most vulnerable residents of the city.

As Chapter 4 will discuss in detail, the *gentrification* or upgrading of once-troubled neighborhoods is not just another stage in a natural process of natural neighborhood evolution. Instead, public officials, real-estate interests, and other corporate actors often *choose* gentrification. They pursue and subsidize actions that aim to gentrify neighborhoods and transform the city.

Before that story can be told, however, we must finish another story that we have already begun: the movement of Americans and political power to the suburbs.

KEY TERMS

annexation (*p. 44*)

balloon payment (*p. 70*)

bedroom communities (*p. 46*)

blockbusting (*p. 67*)

Community Reinvestment Act
  (CRA) of 1977 (*p. 68*)

condominium and cooperative
  apartment conversions (*p. 53*)

demographic factors in urban
  development (*p. 42*)

deregulation (*p. 52*)

disinvestment (*p. 67*)

dual migration (*p. 72*)

economic factors in urban
  development (*p. 42*)

edge cities (*p. 46*)

Fair Housing Act of 1968 (*p. 65*)

federal grant programs for hospitals
  and sewage processing facilities
  (*p. 57*)

Federal Housing Administration
  (FHA) (*p. 49*)

federal tax incentives for the oil and
  gas industries (*p. 57*)

FHA loan insurance (*p. 49*)

Frostbelt (*p. 46*)

GI Bill of Rights of 1944 (*p. 50*)

global cities (*p. 48*)

Great Migration (*p. 44*)

greening strategies (*p. 49*)

hidden urban policy (*p. 41*)

land-use and zoning regulations
  (*p. 60*)

Levittowns (*p. 64*)

mansion subsidy (*p. 53*)

metropolis (*p. 39*)

multicentered metropolis (*p. 46*)

Negro removal, urban renewal as
  (*p. 57*)

Opportunity Zones (*p. 55*)

panic selling (*p. 67*)

political revolt by Brookline,
  Massachusetts (*p. 44*)

predatory lending (*p. 52*)

predatory lending practices,
  examples of (*p. 70*)

racial steering (*p. 51*)

redlining (*p. 50*)

Republican-era deregulation (*p. 52*)

resegregation (*p. 67*)

restrictive covenants (*p. 50*)

right-to-work laws (*p. 61*)

Robin Hood in reverse, homeowner
  tax incentives as (*p. 53*)

second ghetto (*p. 58*)

Shelley v. Kraemer (*p. 63*)

shrinking cities (*p. 49*)

single room occupancy (SRO) hotel
  (*p. 71*)

state action (*p. 40*), the 14th
  Amendment's Equal Protection
  Clause bar on

streetcar suburbs (*p. 44*)

subdividing single-family homes
  (*p. 67*)

Sunbelt (*p. 46*)

NOTES

1. See, for instance, Ted Gayer, Austin K. Drukker, and Alexander K. Gold, "Tax-Exempt Municipal Bonds and the Financing of Professional Sports Stadiums," an Economic Studies report of The Brookings Institution, Washington, DC, September 2016. The Brookings report details how public officials and the federal tax code provide billions of dollars in subsidies for sports stadiums and arenas despite the "weak" (p. 3) evidence that such extensive subsidies for sports arenas provide a worthwhile return to the community. www.brookings.edu/wp-content/uploads/2016/09/gayerdrukkergold_stadiumsubsidies_090816.pdf.
2. Edward C. Banfield, *The Unheavenly City Revisited* (Boston: Little, Brown, 1974), 25–51.
3. A few cities, especially, in the American West, are notable exceptions to the observation that transportation was the dominant factor in a city's location. Communities such as Fort Worth (Texas) and Fort Collins (Colorado) sprouted under the protection of army outposts, as fearful settlers in a hostile territory required military protection.
4. Kenneth T. Jackson, *Crabgrass Frontier: The Suburbanization of the United States* (New York: Oxford University Press, 1985), 14–15.
5. Sam Bass Warner, Jr., *Streetcar Suburbs: The Process of Growth in Boston, 1870–90*, 2nd ed. (Cambridge, MA: Harvard University Press, 1978), 164–165.
6. Warner, *Streetcar Suburbs*, 165.
7. James N. Gregory, *The Southern Diaspora: How the Great Migrations of Black and White Southerners Transformed America* (Chapel Hill: University of North Carolina Press, 2007).
8. Brian J. Miller, "A Small Suburb Becomes a Boomburb: Explaining Suburban Growth in Naperville, Illinois," *Journal of Urban History* 42, No. 6 (2016), 1135–1152. Miller observes how no one theory explains the growth of Naperville. Naperville's growth was not predetermined by natural factors and pressures. Instead, a local policy of boosterism and the joint actions of a business and government "growth coalition" were keys in Naperville's dynamic emergence.
9. Joel Garneau, *Edge City: Life on the New Frontier* (New York: Doubleday, 1991); Robert Fishman, *Bourgeois Utopias: The Rise and Fall of Suburbia* (New York: Basic Books, 1987).
10. Elizabeth Kneebone, "The Changing Geography of US Poverty," testimony delivered before the U.S. House Ways and Means Committee, Subcommittee on Human Resources, February 15, 2017, www.brookings.edu/testimonies/the-changing-geography-of-us-poverty/; Elizabeth Kneebone and Alan Berube, *Confronting Suburban Poverty in America* (Washington, DC: Brookings Institution Press, 2013), esp. chap. 8 "Melting Pot Cities and Suburbs"; William H. Frey, *Diversity Explosion: How New Racial Demographics Are Remaking America* (Washington, DC: Brookings Institution Press, 2014); and Sarah Jackson and Elizabeth Kneebone, "Suburbs on $7.25 an Hour," a report of the Brookings Institution, Washington, DC January 13, 2014, www.brookings.edu/blog/the-avenue/2014/01/13/suburbs-on-7-25-an-hour/; and William H. Frey, "The End of Suburban White Flight," a report of the Brookings Institution, Washington, DC July 23, 2015, www.brookings.edu/blog/the-avenue/2015/07/23/the-end-of-suburban-white-flight/.

11. United States Census Bureau, "Maricopa County Added over 222 People Per Day in 2016, More Than Any Other County, Census Bureau Release CB17–44, March 23, 2017, www.census.gov/newsroom/press-releases/2017/cb17-44.html.

12. Fanny Carlet, Joseph Schilling, and Megan Heckert, "Greening U.S. Legacy Cities: Urban Agriculture as a Strategy for Reclaiming Vacant Urban Land," *Agroecology and Urban Food Systems* 41, no. 8 (2017), 887–906; Winifred Bird, "Hard-Pressed Rust Belt Cities Go Green to Aid Urban Revival," *Yale Environment 360*, a publication of the Yale School of Forestry and Environmental Studies, May 31, 2016, http://e360.yale.edu/features/greening_rust_belt_cities_detroit_gary_indiana; and Daniel Hummel, "Right-Sizing Cities in the United States: Defining Its Strategies," *Journal of Urban Affairs* 37, no. 4 (2014), 397–409. Justin B. Hollander, *Sunburnt Cities: The Great Recession, Depopulation and Urban Planning in the American Sunbelt* (New York: Routledge, 2011) reminds us that in Phoenix, Orlando, and other growing Sunbelt Cities, numerous neighborhoods were victimized by extensive home mortgage defaults and property abandonment. Hollander argues that such Sunbelt cities should consider adopting the various land repurposing and greening strategies that have been utilized by shrinking Rustbelt cities.

13. Janet Rothenberg Pack, ed., *Sunbelt/Frostbelt: Public Policies and Market Forces in Metropolitan Development* (Washington, DC: Brookings Institution Press, 2005), traces the continuing effects of government spending and regulatory actions on the regional population and job shift.

14. Jackson, *Crabgrass Frontier*, 204.

15. The VA program offered no-money-down loans to veterans. In more recent years, the FHA has sought to facilitate homeownership, requiring down payments of around 3 percent or 3.5 percent.

16. Quoted in Jackson, *Crabgrass Frontier*, 207

17. Douglas Massey, "Origins of Economic Disparities: The Historical Role of Housing Segregation," in *Segregation: The Rising Costs for America*, ed. James H. Carr and Nandinee K. Kutty (New York: Routledge, 2008), 72.

18. Richard Rothstein, *The Color of Law: A Forgotten History of How Our Government Segregated America* (New York: Liveright Publishing, 2017), chap 4 "Own Your Own Home" presents an overview of the history of discriminatory actions by the FHA and VA, including vivid examples of how these government agencies promoted racial segregation as the United States entered the suburban age.

19. Massey, "Origins of Economic Disparities," 72.

20. Citizens Commission on Civil Rights, "A Decent Home . . . A Report on the Continuing Failure of the Federal Government to Provide Equal Housing Opportunity" (Washington, DC: 1983), cited in *Critical Perspectives on Housing*, ed. Rachel G. Bratt, Chester Hartman, and Ann Myerson (Philadelphia: Temple University Press, 1986), 299.

21. For a good overview of the evolution of the FHA actions and the variety of governmental practices served to segregate the American city, see Massey, "Origins of Economic Disparities," 39–80, and Rothstein, *The Color of Law*, chaps. 3 and 4.

22. Rothstein, *The Color of Law*, 68–71, 85–86.

23. Citizens Commission on Civil Rights, "A Decent Home," 301.

24. Thomas J. Sugrue, *The Origins of the Urban Crisis: Race and Inequality in Postwar Detroit* (Princeton, NJ: Princeton University Press, 1996), 64.

25. Christopher Bonastia, *Knocking on the Door: The Federal Government's Attempt to Desegregate the Suburbs* (Princeton, NJ: Princeton University Press, 2006), 62–63.

26. Mike Davis, "How Eden Lost Its Garden: A Political History of the Los Angeles Landscape," in *The City: Los Angeles and Urban Theory at the End of the Twentieth Century*, ed. Allen J. Scott and Edward J. Soja (Berkeley and Los Angeles: University of California Press, 1996), 169.

27. Rachael A. Woldoff, *White Flight/Black Flight: The Dynamics of Racial Change in an American Neighborhood* (Ithaca, NY: Cornell University Press, 2011), 142.

28. Roger Biles, *The Fate of Cities: Urban America and the Federal Government, 1945–2000* (Lawrence, KS: University Press of Kansas, 2011), 179–180.

29. David H. Stevens, President and CEO of the Mortgage Bankers Association and Former FHA Commissioner, "Sustainable Housing Finance: Perspectives on Reforming FHA" (written statement prepared for the Subcommittee on Housing and Insurance Services, Committee on Financial Services, U.S. House of Representatives, April 10, 2013), http://financialservices.house.gov/uploadedfiles/hhrg-113-ba04-wstate-dstevens-20130410.pdf.

30. Gregory D. Squires and Charis E. Kubrin, *Privileged Places: Race, Residence, and the Structure of Opportunity* (Boulder, CO: Lynne Rienner, 2006).

31. Jeff Crump, Kathe Newman, Eric S. Belsky, Phil Ashton, David H. Kaplan, Daniel J. Hammel, and Elvin Wyly, "Cities Destroyed (Again) for Cash: Forum on the U.S. Foreclosure Crisis," *Urban Geography* 29, no. 8 (2008): 745–784, quote on 749.

32. U.S. Department of Treasury, "Tax Expenditures," FY 2017 report, www.treasury.gov/resource-center/tax-policy/Documents/Tax-Expenditures-FY2017.pdf.

33. Margery Austin Turner, Eric Toder, Rolf Pendall, and Claudia Sharygin, *How Would Reforming the Mortgage Interest Deduction Affect the Housing Market?* (Washington, DC: The Urban Institute, March 2013), www.taxpolicycenter.org/UploadedPDF/412776-How-Would-Reforming-the-Mortgage-Interest-Deduction-Affect-the-Housing-Market.pdf; Joint Committee on Taxation, U.S. Congress, *Estimates of Federal Tax Expenditures for Fiscal Years 2012–2017* (Washington, DC: U.S. Government Printing Office, 2013), Table 1; Will Fischer and Barbara Sard, "Chart Book: Federal Housing Spending Is Poorly Matched to Need," a report of the Center on Budget and Policy Priorities, Washington DC, March 8, 2017, www.cbpp.org/research/housing/chart-book-federal-housing-spending-is-poorly-matched-to-need.

34. John Iselin and Philip Stallworth, "Who Benefits from Tax Subsidies for Home Ownership?" *TaxVox Blog Posting* of the Tax Policy Center, the Urban Institute and the Brookings Institution, Washington, DC, September 14, 2016, www.taxpolicycenter.org/taxvox/who-benefits-tax-subsidies-home-ownership.

35. J. Brian Charles, "The GOP Tax Law Could Starve Cities of Revenue," *Governing Magazine*, January 9, 2018, www.governing.com/topics/finance/gov-trump-gop-property-taxes-home-values-lc.html.

36. Megan Schrader, "'Opportunity Zones' in Tax Bill Ripe for Abuse," *Denver Post*, December 19, 2017; Jim Tankersley, "A Potential Win for Distressed America," *New York Times*, January 30, 2018.

37. Bruce Katz, "Stirring Market Demand," *The New Localism Blog Posting*, September 5, 2018, www.thenewlocalism.com/newsletter/stirring-market-demand/.

38. See, for instance, Joseph F.C. DiMento, "Stent (or Dagger?) in the Heart of Town: Urban Freeways in Syracuse, 1944–1967," *Journal of Planning History* 8, no. 2 (2009): 133–161.

39. Raymond A. Mohl, "Planned Destruction: The Interstates and Central City Housing," in *The Making of Urban America*, 3rd ed., ed. Raymond A. Mohl and Roger Biles (Lanham, MD: Rowman and Littlefield, 2012), 294–295.

40. Joseph F.C. DiMento and Cliff Ellis, *Changing Lanes: Visions and Histories of Urban Freeways* (Cambridge, MA: MIT Press, 2013), 127–132.

41. Roxanne Warren, *Rail and the City: Shrinking Our Carbon Footprint While Reimagining Urban Space* (Cambridge, MA: MIT Press, 2014).

42. Michael R. Fine, "Realignment: Highways and Livability Policy in the Post-Interstate Era, 178–2014," *Journal of Urban History* 40, no. 5 (2014): 855–869. The quotation can be found on p. 864.

43. John H. Mollenkopf, *The Contested City* (Princeton, NJ: Princeton University Press, 1983), 103–109.

44. Richard M. Bernard and Bradley R. Rice, "Introduction," in *Sunbelt Cities: Politics and Growth Since World War II*, ed. Richard M. Bernard and Bradley R. Rice (Austin: University of Texas Press, 1983), 12.

45. Virginia Mayer and Margaret Downs, *The Pentagon Tilt: Regional Biases in Defense Spending and Strategy* (Washington, DC: Northeast-Midwest Institute, January 1983), 9.

46. Mia Gray, Elyse Golob, Ann R. Markusen, and Sam Ock Park, "The Four Faces of Silicon Valley," in *Second Tier Cities: Rapid Growth Beyond the Metropolis*, ed. Ann R. Markusen, Yong-Sook Lee, and Sean DiGiovanna (Minneapolis: University of Minnesota Press, 1999), 293–299.

47. Margaret Pugh O'Meara, *Cities of Knowledge: Cold War Science and the Search for the Next Silicon Valley* (Princeton, NJ: Princeton University Press, 2005), esp. 4–12.

48. Joe R. Feagin, *Free Enterprise City: Houston in Political and Economic Perspective* (New Brunswick, NJ: Rutgers University Press, 1988), 54–55, 63–71, 186–188, 203–204.

49. For a brief journalistic accounting as to how one southern city used "urban renewal" funds to "destroy" a historic African-American neighborhood, tearing down good homes and commercial businesses as well as structures in dilapidated condition, see Pam Kelley, "How Urban Renewal Destroyed Charlotte's Brooklyn Neighborhood," *Charlotte Observer*, March 18, 2016.

50. Joe W. Trotter and Jared N. Day, *Race and Renaissance: African Americans in Pittsburgh since World War II* (Pittsburgh: University of Pittsburgh Press, 2010), 68–71.

51. Meghan McCarthy, "A History of Urban Renewal in San Antonio," *Planning Forum* 13–14 (2009): 53–56.

52. Melita Marie Garza and Flynn McRoberts, "Addison Settles with Hispanics," *Chicago Tribune*, August 8, 1997.

53. Arnold R. Hirsch, *Making the Second Ghetto: Race and Housing in Chicago, 1940–60* (Chicago: University of Chicago Press, 1983 and 1998) provides the classic statement on the choices underlying the construction of the second ghetto in Chicago. The details of this paragraph and the preceding paragraph are taken form Hirsch.

54. Robert Pear, "New York Admits to Racial Steering in Housing Lawsuit," *New York Times*, July 1, 1992.

55. Robert M. Fogelson, *Downtown: Its Rise and Fall, 1880–1950* (New Haven, CT: Yale University Press, 2001), 160.

56. Jonathan Rothwell and Douglas S. Massey, "The Effect of Density Zoning on Racial Segregation in U.S. Urban Areas," *Urban Affairs Review* 44, no. 6 (June 2009): 779–806; Richard Reeves, "'Exclusionary Zoning' Is Opportunity Hoarding by Upper Middle Class," *RealClear Markets*, May 24, 2017, www.realclearmarkets.com/articles/2017/05/24/exclusionary_zoning_is_opportunity_hoarding_by_upper_middle_class_102706.html.

57. Jonathan Rothwell, "Zoning Out the Poor: Skywalker Ranch Edition," *A Brookings Institution Social Mobility Memo*, July 1, 2015, www.brookings.edu/blog/social-mobility-memos/2015/07/01/zoning-out-the-poor-skywalker-ranch-edition/.

58. Sonia A. Hirt, *Zoned in the USA: The Origins and Implications of American Land-Use Regulation* (Ithaca, NY: Cornell University Press, 2014). William A. Fischel, *Zoning Rules! The Economics of Land Use Regulation* (Cambridge, MA: Lincoln Institute of Land Policy, 2015) presents a somewhat different interpretation, one that emphasizes the fiscal interest that suburbanites often have in maintaining exclusionary zoning.

59. Richard D. Kahlenberg, "An Economic Fair Housing Act," a report of the Century Foundation, August 3, 2017, https://tcf.org/content/report/economic-fair-housing-act/.

60. Michael C. Lens and Paavo Monkkonen, "Do Strict Land Use Regulations Make Metropolitan Areas More Segregated by Income?" *Journal of the American Planning Association*, 82, no. 1 (2016): 6–21,

61. Tom Angotti and Sylvia Morse, eds., *Zoned Out! Race, Displacement, and City Planning in New York City* (New York: Terreform, 2016). In Chicago, one review of the evidence indicates that upzoning led to increases in the price of housing without really doing much to generate an overall increase in the number of dwelling units as developers see the opportunity to construct new luxury units; see Yonah Freemark, "Upzoning Chicago: Impacts of a Zoning Reform on Property Values and Housing Construction," *Urban Affairs Review*, first published January 19, 2019, https://doi.org/10.1177/1078087418824672.

62. Heywood T. Sanders, "The Political Economy of Sunbelt Urban Development: Building the Public Sector" (paper presented at the annual meeting of the American Political Science Association, New York, September 2–5, 1994).

63. Elizabeth Tandy Shermer, *Sunbelt Capitalism: Phoenix and the Transformation of American Capitalism* (Philadelphia: University of Pennsylvania Press, 2013), esp. 87–89.

64. Steven P. Erie and Scot A. MacKenzie, "The L.A. School and Politics Noir: Bringing the Local State Back In," *Journal of Urban Affairs* 31, no. 5 (2009): 545–552.

65. Jackson, *Crabgrass Frontier*, 191.

66. David L. Clark, "Improbable Los Angeles," in *Sunbelt Cities: Politics and Growth since World War II*, ed. Bernard and Rice, 271–272.

67. William Fulton, *The Reluctant Metropolis: The Politics of Urban Growth in Los Angeles* (Baltimore: Johns Hopkins University Press, 1997, 2001 [paperback]), 15.

68. Massey, "Origins of Economic Disparities," 56.

69. Eliot M. Tretter and M. Anwar Sounny-Slitine, "Austin Restricted: Progressivism, Zoning, Private Racial Covenants, and the Making of a Segregated City," final report prepared for the Institute for Urban Policy Research and Analysis, University of Texas, 2012, www.academia.edu/1888949/ Austin_Restricted_Progressivism_Zoning_Private_Racial_Covenants_and_the_Making_of_a_ Segregated_City.

70. *Shelley v. Kraemer*, 334 U.S. 1 (1948).

71. Trotter and Day, *Race and Renaissance*, 66–68.

72. The story of Levittown is presented by Thomas J. Sugrue, "Jim Crow's Last Stand: The Struggle to Integrate Levittown," in *Second Suburb: Levittown, Pennsylvania*, ed. Dianne Harris, 175–199; the quotations appear on pp. 175–179.

73. Margery Austin Turner and Stephen L. Ross, "How Racial Discrimination Affects the Search for Housing," in *The Geography of Choice: Race and Housing Choice in Metropolitan America*, ed. Xavier de Souza Briggs (Washington, DC: Brookings Institution, 2005), 79–100, especially 86 and 92. On the persistence of housing discrimination, see Margery Austin Turner, Todd M. Richardson, and Stephen Ross, "Housing Discrimination in Metropolitan America," in *Fragile Rights Within Cities: Government, Housing, and Fairness*, ed. John Goering (Lanham, MD: Rowman & Littlefield, 2007), 39–60.

74. Nikole Hannah-Jones, "Housing Enforcement Group Sues M&T Bank for Discrimination," *ProPublica*, February 9, 2015, www.propublica.org/article/housing-enforcement-group-sues-mt-bank-for-discrimination; Brena Swanson, "M&T Bank Reaches Settlement Over Discriminatory Lending Charges," *HousingWire*, September 1, 2015, www.housingwire.com/articles/34956-mt-bank-reaches-settlement-over-discriminatory-lending-charges.

75. Kyle DeMaria and Lei Ding, "Federal Reserve Study Finds Evidence of Significant Impact of Community Reinvestment Act," *Cascade* 96 (Summer 2017), www.philadelphiafed.org/community-development/publications/cascade/96/04_federal-reserve-study. *Cascade*, is a publication of the Federal Reserve Bank of Philadelphia

76. This paragraph is based on Rachel L. Swarns, "Biased Lending Evolves, and Blacks Faces Trouble Getting Mortgages," *New York Times*, October 30, 2015.

77. Joseph P. Treaster, "Insurer Must Pay $100.5 Million in Redlining Case," *New York Times*, October 27, 1998.

78. Jessica Silver-Greenberg and Michael Corkery, "Evans Bank Settles New York 'Redlining' Lawsuit," *New York Times*, September 10, 2015; Brentin Mock, "Redlining Is Alive and Well: And Evolving," *CityLab*, September 28, 2015, www.citylab.com/equity/2015/09/redlining-is-alive-and-welland-evolving/407497/.

79. The descriptions in the preceding two paragraphs are based on Douglas S. Massey, Jacob S. Rugh, Justin P. Steil, and Len Albright, "Riding the Stagecoach to Hell: A Qualitative Analysis of Racial Discrimination in Mortgage Lending," *City & Community* 15, no. 2 (June 2016). The references to Wells Fargo are on 128–131. Also see Justin P. Steil, Len Albright, Jacob S. Rugh, and Douglas S. Massey, "The Social Structure of Housing Discrimination," *Housing Studies*, online version published November 3, 2017, https://doi.org/10.1080/02673037.2017.1390076.

80. Timothy Bates and Alicia Robb, "Has the Community Reinvestment Act Increased Loan Availability among Small Businesses Operating in Minority Neighborhoods?" *Urban Studies* 52, no. 9 (2015), 1702–1721.

81. Alex Schwartz, "From Confrontation to Collaboration? Banks, Community Groups, and the Implementation of Community Reinvestment Agreements," *Housing Policy Debate* 9, no. 3 (1998), 631–662. Also see Dan Immergluck, *Credit to the Community: Community Reinvestment and Fair Lending Policy in the United States* (New York: Routledge, 2015; first published by M.E. Sharpe, 2004).

82. Gregory D. Squires, "Predatory Lending: Redlining in Reverse," *Shelterforce Online* 139 (January/February 2005), www.nhi.org/online/issues/139/redlining.html; Traiger & Hinckley LLP, "The Community Reinvestment Act: A Welcome Anomaly in the Foreclosure Crisis-Indications That the CRA Deterred Irresponsible Lending in the 15 Most Populous U.S. Metropolitan Areas," January 7, 2008, www.traigerlaw.com/publications/traiger_hinckley_llp_cra_foreclosure_study_1-7-08.pdf; and Traiger & Hinckley LLP, "The Community Reinvestment Act of 1977: Not Guilty: Mortgage Data Refute Charge That the CRA Is at the Root of the Financial Crisis," January 26, 2009, http://traigerlaw.com/publications/The_community_reinvestment_act_of_1977-not_guilty_1-26-09.pdf.

83. Dan Immergluck, *Foreclosed: High-Risk Lending, Deregulation, and the Undermining of America's Mortgage Market* (Ithaca, NY: Cornell University Press, 2009), esp. 55–58, 162–163, and chap. 3.

84. Darryl E. Getter, "The Effectiveness of the Community Reinvestment Act," a report of the Congressional Research Service, Washington, DC, January 7, 2015, esp. 3–4 and 10–11.

85. Getter, "The Effectiveness of the Community Reinvestment Act," 9.

86. Quoted in Ben Protess and Jessica Silver-Greenberg, "Under Trump, Banking Watchdog Trades Its Bite for a Tamer Stance," *New York Times*, November 15, 2017.

87. Kriston Capps, "It's Time to Rewrite Fair Lending Rules (Just Not Like This)," *CityLab Web Posting*, August 31, 2018, www.citylab.com/equity/2018/08/its-time-to-rewrite-fair-lending-rules-just-not-like-this/568804/?utm_source=twitter&utm_campaign=city-lab&utm_term=2018-08-31T19%3A00%3A15&utm_medium=social&utm_content=edit-promo.

88. Sig Langegger and Stephen Koester, "Dwelling Without a Home: Denver's Splintered Public Spaces," in *Order and Conflict in Public Space*, ed. Mattias De Backer, Lucas Melgaço, Georgiana Varna, and Francesca Manichelli (New York: Routledge, 2016), 141–142.

89. Rachael A. Woldoff and Seth Ovadia, "Not Getting Their Money's Worth: African-American Disadvantages in Converting Income, Wealth, and Education into Residential Quality," *Urban Affairs Review* 45, no. 1 (September 2009): 66–91.

3 | A Suburban Nation

The United States is a suburban nation. This important truth is not exactly a new fact of life. Since the 1960s, the population of the nation's suburbs has exceeded that of its central cities. Even gentrification, the much-celebrated "return" to the cities (a matter that will be discussed in Chapter 4) is only a relatively small countertrend that does little to offset the long-term shift of population, economic activity, and political power to the suburbs.

The United States continues to suburbanize. Between 2000 and 2009, the population of outward-lying suburban areas in the United States grew at three times the rate of central cities and inner suburbs. The nation's fastest-growing communities are locates on the edges of metropolis: North Las Vegas and Henderson (Nevada), Victorville (60 miles northeast of Los Angeles), McKinney and Denton (outside of Dallas), and Gilbert and Chandler (outside of Phoenix) doubles their populations in just seven years! Riverside and San Bernardino (in southern California), Clark (Nevada), and Maricopa (Arizona) experienced similarly explosive growth rates.[1]

Suburban growth slowed in the very early 2000s as a result of the national economic recession and the crisis in housing finance. Popular commentators too quickly jumped to a conclusion that turned out not to be true: that a turning point in urban development has been reached as "Millennials" and other Americans had rediscovered the joys of city living.[2] But the change in growth patterns largely vanished when economic conditions improved. In the 2010s, suburban growth reasserted its dominance, and central cities were once again losing population. Census data from 2016 reinforces the long-term picture: continued suburban growth as contrasted to big-city population stasis and decline.[3] Americans continue to prefer suburban living. Most prefer the "suburbier suburbs."[4] The United States is a suburban nation and will continue to be so.

A number of **boomburbs**—rapidly growing suburbs—have populations as big as more established cities. Mesa (Arizona) has a larger population than does Minneapolis, Miami, or St. Louis. Arlington (Texas) surpasses Pittsburgh, Anaheim, Riverside, Santa Ana. Glendale, Scottsdale, and Tempe are all notable boomburbs in the American Southwest, where the limited availability of water serves to concentrate

Figure 3.1   **A Boomburb: Bellevue, Washington, a City-like Suburb**. A suburb of Seattle, Bellevue is the 5th largest city in the State of Washington, having grown from a mere 13,000 residents in 1960 to more than 141,000 in 2016.

Source: Photo by Jelson25 / Wikimedia Commons, https://commons.wikimedia.org/wiki/File: Aerial_Bellevue_Washington_August_2009.jpg.

patterns of suburban development.[5] Boomburbs like Naperville, Illinois (30 miles west of downtown Chicago) and Bellevue, Washington (the home of Expedia and Eddie Bauer; Figure 3.1), differ radically from the stereotype of a quiet residential suburb. These relatively affluent communities are the site of substantial corporate headquarters and tech-related development.[6]

This chapter describes the politics of an evolving suburbia. The chapter pays special attention to the new diversity of the suburbs and matters of race, inequality, and exclusion. As schools often are at the heart of life in suburban America, this chapter gives special focus to school finance and racial integration. The chapter concludes by assessing contemporary efforts—Smart Growth, urban growth boundaries, and New Urbanism—which promise to build a "better" and more sustainable suburban America.

Suburban Diversity: The Changing Face of Suburbia

A Diversity of Suburban Communities

Contemporary suburbia is quite different from the popular image of suburbia. For decades, television shows and Hollywood movies, with few exceptions, presented suburbia as a homogeneous string of privileged, largely white, middle- and upper-class **bedroom or dormitory communities** (see Box 3.1). The award-winning television series *Mad Men*, for instance, sardonically portrayed suburbia of the 1950s–1960s as an imperfect embodiment of the "familial" ideal: The suburbia of the mid-twentieth century had no room for independent working women, single mothers, gays, and lesbians.[7]

Box 3.1
TV and Hollywood's Schizophrenic View of Suburbia

For much of the latter part of the twentieth century, television and Hollywood presented suburbia as a string of well-to-do bedroom communities. Classic television shows like *The Donna Reed Show, Father Knows Best, Leave It to Beaver*, and *The Dick Van Dyke Show*, and later *The Wonder Years*, all featured conventional two-parent families living the "good life" in large single-family homes. Well-coiffed mothers tended to the children and drank coffee and gossiped with neighbor ladies, awaiting their commuting husbands to return from work. Hollywood movies, including the Christmas classic *Miracle on 34th Street* (1947; remade in 1994) likewise portrayed suburbia as the embodiment of the American Dream: At the end of *Miracle on 34th Street*, a little girl gets her Christmas wish; with Santa's help, she leaves busy New York City for a manorial suburban home with a fireplace and a large backyard. The remake of the film used a spacious house in suburban Lake Forest, Illinois, as the stand-in for its suburban ideal.

Not all filmmakers, however, embraced the suburban ideal. *Rebel Without a Cause* (1955), *The Man in the Gray Flannel Suit* (1956), *Peyton Place* (1957), *The Graduate* (1967), and the Oscar-winning *American Beauty* (1999 Best Picture) all attacked the materialism, conformity, sterility, and hypocrisy of suburban lives, pointing to underside of suburbia that lay beneath its public veneer of normalcy. *The Stepford Wives* (1975; remade 2004) satirized the gender-defined roles, isolation, and vacuity of suburban life, presenting the "ideal" suburban housewife as little more than a robot with no mind or ambitions of her own. Other films showed husbands and wives desperately seeking to escape the boredom of suburbia through alcohol and meaningless sexual affairs, a theme that also runs through more contemporary and tongue-in-cheek TV programming, such as *Desperate Housewives*.

In *Edward Scissorhands* (1990), Tim Burton's charming take on the Frankenstein tale, the boy/monster (played by a young Johnny Depp) speaks to every person who has ever felt out of place amid the enforced conformity of suburbia. In *Pleasantville* (1998), life in mid-century suburbia is presented as so mind-numbingly dull and colorless that portions of the film are shot in black and white. In *The Truman Show* (1998), suburban life is depicted as highly ordered and antiseptic, so much so that Truman Burbank (Jim Carrey) believes that he lives in an ideal suburban community when, in fact, he has spent his entire life on an enormous fabricated and controlled TV studio set.

Do Americans share elite Hollywood's distaste for suburbia? Not really. Polls show that most residents are satisfied with life in the suburbs, a view that is reflected in a countercurrent of films that present a more affectionate portrait of suburbia. Steven Spielberg's *E.T.: The Extra-Terrestrial* (1982) reveals a suburbia of family love and contentment, a place where children grow up in relative safety, with a brimming self-confidence and a freedom to explore.

Ferris Bueller's Day Off (1986) is a mix of positive and negative assessments of suburbia. A hip, fast-talking high school student (played by Matthew Broderick) skips classes in order to taste the vitality of life that can only be found in the big city, Chicago. The father of his best friend is so blinded by the trappings of suburban materialism that he cares more for his luxury sports car than for his son. Yet the film is no caustic anti-suburban diatribe. Bueller clearly enjoys the privileges of being a teenager who lives in, and goes to school in, a top-end, North Shore community. Life in the suburbs is quite good, even though the city beckons with the enticements of ethnic and racial diversity and adventure.

In more recent years, TV and the cinema have begun to offer glimpses into the diversity of suburban communities and their residents. *E.T.* and *Close Encounters of the Third Kind* (1977) were among the first major films that featured single mothers, revealing a suburbia where the two-parent family is no longer the norm. *American Beauty* and the television series *Modern Family* present a suburbia that has become home to same-sex couples. The long-running cartoon *The Simpsons* features a community with a diverse population (including an African-American doctor and a South-Asian store manager), the sort of suburbia that was largely unimaginable at mid-century. *Crazy Rich Asians* (2017) is, in part, based on the personal experiences and tensions of its author who had been raised in the suburban Houston.

The Florida Project (2018) peered behind the scenery of a Florida that is familiar to the tourists who visit Disney World. The film revealed a strip of seedy "welfare motels" outside the Magic Kingdom that are home to low-income women and their children. Hollywood can no longer turn a blind eye to the poverty and diversity that have become an integral part of contemporary suburbia.

Sources: There are numerous commentaries on film and television representation of suburbia, including: Douglas Muzzio and Thomas Halper, "Pleasantville? The Suburb and Its Representation in American Movies," *Urban Affairs Review* 37, no. 4 (March 2002): 542–574; Stanley J. Solomon, "Images of Suburban Life in American Films," in *Westchester: The American Suburb*, ed. Roger Panetta (New York: Fordham University Press; and Yonkers, NY: Hudson River Museum, 2006), 411–441; Timotheus Vermeulen, *Scenes from the Suburbs: The Suburb in Contemporary U.S. Film and Television* (Edinburgh, Scotland: Edinburgh University Press, 2014); and David R. Coon, *Look Closer: Suburban Narratives and American Values in Film and Television* (New Brunswick, NJ: Rutgers University Press, 2014).

But suburbia was never monolithic and uniformly affluent. Even during the 1950s and 1960s, at a time when suburbia was first beginning to flourish, there were a number of **blue-collar and industrial suburbs** centered on manufacturing plants.[8] Over the years, suburban diversity increased still further. The stereotype of suburban homogeneity is hopelessly out of date.

Contemporary suburbia encompasses a wide variety of communities: affluent bedroom or "dormitory" residential suburbs; **privatopias** of **common-interest developments and community associations** with security-controlled gated entrances and rules established by homeowner associations;[9] industrial suburbs centered around factories; **bedroom-developing suburbs**[10] (lower-middle-class communities that lack the tax base to provide quality schools and the infrastructure to keep up with rapid growth); boomburbs, and far-flung **exurbs** located at some distance from a metropolis's center (with residents even commuting 50 miles or more each way to work). **Minority-dominated suburbs** can be found in Prince George's County, Maryland (outside of Washington, DC), and East Chicago Heights. Declining inner-ring suburbs suffer vacant storefronts and have a stock of large antiquated housing—houses with small kitchens, tiny backyards, and no attached garage—that has no great appeal to the present generation of homebuyers. So-called **disaster suburbs**—including East St. Louis (Illinois), East Cleveland, Compton (California), and Camden (New Jersey, just across the river from Philadelphia)—suffer economic and social problems that are usually associated with the central cities they border.[11]

Edge cities—suburban concentrations of office towers, research parks, college campuses, shopping galleries, and entertainment complexes—are lively centers of commercial activity, Edge cities can be found in Valley Forge and King of Prussia (outside of Philadelphia), Monroeville (Pittsburgh), Tyson's Corner (Virginia; see Figures 3.2 and 3.3), Towson (Baltimore), Bloomington (Minneapolis-St. Paul), La Jolla (San Diego), Bellevue (Seattle), Tempe/Scottsdale (Phoenix), North Atlanta, North Dallas, and the Houston Galleria, to name only a few.

Figure 3.2 **Edge City as Corporate Headquarters: The USA Today/Gannett Communications Headquarters at Tyson's Corner in Northern Virginia**. Major corporations like USA Today no longer have to locate in a region's central city. Advances in transportation and telecommunications haves freed businesses to move to the suburbs, including edge cities such as Tyson's Corner, in Northern Virginia, in the Washington, DC, metropolitan area.

Source: Photo by Patrickneal, June 30, 2008/Wikimedia Commons, http://commons.wikimedia.org/wiki/File:USA_Today_building.jpg.

Figure 3.3 **Edge City: The Growth of Tyson's Corner, in Northern Virginia, Outside of Washington, DC.** The suburbs are no longer "sub" in terms of their economic dynamism. The photo also illustrates the degree to which numerous edge cities are designed around the automobile, with multi-lane roads and vast expanses of parking that are almost impossible for a pedestrian to cross on foot.

Source: Photo by BenjPHolm, August 23, 2009 / Wikimedia Commons, http://en.wikipedia.org/wiki/File:2009-08-23_Tysons_Corner_skyline.jpg.

The New York region has multiple centers of edge development, including Morristown (New Jersey); the Route 1 corridor by Princeton (New Jersey); Huntington, Long Island, and White Plains (New York); and Stamford (Connecticut).[12] As evolving patterns of suburban development in metropolitan New York and other regions indicate, the concept of edge cities no longer fully captures the economic dynamism of contemporary suburbia. Substantial commercial growth can also found outside of edge cities in the **edgeless development** of unglamorous strip malls and clusters of offices spread along access roads and side streets near highway interchanges. As seen in the chaotic sprawl of central New Jersey, edgeless development can spill over hundreds of square miles, eating up green space, wetlands, and agricultural acreage.[13]

IMMIGRATION AND THE CHANGING FACE OF SUBURBIA

The changing face of suburbia is evident in its demography. As more recent census counts reveal, African-American families are increasingly finding homes in suburbia. African Americans largely resemble whites in their desire for a home in the suburbs.[14]

A new immigration, too, has increased the diversity of suburban populations. The nation's new arrivals are increasingly settling in the suburbs, skipping the central city. In the Chicago region, first-generation immigrants from Poland and Russia have added to the range of cultures on display in suburban Wheeling, 25 miles northwest of the city. West of Chicago, a continuing stream of newcomers from China, Pakistan, and other countries in Asia has altered the demography of affluent Naperville. In Bolingbrook, located near to Naperville, one-fifth of the local population is foreign born.[15]

In northern California, Cupertino, the home of Apple computers in the heart of Silicon Valley, has a population that is over 60 percent Asian. Across San Francisco Bay, local politics in Fremont have been altered by the arrival of a large Asian-American population intensely concerned with the curriculum of the local schools. In Fremont, wealthy Asian Americans also continue to construct McMansions, despite the opposition of traditionalists who object that such gigantic homes are out of character with traditional development in established neighborhoods. Asian Americans in Fremont and other communities see such large homes as testimony to their success as well as a means to comfortably house a large multigenerational family under a single roof.[16]

Southern California provides particularly vivid examples of how immigration has transformed suburbia. Orange County, the home of Disneyland, was once the iconic ideal of white affluent suburbia. The reality of contemporary Orange County, however, is quite different. Orange County is now "minority majority" with a population that is less than half white (41 percent). In Orange County, minorities—Hispanics (34 percent) and Asians (20 percent)—combine to outnumber whites (in a county where African-Americans are only 2 percent of the county population). "Little Saigon," the self-proclaimed "Capital of Vietnamese America," is located in the Orange County communities of Westminster and Garden Grove.[17]

In numerous suburbs across the country, the arrival of new ethnic populations is often critical to maintaining a strong market for single-family suburban homes.[18] Newcomers have been especially important to the revival of industrial, working- and middle-class suburbs, the faded mill towns of the Northeast and Midwest.[19]

RACIAL IMBALANCE AND RESEGREGATION OF SUBURBIA

As the census trends underscore, minorities and immigrants have enjoyed increased entrance to the suburbs. Yet, a close examination of residential patterns reveals that newcomers and racial and ethnic minorities often live in a different suburbia than do whites. A region's better-off suburbs and more far-off exurbs have populations that are disproportionately white. African Americans and Hispanics, by contrast, are concentrated in declining industrial suburbs and troubled **spillover communities** adjacent to the central city.

In numerous suburbs growing minority populations have led to patterns of resegregation. Covina, California, 22 miles east of downtown Los Angeles, had a population that was only 13 percent Latino in 1980. By 2010, the suburb's Latino population soared to 52 percent. The numbers can be mistakenly read as evidence of the increased racial integration of a suburb that was once overwhelmingly white. Such an interpretation, however, is mistaken, as demographic trends indicate that Covina will soon become a nearly all-Latino community. The racial transformation and resegregation of suburbia accelerates as white homebuyers will tend to avoid communities like Covina where a rapidly growing minority population is gaining dominance.

Cerritos, another L.A. suburb, in 2014 was already 62 percent Asian. The community continues to be home to new arrivals from the Pacific Rim and is on a "path toward Asian segregation."[20]

Heightened racial and ethnic segregation is also evident in the Midwest. The suburbs of Minneapolis and St. Paul show continuing patterns of stratification despite the efforts of the Metropolitan Council (Met Council), a regional governing body, to build subsidized housing in communities throughout the Twin Cities region. The Met Council, however, has had to relax its dispersal policies in the face of resistance from local communities. As a result, low-income families, racial minorities, and new arrivals from other countries tend to be concentrated in the region's central cities and poorer inner-ring suburbs, not in the region's more "opportunity-rich" communities and more far-off exurbs.[21] In terms of the racial integration of the suburbs of the Twin Cities, the glass is, at best, only "half full."[22] In important ways, the region's housing policies in more recent years have served to reinforce residential segregation in the Twin Cities metropolis.[23]

As the Twin Cities experience indicates, strong public policies are necessary to maintain the **stable integration** of suburban communities; but such policy efforts are difficult to sustain over time. In the absence of continuing governmental action, many suburbs will resegregate and become less diverse communities: "Integrated communities have a hard time staying integrated for more than 10 or 20 years."[24] In a suburban nation, public officials often have extreme difficulty in maintaining support for policies that attempt to reduce the segregation of metropolitan areas.[25]

THE NEW SUBURBAN POVERTY

The rise of poverty in America's suburbs is another important dimension of suburbia's increased diversity. No longer are poverty problems found only in the inner city or in remote rural areas. Today, one-third of the nation's poor reside in the suburbs. As census figures further reveal, a greater number of low-income persons live in the suburbs than in central cities! The national economic recession of the early 2000s saw a large growth in the numbers of the suburban poor.[26]

In a couple of important ways, the poor of suburbia differ from the poor of central cities. First of all, the poor of suburbia tend to be whiter. Non-Hispanic whites account for nearly half (44 percent) of the poverty population of suburbia. By contrast, non-Hispanic whites make up only one-fourth (24 percent) of the poor who reside in big cities. Second, the poor who live in suburbia are more likely to be homeowners; 36 percent of the suburban poor own their home as compared to the central city where only 20 percent of the poor are homeowners.[27]

A great many suburbs are not well equipped to respond to the needs of their low-income populations. In many suburbs, transportation poses a particular problem, as buses run infrequently or run on routes that connect only with the downtown and not with decentralized suburban job sites. For a person who does not own an automobile, a suburb-to-suburb work commute may necessitate a number of bus transfers and the investment of an inordinate amount of time. Low-income suburban residents cannot rely on bare-bones public transit to reach employment, especially jobs located in other suburban communities.[28]

The poor of suburbia also often fail to receive the supports and services more commonly found in central cities. Many suburbs offer only minimal local job training programs. Other suburbs lack a sufficient stock of affordable rental units. Still other suburban communities lack counselors and other trained personnel to provide appropriate educational services to poorer children, especially to the children of immigrant and refugee families where English is not spoken in the home. Nonprofit service providers, too, may offer fewer services in suburban locations than in city centers. Numerous suburbs also lack a history of strong cooperation with nonprofit organizations, especially those situated in other communities in the metropolis, who could be helpful partners in joint efforts to alleviate poverty.[29]

The willingness of suburban residents and leaders to tackle the problem of local poverty is further diminished by their view that poverty and social diversity are "urban" phenomena that "are not part of the suburban experience or norm."[30] Indeed, while the number of poor residents in the suburbs is rising, the risk of poverty is greater in central cities. In 2015, the poverty rate of the suburbs stood at 11.2 percent, significantly lower than the 19.6 percent poverty rate for large cities.[31]

GAYS AND LESBIANS IN THE SUBURBS

The numbers of gays and lesbians living in suburbia, too, have increased. While younger gays and lesbians tend to prefer the opportunities and tolerance of central cities, more mature same-sex couples have begun to make their home in the suburbs.[32] Same-sex couples with children, much like more conventional families, also tend to look for suburban homes—although it must be noted that only one-fifth of same-sex couples have children.[33]

Compared to past decades, when the suburbs were viewed as bastions of exclusion and enforced social conformity, contemporary suburbia is increasingly home to nontraditional households, so much so that even television cannot ignore the transformation. The Emmy-winning TV series *Modern Family* features a suburban same-sex couple with an adopted daughter.

Suburbs like Minnesota's Golden Valley celebrate their inclusiveness with an annual gay pride festival. Just across the Hudson River from New York, Jersey City, a once-suffering industrial center now experiencing substantial residential and commercial revival, not only boasts of its pride festival; Jersey City maintains a community center dedicated to serving lesbian, gay, bisexual, and transgender (LGBT) persons. The city also established LGBT liaisons in the mayor's office and the police department.[34] Berwyn, just west of Chicago, is even more explicit in its effort to court same-sex couples as a strategy to bring new vitality to a declining community that was once a blue-collar stronghold.[35]

Of course, not all suburbs are inclusive and welcoming. The Human Rights Campaign, a LGBT advocacy group, awarded low scores to Dallas-Fort Worth suburbs for failing to enact ordinances and initiate other actions to protect gays and lesbians from residential and workplace discrimination.[36]

RACIAL STRATIFICATION IN THE METROPOLIS: IS IT RACE OR INCOME THAT DETERMINES WHERE PEOPLE RESIDE?

Despite the new population diversity of suburbia, metropolitan America is marred by a continuing racial imbalance. Some of the imbalance undeniably reflects differences in money: families with greater wealth can "buy into" better communities while ethnic groups with less buying power tend to wind up in less advantaged communities. Yet, suburban residential patterns do *not* simply reflect differences in buying power. Even when different races and ethnicities have equivalent buying power, they tend *not* to reside in the same community.

Income differences alone do not explain the high degrees of residential segregation in Los Angeles County, especially the geographical segregation of the region's Latino and Asian populations. If income determine where people lived, Los Angeles would have virtually no census tracts dominated by a single racial or ethnic group![37]

Residential patterns are the result of race and ethnicity, not just of income. The extent of discrimination varies by race and ethnicity. An Asian or Hispanic family of higher income seemingly gains the ability to live in a more integrated neighborhood. But increases in the income by African Americans do not produce equivalent gains in terms of their ability to find a home in a racially integrated neighborhood. Even middle-class and upper-income black families confront limits on their residential choice that are not faced by whites of similar income.[38]

Are racial imbalances in the metropolis simply the result of the desire of the members of different racial and ethnic groups to live "among their own"? Actually, survey after survey reveals that a clear majority of African Americans prefer to live in mixed-race, as opposed to all-black, neighborhoods. African Americans tend to value the same suburbs that white desire: communities with high-quality services and single-family detached homes. Whites, however, prefer communities that have lower levels of racial diversity.[39] Patterns of racial segregation in the metropolis largely reflect the residential preferences of whites, not those of African Americans.[40]

Chapter 2 has already reviewed the various government and private-sector actions that, over the years, helped to keep communities racially segregated. The demography of the suburbs, was particularly shaped by a process of **racial steering**, where real-estate agents, home loan and insurance officers, and government home finance and housing officials directed white and minority home seekers to different communities.

Fortunately, federal **fair housing laws** and changed community norms have led to the virtual elimination of the most blatant discriminatory real-estate and rental practices. Today, it is rare that a real-estate agent will show homes in a preferred community to whites while refusing to show the same houses to African-American or Latino home seekers.

Yet housing discrimination in the metropolis continues in the form of more subtle practices that are not easily detected and fought.[41] Real-estate agents, mortgage lenders, and home insurers may not go out of their way to help a minority buyer find appropriate financing for a home when the real estate or finance agent perceives the move to be racially incompatible.[42] There is also some evidence of **linguistic profiling**, where a home seeker's dialect or accent influences how a real-estate agent responds to a phone query about the availability of a home or apartment.[43]

Victimized parties seldom file a complaint when discriminatory actions take such subtle form. Quite simply, a minority homebuyer cannot even know with certainty that an act of discrimination has taken place, as he or she does not know just what home showings and advantageous financing terms are being provided to other home seekers. Individual home seekers, too, seldom have the time and the money to pursue fair housing enforcement through the courts.

Contemporary housing discrimination is primarily detected through a housing audit process known as **paired testing**, where closely matched white and minority individuals pose as home seekers in order to compare the treatment they receive from landlords, real-estate agents, and home financial lenders. The results of paired housing audits conducted across the nation reveal that, despite the Fair Housing Act, discrimination continues. Whites are shown more available homes than are shown to equally qualified African Americans. African-American and Hispanic home seekers are steered to minority communities.[44] An analysis of more than 2,000 paired tests in 20 major metropolitan areas reveals the extent to which differential treatment by race and ethnicity continues to affect the search for housing:

> [I]n roughly one of five visits to a real estate or rental agent, black and Hispanic customers were denied some of the information and assistance that comparable white customers received as a matter of course. Whites were more likely to find out about available houses and apartments, more likely to be given the opportunity to inspect these units, more likely to be offered favorable financial terms, more likely to be steered toward homes for sale in predominantly white neighborhoods, and more likely to receive assistance and encouragement in their housing search.[45]

A 2013 Urban Institute study similarly concluded that "Prejudice by no means has disappeared. . . . (M)inorities still face significant barriers to housing search, even when they are well-qualified as renters or homebuyers."[46] Discriminatory housing practices are not just a thing of the past.

SCHOOLS AND SUBURBIA

A community's schools lie at the focal point of a suburb's identity. Suburbanites often defend their choice of residence by pointing to the quality of the local schools. This section explores the response of suburbanites to two possible "threats" to their schools: school finance reform and efforts to increase metropolitan school integration.

WHY SCHOOL FINANCE REFORM IS SO DIFFICULT TO BRING ABOUT

In the vast majority of the states, the funding of schools is heavily reliant on local property values and property tax levies. Such local reliance produces severe inequalities in school funding; children in poorer communities (that is, children who live in property-poor communities) lack the resources to support their education that are available in districts that have more highly valued homes and commercial property.

Over the past few decades, increased school aid from the states has reduced some of the inequality among school districts. But the opposition from more affluent communities poses a political obstacle to efforts to further equalize school finances. As a result, in virtually all states, the financial resources that are available for a child's education still vary considerably from one school districts to the next.

The situation in Connecticut illustrates the inequalities of school funding. Greenwich, an affluent suburb, spends $6,000 more per pupil each year than does the city of Bridgeport,[47] a disparity that helped lead the Connecticut Coalition of Justice in Education

Funding to bring a lawsuit challenging the state's system of funding its public schools. The State Supreme Court, however, effectively brought the challenge to an end in a ruling that declared the state had met is constitutionally mandated responsibilities of providing a *minimally* adequate education. The court ruled that it was not the judiciary's job to require greater equality in school spending: "Courts are simply not in a position" to determine how "scarce resources" should be allocated or how much a state should invest in poorer districts.[48]

Most states were never enthusiastic players in initiating school finance reform. Early state action legislative action was largely a reaction to the pressures exerted by activist community groups that had won a number of victories in the courts; judicial decisions virtually forced the states to increase the role they played in school finance. The movement gained its greatest impetus when the California Supreme Court in *Serrano v. Priest* (1971) ruled that vast differences in local school spending violated the **equal protection clause** in both the federal and the California state constitutions.[49]

The *Serrano* decision catalyzed legal challenges across the nation that forced the states to modify school finance arrangements. State governments tweaked school aid formulas and increased the amount of aid that school districts received from the state. The system of funding public schools was revolutionized as state assistance came to equal, and eventually narrowly surpass, locally raised revenues for the schools. In 2015 the states provided 47 percent of the funds for K–12 education, while local governments provided 45 percent. The federal government provided only 8 percent.[50] Compared to state and local government, the national government is not a major player in funding public schools, other than to help assure the provision of specialized programs for disadvantaged and disabled children.

The new state funding laws reduced but did *not* eliminate interdistrict disparities in school spending. The amount of funds a school has available still varies considerably by district. In virtually all the states, local property wealth remains an important factor that determines the overall sum of money that a community has to spend on each pupil.

In an all-important decision, the U.S. Supreme Court dealt the movement for greater school finance equalization a major setback. In *Rodriguez v. San Antonio* (1973), the Court ruled 5–4 that reliance on local property taxes for school funding does *not* violate a person's "equal protection" rights guaranteed by the Fourteenth Amendment of the U.S. Constitution.[51] As "education" is nowhere mentioned in the U.S. Constitution, the Supreme Court did not consider spending for education to be a "fundamental right" deserving of special federal protection. The Court was also reluctant to order the equalization of school dollars, as a number of experts contended that money was of no great importance, that school spending was less critical to student learning than were other factors such as parental expectations and student peer pressure.

After the *Rodriguez* ruling, advocates of more equal school funding shifted their action to state courts, arguing that the provisions written into state constitutions barred such great inequality in K–12 schooling. In California, Texas, New Jersey, Ohio, Kentucky, and other states, the courts ruled that the specific language of a state's constitution, such as wording that requires a state to provide a "thorough and efficient" system of education, meant that a state legislature had to enact measures to reduce (but not necessarily eliminate) school finance disparities.

But elected state officials showed little interest in raising taxes and redistributing funds to poorer districts. Legislators from better-off suburbs and other property-rich communities opposed measures that would increase the taxes paid by their constituents or that would jeopardize the quality of education in their own schools. School officials and parents in wealthier communities opposed reform measures that they claimed were **equalizing down** school spending.

Numerous states also responded to populist anti-tax fever by cutting state tax rates, reducing the amount of money available for school programs.[52] In California, the voters's tax revolt led to state-imposed limits on the ability of local governments—including school districts—to raise taxes. When outraged parents complained that the quality of public schools was in jeopardy, the state responded by increasing its funding for public schools. State assistance in California accounts for about 60 percent of the funding of K–12 public schools.[53]

How much does the new state funding make a difference? California's 2013 Local Control Funding Formula provides basic aid to every school district while also dispensing additional "supplemental" and "concentration" grants to give further assistance to poorer districts. One study has found that such targeted aid in California has resulted in increased achievement scores and graduation rates among low-income students.[54] Contrary to the claims that the U.S. Supreme Court asserted four decades earlier in *Rodriguez*, money does matter in public education.

Across the United States, the states have targeted spending increases to low-income districts, seeking to bring low-performing schools up to minimum standards of performance. A review of these efforts concluded that school spending had become more equitable without "leveling down" the funding of schools in better-off districts.[55]

Yet, increases in state school spending do not always have an equalizing impact. Typically, state-elected officials seek to win support from suburban and rural constituencies by writing provisions into school finance measures that act to assure that disproportionate state assistance will continue to go to smaller school districts and even to better-off suburban districts. A "flat grant," for instance, dispenses aid to districts irrespective of need. State aid formulas also often guarantee that a school district receives a certain minimum of "basic aid" no matter a district's small size or large wealth. In North Carolina, the impact of such provisions has been anything but equalizing; in North Carolina more affluent county districts receive just about as much state aid per pupil as do high-poverty districts.[56]

SCHOOLING IN THE METROPOLIS: SEGREGATION, INTEGRATION, AND RESEGREGATION

Suburbs generally do not have to participate in efforts to increase the racial integration of a region's public schools. In the all-important 1974 ***Milliken v. Bradley*** decision,[57] the U.S. Supreme Court ruled that the busing of students across district lines is not required, even if cross-district busing is the only means capable of desegregating overwhelmingly minority central-city schools.

According to *Millikin*, a suburb can be forced to participate in a desegregation plan only if plaintiffs first prove that the suburb intentionally undertook segregative actions.

Racial "intent," however, is nearly impossible to prove. Civil rights advocates can easily document where a suburb's schools have a student body that is vastly different from neighboring districts and the central city. But plaintiffs cannot demonstrate that such imbalances are the result of actions by suburban officials who intended to keep minority enrollments to a minimum. Suburban officials respond that they were not motivated by concerns over race; if a suburban school has an overwhelmingly white student body, it is simply because the suburb itself has an overwhelmingly white population. Racial imbalances in the schools, they argue, are not the result of intentional discrimination but merely reflect population imbalances in the metropolis.

The *Millikin* decision effectively put an end to strong efforts at school desegregation. Residence in a suburb can offer a family an escape from a city program aimed at improving the racial balance in the public schools.

Millikin is not the only Supreme Court decision to lessen the pressure on local school districts to continue desegregation efforts. Other Court rulings have given local districts new leeway to terminate school desegregation programs. The Court's 1991 **Oklahoma City decision** even relaxed the integration requirements on schools districts that had been found guilty of past discrimination. The Court permitted such local districts to halt desegregation efforts that had been attempted for a "reasonable" period of time. That same year, in **Freeman v. Pitts**, a DeKalb County, Georgia, case, the Court placed severe limits on metropolitan desegregation plans, even in instances where "white flight" to the suburbs had undermined court-ordered mandates to integrate central-city schools.

The Supreme Court's rulings led communities across the nation to terminate or diminish metropolitan desegregation efforts. Charlotte, Raleigh, Seattle, Denver, Kansas City, Minneapolis, Indianapolis, Cleveland, Pittsburgh, Buffalo, Dallas, Austin, Savannah, Nashville, Norfolk, and Wilmington (Delaware) all ended programs aimed at school integration.

As a result, resegregation is apparent in Charlotte-Mecklenburg and Wake County (metro Raleigh), two North Carolina "joint" (or "consolidated") city-suburban school districts once renowned for their racial integration efforts. Local officials modified policies governing the assignment of students to schools, abandoning the goal of metropolitan school integration for a new program that emphasized neighborhood schools. The changes led to clear growth in the number of intensely segregated schools, schools with a minority enrollment greater than 90 percent![58]

Florida, too, has turned away from older policies that once promoted racial integration in the state's countywide school districts. The result has been similar to North Carolina: a decline in desegregation and a rise in racial isolation. In 2014–2015, one-fifth of Florida schools were "intensely segregated."[59]

In 2013, Tennessee created a single countywide Shelby County School District, thereby eliminating local school district borders that had previously kept the City of Memphis and its large minority school population apart from schools in the rest of the county. In its first year, the new realignment of attendance zones achieved a small increase in racial exposure levels of students in the county's schools. But just one year later, six predominantly white suburban areas seceded from the countywide school system. With the Supreme Court's retreat from the insistence on school integration, there was no longer judicial oversight to keep such local actions from undermining efforts aimed at school desegregation. In Shelby County, secession led to the creation of suburban school districts that reduced levels of interracial exposure in county classrooms. The new suburban districts also attracted new enrollees that made their schools whiter and wealthier—and other schools in Shelby County more minority and low-income—than they were prior to the suburban pullout.[60]

School resegregation is not limited only to the Old South. In California, white suburban communities have attempted to secede from school districts with sizable working-class Latino populations. In Pleasanton, Walnut Hills, and other East Bay communities across from San Francisco, parental activists (largely white) organized petition drives for secession, which they argued would restore the quality education by emphasizing local control and "community schools." The secessionists did not give attention to the impact that new school district boundary lines would have on increasing the isolation of Latino and low-income students.[61]

Enrollment data across the nation documents a rise in the number of segregated classrooms.[62] While far from a return to the segregation levels of the pre–civil rights era, the data is troubling. Nationwide, 43 percent of Latinos and 38 percent of African Americans attend **intensely segregated schools** that have a student population that is less than 10 percent white. Approximately 15 percent of Latino and African-American students attend **apartheid schools** where whites make up less than 1 percent of the student population![63] "Apartheid" makes the situation analogous to the strict separation by race that once characterized South Africa. In New Jersey, over one-fourth of Black and Latino students attend apartheid schools with a student body that is less than 1 percent white.[64]

Suburban schools are experiencing a **resegregation** of public-school classrooms, where African-American, Latino, and white students have only limited interaction with members of other races and ethnicities. The political borders of suburban school districts reinforce segregation. Latino and African-American students attend schools in suburbs that are quite different from those in communities with overwhelming white enrollments. In suburbia, white students as well as minority students suffer from a lack of substantial exposure to students of different ethnic and racial origins.[65]

Charter schools and other options for "school choice" (school reforms which will be discussed in much greater detail in Chapter 9) have also undercut the overall prospects for school integration. A study of charter schools in 40 states found "strong evidence" of segregation: In virtually every state and metropolitan area, charter schools tended to isolate children by race and class more than did traditional public schools. Seventy percent of African-American students who attended charter academies were enrolled in extremely segregated schools, schools that had a student body that was 90–100 percent minority.[66]

Charter academies can offer white families an alternative to sending their children to public schools undergoing substantial integration. In the Minneapolis-St. Paul area, two-thirds of the charter schools located in the suburbs had enrollments of 80 percent or more white. These suburban schools were "facilitating white flight from increasingly diverse traditional schools."[67] In San Antonio, schools of choice located in the suburbs similarly enabled families to escape local schools experiencing high levels of racial and ethnic diversity.[68]

School desegregation no longer occupies a prominent place on the agenda in most metropolitan areas. As a consequence, leaders in the African-American community in Charlotte-Mecklenburg and Memphis (and, in other parts of the country, leaders in the Latino community) have come to accept the futility of continuing the battle for metropolitan school desegregation. Instead, they have shifted their political efforts to finding the resources to strengthen "neighborhood schools" in their communities.[69]

SUBURBAN LAND USE AND EXCLUSION

THE IMPORTANCE OF LOCAL ZONING POWERS

A suburb can use its zoning and land-use powers to determine just what types of housing and commercial establishments are permitted within its jurisdictional borders. Suburbs do not simply used their land-use and zoning powers as a tool to assure the orderly development of a community. Suburbs also use their land-use and zoning powers to limit what can be built within a community, thereby helping to determine who will and will not be able to reside in a community. Land-use and zoning regulations that limit the construction of multifamily housing structures serve to limit the availability of rental apartments and other forms of more affordable housing in a community.

Exclusionary zoning refers to local zoning and land-use measures that effectively serve to "keep out" people who have a lower income, and who may be of a different race or ethnicity, than the existing residents of a community. A suburb that prohibits the construction of apartment buildings and other multifamily dwellings will tend to exclude the poor, working-class families, racial and ethnic minorities, and even newly marrieds and young workers who cannot afford to buy a detached single-family home.

Of course, suburbs do not enact land-use regulations and zoning ordinances purely for reasons of exclusion. Land-use controls also serve more legitimate purposes. Planning and zoning tools can enhance local livability by keeping manufacturing activities separate from residential areas. Land-use regulations and zoning codes can also help maintain a suburb's hamlet-like appeal, averting "citification" and such problems as school overcrowding and traffic congestion

Strong land-use controls can also reduce the lethality of wildfires. The *absence* of strong land-use regulations contributed to the contagion of wildfires in southern California, in the San Francisco Bay area, and in various communities in Colorado, Arizona, Texas, and Washington. In the absence of strong local zoning and land-use regulations, homeowners may unwisely build residences in highly flammable woodland areas in the brushy "wildland-urban interface," areas where climate change makes the prospect of wildfires virtually unavoidable.[70] In greater Sacramento, an estimated 365,000 persons live in homes in high-hazard suburban areas that are rated has facing a moderate, great, or even higher threat of wildfire. In metropolitan Los Angeles, over a half million homes are at risk.[71] Strong local zoning and land-use controls can also minimize construction on erosion- and slide-prone deep hillside slopes, helping to prevent lethal mudslides such as the disastrous January 2018 slide that killed more than 20 persons in southern California.[72]

Zoning, serves legitimate ends. But suburban zoning can also reflect classist, racist, and nativist sentiments that are not readily voiced in public. In L.A.'s San Gabriel Valley, residents of Monterey Park, San Gabriel, Arcadia, and Alhambra organized "slow-growth" campaigns to limit the construction of new apartments, a move intended to slow the rapid influx of Latino, Chinese, and Vietnamese newcomers.[73]

THE CONSTITUTIONALITY OF LOCAL ZONING AND EXCLUSION

Property-rights activists often claim that zoning is theft, that zoning and land-use regulation deny a property owner the freedom to build whatever he or she wishes on a piece of property. The Supreme Court, however, has upheld the constitutionality of local zoning codes that restrict the use of property. In a ruling that goes back nearly a hundred years ago, the Supreme Court in its 1926 **Euclid decision** (*Village of Euclid, Ohio, v. Ambler Realty Co.*),[74] viewed zoning as a legitimate exercise of the state's **police powers** to protect the public well-being against unwanted noise, congestion, and changes in a community's character.

Yet, as we have already seen, communities do not use their zoning powers solely to maintain public health and safety and curtail noise. Suburban communities also use zoning as a tool to keep out less-advantaged people.

Is such a discriminatory use of local zoning powers constitutional? For the most part, the answer appears to be "Yes." The U.S. Constitution does not bar discrimination on the basis of income or buying power. There is no constitutional violation per se when a poor or middle-class family is unable to "buy into" a wealthier community. The courts will strike down a local zoning ordinance only if a litigant can prove that the community's *intent* to discriminate was racial, not economic, in nature.

The Supreme Court's 1977 **Arlington Heights decision** affirmed the ability of suburbs to administer land-use and zoning measures that have exclusionary impacts.[75] A church group had sought to build subsidized housing units in Arlington Heights, an affluent, overwhelmingly white suburb northwest of Chicago. But Arlington Heights's zoning regulations prohibited multifamily housing in almost all sections of the community. The Supreme Court upheld the constitutionality of the Arlington Heights restrictions, observing the legitimate purposes served by zoning. A community may use its zoning powers to preserve a peaceable environment, promote orderly land development, and protect local property values. The plaintiffs were able to demonstrate that the zoning regulations impeded the ability of less-well-off minority citizens to reside in Arlington Heights. But evidence of discriminatory effect was not enough: The housing advocates could not produce convincing evidence that Arlington Heights enacted its zoning ordinance with a clear intent to discriminate on the basis of race.

The significance of the *Arlington Heights* ruling cannot be overstated. Suburbs are generally under no constitutional obligation to modify their zoning and land-use ordinances in order to promote class and racial integration. A suburb's legal counsel can always argue that land-use regulations have no racial intent but are simply tools that a community uses to protect housing values and preserve a tranquil congestion-free environment.

THE TECHNIQUES OF SUBURBAN EXCLUSION

A suburb has a variety of tools it can use to exclude residents it does not want. Many suburbs simply refuse to apply for assistance to build subsidized housing units for low-income families. These communities prefer that housing for the poor be built elsewhere, beyond their borders.

A suburb's local ordinances can put various impediments in the way of any effort by nonprofit associations and private developers to construct dwellings that are affordable to lower- and even middle-income residents. Most directly, a suburb's zoning and land-use ordinances can effectively **prohibit the construction of multifamily housing**. Such provisions put a suburb beyond the reach of people who can only afford to rent an apartment or buy a small condominium as opposed to a free-standing single-family home.

Exclusive suburbs further drive up the price of entry into their community through **large-lot zoning**, which requires that a home be built on no less than a half acre, one acre, or even two acres of land. Such land requirements greatly add to the price of a home, restricting entry into the community to people who have the wealth necessary to pay the steep price for a large-lot home.[76]

Suburban governments also drive up the price of a home by legislating **minimum room/space requirements** that go beyond concerns for health and safety. **Regulations requiring the use of expensive construction technologies and materials** similarly add to construction costs and home prices. Many suburbs require that homes be built piece by piece on-site, a practice that does not allow for the time and cost savings that come from utilizing preassembled modular home components. Construction regulations can further drive up home prices by requiring the use of expensive copper pipes instead of serviceable plastic pipes.

A **moratorium on the extension of sewer and water lines** effectively limits the supply of land available for new home construction. The designation of **agricultural preserves** and **open-space and green-space areas** likewise limits the acreage available for new homes. Of course, local communities argue that such efforts are motivated by concern for the natural environment, not exclusion.

Suburban jurisdictions can also defeat unwanted development projects through a **strategy of delays** and constantly **shifting development standards**. When a developer meets one set of conditions, a city council or planning commission then imposes additional ones that add new delays and costs to a project. A developer can go to court to challenge the new requirements, but judicial action can take quite a bit of time and be quite costly. A developer cannot make money when a project is ensnared in a seemingly endless sea of entanglements. Good business sense eventually leads many developers to cede to such exclusionary tactics; developers will shift their construction plans to communities more welcoming of new development.

Suburban municipalities can also drive up the cost of entry by imposing thousands of dollars in **developer fees and access charges** that are then passed on to buyers in the form of increased home prices. Developer fees and access charges are levied in addition to local taxes. These fees burden home buyers with having to pay for new streets, sewers, and schools—amenities that other community residents receive as a result of the normal taxes they pay.

Suburbs levy developer fees but are reluctant to raise property tax levies to increase the price of entry into a community. The reason should be obvious. Developer fees and access charges are shouldered by newcomers. In contrast, an increase in local property tax rates would burden a suburb's existing residents, not just newcomers.

Over the years, communities like Petaluma and Livermore (California) have gone so far as to enact **limited-growth and no-growth ordinances**, setting an annual quota or otherwise placing a cap on the permits issued each year for the construction of new residential dwellings. Critics worry about the equity impacts of such measures and their impact on driving up the cost of housing. Ramapo, 35 miles outside New York City, gained fame for its policy of rejecting most new construction requests; the community would issue a permit for new residential development only in cases where a project was especially meritorious and the community had no difficulty in providing supportive municipal services. Decades later, however, Ramapo relaxed its tough antigrowth stance, as local leaders feared that the restrictions were serving to drive desirable new development and jobs to its neighbors.[77]

CAN JUDICIAL POWER "OPEN" THE SUBURBS? THE 40-YEAR TALE OF NEW JERSEY'S MOUNT LAUREL DECISIONS

Activists seeking to "open" the suburbs have turned to litigation in state courts, arguing that exclusionary practices violate a state's constitution and statutes. In most states, the courts are reluctant to play such an active policy role in local land-use decisions, policy matters which they argue should be properly left to elected officials. New Jersey, however, stands out as a notable exception, with an activist state supreme court that has taken steps to force suburbs to accept more affordable housing units than they would otherwise allow.

The advocates of "open suburbs" won their most significant judicial victory when the New Jersey Supreme Court, in a set of rulings known collectively as the *Mount Laurel* **decisions**, struck down the exclusionary practices of a broad range of New Jersey communities. The court ruled that, under the state's constitution, Mount Laurel Township (a New Jersey suburb of Camden and Philadelphia) and all growing communities in the state were obligated to change their land-use and zoning ordinances to allow the construction of their "fair share" of a region's low- and moderate-income housing units.[78]

The court's initial 1975 ruling had little immediate impact. Suburban communities simply dragged their feet and rezoned as few parcels of land as possible.

After eight years, the court again intervened,[79] this time by incentivizing developers to bring legal challenges against local exclusionary practices. Where a developer could demonstrate that local ordinances improperly obstructed new home-building efforts, the court would allow the developer a bonus—permission to construct at higher densities and thereby earn additional profit. The New Jersey Supreme Court also established a special system of housing courts to expedite the legal challenges brought by developers.

Suburban residents were outraged by what they saw as a frontal attack by the courts on their communities. New Jersey's governor and state legislature responded by passing new legislation to narrow the impact of the *Mount Laurel* rulings. New Jersey abolished the special housing courts and created, in their place, an appointed Council on Affordable Housing. Despite its name, the Council did not aggressively promote the construction of affordable housing. Instead, the Council devoted much of its time to hearing appeals from suburbs to reduce the number of affordable housing units that they were expected to build.

Republican Governor Chris Christie refused to obey a court order to have the state establish workable guidelines for local affordable housing. Christie also attempted to abolish the state affordable housing council. But the Court would not back down. Instead, the New Jersey Supreme Court responded by giving lower courts the ability to determine just how many units of low- and moderate-income housing were to be built in communities throughout the state.[80]

For a while, state-elected officials allowed wealthier suburbs an alternative path rather than build their full affordable housing obligation within their borders. State legislation authorized a community to shift up to half of its fair share obligation to other communities that joined in a "regional contribution agreement." A better-off suburb could help pay for new housing units in economically troubled cities like Newark, Paterson, and Jersey City. In 1993, suburban Wayne Township gave $8 million to help low-income Paterson build housing; by doing so, the township avoided having to build an additional 500 units of affordable housing inside its own borders.[81] In 2008, the state revoked its authorization for such agreements.

Continued resistance from the suburbs meant that the *Mount Laurel* decisions could not "open the suburbs" to the extent that its advocates had hoped. Yet, judicial persistence did produce positive results, as numerous middle class and more affluent communities implemented changes in their zoning and land-use regulations to permit the construction of additional affordable dwelling units, especially units intended for seniors and for working- and middle-class families.[82] Even the much criticized regional contribution agreements provided fiscally strapped core cities with tens of millions of dollars in assistance for housing—although such transfers did not actually open the suburbs.

The New Jersey courts would not back down. In 2017, the New Jersey Supreme Court unanimously ruled that localities would have to build an estimated 200,000 or more units of new affordable housing, to make up for the failure to meet their *Mount Laurel* construction obligations.

The battle over housing diversity in the New Jersey suburbs lasted more than four decades. Whatever the weaknesses of court action as a housing strategy, the judicial approach nonetheless has one obvious advantage: Strong judicial action puts pressure on suburbs to build a broader range of housing than they would otherwise allow. Continuing pressure from the judiciary has even led New Jersey suburbs like Mount Laurel, Cherry Hill, and Bridgewater to enter into agreements with housing advocacy groups, nonprofits, and developers to build new affordable units. Suburban communities converted vacant malls, office parks, and industrial sites into new residential communities.[83]

INCLUSIONARY APPROACHES: HOW TO BUILD MORE BALANCED AND AFFORDABLE COMMUNITIES AND SUBURBS

Massachusetts's Chapter 40B **Anti-Snob Zoning law** allows a developer to appeal to a state panel in cases where local land-use controls unreasonably interfere with the construction of low- and moderate-income housing. A developer can go to the state board to argue that a local community has failed to develop a housing plan that allows for the production of a sufficient number of affordable units. The Massachusetts law seeks to place at least 10 percent of the housing stock in each local community within the financial reach of working-class and poorer families. The state can deny development-related assistance to offending municipalities. Connecticut, Rhode Island, New Hampshire, New Jersey, Pennsylvania, Illinois, and California are among the states that have adopted ordinances similar to Massachusetts's 40B.

Anti-snob zoning laws work.[84] The Massachusetts 40B law led to the production of tens of thousands of affordable housing units. Developers in Massachusetts have won appeals against overly restrictive zoning and land-use regulations.

Suburbanites in Massachusetts worry that the law threatens the character of their communities by giving developers a route to bypass local concerns. As a consequence, unsurprisingly, 40B is not always aggressively enforced. In more recent years, the state has also modified 40B to give new weight to the concerns of residents. Overall, Massachusetts 40B has been a fairly effective tool that has prompted suburbs to accept moderate-income families, but not the poor.[85]

Montgomery County (Maryland), Fairfax (Virginia), Orange and San Diego Counties (California), and Seattle all have local **inclusionary programs**. These communities have relaxed zoning ordinances, modified building code requirements, and provided expedited permitting and public financial assistance to developers who commit to building affordable multifamily housing.[86] Some municipalities have gone so far as to purchase a number of dwelling units in a new residential development providing a developer with a guaranteed revenue stream; in return the developer assures that the project will contain a designated number of affordable dwelling units.[87]

Local inclusionary efforts often rely on the award of incentives. The award of **density bonuses** enables a developer to build at greater densities in return for a signed agreement to set aside a specified number of units for low- and moderate-income families. But in Durham, North Carolina, developers were reluctant to participate despite the offer of density bonuses. Developers complained of the administrative costs and hassles of working with government agencies. They were also worried that the inclusion of low-income units would pose a danger to their ability to market a new residential development.[88]

In California, concern for economic growth led Governor Jerry Brown, normally an affordable housing enthusiast, to veto a measure that sought to strengthen the state's requirements that projects be inclusionary. Brown observed that his experience as mayor of Oakland led him to worry that such requirements could impede a city's efforts to attract new development.[89]

Mandates for inclusion are not always popular. In 2016, the Republican state government of Tennessee acted to preempt municipalities from mandating that developers include affordable housing units in new developments. The state-imposed restriction essentially gutted the strong approach to affordable housing that Nashville was considering adopting.[90]

In 2018, the city of Minneapolis (a central city, not a suburb) initiated one of the boldest moves in the nation to counter exclusionary zoning and promote the construction of affordable housing. As part of its newly adopted *Minneapolis 2040* plan, the city council eliminated single-family zoning throughout the city. Approximately half of the acreage of the city, including some of the city's more exclusive residential neighborhoods, would be rezoned to allow the construction of triplexes (three-unit housing structures). Minneapolis sought to increase the supply of affordable housing located in the city, especially in the city's more desirable neighborhoods.[91]

The change in Minneapolis faced intense opposition from residents intent on maintaining the single-family-home character of their neighborhoods. The plan gained passage only as it had the strong backing of Mayor Jacob Frey and affordable housing advocates. The intensity of the opposition and the looming threat of lawsuits from neighborhood homeowners did lead the city to compromise. The changed rules allowed only for the construction of triplexes instead of the four-unit housing structures that planners had initially sought.[92]

Suburban Autonomy and the Fragmented Metropolis

"Metropolitan areas are poorly governed."[93] With only few exceptions, no government exists with the power to act on behalf of the entire region. Instead, a multiplicity of small local governments each rules a part of the metropolitan region. Each local body possesses the political autonomy—that is, the political independence—to follow a course of action that will protect the lifestyles and interests of its residents. A local government does not normally give great consideration as to how its decisions will affect the region's overall development or how its actions will impact its immediate neighbors.

Local communities often act as if they have no ties to one another. Yet, the concept of a **metropolitan area** denotes the economic and social **interdependence** of communities in a region. No city or suburb is an island unto itself. Instead, each community's well-being is dependent on the existence, actions, and resources of its neighbors. Core cities and declining suburbs, for instance, house many of a region's low-wage manual and service workers essential to a region's economy. Central cities and working-class inner-ring suburbs provide much of the warehousing, distribution, and manufacturing activities that sustain economic growth throughout the region. Even the prosperity of a region's most affluent communities is dependent on the support functions, employment opportunities, and the workforces that are situated in other jurisdictions in the metropolis. The economic interdependence of communities in the metropolis is most readily revealed in commuting patterns: the residents of one community travel to other communities for their economic livelihoods.

Metropolitan fragmentation denotes that decision making authority in the modern metropolis is dispersed among numerous, relatively small units or governments; no broader regional governmental body exists with real authority to govern the socially and economically interconnected metropolis. The word *fragmentation* underscores how governmental authority in an urban region is split (some would say "shattered") into many smaller pieces: including autonomous cities and suburbs as well as a large variety of narrow-purpose planning and specialized service districts. Virtually all metropolitan areas have a regional council to help plan transportation development and similar matters. Yet, as Chapter 10 will discuss in greater detail, such regional bodies seldom possess significant power; decision making authority largely resides with the smaller and more localized governments. In the American metropolis, governmental powers are exercised by hundreds of independent cities, towns, villages, townships, counties, special authorities, and narrow-purpose service districts.

The fragmentation of a major metropolitan area can be quite extensive. The greater New York metropolitan area sprawls into three states and is governed by a confusing mosaic of more than 2,200 separate units of government (cities, villages, towns, townships, counties, school districts, and other specialized service districts).[94] Alternative ways of measuring a region's political fragmentation even indicate that metropolitan Chicago, Pittsburgh, and St. Louis may suffer from more extensive fragmentation than does New York.[95]

Especially in the Northeast and the Midwest, the existence of so many local units of government makes effective, coordinated regional action immensely difficult to achieve. No metropolitan area, for instance, can easily develop an effective system of regional mass transit when bus and rail service stops at the boundary lines of a county or community whose residents are unwilling to help pay for the service. The provision of emergency medical services in a region is similarly obstructed when a community's ambulances are not permitted to cross a political boundary line in response to a call for assistance.

Metropolitan fragmentation can be costly. Metropolitan fragmentation also results in a costly **duplication of services** as individual communities each insist on having their own police force, fire station, hospital and CAT scanner. Of course, a variety of intergovernmental agreements enable willing communities in a region to cooperate for cost savings (as will be detailed in Chapter 10). The political fragmentation of metropolitan areas also leads to sprawl, as each autonomous community is free to pursue its own growth. No government in the metropolis has the power to pursue compact development to shorten home-to-work commutes and thereby reduce energy costs and pollution.[96]

THE COSTS OF SUBURBAN SPRAWL

Suburban communities pursue land-use actions in their self-interest; in doing so they exacerbate **urban sprawl** (or, more accurately, "suburban sprawl"), the spread of new development over a wide geographical area.[97] A community on the outer edges of a metropolis, for instance, may offer subsidies and other supports to attract a regional shopping mall or new high-end residential developments that will add to its tax revenues. Looking out for its fiscal self-interest, the rim community will care little about the adverse environmental impacts that often accompany spread development: lost wetlands, increased storm water runoff, and heightened levels of air pollution that result from lengthened automobile trips.

More affluent suburbs located closer to the metropolitan center often adopt a quite different set of zoning and land-use measures that, too, exacerbate sprawl. When an exclusive inner-ring community limits new commercial and housing construction, developers "head for the more rural areas in search of more buildable land."[98]

Sprawled development is expensive; new development requires the construction of infrastructure and facilities that may duplicate what already exists in already-built-up sections of the metropolis. The Salt Lake City region would save an estimated $4.5 billion in transportation, water, sewer, and utility investments if it could override local decisions that lead to continued sprawled development.[99]

Suburban sprawl also has adverse impacts on both the natural environment and human health.[100] Lengthened automobile commutes add to greenhouse gas emissions, degrade air quality, and exhaust nonrenewable energy sources.[101] Runoff from the roadways, parking lots, and paved surfaces of suburbia allows oil, road salts, and other contaminants to flow into lakes and streams. Impermeable roads and parking lot surfaces interfere with the groundwater seepage that replenishes aquifers. Sprawl eats up greenfields and wetlands, destroying animal habitats and diminishing biodiversity. Sprawl also reduces agricultural acreage. In Wisconsin, new residential subdivisions on the edge of the Milwaukee area drove up land prices, prompting farmers to sell their acreage to developers seeking to convert the land to nonagricultural uses.[102] The automobile-reliant lifestyle of suburbia is associated with a higher risk of obesity, high blood pressure, and heart disease.[103]

Urban sprawl also affects racial equity. Sprawled development diminishes the prospects of metropolitan school integration, as white students disproportionately attend more racially homogeneous schools found in the exurbs. Sprawled development hurts the job prospects of inner-city minorities and the poor, as employment concentrations are increasingly found in edge cities and edgeless developments that are not adequately served by public transit.

Can "Smart Growth" Curb Suburban Sprawl?

Can urban sprawl be contained? More than 20 states pursue some variant of **sustainable development, growth management, and Smart Growth** policies that seek compact and transit-oriented development as an alternative to continued sprawl.[104]

Greater Boston has sought to find an alternative to the continued edgeless development occurring beyond the I-495 beltway. The regional transit agency played a key role in pushing plans for **compact development**, targeting growth to new town centers developed around rail stations in older suburbs such as Canton, Medford, Newton, Norwood, Salem, and Waltham.[105] Smart Growth plans often emphasize **transit-oriented development (TOD)**, the construction of high-density clusters of new offices and residences in close proximity to mass transit stations.

For three decades, Florida emphasized a statewide growth management program in an effort to ward off the ecological damage that sprawled development posed to the Everglades and to fragile coastal areas. Florida also sought to manage growth in order to reduce the costs to the taxpayers of new roads and other infrastructure. Florida required localities to formulate comprehensive development plans so that development would take place in areas where the necessary supporting infrastructure already existed.

Florida's growth management program, however, was only partially effective in containing sprawl. Developers pressed local officials to categorize land in ways that would facilitate new growth projects. Municipalities seeking continued growth were complicit in finding ways to circumvent the Florida Growth Management Act. Substantial new growth continued in rim areas of the metropolis where highways had excess capacity. In some cases, the Growth Management Act even slowed development in already-built-up areas where traffic on existing roadways was near capacity.

In 2011, Florida abandoned its system of local growth management. The state greatly modified the Growth Management Act—virtually repealing it—which was renamed the Community Planning Act. Republican Governor Rick Scott and a business-friendly legislature sought deregulation to promote job creation. By revoking the requirement that local governments formulate growth management plans, the 2011 alterations weakened the Act's ability to limit sprawl.[106]

Maryland, like Florida, is another state that gained renown for its Smart Growth policies, first adopted in 1997 as growth pressures threatened farmland and green space in the state. Maryland's Smart Growth Areas Act distributes state funding as an incentive to steer new development to already-built-up areas and to communities in need of revitalization. The State of Maryland targets aid for highways, sewage treatment, new housing, and other programs to already-developed areas. Proposed large-lot subdivisions and projects intended for greenfield sites do not qualify for priority state funding.

Maryland's Smart Growth strategy has received lots of favorable publicity. Yet, the approach has been only moderately successful in curbing sprawled development: "Despite the rhetoric, smart growth still means that growth will happen in the suburbs and on the periphery."[107] The Maryland Smart Growth program has helped preserve farm acreage; but the program has not been as successful in curbing new development in more rural areas on the edge of the metropolis.[108] Despite Smart Growth policy, development in Maryland continues to be low-density and suburban, rather than the infill of existing urban areas.[109]

Maryland and New Jersey (which in 1998 adopted a Smart Growth program similar to that of Maryland) actually do *not* utilize strong state regulations that would prohibit new development in green areas. Instead, the states rely on the offer of incentives (priorities in the award of state aid) in an attempt to steer growth projects to already-built-up areas. Municipalities intent in pursuing growth projects simply ignore the incentives and continue to approve new developments, even in areas that the state has not designated for growth.

In contrast to the Maryland and New Jersey reliance on incentives, Oregon has adopted an alternative, more strong-government approach. In Oregon state regulations restrict unwanted development intrusions into forests, farmland, and other green areas.

Oregon's strong regulatory approach, however, has been challenged by **property rights advocates** who in 2004 turned to the voter initiative process to weaken the state system of land controls. Proposition 37 required the state to pay "just compensation" to owners who claim that growth control measures diminish the value of their properties.[110] Property rights advocates hoped that the prospect of having to bear such an expense would dissuade state officials from continuing to implement strong constraints on local land uses. Three years later, however, voters undid much of the damage done by Proposition 37, when they passed a new measure (Proposition 49) that limited the development of new strip malls and that barred the construction of residential subdivisions on forest lands and high-valued farmland.

Portland's Urban Growth Boundary

One of the most prominent tools in Oregon's growth management approach is the requirement, first adopted in the 1970s, that Portland and other major urban areas formulate growth boundaries. The Portland **Urban Growth Boundary (UGB)** was created to

Figure 3.4 **The Urban Growth Boundary Promotes Compact Development. Orenco Station, Portland.**

Source: Courtesy of user Aboutmovies from Wikimedia Commons, https://commons.wikimedia.org/ wiki/File: HillsboroOrencoStation.JPG.

prevent new residential development from encroaching on green areas and farmland in the Willamette Valley. The UGB is a line drawn on a map; developers are permitted to build new housing only inside, not outside, the designated growth boundary. The UGB averts sprawl while promoting infill development that serves to strengthen downtown Portland, the city's neighborhoods, and the region's older suburbs (see Figure 3.4).

The UGB has clearly succeeded in terms of its major goals. Even in the UGB's early years (the 1980s and early 1990s), over 90 percent of single-family homes and 99 percent of multifamily development in the region took place within the confines of the boundary.[111] The UGB forces compact development, a factor that helps to account for Portland's Number One ranking among the nation's cities in terms of the percentage of people who commute to work by bicycle.[112]

Yet the Portland regulatory approach suffers an important downside: homebuyers get "less house" for their money. Developers often have little alternative but to build townhouses and relatively small homes—"skinny houses" that are "shoehorned" into small plots of land inside the growth boundary. Homes in Portland have tiny backyards and, in many cases, no side yards.

Critics charge that the UGB has an even more damaging effect on housing affordability. According to the critics, the growth boundary constricts the supply of developable land, thereby driving up the costs of housing. Yet the evidence does not clearly support the contention that Portland's UGB has led to steep home price inflation. As Denver and Salt Lake City, two cities that do not have a mandated growth boundary, experienced a rapid increase in home prices during the same years that home prices soared in Portland, blame for home price inflation cannot easily be assigned to the UGB. Home prices in Portland, as in other cities, climb as a result of job and wage growth in the region. Good wages, not the UGB, bear most of the responsibility for high home prices.[113]

Important features of the Oregon law help to explain why the UGB has not led to a shortage of affordable housing. Most significantly, the UGB does not lead to a shortage in the supply of land available for housing, as the Act's critics contend. Oregon state law requires urban communities to adjust the boundary every five years in order to maintain a 30-year supply of land for expected growth. In 2002, Portland's Metro Council widened the boundary by adding 18,000 acres. In 2009 Metro again expanded the boundary, adding a 7 percent increase in developable space.[114] In 2011, at the behest of developers and over the objections of local environmentalist organizations, the Metro Council placed an additional 2,000 acres inside the boundary to facilitate home building.[115] Such expansions accommodate housing needs.

The UGB does not create a shortage of housing sites as much as it shifts the location where new construction takes place. The boundary puts fringe and exurban construction off limits, forcing developers to search for developable sites inside the UGB.[116] The UGB has constrained development on Portland's popular West Side, forcing developers to turn to the eastern portion of the region where developable land inside the boundary is readily available.[117]

Oregon policy makers have muted the impact of the UGB on home prices, by taking additional policy measures to assure the provision of affordable housing. The state promotes the construction of a mix of housing types (and does not allow developers to focus solely on the construction of single-family detached homes) in order to assure that there will dwelling units within the price reach of working- and middle-class families.[118] The state requires local jurisdictions in greater Portland to rezone land so that apartments and multifamily homes will constitute half or more of all new housing.[119] State law prohibits the region's suburbs from placing a cap on new home construction.

Like Oregon, the State of Washington requires metropolitan regions to adopt urban growth boundaries. Evidence from greater Seattle (King County), too, demonstrates how government policies can promote the production of multifamily housing and more affordable dwelling units, offsetting any inflationary pressures on housing prices that a local growth boundary may generate.[120]

THE "NEW URBANISM": CAN WE BUILD BETTER SUBURBS?

The **New Urbanism (NU)** is a movement of designers, developers, and urban planners who have reacted against the automobile reliance and environmental costs of sprawled suburban development. In seeking to build more densely developed, transit-oriented, and more walkable communities, the New Urbanism embodies a commitment to ecological sustainability that has a lot in common with Smart Growth. But the New Urbanism goes still further as it seeks to restore a sense of neighborliness and "community" that its proponents feel has been lost amid the big single-family homes and private backyards of suburbia. New Urbanism seeks to get Americans out of their cars and back on the sidewalk, and out from the seclusion of their homes and into more frequent touch with their neighbors. In short, the New Urbanism seeks to build a better alternative to conventional suburbs. The New Urbanism "is arguably the most influential movement in city design in the last half-century."[121]

THE GUIDING PRINCIPLES OF THE "NEW URBANISM"[122]

Conventional suburbs, designed around the automobile, pose nearly insurmountable barriers to walking. In the conventional suburb, homes are located far from commercial destinations. Side yards and driveways add to the distances that a person must walk to get from one destination to another. Highway approaches and access ramps make it nearly impossible for pedestrians to cross major streets. High schools and office centers are situated on virtual islands surrounded by acres of parking that are not easily traversed by foot. The workers in a suburban office tower who go out for lunch often find that they have no real alternative but to drive from one parking lot to another. Mass-produced homes and a streetscape dominated by high-speed roadways and parking lots also makes suburbia "an incredibly boring place to walk."[123]

The New Urbanism (NU), by contrast, emphasizes compact development and seeks to minimize the acreage lost to roadways, access ramps, and the sea of parking lots that surround shopping centers and office galleries. NU design emphasizes walkability, with homes built close to sidewalks and located within a five-minute pedestrian trip to schools, with convenience stores and other neighborhood facilities located close at hand. Attractive retro-style town centers with fountains, band shells, cafés, and interesting shops and window displays further promote pedestrian traffic (Figure 3.5). Townhomes and garden apartments are essential features of NU communities (or, at least, of certain neighborhoods in NU communities), as multifamily housing provides the population densities to support neighborhood schools and lively town centers.

Front porches on homes restore the "eyes" that watch over streets and make a neighborhood safe and free of crime. **Traffic-calming measures**, such as low speed limits, traffic bumps, and on-street parallel parking, all protect pedestrians and enhance walkability. Tree-lined walkways and bicycle paths provide pleasant alternatives to the automobile. Where central facilities require automobile access, parking is pushed to rear garages so that a pedestrian-friendly environment is maintained.

The New Urbanists emphasizes diversity as opposed to the homogeneity that conventional suburbs enforce through zoning. NU design seeks developments that have a mix apartments, townhomes, and single-family homes. Where government funds for subsidized housing are available, NU will "blend in" subsidized units so that, from the outside, they are not readily distinguishable from market-rate housing.

The New Urbanism's singular achievement has been the construction of aesthetically pleasing communities that offer residents an alternative to automobile-centered conventional suburbia.[124] Commercial developers have also incorporated numerous aspects of

Figure 3.5 **New Urbanism: The Attractive Downtown of Celebration, Florida.** The master-planned community of Celebration in Osceola County, Florida, illustrates a number of features that distinguish New Urbanism design from more typical suburban development: Stores are built close to the street and close to one another to promote walking. Awnings add texture, adding to the "retro" or nostalgic appeal of small-town America. Fountains and places to sit allow people to congregate and meet one another. Streets are narrow and are not built to accommodate high-speed traffic.

Source: From Wikimedia Commons, by Bobak Ha'Eri, February 23, 2006, http://commons.wikimedia.org/wiki/File:022306-CelebrationFL11.jpg.

New Urbanism into "lifestyle centers," the open-air faux-urban shopping and entertainment villages that are more vibrant and fun than the older generation of indoor shopping malls.

More affluent, established suburbs like Upper Arlington, Ohio, just outside of Columbus, have turned to NU-style developments to attract new commercial activity and increase the local tax base. Upper Arlington eased the municipality's height and frontage restrictions and even relaxed parking space requirements in order to facilitate the construction of new office buildings, mixed-use development, and condominiums and apartments, assets that will increase the suburb's attractiveness to young professionals.[125]

New Urbanism is not solely a suburban movement. Its principles have also been applied to center-city shopping districts in an effort to bring 24-hour-a-day life back to a city's downtown. The federal government's **HOPE VI** program even adopted a number of New Urbanism design elements in an effort to create more habitable public housing environments. In Chicago, Atlanta, Baltimore, Charlotte, New Orleans, Louisville, and numerous other cities, HOPE VI sought the physical transformation of public housing, demolishing some of the nation's most distressed public housing structures, replacing them with more attractive low-rise housing communities built according to NU principles.

THE LIMITED NATURE OF THE NEW URBANISM REVOLUTION

New Urbanism developments provide more attractive and walkable alternatives to the traditional suburb. Yet, the New Urbanism does not effectively contain sprawl. Nor can NU be expected to reorganize suburbia. NU cannot undo patterns of single-family homeownership and spread land uses that have become entrenched over the years. Most Americans will continue to seek homes with multicar garages and spacious side yards and backyards, not the more compact developments of the New Urbanism.

New Urbanism values social diversity and mixed-income communities and housing types. But in the absence of public subsidies, NU developers are seldom able to include much housing for the poor. As a result, NU communities are often constructed without the population diversity that is part of the initial NU ideal.[126] Consequently, New Urbanism developments do not often offer an alternative to suburban exclusion. Instead, the NU winds up offering only "a slightly reconfigured suburb," an "automobile-oriented subdivision dressed up to look like a small pre-car-centered town."[127]

CONCLUSION: URBAN AMERICA IN A SUBURBAN AGE

Suburban communities jealously guard their control over schools, zoning, and land uses that define a community's identity. Suburbanites applaud the grassroots nature of small-scale government as embodying the "ideals of Jeffersonian democracy."[128] The value of small-scale and responsive government is undeniable. But suburban power, however, has also compounded problems of sprawled development, suburban exclusion, racially imbalanced schools, and inequality in the metropolis.

The various regional reform movements described in this chapter—school finance equalization, "open suburbs," Smart Growth, growth management, and the New Urbanism—seek to build more equitable and ecologically sustainable communities. Still, none of the movements has the ability to fundamentally reshape suburban and metropolitan development. Home seekers will continue to search for the "good life" in the suburbs. Developers and home builders will continue to profit from the construction of low-density, single-family housing. Together, suburban voters and development interests constitute a quite powerful coalition.

As this chapter has underscored, state action is often critical to the success of inclusionary zoning, smart growth, and other efforts to promote a more balanced, racially integrated, equitable, and ecologically sustainable metropolitan America. But as the population and political power of suburbs continues to grow, it will not be easy to get state legislatures to adopt such solutions. In recent years, numerous states have sought to water down inclusionary requirements and to preempt local actions mandating affordable housing and even more balanced and sustainable development.

Already-built patterns of settlement are nearly impossible to alter. Regional planners and political leaders cannot realistically hope to reverse "facts on the ground." The contemporary and the future American metropolis will continue to be characterized by suburban development, political fragmentation, and sprawl—and the rise of counter-movements to ameliorate adverse effects.

Properly focused public policy can bring improvement. Incentives can catalyze the construction of multifamily and affordable housing. Properly designed, incentives can even spur a degree of voluntary school integration. The states can also prioritize infrastructure investment in already built-up areas as opposed to sparsely green spaces. Regional land-use planning and growth management can help avert—or least reduce—the encroachment of sprawled development into green areas. California has shown renewed interest in transportation-oriented development, concentrating new construction in compact areas close to rail stations

America's politically powerful suburban population will not readily cede to changes that they perceive as a threat to their communities and lifestyles. Politically feasible public policy starts by accepting both the physical and the political reality of suburbia. Politically pragmatic transportation planners, for instance, may do well to recognize that the population densities of many suburban communities are just too small to support conventional light-rail and heavy-rail transit. In lower density areas, dedicated-lane bus rapid transit (BRT) and reinvigorated bus service may be more politically and financially viable alternatives. Paratransit with smaller vehicles can provide flexible service in response to service calls. Safe bicycle paths can be constructed along—but separated from—roadways. Metropolitan regions may also experiment with various forms of congesting pricing and road tolling to reduce automobile commuting during peak times.

American suburbs in the near future will continue to retain their low-density character. Yet, even that is changing, if just a bit. New centers of dense suburban development are emerging, as suburban leaders seek to create active living and work environments that respond to the preferences of young professionals. To develop vital town centers, a suburban municipality can award density bonuses that enable the construction of concentrations of restaurants, grocery stores, and other neighborhood-oriented establishments. The concentration of activities can even encourage walking, as seen in the impacts of such development even in the fabled automobile-oriented suburbs of Los Angeles.[129]

Friendship Heights in Montgomery County, Maryland (just across the border from Washington, DC), has a city-like center of high-density, office development, and quality housing built around a rail station.[130] Friendship Heights is a privileged community, an enclave of wealth. Yet, its evolving development indicates that an increasing number of suburbs are interested in capturing the benefits that come with growth.

Many suburbs, just like central cities, seek to lure new investment, including the offices of major corporations. Just how globalization affects interlocal competition for development is the subject of our next chapter.

KEY TERMS

agricultural preserves as an
    exclusionary tool (*p. 97*)
Anti-Snob Zoning law, the
    Massachusetts (*p. 99*)

apartheid schools (*p. 94*)
Arlington Heights decision (*p. 96*)
bedroom-developing suburbs (*p. 83*)
bedroom or dormitory suburb (*p. 81*)

NOTES

1. Alan Berube, et al., *State of Metropolitan America: On the Front Lines of Demographic Transformation* (Washington, DC: Brookings Institution Press, 2010), 7, www.brookings.edu/~/media/Files/Programs/Metro/state_of_metro_america/metro_america_report.pdf; U.S.

2. See, for instance, Leigh Gallagher, *The End of the Suburbs: Where the American Dream Is Moving* (London, UK: Portfolio and Penguin, 2013). Also see William H. Frey, "A Big City Growth Revival?" *Brookings Institution*, May 28, 2013, www.brookings.edu/research/opinions/2013/05/28-city-growth-frey.

3. Jed Kolko, "Americans' Shift to the Suburbs Sped Up Last Year," *FiveThirtyEight Blog Posting*, May 23, 2017, https://fivethirtyeight.com/features/americans-shift-to-the-suburbs-sped-up-last-year/; William H. Frey, "City Growth Dips Below Suburban Growth, Census Shows," *A Brookings Institution Web Posting*, Washington, DC, May 30, 2017, www.brookings.edu/blog/the-avenue/2017/05/30/city-growth-dips-below-suburban-growth-census-shows/.

4. Jed Kolko, "No, Suburbs Aren't All the Same: The Suburbiest Ones Are Growing Fastest," *CityLab Web Posting*, February 5, 2015, www.citylab.com/equity/2015/02/no-suburbs-arent-all-the-same-the-suburbiest-ones-are-growing-fastest/385183/.

5. Robert E. Lang and Jennifer E. LeFurgy, *Boomburbs: The Rise of America's Accidental Cities* (Washington, DC: Brookings Institution Press, 2007).

6. Lang and LeFurgy, *Boomburbs*, 76; Brian J. Miller, "A Small Suburb Becomes a Boomburb: Explaining Suburban Growth in Naperville, Illinois," *Journal of Urban History* 42, no. 6 (2016): 1135–1152.

7. Stephanie Coontz, "Why 'Mad Men' Is TV's Most Feminist Show," *Washington Post*, October 10, 2010. On suburbia and the "familial ideal," see Lynn M. Appleton, "The Gender Regimes of American Cities," in *Gender in Urban Research*, vol. 42, ed. Judith A. Garber and Robyne S. Turner (Thousand Oaks, CA: Sage Publications, 1994), 44–59.

8. The 1950s stereotype of suburbia as a stream of bedroom communities was the result of such celebrated books as William H. Whyte, Jr., *The Organization Man* (New York: Simon and Schuster, 1956); David Riesman, *The Lonely Crowd* (Garden City, NY: Doubleday, 1957); and J. Seeley, R. Sim, and E. Loosley, *Crestwood Heights* (New York: Basic Books, 1956). Bennett M. Berger's, *Working-Class Suburb* (Berkeley: University of California Press, 1960) was a noteworthy exception: a book that detailed life in a blue-collar suburban community. Suburbia today denotes a quite diverse set of communities, including "first suburbs" and politically progressive communities described in Christopher Niedt, ed., *Social Justice in Diverse Suburbs* (Philadelphia: Temple University Press, 2013).

9. Evan McKenzie, *Privatopia: Homeowner Associations and the Rise of Residential Private Government* (New Haven, CT: Yale University Press, 1994); McKenzie, *Beyond Privatopia: Rethinking Residential Private Government* (Washington, DC: Urban Institute Press, 2011).

10. Myron Orfield, *American Metropolitics: The New Suburban Reality* (Washington, DC: Brookings Institution Press, 2002), 2–3.

11. See, for instance: Marc Joffe, Julie Lark, and Edward Ring, "California's Most Financially Stressed Cities and Counties," a report of the California Policy Center, November 5, 2014, https://californiapolicycenter.org/californias-most-financially-stressed-cities-and-counties/; Alexia Fernández Campbell, "A Suburb on the Brink of Bankruptcy," *The Atlantic*, June 8, 2016, www.theatlantic.com/business/archive/2016/06/a-suburb-on-the-brink-of-bankruptcy/486188/.

12. Joel Garreau, *Edge City: Life on the New Frontier* (New York: Doubleday, 1991).

13. Robert E. Lang, *Edgeless Cities: Exploring the Elusive Metropolis* (Washington, DC: Brookings Institution Press, 2003).

14. William H. Frey, "The 2010 Census: America on the Cusp," *The Milken Institute Review* (Second Quarter 2012), 56–57, www.milkeninstitute.org/publications/review/2012_4/47-58MR54.pdf.

15. Eman Shurbaji, "Chicago's Foreign-Born Population Moving to the Suburbs," *Chicago Monitor*, March 2, 2016, http://chicagomonitor.com/2016/03/chicagos-foreign-born-population-moving-to-suburbs/. The Bolingbrook figure is a 2016 Census Bureau population estimate.

16. Willow S. Lung-Amam, *Trespassers? Asian Americans and the Battle for Suburbia* (Oakland, CA: University of California Press, 2017), describes the political dividing lines between Asian Americans and white residents in Fremont on such matters as reform of the school curriculum and whether or not restrictions should be introduced to bar the construction of McMansions in established neighborhoods.

17. U.S. Census Bureau, *QuickFact*, "Orange County, California." The number represent the Bureau's population estimates for 2016. Also see Karin Aguilar-San Juan, "Staying Vietnamese: Community and Place in Orange County and Boston," *City and Community* 4, no. 1 (2005): 37–65.

18. Lisa Sturtevant, *Home in America: Immigrants and Housing Demand* (Washington, DC: Urban Land Institute, 2017), https://uli.org/wp-content/uploads/ULI-Documents/HomeInAmerica.pdf.

19. Marilynn S. Johnson, "Revitalizing the Suburbs: Immigrants in Greater Boston since the 1980s," in *Immigration and Metropolitan Revitalization in the United States*, ed. Domenic Vitiello and Thomas J. Sugrue (Philadelphia: University of Pennsylvania Press, 2017), 67–79.

20. Michael Bader, "L.A. Is Resegregating: And Whites Are a Major Reason Why," *Los Angeles Times*, April 1, 2016.

21. Myron Orfield, Will Stancil, Thomas Luce, and Eric Myott, "High Costs and Segregation in Subsidized Housing Policy," *Housing Policy Debate* 23, no. 3 (2015), 574–607.

22. Myron Orfield and Thomas Luce, *America's Racially Diverse Suburbs: Opportunities and Challenges* (Institute on Metropolitan Opportunity, University of Minnesota Law School, July 20, 2012), www.law.umn.edu/uploads/e0/65/e065d82a1c1da0bfef7d86172ec5391e/Diverse_Suburbs_FINAL.pdf.

23. Orfield, et al., "High Costs and Segregation in Subsidized Housing Policy."

24. Mary Jo Webster, "Twin Cities Suburbs Diversifying at Rate among Fastest in Nation," *Twin Cities Pioneer Press*, July 19, 2012.

25. Amanda Kolson Hurley, "When Integrating Suburbs Isn't Enough," *CityLab Web Posting*, February 18, 2016, www.citylab.com/equity/2016/02/when-integrating-the-suburbs-isnt-enough/462765/, describes the broad range of community groups that opposed efforts to build affordable housing throughout the metropolitan region.

26. Elizabeth Kneebone and Alan Berube, *Confronting Suburban Poverty in America* (Washington, DC: Brookings Institution, 2013).

27. 2015 census data, reported by Elizabeth Kneebone, "The Changing Geography of US. Poverty," testimony presented before the U.S. House Committee on Ways and Means, Subcommittee on Human Resources, February 15, 2017, www.brookings.edu/testimonies/the-changing-geography-of-us-poverty/.

28. Yonah Freemark, "As Suburban Poverty Grows, U.S. Fails to Respond Adequately," *Next American City*, October 12, 2010, http://americancity.org/columns/entry/2670/; Adie Tomer, Elizabeth Kneebone, Robert Puentes, and Alan Berube, *Missed Opportunity: Transit and Jobs in Urban America* (Washington, DC: The Brookings Institution, May 12, 2011), www.brookings.edu/research/reports/2011/05/12-jobs-and-transit.

29. Melinda D. Anderson, "The Nonwhite Student Behind the White Picket Fence," *The Atlantic*, February 28, 2017, www.theatlantic.com/education/archive/2017/02/the-non-white-student-behind-the-white-picket-fence/518097/; Kneebone, "The Changing Geography of US. Poverty"; Scott W. Allard, *Places in Need: The Changing Geography of Poverty* (New York: Russell Sage Foundation, 2017), 145ff.

30. Allard, *Places in Need: The Changing Geography of Poverty*, 27.

31. Kneebone, "The Changing Geography of US. Poverty."

32. Gary J. Gates, *Geographic Trends among Same-Sex Couples in the U.S. Census and the American Community Survey*, The Williams Institute, UCLA School of Law, November 2007, http://williamsinstitute.law.ucla.edu/wp-content/uploads/Gates-Geographic-Trends-ACSBrief-Nov-2007.

pdf; Associated Press, "Census: More Same-Sex Couples Living in NJ Suburbs," *NBC New York*, August 14, 2011; www.nbcnewyork.com/news/local/Census-More-same-sex-couplesliving-in-NJ-suburbs-127687643.html; Amin Ghaziani, *There Goes the Gayborhood?* (Princeton, NJ: Princeton University Press, 2014), 42–55, 153–155.

33. U.S. Census Bureau, "Same-Sex Couple Households," *American Community Survey Briefs* 10–03, September 2011, www.census.gov/prod/2011pubs/acsbr10-03.pdf.

34. Erin O'Neill, "Where Are the Most LGBT-Friendly Towns in N.J.?," *NJ.com Posting*, November 2, 2016, www.nj.com/entertainment/index.ssf/2016/11/where_are_the_most_lgbt-friendly_towns_in_nj.html.

35. Rex W. Huppke, "Berwyn Pushes to Attract Gay Community," *Chicago Tribune*, September 2, 2010.

36. Lauren McGaughey, "LGBT Equality Rankings Put Dallas on Top, Dallas Suburbs on the Bottom," *Dallas Morning News*, October 17, 2016; Elise Schmelzer, "In Dallas Suburbs, Protections for LGBT Residents Are a Patchwork," *Dallas Morning News*, July 7, 2015.

37. Paul Ong, Chhandara Pech, Jenny Chhea, and C. Aujean Lee, "Race, Ethnicity, and Income Segregation in Los Angeles," *UCLA Center for Neighborhood Knowledge*, June 24, 2016, www.anderson.ucla.edu/Documents/areas/ctr/ziman/Ziman-Segregation-LA-Ong.pdf.

38. Gregory Sharp and John Iceland, "The Residential Segregation Patterns of Whites by Socioeconomic Status, 2000–2011," *Social Science Research* 42 (2013): 1046–1060; Sean F. Reardon, Lindsay Fox, and Joseph Townsend, "Neighborhood Income Composition by Household Race and Income, 10–200," *The Annals of the American as Academy of Political and Social Science* 660, no. 1 (July 2015): 78–77. For a discussion of the evidence on the continuing residential segregation of greater Detroit, see Joe T. Darden and Richard W. Thomas, *Detroit: Race Riots, Racial Conflicts, and Efforts to Bridge the Racial Divide* (East Lansing, MI: Michigan State University Press, 2013), chap. 6.

39. Ingrid Gould Ellen, "Continuing Isolation: Segregation in America Today," in *Segregation: The Rising Costs for America*, ed. James H. Carr and Nandinee Kutty (New York: Routledge, 2008), 265–271.

40. Ester Havekes, Michael Bader, and Maria Krysan, "Realizing Racial and Ethnic Neighborhood Preferences? Exploring the Mismatches Between What People Want, Where They Search, and Where They Live," *Population Research and Policy Review* 36 (2016): 101–126.

41. Margery Austin Turner, Diane K. Levy, Doug Wissoker, Claudia L. Aranda, Rob Pitingolo, and Rob Santos., *Housing Discrimination Against Racial and Ethnic Minorities 2012* (Washington, DC: U.S. Department of Housing and Urban Development, 2013), www.huduser. org/portal/Publications/pdf/HUD-514_HDS2012.pdf.

42. Gregory D. Squires, Samantha Friedman, and Catherine E. Saidat, "Experiencing Residential Segregation: A Contemporary Study of Washington, DC," in *Desegregating the City: Ghettos, Enclaves, and Inequality*, ed. David P. Varady (Albany: State University of New York Press, 2005), 127–144; George Galster and Erin Godfrey, "By Word and by Deed: Racial Steering by Real Estate Agents in the U.S. in 2000," *Journal of the American Planning Association* 71, no. 3 (Summer 2005): 251–268; Margery Austin Turner and Stephen L. Ross, "How Discrimination Affects the Search for Housing," in *The Geography of Opportunity: Race and Housing Choice in Metropolitan America*, ed. Xavier de Souza Briggs (Washington, DC: Brookings Institution Press, 2005), 81–100.

43. John Baugh, "Linguistic Profiling and Discrimination," in *Oxford Handbook of Language and Society*, ed. Ofelia Garcia, Nelson Flores, and Massimiliano Spotti (New York: Oxford University Press, 2017), 349–368. A contrasting view is taken by Meena Bavan, "Does Housing Discrimination Exist Based on the 'Color' of an Individual's Voice?" *Cityscape* 9, no. 1 (2007): 109–130. Bavan finds no real evidence of "linguistic profiling," as measured by the success of members of different racial groups in using the telephone to arrange appointments with real-estate agents.

44. Sun Jung Oh and John Yinger, "What Have We Learned from Paired Testing in Housing Markets?" *Cityscape, a Journal of Policy Development and Research* 17, no. 3 (2015), 15–59.

45. Turner and Ross, "How Discrimination Affects the Search for Housing," 86.

46. Margery Turner, "Housing Discrimination Today and the Persistence of Residential Segregation," *MetroTrends*, June 12, 2013, http://blog.metrotrends.org/2013/06/housing-discrimination-today-persistence-residential-segregation/. For further details, see Turner, et al., *Housing Discrimination against Racial and Ethnic Minorities 2012*.

47. Connecticut State Board of Education 2014–2015 data, cited by Alana Semuels, "Good School, Rich School: Bad School, Poor School," *The Atlantic*, August 25, 2106, www.theatlantic.com/business/archive/2016/08/property-taxes-and-unequal-schools/497333/.

48. Matthew Kauffman and Edmund H. Mahony, "State Supreme Court Overturns Sweeping Ruling in CCJEF Education Funding Lawsuit," *Hartford Courant*, January 17, 2018. The quotations are from Supreme Court of Connecticut, *Connecticut Coalition for Justice in Education Funding v Governor Jodi Rell*, (SC 19768), case decided January 17, 2018.

49. *Serrano v. Priest*, 5 Cal. 3d 584,487 (1971).

50. U.S. Census Bureau, "More than Half of School Expenditures Spent on Classroom Instruction," *Release Number CB17–97*, June 14, 2017. Also see the Census Bureau's *Public Education Finances: 2015*, Report Number G15-ASPEF (Washington, DC: Government Printing Office, 2017).

51. *Rodriguez v. San Antonio Independent School District* 411 U.S. 1 (1973). On the critical impact of the *Rodriguez* ruling, see the collection of essays in Charles J. Ogletree, Jr. and Kimberly Jenkins Robinson, eds., *The Enduring Legacy of Rodriguez* (Cambridge, MA: Harvard Education Press, 2015).

52. Michael Leachman, Kathleen Masterson, and Eric Figueroa, "A Punishing Decade for School Funding," *Center for Budget and Policy Priorities*, Washington, DC, November 2, 2017, www.cbpp.org/research/state-budget-and-tax/a-punishing-decade-for-school-funding.

53. Frank Kemerer and Peter Samson, *California School Law*, 3rd ed. (Stanford, CA: Stanford University Press, 2013).

54. Rucker C. Johnson and Sean Tanner, "Money and Freedom: The Impact of California's School Finance Reform," *A Research Brief of the Learning Policy Research Institute*, Palo Alton, CA, February 2018, https://learningpolicyinstitute.org/sites/default/files/product-files/Money_Freedom_CA_School_Finance_Reform_BRIEF.pdf.

55. Julien Lafortune, Jesse Rothstein, and Diane Whitmore Schanzenbach, "School Finance Reform and the Distribution of Student Achievement," Working Paper 22011, National Bureau of Economic Research, Washington, DC, 2016, www.nber.org/papers/w22011.pdf.

56. "How State Aid Formulas Undermine Educational Equity in the States," in Bruce D. Baker and Sean P. Corcoran, *The Stealth Inequities of School Funding: How State and Local School Finance Systems Perpetuate Inequitable Student Spending* (Washington, DC: Center for American Progress, September 2012), esp. 19, www.americanprogress.org/wp-content/uploads/2012/09/StealthInequities.pdf.

57. *Milliken v. Bradley*, 418 U.S. 717 (1974).

58. Jennifer B. Ayscue, Genevieve Siegel-Hawley, John Kucsera, and Brian Woodward, "School Segregation and Resegregation in Charlotte and Raleigh, 1989–2010," *Educational Policy* 32, no. 1 (2018), 3–54.

59. Gary Orfield, and Jongyeon Ee, "Patterns of Segregation in Florida's Schools," a report prepared for the LeRoy Collins Institute, Florida State University, September 2017, http://collinsinstitute.fsu.edu/sites/default/files/lcitoughchoices.pdf.

60. Erica Frankenberg, Genevieve Siegel-Hawley, and Sarah Diem, "Segregation by District Boundary Line: The Fragmentation of Memphis Area Schools," *Educational Researcher* 46, no. 8 (November 2017): 449–463.

61. Clayton A. Hurd, *Confronting Suburban School Resegregation in California* (Philadelphia: University of Pennsylvania Press, 2014), esp. 2–3; Joyce Tsai, "Northgate Secession: Opponents Rally against What They See as Divisive National Trend," *(San Jose) Mercury News*, June 26, 2017.

62. Sean F. Reardon, Elena Grewal, Demetra Kalogrides, and Erica Greenberg, "*Brown* Fades: The End of Court-Ordered School Desegregation and the Resegregation of American Public Schools," *Journal of Policy Analysis and Management* 31, no. 4 (Fall 2012): 876–904.

63. Gary Orfield, John Kucsera, and Genevieve Siegel-Hawley, *E Pluribus . . . Separation: Deepening Double Segregation for More Students* (Los Angeles: UCLA Civil Rights Project/Proyecto Derechos Civiles, September 2012), 9, http://civilrightsproject.ucla.edu/research/k-12-education/integration-and-diversity/mlk-national/e-pluribus...separation-deepening-double-segregation-formore-students/orfield_epluribus_revised_omplete_2012.pdf.

64. Gary Orfield, Jongyeon Ee, and Ryan Coughlan, "New Jersey's Segregated Schools: Trends and Paths Forward," *UCLA Civil Rights Project/Proyecto Derechos Civiles*, 2017, www.civilrightsproject.ucla.edu/research/k-12-education/integration-and-diversity/new-jerseys-segregated-schools-trends-and-paths-forward/New-Jersey-report-final-110917.pdf.

65. Erica Frankenberg and Gary Orfield, eds., *The Resegregation of Suburban Schools: A Hidden Crisis in American Education* (Cambridge, MA: Harvard Education Press, 2012); Orfield and Kucsera, *E Pluribus . . . Separation*, 57–71; Adai Tefera, Erica Frankenberg, Genevieve Siegel-Hawley, and Gina Chirichigno, *Integrating Suburban Schools: How to Benefit from Growing Diversity and Avoid Segregation* (Los Angeles: UCLA Civil Rights Project/Proyecto Derechos Civiles, 2011), http://civilrightsproject.ucla.edu/research/k-12-education/integration-and-diversity/integrating-suburban-schools-how-to-benefitfrom-growing-diversity-and-avoid-segregation/tefera-suburban-manual-2011.pdf.

66. Erica Frankenberg, Genevieve Siegel-Hawley, and Jia Wang, "Choice Without Equity: Charter School Segregation," *Educational Policy Analysis Archives* 19, no. 1 (2011): 1–92, http://epaa.asu.edu/ojs/article/view/779. The data on school segregation, particularly for the 2007–2008 school years, is discussed on p. 126.

67. Institute on Metropolitan Opportunity, *Charter Schools in the Twin Cities: 2013 Update* (Minneapolis: University of Minnesota Law School, October 2013), 1, www.law.umn.edu/uploads/16/65/1665940a907fdbe31337271af733353d/Charter-School-Update-2013-final.pdf.

68. Jennifer Jellison Home, Anjale Welton, and Sarah Diem, "Pursuing 'Separate But Equal' in Suburban San Antonio," in *The Resegregation of Suburban Schools*, ed. Frankenberg and Oldfield.

69. Laura Simmons and Claire Appaliski, "Mapping de facto Segregation in Charlotte-Mecklenburg Schools," *UNC Charlotte Urban Institute*, September 23, 2010, http://ui.uncc.edu/story/mapping-de-facto-segregation-charlotte-mecklenburg-schools; Wanda Rushing, "School Segregation and Its Discontents: Chaos and Community in Post-Civil Rights Memphis," *Urban Education* 52, no. 1 (January 2017): 3–31.

70. Max A. Mortiz, Enric Batllori, Ross A. Bradstock, A. Malcolm Gill, John Handmer, Paul F. Hessbury, Justin Leonard, Sarah McCaffrey, Dennis C. Odio, Tania Schoennagel, and Alexandra D. Syphard, "Learning to Coexist with Wildfire," *Nature*, November 6, 2014: 58–66.

71. Ryan Lillis, "These Sacramento Suburban Neighborhoods Face the Highest Risk of Wildfire," *Sacramento Bee*, November 13, 2017; Doug Smith and Nina Agrawal, "550,000 Homes in Southern California Have the Highest Risk of Fire Damage, But They Are Not Alone," *Los Angeles Times*, November 13, 2017.

72. David R. Montgomery, "Deadly California Mudslides Show the Need for Maps and Zoning that Better Reflect Landslide Risk," *The Conversation, Anon-Line Journal*, January 16, 2018, https://theconversation.com/deadly-california-mudslides-show-the-need-for-maps-and-zoning-that-better-reflect-landslide-risk-90087.

73. Mike Davis, *City of Quartz* (New York: Random House, 1990), 206–209.

74. *Village of Euclid, Ohio, v. Ambler Realty Co.*, 272 U.S. 365 (1926). Robert H. Nelson, *Private Neighborhoods and the Transformation of Local Government* (Washington, DC: Urban Institute, 2005), 139–152, argues that contemporary communities are less concerned with safeguarding against nuisance land uses and more concerned with using zoning as a tool to maintain income and class segregation, thereby preserving property values.

75. *Arlington Heights v. Metropolitan Housing Development Corporation*, 429 U.S. 252 (1977).

76. Large-lot zoning is not the only tool that a suburb can use to maintain exclusion. For instance, a suburb can impose a residency requirement or charge nonresidents a high entry fee to use the local

park or beach. Intensive police presence at a beach or lake can further communicate that outsiders are not welcome. For an "encyclopedia" of various exclusionary practices used by both cities and suburbs see Tobias Armborst, Daniel D'Oca, and Georgeen Theodore, *The Arsenal of Exclusion and Inclusion* (New York: Acatar, 2017).

77. Alexander Garvin, *The American City: What Works, What Doesn't*, 2nd ed. (New York: McGraw-Hill, 2002), 454.

78. *Southern Burlington County NAACP v. Township of Mount Laurel* 67 N.J. 151,336 A. 2d 713 (1975).

79. *Burlington County NAACP v. Township of Mount Laurel*, 92 N.J. 158, 336A. 2d 390 (1983).

80. Salvador Rizzo, "N.J. Supreme Court Blocks Christie's Plan to Abolish Affordable-Housing Agency," *The Star-Ledger (New Jersey)*, July 10, 2013; Brent Johnson, "N.J. Supreme Court Rebukes Christie Administration, Puts Courts in Charge of Affordable Housing," *NJ.com*, March 10, 21015, www.nj.com/politics/index.ssf/2015/03/nj_supreme_court_rebukes_christie_administration_puts_courts_in_charge_of_affordable_housing.html.

81. Patrick Field, Jennifer Gilbert, and Michael Wheeler, "Trading the Poor: Intermunicipal Housing Negotiation in New Jersey," *Harvard Negotiation Law Review* (Spring 1997): 1–33.

82. Douglas S. Massey, Len Albright, Rebecca Casciano, Elizabeth Derickson, and David N. Kinsey, *Climbing Mount Laurel: The Struggle for Affordable Housing and Social Mobility in an American Suburb* (Princeton, NJ: Princeton University Press, 2013) argue the construction of affordable housing in the community of Mount Laurel has had positive on the lives of its low- and moderate-income residents and has not disrupted surrounding neighborhoods as critics had feared.

83. Laura Denker, "N.J. Court Affirms 'Gap Period' Needs, Rejects Towns' Attempts to Exclude Thousands," *Fair Share Housing Center: Cherry Hill, N.J., Blog*, January 18, 2017, http://fairsharehousing.org/blog/entry/n.j.-supreme-court-affirms-gap-period-needs-rejects-towns-attempts-to-exclu/.

84. Lynn M. Fisher, "State Intervention in Local Land Use Decision Making: The Case of Massachusetts," *Real Estate Economics* 41, no. 2 (2013): 418–447; Ravit Hananel, "Can Centralization, Decentralization, and Welfare Go Together? The Case of Massachusetts Affordable Housing Policy (Ch. 40B)," *Urban Studies* 51, no. 12 (September 2014): 2488.

85. Hananel, "Can Centralization, Decentralization, and Welfare Go Together? The Case of Massachusetts," 2487–2502.

86. Gerrit-Jan Knaap, Antonio Bento, and Scott Lowe, *Housing Market Impacts of Inclusionary Zoning* (College Park, MD: University of Maryland, National Center for Smart Growth Research and Education, 2008); Robert Hickey, "After the Downturn: New Challenges and Opportunities for Inclusionary Housing," *Inclusionary Housing Policy Brief*, February 2013, www.nhc.org/media/files/InclusionaryReport201302.pdf.

87. The Urban Institute and the U.S. Department of Housing and Urban Development, *Expanding Housing Opportunities through Inclusionary Zoning: Lessons from Two Counties* (Washington, DC: HUD, 2013), www.huduser.org/portal/publications/HUD-496_new.pdf.

88. Jim Wise, "'Affordable' Housing Bonus an Incentive to Lose Money," *Durham News (North Carolina)*, December 20, 2013.

89. "Inclusionary Zoning Bill Vetoed in California," *Affordable Housing Finance*, October 2013, www.housingfinance.com/affordable-housing/inclusionary-zoning-bill-vetoed-in-california.aspx.

90. James Fraser, "The Politics of Property and Inclusionary Zoning in Nashville" (paper presented at the annual meeting of the Urban Affairs Association, Toronto, April 5, 2018), https://slate.com/business/2018/12/minneapolis-single-family-zoning-housing-racism.html.

91. Henry Grabar, "Minneapolis Confronts Its History of Housing Segregation," *Slate*, December 7, 2018,

92. Jenny Schuetz, "Minneapolis 2040: The Most Wonderful Plan of the Year," *The Avenue, A Brookings Institution Web Posting*, December 12, 2018, www.brookings.edu/blog/the-avenue/2018/12/12/minneapolis-2040-the-most-wonderful-plan-of-the-year/. Of course, the impact of the Minneapolis 2040 changes would depend on the future details of implementation. What would be the exact language of the zoning changes? To what extent would Minneapolis modify other regulatory barriers

and provide financial incentives to support the construction of affordable housing in the city's more desirable neighborhoods?

93. Myron Orfield and Baris Dawes, "Metropolitan Governance Reform," *Chapman University Local Government Reconsidered*, Paper 8, February 26, 2016, https://digitalcommons.chapman.edu/cgi/viewcontent.cgi?article=1220&context=localgovernmentreconsidered.

94. Laura E. Wiedlocher, "Cities Awash in a Sea of Governments: How Does Political Fragmentation Affect Cities and Their Regions?" (Ph.D. Dissertation, University of Missouri at St. Louis, 2014), 94, https://irl.umsl.edu/cgi/viewcontent.cgi?article=1259&context=dissertation.

95. Rebecca Hendrick and Yu Shi, "Macro-Level Determinants of Local Government Interaction: How Metropolitan Regions in the United States Compare," *Urban Affairs Review* 51, no. 3 (2014): 414–438.

96. Smart Growth America, *Building Better Budgets: A National Examination of the Fiscal Benefits of Smart Growth Development* (Washington, DC), May 2013, www.smartgrowthamerica.org/documents/building-better-budgets.pdf; Daniel Hertz, "Introducing the Sprawl Tax," *CityCommentary Blog Post*, February 6, 2016, http://cityobservatory.org/introducing-the-sprawl-tax/.

97. Of course, the problem of urban sprawl varies considerably from one metropolitan area to the next. Reid Ewing and Shima Hamidi, *Measuring Sprawl 2014* (Washington, DC: Smart Growth America, 2014) rank 221 metropolitan areas and nearly a thousand counties on various indicators of sprawl: www.smartgrowthamerica.org/measuring-sprawl.

98. William A. Fischel, *The Homevoter Hypothesis* Cambridge, MA: Harvard University Press, 2005), 230.

99. American Planning Association, *Planning for Smart Growth: 2002 State of the States* (Washington, DC: APA, 2002).

100. Sarah Gardner, "The Impact of Sprawl on the Environment and Human Health," in *Urban Sprawl: A Comprehensive Reference Guide*, ed. David C. Soule (Westport, CT: Greenwood Press, 2006), 240–259.

101. Christopher Jones and Daniel M. Kammen, "Spatial Distribution of U.S. Carbon Footprints Reveals Suburbanization Undermines Greenhouse Gas Benefits of Urban Population Density," *Environmental Science and Technology* 48, no. 2 (2014): 895–902.

102. Mark Edward Brown, "Subdivision Sprawl in Southeastern Wisconsin: Planning, Politics, and the Lack of Affordable Housing," in *Suburban Sprawl: Culture, Theory, and Politics,* ed. Matthew J. Lindstrom and Hugh Bartling (Lanham, MD: Rowman and Littlefield, 2003), 263.

103. Wesley E. Marshall, Daniel P. Piatowski, and Norman W. Garrick, "Community Design, Street Networks, and Public Health," *Journal of Transport and Health* 1, no. 4 (December 2014): 326–340.

104. Andres Duany, Jeff Speck, and Mike Lydon, *The Smart Growth Manual* (New York: McGraw-Hill, 2010).

105. James C. O'Connell, *The Hub's Metropolis: Greater Boston's Development from Railroad Suburbs to Smart Growth* (Cambridge, MA: MIT Press, 2013), 7–8; also see 225–251.

106. Randall G. Holcombe, "The Rise and Fall of Growth Management in Florida," in *Cities and Private Planning: Property Rights, Entrepreneurship and Transaction Costs*, ed. David Emanuel Andersson and Stefano Moroni (Cheltenham UK and Northampton MA: Edwin Elgar, 2014), 232–246, reviews the history of the Growth Management Act and its eventual repeal.

107. Christopher G. Boone and Ali Modarres, *City and Environment* (Philadelphia: Temple University Press, 2006), 181. See also Jerry Anthony, "Do State Growth Management Regulations Reduce Sprawl?" *Urban Affairs Review* 39, no. 3 (January 2004): 376–397.

108. Amal K. Ali, "Explaining Smart Growth Applications: Lessons Learned from the US Capital Region," *Urban Studies* 51, vol. 1 (January 2014), 116–135.

109. Jason Sartori, Terry Moore, and Gerrit Knapp, "Indicators of Smart Growth in Maryland," The National Center for Smart Growth Research and Education, University of Maryland, January 2011, http://smartgrowth.umd.edu/assets/documents/indicators/2011_smart_growth_indicators_report.pdf.

110. Hannah Gosnell, Jeffrey D. Kline, Garrett Chrostek, and James Duncan, "Is Oregon's Land Use Planning Program Conserving Forest and Farm Land? A Review of the Evidence," *Land Use Policy* 28 (2011): 185–192.
111. Nancy Chapman and Hollie Lund, "Housing Density and Livability in Portland," in *The Portland Edge: Challenges and Successes in Growing Communities*, ed. Connie P. Ozawa (Washington, DC: Island Press, 2004), 210.
112. John Metcalfe, "Portland Ranks First among Major U.S. Cities for Biking to Work," *CityLab Blog*, September 18, 2015, www.citylab.com/transportation/2015/09/portland-ranks-first-in-the-us-for-biking-to-work/406045/.
113. Arthur C. Nelson, Rolf Pendall, Casey J. Dawkins, and Gerrit J. Knapp, "The Link between Growth Management and Housing Affordability: The Academic Evidence" (discussion paper prepared for the Brookings Institution Center on Urban and Metropolitan Policy, Washington, DC, 2002), www.brookings.edu/dybdocroot/es/urban/publications/growthmanagexsum.htm.
114. Peter A. Walker and Patrick T. Hurley, *Planning Paradise: Politics and Visioning of Land Use in Oregon* (Tucson: University of Arizona Press, 2011), 160. Not all of the land encompassed by the expansion of an expanded urban growth boundary is ready for development, as anti-growth localities may refuse to provide the sewers and other infrastructure necessary for development.
115. Eric Mortenson, "Metro Approves Urban Growth Boundary Expansion for the Portland Area," *The Oregonian*, October 20, 2011.
116. Hongwei Dong and John Gliebe, "Assessing the Impacts of Smart Growth Policies on Home Developers in a Bi-State Metropolitan Area: Evidence from the Portland Metropolitan Area," *Urban Studies* 49, no. 10 (August 2012): 2219–2235.
117. William K. Jaeger, Cyrus Grout, and Andrew J. Plantings, "Evidence of the Effects of Oregon's Land Use Planning System on Land Prices," Working Paper WP08WJ1, Cambridge, MA, Lincoln Institute of Land Policy, 2008.
118. Hongwei Dong and Pengyu Zhu, "Smart Growth in Two Contrastive Metropolitan Areas: A Comparison between Portland and Los Angeles," *Urban Studies* 52, no. 4 (2015): 775–792.
119. Rolf Pendall, Arthur C. Nelson, Casey J. Dawkins, and Gerrit J. Knapp, "Connecting Smart Growth, Housing Affordability, and Racial Equity," in *The Geography of Opportunity*, ed. de Souza Briggs, 237–239.
120. Shishir Mathir, "Impact of Urban Growth Boundary on Housing and Land Prices: Evidence from King County, Washington," *Housing Studies* 29, no. 1 (2014): 128–148.
121. Alex Marshall, *How Cities Work: Suburbs, Sprawl, and the Roads Not Taken* (Austin: University of Texas Press, 2000), xix.
122. For a review of the guiding principles of the New Urbanism, see: Andres Duany, Elizabeth Plater-Zyberk, and Jeff Speck, *Suburban Nation: The Rise of Sprawl and the Decline of the American Dream*, 10th anniv. ed. (New York: North Point Press, 2010); and Emily Talen (ed.) and the Congress for the New Urbanism, *Charter of the New Urbanism*, 2nd ed. (New York: McGraw-Hill, 2013).
123. Duany, Plater-Zyberk, and Speck, *Suburban Nation*, 30.
124. Tigran Hass, *Sustainable Urbanism and Beyond: Rethinking Cities for the Future* (New York: Rizzoli, 2012).
125. Glennon Sweeney and Bernadette Hanlon, "From Old Suburb to Post-suburb: The Politics of Retrofit in the Inner Suburb of Upper Arlington, Ohio," *Journal of Urban Affairs* 39, no. 2 (2017): 241–159.
126. Jill L. Grant, "Two Sides of a Coin? New Urbanism and Gated Communities," *Housing Policy Debate* 18, no. 3 (2007): 481–501.
127. Marshall, *How Cities Work*, xx, 6.
128. Royce Hanson, *Suburb: Planning Politics and the Public Interest* (Ithaca, NY: Cornell University Press, 2017), 6.
129. Marlon G. Boarnet, Kenneth Joh, Walter Siembab, William Fulton, and Mai Thi Nguyen, "Retrofitting the Suburbs to Increase Walking: Evidence from a Land-Use-Travel Study," *Urban Studies* 48, no. 1 (January 2011): 12–15.
130. Hanson, *Suburb: Planning Politics and the Public Interest*.

4 Recent Trends

Gentrification and Globalization

This chapter discusses two important recent trends: *gentrification* or the rediscovery of inner-city neighborhoods (a process that is often referred to as the back-to-the-city movement) and *globalization* or the vulnerability of a city to forces from beyond its borders and from beyond the nation's borders. The two concepts are interrelated.

Globalization intensifies pressures toward gentrification as the well-paid employees of an international corporation seek housing close to a firm's headquarters and other downtown facilities. Developers tear down older buildings to make way for upscale rental units and condominiums. The corporate professionals drive up the market price of homes and rental units in suddenly valued areas of the inner city, ousting poorer residents from newly valued neighborhoods. When neighborhoods house a highly talented and technologically skilled work force in close proximity to the downtown, a city becomes increasingly attractive to global corporations.

As the chapter will discuss, gentrification or the upscaling of once-ignored neighborhoods is not a purely natural or free-market phenomenon, the result of home seekers having suddenly discovered undervalued homes in previously overlooked core areas of the city. Instead, civic leaders—private business heads and local elected officials—promote and subsidize neighborhood transformation.

Washington, DC, has witnessed fairly extensive gentrification and revival, an upscaling that has seemingly reversed decades of inner-city stagnation and decline. In just a single decade, from 2000 to 2010, the city gained 30,000 residents. The arrival of younger, upper-status singles and newly marrieds fueled the revival of a number of inner-city neighborhoods. The city's historically black—and, in recent years, poor—Shaw/U-Street corridor became the site of new condominiums, apartments, and trendy restaurants and coffeehouses. The upscaling of U-Street and other DC neighborhoods was promoted by government policies. In a city that had suffered a half-century of population losses, civic leaders "made growing the District's population a priority." The attraction of new upper- and middle-class professionals was seen as critical to the District's future. Mayor Anthony Williams, an African-American mayor governing a black-majority city, announced that he would launch policy efforts intended to attract 100,000 new residents to the city in just ten years.[1]

In DC and other cities, gentrification has contributed to local economic prosperity. Yet, the impacts of gentrification have not been all for the good. Gentrification and globalization have compounded problems of inequality. The displacement of the poor has imposed relocation and hardships on some of the most vulnerable residents of the city. As economist Richard Florida has observed, globalization and gentrification have produced a "New Urban Crisis" where the exaggerated inequality and segregation of contemporary metropolitan areas can no longer be seen solely as the result of long-term central-city decline.[2]

THE SPREAD OF GENTRIFICATION

Gentrification refers to the upgrading of a core urban neighborhood that results when young professionals (and, in some cities, well-off retirees as well) place new value on city living. The term itself denotes the arrival of a relatively well-heeled "gentry" who once may have lived in the suburbs or the countryside (or even in other city neighborhoods) but who now have discovered the virtues of living close to the job, cultural, and entertainment opportunities of cities with an active downtown.

Over the years, urban commentators have used a number of synonyms for gentrification: neighborhood renewal, inner-city revitalization, urban rebirth, neighborhood reinvestment, the back-to-the-city movement, and, more critically, urban invasion.[3] Strictly speaking, gentrification denotes a neighborhood's residential upgrading and transformation. More broadly used, however, the term "gentrification" can also refer to an area's commercial revival—the opening of a new shopping galleria, a multiplex cinema, or a number of upscale fashion boutiques and cafés (Figure 4.1) in a previously overlooked section of the city. On New York's City's Lower East Side, East Village,

Figure 4.1 **Gentrification. Outdoor Tables and a Trendy Cafe Scene in a Once-Gritty Oakland, California, Neighborhood.**

Source: Photo by cdrin / Shutterstock.com.

and the Bowery, trendy cocktail restaurants, hipster bars, and music venues and other nightlife destinations occupy the sites of former factories and working-class "saloons."[4] In New York, Chicago, Los Angeles, San Francisco, and cities across the nation, the opening of a local Starbucks or even a Whole Foods supermarket has come to signify the upscaling and transformation of a once-neglected inner-city neighborhood.

Clearly, not all cities and neighborhoods experience substantial gentrification. Gentrification is most extensive in corporate headquarters cities that offer high-paying jobs and a variety of cultural and nightlife opportunities, that is, in cities that have found their "fit" in the global economy. In declining Rustbelt centers like Detroit, Cleveland, Buffalo, and Pittsburgh, gentrification is more limited and is concentrated in only a small handful of neighborhoods while other nearby neighborhoods continue to decline. In more troubled cities, urban deterioration continues to seep from troubled neighborhoods into abutting areas; the few islands of gentrification stand out as exceptions.[5]

Still, it is remarkable to observe that gentrification is now occurring even in the nation's more troubled Rustbelt cities, even if reinvestment is largely limited to a select few neighborhoods. In Cleveland, the return of corporate jobs to the city center led younger workers to seek homes in Ohio City and Tremont (two neighborhoods virtually abutting the downtown) and a bit further out in Old Brooklyn (by the Cleveland Zoo).[6] In post-bankruptcy Detroit, young white professionals have begun to take up residence in the city's downtown and in the central Midtown, Woodbridge, and Corktown neighborhoods. In Detroit, the arrival of these new residents has even led to an upsurge in urban bicycling.[7]

Still, as the Cleveland and Detroit experiences clearly underscore, gentrification does not denote the revival of all poor inner-city communities. Areas of the city with the highest concentrations of poverty and social disorganization are the least likely areas to experience revival.[8] Evidence from New York and Chicago confirms that white gentrifiers are attracted to near-downtown areas but not to those that have a high concentrations of African Americans.[9]

Yet, sometimes gentrifying pressures do hit minority communities. In Los Angeles, white home seekers and art galleries priced out of the city's downtown suddenly discovered Boyle Heights, the poor Latino neighborhood located immediately east of the city's central business district. The encroachment of development provoked a counter-mobilization by Defend Boyle Heights, a local activist group that, among its actions, sought to close the new art galleries that were threatening to transform the area.[10] In another part of L.A's Latino East Side, El Sereno Against Gentrification, another grassroots organization, has similarly sought to resist the incipient "colonization" of the neighborhood by organizing protests against new developments, rent increases, and the displacement of family-owned businesses.[11] The group fought to preserve the area's Chicano culture, initiating action to prevent the destruction of street and alley murals threatened by new construction.

In smaller cities where high-paying corporate job and nightlife are more limited, the rebirth of inner-city neighborhoods is often less extensive. Still, gentrification has taken place in neighborhoods in numerous small- and medium-sized cities in the American heartland.[12] In the South, Charlotte, Asheville, Nashville, Richmond, and Austin have all witnessed extensive new investment in previously overlooked neighborhoods.[13]

Oftentimes, gentrification entails racial **displacement**, with young white professionals and retirees moving into predominantly minority areas of the city. Tenement buildings are converted to condominiums or are torn down to make way for new upscale dwelling units. As rents and home prices in the area rise, poor families are forced to move elsewhere. Gentrification can dramatically alter the racial composition of a neighborhood.[14]

Black-on-black gentrification also occurs in cities where more affluent African Americans have sought homes in central locations. In Chicago, black professionals bought houses in the city's historic Bronzeville neighborhood and in areas of the near South Side bordering the lakeshore, transforming neighborhoods that, not too long ago, were overwhelmingly poor.[15] In New York City, black middle-class families transformed the Clinton Hill and Fort Greene sections of Brooklyn, moving into newly constructed condominiums and upscale apartments.[16]

Derek Hyra uses the phrase **black branding** to refer to how developers use references to black heritage to promote the marketability of a black neighborhood to a culturally "hip" clientele. In Washington, DC, the Langston Lofts condominiums (named after renown poet Langston Hughes), the Ellington apartments (named after the "Duke" of jazz), and Marvin's restaurant (named after pop legend Marvin Gaye) all appealed to a larger audience.[17] In Chicago's Pilsen district, the center of the city's Mexican and Mexican-American population, real-estate interests touted the community's many Mexican restaurants and its culture in an effort to sell homes to outside professionals.[18]

Does Gentrification Mean That the Urban Crisis Has Come to an End?

Urban journalist Alan Ehrenhalt argues that the term "gentrification" fails to capture the full extent of the inner-city revival that has occurred in American cities. According to Ehrenhalt, the turnaround of urban areas is the result of "a much larger force than the coming of 'gentry' to previously dilapidated neighborhoods. . . . 'Gentrification' is too small a word for it."[19] Ehrenhalt argues that a "great inversion" is taking place in the American metropolis, with central cities increasingly becoming home to well-paid professionals and technologically skilled workers while the poor and the working class are increasingly consigned to a city's outer neighborhoods and the suburbs.

Yet, the extent of the urban revival is not nearly as great as Ehrenhalt proclaims. Certainly, a large number of core-city neighborhoods have gentrified, and the American city is increasingly home to more affluent professionals. Census numbers also reveal a growth in number of suburbanites who live in poverty. As we reviewed in Chapter 3, contemporary suburbia is more diverse than is commonly believed. Yet, these recent trends do not alter the fundamental picture of suburban affluence and central-city disadvantage.

Despite gentrification, central cities suffer poverty rates considerably higher than those of the suburbs. In 2016, the poverty rate of United States central cities (18.7 percent) was nearly twice the poverty rate of the suburbs (10.8 percent).[20] In 2012, Philadelphia had a poverty rate of 24 percent, over three times the 7.4 percent poverty rate of its suburbs. In New York City, substantial gentrification did little to alter the metropolitan imbalance: New York City's poverty rate (21 percent) was over twice the poverty rate (9 percent) of the region's suburbs.[21]

Despite gentrification, central cities are not "catching up" to their suburbs. The United States is not entering a future of wealthy cities and a poor suburbs. Gentrification represents a comparatively small trickle that does not offset the more dominant wave of the outmigration of population—notably the American middle class—and taxable wealth from central cities to the suburbs.[22]

The gentrification of select inner-city neighborhoods does not signify the end of the urban crisis. In the least fortunate Rustbelt cities, urban problems continue to be particularly severe despite select pockets of gentrification. Detroit's post-bankruptcy revival has been confined to a select few neighborhoods that enjoy good proximity to the downtown, to Wayne State University, and to the region's Medical Center. The vast majority Detroit's poor communities continue to suffer advanced decline.[23]

As we have already noted and shall soon discuss in greater detail, gentrification and neighborhood transformation have also compounded problems of housing affordability and inequality in the city.

WHO RESHAPES AMERICAN NEIGHBORHOODS? FROM URBAN PIONEERS TO FINANCIFIERS: THE CHANGING NATURE OF GENTRIFICATION

Urban commentators began to take note of gentrification in the late 1970s and early 1980s, when so-called **urban pioneers** began to buy and renovate housing in distressed areas of the inner city. At the time, such investments were viewed as rather extraordinary. The urban pioneers represented a small back-to the-city countermovement that was contrary to the long-term story of suburban growth and central-city decline.

Gentrification is often portrayed as an individualized and market-driven process shaped by the preferences of individual home seekers. The narrative has its roots in the early stages or first wave of gentrification. It does not describe the full set of actions and decisions that are transforming inner-city neighborhoods.

According to the narrative, urban pioneers "discovered" long-overlooked core areas of the city in which they bought homes at bargain prices, often rehabilitating the dilapidated structures through their own hard work or **sweat equity**. In a number of cities, artists helped lead the rediscovery of the city, moving into aging lofts and vacant warehouses in former industrial areas of city—even where municipals laws at the time prohibited residency in industrial structures. The artists prized the large workspaces they found at quite affordable rents.[24]

Many of the early newcomers prized urban living and valued the population diversity and cultural "authenticity" they found in inner-city neighborhoods.[25] Other gentrifiers, however, sought only the convenience of living in close proximity to the jobs and nightlife areas of the city; they had little appreciation for the poor and minorities who lived around them.[26]

A tale of gentrification that focuses on urban pioneers and "sweat equity" overlooks the role that developers and financial institutions played in neighborhood upgrading and transformation. Bankers may have initially been somewhat unwilling to extend loans to buyers who were seeking to move into portions of the city that were generally seen as undesirable. As a result, the initial pioneers often had to resort to creative financing and their own hard work to acquire and improve the properties they acquired. However, the members of the city's growth coalition—developers, real-estate agents, landlords, and insurance companies—came to see the profits that they could gain from neighborhood transformation. In city after city, financial and real-estate interests began to play a more vigorous role promoting neighborhood transformation.

Real-estate companies and developers "branded" communities with names that added to the cachet of takeoff areas. In New York City, developers, landlords, and real estate agencies marketed a fashionable SoHo (the South of Houston Street neighborhood), portraying an area of old factories and warehouses as the equivalent of active SoHo in London. SoHo was promoted as a "destination" for younger and more upscale consumers. Contemporary SoHo is the site of expensive residences, high-end boutiques such as Chanel, retail giants such as Banana Republic, and an Apple computer store (with its "genius bar" in back). The corporate-led developments attracted still additional new residents and commercial investors—driving out many of the art galleries, individually owned boutiques, and dance companies that had dominated SoHo during the early years of its revival. In SoHo, many of the artists who had converted empty industrial lofts into live/work spaces were themselves forced out when developers and landlords sought to lease properties and build new housing for more profitable clienteles (see Box 4.1).

Neighborhood transformation in New York was not limited to SoHo. Other areas, once dominated by warehouses and tenement buildings, were similarly rebranded with newly created and fashionable acronyms: NoHo (north of Houston), NoLita (north of Little Italy), and DUMBO (down under the Manhattan-Brooklyn Bridge overpass).

New York City's government facilitated neighborhood transformation by **upzoning** an area to allow new residential construction in what were formerly commercial and industrial zones. In New York, upzoning also permitted more dense residential development, necessary for the construction of new high-rise condominiums and apartments. The policy changes were critical to the transformation of Greenpoint, Williamsburg, Crown Heights, and other poorer sections of Brooklyn.[27]

The arrival of African-American corporate managers and professionals similarly transformed historic Harlem in upper Manhattan. But in Harlem, too, upscaling was facilitated by a change in government policy, with rezoning serving to accelerate the pace of the neighborhood's transformation. Zoning changes allowed new residential construction (including the construction of luxury homes). Zoning changes also brought mixed-use development along Harlem's historic 125th Street commercial strip, allowing national retailers to move in and drive out locally owned businesses.[28]

Loretta Lees uses the terms "financifiers" and "supergentrifiers" to denote the quite different character of the later neighborhood invasion waves that succeeded the initial pioneer phase of gentrification.[29] The **financifiers**, who earned substantial income from their corporate jobs, have the money to buy housing in neighborhoods that offered good access to work. The financiers and other late-stage **supergentrifiers** valued the convenient location and fashionableness of upwardly trending neighborhoods. They built new houses and sought luxury high-rise apartments and condominiums out of character with the historic patterns in a neighborhood. They sought the convenience of strip shopping stores and superstores with on-site parking lots, even though such suburban-style development is often incongruent with an area's more traditional cityscape.[30]

Box 4.1
Chicago and Los Angeles: Neighborhood Changes, as Seen in Its Coffeehouses

In the Wicker Park section of Chicago, a change in local coffeehouses stands as testimony to how different waves of gentrification transformed the population of this inner-city neighborhood. When Wicker Park was still a Polish working-class neighborhood, residents gathered at Sophie's Busy Bee, the local "greasy spoon" that had a photograph of the Pope prominently displayed on the wall. When the neighborhood declined and many of the Poles moved to the suburbs, the area became home to low-income Puerto Ricans and other Latino families. In 1998, after 33 years, Sophie's Busy Bee closed its doors.

The first wave of gentrification saw the appearance of a new neighborhood coffeehouse, the neo-bohemian Urbus Orbis, which served as a hangout for the area's newly arrived artists and young "hipsters." The presence of these newcomers also served to signify that the neighborhood was "in" and open to other newcomers whose arrival would further transform the neighborhood and its population.

As a result of its near-downtown location and "Blue Line" rail access, Wicker Park was soon "discovered" by newcomers who worked in the city's downtown offices. These new arrivals, in contrast to the earlier wave of artists and pioneers, had less fondness for the area's authentic gritty texture. Developers built new housing for young professionals who cared little about the neighborhood's history and ethnic heritage. The new arrivals visited Starbucks and other newly opened corporate coffeehouses. The arts-crowd-dominated Urbus Orbis closed. Sophie's Busy Bee was eventually transformed into a trendy cocktail bar, part of Wicker Park's nightlife scene. Today, the population of Wicker Park differs greater from the days when the Poles and Puerto Ricans dominated the neighborhood and Sophie's Busy Bee and Urban Orbis were neighborhood treasures.

Across the continent, in Los Angeles, the opening of a new coffeehouse similarly signaled a neighborhood's transformation and the change in ownership became a source of contention. In Boyle Heights, a low-income Latino section of L.A. just east of the downtown, community activists protested the arrival of both Weird Wave Coffee, a hipster-oriented coffee shop, and the growing number of art galleries in the neighborhood. These businesses threatened to accelerate the transformation of a neighborhood which was already under pressure as the opening of a Metro Gold Line subway station had improved the area's accessibility. Continued development, they feared, would come at a severe price: the displacement or ousting of poorer residents from the community.

Source: Richard Lloyd, *Neo-Bohemia: Art and Commerce in the Postindustrial City* (New York: Routledge, 2006), 107; Ruben Vives, "A Community in Flux: Will Boyle Heights Be Ruined by One Coffee Shop?" *Los Angeles Times*, July 18, 2017.

Figure 4.2   **New Condominiums in the Gentrifying Williamsburg Section of Brooklyn, New York City.** The once rather poor Williamsburg section of New York is undergoing a significant transformation as the result of new corporate investment in condominiums and other upscale development. The new condominiums pictures in the photo abut an older industrial structure, the sort of facility that once dominated this portion of Williamsburg. Such a transformation cannot be attributed solely to the actions of "urban pioneers" who "discovered" the virtues of living in a previously overlooked and neglected sections of the city. Instead, corporate institutions and city planners play an important role in arranging and financing the construction of projects associated with late-stage gentrification.

Source: Photo by Leonard Zhukovsky/Shutterstock.com.

The phrase **new-build gentrification** (Figure 4.2) points to how corporate investment in major projects—high-rise residential towers, inner-city shopping centers, and big-box retails stores—is transforming core urban communities. Such projects increase the attractiveness of inner-city living, resulting in an escalation of rents in nearby areas that further serves to push out the working class and the poor.[31]

The far-reaching transformation of inner-city neighborhoods cannot be attributed solely to the venturesome actions, sweat equity, and "incumbent upgrading" by individual homeowners. Instead, major private institutions, working with the cooperation of local governments, made extensive capital investments and received the zoning changes and financial support necessary to reshape inner-city neighborhoods[32] (see Box 4.2).

Box 4.2
3CDC: A Civic Elite Remakes Cincinnati's Riot Corridor

In 2001, Cincinnati's Over-the-Rhine (OTR) neighborhood was the site of a major civil disturbance, an event that scared off investors and sent the already distressed community spiraling into further decline. The riot brought to a virtual halt the limited pioneer gentrification and incumbent upgrading that had been occurring in the area.

But the area's decline did not last forever. In the decades that followed, Over-the-Rhine, especially the southern portion of the area located on the edge of the Cincinnati's central business district, came back. Vacant properties and boarded-up storefronts in OTR gave way to expensive new condominiums, fashionable bars and eateries, boutique stores, and a flourishing nightlife.

The leaders of Cincinnati's top corporations orchestrated the area's rebirth. Pulling together investment funds and working with the advantage of federal tax credits, the city's top business leaders created a nonprofit corporation that pursued a strategic plan for the block-by-block transformation of the troubled area. Cincinnati's civic elite believed that conditions of distress in OTR, which adjoined the city's downtown on its northern edge, had to be changed as they were scaring major corporations away from the city's central business district. These leaders saw a renewed, "safe," and "clean" OTR as essential to changing Cincinnati's image, a necessary step to bring conventions, new investment, and development to the city's central business district.

Population figures underscore the steep decline that had previously taken place in OTR. OTR had shrunk from a population of 44,500 in 1900 to a mere 7,600 in the year 2000. Eighty percent of OTR's residents were African American. The area was marred by extensive vacancies: an estimated 500 vacant residential buildings and 700 vacant land parcels.

The Cincinnati Center City Development Corporation (or 3CDC, as it is commonly called) was created in 2003 to spur real-estate development and new investment in Cincinnati's downtown and in the adjacent OTR neighborhood. 3CDC is a corporate-led organization with a board of directors that included the top executives of the Western & Southern Financial Group, the Kroger Company, Proctor and Gamble, PNC Bank, Fifth Third Bank, and Cincinnati Bell.

3CDC spent $30 million to become the owner or "preferred developer" of over 200 vacant properties acquired as part of a "land banking" strategy to give the organization greater control over new construction in the neighborhood. The corporation also bought up and closed liquor stores and other "hot spot" properties that had been an impediment to new development. 3CDC also managed streetscape improvements, financed with city assistance, to build an attractive new restaurant strip. As the popularity of the area increased and crime in 3CDC's target area declined, developers began to use the Over-the-Rhine name once again, no longer marketing the area as Cincinnati's Gateway District. "Over-the-Rhine" had cachet and urban context. It was a brand that reflected the urban feel of the city's newly hip area.

Municipal agencies aided efforts to reposition the southern section of OTR, an area that had a number of small theater companies and galleries, as an emerging arts district. The city built a gleaming, modern School for the Creative and Performing Arts to connect the district with the Music Hall, the city's German-style opera house situated on OTR's western edge. Across from Music Hall, the Parks Department reconstructed Washington Park to serve as a new "civic lawn" for music, outdoor film showings, and festivals. 3CDC, which had pushed for construction of the new park and its underground garage, was given charge of programming events to make Washington Park an entertainment destination. The City Parks Department and 3CDC partnered in a $40 million effort to turn the neglected park, a haven for drug abusers and the homeless, into an active public space that served the larger city and not just area residents. 3CDC also managed the distribution of Cincinnati Equity Funds and New Market Funds, $400 million in gap financing and below market-rate loans that were used as an impetus for its projects.

3CDC worked to relocate the Drop Inn Center, the city's largest shelter for the homeless just a block away from Washington Park, to a less central location elsewhere in the city. Before the move, Drop Inn residents had often spilled from the shelter into the park, with a boisterous behavior that decreased the area's attractiveness to visitors and homebuyers.

The transformation of Over-the-Rhine was a well-financed and carefully coordinated enterprise where planners even paid close attention to the construction of parking lots and garages to support the area's new commercial enterprises and condominiums. As 3CDC reclaimed one block, the organization shifted its attention to the next block.

The 3CDC approach worked. Over-the-Rhine was transformed and became an asset that helped promote new investment in Cincinnati's city center. Local activists, however, criticized the city for its willingness to invest in OTR's streetscape and parking garages rather than fund programs aimed at improving the lives of the neighborhood's poor residents.

Source: Original case study, based on 3CDC annual reports and various other 3CDC documents and presentations, www.3cdc.com Web postings, personal interviews, and attendance at community meetings.

WHY CITIES PROMOTE GENTRIFICATION

Cities promote gentrification to stabilize declining areas and to bring new vitality to troubled core neighborhoods. Even more important, city leaders believe that gentrification helps attract future investment to the city.[33] Gentrified areas attract workers with advanced technological and specialized skills, the sort of talented workforce that a city needs to compete for high-tech, legal, and financial service firms. Cities also desire the tax revenues that accompany higher level property uses.

Private interests garner support for gentrification. In Charlotte, the Bank of America (then known as North Carolina National Bank) pushed gentrification as a key part of a corporate-oriented strategy to transform a fading mill town into a dynamic regional banking and financial center. The bank played the lead role in a series of public-private partnerships that converted the city's blighted Fourth Ward into a "vibrant center-city neighborhood" that could attract "globally competitive financial service workers to the city and to the employment rolls of the ascendant corporations headquartered" in the city's downtown.[34]

The extensive transformation of numerous core urban neighborhoods would not have occurred without the actions of corporate actors.[35] In New York, the reshaping of SoHo by a "tidal wave of new luxury apartments and chain stores" was largely willed into being by the actions of major corporations. Sociologist Sharon Zukin describes the role played by corporations in the neighborhood's change: "Global investment firms have bought thousands of low-cost apartment houses and prepare to raise the rent or sell them as condos, driving out older and poorer residents," including "tenement dwellers, mom and pop store owners, whole populations of artists and workers, and people of color." New York, according to Zukin, had "lost its soul."[36]

In New York, developers and real-estate interests lured middle-class home seekers by marketing an appealing but highly sanitized vision of the city's Lower East Side and East Village. Their sales campaigns pitched the "local color" of neighborhoods while also portraying the areas as high-amenity communities that were safe, modern, primarily white, and largely insulated from "the risks and inconvenience of poverty." The new developments did little to improve the lives of the Puerto Ricans, Dominicans, and other Latinos living in the vicinity. New construction and rising rents threatened to oust the working class and the poor.[37]

Developers also played to racial stereotypes that outsiders have of urban ghettos in gaining public approval for their projects. In Chester, Pennsylvania, a small and impoverished city just 20 or so miles south of Philadelphia, developers resorted to racialized perceptions of inner-city poverty conditions in order to gain governmental permissions and subsidies for a new casino, a major-league soccer stadium for the Philadelphia Fury, and other waterfront development projects. Developers stressed the urgency of "doing something" to turn around conditions in deindustrialized Chester, a city with a population that is 80 percent African American. Their rhetoric emphasized the progressive nature of urban change. But the attractive new waterfront enclave that they built largely served visitors and tourists and brought few benefits to the residents of Chester's poorer neighborhoods. Casino gamblers and other visitors travel via interstate highways, enter guarded parking garages, and seldom patronize establishments in other areas of the city.[38]

Municipal governments utilize a variety of actions, big and small, to catalyze neighborhood upgrading and transformation. Notably, as we have already seen, cities can upzone a neighborhood to permit the construction of luxury apartments, high-rise condominiums, and new commercial centers. New York City also modified the area's zoning in order to give birth to **"Silicon Alley,"** an emerging "technobohemian" of "new media" firms established in a Lower Manhattan district of small offices and aging warehouses."[39]

Local governments also used federal **HOPE VI** funds to demolish hulking public housing projects that inhibited the upscaling of nearby areas.[40] By tearing down the infamous high-rise towers of the Cabrini-Green housing project, Chicago opened the surrounding area to investors seeking to build new townhouses and condominiums in close proximity to the city's Gold Coast and Magnificent Mile.

The City of Chicago undertook numerous actions to support the transformation of various parts of the city. Chicago granted historic landmark status to Wicker Park and other neighborhoods, a designation that developers and real-estate firms had sought in order to enhance their efforts to rebrand the area. Historic landmark designation also provided their projects with an important source of subsidies, as homebuyers could now receive tax credits for housing rehabilitation.[41] Developers in Wicker Park and in the surrounding area also went to the city council to block efforts by a nonprofit group to rehabilitate housing units for the poor. Developers worried that new low-income housing would anchor the poor in the neighborhood, diminishing the area's attractiveness to market-rate homebuyers.[42]

Cities can also provide improved transportation in order to facilitate gentrification. In Los Angeles, the opening of new rail stations improved the accessibility of hard-to-get-to neighborhoods, stimulating investment and gentrification.[43] In Austin, Texas, the opening of a new light-rail line brought higher density condominium, apartment, and mixed-use development to neighborhoods on the city's east side. Housing advocates worried that rents would rise in areas of the city that had traditionally provided very affordable housing.

THE BENEFITS OF GENTRIFICATION

New supermarkets and upgraded stores and restaurants improve the quality of urban living. Even low-income African-American residents of transition areas generally report that they are happy with how their neighborhood is improving. Gentrifiers often have the political clout to demand more intensive police protection, trash pickup, street lighting, and other municipal services. Long-time residents appreciate the gains that accompany a neighborhood's takeoff.[44] Gentrification brings once-neglected neighborhoods more into the mainstream of American life.[45]

Gentrification can also increase the physical safety of an inner-city community. Statistics reveal that gentrified areas generally experience a reduction in homicide rates. The gains in physical safety, however, are more clearly found in areas experiencing white gentrification as opposed to black-on-black gentrification. Gentrification does not necessarily reduce property crimes; the new wealth in an area creates new opportunities for burglaries.[46]

PROBLEMS WITH GENTRIFICATION: DISPLACEMENT AND AN INCREASING CLASS AND RACIAL DIVIDE IN CITIES

Critics argue that the disadvantages brought by neighborhood transformation outweigh the benefits. They see gentrification as a process of **"neighborhood invasion"**[47] where upper-status arrivals expropriate a low-income neighborhood. The result, too often, is **displacement**, where the new arrivals wind up pushing out existing residents, oftentimes the poor and racial minorities. Gentrification raises home prices and rents, making an area increasingly unaffordable to the working class and the poor.[48] In some instances, displacement is the result of the manipulations of private actors. More unscrupulous landlords and developers can seek to oust low-income tenants by failing to maintain properties or fix locks on a building's outer doors. In extreme cases, a building owner may even resort to arson and other illegal actions in order to force tenants out so that a property can be converted to more profitable uses.[49]

Gentrification often entails cultural clashes between newcomers and long-term residents, especially when gentrifiers demand policies to "manage neighborhood behaviors" such as public drinking, the blaring of loud music, and playing basketball at night.[50] Not surprisingly, African Americans tend to be less positive than whites in their assessment of the changes being brought to gentrifying communities (see Box 4.3).[51]

Gentrification seldom delivers the benefits that its proponents claim that neighborhood newcomers will bring to low-income children and neighborhood schools. A study of Chicago found that gentrification did little to increase math and reading test scores in neighborhood schools. Why did gentrification have so little impact on the educational growth of low-income children? Quite simply, the upscale new arrivals chose to opt out of city's neighborhood schools, and instead enrolled their children in private academies or in the more select public schools created by school choice programs. The children of the gentrifiers did not attend classrooms with poorer children. As their children largely did not attend the neighborhood school, upscale parents did not become a force for change in their neighborhood's school.[52]

Even when gentrifiers and low-income residents live in the same neighborhood, they still inhabit vastly different worlds. In the Shaw/U-Street section of Washington, DC, white and African-American customers both patronize the neighborhood's new coffee shops and bookstore. But the result is far from the ideal of class- and race-integration that supporters of mixed-income mixed-race neighborhoods had hoped to achieve. More often than not, gentrification is characterized by within-neighborhood separation. Gentrification generally fails to produce new social networks and friendships that would allow upscale residents to share job advice and offer educational guidance.[53] A local observer describes the degree of separation that remains in a gentrifying neighborhood in Washington, DC:

> Over time the neighborhood's revitalization engineers a rigid caste system eerily reminiscent of pre-1965 America. You see it in bars, churches, restaurants and bookstores. You see it in the buildings people live in and where people do their shopping. In fact, other than public space, little is shared in the neighborhood. Not resources. Not opportunities. Not the kind of social capital that is vital for social mobility. Not even words.[54]

In New Orleans, after the destruction wrought by Hurricane Katrina, officials in the city and the U.S. Department of Housing and Urban Development promoted gentrification as a means to attract new residents and investment to the city. However, the arrival of the newcomers resulted in little positive intermixing and community building. City "insiders" (New Orleans's long-term residents) and "outsiders" (the professionals who moved to New Orleans to help rebuild the city) seldom crossed lines of class and race.[55]

Gentrifiers also tend to define the boundaries of their neighborhood in such a way as to deny connections to many of the nearby poor. In Philadelphia, white gentrifiers who moved south of the downtown felt no responsibility to "South Philly." Instead, the gentrifiers defined their neighborhood much more narrowly as "Graduate Hospital,"

Box 4.3
Gentrification and the Movies of Spike Lee

For much of his career, celebrated American movie director Spike Lee has sought to highlight the ills of gentrification and the danger it poses to inner-city African-American communities. His 1989 classic *Do the Right Thing* traces how simmering racial tensions coupled with police brutality on a hot summer day can explode into a race riot. In an early scene in the film, set in the predominantly black Bedford-Stuyvesant section of Brooklyn, Lee gives voice to the resentments over gentrification which, at the time, was still in its early pioneering phase in Brooklyn. In the film, a minor altercation ensues when Clifton, maybe the first young white person to move into the neighborhood, accidently scuffs the "Jordans" basketball sneakers worn by Buggin' Out (played by Giancarlo Esposito), a young man with a strong sense of Black Pride:

Buggin' Out: Who told you to step on my sneakers? Who told you to walk on my side of the block?
Clifton: I own this brownstone.
Buggin' Out: Who told you to buy a brownstone on my block, in my neighborhood on my side of the street? Yo, what you wanna live in a black neighborhood for, anyway? Man, motherfuck gentrification!

Over the years, the pace of gentrification accelerated, transforming a number of Brooklyn neighborhoods, including Cobble Hill, and Fort Greene (Lee's childhood home) as well as Bedford-Stuyvesant. The influx of whites meant a diminished presence of the African-American poor. With the opening of wine bars and organic markets, the poor increasingly felt like aliens in their own neighborhood.

In a series of interviews produced for YouTube and other platforms, Spike Lee in 2013 enunciated his concerns over the changes being brought to Brooklyn. Lee professed to having "mixed" feelings about gentrification. Lee recognized that gentrification can lead to a greater police presence, improved public schools, and better garbage pickup. But he is troubled by what he labeled the "Christopher Columbus syndrome," where the new arrivals show little respect for the people who already live there. The gentrifiers impose their behavioral expectations on their neighbors.

Spike Lee laments the disappearance of African drummers who had for decades played on Sunday mornings in a Harlem park in Upper Manhattan. He also describes the disrespect shown his father, a noted jazz musician who for decades had played music in his Fort Greene brownstone, when newcomers called the cops to complain about the noise: "That's not making good neighbors. That's not coming in a neighborhood and being humble."

Not all filmmakers, however, portray gentrification in such a harsh light. Amanda Marsalis's *Echo Park* (2014) presents a mixed but largely positive view of gentrification, focusing on the quality of life (and the prospects for romance!) in a quickly changing, mixed-race section of Los Angeles. The movie, intended for a young white audience, includes scenes set in hipster coffeehouses and art galleries. Although the characters in the film voice some concerns about neighborhood transformation, the film does not focus on the neighborhood but on the fate of the two main characters and their budding romance. The film's warm and fuzzy portrayal of life in a racially diverse gentrifying neighborhood gives little focus to the problems posed by the displacement of residents and disrespect for the neighborhood's Latino culture.

Sources: Spike Lee, *Do the Right Thing: A Spike Lee Joint* [includes the movie script] (New York: Fireside, 1969), 167; the dialogue presented above is how it was spoken on screen, in a dialect that differs slightly from the words found in the original script. "Spike Lee Keeps It Funky About Gentrification & the 'Christopher Columbus Syndrome'" (video), July 21, 2013, http://hiphopwired. com/2013/07/31/spike-lee-keeps-it-funky-about-gentrification-the-christopher-columbus-syndrome-video/.

"South Center City," "South Center," and "South Rittenhouse," excluding areas of South Philly with high concentrations of the minority poor.[56]

Chicago, built new mixed-income and mixed-race housing developments on the sites where high-rise public housing once stood. But the new developments resulted in very little community-building and class- and race-mixing. Instead, the new developments were characterized by a continuing "social compartmentalization" by class and by race. The buyers of market-rate units and the former tenants of public housing tended to live separate lives even though they shared a common physical structure.[57]

Gentrification can also disrupt the **neighborhood networks** upon which poor people depend.[58] Low-income residents who are displaced, may lose contact with their local church, neighborhood youth groups, and various community-based organizations, and self-help ethnic associations. These are the organizations upon which low-income families, especially female-headed families, rely for assistance.

CAN WE MITIGATE SOME OF THE ILL EFFECTS OF GENTRIFICATION?

The critics of gentrification often call for vulnerable communities to mobilize and resist gentrification. Indeed, local organizing efforts have at times succeeded in stopping a major development project that threatens to hasten the pace of neighborhood change.[59]

But neighborhoods undergoing gentrification often are not unified in opposing further new development. Longer-term residents tend to oppose such development, but families who have more recently bought into a neighborhood tend to look favorably upon new projects that that promise to upgrade the community and improve safety. In the blue-collar Fishtown section of Philadelphia, community action failed to stop the siting of a casino. Residents with long-term roots in the community tended to oppose the project.

Yet a number of long-term residents supported the project as they were persuaded by the prospects of casino-related jobs and the promises by developers to help fund community projects. More recent arrivals to the area saw the casinos as providing an attraction that would increase the value of their homes.[60]

In most cities community activism is unlikely to be able to hold back the tide of gentrification, especially as private- and public officials continue to launch one development project after another. In a privatist United States, private investment decisions and municipal growth agendas will continue to reshape neighborhoods.

If gentrification cannot be brought to a halt, can it at least be tamed? There are strategies that can promote more equitable development and temper some of the ill effects of unbridled market- and government-led gentrification.

Grassroots organizing efforts remain important as they can force cities to consider alternatives to unfettered gentrification. In Washington Heights in New York's Upper Manhattan, a multiethnic coalition of community groups battled to ensure that housing opportunities for the poor were included in institutional plans for new development in the area. In contrast, in the Park Slope section of Brooklyn, grassroots groups were weakly organized. As a result, property developers in Park Slope enjoyed more extensive freedom in condominium conversions and other development decisions that resulted in substantial displacement.[61]

In Bernal Heights in southern San Francisco, progressive community organizations pressed the city government to acquire land for new public housing, in order to assure the continued income diversity of an area facing gentrifying pressures.[62] In San Diego, a coalition of community groups mobilized to oppose the construction of Ballpark Village, a mixed-use bayfront development located just outside the fences of the new Padres baseball stadium. The grassroots groups were able to force a compromise, with the city and the developer agreeing to increase the number of affordable housing units built on-site and elsewhere in San Diego's downtown.[63]

In central San Francisco, grassroots organizations fought for **measures to limit the conversion of single room occupancy (SRO) hotels**. Advocates for the homeless sought to preserve dwelling units that are home to the more transient poor and the most vulnerable residents of the city's Tenderloin district.[64] In Philadelphia, Registered Community Organizations (RCOs) gained the legal right to review development plans that require zoning variances, a process that gave them the ability to insist on more inclusive development.[65]

In Boston, activists sought regulations to prohibit large-scale luxury development in at-risk neighborhoods.[66] Such regulations, however, are not popular. The home construction and real-estate industries argue that such regulations destroy jobs by making new housing construction financially unviable.

On Chicago's South Side, African-American activists pursued a strategy of "defensive development." Community activists promoted black-owned restaurants and African-American heritage tourism in the city's historic Bronzeville neighborhood as alternatives to new development controlled by outsiders. The activists argued that community-rooted projects were more likely to deliver jobs to neighborhood residents and would be more responsive to community concerns. But, too often, even projects led by African-American developers wind up accelerating rent increases and fueling displacement. Politically wise development interests also seek out African-American partners for political reasons—to mute the criticisms of transformative development.[67]

Cities can assist **community development corporations (CDCs)**, local-based groups that build affordable housing, as a means of lessening displacement in neighborhoods undergoing change. CDCs are neighborhood-based organizations that work with bankers, public officials, and other partners in order to provide quality housing units that are within the financial reach of low-income and working-class tenants. (Chapter 8 describes the bridge-building strategy of CDCs in further detail.) In Chicago, the Bickerdike Redevelopment Corporation worked with various partners to amass the funds necessary to acquire and rehabilitate low-income rental units in the city's Humboldt Park neighborhood. In Atlanta, the Reynoldstown Redevelopment Corporation (RRC) moved beyond rental housing; the community development corporation constructed owner-occupied homes on vacant lots, part of the organization's strategy to provide good homes as low prices.[68] Municipalities can assist such efforts by providing city-held vacant properties to CDCs at a greatly discounted price.

Affordable housing advocates also argue for **mandatory set asides**, a legislative requirement that new residential developments include a certain percentage of affordable units. New York has a "mandatory inclusionary housing" program, initiated by Mayor Bill de Blasio, that requires new residential developments in designated neighborhoods to have a certain percentage of dwelling units within the financial reach of low- and middle-income families.[69] The mayor's ten-year housing plan also provides increased subsidies for affordable housing and permits housing to be built at higher densities, a move intended to increase housing supply and thereby alleviate rent inflation.[70] Critics feared higher density construction would lead to the production of new upscale housing development that would serve to fuel gentrification and displacement pressures.[71]

Boston, San Francisco, Sacramento, Seattle, and Boulder impose **linkage fees** on the construction of new office buildings and other commercial development in order to generate funds to support affordable housing projects elsewhere in the city. Boston's program has provided assistance for thousands of units of affordable housing.[72] Seattle has a special **housing levy** that raises tax money to support the preservation of rental apartments, the construction of new affordable rental units, and the development of mixed-income residential projects.[73]

Direct residential displacement can be minimized if a city adopts a clear policy of awarding tax credits and other concessions only when a project entails the conversion of commercial structures to residential use. Public subsidies would be denied to projects that upscale residential properties.[74]

Economists tend to argue that cities need to relax zoning and land-use policies in order to promote the increased production of housing at all income levels. In San Francisco and Boston, local measures intended to preserve the low-rise and historic character of neighborhoods have acted to constrict the supply of housing. In San Francisco, a city that is home to Google, Twitter, Yelp, LinkedIn, Adobe, Intuit, and other tech-related firms, the high salaries paid tech workers coupled with limits on construction have resulted in skyrocketing housing prices, eviction,[75] and displacement.

As an alternative to deregulating land uses and rents to promote new construction, the targeting of subsidies to low-income families may produce even better results.

One study of the San Francisco Bay Area reports that when strategies that targeted the construction of affordable housing resulted in less displacement as compared to strategies that simply sought to expand the supply of market-rate housing.[76] The construction of subsidized housing units is especially necessary if low-income families are going to continue to reside in neighborhoods experiencing the "take off" of gentrification.

Other municipal actions seek to promote residential stability in transition neighborhoods.[77] Boston, Philadelphia, Pittsburgh, and Washington, DC are among the cities that have placed a **freeze on property taxes** for working- and lower-middle-class homeowners who reside in areas where gentrifying pressures have led to soaring property values and tax bills, financial pressures that could force working-class owners to sell their homes.[78]

GLOBALIZATION: THE POSITION OF CITIES IN A GLOBAL ECONOMY

Gentrification, especially new-build gentrification, is to a large extent a response to globalization. Developers seek to build residences for the well-paid workers of global firms. Municipal governments often promote the upscaling of core neighborhoods, refashioning them as attractive communities for the professional workers of the global economy. Cities even build museums and other cultural facilities in an effort to project an image that will attract skilled creative workers and major corporations.[79]

Only a relatively few cities serve as the key centers of an increasingly integrated world economy. The phrase **Global City** (or **world city**) denotes that a city has become a critical **command-and-control center** of an interconnected global economy. A Global City has a dense concentration of corporate headquarters, banks, and other financial institutions. The decisions made by major corporations and financial institutions located in a Global City have an impact on the well-being of cities around the world. A world city is also a hub of telecommunications technology.

All cities are affected by **globalization** as forces generated from beyond a nation's borders (i.e. corporate siting decisions; immigration; and the sharing of innovative entrepreneurial ideas and managerial practices via new media technology) influence local economic health and politics. Yet, while all cities are influenced by globalization, few are true centers of global finance, commerce, transportation, and communications.

A **world cities hierarchy** sorts cities according to the degree to which a city occupies a central position in the global economy. New York, London, and Tokyo are generally seen to be at the very top of the hierarchy; each has an extensive concentration of corporate headquarters, financial offices, and telecommunications that makes the city an important hub in the global economy.[80] Decisions made in these cities affect businesses and communities around the world. Los Angeles (Box 4.4), Chicago (Figure 4.3), and Washington, DC lack an equivalent density of corporate headquarters and top financial institutions and hence rank below New York in terms of their significance on the world economic stage. Still, these cities have global connections. Los Angeles is an important center of Pacific Rim banking and multicultural media. The growth of textile manufacturing in L.A. has been abetted by the immigration of low-wage workers from Mexico,

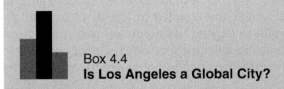

Box 4.4
Is Los Angeles a Global City?

New York, London, and Tokyo clearly meet anyone's definition of a Global City. But is Los Angeles, the second largest city in the United States, also a Global City?

The answer would seem to be an obvious "Yes!" The management consulting firm A.T. Kearney in 2017 ranked Los Angeles as Number 8 in the world on its "Global Cities Index."[1] Los Angeles's position was the result of the pivotal connections that the city, its businesses, and its people have to the Pacific Rim nations, especially China, Japan, and Korea. L.A.'s downtown is a center of banking and finance where financial decisions made in Los Angeles influence development on both sides of the Pacific. The economic health of Los Angeles is dependent on foreign capital, as seen in the deep investment by Japanese corporations and other overseas corporations that has helped to drive up home prices in the region.[2]

Los Angeles mayors have led trade missions abroad to tout L.A. as the "gateway for the Pacific Rim." Mayor Eric Garcetti met with business leaders and public officials in China, South Korea, and Japan in order to promote tourism and investment in his city. He even signed an agreement to facilitate medical travel of patients from China for surgery at Los Angeles hospitals.

The Los Angeles region expanded its port and airport facilities to accommodate increased international commerce. Municipal leaders encourage immigrants to maintain business contacts in their countries of origin, connections that can facilitate new trade opportunities for, as well as investment in, Los Angeles.[3] L.A. is also a multicultural mecca, where the region's dining opportunities[4] and culture have been enriched by arrivals from Mexico, El Salvador, Guatemala, India, Pakistan, China, Korea, Japan, and other nations.

Yet despite these international connections and influences, sociologist Michael Peter Smith argues that Los Angeles should *not* be regarded as a Global City, as L.A. does not occupy a position at the top of the Global City hierarchy. Los Angeles, he explains, is more "a receiver rather than a sender of global commands and controls."[5] L.A. lacks the density of corporate headquarters and banking firms found in a true command-and-control city like New York. The A.T. Kearney firm in its ranking of global cities observes that Los Angeles risks being eclipsed by San Francisco as a hub of Pacific Rim capital investment and economic entrepreneurship.

Yet, such a view of Los Angeles as something less than a top-tier Global City may result from the excessive weight give to a single factor, the relative absence of command-and-control corporate headquarters in L.A. As political geographer Edward Soja argues, other aspects of globalization clearly point to Los Angeles's position as a global center, especially as 40 percent of its population is foreign born and a vast number of L.A. residents maintain cross-national ties and bicultural identities.[6] When other dimensions of globalization are taken into account, L.A. is clearly a Global City. As The Brookings Institution observes, "there is no one way to be a global city."[7]

1. *Global Cities 2017: Leaders in a World of Disruptive Information*, a report of J.T. Kearney, 2017, www.atkearney.com/documents/20152/436055/Global+Cities+2017.pdf/f68ca227-48a0-2a74-96b9-0989ce3ce321.

2. Roger Vincent, "Los Angeles Ranks as the Top Choice in the U.S. for International Real Estate Investors," *Los Angeles Times*, March 21, 2017.

3. Steven P. Erie, *Globalizing L.A.: Trade, Infrastructure, and Regional Development* (Stanford, CA: Stanford University Press, 2004), 224–227.

4. Food critic Jonathan Gold has played a particularly noteworthy role in drawing national attention to the amazing cultural diversity of Los Angles as seen in its ethnic restaurants. See the video *City of Gold* (2016), distributed by MPI Home Video.

5. Michael Peter Smith, "Looking for Globality in Los Angeles," in *Articulating the Global and the Local*, ed. Ann Cvetkovich and Douglas Kellner (Boulder, CO: Westview, 1997), 55–71; the quotation appears on p. 55.

6. Edward W. Soja, *Postmetropolis: Critical Studies of Cities and Regions* (Maiden, MA: Blackwell, 2000), 222–232.

7. Jesus Real Trujillo and Joseph Parilla, *Redefining Global Cities: The Seven Types of Global Metro Economies*, a joint report of The Brookings Institution Metropolitan Policy Initiative and J.P. Morgan Chase, Washington DC, 2016.

Figure 4.3   **"The Bean," Chicago.** Chicago leaders built the lakefront Millennium Park on the site of underutilized property that once served as the downtown rail yards for the city's old commuter lines. Millennium Park was a key element in the effort of civic leaders to transform the image of Chicago and promote a new Chicago as a "world class" city. "The Bean," the popular name that Chicagoans and tourists use when referring to the park's unique Cloud Gate sculpture, has proved to be a popular success. It provides a visual icon that civic leaders have used in their efforts to brand Chicago as a dynamic, forward-thinking, and fun city.

Source: Photo by elesi / Shutterstock.com.

Central America, and Asia. Chicago similarly enjoys a "global connectivity" that has enabled the region to attract the headquarters of a number of national and international firms.[81]

Other U.S. cities occupy more limited or niche positions in the global economic hierarchy. Third-tier global cities include Houston (with its connections to Mexico and Latin America), Miami (with its Cuban enclave and its emergence as a center of Caribbean banking and finance; Figure 4.4), and San Francisco (which competes with Los Angeles as a Pacific Rim financial center). Boston, Dallas, and Philadelphia can be viewed as fourth-tier cities, important in their regions but with limited international ties. J.T. Kearney, however, ranks Boston much higher as the Boston area has gained global prominence as a result of its universities and academic connections. Boston is also a central information source for business and technological innovation. A

Figure 4.4   **Miami's Downtown. The City Has Grown as a Global Corporate Finance Center for Central and South America**.

Source: Copyright © by Tom Schaefer. http://commons.wikimedia.org/wiki/File: Miami_downtown_ by_Tom_Schaefer_-_ Miamitom.jpg.

fifth tier includes such cities as Atlanta, Charlotte (an important regional banking center), Columbus, Denver, Minneapolis, San Diego, San Jose, and Seattle, cities where business leaders have not yet established a full range of global connections.

THE VULNERABILITY OF CITIES IN A GLOBAL AGE

In a global age, a city's economic growth and well-being are often dependent on the decisions made by corporations and institutions overseas.[82] Investment from overseas can help nourish a city's economy. But global influences are not always positive.

Globalization adds to a city's sense of vulnerability, as no community has the total ability to control the overseas events and decisions that have such a great impact on a community's well-being. Overall, five sets of factors have served to compound city vulnerability in a global age.

ADVANCES IN TRANSPORTATION AND TELECOMMUNICATIONS INTENSIFY THE REGIONAL AND GLOBAL ECONOMIC COMPETITION

Telecommunications, satellite uplinks and downlinks, fiber optics, and advances in computerization and information technology have joined with the speed of jet travel to give a corporation the ability to locate its headquarters and financial services divisions at some distance from its production facilities and back-office support operations. A multinational firm can locate its headquarters at a prestigious address in New York, Chicago, Los Angles, or other big city while siting manufacturing plants and support operations in lower-cost sites in smaller cities and suburbs—and even overseas. Automobile companies have established supply chains allowing parts manufactured in Mexico, Brazil, and even South Africa and Central Europe to be shipped to the United States for final assembly. In India, Mumbai, Bangalore, and Hyderabad (Figure 4.5) have become important centers of software engineering and information technology development.

Multinational firms engage in **offshoring**, where they shift production and support tasks to lower-cost subsidiaries located overseas. **Outsourcing**, is a variation of offshoring; a company does not establish its own branches overseas but instead signs contracts to have work performed by firms located in other countries. Major retailers, for instance, have established customer service **call centers** in India; English-speaking phone operators in Mumbai, Bangalore, and Hyderabad respond to questions from

Figure 4.5 **The Outsourcing of Work and the Rise of New Competitors to U.S. Cities: MindSpace Campus, HiTec City, Hyderabad, India**. U.S. cities are losing jobs as American firms digitalize and outsource work to well-educated workers in lower-wage nations. Hyderabad is an Information Technology center of India. The product can be prepared overseas and the submitted electronically to finance firms, law offices, and other corporate business in the United States.

Source: From Wikimedia Commons via Flickr by user peculiar235, http://commons.wikimedia.org/wiki/File: Hydabada.jpg.

a retailer's customers in the United States (and in other countries around the globe). Mexico, China, the Philippines, and the former communist countries of Eastern Europe, too, offer low-wage, low-tax sites as an alternative to U.S. cities. Technology-oriented corporations can threaten to shift work overseas should a city prove hesitant in ceding to a firm's demands for rezoning, tax abatements, and other concessions.[83]

Of course, not all firms can easily relocate production and support activities overseas. Many firms find it important to be located close to suppliers, customers, and skilled labor markets in the United States. The mobility of capital can be exaggerated. Yet, one fact remains undeniable: Major firms have a greater variety of geographical options today than at any time in the past.

U.S. localities increasingly compete for economic development not just with one another but also with communities overseas. Cities invest in airport expansion and modernization in order to maintain their gateway to the global economy. A city that has an airport hub gains the benefits that come with being a convenient site for business meetings, conventions, tourism, and even the location of corporation headquarters and front offices.[84]

WINNING THE ECONOMIC COMPETITION: CITIES SEARCH FOR NEW GROWTH OPPORTUNITIES

In a postindustrial age, cities and suburbs can no longer stake their futures solely on "smokestack chasing" and the hope of winning a share of a revived manufacturing sector. Communities have responded by increasing their efforts to attract "new technology" firms and nurture start-up ventures. To "win" such industries, a city must do more than simply offer tax incentives.

Cities across the United States invest heavily to upgrade their telecommunications infrastructure, a necessary step to make a locality attractive to creative and technology-oriented firms. Cities have also invested in human resource development—that is, in education and job training—in order to provide the skilled and capable workforce that can attract tech and creative firms. Numerous municipalities offer programs of entrepreneurial assistance, providing technical advice and business support services in an effort to "incubate" homegrown firms. Local economic development officials introduce the heads of newly established firms to a network of more experienced business executives who can serve as mentors and offer advice on such matters as how to expand the scale of production or how to introduce their products into new markets. Improved municipal services and quality public schools, too, can help make a city attractive to postindustrial business firms and their workforces.[85]

Silicon Valley, the area south of San Francisco, emerged as a global center of computer development, programming, and information technology. The region's dynamic economic growth was largely due to the region's high-quality workforce. Stanford University anchors Silicon Valley, which is home to highly educated professionals with advanced skills in mathematics, computer programming, and digital technologies. Across the continent, New York City sought to emulate the Silicon Valley model by upgrading teleport facilities and other telecommunications infrastructure to create *Silicon Alley* in an area of Manhattan previously known as the Garment District.[86] Austin, Texas, similarly has built on the advantages the city enjoys as the home of both the University of Texas and Dell Computers. Omaha, Nebraska, touts itself as the "Silicon Prairie"; the city offers financial support to start-up firms as well mentoring provided by a network of Fortune 500 executives.[87]

Advances in telecommunications and the increased reliance on air travel have freed multinational corporations (MNCs) to choose facility locations in the suburbs, with the result that the suburbs, too, have joined in the competition for global firms. An MNC can choose to site its headquarters or branch-offices and back-office support operations in the office parks of "self-contained high-end suburbs," the so-called suburban **nerdistans** with their "concentrations of skilled workers."[88]

Advances in telecommunications and technology also enable firms to site activities in smaller cities and communities located at seemingly great distances from major global hubs. International law firms, for instance, have moved back-office operations (including financing, accounting, human resource support, information technology and even legal support services) to lower-wage cities such as Kansas City and Louisville.[89]

Civic leaders in Utah recognized the importance of upgraded technology to the region's future. Salt Lake City joined with a dozen or so other communities to build the UTOPIA (Utah Telecommunication Open Infrastructure Agency), a publicly owned fiber-optic network. The region's boosters promoted UTOPIA to corporate heads as one of the largest capacity ultra-high-speed digital networks in the world: "The best network in the U.S. will be in Utah—not in New York, not in Chicago, not in Los Angeles."[90]

Chattanooga, Tennessee, has similarly built an ultra-fast connection as part of the city's efforts to attract young entrepreneurs and business start-ups and shed Chattanooga's "smokestack" past. Chattanooga's Innovation District claims to offer the fastest fiber-optic Internet service in the nation, transferring data at one gigabit per second—50 times faster than the average speed for home networks.[91]

ATTRACTING PROFESSIONALS IN ORDER TO ATTRACT BUSINESSES

Municipal officials have come to recognize that tax inducements—the promise to cut a business's taxes—will not always succeed in winning a business firm that has such a wide variety of locations. The offer of a tax cut can easily be met by a similar offer from other communities. As a result, cities have had to turn to alternative development approaches.

Numerous cities have made investments to improve the quality of local life—upgrading both the road network and public transit and providing good schools, parks, and recreational and cultural facilities to attract a high-quality workforce. High-quality workers, in turn, help attract corporations especially in the creative and technology-related sectors.[92]

The continued growth of North Carolina's "Research Triangle"—the Raleigh, Durham, and Chapel Hill region—is in no small part due to planning efforts that maintained the region's high quality of life. The region's planners guided new development into mixed-use activity centers along highways. The centers provided the population densities to support businesses and entertainment. The centers also served to preserve the region's highly regarded green spaces and recreational areas in the face of growth pressures in the region.[93]

THE NEW IMMIGRATION AND ITS IMPACT ON CITIES AND SUBURBS

Capital in a global age is mobile; so too is labor! Media images of American prosperity cross national borders, luring families from other countries in search of jobs. Advances in transportation enable people seeking refuge from violence and escape from war-torn countries to reach safety in the United States. U.S. foreign policy, with the various commitments that it has made over the years, has promoted immigration from such countries as Vietnam, Laos, the Philippines, Russia, El Salvador, and Cuba.

Technology and transportation have resulted in the creation of **transnational communities**; e-mail, Skype, cheap telephone calling cards, satellite television, and even fairly frequent visits back home enable new arrivals in the United States to maintain a bicultural identity. The new arrivals seek economic opportunity in the United States but do not necessarily relinquish their home ties. Chicago's Pilsen and Little Village neighborhoods and Detroit's Mexicantown are only a few of the Latino communities where workers send part of their paychecks to family members in Mexico.

The new arrivals to cities form a pool of low-paid labor in the food, health care, and construction industries. "Day laborers" are hired to assist on jobs that may be of very short duration. Immigrants are part of the informal economy, where worker are often paid "off the books" and receive no fringe benefits. Such employment conditions—low pay, little guarantee of full-time or permanent work, and poor working conditions— characterize the **informalization** or **casualization of work** in the global postindustrial economy.[94]

In Los Angeles, the casualization of work is especially apparent in the garment industry, where the city's large population of Asian Americans and Latinas have provided a labor force of women that has allowed the resurgence of the city as a low-wage, textile manufacturing center (see Box 4.5). Los Angeles is just one of many cities where immigrant labor has helped to incubate new manufacturing.[95]

A **new immigration** to the United States from the Caribbean, Latin America, the Pacific Rim, and Africa to U.S. communities is sharply different from the "old" immigration of an early era where new arrivals came largely from Europe. What factors help explain the shift in immigration?

In part, the United States in the late twentieth century revised its immigration laws, abolishing the old system of country-by-country quotas that had favored immigration from Europe while sharply limiting arrivals from other regions of the world. New rules also facilitated family reunification, enabling family members from overseas to join a breadwinner working in the United States. Provisions that regularized the status of undocumented families already living in the United States, so that families already living in the country did not have to live in fear, may have also served to spur an influx of new arrivals, especially from Mexico.[96] Civil war and political conflicts overseas also led families fearful of religious, ethnic, and political persecution to seek safety in the United States. In 2016, refugees seeking political asylum came to the United States from the Democratic Republic of the Congo, Syria, Burma, Iraq, and Somalia. In some years, nearly half of the refugees seeking safety have been Muslim, a fact that is unsettling to some Americans and that led to President Donald Trump's efforts to curtail immigration from Iran, Libya, Syria, and other volatile Muslim-majority nations.

Box 4.5
Film Images of the City—Immigrant Los Angeles: *Real Women Have Curves* **and** *Bread and Roses*

Director Patricia Cardoso's *Real Women Have Curves* (2002) focuses on the struggles of Ana, an 18-year-old Latina (played by America Ferrera) in Los Angeles who attempts to cope with the conflicting demands of her Mexican and U.S. worlds. Should she defy the expectations of her family and take a scholarship to attend Columbia University in far-off New York City? Or should she remain in Boyle Heights and play the traditional supportive role expected of Latina women? Initially, Ana bows to her family's wishes and helps out in the small dressmaking business run by her sister.

The film points to the casualization of work in a Global City, especially the low-paid jobs often performed by women. The small factory is literally a sweatshop where the ladies strip down to their underwear in order to cope with the suffocating heat. Ana rails against the exploitation of the immigrant women; corporations sell the women's hand-crafted gowns for hundreds of dollars but pay the women only a pittance for their work.

Ken Loach's *Bread and Roses* (2000) is a more strident, unvarnished indictment of the social and work conditions suffered by immigrants who occupy the bottom-rung positions in global Los Angeles. Loach starts by showing the dangers that the migrants face in crossing the border, including the possibilities of rape. The undocumented migrants pay a "coyote" high fees to smuggle them across the U.S. border. The coyotes, however, abandon their human cargo when things go wrong; the human-cargo smugglers often "rip off" their paying customers.

Maya (played by Pilar Padilla) escapes the coyotes and, with the help of her sister, finds a job cleaning offices in one of Los Angeles's gleaming downtown office towers. The film reveals the low-wage, no-benefits, no-employment-security jobs that make up the underside of the city's glitzy global economy. The women put up with all sorts of abuse on the job for fear of losing their livelihood. The city's downtown corporations contract with smaller firms to clean their offices. The contracted firm stands as a buffer between the women and the city's giant corporations which, by outsourcing janitorial tasks, can deny responsibility for the low pay and poor work conditions of the Latina workers. Even the cleaning firm run by Mexican Americans exploits the women, with the men in charge demanding a portion of the women's wages and sexual favors in return for giving them work. The film underscores the **dualism** of the Global City, contrasting the harsh lives of the workers with scenes of the flamboyant excesses of a lavish Hollywood party.

Source: For further reading: Juanita Heredia, "From the New Heights: The City and Migrating Latinas in *Real Women Have* Curves and *Maria Full of Grace*," *Mester*, 42, No. 1 (2013): 1–24; Celestino Deleyto, *From TINSELTOWN to BORDERTOWN: Los Angeles on Film* (Detroit: Wayne State University Press, 2016), 247–266.

The surge of immigration from China and South Asia, especially India, has had helped to reshape urban areas in the United States. Arrivals from Mexico no longer dominate each year's immigration numbers to the extent they once did. From 2009 to 2015, arrivals from Asia actually surpassed the number from Mexico. In 2013, China was the Number One country of origin for new arrivals to the United States; in 2015, India was Number One.[97]

The new immigration has altered both the demography and the politics of the American metropolis. Phoenix, located near the international border with Mexico, has been a center of both legal and undocumented (that is, unauthorized) immigration—and, as a result, a hot spot of the political reaction against the new immigration. In just two decades (from 1980 to 2000), Phoenix saw its population grow by two-thirds, primarily due to the surge in arrivals from Mexico. By 2010, over 40 percent of Phoenix's population were of Hispanic or Latino ancestry. The immigration pressures on Phoenix eased just a bit in the early 2000s as the United States suffered an economic downturn and cities like Phoenix no longer had a ready supply of job opportunities to attract newcomers.[98]

The new immigration has even had considerable impact on cities and suburbs located at considerable distance from the United States's southern border. In 1970, only 17 percent of the population of New York City was foreign born. Over the decades, the figure more than doubled: today, nearly two in five New Yorkers (37 percent) were born in other countries.[99] As arrivals from Asia continued to come to the city, the informal borders that defined New York's Chinatown on Manhattan's Lower East Side largely crumbled, with Chinatown spilling into neighboring Little Italy. New Chinatowns emerged in the city's outer boroughs, notably in Jackson Heights and Flushing (Queens) and in Sunset Park (Brooklyn).[100]

In Chicago, the city's Chinese population swelled well beyond the traditional borders of the city's South Side Chinatown, encroaching into the adjoining Bridgeport neighborhood. A second Chinatown has expanded on Chicago's North Side, along Argyle Street and Broadway (Figure 4.6), an area of the city that is a port-of-entry for new arrivals from China, Vietnam, and other countries in Southeast Asia.

The new immigration has also reshaped midsized and small cities, communities that have not traditionally been destinations for new arrivals. Denver, Nashville, Oklahoma City, Wichita, and St. Paul are among the heartland cities that have seen a sizable increase in their foreign-born populations.[101] Nearly one-fifth of Denver's population is foreign born. As early as 1983, the city's burgeoning Latino population led to the election of a Mexican-American, Federico Peña, as mayor![102] In the Upper Midwest, small cities in Minnesota (Rochester) and Wisconsin (Wausau, Green Bay, Sheboygan, Appleton, La Crosse, and Eau Claire) have seen substantial growth in the local Hmong population, an ethnic group from Laos that resettled in the United States as a result of the Vietnam War.[103]

In Minneapolis, a growing Somali population is concentrated in the Cedar-Riverside neighborhood, an area that is often referred to as "Little Mogadishu."[104] On the nation's east coast, hundreds of Somalis, a largely black and Muslim population, were resettled in Lewiston, Maine, a working-class community that was 94 percent white. Local schools were suddenly confronted with the difficult task of having to teach large numbers of students who had limited English proficiency. The ethnic tensions that accompanied Lewiston's changing demography likely help explain how Donald

Figure 4.6   **The New Immigration Creates a New Chinatown in Chicago's "Uptown"**
Neighborhood. Argyle Street is the commercial center of Chicago's Uptown
neighborhood on the city's North Side. The low-income neighborhood serves as a
port of entry for new arrivals from China, Vietnam, Thailand, and other countries
in Asia. Locals refer to the area as the "New" Chinatown as it is located at quite
a distance from Chicago's more established and historic Chinatown on the city's
South Side.

Source: Author's original photo.

Trump was able to win a majority of the vote in a community that traditionally voted
Democrat; 2016 was the first time in three decades that this working-class city voted
Republican for president.[105]

The new immigration is a suburban as well as a city phenomenon.[106] The immigrants
of a century or so ago from Europe largely settled in the industrial centers of the East
Coast and the Midwest. In contrast, many of the new immigrants "skip" the central
city and move directly to the suburbs where they often have the support of established
residents who are members of their extended family. Immigrants come to the United
States in search of economic opportunity. In a postindustrial age, jobs are increasingly
likely to be found in the suburbs.

The diversity of the population of Los Angeles's suburbs is impossible to miss. Los
Angeles is ringed by various communities with large Mexican, Korean, Chinese, and
Vietnamese populations. Suburban strip malls feature cuisines from around the world.
Westminster, south of Los Angeles in Orange County, advertises itself as "Little Saigon"
(Figure 4.7). Across the continent, outside of New York City on suburban Long Island,
Hempstead and Hicksville are noteworthy centers of the region's South-Asian popu-
lation. Hicksville is often referred to as "Little India." In the greater Chicago region,

Figure 4.7   **Westminster, California: "Little Saigon" in the Los Angeles Suburbs. Parade Celebrating the Tết Lunar New Year.**

Source: Photo by Joseph Sohm / Shutterstock.com.

Naperville, Schaumburg, Skokie, Hoffman Estates, Glendale Heights, Hanover Park, and Palatine all have large concentrations of South Asians.[107]

Census data underscores that an increasing number of immigrants call the suburbs their home. Still, newcomers to the United States continue to be disproportionately concentrated in central cities. **Port-of-entry or gateway cities** have especially large concentrations of new arrivals. Over half Miami's population is foreign born, as is half the population of Santa Ana (California). San Jose (39 percent), Los Angeles (38 percent), New York (37 percent), and San Francisco (35 percent) all have immigrant populations that are nearly as large. Boston, Houston, Dallas, El Paso, Phoenix, and San Diego are cities where more than one-fourth of the local population was born outside the United States.[108]

In port-of-entry cities, immigrants—especially immigrant women—work at low-paid clerical, janitorial, and assembly jobs. Their jobs help to fill the void left by behind by the disappearance of the better-paid factory jobs of the Industrial City. Too often, such manufacturing is accompanied by the reemergence of exploitive practices associated with cities during the early Industrial Revolution: **piecework** (where workers are paid according to the number pieces of cloth or other pieces of work they finish, not by the hour), **sweatshops** (with overcrowded, poorly ventilated, and unsafe facilities), and even manufacturing done at home.[109] In cities like New York and Los Angeles, immigrant laborers and small migrant-owned firms provide the basis for a new manufacturing sector.

Critics point to the costs borne by municipalities and school systems that have large numbers of immigrants. The costs can be particularly severe in communities in the Southwest near the nation's southern border.[110]

Yet, many cities have discovered that the new arrivals are also assets who contribute to both local economic growth and community well-being. The University of Pennsylvania's "Penn Wharton budget model" points to the overall positive impact of immigration: "immigration leads to more innovation, a better educated workforce, greater occupational specialization, better matching of skills with jobs, and higher overall economic productivity."[111] Economist Edward Glaeser argues that immigration has been "essential" to the renaissance of New York, Chicago, and other major cities: "Cities are good for immigrants and immigrants are good for cities."[112] Immigrant entrepreneurs take advantage of ethnic networks that connect their new city with their home country, providing access to foreign markets. Ethnic networks also offer access to alternative sources of capital for ethnic-owned business start-ups.[113] More skilled immigrants help drive technology-oriented industries.[114] Were it not for the arrival of newcomers from other countries, most metropolitan areas in the United States—and their core cities— would have suffered population decline,[115]

Houston has recognized the advantages offered by immigration and has chosen to be a "welcoming city" that celebrates the ethnic diversity that has been a critical factor in Houston's economic rebound.[116] In Houston, younger people tend to have more positive perceptions of immigration, perhaps as they have grown up in an age of diversity and are more accustomed to diverse cultures. Older Houstonians, by contrast, maintain fond memories of a Houston at a time when its population was largely Anglo.[117]

Immigration has been especially crucial to the revival of a number of Rustbelt cities in the Northeast and the Midwest.[118] In New Jersey, a multiethnic blend of Puerto Ricans (the dominant Spanish-speaking group in New Jersey), Dominicans, Columbians, Cubans, Peruvians, and Mexicans helped to rejuvenate Paterson and other former industrial centers that had fallen on hard times.[119]

Immigration also helps stabilize economically frail inner-city and suburban neighborhoods, propping up the demand for housing in weak housing markets.[120] In more vulnerable neighborhoods, the arrival of newcomers helps to maintain the occupancy of houses that would otherwise lie vacant and slip into disrepair.

President Trump and his first Attorney General, Jeff Session, pointed to illegal or undocumented immigrants as the source of crime. Yet, academic examinations of crime data often reach the exact opposite conclusion: Rather than increasing crime, immigration is often associated with decreased crime rates, especially in homicides, robberies, and burglaries (although, in some cases, the decreases are rather small). Even communities with high numbers of illegal immigrants do not suffer higher rates of violent and property crimes as compared to similar communities that have a smaller presence of undocumented immigrants.[121] First-generation immigrants tend be committed to work as the path to success. In neighborhoods suffering decline, the arrival of immigrants reduces the number of vacant houses while adding to the number of people on city streets, factors that increase residents's sense of safety (see Box 4.6).

Box 4.6
Are Cities Better Off as a Result of Immigration? Chicago's Killer Heat Wave and "Little Village"

Does immigration help or hurt a city? Immigration can actually add to a city's well-being, as demonstrated by a review of the death toll of Chicago's 1995 killer heat wave. That summer, over 485 people died in the city from heat-related causes. Low-income elderly persons were especially vulnerable.

But not all lower-income communities suffered high death rates. The mortality rate was actually fairly low in the predominantly poor Mexican-American community of South Lawndale, an area commonly called "Little Village." After the crisis passed, public-health authorities sought to find out why the death rate in Little Village was so low, especially when the death rate in neighboring North Lawndale, a poor African-American area, was so high.

Continuing immigration from Mexico had made Little Village a lively neighborhood, with an active shopping district and a well-supported network of churches. The elderly in Little Village were able to escape the heat of their old apartments by frequenting the area's air-conditioned stores. The elderly were not scared to venture into the busy 26th Street shopping district, with its stores, bakeries, restaurants, and pushcart vendors selling juices and churros. The community's well-financed and socially active churches also provided outreach services, with church members visiting homes and tending to the needs of the elderly.

North Lawndale, by contrast, was a distressed community pockmarked by boarded-up buildings, abandoned lots, and drug dealing on the streets. North Lawndale had few air-conditioned stores that the elderly could frequent to escape the blast-furnace conditions of their apartments. The elderly in North Lawndale lived in fear; even in the heat, they were reluctant to open first-floor windows, venture out into the streets, or even unchain the door when municipal officials inquired as to their health. The elderly were afraid to open the door to strangers. The elderly died in their apartments, behind locked doors and oftentimes with windows bolted shut.

Both Little Village and North Lawndale are poor neighborhoods, and both suffer problems of gang activity. Yet there is a vast difference between the two communities. Continuing immigration gave Little Village a vital street life and an active network of churches. North Lawndale experienced no such immigration and, as a result, suffered an exodus of population that emptied streets, closed churches and stores, and diminished residents's sense of personal safety. Without new arrivals, North Lawndale suffered abandonment and steep decline.

Even the churches of North Lawndale exhibited extreme distress. They lacked the stream of new members that immigration provided, the person-power upon which churches rely to provide the home visits and networks of support that proved so crucial in Little Village.

Source: Eric Klinenberg, *Heat Wave: A Social Autopsy of Disaster in Chicago* (Chicago: University of Chicago Press, 2002), chap. 2. A. K. Sandoval-Strausz, *"Migrantes,* Barrios, and *Infraestructura*: Transnational Processes of Urban Revitalization in Chicago," in *Immigration and Metropolitan Revitalization in the United States*, ed. Domenic Vitiello and Thomas J. Sugrue (Philadelphia: University of Pennsylvania Press, 2017), 133–153, similarly looks at Little Village and concludes that immigration serves to reduce crime rates and social disorder, contributing to neighborhood health and safety.

Baltimore, Chicago, Philadelphia, Pittsburgh, Detroit, Cleveland, and Dayton are among the cities that proclaim to be a **Welcome City**. These cities see immigrants as a means to reverse population decline, fill vacant properties, and promote economic growth, Baltimore Mayor Stephanie Rawlings-Blake announced her hopes to recruit 10,000 immigrant families to Baltimore. Her successor, Catherine Pugh, reaffirmed the city's overall policy, that Baltimore was a Welcoming City that would provide services and seek to attract immigrants. Baltimore police officers would not routinely ask people from where they came.[122] Chicago Mayor Rahm Emanuel observed that a city ordinance prohibited his city's police from detaining undocumented immigrants unless they were involved in a serious crime. Chicago, Emanuel explained, intended to be the most immigrant-friendly city in the United States.[123] The Pittsburgh Promise saw a nonprofit organization award $40,000 college scholarships to lure immigrant families in the region to Pittsburgh where their children would help fill the city's schools.[124]

THE VULNERABILITY OF CITIES IN AN AGE OF DIMINISHED BORDERS

Global tensions and resentments heighten the vulnerability of cities, a reality underscored by the 9/11 terrorist attacks on New York City and by the 2016 mass shooting at an Orlando night club. Even cities that have not been the targets of terrorist assaults have had to divert spending for activities related to homeland defense.

Cities are also vulnerable to cyber-attacks by malcontents. Cyber-attacks are seen as inevitable, and cities have little choice but to devote resources to cybersecurity in order to prevent e-attacks from compromising and paralyzing a city's digital enterprises.[125]

Cities are also susceptible to pandemics. With modern jet travel, diseases such as AIDS and Ebola can quickly cross from one continent to another.[126] International crises—famine, civil war, and political turmoil—can produce a wave of refugees and immigration.

Climate change also produces costly problems over which a city has no direct control. Cities like New York, Miami, Ft. Lauderdale, and other Florida cities must deal with heightened coastal flooding due to climate change.[127] Chicago similarly must cope with rising lake levels as global warming continues to melt arctic and Antarctic ice shelfs. Climate change also makes weather more unpredictable and extreme. The human toll and multibillion-dollar costs that climate change imposes on cities are evident in virulent "heat island" effects, killer summer heat waves, and the extreme destructiveness of uncontrollable wildfires such as those that ravaged northern and southern California.[128]

This book's concluding chapter reviews the various steps that cities and suburbs are taking to cope with sustainability problems including global warming. As the next section of the present chapter describes, cities have also increased their activism on the global stage in an effort to mitigate the expected costs of climate change.

CITIES AND THEIR NEW PROMINENCE ON THE INTERNATIONAL STAGE

City leaders are no longer content to confine their attention to traditional questions of municipal service delivery, leaving "big picture" policy matters in the hands of others. Instead, local leaders have entered into a relatively new arena, one of "local diplomacy." Cities forge cross-border alliances to enhance local economic development. Cities also join the efforts of United Nations agencies and other international organizations to address such matters as climate change, the protections offered refugees and children, and other questions of human rights—all policy matters that, if ignored, impose costs on cities and their residents. Such local diplomacy has gained special prominence at a time when recalcitrant state and national governments have been unwilling to join in cooperative global actions to cope with the problems that afflict cities.

Mayors venture overseas on missions to seek markets for products produced by a city's firms. International meetings also pave the way for foreign investment that will enhance job creation back home. The mayors of Chicago and Mexico City formalized a "Global Cities Economic Partnership" to expand investment and job creation in both communities, for instance by facilitating the knowledge exchange between business incubators in the two cities. Los Angeles Mayor Eric Garcetti announced a similar effort to provide counseling and training programs to help Los Angeles firms expand their markets overseas.

In more recent years, however, the heightened international profile of mayors extends beyond economic development. The 2017 North American Global Climate Summit in Chicago was only one of a number of meetings that allowed mayors to learn about the "green" strategies of cities in other countries, Such international sessions also provide a forum to mayors to press for more extensive action by the U.S. national government. Local participation in international forums took on even greater importance in the wake of President Trump's announcement that the federal government would not abide by the global warming reduction strategies set in motion by the 2015 Paris Climate Change accords. Trump withdrew, and the mayors mobilized. Eric Garcetti (Los Angeles), Martin Walsh (Boston), Bill de Blasio (New York), Sylvester Turner (Houston), Rahm Emanuel (Chicago), Ed Murray (Seattle), and Jim Kenney (Philadelphia) headlined a list of 386 mayors of self-proclaimed "U.S. climate cities" who reaffirmed their commitment to reduce climate risks.[129] The nation's mayors had stepped into the "high politics" of foreign policy, an action that would have been almost unconceivable just a generation or two earlier. City diplomacy had become part of a mayor's job description.[130]

The story of local activism regarding immigration matters is quite similar. When President Trump announced that the United States would no longer participate in a United Nations-backed process to address migration issues and protect the human rights of immigrants, the cities stepped in. New York, Los Angeles, Chicago, Atlanta, Philadelphia,

Providence, Dallas, and the District of Columbia even petitioned the United Nations High Commissioner for Refugees asking to be a formal part of the talks concerning the development of an immigration compact.[131]

The impact of local activism in the international arena can be easily exaggerated. Constitutional constraints limit local action, and cities are not interested in the broad panoply of foreign affairs. U.S. cities enter the diplomatic arena only when matters directly affect municipal service provision and city well-being.[132] Cities step into the global arena and act when the national government shows its distain for arranging international action.

CONCLUSION: GLOBALIZATION, POWER, AND DEMOCRACY

Globalization magnifies the competitive pressures that lead cities to prioritize local economic development, including gentrification, over concerns for other matters including the provision of social programs and affordable housing. As Thomas Friedman provocatively proclaims, in the face of global pressures, "Your politics shrinks."[133]

Still, local politics *does* count. In Seattle, neighborhood groups play a vigilant role, ensuring that corporations will not dictate the exact shape of Seattle's postindustrial transformation.[134] Portland has chosen to pursue new economic growth while also pursuing environmental protection and livability, a balanced local agenda that growth advocates have attacked as anti-business.[135] In Boston, Seattle, and other cities with large numbers of well-educated and affluent professionals who value ecological sustainability and quality-of-life concerns, public officials do not simply cede to the demands of multinational corporations. The political activism of gay and lesbian and other countercultural groups further leads local officials to pursue policies that deviate from a growth agenda set by global corporate interests.[136]

In a globally competitive age, "smart" cities recognize the critical importance of investing in human resource development, not just in cutting taxes levied on businesses. Cities that are the home of well-educated, technologically capable and adaptable workers have the best chances of attracting knowledge-based industry.

Improvements in the local quality of life help make a community attractive to both professional workers and technology-oriented firms. New York and Chattanooga, are among the cities that have invested in improved parks, bicycle and hiking trails, recreational opportunities such as river rafting, and the upgrading of concert halls and cultural and entertainment facilities in order to attract creative workers and their employers. In San Francisco, city planners helped to transform the area of aging warehouses in SOMA (South of Market Street) into a "hip" and "trendy" neighborhood that has been able to attract "new media" start-ups and other creative business firms.[137] San Francisco faces the difficult choice of finding the right balance: How can the city promote affordable housing, constrain gentrification, and maintain the city's fabled population diversity while also providing for technology-oriented growth in a postindustrial global economy?

The competitive forces that constrain city power are very real. Globalization intensifies those forces. Yet, as this chapter has already begun to describe, and as the next chapter will further observe, each locality determines how it will respond to competitive pressures.

KEY TERMS

black branding of a neighborhood
 by minority developers (*p. 123*)
call centers, overseas (*p. 141*)
casualization of work (*p. 144*)
command-and-control center in a
 global economy (*p. 137*)
community development
 corporations (CDCs) (*p. 136*)
displacement (*p. 123*)
dualism (*p. 145*)
financifiers (*p. 125*)
freeze on property taxes as a means
 to reduce displacement pressures
 (*p. 137*)
gateway cities (*p. 148*)
gentrification (*p. 121*)
Global City (*p. 137*)
globalization (*p. 137*)
grassroots organizing efforts (*p. 135*)
HOPE VI (*p. 130*)
housing levy, Seattle's (*p. 136*)
informalization of the economy (*p. 144*)
linkage fees (*p. 136*)
mandatory set asides as an affordable
 housing strategy (*p. 136*)

measures to limit the conversion of
 single room occupancy (SRO)
 hotels (*p. 135*)
neighborhood invasion,
 gentrificiation as (*p. 131*)
neighborhood networks (*p. 134*)
nerdistans (*p. 143*)
new-build gentrification (*p. 127*)
new immigration (*p. 144*)
offshoring (*p. 141*)
outsourcing (*p. 141*)
piecework (*p. 148*)
port-of-entry city (*p. 148*)
Silicon Alley (*p. 130*)
Silicon Valley (*p. 142*)
supergentrifiers (*p. 125*)
sweat equity (*p. 124*)
sweatshops (*p. 148*)
transnational communities (*p. 144*)
upzoning (*p. 125*)
urban pioneers (*p. 124*)
Welcome City (*p. 151*)
world cities hierarchy (*p. 137*)
world city (*p. 137*)

NOTES

1. Lisa Sturtevant, "The New District of Columbia: What Population Growth and Demographic Change Mean for the City," *Journal of Urban Affairs* 36, no. 2 (May 2014): 276–299. The quotations can be found on 279.
2. Richard Florida, *The New Urban Crisis: How Our Cities Are Increasing Inequality, Deepening Segregation, and Failing the Middle Class: And What We Can Do About It* (New York: Basic Books, 2017).
3. See Japonica Brown-Saracino, ed., *The Gentrification Debates: A Reader* (London and New York: Routledge, 2010); and Loretta Lees, Tom Slater, and Elvin Wyly, eds., *The Gentrification Reader* (London and New York: Routledge, 2010).
4. Richard E. Ocejo, *Upscaling Downtown: From Bowery Saloons to Cocktail Bars in New York City* (Princeton, NJ: Princeton University Press, 2014).
5. Daniel Hartley, "Urban Decline in Rust-Belt Cities," *Economic Commentary*, a newsletter of the Federal Reserve Bank of Cleveland, May 20, 2106, www.clevelandfed.org/newsroom-and-events/publications/economic-commentary/2013-economic-commentaries/ec-201306-urban-decline-in-rust-belt-cities.aspx.
6. Richey Piiparinen and Jim Russell, "From Balkanized Cleveland to Global Cleveland: A Theory of Change for Legacy Cities" (2013). Urban Publications, a white paper of the Maxine Goodman

Levin College of Urban Affairs, Cleveland State University, http://engagedscholarship.csuohio.edu/urban_facpub/1165

7. Brian Doucet and Edske Smit, "Building an Urban 'Renaissance': Fragmented Services and the Production of Inequality in Greater Downtown Detroit," *Journal of Housing and the Built Environment* 31, no. 4 (December 2016): 635–657, https://link.springer.com/article/10.1007/s10901-015-9483-0.

8. George C. Galster, Roberto G. Quercia, Alvaro Cortes, and Ron Malega, "The Fortunes of Poor Neighborhoods," *Urban Affairs Review* 39 (November 2003): 205–227.

9. Jeffrey M. Timberlake and Elaina Johns-Wolfe, "Neighborhood Ethnoracial Composition and Gentrification in Chicago and New York, 1980 to 2010," *Urban Affairs Review* 53, no. 2 (2017): 236–272.

10. Natalie Delgadillo, "The Neighborhood That Went to War against Gentrifiers," *CityLab Web Posting*, March 1, 2017, www.citylab.com/equity/2017/03/the-neighborhood-that-went-to-war-against-gentrifiers/518181/.

11. El Sereno Against Gentrification, Facebook page, downloaded November 14, 2017.

12. Sean Tierney and Clint Petty, "Gentrification in the American Heartland? Evidence from Oklahoma City," *Urban Geography*, 36, no. 3 (2015): 439–345.

13. Yuqinkg Pan, "The U.S. Cities That Are Gentrifying the Fastest: You'll Never Guess No. 1," *Realtor. com*, January 23, 2017, www.realtor.com/news/trends/10-surprising-cities-that-are-gentrifying-the-fastest/; Graves and Smith, ed., *Charlotte, NC*.

14. Displacement usually, but does not always, accompanies gentrification. In Charlotte, North Carolina, new businesses and urban places were created on vacant former mill sites, with minimal direct displacement. See Tyrel G. Moore and Gerald L. Ingalls, "A Place for Old Mills in a New Economy: Textile Mill Reuse in Charlotte," in *Charlotte, NC: The Global Evolution of a New South City*, ed, William Graves and Heather A. Smith (Athens, GA: University of Georgia Press, 2010), 119–140, esp. 127.

15. See Derek S. Hyra, *The New Urban Renewal: The Economic Transformation of Harlem and Bronzeville* (Chicago: University of Chicago Press, 2008); and Lance Freeman, *There Goes the 'Hood: Views of Gentrification from the Ground Up* (Philadelphia: Temple University Press, 2006), esp. 40–48.

16. Themis Chronopoulos, "African Americans, Gentrification, and Neoliberal Urbanization: The Case of Fort Greene, Brooklyn," *Journal of African American Studies* 20, no. 3–4 (December 2016): 294–322.

17. Derek S. Hyra, *Race, Class, and Politics in the Cappuccino City* (Chicago: University of Chicago Press, 2017), chap. 4.

18. Mathew B. Anderson and Carolina Sternberg, "'Non-White' Gentrification in Chicago's Bronzeville and Pilsen: Racial Economy and the Intraurban Contingency of Urban Redevelopment," *Urban Affairs Review* 49, no. 3 (May 2013): 435–467; Jon J. Betancur and Janet L. Smith, *Claiming Neighborhood: New Ways of Understanding Urban Change* (Urbana: University of Illinois Press, 2016), chap. 3. In Chapter 6 Betancur and Smith observe how public officials and business leaders in Chicago marketed caricatures of ethnic neighborhoods (of Puerto Rican Humboldt Park as well as Mexican Pilsen) to attract visitors and new upscale investment.

19. Alan Ehrenhalt, *The Great Inversion and the Future of the American City* (New York: Alfred A. Knopf, 2012), 233.

20. 2016 American Community Survey figures, Bureau of the Census, reported by Alan Berube and Cecile Murray, "Three Charts Showing You Poverty in U.S. Cities and Metro Areas," web newsletter of the Brookings Institution's Metropolitan Policy Program, September 14, 2017, www.brookings.edu/blog/the-avenue/2017/09/14/three-charts-showing-you-poverty-in-u-s-cities-and-metro-areas/.

21. 2012 American Community Survey figures, reported by Michael Lewyn, "Gentrification, Shmentrification," *Planetizen*, October 1, 2013, www.planetizen.com/node/65386.

22. William H. Frey, "Census Shows a Revival of Pre-Recession Migration Flows," The Brookings Institution web newsletter of the Metropolitan Policy Program, March 30, 2017, www.brookings.edu/blog/the-avenue/2017/03/30/census-shows-a-revival-of-pre-recession-migration-flows/.

23. Brian Doucet and Edske Smit, "Building an Urban 'Renaissance': Fragmented Services and the Production of Inequality in Greater Downtown Detroit," *Journal of Housing and the Built Environment* 31, no. 4 (December 2016): 635–657, https://link.springer.com/article/10.1007/s10901-015-9483-0.

24. Aaron Shkuda, *The Lofts of SoHo: Gentrification, Art, and Industry in New York, 1950–1980* (Chicago: University of Chicago Press, 2016).

25. Suleiman Osman, *The Invention of Brownstone Brooklyn: Gentrification and the Search for Authenticity in Postwar New York* (New York: Oxford University Press, 2011), especially 13–16, 23–37, 192–206.

26. Japonica Brown-Saracino, *A Neighborhood That Never Changes: Gentrification, Social Preservation, and the Search for Authenticity* (Chicago: University of Chicago Press, 2009). Newcomers in numerous ways impose their cultural norms and preferred lifestyle on inner-city communities. Also see Sylvie Tissot, *Good Neighbors: Gentrifying Diversity in Boston's South End*, trans. David Broder and Catherine Romatowski (Brooklyn, NY: Verso Books, 2015).

27. Jerome Krase and Judith N. deSena, *Race, Class, and Gentrification in Brooklyn: A View from the Streets* (Lanham, MD: Lexington Books, 2016).

28. Alessandro Busà, "After the 125th Street Rezoning: The Gentrification of Harlem's Main Street in the Bloomberg Years," *Urbanities* 4, no. 2 (November 2014): 52–68.

29. Loretta Lees, "A Reappraisal of Gentrification: Towards a 'Geography of Gentrification'," *Progress in Human Geography* 24, no. 3 (2000): 389–408.

30. For a description of different types of gentrifiers and their values, see Brown-Saracino, *A Neighborhood That Never Changes: Gentrification, Social Preservation, and the Search for Authenticity*, and Osman, *The Invention of Brownstone Brooklyn*.

31. Patrick Rérat, Ola Söderström, and Etienne Piguet, "New Forms of Gentrification: Issues and Debate," *Population, Space and Place* 16, no. 5 (2010): 335–343; Mark Davidson and Loretta Lees, "New-Build Gentrification: Its Histories, Trajectories, and Critical Geographies," *Population, Space and Place* 16, no. 5 (2010): 395–411.

32. Jason Hackworth, *The Neoliberal City* (Ithaca, NY: Cornell University Press, 2007); Harley F. Etienne, *Pushing Back the Gates: Neighborhood Perspectives on University-Driven Revitalization in West Philadelphia* (Philadelphia, PA: Temple University Press, 2012), especially 90–92. Etienne reveals how the University of Pennsylvania and the City of Philadelphia worked together to upgrade the much-troubled and crime-ridden inner-city area that surrounded the university's campus.

33. Ocejo, *Upscaling Downtown*, 62–63.

34. Heather A. Smith and Emily Thomas Livingstone, "Banking on the Neighborhood: Corporate Citizenship and Revitalization in Upscale Charlotte," in *Charlotte, NC: The Global Evolution of a New South City, op. cit.*, 142.

35. Jason Hackworth, "Post-Recession Gentrification in New York City," *Urban Affairs Review* 37, no. 6 (2002): 815–843, esp. 835–838.

36. Sharon Zukin, *Naked City: The Death and Life of Authentic Urban Places* (New York: Oxford University Press, 2010). The quotations appear on pp. x and xi.

37. Christopher Mele, *The Selling of the Lower East Side: Culture, Real Estate, and Resistance in New York City* (Minneapolis: University of Minnesota Press, 2000). The quotations appear on pp. 3–6.

38. Christopher Mele, *Race and the Politics of Deception: The Making of an American City* (New York: New York University Press, 2017).

39. Michael Indergaard, *Silicon Alley: The Rise and Fall of a New Media District* (New York: Routledge, 2004), 26–27, 102–112.

40. Edward G. Goetz, "Where Have All the Towers Gone? The Dismantling of Public Housing in U.S. Cities," *Journal of Urban Affairs* 33, no. 4 (2011): 267–287.

41. Susan J. Popkin, Bruce Katz, Mary K. Cunningham, Karen D. Brown, Jeremy Gustafson, and Margery A. Turner, *A Decade of Hope VI: Research Findings and Policy Challenges* (Washington, DC: Urban Institute and Brookings Institution, 2004), 44–45.

42. John J. Betancur, "The Politics of Gentrification: The Case of West Town in Chicago," *Urban Affairs Review* 37, no. 6 (July 2002): 780–814, esp. 787–789 and 801–803.

43. Anne E. Brown, "Uneven Effects: The Mixed Story of Transit-Oriented Gentrification in Los Angeles," *Critical Planning*, 22, no. 1 (2015): 179–187.

44. Brown-Saracino, *A Neighborhood That Never Changes*, 213–248.

45. Freeman, *There Goes the 'Hood*, esp. 62–74, 92–94, 190–202.

46. Andrew V. Papachristos, Chris M. Smith, Mary L. Scherer, and Melissa A. Fugiero, "More Coffee, Less Crime? The Relationship between Gentrification and Neighborhood Crime Rates in Chicago, 1991–2005," *City & Community* 10, no. 3 (2011): 215–240.

47. Neil Smith, *The New Frontier: Gentrification and the Revanchist City* (London: Routledge, 1996).

48. Kathe Newman and Elvin K. Wyly, "The Right to Stay Put, Revisited: Gentrification and Resistance to Displacement in New York City," *Urban Studies* 43, no. 1 (January 2006): 23–57.

49. Betancur, "The Politics of Gentrification."

50. Mary Pattillo, *Black on the Block: The Politics of Race and Class in the City* (Chicago: University of Chicago Press, 2007), 284.

51. Daniel Monroe Sullivan, "Reassessing Gentrification: Measuring Residents' Opinions Using Survey Data," *Urban Affairs Review* 42, no. 4 (2007): 589–591.

52. Micere Keels, Julia Burdick-Will, and Sara Keene, "The Effects of Gentrification on Neighborhood Public Schools," *City & Community*, 12, no. 3 (September 2013): 238–259.

53. A number of scholars doubt that such "role model" effects exist. They argue that there is no convincing evidence that mixing social groups in a neighborhood will lead the poor to better life choices and habits. See David Manley, Maarten van Ham, and Joe Doherty, "Social Mixing as a Cure for Negative Neighbourhood Effects: Evidence-Based Policy or Urban Myth?" in *Mixed Communities: Gentrification by Stealth?* ed. Gary Bridge, Tim Butler, and Loretta Lees (Bristol, England: The Policy Press, 2012), 151–168.

54. Dax-Devlon Ross, "Separate and Unequal in D.C.," *Next City*, April 8, 2013, http://nextcity.org/daily/features/view/separate-and-unequal-in-D.C.

55. Renia Ehrenfeucht and Marla Nelson, "Young Professionals as Ambivalent Change Agents in New Orleans after the 2005 Hurricanes," *Urban Studies* 50, no. 4 (2013): 825–841.

56. Jackelyn Hwang, "The Social Construction of a Gentrifying Neighborhood: Reifying and Redefining Identity and Boundaries in Inequality," *Urban Affairs Quarterly* 52, no. 1 (2016): 98–128.

57. Robert J. Chaskin and Mark L. Joseph, "Building 'Community' in Mixed-Income Developments: Assumptions, Approaches, and Early Experiences," *Urban Affairs Review* 45, no. 3 (2010): 299–335; the quotation appears on 323. Also see Pauline Lipman, "Mixed-Income Schools and Housing Policy in Chicago: A Critical Examination of the Gentrification/Education/'Racial' Exclusion Nexus," in *Mixed Communities: Gentrification by Stealth?* ed. Gary Bridge, Tim Butler, and Loretta Lees (Bristol, England: Policy Press, 2012), 105–107.

58. John Betancur, "Gentrification and Community Fabric in Chicago," *Urban Studies* 48, no. 2 (2011): 383–406.

59. Loretta Lees and Mara Ferreri, "Resisting Gentrification on Its Final Frontiers: Learning from the Heygate Estate in London (1974–2013)," *Cities* 57 (2016): 14–24 reviews resistance to state-led gentrification projects in cities in the United States, Great Britain, and in other countries around the globe. Also see Loretta Lees, Sandra Annunziata, and Clara Rivas-Alonso, "Resisting Planetary Gentrification: The Value of Survivability in the Fight to Stay Put," *Annals of the American Association of Geographers*, published online October 16, 2017, http://dx.doi.org/10.1080/24694452.2017.1365587.

60. John E. Balzarini and Anne B. Shlay, "Gentrification and the Right to the City: Community Conflict and Casinos," *Journal of Urban Affairs* 38, no. 4 (October 2016): 503–517.

61. Joyce Gelb and Michael Lyons, "A Tale of Two Cities: Housing Policy and Gentrification in London and New York," *Journal of Urban Affairs* 15, no. 4 (1993): 345–366.

62. Maureen Kennedy and Paul Leonard, "Dealing with Neighborhood Change: A Primer on Gentrification and Policy Choices" (discussion paper prepared for The Brookings Institution Center on Urban

and Metropolitan Policy, Washington, DC, 2001), 30, www.brookings.edu/es/urban/gentrification/gentrification.pdf.

63. Murtaza H. Baxamusa, "Empowering Communities through Deliberation: The Model of Community Benefits Agreements," *Journal of Planning and Education Research* 27, no. 3 (March 2008): 261–276.

64. Tony Robinson, "Gentrification and Grassroots Resistance in San Francisco's Tenderloin," *Urban Affairs Review* 30, no. 4 (1995): 483–513.

65. Sandy Smith, "3 Ways Communities Can Take Control of Gentrification," *Next City Web Posting*, December 4, 2014, https://nextcity.org/daily/entry/gentrification-solutions-affordable-housing-ideas.

66. David Price, "7 Policies That Could Prevent Gentrification," *Shelterforce, Web Posting* May 23, 2014, https://shelterforce.org/2014/05/23/7_policies_that_could_prevent_gentrification/.

67. Michelle Boyd, "Defensive Development: The Role of Racial Conflict in Gentrification," *Urban Affairs Review* 43, no. 6 (July 2008): 751–776.

68. Diane K. Levy, Jennifer Comey, and Sandra Padilla, *In the Face of Gentrification* (Washington, DC: The Urban Institute, 2006), 33–43, www.urban.org/UploadedPDF/411294_gentrification.pdf.

69. New York City, Department of Planning, *Mandatory Inclusionary Housing*, March 22, 2016 update, www1.nyc.gov/site/planning/plans/mih/mandatory-inclusionary-housing.page.

70. City of New York Mayor Bill de Blasio, *Housing New York: A Five-Borough 10-Year Plan* (New York: Office of the Mayor, 2014), www.nyc.gov/html/housing/assets/downloads/pdf/housing_plan.pdf; the "mandatory" quote appears on p. 8. Also see Mireya Navarro and Michael M. Grynbaum, "De Blasio Makes Push for Affordable Units in His $8.2 Billion Housing Plan," *New York Times*, May 6, 2014; and Charles V. Bagli, "Plan to Redevelop Brooklyn Sugar Refinery Hits Roadblock: New Mayor," *New York Times*, February 24, 2014.

71. Abigail Savitch-Lew, "Everything You Need to Know about Mandatory Inclusionary Housing but Were Afraid to Ask," *City Limits Web Posting*, November 18=7, 2016, https://citylimits.org/2016/11/17/everything-you-need-to-know-about-mandatory-inclusionary-housing-but-were-afraid-to-ask/.

72. NYU Furman Center, *Gentrification Response: A Survey of Strategies to Maintain Neighborhood Economic Diversity*, New York, October 2016, pp. 13–14, NYU Furman Center, *Gentrification Response: A Survey of Strategies to Maintain Neighborhood Economic.*

73. Levy, Comey, and Padilla, *In the Face of Gentrification*, 53–65.

74. Stephanie Ryberg-Webster, "The Landscape of Urban Preservation: A Spatial Analysis of Federal Rehabilitation Tax Credits in Richmond, Virginia," *Journal of Urban Affairs* 37, no. 4 (October 2015): 410–435.

75. San Francisco Anti-Displacement Coalition, *San Francisco's Eviction Crisis*, 2015, http://nonprofithousing.org/wp-content/uploads/SFADC-Eviction-Report-2015.pdf.

76. Miriam Zuk and Karen Chapple, "Housing Production, Filtering and Displacement: Untangling the Relationships," a research brief of the Institute of Government Studies, University of California, Berkeley, May 2016, www.urbandisplacement.org/sites/default/files/images/udp_research_brief_052316.pdf.

77. David Imbroscio, "From Redistribution to Ownership: Toward an Alternative Urban Policy for America's Cities," *Urban Affairs Review* 49, no. 6 (2013): 787–820, esp. 800–801.

78. Timothy Williams, "City Helping Residents Resist the New Gentry," *New York Times*, March 4, 2014.

79. The use of the arts to promote city rejuvenation and competitiveness is not confined to the United States. Cities in Asia and other parts of the world have been aggressive in investing in the arts and culture to promote local competiveness. See Lily Kong Ching Chia-ho and Chou Tsu-Lung, *Arts, Culture and the Making of Global Cities: Creating New Urban Landscapes in Asia* (Northampton MA: Edward Elgar, 2015).

80. Of course, the exact ranking of a city in the world hierarchy depends on just how a researcher weighs each aspect of a city's being "global." One "globalizing cities index" ranked Tokyo only as the world's 6th most important city on its "Financial Control Index"; see Peter J. Taylor, Pengfei Ni,

Ben Derudder, Michael Hoyler, Jin Huang, and Frank Witlox, *Global Urban Analysis: A Survey of Cities in Globalization* (London, UK: Earthscan, 2011). The ranking of United States global cities presented in this chapter relies heavily on the two separate studies: Paul K. Knox, "Globalization and Urban Economic Change," *Annals of the American Academy of Political and Social Science* (May 1997), 22–23; and the Globalization and World Cities (GaWC) Research Network at Loughborough University, "The World According to GaWC 2016," Loughborough University, Leicestershire, UK, 2016, www.lboro.ac.uk/gawc/world2016t.html.

81. Peter J. Taylor and Robert E. Lang, *U.S. Cities in the "World Cities Network"* (Washington, DC: Brookings Institution, February 2005), www.brookings.edu/~/media/Files/rc/reports/2005/02cities_taylor/20050222_worldcities.pdf.

82. John Rennie Short, *Globalization, Modernity, and the City* (New York: Routledge, 2012), 7.

83. Robert Atkinson and Howard Wial, *The Implications of Service Offshoring for Metropolitan Economies* (Washington, DC: Brookings Institution, February 2007), www.brookings.edu/~/media/Files/rc/reports/2007/02cities_atkinson/20070131_offshoring.pdf.

84. Zachary P. Neal, *The Connected City: How Networks Are Shaping the Modern Metropolis* (New York: Routledge, 2013), 137–142, 159–161.

85. Susan M. Wachter and Kimberly A. Zeuli, eds., *Revitalizing American Cities* (Philadelphia: University of Pennsylvania Press, 2014).

86. Indergaard, *Silicon Alley*.

87. Sujan Patel, "25 Cities Worth Moving to If You Want to Launch a Business," *Entrepreneur*, August 20, 2105, www.entrepreneur.com/article/249735.

88. Joel Kotkin, *The New Geography: How the Digital Revolution Is Reshaping the American Landscape* (New York: Random House, 2000), 9.

89. Staci Zaretsky, "Yet Another Firm to Move Back-Office Operations Offsite; Will There Be Layoffs?" *Above the Law Website*, February 26, 2016, https://abovethelaw.com/2016/02/yet-another-firm-to-move-back-office-operations-offsite-will-there-be-layoffs/?rf=1.

90. Matt Richtel, "In Utah, Public Works Project in Digital," *New York Times*, November 17, 2003. While Utah's growth coalition supports continued investment in the region's technological infrastructure, critics, respond that UTOPIA is an expensive "drain" on taxpayers. See Vince Horiuchi, "Lawmakers: Is It Time to Let UTOPIA Die?" *Salt Lake City Tribune*, September 19, 2012. Some critics argue that the private sector, not the government, should pay for the region's extensive infrastructure upgrade. See Colin Wood, "Now 10 Years Old, Utah's UTOPIA Tries to Beat the Odds," *Government Technology*, April 21, 2014, www.govtech.com/network/Now-10-Years-Old-Utahs-UTOPIA-Tries-to-Beat-the-Odds.html.

91. Edward Wyatt, "A City Wired for Growth," *New York Times*, February 4, 2014; Keith Schneider, "Chattanooga's Innovation District Beckons to Young Entrepreneurs," *New York Times*, August 16, 20016; David Flessner, "Chattanooga's Innovation District Revived the City: But Is It Sustainable?" *(Chattanooga) Times Free Press*, August 9, 2017.

92. Daphne T. Greenwood and Richard P.F. Holt, *Local Economic Development in the 21st Century: Quality of Life and Sustainability* (New York: Routledge, 2010 and 2015).

93. William M. Rohe, *The Research Triangle: From Tobacco Road to Global Prominence* (Philadelphia, PA: University of Pennsylvania Press, 2011), 96–105, 178–190.

94. Saskia Sassen, *Cities in a World Economy*, 4th ed. (Los Angeles: Pine Forge Press and Sage Publications, 2012).

95. Jacob L. Vigdor, "Immigration and the Revival of American Cities: From Preserving Manufacturing Jobs to Preserving the Housing Market," a report of the Partnership for a New American Economy and the Americas Society/Council of the Americas, September 2013, www.as-coa.org/sites/default/files/ImmigrationUSRevivalReport.pdf.

96. Robert Courtney Smith, "Mexicans: Civic Engagement, Education, and Social Progress Achieved and Inhibited," in *One Out of Three: Immigrant New York in the Twenty-First Century*, ed. Nancy Foner (New York: Columbia University Press, 2013).

97. Figures in the preceding two paragraphs are from Gustavo López and Kristen Bialik, "Key Findings about U.S. Immigrants," *Fact Tank: News in the Numbers*, a publication of the Pew Research Institute, May 3, 2017, www.pewresearch.org/fact-tank/2017/05/03/key-findings-about-u-s-immigrants/.

98. Brookings Institution, *Phoenix in Focus: A Profile from Census 2000* (Washington, DC, November 2003), www.brookings.edu/reports/2003/11_livingcities_Phoenix.aspx; Audrey Singer and Jill H. Wilson, *The Impact of the Great Recession on Metropolitan Immigration Trends* (Washington, DC: Brookings Institution, December 2010), www.brookings.edu/~/media/Files/rc/papers/2010/1216_immigration_singer_wilson/1216_immigration_singer_wilson.pdf; U.S. Census Bureau, "State & County QuickFacts: Phoenix (city), Arizona," revised June 28, 2013.

99. U.S. Census Bureau, "State & County Quick Facts: New York City, New York; Foreign-Born Population, 2012–2016."

100. Min Zhou, "Chinese: Diverse Origins and Destinies," in Foner, *One Out of Three*, 120–127.

101. Richard C. Jones, ed., *Immigrants Outside Megalopolis: Ethnic Transformation in the Heartland* (Lanham, MD: Lexington Books, 2008).

102. Chicano electoral victory in Denver, however, was not sustained. The four mayors who succeeded Peña were not Hispanic. Two of the mayors, Wellington Webb (1991–2003) and Michael Hancock (elected 2011, reelected 2015), were African American.

103. Jeremy Hein, *Ethnic Origins: The Adaptation of Cambodian and Hmong Refugees in Four American Cities* (New York: Russell Sage Foundation, 2006); Karl Byrand, "The Quest for Home: Sheboygan's Hmong Population," in *Immigrants Outside Megalopolis*, ed. Jones, 189–211.

104. Allie Shah, "Go Inside 'Little Mogadishu,' the Somali Capital of America," *(Minneapolis) Star-Tribune*, March 2, 2017.

105. Claire Galofaro, "How a Community Changed by Refugees Came to Embrace Trump," *AP News Release*, April 19, 2017, www.apnews.com/7f2b534b80674596875980b9b6e701c9.

106. Jill H. Wilson and Nicole Prchal Svajlenka, "Immigrants Continue to Disperse, With Fastest Growth in the Suburbs," a report of The Brookings Institution, Washington, DC, October 29, 2014, www.brookings.edu/research/immigrants-continue-to-disperse-with-fastest-growth-in-the-suburbs/.

107. Padma Rangaswamy, "Asian Indians in Chicago," in *The New Chicago*, ed. Koval, et al., 130–131.

108. 2016 population estimates are from the individual city profiles provided by the U.S. Census Bureau, *Quick Facts*, at the Bureau's interactive Web site, www.census.gov/quickfacts/.

109. Sassen, *Cities in a World Economy*, chap. 6.

110. U.S. Congressional Budget Office, *The Impact of Unauthorized Immigrants on the Budgets of State and Local Governments* (Washington, DC, December 2007).

111. Penn Wharton Budget Model, "The Effects of Immigration on the United States' Economy," University of Pennsylvania, June 27, 2016, http://budgetmodel.wharton.upenn.edu/issues/2016/1/27/the-effects-of-immigration-on-the-united-states-economy.

112. Edward Glaeser, *Triumph of the City* (New York: Penguin, 2011), 252. Also see Ted Hesson, "Why Cities Are Fighting to Attract Immigrants," *The Atlantic*, July 21, 2015, www.theatlantic.com/business/archive/2015/07/us-cities-immigrants-economy/398987/.

113. See, for example, Jin-Kyung-Yoo, *Korean Immigrant Entrepreneurs: Networks and Ethnic Resources* (New York: Routledge, 2013).

114. Richard Florida, "America's Leading Immigrant Cities: Trump Has It Backwards: Large Immigrant Populations Boost Rather Than Hurt U.S. Metros," *CityLab Web Posting*, September 22, 2015, www.citylab.com/equity/2015/09/americas-leading-immigrant-cities/406438/.

115. William H. Frey, "Immigration Levels Continue to Fuel Most Community Demographics Gains," *The Avenue*, a newsletter of The Brookings Institution, Washington, DC, August 3, 2017, www.brookings.edu/blog/the-avenue/2017/08/03/u-s-immigration-levels-continue-to-fuel-most-community-demographic-gains/.

116. Anthony Knapp and Igor Vojnovic, "Ethnicity in an Immigrant Gateway City: The Asian Condition in Houston," *Journal of Urban Affairs* 39, no. 3 (August 2016): 344–369.

117. Leah Binkovitz, "Why Houston Is Becoming More Accepting of Immigration," *Houston Chronicle*, May 2, 2017; Stephen L. Klineberg, *The Kinder Houston Area Survey: Thirty-Six Years of Measuring Responses to a Changing America*, a report of the Kinder Institute for Urban Research, Rice University, Houston, May 2017, https://kinder.rice.edu/uploadedFiles/Kinder_Institute_for_Urban_Research/HAS/2017%20Kinder%20Houston%20Area%20Survey%20FINAL.pdf.

118. Will Connors, "Cities in Midwest, Rustbelt Say They Need Immigrants," *Wall Street Journal*, January 31, 2017.

119. David Gladstone and Peter Marina, "Stemming Urban Decline in the Most Urbanized State in the United States: Latino Immigration and Urban Revitalization in New Jersey," paper presented at the annual meeting of the Urban Affairs Association, San Antonio, Texas, March 20, 2014. Gladstone and Marina's work is also being developed as a book, *New Hispanic Places: Immigration, Revitalization, and Urban Change in Post-Industrial New Jersey* (New York: Routledge, forthcoming).

120. Partnership for a New American Economy, "Immigrants Boost U.S. Economic Vitality through the Housing Market," *Press Release*, June 20, 2013, www.renewoureconomy.org/research/immigrants-boost-u-s-economic-vitality-through-the-housing-market/; and Vigdor, "Immigration and the Revival of American Cities." Also see "Do Immigrants Present an Untapped Opportunity to Revitalize Communities?' a joint report of the Welcoming Economies Global Network and the Fiscal Policy Institute, 20176, www.weglobalnetwork.org/wp-content/uploads/2016/10/WE_Distressed-Housing-Report_H.pdf. The Welcoming Economies Global Network is an immigration advocacy group.

121. For a review of the key studies on the impact of immigration on crime, see Robert Adelman, Lesley Williams Reid, Gayle Markle, Saskia Weiss, and Charles Jaret, "Urban Crime Rates and the Changing Face of Immigration: Evidence across Four Decades," *Journal of Ethnicity in Criminal Justice* 15, no. 1 (2017): 52–77. For the data that indicates a presence of unauthorized immigrants does not lead to higher crime rates when similarly communities are compared, see Anna Flagg, "Is There a Connection between Undocumented Immigrants and Crime?," a research report of The Marshall Project, New York, May 13, 2019, www.themarshallproject.org/2019/05/13/is-there-a-connection-between-undocumented-immigrants-and-crime.

122. Carol Morello and Luz Lazo, "Baltimore Puts Out Welcome Mat for Immigrants, Hoping to Stop Population Decline," *Washington Post*, July 24, 2012; Yvonne Wenger, "Mayor: Baltimore Is a 'Welcoming City" for Immigrants and Refugees," *Baltimore Sun*, November 17, 2016; Jayne Miller, "Baltimore: 'Welcoming" City for Immigrants, Not 'Sanctuary,'" *WBAL-TV News Report*, January 25, 2017, www.wbaltv.com/article/mayor-baltimore-welcoming-city-for-immigrants-not-sanctuary/8639210.

123. Fran Spielman, "Emanuel: Police Won't Detain Undocumented Immigrants Except for Serious Crime," *Chicago Sun-Times*, July 10, 2012.

124. Joe Smydo, "Pittsburgh Promise Aims to Lure Hispanics with Financial Aid," *Pittsburgh Post-Gazette*, September 27, 2012.

125. William J. Mitchell and Anthony M. Townsend, "Cyborg Agonistes: Disaster and Reconstruction in the Digital Electronic Era," in *The Resilient City: How Cities Recover from Disaster*, ed. Lawrence J. Vale and Thomas J. Campanella (New York: Oxford University Press, 2005), 313–334; Scott Calvert and Jon Kamp, "More U.S. Cities Brace for 'Inevitable' Hackers," *Wall Street Journal*, September 4, 2018.

126. Randy Shilts, *And the Band Played On: Politics, People, and the AIDS Epidemic* (New York: St. Martin's Press, 1987).

127. Climate Central, "These U.S. Cities Are Most Vulnerable to Major Coastal Flooding and Sea Level Rise," October 25, 2017, www.climatecentral.org/news/us-cities-most-vulnerable-major-coastal-flooding-sea-level-rise-21748.

128. Union of Concerned Scientists, "Is Global Warming Fueling Increased Wildfire Risks?" *Web Posting*, downloaded December 29, 2017, www.ucsusa.org/global-warming/science-and-impacts/impacts/global-warming-and-wildfire.html. Also see Rachel Cleetus and Kranti Mulik, *Playing with Fire: How Climate Change and Development Patterns Are Contributing to the Soaring Costs of Western*

Wildfires, a report of the Union of Concerned Scientists, July 2014, www.ucsusa.org/sites/default/files/legacy/assets/documents/global_warming/playing-with-fire-report.pdf.

129. "386 US Climate Mayors Commit to Adopt, Honor and Uphold Paris Climate Agreement Goals; Statement by the Climate Mayors in Response to President Trump's Withdrawal from the Paris Climate Agreement," June 1, 2017, https://medium.com/@ClimateMayors/climate-mayors-commit-to-adopt-honor-and-uphold-paris-climate-agreement-goals-ba566e260097.

130. Kristen Ljunkvist, *The Global City 2.0: From Strategic Site to Global Actor* (New York: Routledge, 2016).

131. Bethany Allen-Ibrahimian, "U.S. Cities Want to Join U.N. Migration Talks That Trump Boycotted," *Foreign Policy*, December 5, 2017, http://foreignpolicy.com/2017/12/05/u-s-cities-want-to-join-u-n-migration-talks-that-trump-boycotted/.

132. Rodrigo Tavares, *Paradiplomacy: Cities and States as Global Players* (New York: Oxford University Press, 2016).

133. Thomas L. Friedman, *The Lexus and the Olive Tree: Understanding Globalization* (New York: Anchor Books, 2000), 105.

134. Mark Purcell, *Recapturing Democracy: Neoliberalization and the Struggle for Alternative Urban Futures* (New York: Routledge, 2008), 109–152.

135. Dan Cook, "Is Oregon Good for Business?" *Oregon Business*, January 5, 2016, www.oregonbusiness.com/article/regional-report/item/16045-is-oregon-good-for-business.

136. Donald Rosdil, *The Cultural Contradictions of Progressive Politics: The Role of Cultural Change and the Global Economy in Local Policymaking* (New York: Routledge, 2012). Terry Nichols Clark, in *The City as an Entertainment Machine* (Lanham, MD: Lexington Books, 2011), 209–236, describes the emergence of a "new political culture" where cities give new emphasis to the lifestyle amenities and maintaining ecological sustainability. The new political culture often serves as a counterweight to the demands of the local growth coalitions.

137. Rosdil, *The Cultural Contradictions of Progressive Politics*, 10.

5 | Who Has the Power?

Decision Making and Economic Development in Cities and Suburbs

Who has the power to "get things done" in the urban arena? Whom do local governments serve? Why do cities subsidize sports stadiums despite numerous academic studies that point to the waste and economic inefficiency of such investments?

A review of the formal structure of local government—the formal authority of mayors, managers, and council members—cannot provide a full answer to these questions. A thorough examination of urban power requires a look "behind the scenes" to determine the extent to which offstage actors and economic and other considerations constrain the actions of municipal officials.

MOVING BEYOND THE OLD "POWER ELITE" VERSUS "PLURALISM" DEBATE

For too many years, two schools of thought—*power elite theory* and *pluralism*—dominated the debate over urban power. **Power elite theory** argues that "big business," wealthy families, and other behind-the-scenes notables effectively control the local arena. Elite theory views politics as inherently undemocratic, with elected officials acting to implement courses of action that business leaders and other local notables have already decided in private—in corporate boardrooms, country clubs, and other venues that are closed to public participation. Elite theory views public debate and the action of city councils and mayors to be of little importance, other than to provide the rituals of democracy that serve to build public acquiescence to the decisions that private powers have already made.[1] American popular culture continues to portray politics through the lens of elite theory, with numerous films pointing to the vast injustices that result when moneyed interests and corporate officials have a stranglehold over public decisions (see Box 5.1).

Pluralism (also called **pluralist theory**) rejects the view that businesses and other behind-the-scenes elites exert such a tight chokehold on local politics. Pluralists argue that elite theory too often reflects political paranoia and unsubstantiated conspiracy scenarios based only on anecdotal evidence. More comprehensive study, they argue, shows that numerous groups are able to influence government decisions.[2] Pluralism does not

Box 5.1
**Urban Films—A Corporate Power Elite: *Roger and Me*
and the Films of Michael Moore**

Michael Moore's "guerilla" documentary *Roger and Me* (1989) is one of the clearest
film statements ever of the immense and unaccountable power that corporate elites
possess in the local arena. Moore, a native of Flint, Michigan, traces the steep slide
of his beloved community, once known as an auto factory worker's paradise, into
postindustrial decline. Postindustrial Flint, according to Moore, was brought to ruin
by the self-serving actions of General Motors (GM). GM shifted automobile production to lower-wage assembly sites overseas, leading to the shutdown of assembly
lines and to extensive joblessness, poverty, housing foreclosures, evictions, and
property abandonment in Flint. Moore points to the villains responsible for Flint's
descent: General Motors and its then-CEO Roger Smith who cared more about the
corporation's bottom line than the communities in which GM was located. The top
managers of giant national global corporations even lack the sense of local loyalty
and roots exhibited by business elites in an earlier age, when major firms in a city
were run by homegrown owners and managers. Moore presents GM officials as
highly isolated, as living and operating in an environment removed from the working people of Flint. Ensconced in security-guarded corporate headquarters and
playing golf in private clubs, the contemporary corporate elite has little familiarity
with the people of the city and their daily lives and sufferings.

Moore's overall assessment of local politics is clear: The "people" have no
meaningful control over what happens in local communities like Flint—and in the
United States as a whole. In his films that followed, Moore repeats his indictment
of the undemocratic and unaccountable nature of elite power. *Bowling for Col-
umbine* (2002) highlights the self-serving actions of the American gun industry.
Sicko (2007) reveals extensive profit-taking by pharmaceutical giants and health
insurers and providers. *Capitalism: A Love Story* (2009) charges that hard-working
Americans lost their jobs and homes in Miami, Detroit, and other cities as a result
of the financial manipulations and profit-taking of the nation's banks and corporate
financial giants. Wall Street financial firms have big-money ties to both political
parties, which enable them to secure favorable legislative action from both the
Democratic and the Republican parties.

portray the United States and its cities as perfectly democratic. Pluralists accepts the
fact that power in the United States and in the American city is not distributed equally;
no one can seriously assert that the average citizen has the same political influence as
the CEO of a major corporation or a big-money campaign donor. But the recognition of
inequality is only a starting point for meaningful observations concerning the distribution of power in the American city.

Pluralists contend that power in the American city is spread more widely than elite theorists admit. Big businesses and established families are not the only ones who have power. Small business owners, environmentalist groups, coalitions of middle-class home-owners, anti-tax associations, poor people's groups, and growing immigrant populations all possess varying degrees of power that they can mobilize, especially when they feel threatened. Middle-class neighborhood groups and environmental activists in numerous communities, for instance, have been able to block a new commercial development or the construction of a costly new stadium, projects wanted by elite interests. In poorer portions of the city, neighborhood groups have been able to fight for community health clinics, preschool programs, and partnerships with the city to build affordable housing. Immigrant groups have been able to get cities to declare themselves as sanctuary cities or welcoming cities, with mayors and police chiefs vowing not to cooperate with the federal government's efforts to detain and expel undocumented residents who have committed no crime other than their immigration status.

Both elite theory and pluralism suffer as overstatements; each theory views local politics through a rather rigid ideological lens that fails to provide a more nuanced and accurate description as to how decisions are made in America's cities and suburbs.[3] Elite theory overstates the power of corporate interests to "govern" or rule over a city. Despite the contention of elite theorists, corporate interests are not all-powerful, and municipal officials are not their mere puppets. In most cities, "business" does not even denote a unified bloc of interests capable of coordinated political action. Major downtown revitalization projects, for instance, often face considerable opposition from small business owners and from businesses located outside the city center. Globaliza-tion, too, has pluralized business interests; corporate managers sent on assignment to a city by a multinational firm do not always share the perspectives of locally rooted business leaders.

In Houston, a city where local business interests have historically dominated city politics, immigration has altered the demography and politics of the city, leading munici-pal officials to give a new level of responsiveness to the concerns of Latinos, gays and lesbians, and other new arrivals to the city. This responsiveness is apparent even at a time when business interests pushed development projects that led to the virtual disap-pearance of historic ethnic sections of the city, including Chinatown, Little Saigon, and the African-American "Freedmen's Town."[4]

Pluralist theory suffers its own serious shortcomings. Corporations may lack the power to simply dictate a course of action to municipal officials. Still, cities and suburbs nonetheless wind up pursuing business growth and courses action heavily tilted toward business needs.

The pluralist perspective fails to recognize the influence of the urban **growth machine**—the coalition of businesses, real estate and financial firms, and even labor unions in the construction trades that benefit from continued governmental approval of, and subsidies for, growth projects.[5] The members of the growth machine always claim that growth projects are in the public interest, that new construction and growth will provide the jobs and tax base that will be of benefit to the entire community. Especially in big and medium-sized cities, the members of the growth machine make sizable campaign donations that give them access to elected officials. In the suburbs, local growth machines

Box 5.2
Elite Control or Reshaping the City for Competition? New York Constructs a New Economic Center at Hudson Yards

In 2019, New York City unveiled the commercial and culture facilities of the city's new and massive 26-acre economic center—a megaproject of soaring office towers, luxury residences, and high-end retail built on the West Side of Manhattan (just a bit south and west of Times Square). The project's central skyscrapers were constructed on platforms (weighing 37,000 tons!) above the Hudson Yards rail tracks of the MTA, the Metropolitan Transit Authority (Figure 5.1). With its luxury shops (Rolex; Cartier), fashionable restaurants (David Chang's Kawi), and exorbitantly priced condominiums (with prices reaching $4.3 million for a two-bedroom apartment and $32 million for a penthouse[1]), the project was clearly intended as a world-class center of office space and fine living.

Figure 5.1   **Hudson Yards, 2018: New York Builds a Dynamic New Economic Center on the West Side of Manhattan.** Just west of midtown Manhattan and Broadway, New York City is seeing the development of a new center of corporate skyscrapers and condominium towers that will change the city's skyline and provide first-class office space for the city's continued economic growth.

Source: Photo by art4stock / Shutterstock.com.

The gigantic development was built in the last remaining large area available for development near the heart of New York City. The Hudson Yards project sought to provide the sort of upscale and high-density spaces that would attract major corporations and "smart city" development to what had been a gritty edge of Manhattan, an area of rail yards, parking lots, aging warehouses and tenement buildings, and traffic congestion from nearby Lincoln Tunnel and the city's regional bus terminal,.

Government action and extensive public subsidies were critical to the area's upscaling and transformation. The city rezoned areas that had previously been designated for manufacturing. Further changes allowed developers to build at increased densities and soaring heights way above what was already permitted in the area. The city spent more than $2 billion to open a new subway station to enhance the accessibility of the area. The city also helped develop new green spaces in the Hudson Yards area, even extending the popular High Line elevated walkway to the project's core facilities. These supportive actions were vital to the livability and marketability of the new district. The city's expansion of the nearby Javits Convention Center further added to the attractiveness of the Hudson Yards location.

The construction at Hudson Yards offers much evidence to support the view that elite power makes many of the most important decisions in the modern city. Global businesses and other elites occupy the project's world-class offices and luxury residences. Only the super-rich can afford to pay $800 for a haircut at Sally Hershberger at "her over-the-top luxury salon for the chic, sophisticated consumer"[2] at Hudson Yards. Construction at Hudson Yards brought huge profits to property developers, real estate interests, the construction industry, and the financial firms and bondholders who provided the loans to help finance the massive project.

An examination of the project's financing further underscores aspects of elite power theory. Taxpayers paid for the infrastructure improvements that opened a new area of Midtown Manhattan to the investment class and other elite interests. Two creative financing mechanisms—Payments in Lieu of Taxes (PILOTs) and Tax Increment Financing (TIF)—operated in similar fashion. The city essentially borrowed money (by issuing bonds) to pay up front for infrastructure improvements essential to the project's construction. The city argued that high-value land uses would generate increased property tax receipts that would enable the city to pay off the incurred debt. Citizens were told that the Hudson Yards project would be "self-financing," that the project would pay for itself and require no subsidies from taxpayers.

The promise that the project was self-financed was never credible. The city paid for certain infrastructure improvements without even attempting to negotiate arrangements to insure that the city and its taxpayers would be reimbursed. In their efforts to recover as much property tax revenue as possible, city leaders approved other elite-oriented features of the project, such as high-density development and the construction of office and condominium towers at soaring heights. Officials virtually ignored objections from neighborhood groups that such a giganticized project threatened to transform the neighborhood into a wall of glass towers. The TIF arrangement also effectively tied much of the revenue gains from the project to future improvements in the immediate project area; the city could not use much of the property tax receipts from Hudson Yards to pay for improved public schools, senior centers, and municipal services in low-income and working-class sections of the city.[3]

But it is too reductive to view the construction of the Hudson Yards megaproject solely through the lens of elite power theory. The project did contain a few important spaces geared more to the general public than to private elites. The project's culture "Shed" was built with a telescopic outer wall set on rails to accommodate arts activities as small as poetry readings and as large as rock-oriented concerts and Fashion Week shows. Located at the center of the development, the "Vessel" (often referred to as the "Hive" or Beehive) was a honeycomb-shaped structure with spiraling steps that visitors could climb, at no charge, and take attractive cellphone photos of New York and neighboring New Jersey.

Even more significant, the Hudson Yards undertaking was a long time in the making and reflected the desires of public actors—not just private elites—intent on maintaining New York's global competitiveness. The project reflected the "let 'er rip" economic growth ideology of Mayor Michael Bloomberg. Bloomberg had Wall Street ties (Bloomberg News!) and an agenda of his own. The Mayor used the terrorist attacks of 9/11 to gain political leverage behind his project as he sought to transform New York City's West Side. Bloomberg argued that the gigantic project could serve as the city's global signature, enabling the city to rebound from the terrorist assault and to provide the high-end office and residential space necessary to the city's future economic dynamism.

Further details of the history of the West Side project reveal a number of inconsistencies with the view that elites governed and easily got their way. Elite interests actually faced extreme difficulty over the years in their efforts to win municipal approval for a massive and transformative West Side project, an idea that first emerged in the 1960s under Mayor John Lindsay. Neighborhood activists mobilized to thwart various projects aimed at upscaling Manhattan's West Side. Neighborhood groups succeeded in winning legislative protection of the area's low-rise residential character. The fervent opposition of the local community board and nearby citizen groups thwarted a much-publicized effort to build a new West Side football stadium for the New York Jets, a stadium that was to serve as a centerpiece in the city's bid to land the Summer Olympics. In these efforts, moneyed interests—even with the backing of the mayor—were unable to reshape Manhattan's West Side as they desired.[4]

The Hudson Yards development area that eventually won approval contains a sizable stock of affordable housing, built both on-site and off-site. The inclusion of affordable units underscroes the city's responsiveness to a wider set of constituencies than just a global elite. One-fourth of the residential units in the Hudson Yards area are dedicated to affordable housing. But housing activists lament that many of the affordable units are only small studio apartments that are not suitable for families.[5] Nonetheless, the project area contains a number of residential units that are truly affordable, especially when compared to prevailing housing prices on Manhattan. The 56-story residential tower at 555 Ten set aside 90 units as affordable housing to be awarded by lottery to eligible families. A two-person couple earning less than $35,500 a year would pay a monthly rent of only $660 for a one-bedroom apartment, a virtual steal by New York standards.[6]

Mayor Bloomberg initially proposed that 16 percent of the residential units be designated for affordable housing. But pressure from neighborhood groups and affordable housing advocates soon led the mayor to increase this number. To move the contentious project forward, the mayor in 2005 agreed to a deal with the City Council increasing the percentage of affordable units in the Hudson Yards area: 25 percent of the 13,600 new dwelling units in area would be affordable to moderate- and low-income New Yorkers. The ensuing election of Bill de Blasio, a self-styled progressive mayor, led to an even greater emphasis on housing affordability, resulting in additional affordable units built in the areas abutting the Hudson Yards district.[7] Non-elite actors had forced the inclusion of affordable housing at Hudson Yards!

The megaproject at Hudson Yards was *not* simply imposed on the city by elite actors. Affordable housing forces had an impact. The development of Hudson Yards was also the result of initiatives undertaken by local officials intent on expanding the New York City's competitiveness. Mayor Bloomberg and his deputy mayor for economic development, Daniel Doctoroff, played critical roles. Doctoroff proclaimed that New York, like any city, must increase its capacity to attract continued development in order to attract the quality work force, high-end investments, and ultimately the tax revenues that enable the city to meet its many service obligations.[8]

1. Matthew Schneier, "If You Guild It, Will They Come? Opening This Week" A New "Vertical Retail" Palace at Hudson Yards, *New York Times*, March 14, 2019.

2. The description is from "NEWS PROVIDED BY Sally Hershberger: Celebrity Hairstylist Sally Hershberger Unveils Sally Hershberger Hudson Yards, her New Flagship Salon at Hudson Yards in New York City," May 15, 2019, www.prnewswire.com/news-releases/celebrity-hairstylist-sally-hershberger-unveils-sally-hershberger-hudson-yards-her-new-flagship-salon-at-hudson-yards-in-new-york-city-300813044.html. The $800 price tag is reported by Schneier, "If You Guild It, Will They Come?

3. Bridget Fisher, "The Myth of Self-Financing: The Trade-Offs Behind the Hudson Yards Redevelopment Project," Schwartz Center for Economic Policy Analysis, The New School for Social Research, Working Paper #4, 2015, www.economicpolicyresearch.org/images/docs/research/political_economy/Bridget_Fisher_WP_2015-4_final.pdf.

4. Julian Brash, *Bloomberg's New York: Class and Governance in the Luxury City* (Athens, GA: University of Georgia Press, 2011) provides a critical analysis of Mayor Bloomberg's investment ideology, Brash observes the role played by community groups in stopping the proposed West Side New York Jets football stadium.

5. Shannon Mettern, "Instrumental City: The View from Hudson Yards, circa 2019," *Places* journal, April 2016, https://placesjournal.org/article/instrumental-city-new-york-hudson-yards/.

6. Laura Vecsey, "Housing Lottery Open at Luxe 555Ten in Hudson Yards," *StreetEasy* blog posting, August 22, 2017, https://streeteasy.com/blog/555-ten-affordable-housing-lottery-hudson-yards-apartments/.

7. Charles V. Bagli and Mike McIntier, "Mayor and Council Reach Deal on West Side Development," *New York Times*, January 11, 2005; "NYCEDC and HPD Release Plans to Bring Affordable Housing, Mixed-Use Development to Former Slaughterhouse Site on Far West Side of Manhattan," New York City Economic Development Corporation press release, May 8, 2017, www.nycedc.com/press-release/nycedc-and-hpd-release-plans-bring-affordable-housing-mixed-use-development-former.

8. Daniel L. Doctoroff, *Greater Than Ever: New York's Big Comeback* (New York: PublicAffairs, an imprint of Perseus Books, 2017).

provide the political impetus for the continuing development of "edge cities" such as Tyson's Corner, Virginia, outside Washington, DC.[6]

Newer theories of urban power recognize that local officials have the ability to make decisions on behalf of their communities—as pluralists often contend—but nonetheless still tend to pursue policy actions favored by the growth coalition. Cities and suburbs often compete to be the location of desirable businesses, a competition that even leads municipal officials to anticipate the needs of corporate leaders by proffering extensive tax breaks and other subsidies. As this chapter shall describe, a "newer" theory of urban power, urban **regime theory**, recognizes both the autonomy possessed by local elected officials and the need for local officials to turn to private-sector partners whose cooperation is essential to get "big things" done.

The contemporary city is a complex entity that no private elite can rule by mere command. Nonetheless, business entities often occupy a privileged place in local decision making (see Box 5.2).

CITY LIMITS: HOW ECONOMIC COMPETITION SHAPES LOCAL POLITICS

Why do many cities and suburbs pay so great attention to the concerns of business leaders? Paul Peterson, in his important book *City Limits*, offers one possible explanation.[7] According to Peterson, business influence in the local arena derives from the **mobility of capital**. The owners of a business can locate their facilities in another town or state. Municipal officials, fearing the loss of local jobs and tax contributions, take whatever actions are necessary to attract new businesses and retain existing businesses, actions that are necessary for the city's economic and fiscal health. Business executives can use the threat of siting their facilities elsewhere in order to leverage substantial tax abatements and other important concessions from municipal officials. The fierceness of intercity competition leads municipal leaders to pay great deference to the concerns of major corporations—a fact that was shamelessly put on display when more than 200 U.S. cities and suburbs offered Amazon very generous—in some cases absurdly generous—concessions when the giant Internet retailer announced that it was holding an open competition to see just where it would site its second national headquarters, Amazon's HQ2 (see Box 5.3).

Business leaders, however, do not exert control over the entire range of municipal affairs; instead, they focus on those public decisions that most directly affect their enterprises. Corporate executives are most concerned with **developmental policy**, that is, with redevelopment plans, infrastructure provision, and other public decisions that directly affect business investment and growth. Cities, according to Peterson, have little choice but to cater to business needs in the development arena. Cities provide the land-use plans, regulatory approvals, tax abatements, subsidies, and roads, sewers and other physical infrastructure improvements desired by business—or else face the prospect that a business will locate elsewhere.

Each city and suburb strives to maintain a reputation for being a place that is "good for business." Even an older suburb, such as affluent Arlington, Ohio, pursues new

Box 5.3
**238 Cities Attempt to Outdo One Another in the Amazing
Race to Win Amazon HQ2**

In 2017 and 2018, 238 cities and suburbs scrambled to outdo one another in an effort to win the location of Amazon's second North American headquarters, popularly referred to as Amazon HQ2. Amazon officials claimed the project would yield 50,000 local jobs.

The scale of the municipal offers was awe inspiring, as cities and states teamed jointly to piece together a winning incentive package. Chicago Mayor Rahm Emanuel and Illinois Governor Bruce Rauner, normally political antagonists, worked cooperatively to offer Amazon a vast package of incentives, including publicly provided workforce training and $2 billion in tax credits and other tax breaks—with the promise that they could offer Amazon still more if the city were chosen as one of the finalists in the HQ2 competition. As part of its package of inducements, Illinois even promised to give the income taxes collected from Amazon workers directly back to the company! The firm's workers would pay their full income tax obligation, but the money would be turned over to Amazon corporate officials instead of being used to fund schools and other public services.[1]

Maryland Governor Larry Hogan went even further, promising the web giant $3 billion in tax breaks as part of a $5 billion bid to bring HQ2 to suburban Montgomery County (just outside Washington, DC). Not to be outdone, New Jersey Governor Chris Christie offered Amazon an almost unbelievable $7 billion in tax incentives ($5 million in state tax reductions and another $2 million from the city) as Governor Christie worked with Mayor Ras Baraka in their effort to lure HQ2 to much-troubled Newark.[2] Detroit similarly promised to allow Amazon to operate for 30 years without have to pay property levies and various other taxes.[3] Such generous tax concessions virtually guaranteed that the mega development would produce little if any revenues that could be used for literacy and after-school programs or to improve infrastructure, policing, and public service provision in residential neighborhoods.

Fresno, which, like Detroit, did not make it to the second round of the competition, had said that it would put 85 percent of the revenues received from the project into a fund that would controlled by a new board—with half of the board's membership comprised of representatives from Amazon—that would decide just on what projects the city's revenues would be spent. In essence, the city was proposing to cede part of its governing authority to Amazon officials![4]

The competition for Amazon's HQ2 was all-pervasive. Even nominally progressive mayors like Los Angeles's Eric Garcetti and New York's Bill de Blasio helped to arrange very generous bids that were presented to the officials at Amazon.

1. Bill Ruthhart and Monique Garcia, "Illinois, Chicago Letter to Amazon: $2 Billion in Tax Breaks, Maybe More," *Chicago Tribune*, October 25, 2017; Danny Westneat, "This City Hall, Brought to You by Amazon," *Seattle Times*, November 24, 2017 (updated December 28, 2017).

2. Erin Cox, "Maryland Gov. Larry Hogan Details Amazon Pitch with $3 Billion in Tax Credits, $2 Billion in Transportation Projects," *Baltimore Sun*, January 22, 2018; Sarah Holder, "The Extreme Amazon Bidder Just Got Real," *CityLab web posting*, Nov 28, 2017, www.citylab.com/life/2017/11/the-extreme-amazon-bidder-just-got-real/546857/; Issie Lipowksy, "What's at Stake with Amazon's New HQ? Ask Newark," *WIRED*, January 19, 2018, www.wired.com/story/amazon-hq2-finalist-cities-newark/.

3. Nick Wingfield, "How Amazon Benefits from Losing Cities' HQ2 Bids," *New York Times*, January 28, 2018.

4. Westneat, "This City Hall, Brought to You by Amazon"; Holder, "The Extreme Amazon Bidder Just Got Real."

development projects in order to provide the types of housing and leisure activities that would increase the community's appeal to young professionals and technologically oriented businesses.[8]

Business leaders are also concerned with **redistributive policy**, which encompasses social welfare, health, housing, and other programs of assistance to the poor. Corporate executives do not wish to have their facilities taxed in order to support welfare-type programs. Peterson argues that American cities have little choice but to meet the concerns of business even at the price of ignoring the needs of more vulnerable residents:

> [T]he pursuit of a city's economic interests, which requires an efficient provision of local services, makes no allowance for the care of the needy and unfortunate members of the society. Indeed, the competition among local communities all but precludes a concern for redistribution.[9]

Peterson posits a **theory of "city limits"**: The need to maintain a city's economic competitiveness imposes severe constraints on the city's ability to pursue a broad range of social welfare and housing programs.

Corporate officials, however, have no great stake in issues of **allocational policy**, decisions that municipalities make regarding just how various services—such as fire stations, library books, and computer facilities—are distributed among neighborhoods. Such service decisions seldom have a great impact on business well-being. Corporate elites pay little attention to such matters, leaving local officials great freedom to act on matters that lie in this broad policy area.

BUILDING NEW STADIUMS: WHY CITIES IGNORE THE STUDIES OF ECONOMISTS AND OTHER ACADEMICS

Intercity competition helps to explain why local authorities continue to spend vast sums of taxpayer money to aid the multimillionaire owners of sports franchises who seek new arenas with luxury skyboxes, restaurants, and computerized state-of-the-art scoreboards. Cities provide team owners with generous tax abatements and other subsidies for stadium construction. Signed contracts often commit the city to costly land giveaways and cede to team owners the revenues from stadium-naming rights, parking, and other concessions. Stadium deals further saddle taxpayers with the costs of various hidden subsidies that only become fully apparent during the post-construction operation of a facility.[10]

Numerous economic studies show that public investment in sports arenas is a very expensive and inefficient way to create new jobs and that stadium construction seldom produces strong economic benefits for a city.[11] Sports-related development suffers from a **substitution effect**; the increased economic activity around a new ballpark is offset by the displacement of existing businesses in the area and a decline in entertainment and dining activity elsewhere in the city.[12] A new downtown stadium may generate new activity and increased property values in the immediate vicinity of the arena; but such projects seldom contribute to a rise in incomes throughout the city. Stadiums do not host major events 365 days a year; a football or professional soccer stadium or ice hockey arena may be open for a relatively few days (or nights) each year. On days when there are no sports events, the stadium area is a lifeless "black hole" rather than a revenue producer.

So, why do cities pursue such seemingly unwise sports investments? It is not simply that team owners make large political campaign donations or that local elected officials fear the wrath of fans if a team leaves town. A city also gains certain competitive advantages from having a major sports franchise, a presence that tells the global business community that the city is "major league" and worthy of major private investment. A new stadium also provides "intangible benefits" in terms of community pride and heightened image of a city, making a community more attractive to residents as well as to business.[13] In contrast, the loss of a sports franchise signals that a city is in decline and maybe even that the city is not a particularly "good place for business." Municipal officials fear the local economic repercussion if business officials begin to perceive a community as irresponsive to business needs.

Fiscally ravaged Detroit cut a deal with the NBA Pistons, reducing the tax on tickets and agreeing to subsidize a new practice arena and garage, in order to lure the professional basketball team back from suburban Auburn Hills to a reconstructed downtown Little Caesars Arena. The city and the downtown development authority further agreed to commit $34.5 million in bond proceeds to modify the hockey-oriented Little Caesars Arena so that it could also be used for pro basketball. Under the "community benefits agreement" which was part of the deal, the Pistons agreed to hire local residents for half of the construction jobs on the project. The team also agree to refurbish more than 60 basketball courts in parks located throughout the city and to provide 200,000 free tickets to Detroit youth each season.[14]

Sports franchises use their mobility to leverage lucrative municipal subsidies. Team owners can hint at moving elsewhere and underscore the "better deal" offer that they have received from a competitor city. The threat to relocate can be real. The NBA Seattle Supersonics became the Oklahoma City Thunder. The basketball Nets moved from New Jersey to the showcase Barclays Center in downtown Brooklyn in New York City. The NFL Rams moved from Los Angeles to St. Louis, only to return to L.A. two decades later (2016), and then to leave the City of Angels once again for an anticipated 2020 move to a new stadium in suburban Inglewood. The Oakland Raiders are especially footloose, having moved to Los Angeles in 1982 only to return to Oakland in 1995—with the football team later announcing a scheduled 2020 move to Las Vegas.

In many cases, however, the threat of franchise relocation is highly exaggerated. The mobility of a great many franchises is overstated, as a team must rebuild its fan base if it relocates to a new metropolitan area. In such cases, the threat to leave is simply a "card" that franchise owners play in their effort to gain maximum public concessions. As Pittsburgh Penguins owner and former NHL superstar Mario Lemieux candidly revealed after the city agreed to fund a new hockey arena:

> Our goal was to remain here in Pittsburgh all the way. Those trips to Kansas City and Vegas was [sic] just to go, and have a nice dinner and come back. . . . That was just a way for us to put more pressure, and we knew it would work at the end of the day.[15]

Hints that the Chicago Cubs might possibly leave Wrigley Field for a possible facility in Rosemont or another suburb helped team owners to gain city approval of development plans that included a nearby hotel as well as the addition of a video screen, new advertising space, and other upgrades that would alter the appearance of landmarked Wrigley Field, the oldest ballpark in the National League.

Public officials can never be sure if a team's threat to leave is real or not. Nor do they know just what concessions franchise owners truly require to keep the team in a city. As a result, elected officials tend to err on the side of safety, agreeing to more generous concessions than what is absolutely necessary to retain a franchise.

Franchise relocation is not always profitable, at least in the short term. The Chargers had the lowest attendance in the National Football League in 2017 after relocating from San Diego to Los Angeles and having to play in an undersized facility while awaiting the construction of a new Inglewood stadium. Crowds at their temporary home were so sparse that empty seats were readily visible even though the temporary facility could only seat 27,000. The club placed black tarp over some seating sections, a visual trick to make the stadium appear to be more full than it actually was. The Chargers, in their move north, alienated fans from San Diego and had not yet built an enthusiastic fan base in Los Angeles.[16]

The members of a city's growth machine add to the lobbying pressures for new stadium construction. Labor union leaders point to the jobs that new construction will generate. Consultant studies emphasize the new revenue stream that a city will tap as a result of stadium development. These forecasts, often paid for by members of the growth coalition, tend to underestimate the costs of a new stadium while overestimating the future revenues that the project will yield. All of this leads local officials to sign legally binding, **one-sided stadium contracts** where local taxpayers, not the team owners, are left "on the hook" when costs rise and revenues are less than what had been predicted.

Cincinnati provides a clear illustration of a one-sided stadium deal. Amid talk that the city could lose it professional football team, citizens in Hamilton County (greater Cincinnati) voted to increase the local sales tax in order to fund two new riverfront stadiums—one for the football Bengals and the other for the baseball Reds. To convince voters to approve the ballot measure, the growth machine promised that revenues from the new sales tax would not only pay for the stadiums but would also provide tax relief for the homeowners and provide for additional spending for the area's public schools. Downtown business interests created a pseudo-grassroots organization to garner public support behind the measure, purchasing a million dollars in television ads to overcome what polls revealed to be great public resistance to the giveaways.

The ballot measure passed, and the two stadiums were built. But when the economy slumped and the sales tax failed to yield the revenues that the consultants had projected, it was only the public schools, county services, and the promise of homeowner relief—and not the subsidies provided the sports franchises—that suffered cutbacks. The one-sided contract committed the government to paying for such upgrades to the Bengals's stadium as a multimillion-dollar state-of-the art holographic replay machine. The contract even barred the county from placing new taxes on tickets, parking, and concessions in an effort to generate additional monies to help to defray the costs of the public's obligations.[17] In the years that followed, continued talk that the Bengals could leave Cincinnati was used to thwart any effort to impose new fees on stadium-related activity.

In Georgia, Cobb County's decision to build a suburban ballpark to woo the Braves from central Atlanta provides an even more recent example of a one-sided deal that saddled area taxpayers with large and often hidden obligations (see Box 5.4). But a municipality cannot be certain that the provision of extensive subsidies will bind a team to the city. The NBA Miami Heat demanded construction of a new arena with increased seating capacity and a greater number of luxury suites to replace the "obsolete" Miami Arena that local authorities had opened just eight years previous.[18]

Not every stadium deal is bad for a city.[19] Indianapolis shows that a city can be among the "major league winners" if its investment in sports facilities is part of a strategic plan to raise the city's economic profile. In San Diego, public authorities and the owners of the baseball Padres formed a public-private partnership to share the costs of a new downtown ballpark.[20] Public authorities paid the bulk of the $450 million costs for land acquisition, infrastructure improvements, and construction. Signed **memos of understanding** with the developers ensured that team owners would make a financial commitment to construct a "Ballpark Village" of shops and activities in the underdeveloped 26-block area lying just beyond the fences of Petco Park.

Although the San Diego partnership is held out as a model, the stadium deal has also received intense criticism. Taxpayers paid the up-front costs of the stadium; but the contract gave the private developers—not the public—the profits from the Ballpark Village project. As construction proceeded, the developers scaled back their earlier promise to build affordable housing. The developers also built a smaller green park than the one that was pictured when they initially presented the project design to the voters. The costs borne by city taxpayers also increased when the development did not generate the revenues that the project's enthusiasts had projected. Tax Increment Financing arrangements served to ensure that any gains in property tax revenues in the project area would be used to finance additional improvements in the immediate project area; the revenue gains could not be used to improve city schools or to improve public services in residential neighborhoods across the city.[21]

Memos of understanding and more formalized **community benefit agreements (CBAs)** are useful tools to help assure that a new development will provide jobs, training opportunities, funds for parks development and affordable housing, and other activities that will benefit poorer residents in the immediate vicinity of the project. In Los Angeles a coalition of activist labor unions, community-based organizations, and advocates for the homeless successfully challenged the city's growth coalition, demanding a CBA as the price for consenting to the construction of the downtown Staples sports arena and entertainment district.[22]

Box 5.4
**Cobb County Pursues the Atlanta Braves—and
the Braves Win**

In 2013, the Atlanta Braves announced that they were moving to suburban Cobb
County, leaving Turner Field, their 20-year home in central Atlanta that was built as
part of the city's construction program for the 1996 Summer Olympics. Cobb County
offered a reported $450 million (some reports put the figure as high as $672 million) in subsidies and infrastructure improvements. Still additional public costs were
incurred as public authorities needed to upgrade highway access and bus service
to a stadium that was not situated on a MARTA rail line. Critics surmised that
the Braves were looking for a new state-of-the art facility and wished to leave the
inner-city African-American neighborhood that surrounded Turner Field.[1]

The initial Sun Trust Stadium deal was so advantageous to the Braves that it even
gave team owners a monopoly on parking, barring other privately-run game-day
parking on major streets within a half mile of the stadium. Howls of protest, however,
soon led the County to remove the parking lot ban.[2] Still Cobb County taxpayers were
on the hook for more than $6 million in subsidies for the bonds issued for stadium
construction, another $1.2 for stadium operations and maintenance, $1.6 million for
police overtime and traffic management for stadium events, and tens of millions of
dollars in transportation improvements and other infrastructure upgrades to support
the stadium.[3] Taxpayer outrage over the extensive subsidies resulted in the 2016
landslide defeat of the chair of the Cobb County Commission, the public official who
had been a prime mover behind the stadium deal.

Intraregional competition had allowed the owners of the Braves to find a better
deal in suburban Cobb County. Cobb County's taxpayers assumed much of the
costs of the Braves's move.[4]

1. Bill Torpy, "Stadium Move Angers Its Neighbors," *Atlanta Journal-Constitution*, November
13, 2013. Also see the comments of former Atlanta Braves pitcher John Rocker, "Who Wants to
Fight Crime on the Way to the Ballpark?" *WND: Commentary*, November 20, 2013, www.wnd.
com/2013/11/who-wants-to-fight-crime-on-way-to-ballpark/.

2. Dan Klepal, "SunTrust Parking Restricted Near Cobb County Stadium," *Atlanta Journal-
Constitution*, June 29, 2016; Meris Lutz, "Cobb to Suspend Parking Ban on Private Property Near
Braves Stadium," *Atlanta Journal-Constitution*, July 12, 2016.

3. Meris Lutz, "Braves' New Stadium Hardly a Home Run for Cobb County Taxpayers," *Atlanta
Journal-Constitution*, December 26, 2017.

4. Neil deMause, "Cobb County Chair Who Masterminded Braves Deal Gets Booted in Landslide,"
Field of Schemes blog, July 27, 2016, www.fieldofschemes.com/2016/07/27/11396/cobb-county-
chair-who-masterminded-braves-deal-gets-booted-in-landslide/.

There are still other ways to make stadium projects more equitable. The imposition of
a tax on hotel rooms, for instance, has an industry that benefits from stadium development share in its costs rather than burdening city residents with the costs of subsidizing
the facility (see Box 5.5).

Box 5.5
Are There Better Ways to Finance a New Stadium?
San Francisco and Minneapolis

Stadium deals are not all equally one-sided and bad for taxpayers. Some cities negotiate a better deal than others.

In San Francisco, the history of citizen opposition to corporate-oriented growth projects strengthened the hand of municipal officials in their negotiations with sports team owners. As a result, public authorities in San Francisco were able to strike a deal where they paid only 14 percent of the capital costs of a new Giants ballpark—much less than the 44 percent of capital costs shouldered by the public in Detroit and the 95 percent paid by the public in Baltimore for new ballparks!

Santa Clara, in the heart of affluent Silicon Valley, took a similarly strong posture in its negotiations with the NFL football 49ers who sought to move to a state-of-the-art stadium just 25 miles south of San Francisco. The bargaining position of public officials was strengthened by a voter initiative that barred Santa Clara from levying new taxes to support the stadium. Team owners could only get their desired Silicon Valley stadium by agreeing to pick up a greater share of project costs than was typical in other cities. The new stadium was built in the center of a region where information and digital technology workers received extraordinarily high salaries. Consequently, the owners of the 49ers agreed to pick the costs, knowing that the team could easily raise $40 million through the sale of **seat licenses**—where willing fans each paid thousands of dollars for the right to purchase tickets to future games. The sale of **naming rights** to Levi Strauss & Sons generated an additional $220 million over five years, with the facility called Levi's Stadium.

In Minnesota, voter reluctance to approve subsidies for a new stadium similarly strengthened city officials in their bargaining sessions with the city's major league baseball team. The owners of the Minnesota Twins had hinted they would consider relocating the team to Charlotte or another city if they could not get a new ballpark to replace the aging Metrodome. But local citizens objected to the use of taxpayer money. In the face of local resistance, team owners and their growth-coalition allies shifted their lobbying efforts to the state capitol. The state government intervened to assure the construction of Target Field, but without the expensive retractable dome that team owners had sought.

The Minnesota Vikings then hiked (pardon the pun) their own demands for a new state-of-the-art downtown football facility to replace the three-decades-old Metrodome (also know as Mall of America Field). Team owners intimated that, if a new stadium were to be rejected, hey would sell the franchise and have the team move out of state. Again, the state government intervened and arranged the financing for the new stadium. Similar to the 49ers and Levi's Stadium, the owners of the Vikings sold seat licenses, essentially having fans help pay for the franchise's share of the stadium's costs.

Compared to one-side deals struck in cities like Cincinnati, the Santa Clara deal is more balanced and places less of a financial burden on homeowners and ordinary citizens. But even in "good" stadium deals, the general public still incurs substantial costs, having to pick up roughly half the costs of the construction. In Minneapolis, the city was also responsible for building 1,400 parking spaces for the Vikings. The Minnesota state legislature authorized a citywide sales tax surcharge to help cover the public's costs of the new Vikings stadium. A sales tax is a regressive revenue instrument that places a disproportionate burden on a city's poorer residents—residents who cannot afford the price of attending a game. Minnesota also enacted a new state tax on "pull tab" gambling to generate additional revenues for the stadium without directly burdening homeowners with increased property taxes. When pull-tab gaming failed to produce the proceeds that team consultants had so confidently projected, the taxpayers had to cover the difference.

The San Francisco, Santa Clara, and Minnesota cases illustrate two of the guiding principles for a more fair or equitable stadium deal. First, financing should, follow the **benefit principle**: Persons and interests who benefit from a project should directly contribute to the project. The benefit principle justifies the imposition of seat license fees, a tax surcharge on tickets, and the levy of special hotel, restaurant, and bar taxes on enterprises that enjoy greater patronage as a result of stadium events. Santa Clara placed a room surcharge on hotels located within two miles of the stadium.

Second, **spread the responsibility for financing a new stadium over a large geographical area** rather than place the financial burden for construction on a single city. If a new stadium truly contributes to the "major league" image and economic marketability of a state or metropolitan area, then the state or metropolitan region should share in the costs of construction. State action is often necessary to set up financing arrangements that extend beyond the borders of a single city or county.

Sources: The San Francisco, Detroit, and Baltimore figures are cited by Judith Grant Long, *Public-Private Partnerships for Major League Sports Facilities* (New York: Routledge, 2013), 14; also see chap. 7. For further discussion of the Santa Clara and Minnesota and stadium deals, see: Richard Meryhew, "Doubts, Controversy Exist over $975 Million Vikings Stadium Deal," *Minneapolis Star Tribune*, September 27, 2013; Michael Powell, "Sniffing for Dollars at Home of the Vikings," *New York Times*, October 3, 2014; and "Levi's Stadium Is a Model for Privately Financed Stadiums," *San Francisco Chronicle*, February 4, 2016.

However, the efforts to reform stadium finance do not always work as anticipated. Even a CBA may not serious alter the balance of benefits and costs in a stadium's construction. Too often, key provisions in a CBA are phrased only as goals and are not legally binding on franchise owners. City administrators are often reluctant to release financial data that would allow community members to see just where team owners are and are not living up to the promises they made. The seeming commitments of a CBA can often be evaded or watered down during a project's implementation.[23]

Critics charge that the negotiation of a CBA may provide political "cover" that enables team owners and developers to win approval for their projects. In New York City, developers pointed to the existence of community benefits agreements to argue that it was safe to approve a number of controversial development projects, including the construction of Atlantic Yards (with Barclay's Arena as its centerpiece), a new Yankee Stadium, and even the expansion of Columbia University's footprint into historic sections of black Harlem.[24]

Sports interests can circumvent strident local opposition by arranging approvals and subsidies through the state government. In Chicago, Atlanta, Minneapolis (see Box 5.5), and a number of other cities, state officials intruded to keep stadium projects alive when local official refused to cede to the requests of franchise owners. The states essentially took key decisions on stadium construction from the hands of local elected officials and placed important finance powers (such as the authority to issue bonds to finance construction) in the hands of a state-created board or authority.

As this brief review of stadium politics reveals, no behind-the-scenes elite exists with the power to dictate the construction of a new stadium. Stadium construction and public subsidies for new arenas are proving increasingly controversial. While team owners often "win," they seldom get the full subsidies they desire; not all cities are inept and amateurish bargainers. Even where local officials view a new stadium as a key to economic development, the negotiations between franchise owners and public officials can be lengthy and protracted.

Still, team owners in general are able to get what they want—or, to be more accurate, more of what they want. The power of franchise owners is rooted in the perceived threat inherent in the team's geographical mobility and their ability to convince local—and state—leaders that the threat to relocate is real.

WHAT DRIVES THE OVERINVESTMENT IN CITY AND COUNTY CONVENTION CENTERS?

Downtown businesses and their growth machine allies push cities to build and enlarge convention centers. City boosters argue that an updated convention center is essential for a healthy local economy, that only the construction of new facilities can prevent the loss of conventions and tourism-related patronage to other communities. Prestigious consulting firms (such as KPMG Peat Marwick, Price Waterhouse, and Conventions, Sports and Leisure International) prepare detailed analyses with extensive charts, tables, and statistics that purport to clearly demonstrate the economic benefits that a city will derive from investing in a new convention center.

But is expansive public investment in a new or expanded convention center really that good for a city? In most cases, convention centers fail to produce the jobs and extensive economic benefits that growth advocates had predicted. Convention centers that cannot run a full calendar of events do not produce the economic impacts that the consultants had envisioned. Center managers offer discounts and other incentives in an effort to fill "dark" days where no activity is scheduled. As Heywood

T. Sanders, an urbanist who compared the promises with the reality of convention centers, observes:

> But while communities have proven remarkably capable of building new and larger centers, they have proven remarkably unsuccessful in filling them. From Atlanta to Seattle, Boston to Las Vegas, the promises of local officials and the forecasts of consultants have come up short. State and local governments have built modern new centers, only to see half or less of the convention attendees promised by the consultants. Other cities have expanded their existing centers, yet failed to see any consistent increase in business. Indeed, there is substantial evidence that the supply of convention center space substantially exceeds demand (a "buyer's market"), with cities desperately competing by offering their center space rent free.[25]

As the result of dark nights and discounted prices, convention centers underperform and require additional monies from taxpayers.

The growing competition for the convention business means that even in a major city like Chicago, a convention center will have difficulty in filling its schedule with top-rate conventions. McCormick Place, Chicago's premier tradeshow venue, faced declining business and attendance despite the expenses undertaken for facility's modernization and expansion. Chicago faces competition from Las Vegas, Orlando, and other cities that upgraded their tradeshow facilities. In 2008, the number of major tradeshows at Chicago's McCormick Place dwindled to only two. The State of Illinois offered tradeshow organizers $10 million in incentives and rebates, an effort to lure major tradeshows to an underperforming McCormick Place.[26]

The rise of the Internet poses an important threat to convention attendance. Professionals are beginning to discover that they can update their credentials by completing online courses without having to incur the expense of attending a national conference. Convention centers are a less productive investment for a city than they once were.[27]

Why do cities—big and small and many suburbs as well—invest lavishly in new and upgraded convention facilities when there is too little convention and tradeshow business to fill all of the convention center space that has already been built across the nation? In many cities, local officials are convinced by the market analyses provided by the hired-gun consulting firms of the growth coalition. The analyses often contain very precise figures of the economic return that a city will receive on its investment. However, such figures often are little more than guesses based on overly optimistic assumptions regarding tradeshow attendance and just how much visitors will spend in the city.[28]

HOW CITIES CAN WOO BUSINESSES: MOVING BEYOND A STRATEGY OF TAX CUTS

Paul Peterson's theory of "city limits" points to the constraints that economic competition imposes on local officials. But Peterson overstates the case, especially in his contention that cities have no real choice but to maintain their economic competitiveness by keeping taxes low and by minimizing social spending and other redistributive programs.

A policy of low taxes does not provide the only path—or even the most viable path—to local economic prosperity. Technology-oriented firms do not always desire locations in low-tax, low-service communities. "Knowledge" enterprises look favorably on communities that have quality schools and effective job training programs. The provision of quality recreational facilities and lifestyle amenities also helps a community attract creative workers and other professionals.

Peterson overstates the mobility of businesses.[29] Not every business is free to pick up and relocate to a community that offers more extensive subsidies and tax abatements. Local tax rates are *not* the Number One factor in a business-siting decision. Businesses give greater consideration to the quality of the local labor force and a site's transportation infrastructure, as well as a community's accessibility to suppliers and markets. A business may also be hesitant to uproot—and possibly lose—top executives and talented personnel.

In cases where firms are not totally free to relocate, municipal leaders have much greater policy discretion than Peterson assumes. Cities and suburbs can pursue more balanced priorities—including spending on housing and social services—without worrying that each spending choice will lead to an exodus of business.

Many communities adopt programs that offer support services to existing businesses and that nurture the growth of smaller and more entrepreneurial firms.[30] Cities can provide locally owned businesses a variety of supports, including managerial assistance and mentoring partners, low-interest loans, space in new projects (and even the adaptive reuse of vacant buildings), and preferences in city purchasing.[31] A number of cities welcome immigrants and seek to assist immigrant entrepreneurs, a much different development strategy than focusing solely on efforts to attract major corporations.[32]

REGIME THEORY: POWER AS SOCIAL PRODUCTION

Urban theorist Clarence Stone asks, "Why, when all of their actions are taken into account, do officials over the long haul seem to favor upper-strata interests, disfavor lower-strata interests, and sometimes act in apparent disregard of the contours of electoral power?"[33] To a great extent, the answer can be found in the dependence of municipal leaders on private business to "get things done," what Stone has called **social production**. Even when no all-powerful elite rules a city, top elected officials eventually come to recognize that they need the cooperation of business leaders to get important things done for the community. Business leaders can be important partners to a city that seeks to reenergize its downtown, create new jobs, redevelop troubled neighborhoods, and provide mentoring and employment opportunities for at-risk youth. In these and a great many other policy areas, city and suburban officials can hardly accomplish much without the cooperation of the private sector.

Business executives, in turn, find that they often need the cooperation of public officials to realize their own goals. Business growth and expansion requires government
approvals (i.e. zoning and land-use approvals and the issuance of business licenses and
permits) and the provision of public subsidies. As city-business cooperation provides
mutual benefits, public-private partnerships can even emerge in a city where government
leaders and business heads have different political philosophies and different partisan
allegiances.

In some instances, business cooperation is so crucial to the success of a civic project
that a project cannot be completed without their help. Business leaders have **preemptive
power**; their refusal to cooperate can effectively doom a course of action they disfavor.
However, while business leaders may effectively hold veto power over a project, they
do not necessarily possess the ability to force a city to do their bidding across a broad
range of policy areas. To accomplish their ends, business leaders forge a working accommodation with public officials.[34]

LOOKING BEYOND ELECTIONS TO GOVERNING REGIMES

Elections by themselves do not determine power and what gets done in a city. A newly
elected mayor cannot do whatever he or she pleases. To get important things done, the
mayor will often find it necessary to gain the cooperation of actors who were not a part
of the mayor's electoral base.

An **urban regime** (also called a **governing regime**) exists when an informal working coalition of governmental and nongovernmental actors persists over a significant
number of years with the capacity to decide the overall policy direction that a city will
pursue. The concept of an urban regime denotes the formation of a public-private alliance of considerable significance that lasts from one municipal administration to the
next. Public-private partnerships that are only temporary and fail to endure beyond a
single mayoral term do *not* constitute an urban regime.

Regime theory shifts the focus when studying urban politics. Regime analysis gives
less attention to elections and pays greater attention to the post-election arrangements
that govern a city. The election of an African-American or Latino mayor and city council, for instance, does not guarantee the emergence of Black Power or Latino Power;
election results provide no guaranty that municipal officials will be able to produce
policy actions that respond to the needs and concerns of African-American and Hispanic
residents. After winning office, African-American and Latino officials often discover
the necessity of their working cooperatively with business leaders and other influentials
who control investment capital and other resources critical to the health of the city and
its communities.[35]

The composition of a city's governing regime can be quite different from the electoral
coalition that put the mayor and city council into office. In Atlanta the city's black popular
majority has dominated municipal elections in recent decades. But an examination of
what happens in Atlanta after an election is over reveals that local business leaders have
been able to maintain a privileged position in the biracial regime that governs Atlanta
(see Box 5.6).

Box 5.6
Atlanta's Biracial Governing Regime Under Pressure

During the civil rights era in the middle of the twentieth century, Atlanta remained relatively calm, especially when compared to the turmoil taking place in other cities in the South. Atlanta proclaimed itself to be the "City Too Busy to Hate." Even during the later years of segregation, a biracial governing regime ruled Atlanta. Whites held elected municipal offices and responded to the concerns of local business leaders. Business leaders, however, recognized the advantages of forging cooperative arrangements with black leaders, especially with leaders of the city's large African-American middle-class community.

Blacks and whites in Atlanta did not see eye to eye on a great many issues, and the informal cooperative arrangement that emerged was far from an equal partnership. Nonetheless, Atlanta's business leaders and spokespersons from the African-American community recognized that their mutual interests could be served by having the city pursue a path of moderate progress on civil rights, a course of action that averted the civil unrest that scared away customers from the downtowns other cities in the South.[1]

Atlanta has changed considerably since the civil rights era. Since that time, African Americans have gained effective control of city hall; a majority black electorate has consistently chosen a black mayor and a black-majority city council. Demographic changes—including the exodus of whites to the suburbs—helped to cement the electoral hold that African Americans in Atlanta have on city hall. Still, despite the outward appearance of "black power," African-American officials in Atlanta routinely seek to work cooperatively with major businesses. As a result, members of the business community continue to maintain considerable influence in the governance of the New Atlanta despite the dwindling number of white elected officials in the city.

Public-private arrangements have not always come about easily, and intergroup suspicions remain. Yet, public-private accommodation was already evident during the years of the city's first two African-American mayors, a time when the city politics was otherwise plagued by sharp racial division. Maynard Jackson (serving 1974–1982 and 1990–1994) was a political outsider who initially challenged the Atlanta system of elite-led accommodation. Much to the horror of white business leaders, Jackson insisted on strong affirmative-action hiring policies, including a requirement that 20 percent of the contracts on development projects be awarded to minority firms. White business leaders disliked Jackson but still recognized the necessity of maintaining a working relationship with city hall. Jackson, in turn, discovered that he needed the assistance of the business community on important civic projects. The city approved the construction of a new international airport, the business community's Number One priority. In return, businesses acceded to affirmative-action requirements in hiring and contracting. Mayor Jackson gave renewed attention to Atlanta's economic redevelopment, backing away from his earlier focus on neighborhood-oriented planning.

Jackson's mayoral successor, Andrew Young (1982–1990), a political associate of the late Martin Luther King, Jr., gave still greater emphasis to working with businesses for the city's economic growth. Young even backed efforts to bring the Summer Olympics to Atlanta, a project that necessitated the demolition of homes in a low-income section of the city in order to clear space for Olympics facilities, including a new ballpark (which later became the home of the Atlanta Braves).[2]

Does a biracial regime still govern Atlanta today? Globalization and demographic shifts have weakened the biracial arrangement that had governed Atlanta for so many years. Corporate managers assigned to Atlanta lack the familiarity necessary to maintain smooth working relations with local black leaders. The African-American community has splintered along class lines, with leaders in the city's poorest neighborhoods arguing that the biracial governing partnership has largely forsaken poor neighborhoods for growth projects favored by the city's large population of black professionals.[3]

Low black voter turnout, the outmigration of black middle-class voters to the suburbs, the growth of the city's Hispanic population, and the arrival of white gentrifiers have all served to diminish black electoral power in the city. As a result, in 2009, the outspoken Kasim Reed, an African American, was able to win the mayoralty by a mere margin of only 714 votes over a white challenger. As mayor, Reed worked with corporate leaders and even Georgia's Republican governor in the pursuit of various local economic growth projects. Reed even supported the construction of a billion-dollar Atlanta Falcons football stadium to replace the Georgia Dome. In 2013, Reed coasted to reelection victory, having declared that "growing business" would be the Number One priority of his second term as mayor.[4]

The fragility of "black power" in a changing Atlanta was further underscored in the 2017 runoff election for mayor. Keisha Lance Bottoms, a black woman, squeaked into office after a recount of the ballot declared her the victor by a paltry 832 votes over Mary Norwood, a white challenger and a political independent with Republican ties. In her campaign, Bottoms, much like her predecessors, emphasized an agenda of economic development and job growth.

In an evolving Atlanta, the concerns of businesses and corporations continue to occupy an important place on the city's governing agenda. Biracial cooperation in Atlanta persists. But the biracial arrangement no longer possesses the stability, cohesiveness, and authority that it once demonstrated in governing Atalnta.[5]

1. Clarence N. Stone, *Regime Politics—Governing Atlanta: 1946–88* (Lawrence: University of Kansas Press, 1989), esp. 77–159.

2. Cynthia Horan, "Racializing Urban Regimes," *Journal of Urban Affairs* 24, no. 1 (2002): 25–27; Matthew J. Burbank, Gregory D. Andranovich, and Charles H. Heying, *Olympic Dreams: The Impact of Mega-Events on Local Politics* (Boulder, CO: Lynne Rienner, 2001), 81–120.

3. Lawrence J. Vale, *Purging the Poorest: Public Housing and the Design Politics of Twice-Cleared Communities* (Chicago: University of Chicago Press, 2013) describes how some of the city's poorest communities in Atlanta have fared under the city's biracial governing regime.

4. Michael Leo Owens and Jacob Robert Brown, "Weakening Strong Black Political Empowerment: Implication from Atlanta's 2009 Mayoral Election," *Journal of Urban Affairs* 36, no. 4 (October 2014): 663–681; Todd C. Shaw, Kasim Ortiz, James McCoy, and Athena King, "'The Last Black Mayor of Atlanta?' Kasim Reed and the Increasing Complexities of Black Politics," in *21st Century Urban Race Politics: Representing Minorities as Universal Interests*, ed. Ravi K. Perry (Bingley, UK: Emerald Publishing Group, 2013), 201–230.

5. Clarence N. Stone, "Reflections on Regime Politics: From Governing Coalition to Urban Political Order," *Urban Affairs Review*, 51, no. 1 (2015): 101–137.

DIFFERENT REGIME TYPES

Regime theory recognizes that business leaders often occupy key positions in the informal arrangements that govern a city. But regime theory does not portray business interests as all-powerful. A city's elected officials have their own policy agendas and electoral concerns and, as a result, will not always cede to the business community's demands. Business interests do not always get their way in the contemporary city.

There is no guarantee that an informal coalition of city officials and corporate leaders will even emerge to dominate city decision making. City leaders are not always willing to give corporate officials such great deference. Numerous suburbs and small towns resist development proposals that may increase the taxes imposed on homeowners and small businesses. In other communities, a coalition of neighborhood advocates, racial minorities, and environmentalists may win elected office and may be resistant to business-led proposals for growth.

Broadly speaking, there are three alternative types of local governing regimes.[36] A **corporate regime** (also called a **development regime**) pursues the growth projects and policies preferred by major corporations, real-estate firms, labor unions in the construction trades, and a city's "boosters" (often including the local newspaper). A corporate regime tends to slight concerns for equity ("fairness"), protection of the natural environment, and the service needs of more distressed neighborhoods. Booming suburbs, too, are often governed by a coalition of real-estate firms and other pro-development interests who have convinced friendly public officials of the virtues of local growth.[37]

A corporate regime transformed downtown Louisville. The mayor and top municipal staff worked with local businesses, the Chamber of Commerce, the local newspaper, construction unions, and even the NAACP (which saw economic growth as a way to bring new jobs to the city's low-income and minority communities) on a long-term program of stadium construction, waterfront development, and downtown renewal. They shared the goal of "Putting Louisville on the map."[38]

In the United States, corporate regimes are quite commonplace. Yet, they do not emerge in every city and suburb. In many small and medium-size cities and in affluent dormitory suburbs, a **caretaker regime** (also called a **maintenance regime**) reflects the concerns of small business owners and homeowners opposed to growth projects that entail new taxation, traffic congestion, and school overcrowding. Caretaker regimes do not push major new projects but instead focus on basic service provision while keeping taxes low.

The least commonly found governing type is the **progressive regime**, where environmentalists, homeowner associations, community development corporations (CDCs), and various nonprofit organizations and community groups gain a hold on city hall.[39] In San Francisco, Seattle, Boston, and Santa Monica, well-educated and politically active populations demand that local government pursue "green" policies that emphasize environmental protection even at the cost of limiting the scale of new development. Progressive regimes typically emphasize affordable housing, the advancement gay and lesbian rights, and, in some cities, social programs to aid the poor.[40]

There are actually two variants of the progressive regime. A **middle-class progressive regime** represents the concerns of environmentalists and homeowners critical of the ecological harm and the financial costs of growth projects. A **regime devoted to lower-class opportunity expansion**, by contrast, does not emphasize slow-growth policies but instead pursues growth projects that will provide jobs and opportunities for a city's poorer residents.

Progressive regimes are typically unstable—that is, they seldom endure over the years. Progressive alliances fray as middle-class homeowners, environmentalists, poor-people's groups, and minority and gay rights activists do not share common policy preferences. Progressive regimes also lose support during economic hard times when voters demand job creation.

Boston's fabled progressive regime had a relatively short life. In 1983, community activists helped elect the self-styled progressive Raymond Flynn as mayor. Flynn pursued balanced development, including job training for the poor, affordable housing, and restrictions to protect neighborhoods against development incursions. But faced with an economic recession, Flynn soon gave renewed priority to growth projects. Thomas Menino, Flynn's successor who served for 20 years (1993–2013), returned Boston to an even more corporate-oriented posture, with public authorities expediting the approval of growth projects.[41]

Chicago's progressive regime was similarly short lived. Harold Washington, the first African American to be elected mayor of the city, embraced programs of neighborhood equity and empowerment.[42] But when Mayor Washington died in office as the result of a heart attack, Chicago's progressive regime seemingly died with him, as no other leader had the same ability to unite African Americans, Latinos, and white liberals. The two-decades-long-long tenure of Mayor Richard M. Daley (1989–2009) marked the return of a corporate regime to city hall.[43] Daley's refashioned the city to make postindustrial Chicago appealing to global corporations. Rahm Emanuel, Daley's successor, similarly dispense various tax advantages to support downtown development, although the mayor also emphasized school reform, closing underperforming schools, expanding charter schools, and introducing new instructional approaches in the city's low-income neighborhoods.[44]

Numerous cities do not have a governing regime, as no stable public-private governing alliance persists from one mayoral administration to the next. In the absence of a working informal coalition, cities struggle to find the resources to get important things done. In mid-twentieth-century Milwaukee, continuing frictions between municipal officials and downtown business leaders meant that there was no powerful base behind proposed plans to revitalize the city's ailing downtown.[45] In New Orleans, city leaders, suburban officials, and private and nonprofit providers lacked the working relationship and sense of trust that would have enabled communities to work together to practice meaningful disaster relief operations. When Hurricane Katrina struck, there was no practiced set of operations in place that would have enabled governments and nonprofit organizations to work together smoothly to evacuate the carless poor and to provide food, water, and medicine to residents trapped inside the flood-ravaged city.[46]

In the postindustrial era, the executives of multinational corporations often have little familiarity with local business elites and political leaders. An executive who is temporarily assigned to head a corporation's production facilities in a city may be disinterested in taking efforts to help remediate community problems. In a global age, city leaders may find it increasingly difficult to assemble the coalitions of support necessary to sustain major projects.[47]

THE TRANSFORMATION OF SAN FRANCISCO: POWER AND ECONOMIC DEVELOPMENT IN THE POSTINDUSTRIAL CITY

In many ways, San Francisco is a city that is open to emergent political voices—including those of environmentalists, neighborhood activists, the LGBT community, Chinese Americans, African Americans, Hispanics, and various other groups of new immigrants. Over the past few decades, these groups succeeded in enacting a variety of growth-control measures to protect their neighborhoods against aggressive development. Their victories clearly reveal that no corporate elite rules contemporary San Francisco.

Yet, such a portrayal of power in San Francisco fails to adequately denote the influence that technology-oriented corporations and other businesses possess in the development arena. Despite the often celebrated legislative victories won by neighborhood groups and antigrowth forces, new development in San Francisco continues to transform the city. The transformation of the city is even evident in the "Manhattanization" of the San Francisco skyline (Figure 5.2).

The Yerba Buena Center, a large downtown development project, was built to expand the downtown in San Francisco across Market Street into low-income SOMA (the South of Market Area). The project, which featured a convention center as well as important cultural facilities, was built to help lure creative and tech-related "smart" businesses and trade-show attendees to the city. A new district of hotels, offices, and high-end residential development sprouted on what had been a rather grungy area of warehouses located just south of the city's central business district.[48] The revitalization of SOMA soon catalyzed the construction of AT&T Park (the home of the baseball Giants) and the Mission Bay office development immediately to the south.

In the late 1980s, community groups elected mayor Art Agnos who promised to protect the city's neighborhoods from unfettered development. Yet growth interests were not subdued. As mayor, Agnos disappointed many of his grassroots supporters when he endorsed plans for new waterfront development and the Giants ballpark.[49]

In 1995, legendary California political and former state house speaker Willie Brown, a Democrat and an African American, won the mayoralty. Brown was an old-style power broker who maintained political ties to construction unions and other interests that that favored new development projects. The city even approved limited commercial intrusions into the city's cherished Presidio, a large green area and former army base by the Golden Gate Bridge. Brown easily won reelection in 1999, vanquishing neighborhood populist Tom Ammiano, who promised to "declare war" on gentrification and the city's continued transformation. Contributions from business interests and labor unions allowed Brown to outspend Ammiano by more than 10 to 1.[50]

In 2003, Democrat Gavin Newsom won the mayoralty, defeating activist Matt Gonzalez, who had campaigned on a platform of tenant and neighborhood rights. Newsom, by contrast, promised a more balanced approach that would allow downtown and waterfront development to continue but with increased requirements for the inclusion of affordable

Figure 5.2 **The Manhattanization of San Francisco: The Transamerica Pyramid and the City's New Skyline.**

Source: From Wikimedia Commons via Flickr. Copyright © Jesse Garcia, http://commons.wikimedia. org/wiki/File: San_Francisco_skyline_-a.jpg.

housing. Newsom had the support of some of the city's more progressive groups (as he had taken a strong stance in support of gay marriage) as well as the backing of local construction unions and other elements in the city's growth coalition.

When Newsom left the city for state office (he was Lieutenant Governor and later Governor of California), he was succeeded by Ed Lee, the first Asian American to serve as San Francisco's mayor. Lee was a moderate who actively courted dot.com and other digital/technology firms, fueling both the city's dramatic tech boom as well as the soaring price of housing in the city. When Twitter threatened to leave the city, Lee and the Board of Supervisors (San Francisco's city council) responded by offering the digital communications giant $16 million in tax breaks. The city further reduced payroll taxes on businesses that chose to locate in the Mid-Market area which, not coincidentally, was the location of the site that Twitter had chosen for its new facilities.[51] Lee even backed the removal of the homeless from San Francisco's Mid-Market section in order to make the area more desirable to cutting-edge media firms and to housing developers.[52]

Progressive forces did have an impact. Businesses moving into Mid-Market were required to sign a community benefits agreement, detailing the support they intended to give to a variety of community activities, including the provision of day care, grants to small businesses, and financial assistance to nonprofit organizations seeking to aid the large homeless population of Mid-Market.[53] While the CBA spelled out a specific dollar commitments for certain community undertakings, the support for other activities, such as community-based job training, was rather vague. Twitter was to "encourage" its employees to volunteer in the community and to patronize local businesses.[54] San Francisco officials did not enter into the CBA negotiations with Twitter from a position of strength. Fearing that Twitter might choose to leave for a different city, San Francisco committed to granting extensive tax concessions to Twitter even *before* the negotiations over a CBA commenced.

San Francisco is noteworthy for its requirements that new residential developments include affordable units, requirements that are often seen as the strongest in the nation. City residents in 2016 voted for Proposition C virtually doubling—from 12 to 25 percent—the percentage of affordable units to be built in new residential developments. However, the next year the city's Board of Supervisors relaxed the mandate as numerous affordable housing advocates and developers saw the 25 percent requirement as so burdensome that it constituted a serious disincentive to new residential construction. The affordable housing mandate was reduced to 18 percent of rental units and 20 percent of new owner-occupied units. Alternatively a developer could choose to fund the construction of an even higher percentage of affordable units built off site.[55] Developers could earn the right to build up to two additional floors in a high-rise in exchange for the inclusion of residential units. Some neighborhood activists fought the compromise, fearing that more dense construction would accelerate new condominium construction and pressures underlying gentrification.[56]

Ed Lee died in office and in 2018 was succeeded by London Breed, who became the first African-American woman to become mayor. At this point, politics in the city took a strange and confusing twist. Breed's initial tenure as mayor lasted only a brief three weeks as progressives on the city's Board of Supervisors engineered her ouster and replaced with a new interim mayor, Mark Farrell:

> In an only-in-San Francisco tale that involved a mix of tech money, racial tension, and political jockeying, the city's most progressive elected officials spearheaded the ouster of the city's first female African-American mayor, a woman with roots in the city's public housing projects, in favor of a white, male venture capitalist who represents the city's wealthiest neighborhoods.[57]

Farrell, had gained the backing of progressive forces in the city despite his past support of measures to remove the homeless from city sidewalks. Progressive leaders in the city saw Breed, not Farrell, as the greater danger to a progressive agenda, as Breed's candidacy had the backing of wealthy tech investors whose development projects were transforming the city.[58] Breed's critics feared that she would approve future Twitter-style tax deals. In the June special election, Breed won election to the mayor's office, narrowly edging out Mark Leno who had run a campaign against "special interest" money and who had sought to become San Francisco's first avowedly gay mayor.

In San Francisco, major growth projects are built, but no corporate growth regime has emerged to direct the city's politics. Nor have progressive community groups, despite occasional big victories, been able to establish a stable governing regime committed to preserving neighborhoods as opposed to growth. No stable regime governs San Francisco with the ability to organize action in the city. Instead, San Francisco can be viewed as an **anti-regime city** where activist groups have been able to impose restrictions on new development but have not been able to take control of local government and steer San Francisco toward a strong policy of neighborhood protection and preservation (Figure 5.3).[59]

Figure 5.3   **Whose City? Protests Against the Google Bus in San Francisco.** Activists in San Francisco complain that the tech boom and continuing IT-related development is making the city an expensive playground for the highly compensated workers who work in the social media, tech, and creative industries. The rising price of housing threatens to displace working-class and lower-income families and immigrants from neighborhoods that have traditionally been their home. A large number of technologically competent professionals reside in San Francisco and commute south, often in company-provided buses and vans, to jobs in Silicon Valley. Political activists in San Francisco took to the streets to protest the ongoing transformation of their city. On numerous occasions, they attempted to block the private buses that shuttled IT workers living in the city to Google's corporate-campus headquarters located forty miles to the south in Silicon Valley.

Source: From Wikimedia Commons by Chris Martin (Flickr user cjmartin), December 9, 2013, http://en.wikipedia.org/wiki/File: Google_bus_protest.jpg.

CONCLUSION: CONSTRAINED LOCAL POLITICS

Local political systems are not as closed as power elite theory contends. Nor are they as open as pluralist theory avers. A multiplicity of groups influence decision making in cities and suburbs, and public officials retain decision-making autonomy. Yet, on the whole, local governments tend to cater to the concerns of big property developers, the owners of sports franchise owners, and other corporate interests.

In cities like San Francisco, neighborhood activists, racial and ethnic minorities, gays and lesbians, and environmental activists have a strong voice in the local arena. At times, they have succeeded in enacting antigrowth measures or requiring that new residential developments include affordable housing. Yet, despite occasional setbacks, over the years corporate officials have largely been successful in pushing major growth projects that have transformed cities.

While a city's economic fate is dependent on business decisions, more astute municipals officials recognize that businesses are also dependent on the government for project approvals, zoning permissions, and desired subsidies, giving municipal officials a degree of leverage when dealing with private firms.

Tax rates and concession are not the sole—and oftentimes not the dominant—factor when a corporation decides where to site an important facility. Even Amazon in its national search for a second national headquarters did not choose whichever city offered the largest set of tax breaks and subsidies. Corporations also consider other factors: a site's accessibility via roadways and mass transit; its proximity to a major airport; the availability of local labor; the quality and skills of the workforce in a region; and the presence of major universities to provide updated skills training and the cutting-edge research that a business may require.

Rather than simply offer tax concessions to business firms, cities and suburbs can turn to alternative strategies—such as improving the quality of local life and the skills of the local workforce. In a growing number of cases, local elected officials and city planners have joined with residents in negotiating a community benefits agreement where developers agree to affordable housing, neighborhood hiring targets, community-based job training, environmental safeguards, and corporate donations that support day-care provision, the arts, and the activities of community-based organizations.

Grassroots action is important in efforts to counter the power of the growth coalition. In Los Angeles, community-based Latino organizations mobilized against a plan to construct condominiums and upscale retail on sites near a new regional train station that was being built in the poor Mexican and Mexican-American MacArthur Park section of the city. The initial project threatened to gentrify the area and displace the neighborhood's more vulnerable residents. Community-oriented elected officials worked hand-in-hand with neighborhood organizations to force the Metropolitan Transit Authority to make significant alterations to its plans. The result produced a more neighborhood-friendly development project, including the construction of approximately 200 units of affordable housing, local job training programs, and even a place for street vendors (part of the cultural fabric of the Latino neighborhood).[60]

Yet the successes of such community-based movements as the Justice for Janitors "living wage" campaign in Los Angeles often demonstrates only a "modest" ability to reshape a city's long-term policy agenda.[61] City officials seldom take a strong stance in opposition to major business projects. As seen throughout this chapter, corporations continue to receive generous tax abatements, municipal-funded infrastructure improvements, and other expensive concessions.

Public officials cannot easily discern just when a specific concession is or is not absolutely necessary to attract or retain a key business firm. As a result, state and local officials tend to err on the side of political safety, giving corporations much of what they ask, oftentimes without even challenging some of a business's more extravagant claims and demands. Regime theory and the prevalence of corporate regimes serves to underscore the "weakness in the foundation for democratic politics" in the American city.[62]

Still, businesses and their growth-coalition allies do not rule a city by fiat. Mayors and other public officials still possess the "agency" or ability to pursue their own policy agendas, deciding when to cede, and when not to cede, to growth-coalition demands.

Local democracy is further eroded when state officials, often acting in response to the concerns of influential corporations, intervene to override local decisions on matters ranging from stadium construction to charter schools. State political officials, especially governors, have become increasingly active in the local policy arena, intervening in ways that subvert regime formation and local governance.[63]

The next chapter explores how the formal structure and procedures of municipal government continue to determine just whose interests are—and are not—represented in city hall.

KEY TERMS

allocational policy (*p. 172*)

anti-regime city (*p. 190*)

benefit principle to guide the financing of a new stadium (*p. 178*)

caretaker regime (also called a maintenance regime) (*p. 185*)

city limits theory, Paul Peterson's (*p. 172*)

community benefits agreements (CBAs) (*p. 173*)

corporate regime (also called a development regime) (*p. 185*)

developmental policy (*p. 170*)

growth machine (*p. 165*)

memos of understanding (*p. 175*)

middle-class progressive regime (*p. 185*)

mobility of capital (*p. 170*)

naming rights for a stadium (*p. 177*)

one-sided stadium contracts (*p. 174*)

pluralism or pluralist theory (*p. 163*)

power elite theory (*p. 163*)

preemptive power (*p. 182*)

progressive regime (*p. 185*)

redistributive policy (*p. 172*)

regime devoted to lower-class opportunity expansion (*p. 186*)

regime theory (*p. 170*)

seat licenses (*p. 177*)

social production, power as (*p. 181*)

spread the responsibility for financing a new stadium (*p. 178*)

substitution effect (*p. 173*)

urban regime (also called a governing regime) (*p. 182*)

NOTES

1. For classic statements of power elite theory, see Floyd Hunter's studies of Atlanta (which he referred to as "Regional City"): *Community Power Structure* (Garden City, NY: Anchor Books, 1963, originally published in 1953), and *Community Power Succession: Atlanta's Policymakers Revisited* (Chapel Hill: University of North Carolina Press, 1980).

2. For the classic statement of pluralism, see Robert A. Dahl, *Who Governs? Democracy and Power in an American City* (New Haven, CT: Yale University Press, 1961).

3. For criticisms of both power elite theory and the pluralist perspective, see Alan Harding, "The History of Community Power," in *Theories of Urban Power*, 2nd ed., ed. Jonathan Davies and David Imbroscio (Thousand Oaks, CA: Sage Publications, 2009), 27–39; and Alan Harding and Talja Blokland, *Urban Theory: A Critical Introduction to Power, Cities and Urbanism in the 21st Century* (London, UK, and Thousand Oaks, CA: Sage Publications, 2014).

4. Anthony Knapp and Igor Vojnovic, "Rethinking the Growth Machine: How to Erase a Chinatown from the Urban Core," *Urban Geography* 42, no. 1 (2013): 53–85.

5. Harvey Molotch, *Urban Fortunes: The Political Economy of Place*, 20th Anniversary ed. (Berkeley: University of California Press, 2007).

6. Nicholas A. Phelps, "The Growth Machine Stops? Urban Politics and the Making and Remaking of an Edge City," *Urban Affairs Review* 48, no. 5 (September 2012): 670–700.

7. Paul E. Peterson, *City Limits* (Chicago: University of Chicago Press, 1981).

8. Glennon Sweeney and Bernadette Hanlon, "From Old Suburb to Post-Suburb: The Politics of Retrofit in the Inner Suburb of Upper Arlington, Ohio," *Journal of Urban Affairs*, 39, no. 2 2017): 241–225.

9. Peterson, *City Limits*, 37–38.

10. Judith Grant Long, *Public-Private Partnerships for Major League Sports Facilities* (New York: Routledge, 2013).

11. The literature on this subject is vast. See Dennis Coates, "Growth Effects of Sports Franchises, Stadiums, and Arenas: 15 Years Later," Mercatus Working Paper, Mercatus Center at George Mason University, Arlington, VA, September 2015, www.mercatus.org/system/files/Coates-Sports-Franchises.pdf. Also see Mark S. Rosentraub, *Major League Losers: The Real Cost of Sports and Who's Paying for It* (New York: Basic Books, 1997), esp. 129–170; Charles A. Santo, "Beyond the Economic Catalyst Debate: Can Public Consumption Benefits Justify a Municipal Stadium Investment?" *Journal of Urban Affairs* 29, no. 5 (December 2007): 455–479; Geoffrey Propheter, "Are Basketball Arenas Catalysts of Economic Development?" *Journal of Urban Affairs* 34, no. 4 (October 2012): 441–459. Interestingly, in his later works, Rosentraub has given quite positive assessments of local decisions to build sports stadiums to spur downtown revitalization.

12. At times, even a conservative pro-business magazine like *Forbes* has recognized the minimal impacts that are gained from stadium construction, that much of the apparent gains in business are really little more than substitution effects. See Jeffrey Dorfman, "Publicly Financed Stadiums Are a Game that Taxpayers Lose," *Forbes*, January 31, 2015.

13. Mark S. Rosentraub, "The Local Context of a Sports Strategy for Economic Development," *Economic Development Quarterly* 20, no. 3 (August 2006): 278–291.

14. Joe Guillen, "Littler Caesars Arena: How the Cost Nearly Doubled to $863 Million," *Detroit Free Press*, September 7, 2017; City of Detroit, Downtown Development Authority, "Terms of the Proposed Agreement" (with the Detroit Pistons), n.d. (but clearly 2017), www.detroitmi.gov/Portals/0/docs/News/DDA%20Terms%20Pistons.pdf.

15. Neil deMause, "Stop the Subsidy-Sucking Stadiums," *The Nation*, August 5, 2011.

16. Gabe Zaldivar, "The L.A. Chargers Are an Utter Failure," *Forbes*, October 3, 2017; Neil deMause, "No, the Chargers Aren't Moving Back to San Diego, but the NFL Probably Wishes They Could," *Field of Schemes Blog*, September 25, 2017, www.fieldofschemes.com/2017/09/25/12955/no-the-chargers-arent-moving-back-to-san-diego-but-the-nfl-probably-wishes-they-could/. Season attendance figures for 2017 are reported by www.espn.com/nfl/attendance.

17. Reed Albergotti and Cameron McWhirter, "A Stadium's Costly Legacy Throws Taxpayers for a Loss," *Wall Street Journal*, July 12, 2011; Sharon Coolidge, "Tax Rebate from 96's Stadium Plan May Be Gone," *Cincinnati Enquirer*, September 8, 2013. Even the more "balanced" stadium agreement announced in 2014 revealed little real balance. The Bengals consented to higher heights for surrounding downtown buildings; the team also agreed to pick up part of the costs of a new replay system. But public bodies assumed most of the costs for stadium improvements (including new Wi-Fi capacity) and gave the Bengals permission to play two "home" games outside the county without having to compensate the county for lost ticket and parking revenues. See Sharon Coolidge, "Bengals, County Reach Major Deal on The Banks," *Cincinnati Enquirer*, April 17, 2014.

18. Neil deMause and Joanna Cagan, *Field of Schemes: How the Great Stadium Swindle Turns Public Money into Private Profit*, rev. and exp. ed. (Lincoln, NE: University of Nebraska Press, 2008), 106. The *Field of Schemes* Web site provides links to newspaper articles and various other updates concerning stadium deals in cities across the country: www.fieldofschemes.com.

19. Long, *Public-Private Partnerships for Major League Sports Facilities*, chap. 7; Mark S. Rosentraub and David Swindell, "Of Devils and Details: Bargaining for Successful Public/Private Partnerships between Cities and Sports Teams," *Public Administration Quarterly* 33, no. 1 (2009): 118–148.

20. Mark S. Rosentraub, *Major League Winners: Using Sports and Cultural Centers as Tools for Economic Development* (Boca Raton, FL: CRC Press, 2010).

21. Steven P. Erie, Vladimir Kogan, and Scott A. MacKenzie, "'Redevelopment, San Diego Style': The Limits of Public-Private Partnerships," *Urban Affairs Review* 45, no. 5 (2010): 644–678; Steven P. Erie, Vladimir Kogan, and Scott A. MacKenzie, *Paradise Plundered: Fiscal Crisis and Government Failures in San Diego* (Palo Alto, CA: Stanford University Press, 2011), chap. 6.

22. Leland Saito and Jonathan Truong, "The L.A. Live Community Benefits Agreement: Evaluating the Agreement Results and Shifting Political Power within the City," *Urban Affairs Review* 51, no. 2 (March 2015): 263–289. Also see Laura Wolf-Powers, "Community Benefits Agreements and Local Government: A Review of the Evidence," *Journal of the American Planning Association* 76, no. 2 (2010): 141–159.

23. Nicholas J. Marantz, "What Do Community Benefits Agreements Deliver? Evidence from Los Angeles," *Journal of the American Planning Association* 81, no. 4 (Autumn 2015): 251–267. *The New York Times* reports that community development agreement funds resulting from the construction of a new Yankees baseball stadium have largely neglected the neighborhood surrounding the ballpark and were instead awarded to organizations that have common board members with the Yankee Stadium fund. See Micah Hauser, "Yankees Charity Neglects Stadium's Neighbors," *New York Times*, June 27, 2017.

24. Dan Rosenblum, "Building Low, Selling High," *Next City*, February 18, 2013, http://nextcity.org/daily/entry/forefront-excerpt-selling-low-building-high.

25. Heywood T. Sanders, *Convention Center Follies: Politics, Power, and Public Investment in American Cities* (Philadelphia: University of Pennsylvania Press, 2014), x; Heywood T. Sanders, "Institutions, Space, and Time: Approaches to the Study of Urban Politics" (presentation at the annual meeting of the Urban Affairs Association, Minneapolis, April 20, 2017).

26. Sanders, *Convention Center Follies*, 7–8.

27. Heywood T. Sanders, "*Space Available* Revisited: Convention Center Development and Market Realities" (presentation at the annual meeting of the Urban Affairs Association, Toronto, April 5, 2018).

28. Sanders, *Convention Center Follies*, chap. 4, offers persuasive documentation of numerous cases where the economic impact of a new convention center has been far short of what was predicted by the statistical analyses prepared by outside consultants.

29. This is one of a number of criticisms of the "city limits" thesis offered by Richard Schragger, *City Power: City Power: Urban Governance in a Global Age* (New York: Cambridge University Press, 2016), 2–5, 135–174.

30. Edward L. Glaeser and William R. Kerr, "The Secret to Job Growth: Think Small," *Harvard Business Review*, 88, nos. 7–8 (July–August 2010): 26–27; Michael Shuman, "Why Your Community

Should Kick the Subsidy Habit," *Shelterforce Blog Posting*, October 21, 2016, https://shelterforce.org/2016/10/21/why-your-community-should-kick-the-subsidy-habit/.

31. Stacy Mitchell, "8 Policy Strategies a City Can Use to Support Local Businesses," *Institute for Local Self-Reliance Blog*, August 28, 2017, https://ilsr.org/8-policy-strategies-cities-can-use-to-support-local-businesses/.

32. Paul N. McDaniel, *Entrepreneurship and Innovation in Welcoming Cities: Lessons from Chicago, Dayton, and Nashville*, a report of the American Immigration Council, February 2016, www.americanimmigrationcouncil.org/sites/default/files/research/entrepreneurship_and_innovation_in_welcoming_cities.pdf.

33. Clarence N. Stone, "Systemic Power in Community Decision Making: A Restatement of Stratification Theory," *American Political Science Review* 74 (December 1980): 978.

34. Unless otherwise noted, the basic outline of regime theory is taken from Clarence N. Stone's classic work, *Regime Politics: Governing Atlanta: 1946–88* (Lawrence: University of Kansas Press, 1989), 242. For a brief review of the contributions of regime theory, see Karen Mossberger, "Urban Regime Analysis," in *Theories of Urban Power*, 2nd ed., ed. Davies and Imbroscio, pp. 40–54.

35. Cynthia Horan, "Racializing Urban Regimes," *Journal of Urban Affairs* 24, no. 1 (2002): 19–33.

36. The classification of regime types presented here was developed by Clarence N. Stone, "Summing Up: Urban Regimes, Development Policy, and Political Arrangements," in *The Politics of Urban Development*, ed. Clarence N. Stone and Heywood T. Sanders (Lawrence: University of Kansas Press, 1987), 272–273.

37. Brian J. Miller, "A Small Suburb Becomes a Boomburb: Explaining Suburban Growth in Naperville, Illinois," *Journal of Urban History* 42, no. 6 (2016): 1135–1152.

38. H.V. Savitch, Takashi Tsukamoto, and Ronald K. Vogel, "Civic Culture and Corporate Regime in Louisville," *Journal of Urban Affairs* 20, no. 4 (2008): 437–460. The quoted material can be found on p. 452.

39. David L. Imbroscio, *Reconstructing City Politics: Alternative Economic Development and Urban Regimes* (Thousand Oaks, CA: Sage Publications, 1997), 97–138. Imbroscio advocates decentralized, community-based economic development initiatives. See his *Urban America Reconsidered: Alternatives for Governance and Policy* (Ithaca, NY: Cornell University Press, 2010).

40. Donald L. Rosdil, *The Cultural Contradictions of Progressive Politics: The Role of Cultural Change and the Global Economy in Local Policymaking* (New York: Routledge, 2013).

41. Pierre Clavel, *Activists in City Hall: The Progressive Response to the Reagan Era in Boston and Chicago* (Ithaca, NY: Cornell University Press, 2010), 1–95. For a partial listing of Menino's development projects, see Tom Acitelli, "Mayor Menino's Greatest Real Estate Hits," *Curbed*, March 28, 2013, http://boston.curbed.com/archives/2013/03/mayor-meninos-greatest-real-estate-hits.php; and Tom Acitelli, "It's Go Time for Developers as Menino Exits Office," *Curbed*, July 22, 2013, http://boston.curbed.com/archives/2013/07/its-go-time-for-developers-as-menino-leaves-office.php. Also see Casey Ross, "Businesses Hurry to Win Approval in Boston: Mayoral Change Could Slow Projects," *The Boston Globe*, July 22, 2013.

42. Pierre Clavel and Wim Wiewel, eds., *Harold Washington and the Neighborhoods: Progressive City Government in Chicago, 1983–87* (New Brunswick, NJ: Rutgers University Press, 1991); Clavel, *Activists in City Hall*, 96–170.

43. John J. Betancur and Douglas C. Gills, "Community Development in Chicago: From Harold Washington to Richard M. Daley," *Annals of the American Academy of Political and Social Science* 594, no. 1 (2004): 92–108; Dan Immergluck, "Building Power, Losing Power: The Rise and Fall of a Prominent Community Economic Development Coalition," *Economic Development Quarterly* 19, no. 3 (August 2005): 211–224.

44. Political progressives in Chicago sharply criticized Mayor Emanuel's "corporate" school reform agenda. See *Restructuring and Resisting Education Reforms in Chicago's Public Schools,* ed. Rhoda Rae Gutierrez and Federico R. Waitoller, *Education and Policy Analysis Archives* "special issue" 25, no. 53 (June 2017).

45. Joel Rast, "Governing the Regimeless City: The Frank Zeidler Administration in Milwaukee, 1948–1960," *Urban Affairs Review* 42, no. 1 (2006): 81–112.

46. Peter Burns and Matthew O. Thomas, "The Failure of the Nonregime: How Katrina Exposed New Orleans as a Regimeless City," *Urban Affairs Review* 41, no. 4 (2006): 517–527.

47. Clarence N. Stone, "Reflections on Regime Politics: From Governing Coalition to Urban Political Order," *Urban Affairs Review*, 51, no. 1 (2015): 111–112.

48. Chester Hartman and Sarah Carnochan, *City for Sale: The Transformation of San Francisco*, rev. ed. (Berkeley: University of California Press, 2002).

49. Richard Edward DeLeon, *Left Coast City: Progressive Politics in San Francisco, 1975–91* (Lawrence: University of Kansas Press, 1992), 12.

50. Richard E. DeLeon, "San Francisco: The Politics of Race, Land Use, and Ideology," in *Racial Politics in American Cities*, 3rd ed., ed. Rufus P. Browning, Dale Rogers Marshall, and David H. Tabb (New York: Longman, 2003), 168–169, 186–193.

51. Larry N. Gerston, *Not So Golden after All: The Rise and Fall of California* (Boca Raton: FL: CRC Press, 2012), 133–135.

52. Heather Knight, "Swept Off Mid-Market, S.F.'s Homeless Cluster Nearby," *San Francisco Chronicle*, January 11, 2014.

53. Oscar Perry Abello, "S.F. Tax Break Tapped by Twitter Is Intended to Help Struggling Neighborhoods," *Next City Blog*, May 31, 2017, https://nextcity.org/daily/entry/san-francisco-tax-breaks-twitter-community-benefits-agreement.

54. Joshua Sabatini, "SF Citizens Advisory Committee Recommends Revisions to Mid-Market Community Benefit Agreements," *San Francisco Examiner*, January 6, 2014.

55. Kristy Wang, "SF Makes Sweeping Changes to Affordable Housing Requirements," *SPUR (San Francisco Bay Planning and Urban Research Association) News Blog*, August 15, 2017, www.spur.org/news/2017-08-15/sf-makes-sweeping-changes-affordable-housing-requirements.

56. Adam Brinklow, "San Francisco Finally Passes Affordable Housing Law," *Curbed San Francisco Blog*, May 24, 2017, https://sf.curbed.com/2017/5/24/15685126/homes-sf-affordable-housing-bonus-program.

57. Alastair Boone and Benjamin Schneider, "What Just Happened in San Francisco?" *CityLab Blog*, January 25, 2018, www.citylab.com/equity/2018/01/what-just-happened-in-san-francisco/551501/.

58. Thomas Fuller and Conor Dougherty, "San Francisco Ousts a Mayor in a Clash of Tech, Politics and Race," *New York Times*, January 24, 2108.

59. DeLeon, *Left Coast City*, 7–8, 132–133, 142–149.

60. Gerardo Francisco Sandoval, "Transforming Transit-Oriented Development Projects via Immigrant-Led Revitalization: The MacArthur Park Case," in *Immigration and Metropolitan Revitalization in the United States*, ed. Domenic Vitiello and Thomas J. Sugrue (Philadelphia: University of Pennsylvania Press, 2017), 111–130.

61. Michelle Camou, "Labor-Community Coalitions through an Urban Regime Lens: Institutions and Ideas in Building Power from Below," *Urban Affairs Review*, 50, no. 5 (September 2014): 623–647; Michael Jones-Correa and Diane Wong, "Whose Politics? Reflections on Clarence Stone's *Regime Politics*," *Urban Affairs Review*, 51, no. 1 (January 2015): 171–170.

62. Clarence N. Stone, "Looking Back to Look Forward: Reflections on Urban Regime Analysis," *Urban Affairs Review* 40, no. 3 (January 2005): 309–341. The quotation appears on p. 326.

63. Domingo Morel, *Takeover: Race, Education, and American Democracy* (New York: Oxford University Press, 2018).

6 Formal Powers, the Structure of Local Government, and Leadership

Local government is not simply a miniaturized copy of the national or state governments. Local government is quite different, especially as the formal powers that municipalities possess are, in important ways, quite limited. Constitutionally speaking, each state creates (or, to be precise, "charters") its local governments and defines just what powers each municipality may and may not possess. Local governments in the United States have become increasingly active across a range of policy areas. Yet, a city's ability to solve problems is highly dependent on just what powers a state chooses to authorize.

Cities and suburbs do not even possess the full authority to raise the funds necessary to modernize public infrastructure and facilities and to combat local ills. Each state determines just what a locality may and may not tax. A state can impose a ceiling on local tax rates or a limit on the amount of money that a community may borrow to construct new schools, parks, streets, and sewer systems. Private corporations have in many cases filed for bankruptcy protection, a move that places a "freeze" on the demands of creditors and thereby gives a troubled firm an extended period of time to restructure its finances. But a municipal corporation (that is, a local government chartered by a state) is not always permitted similar recourse. Half of the states do not permit municipalities, even in the face of serious budgetary shortfalls, to file for federal Chapter 9 bankruptcy protection in order to find time to take the steps necessary to regain their financial footing.[1]

DILLON'S RULE: THE STATES LIMIT THE POWERS OF LOCAL GOVERNMENTS

The United States Constitution recognizes only two levels of government, the national government and the states. The Constitution contains no mention of local governments and their powers. In terms of constitutional law, strictly speaking, municipalities are the **administrative subunits of a state**. Each state creates local governments and decides just what powers a local government may and may not exercise.

Iowa Judge John F. Dillon in a classic 1868 ruling underscored the quite limited and dependent position of municipal governments in the American constitutional system. **Dillon's Rule**, as the legal doctrine is popularly called, observes that, under the United States Constitution, municipalities are the mere "creatures of the states" and possess only those powers expressly delegated to them by the states.

Dillon's Rule denotes a hierarchical arrangement where a state possesses total authority over the local governments it creates. Should it wish, a state even has the power to eliminate cities, townships, counties, and other municipalities, a power that the states have used over the years to force the closing and merger of tiny school and library districts. As Judge Dillon wrote, the state's power over cities is so complete that "the Legislature might, by a single act, if we can suppose it capable of so great a folly and so great a wrong, sweep from existence all municipal corporations in a state."[2] As a state possesses the authority to destroy a local government, the state also has the right to abridge, amend, or revoke any power that it has granted a city.

Dillon's Rule means that local governments do not possess expansive powers. Dillon's Rule requires that the powers delegated to local government are to be strictly construed, that is, narrowly interpreted. If there is a dispute as to whether or not a local government possesses a particular power, that power is denied to the locality. As Judge Dillon articulated, "Any fair, reasonable, substantial doubt concerning the existence of power is resolved by the courts *against* the [municipal] corporation and the power is denied."[3]

Over the years, the United States Supreme Court has affirmed the underlying principle elaborated in Judge Dillon's ruling.[4] Constitutionally speaking, a local government is a subunit of a state and possesses only those powers granted to it by a state's constitution, state statutes, and a state-approved city charter.

As we shall soon see, however, cities are not quite as limited as a strict reading of Dillon's rule would seem to indicate. Numerous states have chosen to give cities more expansive powers under *home rule charters*.

THE CITY CHARTER: WHAT POWERS ARE GIVEN TO A CITY?

Each state sets the requirements for **municipal incorporation**, the conditions that an area must meet to become a city, village, township, town, or county, a recognized administrative subunit of the state that is then awarded a specified set of governing powers. A **city charter**, issued or approved by the state, is the equivalent of a city constitution. The charter details the geographical boundaries of a municipality, the structure and process of the local government (i.e. whether a city or suburb will operate under the weak-mayor, strong-mayor, or council-manager arrangement), if local elections are conducted on a partisan or nonpartisan basis, and the basic processes of government. A city charter also delineates the responsibilities and powers of a municipality.

During the early years of the American republic, state legislatures wrote **special-act charters** that detailed the unique powers given to each new municipality as it was incorporated. By the mid-1800s, however, states were tired of having to write a unique charter for each new municipality. The states discovered a simple solution, shifting to a system of **general-act charters** (also called **classified charters**): Cities are divided into different general classes based on population (and, in some cases, on the value of the local tax base as well); a different sets of powers is given to each class or category of municipalities. Larger cities are assigned a wider range of service responsibilities and are given greater spending, taxing, and borrowing authority than that accorded smaller municipalities.

Classifying or grouping cities also helps to protect a city from being singled out for arbitrary treatment at the hands of a vindictive state legislature. When cities are put into classes, a state can no longer pass a special act that imposes an obligation or burden only on a single city; instead, the provisions of a state law will apply to all cities that fall into a designated class.

Yet even the classification system does not afford a city complete protection against political discrimination. The history of urban politics is filled with instances where a state has only one city—a Baltimore, Boston, Chicago, Des Moines, New Orleans, or New York—in its top class; a state legislature effectively singles out such a city when it imposes new service responsibilities on its top-tier cities.

PREEMPTION

As a state defines the authority of its local governments, a state possesses the power of **preemption**, the authority to bar localities from taking specified actions or from acting in designated policy areas. Oftentimes, states preempt local action at the request of powerful interests who argue that municipalities have transgressed on political liberty and have intruded unwisely in the operation of local businesses. The political muscle of the gun lobby, for instance, led 45 of the nation's 50 states to ban or limit local gun-control ordinances.[5]

More than 40 states impose limits on the ability of local entities to exercise **eminent domain** powers, that is, to take land for public purposes.[6] Property-rights groups had urged state preemption in order to protect homeowners against overly aggressive local development officials.

For many years, the tobacco lobby was quite successful in its push for state legislation that barred localities from enacting anti-smoking restrictions, even measures intended to reduce tobacco use among minors. However, the tobacco lobby could not sustain its political dominance; pro-health groups countermobilized, leading a number of states to modify or rescind acts that had prevented local governments from implementing and enforcing smoking restrictions. Still, a fair number of states continue to have restrictions that ban local government governments from enacting regulations on tobacco. Some state even have laws that preempt local efforts to restrict tobacco advertising and to bar the sale of cigarettes through vending machines—actions intended to reduce the access that youth have to tobacco.[7]

Associations representing other industries have come to the state capitol to lobby for measures to curb local regulation. In Texas, Louisiana, Colorado, Ohio, and other states, the energy industry pushed state officials to prohibit municipalities from banning "fracking" (hydraulic fracturing), a means of extracting natural gas and oil that may impair local water quality.[8] In Wisconsin and New Jersey, the telecommunications industry secured state measures to prohibit municipalities from taking actions that interfered with the siting of cell phone towers. In California, Nevada, Florida, and other states, Lyft and Uber sought state laws to preempt local governments from imposing additional regulations and fees that would intrude on the operation of ride-hailing platforms.

Republican-controlled state governments have attempted to "rein in" progressive city policy initiatives. By 2017, nearly half the states preempted local municipal action to increase the minimum wage within a locality's borders. Republican-controlled state governments prohibited local action to require employers to pay for sick days and maternity leave. A few states even preempted local prohibitions on free plastic shopping bags at supermarkets. Arkansas, North Carolina, and Tennessee even barred local antidiscrimination legislation that would protect the rights of gay, lesbian and transgender persons.[9]

In more recent years, state intrusion has taken a new and more aggressive form, **super-preemption**, where a state threatens penalties when local officials persist in taking actions contrary to a state's wishes. The Republican-controlled state government of Texas not only barred localities from pursuing "sanctuary cities" measures, the statute threatened to impose fines on local governments and even remove local officials from office in instances where the state law is ignored (Figure 6.1). A 2016 Florida law similarly

Protestors Gather at the State Capitol in Austin as the Texas Legislature Preempts Cities From Adopting Sanctuary City Measures, 2017.

Source: Photo by Vic Hinterland/Shutterstock.com, www.shutterstock.com/image-photo/austin-texas-usa-may-29-2017-688902199?src=X4kTAcmmAXFGLijBPFV89w-1-2.

exposes municipal officials to personal liability and removal from office for continuing to support local restrictions on firearms. Arizona passed a **blanket preemption** law that threatens to withhold shared revenues from a local government that passes any law that the Attorney General views to be in conflict with state law.[10]

State preemption also imposes severe limits on the abilities of local government to raise revenue. Municipalities levy an individual income tax in only 14 states. Why don't a greater number of cities tap this potentially lucrative source of revenue? The answer is simple: more than two-thirds of the states bar localities from taxing individual incomes. Only 13 states permit local governments to impose a tax on fuel. The local taxation of cigarettes is permitted in only ten states. Fewer than half of the states (only 18) permit local taxes on alcoholic beverages.[11] State preemption in the area of taxation denies large and small communities alike important sources of revenue that could help sustain local programs.

HOME RULE

State provisions for *home rule* give a municipality greater freedom to act, easing some (but not all) of the seeming tightness of Dillon's Rule. Virtually every state has enacted some variant of **home rule**, which empowers cities (and, in most cases, counties as well) to make numerous decisions without having to go to the state for explicit permission to act—just as long as the municipal actions do not contradict state law. Some states go further, granting cities home rule charters.

Home rule enables a city or a county to take actions in a wide variety of policy areas, including policy areas that fall outside of traditional municipal service provision. In the 1980s and 1990s, more than 150 communities used their home rule authority to provide domestic partner benefits to municipal workers or took other actions to recognize gay and lesbian unions; local governments were at the forefront of the battle to recognize the rights of same-sex couples.[12] Cities across the country have also relied on their home rule authority to enact "green" building codes that require increased energy efficiency and ecological sustainability in home and office construction. Philadelphia, Cook County (greater Chicago), San Francisco, Oakland, Berkeley, and Seattle are the most notable communities to impose a tax on sodas and other sweetened beverages in an effort to further the battle against childhood obesity.

The extent of local home rule authority varies considerably from state to state. A handful of state supreme courts have ruled that the language of their state's constitution requires that the powers of local government be liberally construed. What exactly does this mean? In strong "home rule states," specific provisions in a state's constitution related to home rule effectively neutralize much of Dillon's Rule. Municipal governments in these states possess a very broad ability to act.

At the other end of the spectrum, in an equivalent number of "Dillon's Rule states," the state constitutional basis for home rule is much weaker. In these states, a municipality must gain the expressed permission of the state government before it can exercise a new power, a requirement that serves to constrain innovative local action.[13] In Nevada, municipalities were hesitant to adopt a vacant property registration ordinance, a tool that would help cities get a handle on the rising tide of abandoned properties; local officials knew that the new regulation on property owners was unlikely to win approval from state officials.[14]

But even in states with a strong home rule tradition, home rule does not totally negate Dillon's Rule: The state government can still intrude into local affairs and reverse a municipal action, although the extent that the state can do so depends on the exact wording of the state constitution. In Ohio and Michigan, public-sector labor unions representing police officers, firefighters, and public-school teachers lobbied to have the state government preempt locally enacted **residency laws** that required a municipality's workers to reside within the geographic borders of a city. The Ohio Supreme Court even upheld a state statute that bars municipalities from enforcing their residency requirements; the court ruled that the state intrusion into local affairs did not violate the specific language of the home rule provisions of the Ohio constitution.

In New York, the state legislature countermanded the efforts of New York City Mayor Bill de Blasio to curtail the expansion of charters schools, alternative schools that de Blasio saw as posing a threat to traditional public-school classrooms. The mayor had sought to end the city's practice of offering free space in public-school buildings to independent charter schools that wished to share a facility with an existing public school. When de Blasio's administration denied space for three charter schools run by Eva Moskowitz, a notable local politico and charter school administrator, Moskowitz responded by going to the state government and organizing a mass rally at the capitol. New York Governor Andrew Cuomo responded by declaring his support for charter schools. A provision was added to the state budget that required a city to provide available space to charter academies or otherwise help a charter school pay for the rental of private space.[15]

Home rule has not prevented states from intruding into the operations of local governments facing crises. Michigan's home rule tradition posed no real barrier to the state's takeover of public schools in Detroit and other troubled communities. The State of Michigan simply revised its laws to give state officials the authority to appoint an emergency fiscal manager to run a city or school district in crisis, superseding the powers of local elected officials.[16] State-appointed emergency managers in Michigan were given the authority to void provisions of municipal labor contracts that had been approved by local elected officials.

Home rule does not entirely free cities from state control and the possibilities of preemption.[17] Dillon's Rule is the dominant doctrine of municipal law in four-fifths of the states.[18] Even in states with a strong home rule tradition, state legislative actions and judicial rulings continue to define local powers.[19] In more recent years, home rule appears a bit more fragile than ever, as the states have "chipped away" at the home rule powers of cities.[20]

STATE REGULATIONS ON LOCAL ANNEXATION AND SECESSION

Each state sets the criteria and procedures that a city must meet in order to expand via **annexation**, that is, to grow by extending its borders, making adjoining territory a part of the city. For decades, North Carolina and Texas gave their major cities liberal authority to grow via annexation. In more recent years, however, protests from suburban areas led state legislatures across the nation to enact new restrictions that have made annexation more difficult (a matter that will be discussed in more detail in Chapter 10).

A state's constitutions and statutes also detail the requirements for **secession**, the conditions that must be met for the residents of an area to separate or detach from a city or a school district. California statutes put severe obstacles in the path of San Fernando Valley residents who sought to break away from the City of Los Angeles and establish what would have been the sixth most populous city in the United States. California state law requires approval by **dual majorities**, that is, the larger city and the seceding area must *both* give their consent for a divorce to proceed. While popular among Valley residents, secession of the Valley was not likely to win approval in the rest of Los Angeles. California law further impeded the Valley's detachment efforts in its requirement that a secession be "revenue neutral," that the detachment must not hurt the larger city financially. Enthusiasm for secession declined as Valley residents discovered that a new Valley city would likely have to pay millions of dollars in "alimony" to Los Angeles, compensating L.A. for past infrastructure improvements and for the revenue losses the larger city would suffer as a result of detachment. On the East Coast, efforts by Staten Island to secede from New York City were similarly stymied by provisions of the state constitution that gave the city the power to veto detachment efforts.[21]

Can white and wealthier areas of a community secede from a school district with a growing minority population in order to establish their own school district, even if the move winds up compounding the racial imbalance of local schools? Here, too, state law helps to determine when secession is or is not a possible course of action.[22]

LOCAL FINANCE: HOW STATES LIMIT THE TAXING AND BORROWING POWERS OF LOCAL GOVERNMENTS

Localities in the United States are not free to levy any tax or fee that they desire or even to borrow large sums of money to finance local projects. Dillon's Rule clearly applies: Each state essentially determines what taxes a local jurisdiction may levy. A state can even set a maximum on the tax rates that a locality may impose. States limit the amounts that school districts and other forms of local government may borrow for infrastructure improvements and other purposes.

State-imposed restrictions distort the shape of local revenue systems. The national government relies heavily on the personal income tax as a result of the vast sums of revenues that such a tax generates. State-imposed restrictions mean that few municipalities can similarly rely on the income tax. Only fourteen states permit local income taxes. Nationwide, localities obtain a meager 2 percent of their revenues from the individual income tax![23]

Even where a local income tax is permitted, a state can cap the maximum tax rate that a municipality may impose. Michigan, for instance, generally imposes a limit of 1 percent on the tax a city can level on the income of local residents. Michigan limits cities to a mere half-of-one-percent tax on the income of commuters who live elsewhere but who work in the city. The State of Michigan provides for four exceptions, allow-ing for somewhat higher tax rates in fiscally distressed Detroit, Highland Park, Grand Rapids, and Saginaw.

Barred from extensive use of an income tax, localities have had to rely on property taxes (which account for nearly 30 percent of local revenues) and the imposition of various small service charges and so-called nuisance fees (which provide 23 percent of local revenues). Where state law permits, a municipality can also adopt a small local add-on to the state sales tax (which, nationwide, accounts for 7 percent of local revenues).

Property and sales taxes are often a source of anger among local residents who resent the unfair burden that such levies impose on lower-income residents and working-class homeowners. Yet, cities, and school districts often have little alterna-tive but to rely so greatly on such taxes, especially the property tax, to finance local operations.

Limited in their ability to raise local revenues, municipalities are dependent on **intergovernmental assistance**, the program assistance provided by the national and state governments. State and federal aid accounts for 36 percent of local budgets and has become the largest single source of revenues supporting local service provision.

THE PROPERTY TAX AND SCHOOL FINANCE

The property tax continues to be a bulwark in providing revenues for K–12 public-school systems. The property tax accounts for over four-fifths of the tax revenues that localities collect for K–12 schools (a figure that excludes state and federal aid).[24] In the great majority of the states, the quality of a local school is dependent on the taxable value of property located within the borders of the local district!

Beginning in the late twentieth century, a virtual revolution in school finance resulted in a dramatic increase in the state assistance provided local schools. Today, the states provide nearly half (45.1 percent) of public-school revenues, narrowly surpassing the 44.8 percent that schools raise through the local property tax. The federal government is *not* that major a player in school finance, as it provides only 10.1 percent of the monies that support K–12 education.[25]

State assistance to K–12 education has helped to reduce, but does not eliminate, the disparate abilities of property-rich and property-poor school districts to spend on behalf of their children. The degree to which to which schools are reliant on local property tax revenues varies considerably from state to state. In Illinois and New Hampshire, a community's property wealth plays a great role in education, with nearly two-thirds of school budgets coming from local taxpayers (2012–2013 figures). In New York, Texas, Maine, and Nebraska, local property tax revenues account for nearly half of all school funds. But in Hawaii and Vermont, local property wealth is not really a factor in local school spending, as these two states assume great responsibility for the funding of K–12 school operations across the state.

"The schools" were once seen as exclusively a local issue. Nowadays, the states have become a major funder and an increasingly influential decision maker in K–12 education.

THE POLITICS OF LOCAL SALES TAXES

Thirty-eight states allow local sales taxes[26] which, as we have seen, account for 7 percent of local spending. Efforts to enact or increase the local sales tax, however, often are met by considerable citizen resistance. To counter such resistance civic leaders often turn to a strategy of **earmarking tax proceeds**, tying the revenues gained from a sales tax increase to a particularly popular project, such as the expansion of a school or its athletic facilities. Yet, earmarking does not always guarantee success. Voters in Pierce County (Tacoma), Washington, in 2016 rejected a very small (one-tenth of 1 percent) sales tax that was earmarked for mental health and chemical dependency programs.

Business advocates worry that a local sales tax can lead customers to shop in neighboring communities. Chicago's whopping 9.25 percent sales tax (the combined city and state taxes on sales) leads consumers to make major purchases in neighboring jurisdictions, even across the state border in Wisconsin. Philadelphia's sales tax serves to drive consumers to Delaware, the self-proclaimed "Home of Tax-Free Shopping," which has no sales tax.[27] In Minnesota, where the combined state and local sales tax rate can reach 7.9 percent, the state decided not to tax the sale of clothing and shoes as part of its effort to lure shoppers to the Mall of America. A number of communities have **sales tax holidays** where, in the weeks preceding a new school year, the tax is temporarily suspended as part of the effort to compete for back-to-school shoppers.

The growing volume of e-commerce threatens to erode the money that a locality can collect from a local sales tax. Internet retailers enjoy a significant competitive advantage in cases where no sales tax is paid for shopping that is done online. New York City in 2013 lost an estimated $235 million in sales tax revenues as a result of its inability to collect the tax on all online transactions. Los Angeles County similarly lost $95 million in foregone revenues. Cook County, Illinois (the county surrounding Chicago) lost more than $55 million.[28] To counter such extensive tax evasion, the National League of Cities, the National Association of Counties, and the U.S. Conference of Mayors joined traditional retailers to demand the enactment of a **Marketplace Fairness Act**, a federal law to require large online retailers to collect sales taxes. Internet enthusiasts and e-commerce retailers, however, countered that making online businesses legally liable for unpaid sales taxes would harm the growth of the e-economy.

In 2018, the U.S. Supreme Court moved to narrow the loophole where many online retail transactions were essentially tax-free. The Court ruled that a state may require the collection of sales taxes on e-sales even in instances where the online seller, located outside the state, lacked a physical brick-and mortar presence inside the state.[29]

NUISANCE TAXES, USER CHARGES, AND DEVELOPMENT IMPACT FEES

Limited in their ability to impose more lucrative taxes, cities by necessity have turned to the imposition of a miscellany of small-yield **nuisance taxes and fees**. Cities levy charges on a variety of activities, including sports and entertainment admissions, hotel room occupancy, and automobile parking in a pay garage. Cities also charge licensing fees to the operators of taxicab limousine service and to establishments that sell alcohol. **User charges and fees**[30] seek to recoup the costs that a city incurs in conducting plumbing and electrical inspections and in operating a public swimming pool, picnic shelters, and the local baseball diamond. **Special assessments** require property owners to pay an additional fee to support street paving, lighting, and other infrastructure upgrades made near their home or business.[31] Revenues from nuisance taxes and user fees and charges constitute a quarter of local own-source collections.[32]

User fees can represent a fair way to finance public services. According to a **benefit principle**, persons who benefit from a municipal service should be asked to help pay for that service. Benefit-related fees are generally seen as fairer than imposing higher taxes on all members of a community, as a tax is paid even if a resident does not use a particular service. Political conservatives further argue that when users pay a sizable fee, they no longer regard municipal services as "free"; such enlightenment should increase the public's demand to curb the growth of costly and poorly provided municipal services.

In more recent decades, local governments have increasingly turned to **development impact fees**, where a property developer is charged a special assessment to help pay for the sewers, roads, parks, schools, and other facilities required by a new residential or commercial project. Development fees are attractive politically as the taxes on existing homeowners in a community are not raised in order to finance the provision of new infrastructure. Instead, a one-time assessment is charged to developers who often wind up passing the charge on to tenants and homebuyers (through higher home prices or higher residential and commercial and rents). The courts have generally upheld the imposition of such development fees as long as the fee is reasonable (that is, "proportional" to the services received) and there is a clear connection between the fees collected and the services provided to a new development.[33]

THE STATES LIMIT BORROWING BY CITIES

State constitutions and statutes restrict how much a municipality may borrow. The New York State Constitution, for instance, limits the total indebtedness of a county, city, town, or village to 7 to 9 percent of its taxable real-estate valuation, with the exact ceiling depending on the size of a community's population. New York State similarly prohibits school districts from borrowing in excess of 9 to 10 percent of a district's property valuation.[34] The Arizona Constitution generally prohibits cities and counties from carrying debt that exceeds 6 percent of the value of taxable property that lies within a municipality's borders.[35] Across the nation, states impose still additional restrictions on municipal borrowing, often requiring voter approval via a public referendum before a city or school district can borrow money through the issuance of bonds. Such referenda are not easily won.

The states see local borrowing or bonding limits as an important device that keeps municipal governments from amassing more debt than they can repay. Such restrictions help to avert avoidable local fiscal disasters. Yet, state-imposed borrowing ceilings and restrictions can be unnecessarily confining, denying local governments the ability to finance important projects, including much-needed infrastructure improvements and the construction of new school facilities.

THE VOTER TAX REVOLT AND ITS IMPACT

A citizens's **tax revolt** that began in California in the 1970s soon spread across the nation, permanently altering patterns of local government and school finance. Californians in 1975 voted for **Proposition 13**, a measure that rolled back local property levies to what they had been a few years earlier and that limited any future annual property increase to just 2 percent. Of greater significance, Proposition 13 required the approval by two-thirds of the voters in a community for additional taxes, fees, and user charges levied by a local government.

In California and other states, tax limitation measures delivered what their backers had promised: tax relief, especially relief from soaring property taxes. In doing so, the measures also impaired the ability of municipalities to find the necessary revenues for municipal service provision. In some cases, the impact on local government was brutal. Michigan voters passed Proposition A to roll back and limit the growth of property taxes. In just a single year (2010), financially strapped Detroit lost an estimated $38 million in much-needed property tax revenues as a result of the ceilings imposed by Proposition A.[36]

State- and voter-imposed caps on property taxes have especially hurt schools that are greatly reliant on property taxation. Proposition 13 led per pupil school spending across California to plummet. Outraged parents in wealthier communities mobilized, and the California legislature responded by mandating that local governments reallocate billions of dollars in local property taxes to the schools. The reallocation of local funds and an infusion of state assistance helped to stem the immediate emergency. But the move did not halt the free-fall of public education in the state, as school districts found it increasingly difficult to raise new money. Once ranked as "Number One" in the nation in terms of the amount of money spent per child in its public schools, California by 2013 tumbled to 34th place in terms of K–12 per pupil spending, with some analyses placing California still further toward the bottom of the rankings.[37]

By ordering local governments to divert funds to education, the state of California weakened the ability of municipalities to fund non-school services. Home rule in California lost much of its significance; state-imposed tax limitation measures and spending mandates "crippled local government finance,"[38] denying local elected officials the flexibility to make meaningful program choices. Even a local government as large as Los Angeles County has been reduced to little more than an "embattled 'service delivery arm' of the State."[39]

Desperate to find alternative sources of funds to maintain local service levels, local leaders searched for loopholes in the state- and voter-imposed limitations. Civic leaders have shifted responsibility for service provision to **special districts**, independent bodies that may not be subject to the taxing and borrowing restrictions placed on general-purpose cities and counties. In Ohio, independent port districts issued revenue bonds and otherwise helped raise the capital necessary for the construction of sports arenas, museum modernization, the Cleveland Rock and Roll Hall of Fame, and the revitalization of abandoned shopping centers—economic development projects not directly related to port activities.[40] Such subterfuges to skirt voter sentiment raise important questions of democratic control and governmental accountability especially when borrowing and spending decisions are placed in the hands of unelected special-district officials (an important matter that is discussed further in Chapter 10).

In California, Florida, and numerous other states, cities have turned to revenue-raising instruments not clearly prohibited by tax limitation measures. Hikes in special assessments, user charges, and service fees help pay for street improvements, fire protection, improvements in solid waste disposal, and other municipal services.[41] In California, local governments increased impact and development fees in order to help pay for the roads, sewers, schools, and other infrastructure improvements provided new subdivisions.[42]

Trapped between the pincers of the tax limitation measure and the public's continued demand for high-quality local service, officials in a number of localities engaged in a **high-risk strategy of borrowing money to invest** in what they believe will be high-return investments. When the strategy works as planned, the investments yield sufficient funds for the municipality to repay the money it borrowed while also providing additional earnings that can support improved local services—without having to ask voters for new taxes! But the market is volatile, and investments do not always fare as predicted. If the value of an investment unexpectedly declines, a municipality may find itself in extreme fiscal distress, unable to repay creditors as the loans become due.

Orange County, California, in 1994, lost nearly $2 billion as a result of its high-risk investment strategy. The county filed for bankruptcy, closed library branches, cut school programs, reduced social programs and policing, and even suspended testing for fecal coliform bacteria at its beaches.[43] In the greater Denver and Milwaukee areas, school districts similarly borrowed money to finance investments that officials hoped would yield earnings that would help the districts meet their costly pension obligations. The school districts wound up in fiscal crisis when the national economy entered a recession, and the investments lost value.[44]

"ACADEMIC BANKRUPTCY" LAWS: THE STATES TAKE OVER SCHOOLS IN CRISIS

School districts are narrow-purpose units of local government subject to Dillon's Rule. Normally, however, school districts possess considerable decision-making latitude, a reflection of the strong value that Americans place on the grassroots control of a community's K–12 schools. Yet, a state government, should it wish, can limit, restructure, and even withdraw a school district's authority. In more recent years, the states have been increasingly willing to intrude on the autonomy of local school districts in order to initiate efforts to turn around academically failing schools and fiscally insolvent school districts.

Two dozen states have **academic bankruptcy laws** that allow the state government to take over the operation of a poorly performing school district. A number of states permit the state government to assume control of individual problem schools rather than an entire school district.[45] Louisiana, Michigan, and Tennessee have created a new statewide "recovery district" that gives state-appointed officials the ability to take over the operations of low-achieving schools no matter their location across the state.[46]

In the typical takeover, the state appoints a "receiver" or a manager (or a management team) to take charge of low-performing schools. The state gives the new manager authority over budgets, personnel, curriculum, educational reform plans, and other important decisions. Such a move effectively strips locally elected school officials of much of their powers.

The state takeover of a local school system was once a fairly rare event. In recent years, however, state takeovers have become quite a bit more commonplace. A partial list of instances where a state has stepped in to force changes in local school operations includes California (with school takeovers, in Compton, Emery, Inglewood, Oakland, and West Fresno), Alabama (Birmingham), Connecticut (Bridgeport and Hartford), Indiana (Gary and Indianapolis), Maryland (Baltimore), Louisiana, Massachusetts (Boston, Chelsea, and Lawrence), Michigan, New Jersey (Newark, Jersey City, and Paterson), New York (Roosevelt on Long Island), Ohio (Lorain and Youngstown), Pennsylvania (Philadelphia), South Carolina (Allendale), Tennessee (Memphis), and Virginia (Hampton Roads).

A brief recounting of a few of the more sizable takeovers will help reveal some of the politics and difficulties that surround a state's attempt to restructure local school operations. In Pennsylvania, the state took charge of troubled schools in Philadelphia, replacing the elected school board with an appointed School Reform Commission and a chief executive officer who, in turn, hired private educational management firms to run the schools.[47] Neighborhood activists, especially in the Philadelphia's African-American community, objected to the loss of local democracy and the shift of authority to private corporations.

In Michigan, the story of state takeovers of local schools is rather complex. In 1999, the state government assumed control of Detroit's public schools, replacing the elected school board, which was facing allegations of mismanagement, with a new board jointly appointed by the state's governor and the city's mayor. Detroit residents objected to the loss of local democracy, that white outsiders had wrested power from the elected school board in an overwhelmingly African-American city. The continued complaints eventually led the state to reverse course, and local school board elections were reinstated in 2005. But new episodes of mismanagement and corruption and the continuing failure of the schools to perform effectively led the state to reverse course yet again, placing the operations of the city's schools under a state-appointed emergency fiscal manager.[48] The see-saw pattern continued, and seven years later, in 2017, the state partially reinstated local control. A locally elected school board took office, and the position of the state-appointed emergency manager was eliminated. Yet, the State of Michigan broadened the oversight authority of the Detroit Financial Review Commission, a body dominated by state officials and their appointees, to review Detroit school budgets, contracts, programs, and the hiring and dismissal of top school officials.[49]

In Michigan, Louisiana, and other states, takeovers by the state also set in motion a process that led to the expanded use of charter schools to replace traditional public schools. (The pros and cons of charter schools will be reviewed in Chapter 9.) In New Orleans, in the wake of the devastation wrought by Hurricane Katrina, state takeover resulted in 100 schools being converted to privately run charter academies; only five schools in the city were left under the city school board. Today, all of New Orleans's public schools are charter academies operated by private and nonprofit providers.[50]

Racial minorities complain that state takeovers target their communities, that white communities are not similarly denied local control of their schools. In Louisiana, Michigan, and Tennessee, 96 percent of the schoolchildren in takeover districts were African American or Latino.[51] State takeovers increase the role played by state officials, technocrats, and philanthropists in school operations while undercutting the power of a city's African-American population.[52]

As Republicans gained increased control of state governments across the nation, school takeovers began to reflect Republicans's distrust of teacher unions and the party's faith in school choice programs and private management. Takeover efforts in Georgia had backing from a Republican governor, education-oriented reform organizations, and the charter school industry. Parents and community organizations in the affected districts, as well as the defenders of the public schools, lined up in opposition.[53] Similar battle lines over school takeovers were observed in Detroit and other cities.[54]

Do state takeovers actually improve education? The evidence is rather mixed. In some cases, a state takeover of a local school district does make a difference. Massachusetts appointed a receiver to take charge of the low-performing Lawrence Public Schools district (located 30 miles north of Boston). The restructuring eventually resulted in the replacement of half of the district's teachers and school principals, the introduction of performance-based pay tied to effective teaching, an increase in the expectations placed on students, and the use of new pedagogical approaches (including small-group instruction for targeted students during week-long vacation breaks). In Lawrence, the changes led to a sizable increase in student math achievement scores and in the number of students in high school who progressed on to the next grade.[55]

Yet, school takeovers do not always produce impressive results. Research by Vanderbilt University reveals that the schools placed into Tennessee's state-run recovery school district did not produce the turnaround that education reformers had predicted. The state-operated takeover schools showed no significant gains in student test scores. The performance of the state-run schools was especially disappointing as it lagged behind that of similar locally run schools that exhibited significant gains in their student test scores.[56] In Indianapolis in 2013, four schools taken over by the state continued to receive "F" grades.[57] In Louisiana and Detroit, the state turnaround programs produced mixed results; despite some successes, the state-managed schools were rated as "failing" according to state standards.[58]

As an alternative to state-appointed managers, some states have given big-city mayors increased authority over troubled local schools. The hope is that a **new breed of "education mayor"** would be a "prime mover" of school reform, with the political muscle to challenge teacher unions and other vested interests.[59] New York, Chicago,

Boston, Cleveland, Harrisburg, Providence, New Haven, Trenton, Hartford, Oakland, and Jackson (Mississippi) are among the cities where mayors have assumed some of the decision-making authority traditionally placed in the hands of elected local school boards.[60]

In Illinois, a Republican-led state legislature was so willing to try something new that it even handed control of the city's schools to Mayor Richard M. Daley, the most powerful Democrat in the state. The state gave the mayor the power to name the school system's chief executive, top financial officers, and a five-member board of trustees. The state further granted the mayor authority to oversee the school system's multibillion-dollar annual budget.[61] Rahm Emanuel, Daley's successor, found that mayoral control of schools could be quite controversial. Emanuel made the reform of city schools and improved student performance a priority. But the changes he instituted evoked strong criticism from the teacher union. The city's teachers went on strike, and the mayor's popularity fell. Nonetheless, Emanuel continued to shut down underperforming schools, create new charter schools, and place greater emphasis on quantitative measures of teacher performance.

THE FORMAL STRUCTURE OF CITY GOVERNMENT

There are three alternative structures of city government in the contemporary United States: the *mayor-council* plan (with its weak-mayor and strong-mayor variants), the *council-manager* plan (which places executive authority in the hands of a professional city manager, not an elected mayor), and the *commission* arrangement (a form that has faded in popularity over the years and is no longer widely used in big cities).

During the first century of U.S. existence, the mayor-council arrangement dominated. Beginning in the 1890s, however, "reformers" had substantial success in getting municipalities to switch to the council-manager plan which places substantial authority in the hands of an expert manager. Today, half of the municipalities in the United States operate under the council-manager arrangement.[62] The council-manager system is particularly popular in the Pacific West.

Most of the nation's biggest cities (including New York, Los Angeles, Chicago, Houston, and Philadelphia), though, have spurned the council-manager arrangement and continue to look to an elected mayor for leadership. Very small communities tend to choose the mayor-council plan, as residents in small communities see little need to pay for a full-time professional manager.

WEAK-MAYOR SYSTEM

Mayors in the early United States lacked strong governing powers. Citizens in the new republic remembered the America's colonial experience and the arrogance of England's King George III; this was reason enough to distrust executive power.

But as the country grew, communities required stronger government capable of providing new streets, sewers, and improved sanitation and protective services. By the

1800s, state legislatures began to experiment with new arrangements to provide necessary local services—but without increasing the power of the mayor! The states created a variety of independent elected offices and appointed boards and commissions, each with the responsibility to provide a specific municipal service. The existence of numerous independent executive offices, boards, and commissions—bodies that compete with the mayor for policy control and administration—is one of the defining characteristic of the weak-mayor system.

In the **weak-mayor system**, a mayor possesses quite limited administrative authority. The weak mayor lacks the ability to direct the operations of executive branch offices. Quite unlike the president of the United States, the mayor of a weak-mayor city does not name the heads of major executive departments. Instead, the mayor must work with a number of other executives whom he or she does not appoint and whom he or she cannot dismiss or readily control: other locally elected executives (i.e. such as a local prosecutor or city treasurer directly elected by the people); appointees to key positions made by the city council and, in some instances, by the state's governor; and the members of various independent boards and commissions (see Figure 6.1). The existence of elected department heads and numerous independent bodies produces a **fragmentation of executive power**; the mayor in a weak-mayor city cannot easily control or provide direction to executive branch agencies.

In a weak-mayor city, the members of local boards and commissions serve long fixed terms of office that insulate the boards from mayoral control. The mayor of a weak-mayor community is often denied the ability to name the majority of an independent board or commission. In the absence of resignations, a mayor may be able to appoint only one member a year to a public board or commission. As a consequence, the mayor must govern with board members who do not necessarily share his or her point of view. In a great many cities, the city council has the right to confirm or reject a mayor's appointments and dismissals. The mayor cannot simply dismiss the uncooperative members of independent boards.

In the classic weak-mayor system, the mayor possesses only the most limited legislative and budgetary responsibilities.[63] Smaller communities (with a population below 25,000) typically do not even give the mayor the ability to veto council-passed legislation.[64] Of even greater significance, in many U.S. communities, the mayor does not control the preparation of a proposed city budget, possibly the single most powerful tool that a mayor could use to set city program priorities. Instead, weak-mayor cities place the power of budget preparation in the hands of an independent administrative officer, not the mayor.

The weak-mayor system was created to shield municipal operations from the ill-advised actions of untrained, power-hungry, and overly partisan mayors. But such a plan does so at the cost of fragmenting the executive branch. The lack of a unified executive branch poses considerable obstacles to the effective governance of modern cities. Just like private corporations, cities and suburbs need a central executive who has sufficient authority to provide clear policy direction and program coordination. The weak mayor lacks such leadership prerogatives. In the weak-mayor city, various independent executives, boards, bodies, and commissions often work at cross-purposes.

Figure 6.1   **The Weak-Mayor System: Two Variants.**

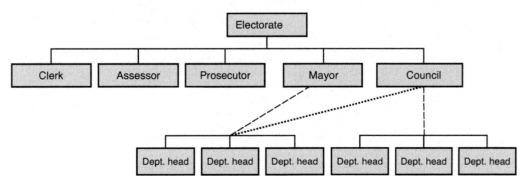

(a) The mayor does not possess total control over the executive branch but shares it with independently elected officials. Other departmental heads are subject to city council confirmation or are appointed directly by the council.

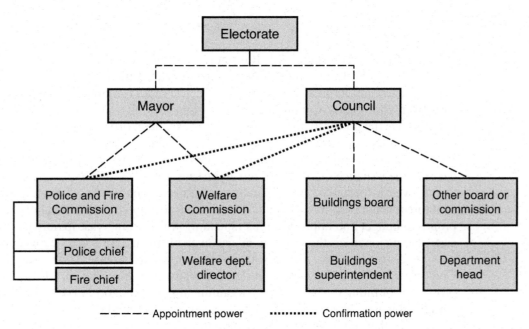

(b) The mayor does not appoint the heads of various departments and the full membership of independent boards and commissions. Even in cities where the mayor can make an appointment to fill a vacant seat, the members of independent local boards and commissions serve long, fixed, and overlapping terms, further reducing their subservience to the mayor.

STRONG-MAYOR SYSTEM

The **strong-mayor system** grants the elected mayor hierarchical authority over important city departments. Similar to the American president, the mayor of a strong-mayor city is clearly the head of the executive branch, with the authority to appoint—and dismiss—top

Figure 6.2 **The Strong-Mayor Structure.**

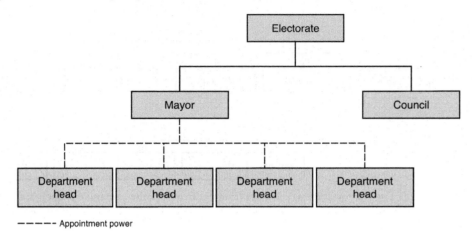

agency officials (see Figure 6.2). Baltimore, Boston, Denver, New York, Philadelphia, Pittsburgh, and St. Louis all have strong-mayor arrangements.

There is no prototypical strong-mayor city. The exact formal powers allotted a mayor vary from community to community according to a city's charter. Generally, strong mayors have the power to hire and dismiss top executive officials, to name the members of key municipal boards and commissions, to set the agenda for public meetings, to prepare the city's budget that establishes a city's spending priorities, and to approve (or decline) the issuance of city contracts to private firms.[65]

But even a formally "strong" mayor is subject to numerous checks. Top mayoral appointees often require city council confirmation. City councils can alter the mayor's proposed budget and appropriations (spending) bills. In the vast majority of medium-sized and major cities, the city council can override the mayor's veto. City councils may also possess the authority to review major municipal purchases and city-issued contracts. Civil service and merit personnel systems (a topic that is discussed in Chapter 7) and the provisions of municipal collective bargaining agreements, too, serve to limit a mayor's command power. Nor can a city's chief executive command the heads of businesses to act in ways that will contribute to a community's well-being.

Even the possession of strong formal powers, then, is not sufficient to guarantee a mayor the ability to lead. Mayors cannot rely solely on the formal prerogatives of office. True leadership also depends on a mayor's ability to build and maintain an effective governing coalitions.

COMMISSION GOVERNMENT

The **commission form** of government has no separation of powers; instead, a five- to nine-member city commission governs the city, with each member having both legislative and executive responsibilities. Different experts each oversee the operations of a

Figure 6.3 **Commission Structure.**

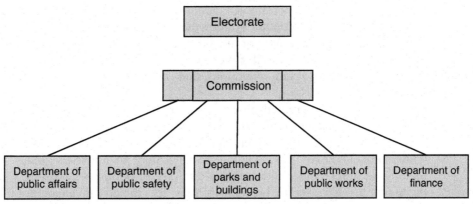

different municipal department, coming together as the city council (referred to as the city commission) to set overall policy. Each commissioner serves both as the head of a city department and as a member of the city's legislature (Figure 6.3). The commission selects one of its members to serve as mayor and preside over commission meetings and ceremonial gatherings. Under the commission arrangement, no real single executive heads the government. The mayor possesses no more authority than does any other commissioner.

In theory, the commission system provides expertise and allows for quick action, as the city's legislators and heads of executive departments are one and the same. There are no checks and balances to slow action.

Yet the disadvantages of the arrangement are often overwhelming. A commissioner may be an advocate of the narrow view of his or her department. A commissioner may be reluctant to scrutinize the budget requests of other departments, fearing that such scrutiny will produce retaliation by other commissioners. An elected commissioner also may not possess the administrative skills needed to manage a large municipal department, especially as voters seldom cast their ballots on the basis of a candidate's administrative abilities.

Portland (Oregon) is the only large city in the United States to retain the commission system. Forest Park (Illinois) and Sunrise (Florida) are notable suburbs with the commission plan. The commission arrangement, though, is more commonly found in county government. More than one-third of U.S. counties are governed under some variant of the commission system.[66]

THE COUNCIL-MANAGER (CITY MANAGER) SYSTEM

A different reform alternative, the *council-manager system*, gained popularity as a result of the value it accorded the expertise and skills of a professional manager. The National Municipal League made the council-manager system a key element in the League's highly influential *Model City Charter*. Dayton, Ohio, in 1913 became the first city of significant size to adopt this "good government" reform. Thousands of communities across the nation quickly followed, adopting the council-manager structure.

Under the **council-manager system**, the city council appoints a professionally trained manager who is given charge of the daily affairs of the city. The city council continues to enact laws and set overall policy; but decisions regarding personnel, day-to-day departmental and program operations, and other matter of administration are handled by the city manager.

The mayor in the council-manager system possesses very limited power. In a great many council-manager cities, the council selects one of its own members to serve as mayor. Alternatively, the city charter may allow citizens to elect the mayor in a city-wide ballot. The mayor in a council-manager may preside over council meetings, sign federal aid agreements, and represent the city in public ceremonies. Other than that, the mayor has few assigned responsibilities. It is the city manager, not the mayor, who is charged with managing the executive branch and running the city on a daily basis. The city manager—not the mayor—appoints key personnel and gives instructions to the various municipal agencies (see Figure 6.4). Department heads report to—and take orders from—the city manager, not to the mayor.

The council-manager system emulates the structure of many private corporations. In a manager-led city, the city council functions much like a private company's board of directors that help set a corporation's overall goals. The city council delegates substantial operational authority to an appointed city manager, just as a private corporation's board of directors appoints a chief executive officer (CEO) and places the day-to-day running of the business in the hands of the CEO.

A city manager is a municipality's CEO. The city council appoints a city manager. Just like a private corporation, the council can also dismiss a chief executive whose service proves disappointing.

Figure 6.4 **Council-Manager Structure.**

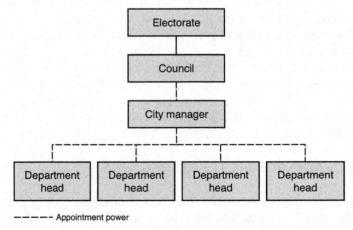

The council-manager system has been widely adopted in medium-sized communities, suburbs, and cities in the South and the West. A number of larger cities, too, have the council-manager arrangement. Phoenix, San Antonio, Dallas, San Jose, Austin, Fort Work, Charlotte, El Paso, Las Vegas, Sacramento, Long Beach, Santa Ana, Tucson, Oklahoma City, Jacksonville, Memphis, Virginia Beach, Kansas City and Wichita are among the noteworthy communities that have a manager-council structure of government.

The advantages of the council-manager plan are obvious: It places the highly complex tasks of government in the hands of a trained professional. City managers possess considerable **expertise** (detailed technical knowledge) in such areas as accounting, budgeting, public finance, long-term planning, personnel management, and civil engineering. City managers also tend to search for long-term policy solutions. In contrast to a mayor who must be concerned with reelection, the decisions made by a manager may be less influenced by short-term electoral and partisan considerations—although the evidence on this point is not overwhelming.[67] City managers also generally exhibit a commitment to high ethical standards.

The council-manager arrangement operates smoothly when officials abide by the roles they are assigned under the plan. The city council establishes a city's overall **mission** or sense of direction, setting forth the city's general philosophy regarding taxing, spending, and growth. The council and city manager jointly decide specific questions of **policy**, for instance, determining the exact level of services that will be provided and just what projects will be built. The city manager, however, has charge of daily program **management and administration**, including personnel assignment and supervision, budget preparation, purchasing, data processing, oversight of the work of private firms contracted by the city, and the day-to-day performance of city agencies. Council members are not supposed to intrude in matters of program administration, a realm assigned to the city manager. Nonetheless, council members often do intervene in administrative matters, especially in response to constituent complaints.[68]

The city-manager model seeks to separate administration (matters of management) from politics. Yet, to get things done, a city manager must exhibit considerable political skill and sensitivity. A city manager cannot sit idly and sidestep controversial issues. The contemporary manager provides project advocacy and policy leadership.[69] The most successful managers often devote considerable time and care to forge a political consensus behind the program initiatives they favor.[70] A city manager commands respect by being "apolitical"; but "being apolitical does not mean avoiding difficult policy issues."[71]

City council members rely on the city manager for research, analysis, and program recommendations. Council members typically serve part-time and are poorly remunerated for their work. Most communities do not provide council members with adequate full-time staff or a well-staffed legislative research bureau. As a result, council members often lack the time and capacity to analyze the complexities of alternative courses of action. The most capable managers present information that helps to shape the choices made by the city council.

Effective city managers try not to take the public stage. Such managers prefer to handle matters quietly rather than engage in visible combat with members of the council.[72]

With its emphasis on expertise and professionalism, the council-manager system can reduce the level of conflict in city hall.[73] Yet in manager-led cities, conflict can still emerge, especially as no clear line separates matters of politics and policy formulation from administration. In some cities, the mayor and manager compete for influence, as the public expects a mayor, especially a mayor who is elected citywide, to lead. City managers often charge that the mayor and council members improperly interfere in administrative matters. Mayors and city council members, in turn, accuse more aggressive city managers of improperly trying to assume policy decisions that should properly be left to elected officials.

Does the ability of the city council to dismiss a city manager give the council effective control over a city manager? Not always! Not every manager lives in fear of being fired. A city council may be hesitant to dismiss the city's top executive, as the city may gain a reputation for being "hostile" place for city managers to work, a reputation that will make it difficult for the city to recruit a truly talented manager. In small- and medium-sized communities, part-time council members are not always willing to commit the extensive time necessary to screen and interview candidates to fill a city manager vacancy.

The nation's biggest cities have, for the most part, spurned the council-manager structure. They believe that an appointed manager will lack important political skills and ability to get things done in a diverse community. In a large contentious city, a mayor may have a difficult task in leading, but at least the mayor enjoys the sense of legitimacy and other advantages that derive from popular election. An unelected manager, by comparison, has less ability to command media attention and rally public support behind a project.

THE HYBRID STRUCTURE OF CITY GOVERNMENT TODAY

Today, few cities strictly abide by the ideal weak-mayor, strong-mayor, and council-manager plans described in this chapter. Instead, the structures of city government have been quite "malleable,"[74] with cities, over the years, making modifications in their initial governing arrangements, borrowing successful structural elements from other communities. Most municipalities today have **hybrid governments** that blend features from alternative governmental structures.

In more recent years, a number of council-manager cities have increased the powers given to the mayor, even though a well-paid city manager is still put in charge of the day-to-day operation of city government. Cincinnati and Toledo sought a strengthened mayor who could deliver on the promises made to business leaders and thereby serve as a more effective bargainer with corporate officials when seeking to steer new job growth to the city. Cincinnati switched to a citywide ballot for mayor, enhancing the mayor's prominence. Cincinnati also gave the mayor additional budgetary authority and the ability to name and replace the city manager as well as the chairs of city council committees. Cincinnati is still largely a council-manager city; yet the mayor is no longer a mere ceremonial figurehead.

San Jose, Oakland, Sacramento, and Hayward (California) and Austin (Texas) all instituted citywide election of the mayor in order to make city government more responsive to the demands of racial minorities and homeowners. Progressive activists hope that direct election of the mayor would help to offset some of the deference that city managers have often shown business elites and members of the local growth machine.[75]

San Diego, once held out as a gleaming model of the council-manager system, shifted to a hybrid governing system before ultimately adopting the strong-mayor arrangement. The long process of transformation began the 1970s when Mayor Pete Wilson (who would later serve as governor of California and U.S. senator) sought to strengthen the mayor's office. Wilson observed that the council-manager system imposed a "structural straitjacket"[76] on the steps that a mayor could take to lead a dynamic growing community. As a result of Wilson's efforts, San Diego granted the mayor's office new authority to set the city council agenda and to name the chairs and members of council committees.

In 2004 (and finalized by a second ballot in 2010), voters approved a total change in San Diego's structure of government: San Diego adopted the strong-mayor system, abandoning its once-celebrated council-manager plan. The mayor gained new powers to appoint department heads and various other city officials as well as the authority to prepare the city budget. San Diego's mayor even gained a power that very few American mayors possess: the **line-item veto power** which serves to increase a mayor's willingness to exercise his or her veto authority. In cities where a mayor can only veto an entire piece of legislation, a mayor may be forced to accept parts of a bill that he or she dislikes in order to sign into law a bill's other important provisions. In San Diego, in contrast, the line-item veto enables the mayor to strike out parts of a budget or spending bill while signing into law the provisions that he or she approves. In 2017 Mayor Kevin Faulconer exercised his line-item veto authority, accepting the bulk of the council-passed budget while striking out increased expenditures for council offices that he deemed unnecessary.[77]

In more recent decades, a fairly large number of other cities have sought to modify or, like San Diego, even abandon the council-manager arrangement in order to provide for more effective mayoral leadership. Oakland turned away from its traditional manager-led system and adopted a strong-mayor plan that gave then-mayor Jerry Brown the authority to dismiss the city manager. Fresno, Spokane, Miami, St. Petersburg, Richmond, and Hartford, too, switched to the mayor-council system.

The changes in municipal government, however, have not all been unidirectional. A few communities—notably El Paso, Topeka, and Cedar Rapids—switched to the council-manager plan. When revelations of local scandal dominate the news, communities pay new attention to the virtues of a manager-led system of government with its avowed commitment to professionalism and to high standards of ethical conduct.[78]

A number of mayor-council cities utilize the professional guidance offered by a city-manager-like figure, a **chief administrative officer (CAO)**. The CAO is an experienced city-hall hand who works with the mayor to oversee the actions of municipal departments. The CAO offers managerial advice and helps tutor a new mayor in the intricacies of budget preparation and other governmental processes. The CAO is usually a careerist who is a source of continuity and institutional memory in city hall.

In cities as diverse as New York, Richmond, and Albuquerque, the mayor names the CAO, with the appointment often subject to city council confirmation. An appointive CAO and a mayor are likely to be able to work together as a team. Mayoral appointment, however, can compromise a CAO's political independence and professionalism.[79] In New York, the CAO (or First Deputy Mayor, as the position is called in New York) functions less like a city manager and more like a top-level mayoral assistant.

CITY COUNCILS: NO MINIATURE REPRODUCTIONS OF THE U.S. CONGRESS

Only in the nation's biggest cities do council members serve full-time and receive more generous compensation. Los Angeles pays the highest council salaries in the nation, an eye-popping $184,610 per year (2015 figures). New York pays council members a base salary of $148,500 (2016 data). Houston pays its full-time council members a more modest $62,983. Other cities pay a lot less.

In Mobile, Alabama, council members receive $19,800 annually plus meeting expenses and a $325 per month expense account. In Irvine, California, a council member receives an annual salary of only $10,560 plus an $8.580 automobile allowance. Fullerton, California, pays a base annual salary of only $9,000.[80] With such low salaries, many council members do not devote extensive time to their legislative work and to providing constituent service. Numerous small- and even a number of medium-sized communities do not even schedule weekly council meetings.

Quite unlike the U.S. Congress and the vast majority of state legislatures, city councils are seldom organized along party lines. In contrast to the U.S. House and Senate, the typical city council has no the majority party leader who exercises great control over legislative proceedings. The overwhelming majority of city councils are formally nonpartisan; members no not run for office as a declared Democratic or Republican. Consequently, city councils generally do not suffer the deep partisan polarizations of the sort that plagued Washington during the Clinton, Obama, and Trump years.

Legislative committees play a much less significant legislative role in city and suburban government than they do in the U.S. Senate and House of Representatives. However, a number of city councils are beginning to make expanded use of **standing committees** (that is, permanent council committees that meet to study proposed legislation in an assigned policy area).[81] Still, the legislative committee system is less developed in city hall than in the U.S. Congress. Most city councils have too few members to be to be able to divide work among a number of specialized committees. Part-time and underpaid council members are also hesitant to devote large amounts of time to committee work. Compared to the U.S. Congress, city councils conduct few committee hearings on proposed legislation.

IMPROVING THE PERFORMANCE OF CITY COUNCILS: ARE TERM LIMITATIONS THE ANSWER?

In contrast to the pattern observed in the U.S. Congress, few city council members serve long legislative careers. The typical city council member stays in office for a relatively short duration of time and then leaves voluntarily in order to return to take a better-paying job in the private sector or to run for higher office. Only half of a newly elected city-council class will on the city council five years later.[82]

The high rate of turnover of city council members results in a lack of experience that can impair council performance. A legislature of short-termers may not have the depth of knowledge necessary for informed and independent legislative action. Amateur, part-time legislators with little experience are not in a strong position to challenge the reports and recommendations presented by a city manager, municipal department heads, a city's hired consultants, and the local business community.

In the 1990s, a grassroots reform movement demanded the enactment of **term limitations** to prohibit a council member from serving more than two or three consecutive terms. The term limitations movement was a call for citizen power. The movement began as a call to change the U.S. Congress, where members easily won reelection and served long legislative careers.

In its early years, local term limitation measures spread like a brushfire. More recently, the demand for term limitations has waned. Only 10 percent of American communities limit the number of terms that a council member may serve.[83]

Why did the movement for municipal term limitations lose steam? There is one obvious explanation: In most communities, where council members to not serve extended legislative careers, there is no real need to impose term limitations! "Term limits" at the local level appears to be medicine for a disease that does not really exist. Term limitation can even diminish legislative performance by forcing a council's few experienced members to leave office.

If term limitations are not the answer, just what can be done to improve the performance of a city council, especially in medium- and large-sized communities? First, city councils need sufficient staff support so that council members can participate as informed and independent voices in local decision making. Second, a city should strive to pay local legislators a level of compensation that will attract members who can devote considerable time to doing the public's business and meeting citizen groups. Third, a city's legislature can make a system of council committees a regular part of the legislative process.

Finally, cities that have two-year terms for council members might consider shifting to four-year terms. The pressures of constant election, including the need to constantly raise campaign funds in large cities for races that are held every two years, can lead talented council members to leave public office.

WOMEN IN LOCAL GOVERNMENT

As of August 2018, 23 of the nation's 100 most populous cities had women mayors. The most prominent women mayors were these: Thelda Williams (Phoenix, the nation's 8th largest city); London Breed (San Francisco, 15th largest); Betsy Price (Fort Worth, 16th largest city); Vi Alexander Lyles (Charlotte, 20th); Muriel Bowser (Washington, DC, 24th); Catherine Pugh (Baltimore, 26th); Jenny Durkin (Seattle, 28th); Carolyn Goodman (Las Vegas, 32nd); Jean Stothert (Omaha, 42nd); Keisha Lance Bottoms (Atlanta, 43rd); Nancy McFarlane (Raleigh, 45th), Elizabeth "Libby" Schaaf (Oakland, 49th), and Betsy Hodges (Minneapolis, 50th). Only one-fifth of the cities with a population greater than 100,000 had a woman as mayor.[84] In 2019, Lori Lightfoot became the first African-American woman and lesbian to be elected mayor of Chicago.

Women are also underrepresented in municipal legislatures where they hold about 30 percent of city council seats. The figure is low but nonetheless compares favorably to the national government where in 2017 only 19.6 percent of House seats and 21 percent of Senate seats occupied by women.[85]

What accounts for the underrepresentation of women in local office? A number of the barriers that once served to bar women from local office actually appear to be eroding. Statistics show that women who run for municipal office actually enjoy about the same victory rate enjoyed by male candidates. In large cities, female office seekers generally are able to raise as much money for their campaigns as do men. The underrepresentation of women in the local arena largely continues as fewer women than men choose to run for public office.[86]

The lower ambitions of women for political office reflects gendered patterns of socialization, as parents do not always communicate to young girls that a political career is appropriate.[87] Women, more than men, see modern electoral campaigns as unduly combative and unfair in the treatment accorded women.[88]

Why are women more willing to seek local positions than state and national office?[89] Here too, entrenched gendered roles continue to affect women's choices. Compared to state and national office, service in local government poses less conflict with the family and child care responsibilities borne by women.[90] Women also have an interest in local office as local governments deals with policy matters—affordable housing, social welfare, health care, and education—of concern to women in their role as family caretaker: "[T]he local level is where many of the problems that are of most concern to women are addressed, and consequently where many women are introduced to political gladiatorial combat."[91]

The ideological climate of a city also affects a woman's chance of electoral success. A study of 239 cities reveals that women are more likely to win city council races in liberal as opposed to more conservative communities.[92]

Once in office, women tend to approach their responsibilities with a political style that differs somewhat from men. A study of city managers, for instance, reveals that female managers are more likely to utilize leadership approaches based on communication and conciliation. Women, more than men, try to bring city officials together when attempting to resolve a dispute. Male city managers, by contrast, tend to rely on their formal authority and are more willing to dismiss an agency head who has lost the confidence of a city's leaders.[93] Other studies similarly underscore the more collegial leadership styles of women.[94] An increase in the number of women serving in local government has the potential to alter the style of operation as well as the policies of local government.[95]

THE DIFFICULT TASK OF MAYORAL LEADERSHIP

Elected officials who wish to lead must look beyond the formal prerogatives of office. Chicago, on paper, has a weak-mayor form of government. Yet, for more than a half century, Chicago mayors were anything but weak. Mayor Richard J. Daley, the legendary "boss" of Chicago (1955 to 1976) and his son Richard M. Daley, the city's longest serving mayor (1989 to 2011), both wielded considerable power, building relationships with developers, corporate heads, and federal officials, as well as using their dominance in the local Democratic Party organization to gain effective control over the city council. Rahm Emanuel (2011 to 2019) proved to be an effective albeit highly controversial leader (see Box 6.1).

Box 6.1
Chicago's Rahm Emanuel: The Challenges Faced by a Self-Styled "Ruthless" Yet "Idealistic" Mayor

Being mayor of a big city is no easy job. Chicago's Rahm Emanuel, formerly a Member of Congress and White House chief of staff to Barack Obama, handily won the city's mayoralty in 2011 despite his abrasive political style and his lack of familiarity with large sections of the city. Emanuel brought a new age of electoral campaigning to Chicago including Hollywood fundraisers. Superior fundraising enabled Emanuel to dominate television and the Internet. Emanuel's ties to Obama enabled him to cruise to victory in every African-American ward in the city, despite running against African-American and Hispanic opponents.

Emanuel was no conventional Chicago politician who emphasized ward politics, patronage, and service particularism. Instead, Emanuel was a "policy wonk," a combative individual who intensely pursued change and who admitted to having little patience when obstructions blocked his path. The mayor pushed school reform, lengthening the school day, closing dozens of underperforming elementary schools, and setting up numerous new charter schools. In his first term as mayor, Emanuel rebuffed the salary and pension demands of the teachers's union, moves which earned the wrath of the union and which precipitated strike.

Emanuel courted continued corporate investment in his Global City. The mayor built strong relations with downtown corporate leaders, with investors from across the nation and even with business executives in Mexico, Poland, and around the world. He offered considerable tax breaks in support of downtown business expansion. The mayor's critics charged that Emanuel's corporate-oriented policies favored big-business interests and tourist-oriented development while slighting conditions in the city's poorer neighborhoods.

Yet Emanuel's governing approach contained a number of populist and progressive elements. He visited black, Hispanic, and white neighborhoods, greeted road crews as they cleared snow from city streets, and talked with passengers as they rode the elevated trains—publicizing these and other mayoral activities on Twitter. He proclaimed Chicago a "sanctuary city" where law enforcement officials would not cooperate with federal efforts to deport undocumented immigrants who had committed no significant crime. Emanuel even launched a free tuition program at the city's colleges for the children of undocumented immigrants who earned a 3.0 grade point average or better in high school. Emanuel emphasized "green" policies, even closing traffic lanes on major streets in order to promote commuting by bicycle.

In a city as big and racially divided as Chicago, it is difficult for a leader to maintain support across the various racial and ethnic groups that make up the city. As mayor, Emanuel initially drew support from whites, Hispanics, and the city's business community. His ties to President Obama helped him among African Americans. But his standing in the polls slipped significantly, especially after his prolonged confrontation with the city's teachers's union. The quite public combat over the city's schools resulted in a drastic drop in the mayor's political standing in Chicago's

African-American community; over 40 percent of Chicago's public-school teachers are black, and the teachers's union was led by a vocal African-American woman.

Emanuel alienated other city labor unions when he declared his intention to renegotiate contracts in order to reduce the city's contributions to municipal pensions, a necessary move, he argued, as the city faced a looming "pension gap." He also raised city taxes, another effort taken, at least in part, to stem the growth of the pension gap.

Events eventually overtook the mayor. The mayor enraged the African-American community when he dawdled in his response to the police killing of Laquan McDonald, a black teen who held a knife but was shot multiple times as he walked away from police officers. Footage from a dash-mounted police camera revealed that the officer in question had lied in his written report; the videotape revealed that the officer had fired an additional dozen shots as McDonald was lying prone in the street. The city was slow to release the dashcam footage, and critics blamed the mayor for being part of an attempted cover-up. Emanuel was attacked for being too protective of a police department that had too many lethal encounters with minority youth.

The mayor was chastened in a surprisingly difficult 2015 reelection campaign, where he received only 45 percent of the popular vote in the initial February contest, falling short of the fifty-plus percent threshold required for victory. Emanuel was forced into a second-round runoff election against the relatively unknown Jesus "Chuy" Garcia. The contest wound up being much tougher than the mayor had anticipated. Backed by his corporate allies, the mayor retained a huge advantage in political spending: Emanuel and his allies spent $23 million, a figure that dwarfed the mere $5 million spent by the Garcia camp. Yet, public opinion polls showed Emanuel trailing throughout much of the race. Emanuel eventually won, but received only 56 percent of the vote, hardly a ringing endorsement of the mayor.

Emanuel began his second term with a more toned-down leadership approach. But he could not escape the city's racial polarizations. Nor could he undo his combative image. The political resentments and racial chasms that appeared during his first term continued to build. When asked about the prolonged bitterness left by the teacher strike, Emanuel said that he had no regrets, that his controversial efforts had markedly improved graduation rates and brought other positive changes to the city's schools:

> "There are certain things that you have [to do], then take the political hit if you think the long-term gain for other people is worth that. You have to be idealistic enough to know why you're doing what you're doing, and then ruthless enough to get it done," he says.

During Emanuel's second term as mayor, the city averted another teachers's strike; the teachers even accepted the city's proposal to no longer contribute to teacher pensions—at least for new hires. The mayor gained national prominence by affirming Chicago's continued commitment to the Paris Accords even after President Trump withdrew the United States federal government from the climate change agreement. Emanuel continued to defy Trump on immigration policies, even declaring Chicago as a "Trump-free zone." His approval ratings doubled, rising from 23 percent to 51 percent.

But new revelations of police misconduct and federal investigations of the shootings of black youth by members of the city police continued. The mayor also alienated homeowners by raising local property taxes, already among the highest in the nation, in an effort to help the city meet its pension obligations.

As the police officer who shot Laquan MacDonald was finally put on trial in 2018, Emanuel surprised local media and city hall observers in suddenly announcing that he would not seek a third term as mayor. Despite his political intensity and his grasp of policy details, Emanuel could no longer maintain "his triangulating balancing act" and continue to win support from African Americans as well as from national and global corporate leaders, poorer communities, and the various ethnic groups that make up Chicago.

Sources: Paul M. Green, "Rahm Emanuel: Beginning a New Mayoral Era in Chicago," in *The Mayors: Chicago's Political Tradition*, 4th ed., ed. Paul M. Green and Melvin G. Holli (Carbondale, IL: Southern Illinois University Press, 2013), 238–261; Kari Lyderson, *Mayor 1%: Rahm Emanuel and the Rise of Chicago's 99%* (Chicago: Haymarket Books, 2013); Bill Snyder, "Rahm Emanuel, 'Be Ruthless and Idealistic,'" web posting of the Stanford Graduate School of Business summarizing its hour-long discussion with Emanuel, posted February 28, 2017, www.gsb.stanford.edu/insights/rahm-emanuel-be-idealistic-ruthless. Campaign spending and polling figures in the 2015 race are reported by Rick Pearson and Hal Dardick, "Emanuel, Allies Spent At Least $22.8 Million to Win," *Chicago Tribune*, April 16, 2015 and Susan B. Glasser, "Trump and Rahm Emanuel Both Love a Fight, Especially Against Each Other," *The New Yorker*, February 14, 2018. The "triangulating balancing act" quotation is from Kim Bellware, "Post-'Rahmbo' Chicago and the Death of Triangulation," *New York Times*, September 8, 2018.

In many cities, however, mayors are denied key prerequisites for leadership. The mayoralty tends to be a full-time time position only in mayor-council cities with a population over 250,000.[96] In council-manager cities and especially in midsized and smaller communities, the mayoralty tends to be only a part-time, poorly paid, and understaffed position. Such a setting does not allow a mayor to develop his or her own policy agenda. Nor is the mayor in such cities in an advantageous position to challenge the recommendations of top managers and planners. Part-time mayors have little time to devote to building effective working relationships with state and local officials, ties that can pay off in increased intergovernmental assistance for local projects. In such circumstances, it is often nearly impossible for a mayor to effectively lead.

The urban setting is difficult political terrain. Effective leadership depends on a mayor's personality, skills, and ability to listen to diverse constituencies. A mayor must also respond to events and crises over which he or she has no control. The formal powers of the mayor's office provide no guarantee of effective leadership.

MINORITY MAYORS AND THE DEBATE OVER DERACIALIZATION

African-American and Latino mayors often confront a particularly difficult tradeoff in governing. Should a minority mayor pursue actions (including programs that seek to improve the conditions in a city's poorer neighborhoods) that will advance the position of his or her core constituency? Or should a minority mayor emphasize broader program goals that promise to benefit the city as whole and that will even win the backing of business leaders, allowing the mayor to forge an effective multiracial and multiethnic governing coalition?

The first generation of big-city African-American mayors were steeped in the activism of the civil rights era and were ready to battle for change in cities that were polarized along racial lines. Cleveland's Carl Stokes in 1967 was the first African American to be elected mayor of a big city. Stokes emerged victorious, winning black votes and a slim sliver of votes from liberal whites that provided the margin of victory. Once in office, Stokes found that undue deference to the concerns of white leaders was stymying his ability to push for far-reaching changes that would improve conditions in Cleveland's poorer neighborhoods. Stokes eventually decided to act as a change-oriented mayor, choosing to pursue redistributive program initiatives that were heavily criticized by the members of other communities.[97] Detroit Mayor Coleman Young (1973–1993), who came to government after years of experience as a labor organizer and civil rights activist who fought police brutality, adopted an even more combative and polarizing "what goes around comes around" political style that irked whites and suburbanites.[98]

In contrast, San Antonio's Henry Cisneros (1981–1989), the first Mexican-American mayor of a major U.S. city, toned down overt racial appeals and instead sought to build support across racial and ethnic lines. Cisneros pursued growth projects to bring much-needed jobs and opportunity for both Latinos and Anglos. Activist Latino organizations including COPS (Communities Organized for Public Services) sometimes complained that Cisneros was overly concerned with the city's central business district and with new stadium construction. Cisneros, they charged, failed to give sufficient attention to the urgent needs of low-income neighborhoods.[99]

In Los Angeles, Tom Bradley during his five terms as mayor (1973–1993) made similar choices and faced similar criticism. An African American, Bradley won the mayoralty with a *deracialized* appeal to diverse ethnic groups. Bradley stressed his reputation for being a "tough cop" in the Los Angeles Police Department. As mayor, Bradley built an effective working partnership with the city's business community and with white liberal groups, including organized labor and the city's Jewish community. Yet more activist critics charged that Bradley, like Cisneros, was too deferential to his coalition partners, including white business interests. The critics argue that the mayors could have done more to help racial minorities and the poor.[100]

Atlanta's Andrew Young, New York's David Dinkins, Philadelphia's Wilson Goode, Detroit's Dennis Archer, Denver's Federico Peña, Seattle's Norman Rice, Charlotte's Harvey Gantt, and Los Angeles's Antonio Villaraigosa were all fabled African-American and Latino mayors who utilized a largely **deracialized approach to leadership** that toned down racial appeals and deemphasized redistribution. These mayors emphasized good-government managerialism, their ability to forge partnerships with business leaders for job growth, and program initiatives that promised benefits across racial lines.[101] Villaraigosa won L.A.'s mayoralty in 2005, having narrowly lost four years previous.

Villaraigosa learned from his earlier failure about the perils inherent in relying solely on Latino votes. In the second campaign, Villaraigosa broadened his appeal and reached out to liberal whites, organized labor, and the city's Jewish community.[102] In office, however, he discovered the difficulties in trying to sustain the support of such a diverse multiethnic coalition.

Deracialized appeals are especially important when a minority candidate seeks office in a city where the city's dominant racial minority group does not constitute a clear majority of the active electorate. Barack Obama's 2008 presidential victory stands as testimony to the electoral advantages of a black candidate's deracialized appeal when running in a majority-white political electorate.

Advocates argue that a deracialized leadership approach represents an evolution or maturing of black and Latino politics. Critics, however, scorn the compromises that black and Latino mayors often make in office. Such critics argue for a minority politics focused on the pursuit of social justice and programs that "improve the quality [of life] of minorities" who reside in the city.[103] Moderate black mayors too often pursue "policies of fiscal conservatism and downtown development"[104] that "appeal to white voters"[105] and wind up slighting the possibilities of more far-reaching transformational change: "Black politics is not maturing and may be degenerating."[106] Constant pressure from community organizations, churches, labor unions, and civil rights groups is often needed to keep a black or Latino mayor from caving to the demands of business leaders and other elite interests.[107]

While the debate over deracialization continues, for many of the current generation of black and Hispanic mayors, the debate does not appear to be practically relevant. They see the debate over deracialization as presenting a false dichotomy. A black mayor or Hispanic mayor recognizes the importance of winning the support of white voters (or, to be precise, the rather slim but politically decisive segment of white voters who may provide the margin of victory) and corporate business leaders whose cooperation is essential to get things done—while also pursuing progressive change to help the city's poor and minority communities.

The 1960s and 1970s "first wave" of big-city black mayors had to confront the obstructionism of white politicians and the hostility of white voters. By contrast, many of today's new generation of **post-racial black mayors** grew up in racially integrated neighborhoods and attended white-dominated schools; some of the new post-racial mayors even attended the nation's best universities. Post-racial minority leaders like Newark's Cory Booker, a graduate of Yale Law School, are comfortable working across racial and ethnic lines.[108] Booker, who would later gain election to the U.S. Senate and run for the presidency, used the mayoralty to bring conditions in Newark to the attention of outside audiences. Booker's skills enabled him to raise project funds for his impoverished city from governmental and nonprofit authorities.[109]

In Sacramento, California, Kevin Johnson (the former pro basketball star) similarly governed by building a moderate cross-racial coalition. Johnson had no other workable choice. His call for fiscal moderation in government appealed to a larger audience in a city where African Americans made up only 20 percent of the local population.[110]

Post-racial black mayors express their commitment to improve conditions in the city's black community. Yet, post-racial black mayors also recognize the necessity of good-government managerialism and reform (both Booker and Johnson endorsed school vouchers), of balancing a city's finances (Booker as mayor even dismissed hundreds of city workers as the city's fiscal position continued to deteriorate), and of partnering with the leaders of corporations and nonprofit organizations in order to bring new project funding and jobs to their city. Booker and Johnson did not justify change in racially divisive terms.

The new-generation black and Hispanic mayors have not forgotten their ethnic "identity"; they do not see race and ethnicity as irrelevant. Post-racial minority mayors respond to the concerns of their core communities; but they also recognize the importance of having an appeal that crosses lines of race and ethnicity.

Black and Hispanic control of city hall also appears to be more fragile than the growing populations of minorities in central cities would seem to suggest. In Detroit and New Orleans (cities where African Americans are a majority of the population) and in Philadelphia, Charlotte, and Jacksonville (cities with a large black population), African-American mayors have been succeeded in office by whites. This political turn of events underscores the electoral importance of a minority mayor's reach across racial lines, to liberal or centrist whites whose votes can be won.

In New Orleans, Hurricane Katrina altered the political demography of the city. The flooding of the city led to an exodus of black residents to other states. The demolition of public housing, and the arrival of white gentrifiers and an ethnically diverse set of laborers who helped in the physical labor of rebuilding the city were all factors that helped Mitch Landrieu win the mayoralty in 2010, the first mayoral victory by a white candidate in over 30 years. Landrieu, a liberal who appealed to African-American voters, handily won reelection in 2014. With the city charter barring the mayor from running for a third term, LaToya Cantrell succeeded him in office to become the first female mayor of New Orleans. An African Americans was once again mayor of the Crescent City. Yet, as a result of the city's changed population demography, the hold that African Americans enjoyed for nearly four decades now seemed somewhat precarious.

A similar story of the fragility of black electoral power in a majority black city is also told in Detroit. As Detroit flirted with insolvency, Mike Duggan, a Caucasian who was the former CEO of the Detroit Medical Center, emerged victorious in the 2013 runoff mayoral election, running a write-in campaign after a city commission had denied him a place on the written ballot as a result of a residency issue. His opponent charged that Duggan was a "carpetbagger" who only recently moved to the city from the suburbs. But in a city thirsting for new leadership in the midst of a dire financial crisis, such complaints fell on deaf ears. Duggan, who had the backing of corporate leaders in the region, carried over 90 percent of the precincts in the city and won the votes of all major demographic groups. Duggan became the Detroit's first white mayor in nearly 40 years. Duggan handily won reelection in 2017, having restored some services in troubled neighborhoods and having Detroit climb its way out of bankruptcy.

The fragility of black electoral gains is also evident in majority-minority Atlanta, where four decades of African-American control on city hall nearly tumbled in two separate elections. In 2009, Kasim Reed, an African American, defeated a seemingly weak white opponent by a quite slim margin of only 700 votes. Reed had been forced into a second round or runoff election against Mary Norwood, a white resident of affluent Buckhead. Reed had won 45 percent of the vote in the initial mayoral contest, but fell short of the 50-percent threshold required in Atlanta for a first-round victory. Norwood's candidacy benefited from a surge in white voter turnout. In the runoff election, white voter turnout (40 percent) once again exceeded black turnout, which stood at a low 30 percent.[111] In 2017, the pattern virtually repeated itself, with Keisha Lance Bottoms, an African-American woman, narrowly survived the first round contest winning only a little more than a quarter of the votes cast. She then defeated Norwood in a runoff election by a mere 750 votes, a margin of less than 1 percent!

In Atlanta and in other cities, African-American mobilization has waned as the excitement that once surround the election of a black mayor seems to have faded into the past. A sizable portion of the black community also sees little point in participating in city elections: past electoral victories did not bring about meaningful changes that improved their daily lives. Political disillusionment and low turnout rates among black voters combine to set a political stage where mobilized white voters can possibly reclaim the mayor's office even in cities where African Americans are a clear majority of the population.[112]

CONCLUSION: CITIES AS ACTIVE—BUT STILL LIMITED—GOVERNMENTS

Each state determines the structure and powers of the various local governments within its borders. The states typically grant a city only limited legislative, taxing, spending, and borrowing authority. Even provisions for home rule do not fully offset Dillon's Rule, the legal doctrine that recognizes the hierarchical control that a state possesses over its cities, school districts, and other forms of local government.

In more recent years, state governments have stepped up their efforts to rein in some of the more expansive and controversial policy actions taken by cities. Republican-controlled state governments have been especially willing to preempt actions undertaken by Democratic-dominated municipalities. The State of Georgia over the years has taken certain decision-making powers from local elected officials and placed the powers in the hands of state-appointed bodies. Georgia created new boards and authorities—most notably an independent hospital authority and the Atlanta Fulton County Recreation Authority—with the authority to make important decisions regarding the financing and location of sports stadiums, convention centers, hospitals, and other key development projects in the Atlanta-Fulton County area.[113]

The existence of numerous independent boards, commissions, and authorities is only one of the many impediments to strong, centralized urban leadership. Municipal mayors seldom possess the full range of formal powers that would enhance the possibilities of leadership. To be effective, a mayor cannot rely solely on the formal authority of the mayor's office, Instead, he or she must also be skillful in assembling and leading a successful governing coalition, gaining the commitment of state and federal officials, corporate heads, and the leaders of nonprofit and community organizations to important projects. Big-city mayors in particular face a difficult balancing act in attempting to juggle the needs and demands of the various constituencies that comprise the modern American city. Proactive mayors will often find that leadership is ephemeral and elusive, given the intractable nature of many urban problems and the paucity of powers that a state has allowed local governments and mayors.

The council-manager system, a popular form of government that has been adopted in communities across the nation, places leadership and the administration of a city's daily affairs in the hands of a trained professional. Governance under the council-manager system emphasizes cooperation more than conflict. However, city council members, mayors, and managers often overstep their roles, which are not clearly demarcated. As a consequence, in some cities the mayor and the manager have emerged as competitors who seek to lead the city. Many of the nation's largest cities have spurned the council-manager arrangement, fearing that a manager will not be able to command the public's attention or otherwise have the sense of legitimacy to provide effective leadership in a tough and diverse political environment. A mayor who is elected citywide can command the attention of the media and claim to speak for the people.

Over the years, cities have altered their governing structures by borrowing elements that have seemed to work well in other communities. As a result, there are relatively few pure mayor-council and council-manager cities in the United States. Instead, many cities have hybrid governing arrangements. The mayors of big cities often govern with the assistance of a professional manager, a city's CAO (chief administrative officer). A fairly large number of council-manager communities now elect the mayor citywide and have increased the formal powers of the mayor's office, moves intended to energize city government and allow a central leader to speak on behalf of the entire community when negotiating with business executives to bring new investments and jobs to a city.

The job of big-city mayor is quite difficult; African-American and Latino mayors face yet an added dilemma. When such mayors forge cross-racial political coalitions and pursue partnerships with businesses for new investment, job creation, and even school reform, they are often criticized by activists who charge that the mayor has been too deferential to the concerns of both whites and business interests. A new generation of post-racial mayors, however, appears to have the comfort level, political skill, and willingness to cross racial lines and work in partnership with business and nonprofit leaders while also maintaining a focus on efforts to improve poorer neighborhoods.

The manager-council plan has proven to be one of the long-lasting contributions of the Progressive Era reformers who sought to bring "good government" to cities. But the council-manager arrangement was not the only reform that the good-government reformers emphasized. As the next chapter describes, the political reformers introduced a number of changes to improve governmental performance and to diminish the hold that political party "machines" and party "bosses" exerted over municipal affairs. As the next chapter details, the reformed rules have shaped power in the city, increasing the access to city hall enjoyed by some groups while diminishing the access and influence of other groups.

KEY TERMS

academic bankruptcy laws (*p. 208*)

administrative subunits of a state, local governments as (*p. 197*)

annexation (*p. 202*)

benefit principle as a justification for user fees (*p. 206*)

blanket preemption (*p. 201*)

chief administrative officer (CAO), a city's (*p. 219*)

city charter (*p. 198*)

classified charters (*p. 199*)

commission form of government (*p. 214*)

council-manager system of government (*p. 216*)

deracialized approach to leadership, a mayor's (*p. 226*)

development impact fees (*p. 206*)

Dillon's Rule (*p. 198*)

dual majorities requirement for an annexation (*p. 203*)

earmarking tax proceeds (*p. 205*)

eminent domain (*p. 199*)

expertise (*p. 217*)

fragmentation of executive power (*p. 212*)

general-act charters (*p. 199*)

high-risk strategy of borrowing money to invest, Orange County's (*p. 208*)

home rule (*p. 201*)

hybrid government (*p. 218*)

intergovernmental assistance (*p. 204*)

line-item veto power (*p. 110*)

management and administration as areas of responsibility assigned to a city manager (*p. 217*)

Marketplace Fairness Act (*p. 205*)

mission, city council role in determining a city's (*p. 217*)

municipal incorporation (*p. 198*)

new breed of "education mayor" (*p. 210*)

nuisance taxes and fees (*p. 205*)

policy, city council and city manager's joint role in setting (*p. 217*)

post-racial black mayors (*p. 227*)

preemption (*p. 199*)

Proposition 13, California's (*p. 207*)

residency laws, municipal (*p. 202*)

sales tax holidays (*p. 205*)

secession (*p. 203*)

special-act charters (*p. 198*)

special assessments (*p. 206*)

special districts (*p. 207*)

standing committees, a city council's (*p. 220*)

strong-mayor system of government (*p. 213*)

super-preemption (*p. 200*)

tax revolt (*p. 207*)

term limitations (*p. 221*)

user charges and fees (*p. 206*)

weak-mayor system of government (*p. 212*)

NOTES

1. Cory Eucalitto, Kristen De Pena, and Shannan Younger, "Municipal Bankruptcy: An Overview for Local Officials," *State Budget Solutions*, February 26, 2013, www.statebudgetsolutions.org/publications/detail/municipal-bankruptcy-an-overview-for-local-officials. Fourteen states require that a municipality receive permission from a state authority before filing for bankruptcy; see National Association of State Budget Officers, "Municipal Bankruptcy & the Role of the States," August 21, 2012, p. 2, www.nasbo.org/sites/default/files/pdf/Municipal%20Bankruptcy%20%26%20the%20 Role%20of%20the%20States.pdf.

2   *City of Clinton v. Cedar Rapids and Missouri Railroad Company*, 24 Iowa 455 (1868).

3. John F. Dillon, *Commentary on the Law of Municipal Corporations*, 5th ed. (Boston: Little, Brown, 1911), vol. 1, sec. 237, emphasis added.

4. *Atkins v. Kansas*, 191 U.S. 207 at 220–221 (1903); and *Trenton v. New Jersey,* 262 U.S. 182. 67LEd93j, 43 S.Ct. 534 (1923).

5. The Law Center to Prevent Gun Violence, "Local Authority to Regulate Firearms Policy Summary," May 18, 2012, http://smartgunlaws.org/local-authority-to-regulate-firearms-policy-summary/, lists Connecticut, Hawaii, Massachusetts, New Jersey, and New York as the only states that do not pre-empt (that is, prohibit) cities from taking local action to implement gun control.

6. David R. Berman, "State-Local Relations: Authority and Finances," in *The Municipal Year Book 2010 (MYB 2010)* (Washington, DC: International City/County Management Association, 2010), 47–49.

7. Center for Disease Control and Preemption, *STATE [State Tobacco Activities Tracking & Evaluation] System Preemption Fact Sheet*, 2017, www.cdc.gov/statesystem/factsheets.html.

8. Lori Riverstone-Newell, "The Rise of State Preemption Laws in Response to Local Policy Innovation," *Publius: The Journal of Federalism* 47, no. 3 (2017): 403–425.

9. National League of Cities, *City Rights in an Era of Preemption: A State-by-State Analysis*, Washington DC, 2017, http://nlc.org/sites/default/files/2017-02/NLC%20Preemption%20Report%202017. pdf; Riverstone-Newell, "The Rise of State Preemption Laws in Response to Local Policy Innovation"; Emily Badger, "Red States and Blue Cities: A Partisan Battle Intensifies," *New York Times*, July 6, 2017.

10. Lori Riverstone-Newell, "Shutting Down Local Control: Conservative States and the Recent Rise in Blanket and Super-Preemption" (paper presented at the annual meeting of the Urban Affairs Association, Toronto, April 7, 2018).

11. John L. Mikesell, *Fiscal Administration: Analysis and Applications for the Public Sector*, 9th ed. (Boston: Wadsworth, 2014), 349.

12. Charles W. Gossett, "Pushing the Envelope: Dillon's Rule and Local Domestic Partnership Ordinances," in *Queer Mobilizations: GLBT Activists Confront the Law*, ed. Scott Barclay, Mary Bernstein, and Anna-Maria Marshall (New York: New York University Press, 2009), 158–186.

13. Jesse J. Richardson Jr., Dillon's Rule Is from Mars, Home Rule Is from Venus: Local Government Autonomy and the Rules of Statutory Interpretation," *Publius: The Journal of Federalism* 41, no. 4 (October 2011): 662–685.

14. Yun Sang Lee, Patrick Terranova, and Dan Immergluck, "New Data on Local Vacant Property Registration Ordinances," *Cityscape: A Journal of Policy Development and Research* 15, no. 2 (2013): 263–264.

15. Kate Taylor, "Mayor Agrees to Accommodate 4 Larger or New Charter Schools," *New York Times*, September 10, 2014. Chapter 8 will present a more detailed discussion of the debate over charter schools.

16. Michelle Wilde Anderson, "Democratic Dissolution: Radical Experimentation in State Takeovers of Local Governments," *Fordham Urban Law Journal* 39 (2012): 577–623.

17. Rick Su, "Have Cities Abandoned Home Rule?" *Fordham Urban Law Journal* 44, no. 1 (2017), 192.

18. Jesse J. Richardson Jr., Meghan Zimmerman Gough, and Robert Puentes, "Is Home Rule the Answer? The Influence of Dillon's Rule on Growth Management" (discussion paper prepared for the Brookings Institution Center on Urban and Metropolitan Policy, Washington, DC, January 2003), www.brookings.edu/~/media/Files/rc/reports/2003/01metropolitanpolicy_jesse%20j%20%20 richardson%20%20jr/dillonsrule.pdf.

19. Su, "Have Cities Abandoned Home Rule?"

20. Berman, "State-Local Relations: Authority and Finances." Also see Su, "Have Cities Abandoned Home Rule?" 181–216.

21. Raphael J. Sonenshein and Tom Hogen-Esch, "Bringing the (State) Government Back In: Home Rule and the Politics of Secession in Los Angeles and New York City," *Urban Affairs Review* 41, no. 4 (March 2006): 467–491.

22. Nikole Hannah-Jones, "The Resegregation of Jefferson County," *New York Times Magazine*, September 6, 2017.

23. Unless otherwise noted, the figures presented here and in the rest of the chapter section are from the Tax Policy Center, *Briefing Book* entry on "State (and Local) Taxes," a publication of the Urban Institute and the Brookings Institution, 2016, www.taxpolicycenter.org/briefing-book/what-are-sources-revenue-local-governments.

24. Institute for Education Sciences, National Center for Education Statistics, *Public School Revenue Sources*, March 2017, https://nces.ed.gov/programs/coe/indicator_cma.asp.

25. National Center for Education Statistics. The data is for 2012.

26. Jared Walczak and Scott Drenkard, *State and Local Sales Tax Rates in 2017*, The Tax Foundation Fiscal Fact Sheet No. 539, January, 2017, https://files.taxfoundation.org/20170131121743/TaxFoundation-FF539.pdf.

27. Scott Drenkard, *State and Local Sales Tax Rates Midyear 2013*, The Tax Foundation Fiscal Fact Sheet No. 392, August 28, 2013, http://taxfoundation.org/article/state-and-local-sales-tax-ratesmid-year-2013.

28. IHS Global Insight, *Impact of "Marketplace Fairness" on Select Jurisdictions: An Update*, report prepared for the National League of Cities, the National Association of Counties, and the U.S. Conference of Mayors, May 2013, http://usmayors.org/metroeconomies/0613/Marketplace FairnessReport.pdf.

29. *South Dakota v Wayfair Inc.*, 585 U.S. __ (2018). Also see Adam Liptak, Ben Casselman, and Julie Creswell, "Supreme Court Widens Reach of Sales Tax for Online Retailers," *New York Times*, June 21, 2018.

30. David L. Sjoquist and Reyna Stoycheva, "Local Revenue Diversification: User Charges, Sales Taxes, and Income Taxes," in *The Oxford Handbook of State and Local Government Finance*, ed. Robert D. Ebel and John E. Petersen (New York: Oxford University Press, 2012), 435–446.

31. For a list of the numerous small nuisance taxes and fees levied by the City of Philadelphia, see Stu Bykofsky, "City Has 100 Ways to Leave You Poorer," *Philadelphia Daily News*, April 6, 2012, http://articles.philly.com/2012-04-06/news/31300570_1_nuisance-taxes-school-taxrealty-transfer-tax. Also see City of Philadelphia, *Taxes & Fees*, http://media.philly.com/documents/Taxes_Fees2_2012.pdf.

32. Berman, "State-Local Relations: Authority and Finances," 54.

33. Larry L. Lawhon, "Local Government Use of Development Impact Fees: More Fallout from a Poor Economy?" in *The Municipal Year Book 2012* (Washington, DC: International City/County Management Association, 2012), 25–35, esp. 28–29.

34. Douglas E. Goodfriend and Thomas E. Myers, *Bond Basics for Towns, Villages, and Cities in New York State* (New York: Orrick, Herrington, and Sutcliffe LLP, 2009), 4, www.orrick.com/Events-and-Publications/Documents/2161.pdf.

35. "Municipal Bonds and Arizona State, Local and County Debt," Arizona State Senate Issue Brief, May 7, 2015, www.azleg.gov/briefs/Senate/MUNICIPAL%20BONDS%20AND%20STATE%20AND%20LOCAL%20%20AND%20COUNTY%20DEBT.pdf.

36. Gary Sands and Mark Skidmore, "Making Ends Meet: Options for Property Tax Reform in Detroit," *Journal of Urban Affairs* 36, no. 4 (2014): 687.

37. U.S. Census Bureau, Educational Research Branch, *Public Education Services: 2013*, June 2015, www2.census.gov/govs/school/13f33pub.pdf, ranked California in 34th place among the 50 states and the District of Columbia in terms of current per pupil spending. Other analysts rank California even lower. See, for example, John Fensterwald, "California Drops to 49th in School Spending in Annual Ed Week Report," *EdSource*, January 14, 2013, http://edsource.org/today/2013/california-drops-to-49th-in-schoolspending-in-annual-ed-week-report/25379#.Uuk_yqQo5gE.

38. David Brunori, *Local Tax Policy: A Federalist Perspective*, 2nd ed. (Washington, DC: The Urban Institute, 2007), 26. For more extensive descriptions of how Proposition 13 and various state ballot initiatives and mandates have diminished or "hollowed out" local authority in California, see Peter

Schrag, *The End of Paradise: California's Experience, America's Future*, rev. ed. (Berkeley, CA: University of California Press, 2004), 163–167.

39. Stephen P. Erie, Christopher W. Hoene, and Gregory D. Saxton, "Fiscal Constraints and the Loss of Home Rule: The Long-Term Impacts of California's Post-Proposition 13 Fiscal Regime," *American Review of Public Administration* 32, no. 4 (December 2002): 423–454.

40. Steven Litt, "Cleveland Cuyahoga County Port Authority Approves $75 Million Bond Issue for Cleveland Museum of Art Expansion," *The Plain Dealer (Cleveland)*, June 8, 2010; James F. McCarty, "Should the Port Authority Be Saved or Dismantled? Critics Say Other Public Entities Could Do the Job Better," *The Plain Dealer (Cleveland)*, January 11, 2010.

41. See Colin H. McCubbins and Mathew D. McCubbins, "Proposition 13 and The California Fiscal Shell Game," *California Journal of Politics and Policy* 2, no. 2 (2010), www.bepress.com/cjpp/vol2/iss2/6/.

42. Jack Citrin, "Proposition 13 and the Transformation of California Government," *California Journal of Politics and Policy* 1, no. 1 (2009), www.bepress.com/cjpp/vol1/iss1/16/.

43. Mark Baldassare, *When Government Fails: The Orange County Bankruptcy* (Berkeley: University of California Press, 1998).

44. Gretchen Morgenson, "Exotic Deals Put Denver Schools Deeper into Debt," *New York Times*, August 5, 2010; Amy Hetzner, "As the Value of Investments Plunge, 5 School Districts Pressured Over Loans," *Wall Street Journal*, January 3, 2010; Amy Hetzner, "Credit Ratings Lowered for 2 School Districts with Risky Investments," *Wall Street Journal*, April 19, 2010.

45. Rutgers University Institute on Education, Law, and Policy, Rutgers University, "50-State Report on Accountability, State Intervention and Takeover," [undated], http://ielp.rutgers.edu/docs/developing_plan_app_b.pdf.

46. Mary L. Mason and Sarah Reckhow, "Rootles Reforms? State Takeovers and School Governance in Detroit and Memphis," *Peabody Journal of Education* 92, no. 1 (2017): 64–75. https://pdfs.semanticscholar.org/6fde/635a40539ebc22344db2c1f068cbb778f049.pdf.

47. Brian Gill, Ron Zimmer, Jolley Christman, and Suzanne Blanc, "State Takeover, School Restructuring, Private Management, and Student Achievement in Philadelphia" (research paper published by the Rand Corporation, Santa Monica, CA, 2007), http://pdf.researchforaction.org/rfapdf/publication/pdf_file/262/Gill_B_State_Takeover.pdf.

48. The earlier stages in the state's fluctuating relations with Detroit schools are described by Wilbur C. Rich, "Who's Afraid of a Mayoral Takeover of Detroit's Public Schools?" in *When Mayors Take Charge: School Governance in the City*, ed. Joseph P. Viteritti (Washington, DC: Brookings Institution Press, 2009), 148–167.

49. Ann Zaniewski, "How Much Control Will New Detroit School District Really Have?" *Detroit Free Press*, August 25, 2016.

50. Brenda Alvarez, "Educators Mobilize as School Takeovers Open Door for Charter Expansion," *neaToday*, August 23, 2016, http://neatoday.org/2016/08/23/school-takeover/.

51. The Alliance to Reclaim Our Public Schools, "The Facts about State Takeovers of Public Schools," undated [downloaded August 7, 2017], www.reclaimourschools.org/sites/default/files/state-takeover-factsheet-3.pdf

52. A.J. Rice, "The Remaking of Black Citizenship: The Takeover of Detroit's Public Schools," (paper presented at the annual meeting of the Urban Affairs Association, Minneapolis, April 19–22, 2017).

53. Richard O. Welsh, Sheneka Williams, Shafiqua Little, and Jerome Graham, "Right Cause, Wrong Method? Examining the Politics of State Takeover in Georgia," *Urban Affairs Review*, forthcoming. Article first published online: July 6, 2017, https://doi.org/10.1177/1078087417714061

54. Rice, "The Remaking of Black Citizenship"

55. Beth E. Schueler, Joshua S. Goodman, and David J. Deming, "Can States Take Over and Turn Around School Districts? Evidence from Lawrence, Massachusetts," *Educational Evaluation and Policy Analysis* 39, no. 2 (June 2017): 311–332.

56. Ron Zimmer, Adam Kho, Gary Henry, and Samantha Viano, "Evaluation of the Effects of Tennessee's Achievement School District on Student Test Scores," a report of Peabody College, Vanderbilt University, Nashville, Tennessee, December 2015, http://mediad.publicbroadcasting.net/p/wpln/files/201512/ASD_Impact_Policy_Brief_Final_12.8.15.pdf .

57. Stephanie Wang, "Four Indianapolis Takeover Schools Get F Grade," *Indianapolis Star*, December 20, 2013.

58. Allie Gross, "Fourteen of the EAA's 15 Schools Are Failing: Can We Finally Say That a State Take-over Didn't Work?" *MetroTimes*, September 2, 1016, www.metrotimes.com/news-hits/archives/2016/09/02/fourteen-of-the-eaas-15-schools-are-failing-can-we-finally-say-a-state-take-over-didnt-work.

59. Kenneth W. Wong and Francis X. Shen, "Mayors Can Be 'Prime Movers' of Urban School Improvement," *Education Week*, October 14, 2009, www.edweek.org/ew/articles/2009/10/14/07wallace-wong.h29.html. The quotations are from Wong and Shen. Also see Jeffrey Henig, "The End of Educational Exceptionalism," in *Education Governance for the Twenty-First Century*, ed. Patrick McGuinn and Paul Manna (Washington, DC: Brookings Institution Press, 2013), 187–192.

60. Jeffrey R. Henig, "Mayoral Control: What We Can and Cannot Learn from Other Cities," in *When Mayors Take Charge*, ed. Viteritti, 19–45; Kenneth K. Wong. Francis X. Shen, Dorothea Agnostopoulos, and Stacey Routledge, *The Education Mayor: Improving America's Schools* (Washington, DC: Georgetown University Press, 2007).

61. Dorothy Shipps, "Updating Tradition: The Institutional Underpinnings of Modern Mayoral Control in Chicago's Public Schools," in *When Mayors Take Charge*, ed. Viteritti, 117–147.

62. James H. Svara and Jennifer Claire Auer, "Perspectives on Changes in City Government Structure," in *The Municipal Year Book 2013* (Washington, DC: International City/County Management Association, 2013), 19.

63. For a good journalistic description how a city council may dominate budgetary and spending decisions in a weak-mayor city, see Marlys Harris, "With Minneapolis' Weak-Mayor System, Does It Really Matter Who Gets Elected?" *Minnesota Post*, August 29, 2013, www.minnpost.com/politics-policy/2013/08/minneapolis-weak-mayor-system-does-it-really-matter-who-gets-elected.

64. Svara and Auer, "Perspectives on Changes in City Government Structure," 24.

65. Richard C. Feiock, Christopher M. Weible, David P. Carter, Cali Curley, Aaron Deslatte, and Tanya Heikkila, "Capturing Structural and Functional Diversity through Institutional Analysis: The Mayor Position in City Charters," *Urban Affairs Review* 52, no. 1 (January 2016): 129–150.

66. Edgar E. Ramirez de la Cruz, "County Form of Government: Trends in Structure and Composition," *The Municipal Year Book 2009* (Washington, DC: International City/County Management Association, 2009), 23.

67. A review of various empirical studies shows that manager-led cities tend not to be that different from mayor-led cities in terms of resisting parochial policies and pursuing the interest of the larger community. See Jered B. Carr, "What Have We Learned about the Performance of Council-Manager Government? A Review and Synthesis of the Research," *Public Administration Review* 75, no. 5 (2015): 673–689. Also see

68. James H. Svara, *Official Leadership in the City: Patterns of Conflict and Cooperation* (New York: Oxford University Press, 1990).

69. John Nalbandian, Robert O'Neill Jr., J. Michael Wilkes, and Amanda Kaufman, "Contemporary Challenges in Local Government: Evolving Roles and Responsibilities, Structures, and Processes," *Public Administration Review* 73, no. 4 (July/August 2013): 567–574; Kimberly L. Nelson and James H. Svara, "The Roles of Local Government Managers in Theory and Practice: A Centennial Perspective," *Public Administration Review* 75, no. 1 (January/February 2015): 49–61.

70. Jerri Killian and Enamul Choudhury, "Continuity and Change in the Role of City Managers," in *The Municipal Year Book 2010* (Washington, DC: The International City/County Management Association, 2010), 10–18, esp. 13; Tansu Demir and Christopher G. Reddick, "Understanding Shared Roles

in Policy and Administration: An Empirical Study of Council-Manager Relations," *Public Administration Review* 72, no. 4 (July/August 2012): 526–535.

71. Ron Carlee, "The Politics of Apolitical Leadership: Professional Management in a Digital and Divided Society," in *The Municipal Year Book 2012* (Washington, DC: International City/County Management Association, 2012), 7.

72. Siegrun Fox Freyss, "Matching City Power Structures and City Managers' Leadership Styles: A New Model of Fit," in *The Municipal Year Book 2009* (Washington, DC: International City/County Management Association, 2009), 3–10.

73. Kimberly L. Nelson and Karl Nollenberger, "Conflict and Cooperation in Municipalities: Do Variations in Form of Government Have an Effect?" *Urban Affairs Review* 45, no. 5 (September 2011): 696–720.

74. H. George Frederickson, Gary A. Johnson, and Curtis H. Wood, *The Adapted City: Institutional Dynamics and Structural Change* (Armonk, NY: M.E. Sharpe, 2004).

75. Rufus P. Browning, Dale Rogers Marshall, and David H. Tabb, *Protest Is Not Enough: The Struggle of Blacks and Hispanics for Equality in Urban Politics* (Berkeley: University of California Press, 1984), 201–202.

76. Glen W. Sparrow, "San Diego: Switch from Reform to Representative," in *More Than Mayor or Manager: Campaigns to Change Form of Government in America's Large Cities*, ed. James H. Svara and Douglas J. Watson (Washington, DC: Georgetown University Press, 2010), 103–120.

77. David Garrick, "Council Fails to Override Faulconer Budget Veto," *San Diego Union-Tribune*, June 13, 2017.

78. See the various case studies in Svara and Watson, eds., *More Than Mayor or Manager*. A list of cities that switched from one form of government to another can be found on p. 12.

79. Kimberly L. Nelson and James H. Svara, "Adaptation of Models versus Variations in Form: Classifying Structures of City Government," *Urban Affairs Review* 45, no. 4 (2010): 552–554.

80. Salary figures from 2015 and 2016 were obtained from the individual cities via their Web sites.

81. Svara and Auer, "Perspectives on Changes in City Government Structure," 29–30.

82. Timothy Bledsoe, *Careers in City Politics: The Case for Urban Democracy* (Pittsburgh: University of Pittsburgh Press, 1993), 113–119 and 126–128.

83. Svara and Auer, "Perspectives on Changes in City Government Structure," 29.

84. Center for American Women in Politics, *Women in Elective Office 2018*, fact sheet, www.cawp.rutgers.edu/women-elective-office-2018. Twenty-one percent of the mayors of cities over 100,000 are women, as initially reported by the United State Conference of Mayors.

85. Rob Richie, "Election of Women in our 1000 Largest Cities: Disadvantaged by Districts," *Fair Vote*, *web posting*, September 11, 2014, www.fairvote.org/election-of-women-in-our-100-largest-cities-disadvantaged-by-districts. Data on women's representation in Congress provided by the Center for American Women in Politics, "Women in Elective Office 2017."

86. Brian E. Adams and Ronnee Schreiber, "Gender, Campaign Finance, and Electoral Success in Municipal Elections," *Journal of Urban Affairs* 33, no. 1 (2010): 83–97.

87. Jennifer L. Lawless and Richard L. Fox, "Girls Just Wanna Not Run: The Gender Gap in Young Americans' Politics Ambition," a report of The American University School of Public Affairs, Washington, DC, January 2012, www.american.edu/spa/wpi/upload/girls-just-wanna-not-run_policy-report.pdf.; Jennifer L. Lawless and Richard L. Fox, *Running from Office: Why Young Americans Are Turned Off to Politics* (New York: Oxford University Press, 2015), chap. 3.

88. Jennifer L. Lawless and Richard L. Fox, "Men Rule: The Continued Under-Representation of Women in U.S. Politics," a report of The American University School of Public Affairs, Washington, DC, March 2013, www.american.edu/spa/wpi/upload/2012-men-rule-report-web.pdf.

89. Jennifer L. Lawless and Richard L. Fox, *It Still Takes a Candidate: Why Women Don't Run for Office* (New York: Cambridge University Press, 2010), 50.

90. Lawless and Fox, *It Still Takes a Candidate*; and Susan J. Carroll and Kira Sanbonmatsu, *More Women Can Run: Gendered Pathways to the State Legislatures* (New York: Oxford University Press, 2013).

91. M. Margaret Conway, Gertrude A. Steuernagel, and David W. Ahern, *Women and Political Partici-pation* (Washington, DC: CQ Press, 1997), 113.

92. Adrienne R. Smith, Beth Reingold, and Michael Leo Owens, "The Political Determinants of Wom-en's Descriptive Representation in Cities," *Political Research Quarterly* 65, no. 2 (2012): 315–329.

93. Robert A. Schumann and Richard L. Fox, "Women Chief Administrative Officers: Perceptions of Their Role in Government," in *The Municipal Year Book 1998* (Washington, DC: International City/County Management Association, 1998), 116–122.

94. Susan Abrams Beck, "Acting as Women: The Effects and Limitations of Gender in Local Govern-ment," in *The Impact of Women in Public Office*, ed. Susan J. Carroll (Bloomington: University of Indiana Press, 2001), 49–67. Also see Laura Van Assendelft, "Entry-Level Politics? Women as Can-didates and Elected Officials at the Local Level," in *Women and Elective Office: Past, Present, and Future,* ed. Sue Thomas and Clyde Wilcox (New York: Oxford University Press, 2014), 199–215.

95. A study of 300 cities found that having a women mayor makes a difference. Especially when work-ing with significant female representation on the city council, women mayors tend to spend more on health and human services, hospitals, social welfare, and community development than do their male counterparts. See Mirya R. Holman, "Sex and the City: Female Leaders and Spending on Social Welfare Programs in U.S. Municipalities," *Journal of Urban Affairs* 36, no. 4 (2014): 701–715.

96. Svara and Auer, "Perspectives on Changes in City Government Structure," 24.

97. Charles H. Levine, *Racial Conflict and the American Mayor* (Lexington, MA: Lexington Books, 1974).

98. The quotation is from Mayor Young.

99. Rodolfo Rosales, *The Illusion of Inclusion: The Untold Story of San Antonio* (Austin: University of Texas Press, 2000), esp. chap. 7.

100. J. Phillip Thompson III, *Double Trouble: Black Mayors, Black Communities, and the Call for a Deep Democracy* (New York: Oxford University Press, 2006), 136–139.

101. See, for instance, Huey L. Perry, ed., *Race, Politics, and Governance in the United States* (Gaines-ville: University Press of Florida, 1997); and Richard A. Keiser, "Philadelphia's Evolving Biracial Coalition," in *Racial Politics in American Cities*, 3rd ed., ed. Rufus P. Browning, Dale Rogers Mar-shall, and David H. Tabb (New York: Longman, 2003), 77–112.

102. Raphael J. Sonenshein and Susan H. Pinkus, "Latino Incorporation Reaches the Urban Summit: How Antonio Villaraigosa Won the 2005 Los Angeles Mayor's Race," *PS: Political Science and Politics* 38, no. 4 (2005): 713–721. Also see Raphael J. Sonenshein, *The City at Stake: Secession, Reform, and the Battle for Los Angeles* (Princeton, NJ: Princeton University Press, 2004), 214–226.

103. Ravi K. Perry, "Deracialization Reconsidered: Theorizing Targeted Universalistic Urban Policies," in *21st Century Urban Race Politics*, ed. Ravi K. Perry (Bingley, UK: Emerald Publishing, 2013), xxiv.

104. David C. Smith, "Recent Elections and Black Politics: The Maturation or Death of Black Politics?" *PS: Political Science and Politics* 23 (June 1990): 161.

105. Georgia A. Persons, "Politics and Social Change: The Demise of the African-American Ethnic Movement?" in *Contours of African-American Politics*, vol. 3, ed. Persons (New Brunswick, NJ: Transaction Publishers, 2014), p. 1.

106. Persons, "Politics and Social Change," 160.

107. Thompson, *Double Trouble*, esp. 15–16, 156, and 265–267.

108. Andra Gillespie, "Meet the New Class: Theorizing Young Black Leadership in a 'Postracial' Era," in *Whose Black Politics? Cases in Post-Racial Black Leadership*, ed. Andra Gillespie (New York: Rout-ledge, 2010); and Andra Gillespie, *The New Black Politician: Cory Booker, Newark, and Post-Racial America* (New York: New York University Press, 2012).

109. Jonathan L. Wharton, *A Post-Racial Change Is Gonna Come: Newark, Cory Booker, and the Trans-formation of Urban America* (New York: Palgrave Macmillan, 2013), esp. 173–190.

110. Corey Cook, "Constructing a Moderate Multiracial Coalition in 'America's Most Diverse City': Kevin Johnson and Coalition Politics in Sacramento," in *21st Century Urban Race Politics* (Research in Race and Ethnic Relations, vol. 18), ed. Ravi K. Perry (Bingley: Emerald Publishing, 2013).

111. Michael Leo Owens and Jacob Robert Brown, "Weakening Strong Black Political Empowerment: Implications from Atlanta's 2009 Mayoral Election," *Journal of Urban Affairs* 36, no. 4 (2014): 663–681.
112. Owens and Brown, "Weakening Strong Black Political Empowerment."
113. Heywood T. Sanders, "Institutions, Space, and Time: Approaches to the Study of Urban Politics and Development," presentation at the annual meeting of the Urban Affairs Association, Minneapolis, April 20, 2017.

7 The Rules of Local Politics and Elections

The Reform and Post-Reform City

This chapter makes a simple but important argument: The rules of city politics are important. The formal rules and processes of local government are not neutral; instead, they help to determine who has access to city and county hall. Consequently, the rules of city politics are often highly contested, with different groups seeking to institute reforms or rule changes that will help advance their interests while diminishing the power of groups they oppose.

Politicians, of course, know the importance of writing rules that work to their advantage. That is why Democrats and Republicans in recent years have fought so strenuously over the details of voter identification and registration requirements. President Donald Trump appointed a Presidential Advisory Commission on Election Integrity to introduce rule changes regarding voter identification and registration, despite the fact that no national studies or review of the data pointed to widespread voter fraud or to large numbers of ballots having been cast by noncitizens. In the absences of such evidence, the commission soon disbanded. But the reasons that motivated the commission's formation were clear, albeit unstated: to advance tales of voter fraud that would justify the enactment of tougher rules that would make it more difficult for Latinos and Democratic-leaning citizens to vote.

As this chapter will observe, many of the more important rules of local politics in U.S. cities have their genesis in the partisan and ethnic battles of an earlier era, the confrontations between the big-city political party *machines* and their antagonists, the self-styled urban *reformers*. The urban **reform movement** sought to institute rules of the game to undercut the power of the political-party machine, an organization the reformers greatly detested. The major battles between the big-city political machines and the reformers occurred during the late 1800s and the first half of the 1900s. In city after city, the reformers emerged victorious. The rules they instituted continue to affect the operations of cities and suburbs today.

The reformers largely succeeded in their efforts to "clean up" much of the corruption and excesses of the old local political machines. But the reforms were far from perfect. As this chapter will detail, the reforms were not neutral; the reformed rules of city government often worked to the advantage of established interests—business leaders and ethnic groups who had arrived in the county in earlier generations—and undercut the representation of poorer neighborhoods and more recent immigrant arrivals to the United States. The reforms also created new problems for the modern city, removing power from the hands of elected officials which was transferred to program bureaucrats.

Eventually, members of the public grew increasingly dissatisfied with the irresponsiveness and even arrogance of "reform" government where their daily lives are affected by the decisions made by faceless and unaccountable administrative officials. Community activists in middle-class as well as low-income neighborhoods began to demand new measures to "reform the reforms" in order to make local government more responsive neighborhood needs. In the contemporary **post-reform city** a relatively new set of rules was introduced to increase citizen participation in decision making and to enhance the responsiveness of municipal service providers to neighborhood concerns. In short, a new generation of reforms sought to de-bureaucratize municipal government. Other new-generation reforms sought to clean up city government by preventing conflicts of interest by public servants and by limiting the influence of money in local elections.

However, as we have already begun to see in the preceding chapter of this book, the reform movement's victory was not total. In the **hybrid city**, older machine-style practices have not entirely disappeared but still can be found even in communities that have adopted a large number of the governmental structures and rules changes advocated by the political reformers.

In more recent years, machine-style practices continue to be seen in such instances as New Jersey Governor's Chris Christie use of jobs at the Port Authority of New York and New Jersey (the vast bi-state agency that runs the region's bridges and tunnels) as a source of patronage that he could dispense to reward his political loyalists.[1] The governor also sought to use the agency to punish local politicians who defied his political will. In 2014, the governor's appointees to the Port Authority closed access lanes to the George Washington Bridge even where there was no road construction project that necessitated lane closings. Christie's acolytes sought to create massive traffic tie-ups that would cause political headaches for the area's local officials who had failed to render the governor their full support. Christie's loyal followers were working according to old political machine maxim: "Reward your friends and punish your enemies!"

HOW THE POLITICAL REFORM MOVEMENT CHANGED THE RULES OF LOCAL POLITICS

For much of the nineteenth and the twentieth centuries, strong political-party organizations or *political machines* dominated big cities, especially in the Northeast and the Midwest. New York, Boston, Philadelphia, Pittsburgh, Jersey City, New Haven, Albany, Kansas City, and Chicago all had political machines at major points of their histories.

While strong political-party organizations were less prevalent in the South and West, "boss rule" (that is, rule by the political machine's leader) also emerged in Memphis, New Orleans, San Antonio, Tampa, and San Francisco.

The big-city **political machine** was a highly structured party organization capable of organizing voters and winning elections. The machine dispensed favors in order to win the support of key voting blocks and businesses. Machine politics was an **exchange process** where the political-party organization traded favors for support and votes. As previously noted, the machine rewarded its friends and punished its enemies. The classic urban political machine relied greatly on the **patronage** or **spoils system**. The winning party distributed government jobs and lucrative contracts to its supporters, following the old adage: "To the victors belong the spoils of war." The political machine denied municipal jobs, building permits, and other benefits to people and businesses who failed to give their support the political organization.

At its peak power, the urban machine was a top-down organization that operated under the **centralized control** of the **political boss** who gave marching orders to city council members and to lesser machine leaders, including ward, precinct, and block captains. The Hague political organization, which ruled Jersey City well into the late 1940s, typified the machine's command structure: "Complete obedience is necessary from the bottom to the top; officials are not supposed to have ideas on public policies, but to take orders."[2] The political boss was not necessarily the city's mayor. The bosses of **Tammany Hall**, the fabled New York City Democratic Party machine of the late 1800s and first half of the 1900s—the legendary William Marcy Tweed, Richard Croker, John Kelly, and Charles F. Murphy—all issued their orders from offstage.

The command nature of the classic machine was still apparent, until quite recently, in Chicago where the city council has functioned less as an independent legislature and more like a "rubber stamp" that approves the decisions made by the city's Democratic mayors. In Chicago, as in other cities, numerous reforms weakened the local political machine. Mayor Richard J. Daley (1955–1976), the legendary "boss" of Chicago, enjoyed a power of command that succeeding mayors, including his son Richard M. Daley (1989–2011) and Rahm Emanuel (2011–2019), could only envy. Still, the city council in Chicago during Richard M. Daley's and Rahm Emanuel's tenure continued to approve the mayor's proposed tax increases and other controversial measures. Dissenting voices on the council did increase, especially during times when the mayor's popularity fell. In his 8 years as mayor, Emanuel did not see the city council reject a single major policy initiative submitted by the mayor or override his exercise of the mayor's veto power.[3]

In obvious ways, the practices of the urban machine and its leaders—trading favors for votes, rewarding political backers with municipal jobs, and using their power to take *graft* for their personal enrichment—do not constitute "good government" The excesses of the political machine led to the rise of the **political reformers** who rewrote the rules of municipal elections and government in order wrest power away from the political machine and to reduce partisanship, parochialism, and graft and corruption in the American city (see Box 7.1).

Box 7.1
Is There Such a Thing as "Honest Graft"? Corruption and the Political Machine

Machine politicians at their worst were notoriously corrupt, taking **graft**, that is, bribes and payoffs, in exchange for dispensing permits and other political favors. Extensive money-grabbing by New York's Tweed Ring (the label that reform-oriented journalists used to refer to Boss William Tweed and his Democratic Party pals) in the late 1800s drained millions of dollars from the municipal treasury and pushed the city to the brink of bankruptcy.

Tammany Hall (another name for New York's Democratic Party organization) district leader George Washington Plunkitt made a fortune in politics and sought to defend the seemingly indefensible practice of taking graft. Plunkitt disingenuously claimed that there was a difference between "honest graft" and dishonest graft, and that no Tammany official (at least according to Plunkitt) ever made a penny through "dishonest graft," by blackmailing saloon keepers or stealing from the public treasury:

> There's an honest graft, and I'm an example of how it works. . . . My party's in power in the city, and it's goin' to undertake a lot of public improvements. Well, I'm tipped off, say, that they're going to layout a new park at a certain place.
> I see my opportunity and I take it. I go to that place and I buy up all the land I can in the neighborhood. Then the board of this or that makes its plan public, and there is a rush to get my land, which nobody cared particular for before.
> Ain't it perfectly honest to charge a good price and make a profit on my investment and foresight? Of course, it is. Well, that's honest graft.[1]

Of course, despite Plunkitt's protestations, "honest graft" is not at all honest. Today, public ethics laws prohibit such practices and officials can be prosecuted for using insider knowledge to gain personal enrichment.

Unfortunately, certain cities and states still seem have a machine-politics culture that makes them vulnerable to instances of influence peddling (selling council votes), bribery, and corruption. In Atlantic City, New Jersey, the mayor and other elected officials were convicted for having accepted bribes from criminal elements associated with the casino industry. In 2013 Detroit's Kwame Kilpatrick, the city's once-promising young mayor, was convicted on federal charges of racketeering and extortion, having steered tens of millions of dollars in municipal contracts to political friends in exchange for kickbacks. In Chicago, the superintendent of city's public-school system, appointed by Mayor Rahm Emanuel, pled guilty in 2015 of having steered no-bid contracts to her former employer in return for more than $2 million in kickbacks.[2]

1. William L. Riordan, *Plunkitt of Tammany Hall*, ed. Terrence J. McDonald (Boston: Bedford Books of St. Martin's Press, 1994), 49.

2. Zbigniew Bzdak, "Prosecutors Seek 7½-Year Prison Term for Ex-CPS Head Barbara Byrd-Bennett," *Chicago Tribune*, June 28, 2017.

The reformers instituted new measures to decrease municipal corruption and enable municipal officials to pursue the "public interest" rather than follow the marching orders of political bosses. The reformers argued that municipal hiring should be based on "merit" and that agencies should be staffed by well-trained expert administrators as oppose to party "hacks." The reformers sought rules to prohibit the dispensation of municipal jobs as patronage, that is, as a reward to individuals who supported the political party in the previous election. The reformers sought to make municipal government more business-like.

The political reform movement instituted a number of political measures that continue to shape city politics today. Most notably, the reformers introduced *civil service systems* (also called "merit systems"), where an applicant for a municipal job is hired according to test scores and qualifications, not because of the work he or she did for a political party. The reformers also emphasized the *nonpartisan ballot, at-large elections*, and the *voter initiative and referendum processes* to give voters a more direct say in government. The reformers also "cleaned up" the electoral process by introducing the *secret ballot* and by requiring *voter registration* in advance of an election. This chapter will review each of these reforms, which are now commonplace features of local governments across the United States.

The reforms, however, were not perfect and in certain ways did not produce good government. Many reformers were as much concerned with their self-interest as with the public interest. Many of the reformers pursued changes in electoral rules to diminish the voting power of urban immigrants, African Americans, and, in more recent years, Hispanics as well.

The reforms decreased municipal corruption and increased the competency and professionalism of local administration. But these achievements came at a cost. The reforms placed decision-making power in the hands of civil service-protected bureaucracies with little assurance that career officials would be responsive to citizens. A number of the reforms also diluted the political influence of ethnic and racial minorities. The public's exasperation with irresponsive and bureaucratic government eventually led to a new generation of municipal reforms—the emergence of a post-reform city where new rules seek to encourage citizen participation and responsive government.

IMMIGRANTS AND THE BIG-CITY POLITICAL MACHINE

The motivations that underlay the reform movement are a bit complex. The reformers certainly sought to reduce corruption and partisan favoritism. Other reformers enacted measures that were intended to undercut the power of the growing immigrant and ethnic populations of cities.

The classic battles between the political machine and the reformers took place in an era of deep-seated ethnic, religious, and class antagonisms (see Box 7.2). Religious intolerance helped shape how the reformers, largely Protestant, perceived the political machine and its largely Catholic immigrant base. The reform movement opposed handing over control of the city to new arrivals who, according to the reformers, did not share the core values of America. In communities across the United States, more

Box 7.2
Film Images of the City: The Tammany Machine and
the Gangs of New York

Martin Scorsese's 2002 film *The Gangs of New York* (starring Leonardo DiCaprio, Cameron Diaz, and Best Actor winner Daniel Day-Lewis) presents pre–Civil War New York at a time when "Boss" William Marcy Tweed was just beginning his rise as the first truly powerful leader of Tammany Hall. In an era when New York had no municipal fire department, both Tweed and his political rivals organized voluntary fire companies that rushed to the scene of a fire in an effort to earn the gratitude of voters. Tammany assistants also "worked the docks," greeting the Irish immigrants upon their arrival in America on the so-called *coffin ships*, a reference to the large number of passengers who died during the perilous trans-Atlantic voyage.

The Gangs of New York documents the extreme poverty and harsh conditions of life in the immigrant slums of the city. Scorsese does not portray the incipient machine's leaders and subleaders as caring or benevolent. The machine's henchmen could be brutal and corrupt. The political machine's sole aim was to win votes and claim power.

Tammany Hall initially started out as a sort of fraternal or social club. But its members soon became active in the competition for power in the local Democratic Party. Tammany's members had no love for the city's newly arrived Irish immigrants. But Tweed and other ambitious Tammany leaders soon recognized that the votes of the city's burgeoning Irish population could provide the key to electoral victory.

The political machines in New York and elsewhere operated during a time of fierce interethnic prejudices and rivalries. The animosities were rooted in differences in social class as well as religious antagonisms. Upper-class Protestant "high society" resented the Irish Catholic newcomers, people who came to America from famine-stricken rural areas and who lacked formal schooling. By comparison, the Tammany political organization, despite its many shortcomings, was more welcoming and willing to meet at least some of the needs of the immigrants.

established social groups enacted new laws—reforms—to "bias the electoral arena in their favor."[4] The upper-class citizens and business owners who dominated municipal reform organizations sought to keep the growing numbers of immigrants from gaining control of city hall, where they could raise taxes to support increased service provision to the urban poor.[5] In Sunbelt cities, business-led reform groups kept taxes low by limiting municipal services provided African-American, Latino, and working-class neighborhoods.[6]

The operations of New York's Tammany Hall even in its early years illustrates the willingness of machine leaders to extend emergency aid and other assistance as part of a strategy to win votes. During the severe winter of 1870–1871, Boss Tweed "spent $50,000 of his personal funds in his own ward and gave each of the city's aldermen

$1,000 out of his own pocket to buy coal for the poor."[7] Between 1869 and 1871 the Tammany-controlled city treasury gave well over a million dollars to the Roman Catholic Church and other religious charities, assistance that helped solidify the machine's hold among the members of this important New York ethnic group.[8] Machine captains attended weddings, funerals, Irish wakes, and Jewish bar mitzvahs, all in the effort to win votes from the city's diverse ethnic groups.

In an age when ethnocentric sentiment was rampant, many of the reformers looked down on the immigrants whom they viewed un-American and a source of indolence and disease. Other reformers objected to spending city resources on behalf of the new-comers. In an era when the United States had no national welfare system to aid people in need, local machine captains offered the new arrivals shelter, emergency assistance, help in securing employment and citizenship, and other assistance. Machine captains demanded only one thing in return for these favors: that the recipients and their families vote for the machine's designated list of candidates.

THE REFORM MOVEMENT'S ATTACK ON PATRONAGE-BASED POWER

The reformers of the Progressive Era (the 1890s through 1920s) pushed for the adoption of **merit employment systems** (also called **civil service systems**) that require governments to hire on the basis of an applicant's test scores and relevant job qualifications. Merit-system hiring eliminated job patronage, depriving the political machine of the most important assets—jobs—that its captains could offer voters in exchange for their votes.

Merit personnel systems transformed local government. Today, almost every city in the United States has merit hiring rules. U.S. Supreme Court rulings further served to squeeze municipal use of job patronage; the Court ruled that partisan-based hiring, firing, and promotion is an unconstitutional denial of an individual's First Amendment rights of freedom of speech, belief, and association. In Chicago, a city with a strong heritage of machine politics, local officials have had to adapt to an age that is increasingly intolerant of classic political patronage[9] (see Box 7.3).

The reformers sought to have cities run a "like a business." The reformers saw politics and political parties as irrelevant to municipal administration. The reform ideology prized **neutral expertise**: trained experts should make decisions as there were no Democratic or Republican ways to pick up the trash, pave streets, or regulate the flow of traffic. Civil service systems enabled a city to recruit capable program managers with the necessary credentials and skills that city administration needed, especially in such areas as budgeting, program planning, accounting, personnel management, and civil engineering. Civil service protections enabled expert administrators to do their jobs free from political interference, free from the threat of being fired if they resisted the requests of party officials.

But merit-system hiring, like other changes advocated by the reformers, is not as neutral and "good government" as their advocates claimed. The rules instituted by the reformers had important class and racial biases. The reforms tended to "tilt" the power struggle of local politics in favor of some interests and away from others.

Box 7.3
Pin-Stripe Patronage in Post-Machine Chicago

Merit-system rules and various Supreme Court decisions meant that Richard M. Daley, the longest serving mayor of Chicago (1989 to 2011), could not amass the patronage armies of his father, the legendary "Boss" Richard J. Daley (1955 to 1976). Still, Richard M Daley found ways to skirt civil service and competitive bidding laws in order to steer jobs and important favors to his political supporters.

Richard M. Daley's governing style was "part machine/part reform." He cast himself in the role of a good-government reformer, a capable city executive who could effectively manage the city. He promoted Chicago's downtown as a major center of global businesses. He leased parking garages to private operators and privatized parking meter collections in order to take advantage of new service efficiencies and the technological know-how of private firms in the field.

The privatization of municipal services added to Daley's stock of **pin-stripe or contract patronage**; the mayor rewarded his political friends with no-bid consulting contracts and legal work. Daley received millions of dollars in campaign donations from members of the financial services industry, insurance companies, construction firms, and labor unions.

Rahm Emanuel, Daley's successor, came to the mayoralty sharply critical of the patronage practices. He pushed for the enactment of an ethics law that he stated would bar municipal officials from receiving campaign donations from persons seeking contracts with the city. Yet, throughout his years in office, Emanuel benefited from extensive campaign donations from the leaders of major corporations, including the CEO and top executives of the Magellan Dearborn Group who sought the necessary government approvals to build new developments in the city's downtown and near-north neighborhoods. Emanuel's aides solicited donations from business executives and their legal representatives who, of course, expected city officials to give favorable consideration to their requests for tax concessions, zoning changes, and development permissions.

Jesus "Chuy" Garcia, in his unsuccessful 2015 mayoral insurgency, charged that Emanuel had even used charter schools as a new source of pin-stripe patronage, that Chicago politicians steered charter school contracts to community organizations that actively supported Emanuel's reelection bid. Juan Rangel, the co-chair of Emanuel's 2011 election campaign, served as director of United Neighborhoods Organization (UNO), a community organization that received tens of millions of dollars in public assistance for its operation of local charter schools.

Emanuel, like his predecessor, could steer lucrative legal and financial contracts to his backers. In modern Chicago, corporate pin-stripe patronage substitutes for the job patronage doled out by the classic political machine.

Sources: William J. Grimshaw, *Bitter Fruit: Black Politics and the Chicago Machine* (Chicago: University of Chicago Press, 1992), 206–224); Dick Simpson and Constance A. Mixon, eds., *Twenty-First Century Chicago* (San Diego: Cognella, 2013); John Chase, Jeff Coen, and Bill Ruthhart, "Rahm Emanuel Counts on Big Donors, with Many Getting City Hall Benefits," *Chicago Tribune*, June 14, 2016; Anthony Cody, "Chicago Mayoral Candidate Jesus 'Chuy' Garcia Talks about Schools," *Living in Dialogue* blog post, February 2, 2015, www.livingindialogue.com/chicago-mayoral-candidate-jesus-chuy-garcia-talks-schools/; Dan Mihalopoulos, "Leader of Clout-heavy UNO Quits" *Chicago Sun Times*, March 25, 2016.

LOOKING BACK: WAS THE BIG-CITY POLITICAL MACHINE A "RAINBOW COALITION"?

Without a doubt, machine leaders provided benefits to a diverse collection of residents who needed assistance. As a result, some urban analysts have had a tendency to portray the urban political machine as a **rainbow coalition** of the "outs," a diverse coalition of ethnic and racial groups and the poor who gained jobs, housing, and other assistance though the political machine.

Such a romanticized assessment contains an important element of truth, as the political machine did provide aid to the city's immigrant newcomers and the poor. Yet, such an assessment overly glorifies machine politics. It would be a mistake to view political machines uncritically as the kindly friend of the immigrants, the industrial-age working class, and the poor. The assistance that machine leaders provided persons in need was often quite limited. The provision of jobs was very important. But other benefits dispensed by machine leaders—a Christmas turkey or a bucket of coal to heat their apartments in the dead of winter—were hardly of a scale to lift people out of poverty.

Nor did the political machine fight for social justice. Actually, machine leaders often protected slumlords and the owners of factory sweatshops, taking payoffs in return for overlooking violations of health and safety standards. Machine leaders did *not* lead the fight for workplace safety and habitable housing. Instead, in New York and other cities during the industrial age, party officials turned a blind eye to the unhealthy and dangerous working conditions of urban sweatshops and to the lack of toilets, lighting, and adequate ventilation in overcrowded slum tenement dwellings.

The leaders of most big-city machines did not share benefits as widely as the rainbow coalition thesis avers; instead the leaders of the machine tended to favor their own racial and ethnic group. The Irish-led machine of Boston's Michael J. Curley dispensed patronage jobs largely to the city's working-class Irish; the Boston machine provided relatively few good jobs to the members of other ethnic groups. The Irish-led Democratic organization in Chicago similarly reserved the lion's share of municipal jobs and other benefits for the city's Irish, dispensing much lesser benefits to the machine's Polish, Italian, and African-American supporters.[10]

In cities like Memphis and Chicago, machine leaders sought the votes of African Americans in an era when blacks were otherwise discouraged from participating in politics. The benefits that African Americans received in exchange for their votes, however, were quite limited (see Box 7.4).

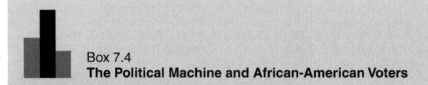

Box 7.4
The Political Machine and African-American Voters

At a time in United States history when African Americans were largely excluded from politics, a number of the big-city machines encouraged black voter registration and dispensed rewards to win the votes of black supporters. Still, the political machines were not inclusive. Even when black votes were crucial to the political organization's electoral success, machine leaders seldom, if ever, dispensed a commensurate share of benefits to African Americans.

In Memphis in the early and mid-twentieth century, "Boss" E.H. Crump astutely recognized that African Americans could provide his margin of victory. He maintained a degree of civility in his relations with the city's African-American community. He appointed African Americans to positions in the municipal bureaucracy. The Crump organization also improved black schools and the streets in black neighborhoods. The city under his direction even erected a monument to a heroic black citizen—an action that was a rarity in the segregationist Old South. Crump's political lieutenants encouraged African-American voter registration; the Crump organization even paid the poll tax so that a selected number of blacks would be able to vote. Yet once Crump cemented his power in office, he had less need to cater to black voters. His organization reduced the numbers of African Americans permitted to register to vote; the Crump organization also drew back on the benefits it dispensed to the black community.[1]

The Chicago Democratic organization, led in the 1950s and 1960s by the legendary Richard J. Daley, dispensed jobs, housing assistance, and welfare-style benefits to its African-American supporters. The Daley organization also had a number of black lieutenants who were rewarded with important privileges, even a seat in Congress. But the white ethnic-dominated machine would not push for housing and school desegregation. Chicago built a **second ghetto**, a virtual "wall" of high-rise public housing structures to keep the city's black population, displaced by urban renewal projects, from spilling into white neighborhoods.[2] The city's public housing policies virtually mandated racial segregation. The Dan Ryan Expressway "was shifted several blocks during the planning stage to make one of the ghetto walls."[3] According to critics, "The Daley political machine functioned not as a ladder of political empowerment but as a lid blocking African-American political empowerment."[4]

1. Marcus D. Pohlmann and Michael P. Kirby, *Racial Politics at the Crossroads: Memphis Elects Dr. W.W. Herenton* (Knoxville: University of Tennessee Press, 1996), 62–63 and 100–104; Elizabeth Gritter, *River of Hope: Black Politics and the Memphis Freedom Movement, 1865–1954* (Lexington: University Press of Kentucky, 2014).

2. William J. Grimshaw, *Bitter Fruit: Black Politics and the Chicago Machine, 1931–1991* (Chicago: University of Chicago Press, 1992). Arnold R. Hirsch, *Making the Second Ghetto: Race and Housing in Chicago Politics, 1940–1960*, rev. ed. (Chicago: University of Chicago Press, 1998), describes the complicity of the Chicago machine in building and maintaining public housing and residential segregation.

3. Mike Royko, *Boss: Richard J. Daley of Chicago* (New York: Signet, 1977), 137

4. Richard A. Keiser, "Explaining African-American Political Empowerment: Windy City Politics from 1900 to 1983," *Urban Affairs Quarterly* 29 (September 1993): 84–116; quotation on p. 112.

The Political Machine, Sweatshops and Child Labor: Cigar Makers and Children at Work in a Tenement Home Workshop, New York City, 1890. Political-party machine leaders often took kickbacks and bribes from industrialists and landlords. As a result, the machine did little to combat the unhealthy and dangerous conditions of the slum tenements and sweatshops of the immigrant city. While many reformers had little sympathy for the immigrants, photographer Jacob Riis, who took this photo, was among the *social reformers* who sought safer work and housing conditions, upgraded sanitation, expanded public education, and an end to child labor.

Source: Photo taken by Jacob Riis, http://commons.wikimedia.org/wiki/File: Bohemian_Cigarmakers.jpg.

THE REFORMS AND THEIR IMPACTS

Over the decades, political machines declined. Increases in prosperity and gains in education meant that citizens could increasingly ignore the limited benefits that big-city political organizations offered for their votes. Federal laws that restricted immigration, especially in the 1920s, denied the machine a pool of potential supporters. The rise of the welfare state, beginning with President Franklin Roosevelt's New Deal, also undercut the machine's power, as Americans could now obtain public assistance and social services without having to please machine captains.

Yet these societal trends do not fully explain the decline of big-city political organizations. The various reforms introduced by political reform movement, too, served to undercut the power of the big-city political machines.

Chapter 6 previously reviewed two reforms in the structure of local government: the council-manager and commission plans. We now examine other structural reforms and rules changes that have had a lasting influence on city politics.

THE DEBATE OVER VOTER REGISTRATION

As early as the Progressive Era, the reformers introduced **voter registration requirements** to eliminate fraudulent voting. Before the introduction of laws that required a person to register in advance before he or she could vote, citizens simply showed up on Election Day and cast a ballot. The new voter registration systems served to protect the integrity of elections. But the new registration requirements have a less desir-

Box 7.5
Who Shall Be Allowed to Vote? The Past and Current Debate Over Voting Rules

Should laws and regulations on voting be modified to make it easier for more citizens to vote? Not all political actors seek to maximize voter turnout. Progressive Era-like **voter registration** requirements clearly reduce voter participation. The introduction of voter registration in the United States "cleaned up" elections by making it impossible for ineligibles to vote and for political organizations to pay for **repeaters** to go from poll to poll to cast multiple votes (to "vote early and often," as the saying goes). Requiring advance registration was a simple way to eliminate such corrupt practices and protect the integrity of the ballot box.

But voter registration is also a political weapon that entrenched interests use to diminish the ballot-box power of emergent political groups, including the poor and newly arrived immigrants. As far back as the Progressive Era, as political scientist Walter Dean Burnham observed, voter registration requirements reflected the "old-stock nativist and corporate-minded hostility to the political machine, the polyglot city, and the immigrant which was so important a component of the progressive mentality." Registration requirements were not initially introduced everywhere. Pennsylvania and other states in the early 1900s required advanced voter registration only in the state's largest cities, communities with a growing immigrant and Catholic populations. Citizens in Protestant small towns and rural areas, by contrast, could continue to go to the polls and vote on Election Day without having to register in advance.[1]

Voter registration requirements have a clear class impact. Lesser-educated, low-income voters often fail to make the attempt to register in advance of Election Day and hence are not permitted to vote. Higher status voters, who have the education and civic awareness to register, enjoy greater electoral strength than their numbers in the population would otherwise merit. Simple changes the voter registration rules can help correct this bias. As one classic study of voter turnout concluded, "Liberalizing registration provisions would have by far the greatest impact on the least educated."[2]

A new generation of pro-democracy advocates urge the adoption of a series of measures to make it easier for people to vote. **Motor voter** legislation offers citizens the convenience of registering to vote when they receive or renew their driver licenses; citizens do not need to make a separate trip to city hall. **Mobile registrars** can register people to vote where they live, shop, or work. As of 2016, 13 states and the District of Columbia went still further, adopting **Election Day registration** (also called **same-day registration**) that allows citizens to prove their eligibility and add their names to the voter rolls as they show up at the polls to cast a ballot.

One increasingly popular innovation promotes early voting, allowing voters to cast a ballot days or even weeks before Election Day. Thirty-two states and the District of Columbia allow early voting. **Vote by mail (VBM)** systems eliminate the inconvenience of having to show up at a polling site to vote in person. In Washington, Oregon, and Colorado, all citizens cast their ballots by mail, a process that spreads the act of voting over a period of weeks; Election Day is no longer the sole day for a person to vote. An additional 19 states permit certain specified state and local contests to be conducted by mail.[3] Mail balloting eliminates the difficulties that citizens face in rearranging their work schedules and even in finding their assigned polling site when an election takes place on a single day.

Critics contend that such relaxations of the rules can lead to election fraud. Not all the critics of these innovative voting systems, however, are motivated solely by a desire to protect the integrity of the electoral process. Republican and conservative activists often worry about the partisan leanings of new voters, especially as newly registered black and Latino voters have a tendency to vote Democratic.

"Talk radio" hosts and activist conservative political groups have joined with Republican strategists in asserting that the new efforts to promote voting enable Democratic Party leaders and their allies to march "phantom voters" to the polls, ineligibles whom Democrats will fraudulently sneak into the ballot booth.[4]

But despite the howls of talk-radio hosts and the claims tweeted by President Trump, a review of the statistical evidence shows that voter fraud in the United States is quite rare; existing penalties, including the threat of jail, effectively deter registration fraud. A Brennan Center survey of local officials in charge of administering elections underscored the virtual absence of fraudulent voting by noncitizens in 2010; in the jurisdictions surveyed, only one in every 10,000 ballots was cast by a noncitizen![5] Nonetheless, Republican-controlled state legislatures continue their attempts to tighten the restrictions on voting, adding requirements that are likely to deter voter registration by younger voters, college students, minorities, and the poor, all groups whose members have tended to support Democratic candidates.[6]

More than 30 states enacted laws to strengthen the requirements for identification before a person can be issued a ballot. The more strict states require that a voter produce an official government-issued photo ID. A federal judge in 2017 struck down Texas's tight Voter ID law as discriminatory, accepting the contention of plaintiffs that the law placed an unnecessary burden on poor people and minorities who lacked a state driver's license or other approved photo ID but who, in past elections, had voted as they had offered alternative proof of residence, including bills mailed to their home address from a public utility. The court ruled that the strengthened Texas ID requirement violated the federal Voting Rights Act, that the statute was enacted with the intention to discriminate against Blacks and Hispanics.[7]

In Ohio in 2016, the Republican-controlled legislature eliminated "Golden Week," the week-long period just before the election that enables one-stop registration and voting. Evidence from the 2008 and 2012 presidential elections revealed that African Americans were, respectively, 3.5 and 5 times more likely than whites to take advantage of Golden Week. The Republican-imposed change also effectively closed local election offices on the Sunday before an election, the day on which African-American church leaders at the conclusion of services had bussed members of their congregations to county hall to register and vote.[8] The courts approved some, but not all, of the Republican efforts in Ohio to narrow the voting period.

The federal courts have not provided clear and consistent guidelines concerning what exact voter ID requirements and restrictions on early voting a state may—and may not—enact. U.S. Supreme Court action will likely eventually be required to sort out matters.

Academic studies, however, are rather clear: Republican-controlled state governments have tended to enact strict photographic ID laws and other voting restrictions that have a disproportionate impact that discourages voting by racial minorities and thereby skews voting power toward the "political right."[9] The *Harvard Law Review* concluded: "Whatever the motivations behind them, these new requirements have had a distinctly partisan and—in many cases—racial impact."[10] This was also the logic of a federal court decision that struck down North Carolina's strict voter ID law: the court ruled that changes made by North Carolina amounted to an unconstitutional "effort to target African-Americans with almost surgical precision."[11]

1. Walter Dean Burnham, *Critical Elections and the Mainsprings of American Politics* (New York: W.W. Norton, 1970), 79–65.

2. Raymond E. Wolfinger and Steve Rosenstone, *Who Votes?* (New Haven, CT: Yale University Press, 1980), p. 79.

3. Figures for state adoption of the Same-Day Registration and Vote-by-Mail (VBM) systems are provided by the National Conference of State Legislatures, 2016.

4. Radio talk show host Rush Limbaugh viewed measures to reduce the long lines at the polls and other measures to ease voting as little more than a partisan power grab by Democrats intent on allowing noncitizens to cast ballots. See the transcript of the segment "Democrats Move to Make Voter Fraud Easier," *The Rush Limbaugh Show*, February 5, 2013, www.rushlimbaugh.com/daily/2013/02/05/democrats_move_to_make_voter_fraud_easier.

5. Lorraine C. Minnite, *The Myth of Voter Fraud* (Ithaca, NY: Cornell University Press, 2010); Jane Mayer, "The Voter Fraud Myth," *New Yorker*, October 29, 2012; "Myth of Voter Fraud," *New York Times* editorial, October 9, 2011; Christopher Famighetti, Douglas Keith and Myrna Pérez, *Noncitizen Voting: The Missing Millions* (New York: Brennan Center for Social Justice, New York University School of Law, 2017), www.brennancenter.org/sites/default/files/publications/2017_NoncitizenVoting_Final.pdf.

6. Wendy R. Weiser and Lawrence Norden, *Voting Law Changes in 2012* (New York: Brennan Center for Social Justice, New York University School of Law, 2011), www.brennancenter.org/publication/voting-law-changes-2012; Stephanie Saul, "Looking, Very Closely, for Voter Fraud: Conservative Groups Focus on Voters in Swing States," *New York Times*, September 16, 2012.

7. "Fifth Circuit Court Strikes Down Voter ID Law Based on Disparate Impact—*Veasey v. Abbott*, 796 F.3d 487 (5th Cir. 2015)," *Harvard Law Review* 129 (2016): 1128–1134; Manny Fernandez, "Federal Judge Says Texas Voter ID Law Intentionally Discriminates," *New York Times*, April 10, 2017

8. Darrel Roland, "Judge Rules Ohio Voter Rights Violated," *Columbus Post-Dispatch*, May 25, 2016.

9. Zoltan Hajnal, Nazita Lajevardi, and Lindsay Nielson, "Voter Identification Laws and the Suppression of Minority Voters," *Journal of Politics* 79, no. 2 (April 2017): 363–379. Daniel R. Biggers and Michael J. Hanmer, "Understanding the Adoption of Voter Identification Laws in the American States," *American Politics Research* 45, no. 4 (2017). 516–88; Mark P. Jones, Jim Granato, and Renée Cross, "Voter ID Law and the 2014 Election: A Study of Texas's 23rd Congressional District," University of Houston Hobby Center for Public Policy and Rice University Baker Institute for Public Policy, August 2015, further reports that the Texas law had the impact of confusing and thereby discouraging participation by Latino voters who actually possessed state-approved forms of identification: http://bakerinstitute.org/research/he-texas-voter-id-law-and-2014-election-study-texass-23rd-congressional-district/.#sthash.dkHmunxq.dpuf.

10. "It's About Time (Place and Manner): Why and How Congress Must Act to Protect Access to Early Voting," *Harvard Law Review* 128, no. 4 (2015): 1229.

11. Adam Liptak and Michael Wines, "Strict North Carolina Voter ID Law Thwarted After Supreme Court Rejects Case." *New York Times*, May 15, 2017.

able secondary impact: registration requirements diminish the ballot-box power of lower-class citizens and minorities. While middle-class and well-educated persons have little difficulty in registering to vote, the requirement for advance registration poses a barrier to the participation of lower-income and lesser-educated persons who do not plan in advance. As a consequence, voter registration can properly be viewed as both a "good government" reform *and* a partisan political weapon that has a clear class and ethnic bias.

The debate over voter registration requirements continues to the present day. Pro-democracy reformers have sought to relax unnecessary voter restrictions in order increase participation. Pro-democracy advocates seek to expand voter turnout through such innovations as **early voting**, giving citizens the option to vote by mail or otherwise cast ballots during the weeks preceding Election Day Tuesday. Other political actors, however, resist such efforts and continue to seek laws that move in the exact opposite direction, tightening the rules governing voting by shortening the early voting period and by demanding that voters meet more strict identification requirements (see Box 7.5).

AT-LARGE ELECTIONS

The reformers disliked **district elections**, whereby candidates were elected from relatively small geographical areas of the city and did not have to win the approval of voters throughout the city. The reformers argued that a system of districts (also called wards) results in parochialism and overspending, as each council member fights for projects that benefit his or her geographic ward instead of considering the larger good of the city as a whole. The reformers sought to replace district elections with a system of **at-large elections**, where legislative candidates run citywide (or countywide), leading them to seek out policies that serve the entire city (or county). The reformers also argued that an at-large system enables and increased number of more high-quality candidates to serve on the city council, as the best-qualified candidates are not scattered, one per district or ward, throughout the city.

The system of at-large elections has gained great popularity in local government. Nearly two-thirds of all local governments in the United States use some variation of at-large ballot rules. About one-fourth of U.S. cities elect their entire city council in at-large contests. Another 20 or so percent of municipalities use a **combination or mixed electoral system**, where some council members run citywide while others are elected from narrower voting districts. Only 14 percent of U.S. communities elect all council members by district.[11]

At-Large Elections and the Dilution of Minority Power: The Voting Rights Act (VRA)

At-large systems can make it difficult for a geographically concentrated or ghettoized minority to elect one of its own members to office.[12] When electoral contests are conducted city- or countywide, a geographically concentrated minority can be easily outvoted by the city- or countywide majority. In contrast, where a city or county is carved into smaller council districts, a minority group that dominates a relatively small geographical area can be expected to elect one of its own to the city or county council.[13]

At-large election can produce outcomes quite different from ward-based voting, as clearly seen in the political history of San Francisco. For many decades, San Francisco utilized a system of at-large elections, and minorities won no seats on the city's Board of Supervisors (San Francisco's city council): With their population concentrated in only a portion of the city, minorities were outvoted in supervisor races run citywide. When the city in 1977 switched to the "unreformed" system of district elections, the composition of city's Board of Supervisors was transformed; for the first time, a black woman, a Chinese American, and a gay activist—Harvey Milk—all won seats. Harvey Milk won easily in a district that embraced "the Castro," the center of San Francisco's growing gay population. He had lost earlier electoral contests that were conducted at-large.

Neighborhood activists are disadvantaged when electoral contests are run city- or countywide. A neighborhood activist may be well known in his or her immediate community but will have difficulty in raising the vast sums of money required for a citywide campaign that requires great reliance on paid advertising. At-large systems favor office seekers who are visible citywide and who gain support from big donors. A system of district elections, by contrast, provides a more likely route to office for grassroots activists who have strong neighborhood backing.

In Florida, metropolitan Miami-Dade County's system of nonpartisan, at-large elections similarly served to dissuade "candidates from running as strong advocates of minority political interests."[14] Inner-city community activists and racial minorities faced great difficulty winning support from voters living in the suburban portions of the county. Racial minorities went to court to challenge the voting systems as discriminatory. When, in the 1990s, Dade County under judicial pressure switched to a system of district elections, the results were dramatic: The change to district representation produced an immediate increase in the number of Hispanics and African Americans elected to the Miami-Dade Metro Commission. Today, however, the choice of at-large versus district-based voting in Miami-Dade County may be less consequential, as the electoral influence of the area's growing Cuban population is felt even in contests that are conducted countywide.[15]

In cities in the South, and in a number of cities in the North as well, whites resorted to at-large voting systems as a weapon of discrimination, a means to undermine minority voting rights. In the 1960s, at a time when African Americans in the South were gaining the right to vote, 20 county governments and boards of education in Georgia suddenly switched from district to at-large voting rules, a rules-switch designed to minimize the likelihood of electing black candidates. The State of Mississippi, a bastion of segregation in the Civil Rights era, even passed legislation requiring that all county boards of supervisors and county school boards be elected at large.[16] In some cities, whites even looked to the annexation of white suburbs to dilute black voting power; when coupled with at-large voting rules, annexation increased the white share of the electorate, with whites in the newly attached suburban portions helping to outvote a city's growing African-American population.

The national government responded to such manipulations of electoral rules by passing the **Voting Rights Act (VRA) of 1965**. One important section of the VRA prohibits cities with a history of discrimination from implementing voting rules that diminish the possibilities of electing minority candidates.

Armed with the VRA, civil rights groups went to courts to challenge at-large voting systems. Dallas in the 1990s responded to the continuing threat of legal action by replacing its at-large electoral system with a new "14–1 plan," a dramatic change under which 14 members of the new city council were elected by district and only the mayor was elected citywide. The switch to district voting rules helped enable four African Americans and two Latinos to gain seats on the Dallas city council in the elections that immediately followed the switch.

There are even more contemporary examples of the battle over voting rules and voting rights. Legal action brought by voting rights groups led the Irving (Texas) Independent School District in 2012 to switch from an at-large system to a mixed system of representation (with five school board members elected from districts and two elected at-large). Minority parents had argued that Irving's older system of at-large electoral contests produced an all-white school board that was incapable of responding to the needs of the district's growing number of Hispanic children. Judicial pressure similarly led suburban Grand Prairie Independent School District, just outside of Dallas, to abandon its at-large voting system for a 5–2 mixed system similar to that instituted in Irving. In Grand Prairie, as in Irving, the system of at-large elections had helped maintain an all-white school board.[17] Numerous communities in California, too, have responded to judicial pressure by increasing the number of council and school board members elected by district.[18]

Recent changes, however, have weakened the Voting Rights Act. For four decades, the Voting Rights Act required **preclearance** by the U.S. Justice Department: If a community had a past record of discriminating against minority voters, it could not institute changes to is voting rules, including the introduction of at-large voting systems, without first gaining the consent of the Justice Department. Preclearance review sought to prevent local manipulations of the voting rules that would dilute minority voting power.

Cities, particularly in the South, chafed under such supervision by the national government. Local leaders argued that their city should not be forever denied the freedom to make decisions on their representational systems permitted in other communities, simply because of discriminatory actions that occurred in the distant past.

A divided U.S. Supreme Court relaxed some of the more important constraints imposed by the Voting Rights Act. *Shelby County v. Holder* (2013) freed communities in nine states from preclearance requirements. The Court ruled that the Justice Department would need more "current" evidence of local discrimination before the Department could mandate that a locality submit a proposed change in voting rules for the Department's approval.[19]

Voting rights activists were troubled by the Court's ruling. They worried that *Shelby* would give cities and counties the ability to institute rules changes that would adversely affect minority voting power. Maricopa County in Arizona in 2016, for instance, slashed the number of polling places by 70 percent, a decision that led to voting lines in Phoenix that circled a city block; wait times of up to three hours discouraged people from casting a ballot. County officials claimed that the reduction in the number of polling places was necessary to save money. The federal Justice Department likely would not have given preclearance approval to a move that was likely to have such an impact on inner-city voting stations; but after *Shelby* such oversight was no longer required.[20]

Voting rights advocates worried that cities, especially Republican-controlled communities in the South and the Southwest, would use their newfound latitude to return to at-large voting systems that dilute the ballot-box power of African Americans and Latinos.[21] Immediately after the *Shelby* decision, Pasadena (Texas), a suburb of Houston facing a large surge in its Latino population, switched to a mixed system of representation, converting two of its eight council seats to election-at-large, altering the district-election plan that the community had previously adopted to increase Latino representation.[22] A U.S. District Court, however, struck down Pasadena's move, with the presiding federal judge citing both historical and more contemporary discrimination in Pasadena. The judge ordered the municipality to revert back to its system of district elections.[23]

Outside the South, the courts ruled the at-large electoral system of Yakima, Washington, similarly had impermissible discriminatory effects; no Latino was able to win election to the city council in 40 years, despite the fact that Latinos comprise one-third of Yakima's population. In Santa Barbara, California, a community where Hispanics make up 40 percent of the local population, plaintiffs similarly argued that the city's system of at-large council elections resulted in the gross underrepresentation of Hispanics. Santa Barbara settled the lawsuit out of court, agreeing to create a new system of district-based elections.[24]

District voting systems help promote the election of Latino officials in communities where the Latino population is geographically concentrated or ghettoized.[25] But in many cities, the Latino population is less concentrated or ghettoized than is the African-American population. In such cities, a switch to district elections will not likely produce the equivalent political gains for Latinos as such a switch often does for African Americans.[26]

The Impacts of "Positive" Gerrymandering

Throughout the history of the United States, the political party in power has resorted to **gerrymandering**, drawing strangely shaped voting districts in an effort to diminish the number of seats that an opposing party will likely win in ensuing elections. Gerrymandering is often criticized for being crudely partisan. In more recent years, however, gerrymandering has served a new purpose. In a process that can be labeled **positive racial gerrymandering** or **race-conscious redistricting**, political boundary lines are drawn to create **majority-minority districts** that *increase* the likely election of racial and ethnic minorities to public office.

A good example of "positive" race-conscious redistricting can be found in Chicago. In Chicago, the Latino population is spread out over large portions of the city, making it difficult for a Latino to win election in any United States congressional district. Chicago at long last elected its first Latino, Luis Guttiérrez, to Congress only after redistricters fashioned a very strange C-shaped congressional district: Two separate Latino sections of the city were connected by a very narrow strip of land that ran along an interstate highway in order to create a Latino-majority district (see Figure 7.1).

The Supreme Court has put some limits on the extent to which state and local officials may take race into account when drawing the lines of a district to increase the

Figure 7.1   **Chicago's C-Shaped Hispanic Congressional District.** The Fourth
Congressional District continues to retain the C-shape the district was given
when two Latino areas of the city were fused together to create a district that
could elect a Latino to Congress. In 2018, Jesus "Chuy" Garcia easily won
election to Congress from the district, receiving 86 percent of the votes cast.

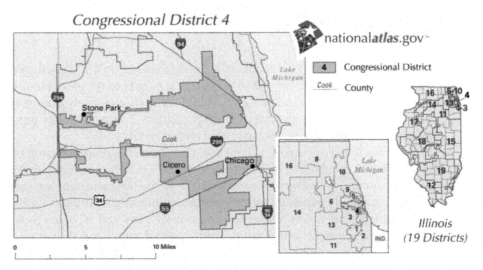

Source: Department of the Interior, U.S. Geological Survey, https://nationalmap.gov/small_scale/
printable/images/pdf/congdist/IL04_110.pdf.

likelihood of the election of a member of a racial minority group. In several instances,
the Court struck down districts with overly "bizarre" shapes[27] where race appeared to
be "the overriding or predominant factor" in drawing district lines.[28] Yet, the Court did
not ban the drawing of oddly shaped districts. State and local officials can consider
minority representation as *one* of a number of factors when drawing a district's boundary lines. Unless new Court rulings provide even more precise guidance as to just what
is and is not permissible, governments can continue to shape districts to increase the
election of underrepresented African Americans and Latinos. White voters residing in
such a majority-minority district object that their power is undermined by such a race-
conscious practice.

Somewhat surprisingly, the creation of minority-dominated voting districts actually
works to the long-term advantage of Republicans! When district lines are creatively
drawn to pack as many minority voters as possible into a single legislative district, the
newly created district increases the chances of victory by a candidate who is likely be
a Democrat. However, neighboring districts become increasingly likely to be won by
Republicans as those districts have been "bleached" or drained of nonwhite voters who
were packed into the majority-minority district. Positive racial gerrymandering increases
the number of racial minorities elected to the U.S. House of Representatives, at the price
of increasing Republican power in Congress.[29]

The U.S. Supreme Court struck down a congressional district map drawn by North
Carolina's Republican-dominated state government. The Court was troubled by the fact

that state Republican leaders had removed blacks from neighboring districts and packed thousands of black citizens into districts that already had a record of electing Democratic candidates. Such a move did not increase black representation but did reduce the electoral influence of African Americans in surrounding districts.[30]

Do At-Large Voting Systems Discriminate Against Women, Gays, and Lesbians?

At-large voting rules do *not* necessarily discriminate against all underrepresented groups. At-large systems do *not* appear to pose a great barrier to the election of women to local office. The evidence is inconsistent: While some studies show that women candidates fare better when races are run in smaller districts,[31] others studies report that women actually do a bit better when races are conducted citywide.[32]

Why is it that a system of at-large elections hurts the representation of racial minorities but has no equivalent bias against women? The reason is simple: At-large election systems hurt geographically concentrated minorities, and women (especially white women) are neither spatially segregated nor a minority of the population.

Do at-large elections hinder the election of gays and lesbians to local legislative office? It depends. In cities where lesbians and gays tend to live in a concentrated area (a city's so-called "gay ghetto"), a system of district election acts much as it does for African Americans and can promote the chances of electoral success.[33] But in cities where the gay and lesbian population is more geographically dispersed, the situation is more analogous to that of women, with district elections providing no clear and consistent advantage.[34] As referred to earlier, San Francisco's switch to district elections led to the 1977 election of gay activist Harvey Milk. Today, however, San Francisco's gay and lesbian population is so large, politically active, and spread geographically throughout the city that gays and lesbians can win races that are conducted citywide.

Annise Parker served three terms (2010–2016) as mayor of Houston, further indicating that citywide contests are not a barrier to an openly gay or lesbian candidate who meets other important political criteria. Parker won by emphasizing her fiscal moderation and experience as controller, qualifications that helped her gain support from moderate conservatives and the city's leading newspaper, the *Houston Chronicle*. Lori Lightfoot in 2019 became the first African-American woman and openly lesbian candidate to be elected mayor, Lightfoot won the citywide race by emphasizing her managerial credentials as an alternative to her opponent's tolerance of patronage and other political-machine practices.

Should At-Large Elections Continue to Be Viewed as "Good Government"?

The reformers argued that at-large elections would lead elected officials to adopt a broader, long-term vision for the city rather than adopt more parochial concerns of council members elected by district.[35] Even if true, at-large elections do not necessarily make for "good government," if by "good government" we mean government that is responsive to citizens, including racial minorities. When these concerns are taken into account, district elections actually have a number of quite positive impacts, as Amy Bridges found in her review of southwestern cities:

> Dramatic political changes appeared in the immediate aftermath of changes to district elections. More candidates ran for open seats; issues were more prominent in campaigns; portraits of districts, neighborhoods, and the concerns of their residents appeared in the news; candidates boasted their familiarity with neighborhoods they hoped to represent. Newly elected city councils were more racially diverse than the councils of big-city reform.[36]

NONPARTISAN ELECTIONS AND OFF-TIME ELECTIONS

Nonpartisan election is another of the lasting legacies of the reform movement. In a system of **nonpartisan elections** candidates run for office without a party label listed next to their names on the ballot. Nonpartisan ballots force voters to focus on the qualifications of the individual candidates and on local issues, not on a candidate's party affiliation or reaction to the statements of a national political figure who may dominate media coverage.

Over three-fourths of the local governments in the United States use the nonpartisan ballot.[37] In the West, virtually all local contests for office are nonpartisan. The State of Arizona mandates that its cities and towns use nonpartisan ballot systems.

Even many of the nation's largest cities have turned to nonpartisan voting systems: 22 of the 30 most populous cities have nonpartisan contests.[38] New York, Houston, Philadelphia, Indianapolis, and Charlotte are among the noteworthy outliers, big cities that employ partisan ballots. Even in Chicago, where local politics for decades was dominated by the city's legendary Democratic political machine, contests for the city council are formally nonpartisan. By the end of the twentieth century, Chicago made the contest for mayor nonpartisan as well.

As the Chicago experience indicates, the actual operations of a nonpartisan system vary greatly from city to city. In communities with a strong nonpartisan tradition, political-party organizations play little or no role in the election process. In cities like Chicago, however, partisan activity lurks just below the nonpartisan surface, and party leaders and organizations play important roles in slating candidates, raising campaign funds, and turning out the vote.

Houston is another city where a political-party presence lies below the surface of local elections that are formally nonpartisan. The Harris County Democratic and Republican parties endorse mayoral candidates, and political-party operatives assist local campaigns.[39] In 2015, Sylvester Turner narrowly won the mayoralty, running with the help of the local Democratic organization.

Nonpartisan election systems have their virtues but also suffer important shortcomings. The absence of party labels often confuses voters; especially in races for lower offices, a political-party label may help voters to choose among candidates about whom the voters know very little. In low-visibility city council and county board races, a party label can provide a clue or hint as to the basic policy orientations of a candidate.

By adding to voter confusion, nonpartisan ballot systems aggravate the **class bias in voting turnout**. Better-educated middle- and upper-class citizens are political self-starters who can sort through the basic records or promises of a candidate and then go out to vote. In contrast, lesser-educated and lower-class voters, when denied the hints provided by party labels, are more likely to be confused and stay home. In cities where elections are truly nonpartisan, there also is no organization of local party workers to telephone, text, knock on doors, and drive lower-class citizens to the polls on Election Day.

By reducing the turnout of lower-class voters and minorities who tend to vote Democrat, nonpartisan elections are generally seen as having a partisan bias. Hence few political observers were surprised when Arizona's Republican-controlled state legislature in 2010 passed a measure that forced Democrat-dominated Tucson to remove party labels from the local ballot.

Nonpartisan elections for school board are often marred by extremely low voter turnout. Turnout is further reduced when school contests are scheduled for a date when there are no races for other offices on the ballot. Reformers argued that the **off-year** or **off-time** (or **off-cycle**) **scheduling of elections** for school board and other local offices allows voters to focus on the issues unique to the race at hand. The reformers argued that candidates for offices such as a school board should not have to answer questions that arise from more prominent contests or the behavior of candidates for national office.

Yet when nonpartisan local elections are held on dates when no other electoral contests are scheduled, turnout can run as low as 10 or 15 percent—at times even lower! Such poor voter turnout undermines the use of elections as a tool of democracy. The off-time March 2017 Los Angeles school board elections had a turnout rate of only 12 percent.[40] When voter turnout is extremely low, organized interest groups with a material stake in an issue enjoy increased power. Teachers and other employees of the school system and their immediate families, for instance, often make up much of the actual turnout in off-cycle local school elections and bond referenda. Such effective voting power in low-turnout contests serves as a factor that can promote higher pay levels for teachers.[41]

A change to schedule elections for school board and other local offices on the same day as national or even state races would help increase voter participation in local contests.[42] Changes to allow early voting and online voting, as we have previously discussed, too, can be expected to result in small improvements in voting turnout. But, Democrats and Republicans continue to be divided when it comes to adopting measures to promote greater voter turnout.

In Ferguson, Missouri, the site of protests and riots after the 2014 fatal police shooting of an unarmed young black male, Michael Brown, a system of nonpartisan elections held in off-years virtually assured anemic rates of African-American participation, diminishing black representation in city hall. Ferguson's elections were held in April in odd-numbered years, times when there were no other elections of importance to attract voters to the polls. Ferguson has a population that is majority African American; but the anti-participation nature of the city's off-year off-time elections helped enable whites to control the city council (five of six seats) and the city's mayoralty.

In San Diego, municipal elections are nominally nonpartisan, but Democratic and Republican operatives work actively behind the scenes. Here, too, the scheduling of local elections in non-presidential years has served to reduce voter turnout, especially among the growing number of lower-income and minority voters who normally vote Democratic. The off-time system has helped Republicans in their efforts to hold onto city hall.[43]

REFORMS FOR DIRECT DEMOCRACY: THE DIRECT PRIMARY AND THE INITIATIVE, REFERENDUM, AND RECALL

Reformers of the Progressive Era argued that the railroad barons and other special interests had effectively seized control of state and local legislatures. Despite popular election, elected officials were not serving the people. The Progressives argued for a **direct primary**, that the voters themselves—and not political-party leaders—should select a party's candidates for public office. In a direct primary, the voters themselves—not party leaders—determine just who will be on the party's slate of candidates in the ensuing general election

For state and local governments, the reformers instituted three additional changes that have come to be known as the **direct democracy reforms**—the *initiative, referendum,* and *recall*—in an attempt to give citizens more direct say in policy making, weakening the grip of powerful private interests on the political process.

Today, the tools of direct democracy are found in states and communities across the United States. Twenty-six states and the District of Columbia allow citizens to vote on issues through the ballot initiative and referendum processes.[44] Thirty-eight states permit local recall elections, a special ballot to remove an officeholder before his or her term of office is completed.[45]

The popularity of the three institutions of direct democracy—especially the initiative and referendum—varies greatly by region. The institutions of direct democracy are nearly a universal feature of local governments in the Southwest and the West, but are less commonplace in the East. While 90 percent of cities in the West allow for the initiative and recall, only a third of Mid-Atlantic states permit such processes.[46]

To a great degree, the direct democracy reforms have delivered on their promise. Citizen groups use the initiative, referendum, and recall to force government officials to be more responsive to citizens's needs. Yet each of the three direct democracy tools is imperfect and has received vast criticism. In recent years, powerful interest groups have demonstrated their ability to use the tools of direct democracy to advance their own interests rather than the people's interests.

The Initiative and Referendum

Under the **citizens's ballot initiative** (or, more simply, the **initiative process**), the citizens themselves write and then cast ballots on a proposed piece of legislation, bypassing a legislature that has lost touch with the people. Where the initiative is permitted, the laws (or constitution) of each state and locality specify the number of signatures that citizens must gather to put a proposed piece of legislation or a city charter amendment before the voters.

Critics argue that the initiative process is fundamentally flawed. Initiatives are often poorly drafted and subject to legal challenge. More important, the initiative bypasses the processes of **representative government** that allow elected officials to balance the competing perspectives of different groups of voters. Legislation by initiative does not allow for fine-tuning and compromise; voters simply cast their ballots "Yes" or "No" on the measure as it is written on the ballot. A proposal's backers are likely to exaggerate the measure's benefits. Opponents, in their televisions advertising and social media campaigns, likewise exaggerate the ills that will to result from voter passage of a ballot measure. Amid a flurry of specious claims, popular passions and half-truths may dominate the vote on a ballot initiative.

California's **Proposition 13**, the very important 1978 measure that limited property taxes in the state, illustrates both the virtues and the shortcomings of legislation by the ballot initiative.[47] Voters took the necessary steps to enact Proposition 13 after the state legislature proved irresponsive to the demands of Californians for much-needed relief from soaring property taxes. The tax reductions brought about by Proposition 13 and similar direct measures in the years that followed garnered strong public approval.

Yet California's voters did not foresee numerous adverse impacts that resulted from Proposition 13. Homeowners were not the only ones who received tax relief; Proposition 13 gave the lion's share of the tax reductions to big corporations and other large property holders. The resulting constriction of tax revenues sharply limited local governments, forcing cutbacks in infrastructure investment, municipal services, and the public schools.[48] In an effort to find new ways to fund basic services, local governments raised user charges and fees, a move that further hurt lower- and middle-income residents and schoolchildren.[49] Proposition 13 even wound up diminishing local control of education: Caught in a fiscal bind, school districts accepted additional fiscal assistance and accompanying regulations from the State of California. Education in California became increasingly dependent on decisions made in the state capital.[50]

In San Diego, Proposition 13 virtually paralyzed the city, as municipal officials found that they could not raise revenues to support popular services. Local officials responded with "creative financing schemes," including the use of city pension funds to fund day-to-day service provision, a "dubious practice" that put pensions at risk and led to a municipal financial crisis.[51]

Modern-day initiative campaigns can be quite expensive, which means that this supposed tool of direct democracy can be dominated by moneyed interests. Business-backed groups hire **paid petition circulators** who secure the required number of signatures to place a measure on the ballot; signature gathering no longer serves as a proxy indicator for the people's genuine interest in a proposed measure.[52] The costs of pollsters, advertising specialists, and other members of a highly paid, professional "**initiative industry**"[53] further diminish the grassroots direct-democracy ideal of the initiative process. The U.S. Supreme Court legitimized the role played by moneyed interests in initiative campaigns, declaring that state laws that ban paid petition circulators are a violation of citizen First Amendment freedom-of-speech rights.[54]

The gambling industry effectively financed ballot campaigns that brought a state lottery to California and casinos to Atlantic City (New Jersey) and major cities in Ohio. In the state of Washington, Microsoft cofounder and billionaire Paul Allen, owner of the Seattle Seahawks, spent over $10 million on an initiative drive to have state taxpayers fund a new football stadium. The measure narrowly passed with 51 percent voter approval.[55]

The **referendum** is similar to the ballot initiative, except that the process typically starts not with voter signatures but with a decision of the legislature to put an item before the citizens for their approval. In some cities and states, citizens can petition for a referendum or public vote on a bill that has previously been passed by the city council or state legislature.

In numerous cities, especially in the Sunbelt, neighborhood, taxpayer, and environmental groups have used the initiative and referendum processes to counter the power of local growth coalitions. Commentators use the terms **ballot-box planning** and **electoral land-use planning** to denote instances when voters, angered by classroom overcrowding, increased pollution, traffic congestion, and the prospects of additional taxation, turned to the initiative and referendum processes to stop unwanted development projects. In Seattle, grassroots activists pushed for Initiative 31, the Citizens' Alternative Plan to slow the pace of downtown skyscraper and office development. Seattle activists also turned to the initiative and referendum routes to commit the city to the construction of a monorail, a system that would be financed by a new tax levied on automobiles.[56]

In San Francisco in 2014, Proposition K, the so-called Housing Affordability Initiative, sought to gain voter endorsement for the construction of 30,000 units of new housing, with at least one-third set aside for low- and middle-income tenants. Housing in this price range was quickly disappearing amid San Francisco's tech boom. But a number of local housing activists decried that the measure was advisory only and actually would do little to slow the pace of neighborhood transformation.[57]

Voter-imposed antigrowth measures are often more restrictive than the regulations that city councils place on growth.[58] In San Francisco, voters approved Proposition M, which capped annual new construction and required developers to pay various **linkage fees** to support affordable housing and other public services. Proposition M is one of the toughest antigrowth measures in the United States. Developers and advocates of new construction have, over the years, proposed a number of modifications to Proposition M. Yet in San Francisco, as well as in San Diego and other California cities, seemingly tough measures like Proposition M have not brought a halt to new development. When the market demand is there, developers build; they simply provide additional public amenities required by the statutes.[59]

Developers and growth-oriented elites have discovered that they can use the tools of direct democracy to gain approval for development projects and even subvert some environmental restrictions! Under California law, projects approved by the ballot initiative process cannot be challenged by lawsuits brought under the state's Environmental Quality Act (which is generally seen as tougher than federal environmental laws). Such special protection is offered even when voters have noted voted on a proposed project, that is, where a city council votes to accept the provisions of a citizens's petition, negating the need to conduct an actual public ballot. Across a wide range of cases—from the development of a vast 40-million-square-foot warehouse complex (the World Logistics Center) in Moreno Valley to the construction of a new Inglewood stadium for the Los Angeles Rams in Inglewood (a project of over 200 acres)—development forces wrote the proposed ballot measures for the zoning changes and other provisions that "fast-tracked" new construction. Development interests also helped pay for the canvassing campaigns to gather the necessary number of signatures required for an initiative petition.[60]

Such developer manipulated campaigns illustrate the ability of corporate interests to "capture" the initiative process, subverting the citizen-power intent of direct democracy. Developer-led initiatives often seek to deny the people's representatives a chance to rule on a controversial project. Developer-led initiatives also undercut the transparency of state environmental reviews.[61]

In San Antonio, civic leaders have turned to bond referenda to provide funding for uncontroversial projects—such as streets and drainage projects—but not for "equity" oriented projects such as the provision of mass transit or the construction of affordable housing. In San Antonio, project funding via ballot referendum generally serves to reinforce the status quo rather than provide funds for projects to promote greater equality.[62]

The Recall

In a **recall process**, citizens sign petitions to hold a special vote to decide whether an official will be removed from office before the normal expiration date of the official's term. Even in instances when an elected official is not removed, the mere threat of a recall election may push an elected official to pay greater heed to the wishes of constituents.

Fewer than half the states allow recall elections. Each state's laws determine just when local recalls are and are not allowed.

Local recall efforts are fairly commonplace in California, Oregon, and Michigan.[63] In Omaha, Nebraska, efforts to recall the mayor are so frequent that they are viewed as a routine aspect of the local political landscape.[64]

Oftentimes, voter dissatisfaction with an official's vote on taxes provides the impetus for a recall effort. Recall campaigns are also launched in response to revelations of local corruption. But in some cases the precipitating offense is less momentous. In 2008, the citizens of tiny Arlington, Oregon (population 600), decided by a narrow vote to remove Mayor Carmen Kontur-Gronquist from office after social media photos showed the scantily clad single mother posing on a fire truck. In San Jose, a special 2009 local election was scheduled to remove Councilwoman Madison Nguyen from office as she had referred to the local commercial strip as "the Saigon business district" instead of "Little Saigon,"[65] the name preferred by many of the city's Vietnamese refugees who had fled communism. The councilwoman survived the attempted recall.

Big-city mayors have on occasion had to deal with the threat of removal. Billionaire Norman Braman helped fuel the 2011 effort that recalled Miami-Dade Mayor Carlos Alvarez. The campaign was prompted by the county's award of a large pay hike to Dade employees and members of the mayor's staff at a time when the city had raised property taxes in response to a budgetary shortfall.[66] Under the threat of a recall effort resulting from allegations of sexual harassment allegations brought by a number of women, San Diego Mayor Bob Filner in 2013 resigned from office.

Critics contend that recall efforts intrude on responsible, representative government. Facing the threat of removal, an elected official may be more responsive to the demands of recall organizers than to the needs of the general public. Recall efforts can provide an important check on government malfeasance. But in some communities, resort to the recall is overused, with anti-tax activists mounting a recall effort any time a local official considers raising taxes, even when a revenue increase is needed to keep schools open or to get a community out of a tight fiscal squeeze.

Given the anti-government mood of citizens in the early twenty-first century, public officials did not have to do much in order to prompt a recall effort. In 2016, a recall effort in Austin sought to remove Councilmember Ann Kitchen for her support of regulations on Lyft and Uber and other ride-sharing companies. Recall organizers saw Kitchen's stance as being inconsistent with an innovation- and growth-oriented Austin. The recall effort floundered on a technicality, when the city clerk refused to accept signatures on petition pages that lacked the required notary stamp.[67]

NIMBY ("Not In My Backyard") activists have used the recall process to reinforce local exclusion. In 2008 anti-immigrant forces attempted to oust Phoenix Mayor Phil Gordon for failing to take aggressive steps against undocumented arrivals. But the effort fizzled when recall organizers failed to submit the necessary number of signed petitions.[68] In Plano, Texas, citizens in 2015 launched a recall campaign to remove from office members of the city council who had approved a plan for higher density development in the city. Here, too, the recall effort stalled on a technicality, as petitions were not properly prepared according to state law.

The nation's most dramatic instance of a successful recall election occurred not at the local level but at the state level. In 2003, Californians removed Gray Davis from the governorship, only a year after he had won reelection, replacing him with Arnold Schwarzenegger. Recall advocates argued that Davis had covered up the extent of the state's fiscal difficulties and had failed to initiate steps to alleviate the state's fiscal crisis.

CIVIL SERVICE RULES AND MERIT-BASED HIRING AND PROMOTION

As we have already seen in our earlier discussion of the reform movement, **civil service personnel systems** provide for the recruitment and promotion of municipal workers on the basis of skills and experience. Merit-system rules reduce the ability of political officeholders to dispense municipal jobs as patronage rewards to campaign workers. Civil service laws also afford career public servants the protection they need to do their jobs free from improper political intrusion; elected officials can no longer fire municipal workers for partisan reasons.

The introduction of civil service systems clearly changed local government for the better. Still, the changes that civil service brought came at a high cost: Civil service protections compound problems of governmental performance and accountability. Managers find that they cannot easily dismiss an underperforming civil servant or even transfer a worker to an assignment where he or she is more greatly needed. Critics charge that too many workers in civil service enjoy the equivalent of lifelong tenure on their jobs, with the result that they do not work especially hard or exhibit great willingness to follow the directives of superiors.

Management experts often recommend that civil service protections be relaxed in order to improve the performance and efficiency of government operations. Cities with a strong good-government ethos and an active investigatory media are often able to modify civil service rules with little risk. However, in Rhode Island, Delaware, Illinois, Maryland, West Virginia, and New Jersey—states with a relatively current history of political corruption and cronyism—a relaxation of civil service protections could open the door to machine-style abuses.[69]

Nor do municipal hiring systems in all cities truly reward merit? Municipalities that award "bonus points" to veterans, a commonplace practice, effectively discriminate

Box 7.6
Los Angeles and the Rodney King Riots: Can Anyone Fire Chief Gates?

Los Angeles provides a dramatic illustration of the insularity of powerful municipal agencies and the inability of elected officials to control important courses of action undertaken by professional city administrators. In 1992, a tense Los Angeles awaited the verdict in the trial of four police officers accused of beating a black motorist, Rodney King. The beating had been recorded on videotape. Dramatic footage that showed a circle of officers repeatedly kick and club the fallen King was aired again and again on television. The trial was move to white suburban Simi Valley, to avoid the turmoil and emotions swirling around Los Angeles.

A tense Los Angeles awaited the verdict. A potential riot situation was in the making. But Los Angeles police chief Daryl Gates chose not take direct charge of the situation and, instead, attended a political fundraiser. When the jury announced its "Not guilty!" verdict, inner-city areas of Los Angeles were rocked by spasms of violence. The police quickly withdrew from the South Central riot area, for fear that their continued presence would only precipitate new incidents of violence. The police withdrawal, however, was counterproductive, as it allowed the violence to escalate.

After the disturbance, Mayor Tom Bradley and other critics sought to remove Chief Gates from office, as the chief had refused to discuss riot preparations with the mayor. Mayor Bradley and Chief Gates did not get along. As Gates later revealed in his memoir, he and the mayor "were scarcely on speaking terms"; they had learned over time "to tolerate each other, barely speaking only when we had to, mainly by telephone."[1] The mayor lacked the formal authority to fire the city's "top cop."

Los Angeles is known as America's most reformed big city. The political reform movement in Los Angeles wrote a charter that gave professional department heads virtual independence from elected leaders. Chief Gates's successor, Willie Williams, observed that the city's top cop was under no legal obligation to meet with the mayor: "I don't have one operating superior. . . . The first six months I thought I was mayor!"[2] The city's reformed founders had gone too far in insulating top administrators from the city's electorally chosen leaders.

Gates's mishandling of the South Central disturbances coupled with the revelation of other scandals in the Los Angeles Police Department soon led voters to change the city charter. New rules made the police chief subject to reappointment every five years.

1. Daryl F. Gates, *Chief: My Life in the LAPD* (New York: Bantam Books, 1992); see also: Raphael J. Sonenshein, *Politics in Black and White: Race and Power in Los Angeles* (Princeton, NJ: Princeton University Press, 1993), 210–226; and Lou Cannon, *Official Negligence: How Rodney King and the Riots Changed the LAPD* (New York: Books/Random House, 1997), 121–122; Raphael J. Sonenshein, "Memo to the Police Commission: Govern Now and Spin Later," *Los Angeles Times*, December 10, 2001.

2. Los Angeles police chief Willie Williams, comments to the annual meeting of the National Civic League, Los Angeles, November 13, 1992.

against the hiring of women,[70] even though the increased number of women with military service is beginning to reduce the extent of the discrimination. In Los Angeles, certain provisions of the city's hiring process discriminate against the hiring of minorities. Mayor Eric Garcetti suspended recruitment by the city's fire department amid revelations that LAFD family members were given special exam-coaching sessions, sessions that gave the relatives of existing departmental personnel a considerable advantage over other applicants. Firefighters argued that the coaching sessions were necessary to continue traditions of family service. Critics charged that the practice amounted to **nepotism**, the hiring of family members instead of the most qualified applicants. Mayor Garcetti further criticized the program for undermining the city's efforts to increase racial and gender diversity in the department, as minorities and women tended to lack an insider connection when seeking careers with the LAFD.[71]

THE POST-REFORM CITY AND THE PROBLEM OF BUREAUCRATIC POWER

Merit-based personnel systems and systems that enshrined the power of expert "professionals" had the unfortunate consequence of bureaucratizing city government. By providing public servants with civil service safeguards against political interference, the reformers created a city that is "well-run but ungoverned." Mayors and city managers discovered that they could not easily dismiss officials who refused to follow their policy leads or who performed poorly (see Box 7.6). Too often, municipal agencies became uncontrollable "'islands of functional power' before which the modern mayor stands denuded of authority."[72]

The reformers had killed the old political-party machines. But in doing so, they made the civil service protected bureaucracies the new centers of decision-making power, so much so that political scientist Theodore Lowi referred to them as the **New Machines**.[73] Citizens soon began to express their dissatisfaction with the insularity, lack of responsiveness, and arrogance of bureaucratic government. They demanded a new generation of reforms to de-bureaucratize local government and to make public service provision more flexible and responsive to the needs of individual citizens and neighborhoods.

A NEW GENERATION OF REFORMS: SEARCHING FOR RESPONSIVENESS IN THE POST-REFORM CITY

Racial minorities, middle-class taxpayers, school parents, grassroots activists, and environmentalists have all at various times complained about the lack of responsiveness of city officials. Over the past decades, their complaints led to a new generation of reform legislation. In contrast to the earlier Progressive Era reformers, the new generation of reformers do not focus so narrowly on improving governmental efficiency and reducing spending. The new generation of reformers also sought to enhance the democracy, responsiveness, and fairness of the modern city. The new reformers also enacted new measures to increase citizen participation in urban decision making, participatory mechanisms that we will review in greater detail in Chapter 8.

Numerous cities turned to city council election by districts (or added a few seats elected by district atop of contests where council members are chosen in at-large contests) to make government more responsive to neighborhood needs. San Jose, Long Beach, Sacramento, Stockton, Oakland, Watsonville, Escondido, Tacoma, San Antonio, Dallas, Fort Worth, El Paso, Albuquerque, Richmond, Montgomery, Charlotte, and Raleigh all reinstituted district elections or created new hybrid systems of elections. In many instances, cities changed their electoral systems in response to lawsuits brought by ethnic and racial minorities. San Mateo County, south of San Francisco, settled a lawsuit brought by Latino and Asian plaintiffs, ending its holdout status as the last California county still running countywide electoral contests. In 2016, Anaheim finally switched to a system of council districts, a change the city instituted to settle a lawsuit brought by Latino voters. Seattle voters in 2013 voted for a mixed system of representation, with seven of nine city council members elected by district, a move to increase the council's responsiveness to neighborhood concerns.[74] California school districts, too, switched to district elections, as the California Voting Rights Act of 2001 prohibits all local governments, including school districts, from using a system of at-large elections that "impairs" the ability of a minority group "to elect candidates of its choice" or "to influence the outcome of an election."[75]

San Diego, San Jose, Oakland, Sacramento, Stockton, Spokane, Richmond (Virginia), Cincinnati, and Kansas City are cities that increased the power of the mayor, a move that contradicts the faith that Progressive Era reformers had placed in an expert city manager.[76] Kansas City Mayor Emanuel Cleaver explained the reason for the move: A modern big city needs real leadership rather than a mayor who, under the council-manager system, is only a glorified member of the city council who performs additional ceremonial duties:

> Kansas City is now a big-league city, and when the mayor of the city sits around with the president and CEO of a major corporation trying to get them to relocate here, the mayor is at a disadvantage, because other mayors can cut the deal at the table. We are at a disadvantage in many instances when we are out competing.[77]

ETHICS LAWS, SUNSHINE LAWS, AND CAMPAIGN FINANCE REFORM

The new generation of reformers further sought ethics laws and campaign finance regulations in order to reduce the influence of "big money" in the local arena. **Conflict-of-interest laws** and **requirements for financial disclosure** seek to increase public awareness of the ties that public officials may have to business interests and big campaign donors. It is then left up to the voters to decide if they are willing to elect a candidate with such ties.

Competitive bidding laws limit the ability of politicians to steer no-bid contracts to their political backers. Competitive bidding requirements assure that contracts are awarded to capable firms willing to do work for the city at the lowest price.

Open-meeting laws, often called **sunshine laws**, are another tool that seeks to enhance the transparency of government. Sunshine requirements prohibit government officials from conducting public business in unofficial gatherings that are closed to the public. Yet, in numerous cities, officials have been able to evade legal requirements for transparency. California state law bars public officials from doing business in closed forums. Yet, for a number of years, the members of the Los Angeles County Board of Supervisors often met in informal sessions, without citizen participation and public review, where they reached a consensus on 90 percent of the board's business that was later formalized in a public vote.[78]

In New York, loopholes in the state's ethics laws allow officials in small communities to evade requirements for public disclosure. In New York, officials in small towns and municipalities voted to support controversial "fracking" (that is, hydraulic fracking or the insertion of water into cracks in rock formations in order to recover more natural gas and oil) without first informing the public of the various financial ties that the officials had with gas and oil companies. Small communities lacked training sessions where elected officials are instructed as to their conflict-of-interest and disclosure obligations under state ethics laws. Local officials paid little heed to ethics requirements as the penalties for failing to disclose a conflict of interest were "anemic." State laws also suffered from loopholes. The New York law did not require lobbyists to publicly report their spending when targeting the officials of a village or municipality with a population of less than 50,000.[79]

Local **campaign finance reform** measures often seek to more directly limit the influence of private money in politics. Albuquerque, New Mexico, imposes a **limit on campaign spending**, setting a ceiling on the total amount that a candidate can spend in a local electoral race. New York, San Francisco, and Austin (Texas) are among the cities that impose a limit or **ceiling on political contributions**. New York City set a 2017 limit of $2,750 for the total amount that an individual can contribute a city council candidate; an individual donor was also limited to a maximum $4,950 contribution to a candidate for mayor or other citywide office. Contractors and people "doing business" with the city face even more stringent restrictions: a maximum of $250 in donations to a city council candidate and $400 to a mayoral hopeful.

Pasadena, Claremont, and Santa Monica (all in California) and Madison (Wisconsin) are among the cities that impose very strict **limits on the acceptance of gifts by city officials**.[80] Yet, not all cities have tough gift restrictions. San Jose in 2017 raised the maximum permitted gift to a public official from $50 to $470, a change that effectively allowed city officials to receive free tickets to sports events.[81] The Oakland Alameda Coliseum Authority gives county supervisors and local officials (including the mayor, city council members, and other key city officials) free luxury suite access and tickets to all events, including Warriors NBA playoff tickets, benefits that were worth tens of thousands of dollars (if not more) in 2016 and 2017, exceeding the $470 ceiling of gifts allowed under state law. Local officials conveniently failed to report the tickets. Alternatively, officials justified their attendance at arena events as necessary to their work in overseeing the operation of the facility.[82]

Ceilings on the amount of money that an individual can contribute to a political campaign can act to force office seekers to search for a broad funding base, decreasing the obligations that a candidate may have to a few wealthy donors. Beyond that, however, such campaign reform measures have not had a great impact on local politics. Measures that limit the role of money in public races have not been very successful in stimulating new electoral competition.[83]

Ceilings on campaign donations and spending that are set unduly low may wind up lessening the ability of a campaign to reach and educate voters. Austin, Texas, in 2014 set a limit of only $350 on the amount that an individual or political action committee can contribute to a candidate for municipal office. Austin also limits the **bundling** of individual campaign contributions to $1,750, the total amount in individual donations that a lobbyist can assemble and then present to a candidate. Austin enacted its restrictions on bundling after discovering that that a handful of lobbyists had each assembled more than $60,000 in contributions from individuals that they then delivered to local candidates.[84] Such severe ceilings on campaign donations may also help to account for the apparent rise of independently wealthy candidates seeking office in Austin—as wealthy candidates already have the personal wealth to pay for a modern political campaign and are not greatly hampered by limitations on donations.

Albuquerque adopted an even stronger approach in its effort to minimize the influence of private money. Albuquerque provides **full public funding** of citywide campaigns: the city's taxpayers pay for each candidate's entire campaign bill. Portland, Oregon, similarly had a system of public funding for local candidates, but voters in 2010 terminated the system, concerned about its costs. But if the amount a city offers a candidate is relatively small (Albuquerque offered only $379,000 to each candidate for mayor in 2017), candidates for local office may simply reject public funds in order to raise and spend as much money as they wish—just as nearly all major presidential candidates have done in recent years.

Full public funding of local elections is a rarity as it is expensive. A bit more commonplace is the *partial* taxpayer funding of races for local office. About a dozen communities (including Austin, Boulder, Long Beach, Los Angeles, Miami-Dade County, New York, Oakland, Petaluma, San Francisco, and Tucson) provide for the **partial public funding** of elections, where taxpayer funds pay for part of a candidate's campaign costs, reducing—but not eliminating—an office seeker's reliance on special interest money. Candidates who choose to accept public money voluntarily agree to limit their overall campaign spending and to abide by various accompanying campaign regulations. New York City requires candidates who accept public funds to engage in a series of public campaign debates. The city offers a generous 6:1 match of public money for individual donations up to $175, a hefty incentive for candidates to accept public funding and abide by its accompanying rules. When a candidate voluntarily chooses to accept public funds and the accompanying rules, the spending limitations do not infringe on a candidate's free-speech rights.[85]

Over the years, a number of U.S. Supreme Court rulings have severely undermined the ability of governments, including municipalities, to reduce the influence of money in political campaigns. The Court's very important 1976 *Buckley v. Valeo* decision created an **independent expenditures** loophole in campaign finance laws. Candidates and citizens have a First Amendment right of free speech, including the ability to spend money to advance their ideas, that they cannot be compelled to surrender.

The Court's ruling on independent expenditures essentially gave super-rich candidates like billionaire New York Mayor Michael Bloomberg the right to spend vast sums of money on their political campaigns, making a mockery of municipal attempts to rein in and equalize campaign spending. In 2001, Bloomberg spent $75 million of his own funds in his race for mayor, outspending his opponent's campaign by $50 million. Bloomberg spent $90 for each vote he received.[86] As his opponent's campaign manager observed, Bloomberg "bought it [the mayoralty] fair and square." Running for a third term in 2009, the billionaire mayor spent over $100 million of his own money—$174 for every vote he received.[87]

The Supreme Court has also overturned federal laws that bar corporations and labor unions from making campaign contributions.[88] The Court's 2011 ruling in *Arizona Free Enterprise v. Bennett* (2011) casts doubts as to the constitutionality of the "trigger" provisions used by New York City and a number of states and cities in their campaign funding systems. The Court essentially ruled that governments cannot attempt to equalized campaigns by providing additional funds to a candidate who is dwarfed by the campaign expenditures of a wealthy or well-financed opponent who refuses to abide by a government's limits on spending.

The various judicial rulings have allowed a virtual explosion of spending in local elections. Large sums of money from billionaires and wealthy donors entered local races as Super PACs (political action committees) were organizations that the Court declared have free-speech rights to spend as they wish. In Los Angeles, independent expenditures reached "unprecedented levels" as spending by businesses, political parties, and labor unions all gained heightened prominence in the local arena. In the Midwest, the "Chicago Forward" super PAC spent $2.7 million to support the 2015 reelection of Mayor Rahm Emanuel.

Super PACs have even contributed millions of dollars to school board races, as national political groups attempt to shape local decisions on such matters as the expansion of charter schools and the introduction of a Common Core curriculum.[89] The surge in donations from outside a school district marks a "nationalization" of local school board elections. School board matters are no longer a low-profile locally rooted affair.[90]

Despite campaign finance reform laws, "interested money" finds its way into the political arena. Decades before he became president, real-estate tycoon Donald Trump testified how he easily circumvented the New York statutes that sought to reduce the influence of money in local politics. At the time, state law limited a corporation's contributions to $5,000. Trump reported that he simply made the campaign contributions through 18 separate subsidiary corporations.[91]

CONCLUSION: THE CONTINUING IMPORTANCE OF THE RULES OF CITY POLITICS

The changes introduced by the reform movement permanently reshaped local politics and government. Many of the changes were clearly for the better, as the reforms reduced municipal corruption, patronage, partisan favoritism, and other machine-style practices. The reforms also increased the levels of technical competence and professionalism of municipal agencies. The reforms were so successful that even nominally "unreformed" cities adopted civil service systems, competitive bidding, ethics requirements, and other reformed practices.

Yet, the reforms were not perfect. At-large and nonpartisan elections and civil service systems were introduced by political groups intent on preserving their political power by diluting the power of immigrant groups and lower-class and minority citizens. Civil service systems further vested decision-making power in the hands of highly insulated municipal agencies and officials. City residents complain of the irresponsiveness of depersonalized, bureaucratized program administration.

The dissatisfaction eventually led to a new generation of reforms to increase the responsiveness and performance of municipal agencies and school systems. The new generation of reformers is not committed only to managerialism, cost-efficiency, and saving money. The new reformers are also committed to democracy, to increasing citizen participation, and to creating municipal governments that serve the diversity of populations of the contemporary city.

The chapters that follow discuss various efforts in the post-reform city to increase citizen participation, improve service provision, increase government's concern for the natural environment, and expand local job growth.

KEY TERMS

at-large elections (also known as
  at-large voting systems) (*p. 253*)
ballot-box planning (*p. 263*)
Buckley v. Valeo (*p. 270*)
bundling (*p. 270*)
campaign finance reform (*p. 269*)
ceiling on political contributions
  (*p. 269*)
centralized control, political
  machine as (*p. 241*)
civil service personnel systems
  (also known as merit employment
  systems) (*p. 265*)
class bias in voting turnout, the
  impact of nonpartisan elections
  on (*p. 259*)
combination or mixed electoral
  system (*p. 253*)
competitive bidding laws (*p. 268*)
conflict-of-interest laws (*p. 268*)
direct democracy reforms (*p. 261*)
direct primary (*p. 261*)
district elections (also known as
  ward-based elections) (*p. 253*)
early voting reforms (*p. 253*)
Election Day registration (*p. 250*)
electoral land-use planning (*p. 263*)
exchange process, machine politics
  as an (*p. 241*)

full public funding of election
  campaigns (*p. 270*)
gerrymandering (*p. 256*)
graft (*p. 242*)
hybrid city (*p. 240*)
independent expenditures, campaign
  finance reform and (*p. 270*)
"initiative industry" (*p. 262*)
initiative process (also known as
  citizens's initiative or the ballot
  initiative) (*p. 261*)
limits (or ceilings) on campaign
  spending (*p. 269*)
limits on the acceptance of gifts by
  city officials (*p. 269*)
linkage fees (*p. 263*)
majority-minority districts (*p. 256*)
merit employment systems
  (*p. 245*)
mobile registrars (*p. 250*)
motor voter laws (*p. 250*)
nepotism (*p. 267*)
neutral expertise, the reform
  movement's emphasis on
  (*p. 245*)
New Machines, civil service
  bureaucracies as the (*p. 267*)
nonpartisan elections (also known as
  nonpartisan systems) (*p. 259*)

NOTES

1. Bob Dreyfuss and Barbara Dreyfuss, "Inside the Port Authority: Governor Christie's Vast Patronage Machine," *The Nation*, February 14, 2014.
2. Dayton David McKean, *The Boss: The Hague Machine in Action* (Boston: Houghton Mifflin, 1940), 271.
3. Dick Simpson, Ion Nimerencu, Maria Estrada, Catie Sherman, and Thomas J. Gradel, "A More Active City Council: June 17, 2015–April 13, 2016," Chicago City Council Report #8, University of Illinois at Chicago, Department of Political Science, May 13, 2016, https://pols.uic.edu/docs/default-source/chicago_politics/city_council_voting_records/city_council_report_8.pdf?sfvrsn=8; "What If Chicago Aldermen Actually Challenged a Mayor?" *Chicago Tribune* (editorial), September 14, 2018. For the classic description of the Chicago city council as a rubber stamp, see Dick Simpson, *Rogues, Rebels, and Rubber Stamps: The Politics of the Chicago City Council from 1863 to the Present* (Boulder, CO: Westview Press, 2001).
4. Jessica Trounstine, *Political Monopolies in American Cities: The Rise and Fall of Bosses and Reformers* (Chicago: University of Chicago Press, 2008).
5. Amy Bridges and Richard Kronick, "Writing the Rules to Win the Game: The Middle-Class Regimes of Municipal Reformers," *Urban Affairs Review* 34, no. 5 (May 1999): 691–706.
6. Amy Bridges, *Morning Glories: Municipal Reform in the Southwest* (Princeton, NJ: Princeton University Press, 1997), esp. 151–174.
7. Martin Shefter, "The Emergence of the Political Machine: An Alternative View," in *Theoretical Perspectives on Urban Politics*, ed. Willis D. Hawley and Michael Lipsky (Englewood Cliffs, NJ: Prentice Hall, 1976), 22.

8. John M. Allswang, *Bosses, Machines, and Urban Voters* (Port Washington, NY: Kennikat Press, 1977), 52.

9. For a review as to how Chicago responded to court rulings on patronage, see Dick Simpson and Constance A. Mixon, eds., *Twenty-First Century Chicago* (San Diego, CA: Cognella, 2013), esp. 85–94.

10. Steven P. Erie, *Rainbow's End: Irish Americans and the Dilemmas of Urban Machine Politics, 1840–1985* (Berkeley: University of California Press, 1988); Tomasz Inglot and John P. Pelissero, "Ethnic Political Power in a Machine City: Chicago's Poles at Rainbow's End," *Urban Affairs Quarterly* 28, no. 4 (June 1993): 526–543.

11. National League of Cities, *Municipal Elections*, 2013 posting, www.nlc.org/build-skills-and-networks/resources/cities-101/city-officials/municipal-elections.

12. See Jessica Trounstine and Melody E. Valdini, "The Context Matters: The Effects of Single-Member versus At-Large Districts on City Council Diversity," *American Journal of Political Science* 57 (July 2008): 554–569.

13. Even where the choice of a voting system affects group representation is very real, the choice of election system may not greatly affect the policies that a city council pursues. A recent statistical study of cities concludes that "cities with at-large elections are somewhat less responsive to their citizens' policy preferences. But this difference in responsiveness is relatively small." See Chris Tausanovich and Christopher Warshaw, "Representation in Municipal Government," *American Political Science Review* 108, no. 3 (August 2014 2008): 605–641. The quotation appears on p. 619.

14. Christopher L. Warren, John G. Corbett, and John F. Stack Jr., "Hispanic Ascendancy and Tripartite Politics in Miami," in *Racial Politics in American Cities*, 2nd ed., ed. Rufus P. Browning, Dale Rogers Marshall, and David H. Tabb (New York: Longman, 1990), 158.

15. Elizabeth M. Aranda, Sallie Hughes, and Elena Sabogal, *Making a Life in Multiethnic Miami: Immigration and the Rise of a Global City* (Boulder, CO: Lynne Rienner, 2014), 171.

16. Chandler Davidson, "Minority Vote Dilution: An Overview," in *Minority Vote Dilution*, ed. Chandler Davidson (Washington, DC: Howard University Press, 1989), 11.

17. Jackie Hardy, "The Verdict Is Finally in as Irving ISD Moves to Adopt a 5–2 Single-Member/At-Large Mixed Voting System," *North Dallas Gazette*, January 19, 2012.

18. Chris Haire, "Local Voting Systems in Historic Upheaval as Cities Change How Officials Are Elected," *Orange County Register*, October 23, 2016; Phil Diehl, "District Elections Spreading to More Cities," *San-Diego Union-Tribune*, May 5, 2017.

19. *Shelby County v. Holder*, 570 U.S. (2013). Shaun Bowler and Gary M. Segura, *The Future Is Ours: Minority Politics, Political Behavior, and the Multiracial Era of American Politics* (Los Angeles: SAGE/CQ Press, 2012), 155–165, reviews the importance of the Voting Rights Act, and how the VRA sought to combat "cracking," "packing," and other techniques that localities use to dilute minority voting power.

20. Fernanda Santos, "Angry Arizona Voters Demand: Why Such Long Lines at Polling Sites?" *New York Times*, March 24, 2016.

21. Jonathan Martin, "New Face of South Rises as an Extralegal Force," *New York Times*, June 26, 2013.

22. Kira Lerner, "Voters Sue Texas Town for Diluting Hispanic Vote," *Think Progress Blog*, January 5, 2015, https://thinkprogress.org/voters-sue-texas-town-for-diluting-hispanic-vote-40af01178ab8.

23. Gabrielle Banks and Mihir Zaveri, "Pasadena Deliberately Diluted Hispanic Vote, Judge Rules in Voting Rights Case," *Houston Chronicle*, January 6, 2017; Alex Ura, "Voting Rights Battle in Pasadena Could Have Texas-Wide Legal Ramifications," *Texas Tribune*, July 11, 2017, www.texastribune.org/2017/07/11/voting-rights-battle-pasadena-could-come-wide-legal-ramifications/.

24. Kira Lerner, "Cities Are Quietly Reviving a Jim-Crow Era Trick to Suppress Latino Votes," *Think Progress*, March 5, 2015, http://thinkprogress.org/politics/2015/03/05/3629788/at-large-systems-latino-vote-suppression/.

25. Timothy B. Krebs and John P. Pelissero, "City Councils," in *Cities, Politics, and Policy*, ed. John P. Pelissero (Washington, DC: CQ Press, 2003), 174; David L. Leal, Valerie Martinez-Ebers, and Kenneth J. Meier, "The Politics of Latino Education: The Biases of At-Large Elections," *Journal*

of Politics 66 (November 2004): 1224–1244; Belinda I. Reyes and Max Neiman, "System of Elections, Latino Representation, and School Policy in Central California Schools," in *Latinos and the Economy: Integration and Impact in Schools, Labor Markets, and Beyond*, ed. David L. Leal and Stephen J. Trejo (New York: Springer, 2011), esp. 43–53.

26. Trounstine and Valdini, "The Context Matters," 563–565.
27. *Shaw v. Reno* 509 U.S. 630 (1993).
28. *Miller v. Johnson* 515 US 900 (1995). See also *Shaw v. Hunt* 517 US 899 (1996).
29. Kim Soffen, "How Racial Gerrymandering Deprives Black People of Political Power," *Washington Post*, June 9, 2016.
30. *Cooper v. Harris*, 581 US (2017). David G. Savage, "Supreme Court Finds the GOP Packed Black Voters into Two North Carolina Districts to Help Win More House Seats," *Los Angeles Times*, May 22, 2017; Michael Wines and Richard Fausset, "North Carolina Is Ordered to Redraw Its Gerrymandered Congressional Map: Again," *New York Times*, August 27, 2018.
31. Melody Crowder-Meyer, Shana Kushner Gadarian, and Jessica Trounstine, "Electoral Institutions, Gender Stereotypes, and Women's Local Representation," *Politics, Groups, and Identities* 3, no. 2 (2015): 318–334.
32. Trounstine and Valdini, "The Context Matters," 560–562, find that the type of election, at-large or by district, appears to have only a very small impact on the election of women to local councils. White women actually fare a bit better in at-large races. The authors further report that women in office share no consensus opinion when it comes to election type; some women feel that women fare better in district systems, while others feel that women are more likely to succeed under at-large arrangements.
33. James W. Button, Kenneth D. Wald, and Barbara A. Rienzo, "The Election of Openly Gay Public Officials in American Communities," *Urban Affairs Review* 35, no. 2 (November 1999): 188–209, esp. 199–203.
34. Gary M. Segura, "Institutions Matter: Local Electoral Laws, Gay and Lesbian Representation, and Coalition Building across Minority Communities," in *Gays and Lesbians in the Democratic Process*, ed. Ellen D.B. Riggle and Barry L. Tadlock (New York: Columbia University Press, 1999), 225.
35. A study of the Los Angeles city council, however, disputes the contention that members elected by district tend to ignore the larger interests of the city. See Craig M. Burnett and Vladimir Kogan, "Local Logrolling? Assessing the Impact of Legislative Districting in Los Angeles," *Urban Affairs Review* 50, no. 5 (September 2014): 648–671.
36. Bridges, *Morning Glories*, 200.
37. The data is from a 2001 survey of communities. See National League of Cities, *Partisan vs. Nonpartisan Elections*, www.nlc.org/build-skills-and-networks/resources/cities-101/city-officials/partisan-vs-nonpartisan-elections.
38. National League of Cities, *Partisan vs. Nonpartisan Elections*, Downloaded July 13, 2017, www.nlc.org/partisan-vs-nonpartisan-elections.
39. Rebecca Elliott, "Mayor's Race Looking Anything but Nonpartisan," *Houston Chronicle*, November 21, 2015.
40. Julia Payson, "Test Scores and School Boards: Why Election Timing Matters," a Brown Center "Chalkboard" posting of The Brookings Institution, Washington DC, March 22, 2017, www.brookings.edu/blog/brown-center-chalkboard/2017/03/22/test-scores-and-school-boards-why-election-timing-matters/.
41. Sarah F. Anzia, "Election Timing and the Electoral Influence of Interest Groups," *Journal of Politics* 73, no. 2 (April 2011), 412–427; Julia A. Payson, "When Are Local Incumbents Held Accountable for Government Performance? Evidence from US School Districts," *Legislative Studies Quarterly* 42 (2017), forthcoming.
42. Zoltan L. Hajnal and Paul G. Lewis, "Municipal Institutions and Voter Turnout in Local Elections," *Urban Affairs Review* 38, no. 5 (May 2003): 645–668; Neal Caren, "Big City, Big Turnout? Electoral Participation in American Cities," *Journal of Urban Affairs* 29, no. 1 (2007): 31–46. Interestingly,

Caren finds that council-manager cities suffer depressed turnouts, as voters apparently see less at stake in municipal elections when a manager is given substantial authority in a city's affairs.

43. Steven P. Erie, Vladimir Kogan, Nazita Lajevardi, and Scott A. MacKenzie, "Paradise Regained? Nonpartisan Appeals and Special Election Rules in San Diego's 2013–2014 Mayoral Race," in *Local Politics and Mayoral Elections in 21st Century America: The Keys to City Hall*, ed. Sean D. Foreman and Marcia L. Godwin (New York and London: Routledge, 2014), 184–202.

44. Ballotpedia, *States with Initiative or Voter Referendum*, 2017, https://ballotpedia.org/States_with_initiative_or_referendum.

45. Ryan Holeywell, "The Rise of the Recall Election," *Governing*, April 2011, www.governing.com/topics/politics/rise-recall-election.html.

46. Tari Renner and Victor S. DeSantis, "Contemporary Patterns and Trends in Municipal Government Structures," *The Municipal Year Book 1993* (Washington, DC: International City/County Management Association, 1993), 68–69.

47. Jack Citrin and Isaac William Martin, eds., *After the Tax Revolt: California's Proposition 13 Turns 30* (Berkley, CA: Institute of Government Studies Press, 2009).

48. Peter Schrag, *Paradise Lost: California's Experience, America's Future* (New York: Norton, 1998), 188–256; Sasha Abramsky, "Have California Voters Finally Had Enough of Proposition 13?" *The Nation* magazine, December 22, 2015.

49. Christopher Hoene, "Fiscal Structure and the Post-Proposition 13 Fiscal Regime in California's Cities," *Public Budgeting and Finance* 24, no. 4 (December 2004): 51–72.

50. Hoene, "Fiscal Structure and the Post-Proposition 13 Fiscal Regime in California's Cities," 70-72.

51. Steven P. Erie, Vladimir Kogan, and Scott A. MacKenzie, *Paradise Plundered: Fiscal Crisis and Governance Failures in San Diego* (Stanford, CA: Stanford University Press, 2011). The quotations, respectively, appear on pp. 66 and 70.

52. Richard J. Ellis, *Democratic Delusions: The Initiative Process in America* (Lawrence: University Press of Kansas, 2002), 49–61; Dennis F. Thompson, *Just Elections: Creating a Fair Electoral Process in the United States* (Chicago: University of Chicago Press, 2002), 139.

53. Mark Baldassare and Cheryl Katz, *The Coming Age of Direct Democracy: California's Recall and Beyond* (Lanham, MD: Rowman & Littlefield, 2008), 17.

54. *Meyer v. Grant*, 486 US 414 (1988). See Jessica A. Levinson, "Taking the Initiative: How to Save Direct Democracy," *Lewis & Clark Law Review* 18, no. 3 (2014): 1019–1061.

55. Galen Nelson, "Putting Democracy Back into the Initiative and Referendum," in *Democracy's Moment: Reforming America's Political System for the 21st Century*, ed. Ronald Hayduk and Kevin Mattson (Lanham, MD: Rowman and Littlefield, 2002), 159.

56. Anne F. Peterson, Barbara S. Kinsey, Hugh Bartling, and Brady Baybeck, "Bringing the Spatial In: The Case of the 2002 Seattle Monorail Referendum," *Urban Affairs Review* 43, no. 3 (January 2008): 403–429.

57. John Coté, "Prop. K Will Do Little to Ease S.F.'s Housing Crisis," *San Francisco Chronicle*, September 24, 2014.

58. Elisabeth R. Gerber and Justin H. Phillips, "Evaluating the Effects of Direct Democracy on Public Policy: California's Urban Growth Boundaries," *American Politics Research* 33, no. 2 (2005): 310–330.

59. Elisabeth R. Gerber and Justin H. Phillips, "Direct Democracy and Land Use Policy: Exchanging Public Goods for Development Rights," *Urban Studies* 41, no. 2 (2004): 463–479.

60. Paloma Esquivel, "Moreno Valley Leaders OK Initiatives for 40-million-square-foot Warehouse Project," *Los Angeles Times*, November 25, 2015; Ian Lovett, "Builders Pierce California's Environmental Shield: Speeding Developments and Sidestepping Laws through Initiative System," *New York Times*, June 8, 2016.

61. Kellen Zale, "How the NFL Ducked CEQA," *Environmental Law Prof Blog*, January 19, 2016, http://lawprofessors.typepad.com/environmental_law/2016/01/how-the-nfl-ducked-ceqa.html.

62. Jacqueline Peterson, "Do Municipal Bond Elections Privilege Certain Infrastructure Investments over Others?" (paper presented at the annual meeting of the Urban Affairs Association, Minneapolis, April 19–22, 2017).

63. Joseph F. Zimmerman, *The Recall: Tribunal of the People*, 2nd ed. (Albany, NY: State University of New York Press, 2013) provides an overview of the history of recall elections and the various arguments for and against the use of the recall process.

64. A.G. Sulzberger, "For Omaha Mayors, Recall Elections Are Almost Routine," *New York Times*, January 26, 2011.

65. John Woolfolk, "Both Sides in San Jose's 'Little Saigon' Furor Plotting Next Moves," *San Jose Mercury News*, October 10, 2008.

66. Matthew Haggman and Martha Brannigan, "In Dramatic Revolt, Miami-Dade Voters Fire Mayor Carlos Alvarez over Pay Hikes, Tax Increase," *Miami Herald*, March 15, 2011.

67. Ballotpedia, *Ann Kitchen Recall, Austin, Texas*, 2016, https://ballotpedia.org/Ann_Kitchen_recall,_Austin,_Texas_(2016).

68. Casey Newton, "Group Organizes Recall Against Gordon," *Arizona Republic*, April 30, 2008.

69. Robert Maranto and Jeremy Johnson, "Bringing Back Boss Tweed: Could At-Will Employment Work in State and Local Government and, If So, Where?" in *American Public Service: Radical Reform and the Merit System*, ed. James S. Bowman and Jonathan P. West (Boca Raton, FL: CRC Press, 2007), 77–100.

70. Gregory B. Lewis and Rahul Pathak, "The Employment of Veterans in State and Local Government Service," *State and Local Government Review*, 46, no. 2 (June 2014): 91–105.

71. Robert J. Lopez and Ben Welsh, "LAFD Recruitment Program Is Suspended," *Los Angeles Times*, March 20, 2014; Ben Welsh, "LAFD Gets New Anti-Nepotism Rules in Wake of Hiring Controversy," *Los Angeles Times*, September 16, 2014.

72. The quotations are from Theodore Lowi, "Machine Politics-Old and New," *Public Interest* 9 (Fall 1967): 86–87.

73. Lowi, "Machine Politics-Old and New," 86–87.

74. Bob Egelko, "San Mateo County Shifts to District Elections," *San Francisco Chronicle*, February 20, 2013.

75. California Voting Rights Act of 2001, Election Codes Section 14027. Also see Nora Fleming, "Districts Abandoning At-Large School Board Elections," *Education Week*, May 17, 2013.

76. Rufus P. Browning, Dale Rogers Marshall, and David H. Tabb, *Protest Is Not Enough* (Berkeley: University of California Press, 1986), 201–202, in their study of ten communities in northern California, found that "minority incorporation" was strengthened in cities that modified their old reformed structures of government.

77. Rob Gurwitt, "Nobody in Charge," *Governing* (September 1997): 20–24.

78. Evelyn Larrubia, "Supervisors' Decisions Made Mostly Behind Closed Doors," *Los Angeles Times*, March 26, 2002.

79. New York Public Interest Research Group (NYPIRG), *Drilling Down: Local Fracking Decisions Highlight Failures in New York's Municipal Ethics Laws*, December 2013, www.nypirg.org.

80. For a more full discussion of limits on gift giving, disclosure requirements, requirements for transparency, and other local government ethics laws, see Institute for Local Government (ILG), *Understanding the Basics of Public Service Ethics Laws: Principles and California Law* (Sacramento, CA: ILG, 2013), www.ca-ilg.org/sites/main/files/file-attachments/understandingbasicsethicslaws_finalproof_0.pdf.

81. Ramona Giwargis, "San Jose Politicians Can Soon Accept Gifts Up to $470, a Major Change in City Rules," *(San Jose) Mercury-News*, June 22, 2017.

82. Mark Hedin, "Oakland Ethics Panel Slams Lax Oversight of Free Warriors, Raiders, and A's Tickets," *East Bay Times*, April 14, 2017.

83. Jeffrey Kraus, "Campaign Finance Reform Reconsidered: New York City's Public Finance Program at Twenty," in *Public Financing in American Elections*, ed. Costas Panagopoulos (Philadelphia: Temple University Press, 2011), 147–175.

84. Sarah Coppola, "Austin Approves New Campaign Finance Rules," *Austin American-Statesman*, April 26, 2012.

85. Michael J. Malbin, Peter W. Brusoe, and Brendan Glavin, "Small Donors, Big Democracy: New York City's Matching Funds As a Model for the Nation and States," *Election Law Journal* 11, no. 1 (2012), 3–20, www.cfinst.org/pdf/state/NYC-as-a-Model_ELJ_As-Published_March2012.pdf.

86. Michael Cooper, "At $92.60 a Vote, Bloomberg Shatters an Election Record," *New York Times*, December 4, 2001; Michael Cooper, "Final Tally: Bloomberg Spent $75.5 Million to Become Mayor," *New York Times*, March 30, 2002. For a more detailed analysis, see New York City Campaign Finance Board, *An Election Interrupted . . . The Campaign Finance Program and the 2001 New York City Elections*, Part I (New York, 2002).

87. Michael Barbaro, "Bloomberg Spends $102 Million to Win 3rd Term," *New York Times*, November 27, 2009.

88. *Citizens United v. Federal Election Commission,* 558 US 876 (2010).

89. Los Angeles City Ethics Commission, *Campaign Finance Reform in Los Angeles: Lessons from the 2001 City Elections*, Executive Summary, October 2001, 3, http://ethics.lacity.org/news.cfm; Paul Blumenthal, "Your State and Local Elections Are Now a Super PAC Playground," *The Huffington Post*, October 31, 2015, www.huffingtonpost.com/entry/2015-elections-super-pac_us_5633d165e4b0c66bae5c7bbb.

90. Sarah Reckhow, Jeffrey R. Henig, Rebecca Jacobsen, and Jamie Alter Litt, "'Outsiders with Deep Pockets': The Nationalization of Local School Board Elections," *Urban Affairs Review* 53, no. 5 (2017): 783-811.

91. Joyce Purnick, "Koch to Limit Contributions in Race," *New York Times*, June 21, 1988.

8 | Citizen Participation

Citizen participation refers to the variety of arrangements—including open public forums, joint planning sessions, user surveys, street protests, and the use of social media for interactive engagement with public officials—that enables people to be heard in the period between elections when a municipal decision is likely to have an important impact on their neighborhood or on their daily lives. Ordinary residents have knowledge—a "practical wisdom"[1]—gained from their life experiences and daily living.

Participatory processes enhance democracy. Democracy entails more than the opportunity to vote in an election every two or four years; people expect to have a say in decisions that directly affect their lives and their neighborhoods. Participatory governance can also enhance social justice by making local government more aware of, and responsive to, the concerns of minority communities. Procedures that provide for citizen participation in decision making can ease some of the grip that powerful economic and elite groups have on city hall.[2] Citizen participation makes a difference. Statistical analysis, for instance, reveals that the actions of local housing advocacy groups often lead public decision makers to increase the funding of affordable housing programs.[3]

Private businesses know the importance of citizen participation; private firms utilize scientific surveys, customer satisfaction questionnaires, focus groups, and E-questionnaires to find out what their targeted audiences want. Municipal agencies, to a great extent, have copied the most successful practices that private businesses have used to respond to their customers's concerns. To serve a neighborhood well, a city must likewise find out what residents want.

In a democracy, the rationale for citizen participation goes way beyond consumerism, where businesses seek customer input as an aid in marketing strategies. The residents of cities and suburbs are not merely *customers* or consumers. Instead, the residents of a community are *citizens* who have a democratic right to have a say in decisions that affect their lives.[4] The formal channels for citizen participation—such as neighborhood meetings with public officials—and informal participatory channels—such as the organization of a political protest—both serve to offer residents an opportunity to make their voices effectively heard.

As this chapter describes, public officials over the years have indeed come to recognize the importance of structuring citizen participation into public decision making. As we shall see, the style of community action, too, has changed. Community groups are less interested in protest actions and more interested in initiating partnerships with municipal officials, the heads of nonprofit organizations, and key business leaders in order to provide increases in affordable housing, a new community health-care facility, and community-oriented jobs training and crime reduction programs.

THE EVOLUTION OF CITIZEN PARTICIPATION

Citizen participation has not always been a regular and commonly accepted part of municipal decision making. For much the nation's history, federal, state, and local officials shaped and implemented public programs in top-down fashion with little involvement of those citizens who lived in the path or government projects or who were directly affected by a government action.

The ills of top-down decision making, however, became all too evident in the 1950s and 1960s when government slum clearance and urban renewal programs tore down more housing than they built, displacing working-class residents and the poor in order to build expanded downtown business districts and new university campuses. The displacees were shunted into overcrowded housing in adjoining neighborhoods or rehoused in high-rise housing projects where social conditions soon proved worse than in the low-rise "slums" they replaced. The construction of new highways through residential areas physically divided and weakened inner-city neighborhoods, walling off neighborhood stores from a large portion of their customer base. The federal, state, and local planners and other officials who administered the urban renewal and highway programs did not foresee the ills that their programs would cause. Highway planners, redevelopment officials, and most the city's elected officialdom did not live in or fully understand the communities that their programs were reengineering.

In the 1950s and 1960s, Americans still gave undue deference to municipal "experts and their mystique."[5] Few Americans challenged the harmful decisions made by highway planners, urban renewal administrators, and civil engineers. Citizen participation would provide a much-needed corrective.

The social ills wrought by indiscriminate urban highway construction and land-clearance urban renewal led to a revolt. All besieged communities, however, did not receive equivalent public sympathy. Media coverage and the public's response were largely "racialized," with protests gaining the most political traction in cases where white middle-class communities—in parts of Cambridge (Massachusetts), Lower Manhattan (New York City), and Georgetown (Washington, DC)—rose up in protests against the urban bulldozer. Protests in poor black and Latino neighborhoods did not gain an equivalent response. The "whiteness" of the highway revolt in New Orleans was evident when "upper crust" southerners and urban preservationists mobilized to protect the charm of the city's historic French Quarter (the Vieux Carré) against the proposed construction of a Riverfront Expressway but "remained silent" when Interstate 10 was routed though Faubourg Tremé, the historic African-American center of the city.[6]

Beginning in the 1960s, new federal legislation gave affected residents a more substantial voice in program decisions that would impact their neighborhoods and their daily

Jane Jacobs, a Critic of Highways and a Fighter for Neighborhoods. In 1950s and 1960s New York, Jane Jacobs led the fight against various urban renewal projects, including a proposed new highway that would cut through her Lower Manhattan East Village neighborhood. Jacobs argued for the importance of bringing citizen voices into the decision-making process. She argued that highway and redevelopment projects conceived by outsiders often destroyed communities and the vitality of community and interpersonal networks that existed in poorer and working-class neighborhoods. Jacobs helped to organize protests against various urban highway and urban renewal projects. She argued for the preservation of urban neighborhoods and their vitality. She wanted a city build for people, not for corporate investors and automobiles.

Source: Photo by Phil Stanziola, December 6, 1961. From the Library of Congress, Prints and Photographs Division, Washington, DC 20540 U.S.A., www.loc.gov/pictures/item/2008677538/.

lives. Participatory requirements were made a part of federal programs in numerous policy areas. The 1960s War on Poverty required the "maximum feasible participation of the poor" in antipoverty programs.[7] The Community Development Block Grant (CDBG) program required cities to develop processes that would allow citizens to help determine just how a city would spend its community development monies. Today, requirements for citizen participation are a part of virtually every major federally funded urban and environmental program.

Given the early history of the citizen participation movement in the United States, casual observers often mistakenly assume that new participatory mechanisms are only for the disadvantaged and urban minorities. The reality is quite different. Middle- and upper-class groups are often the primary beneficiaries of participatory processes. In cities and suburbs alike, better-off citizen and professionals have the education, skills, and motivation to take maximum advantage of the processes that governments create to enhance citizen engagement (see Box 8.1). Suburban residents have utilized participatory mechanisms to force changes in the local school curriculum, to stop the construction of new development that they deem harmful to the natural environment,

Box 8.1
Who Participates in Citizen Participation? Evidence From Chicago, New York, the Twin Cities, and Los Angeles

Do citizen participation requirements empower racial minorities and the urban poor? Or do such participatory requirements give upper-middle-class citizens and highly educated professionals a tool that they can use to safeguard their own interests? A review of the evidence reveals that, in numerous instances, upper-status groups are the primary beneficiaries of processes designed to promote citizen engagement.

In Chicago, a statistical review of neighborhood participation indicates the extent to which upper-status individuals—especially persons with higher levels of education—have the highest rates of participation in local problem-solving efforts. African Americans and recently arrived immigrants, by comparison, exhibit relatively low rates of neighborhood engagement.[1]

A similar pattern was observed when New York City instituted 59 community boards to enhance citizen influence in decisions concerning neighborhood land use, budgeting, and service delivery. Although the boards are only advisory, municipal agencies often heed the recommendations of a local board. The community boards, however, have been a vehicle that better-off groups in the city have used to advance their concerns, such as limiting the issuance of liquor licenses in the neighborhood. Activist community boards have also been able to force developers to scale back the size of a development or to add off-street parking and a number of community amenities in return for a favorable board recommendation.[2] At least 22 of New York City's community boards voted against Mayor Bill De Blasio's plan to increase the construction of affordable housing.[3] The community boards feared that increased building densities and affordable housing would bring new and undesirable social change to their neighborhoods.

Evidence from other cities further points to the class bias inherent in many participatory systems. In Minnesota's Twin Cities, lower-class residents were generally less effective than more upscale residents in using participatory processes to win program funding. In St. Paul, the citizen engagement process even resulted in the award of funds to a white middle-class homeowner association that resisted participation by low-income tenants.[4] Los Angeles created a system of 86 neighborhood boards in an effort to decentralize government in a gigantic and sprawling city. Homeowners wound up dominating the boards, which did not adequately reflect the region's considerable diversity: "Latinos are underrepresented, and boards are disproportionately wealthy, white, and highly educated."[5]

Upper-status neighborhood associations have certainly taken advantage of participatory processes to advance their own interests. Still, in numerous instances, participatory mechanisms have provided an important channel by which disadvantage residents have aired their concerns. In New York City, both working-class residents and middle-class professionals both took to community board meetings to fight the pace of gentrification in the gritty industrial Gowanus Canal section of Brooklyn.[6]

Overall, what can we conclude? While participatory mechanisms do help empower marginalized groups, participatory vehicles may serve the urban middle and professional classes even more.

1. Megan E. Gilster, "Putting Activism in Its Place: The Neighborhood Context of Participation in Neighborhood-Focused Activism" *Journal of Urban Affairs* 36, no. 1 (2014): 13–32.

2. Julian Brash, *Bloomberg's New York: Class and Governance in the Luxury City* (Athens, GA: University of Georgia Press, 2011), 161–195; Richard E. Ocejo, *Upscaling Downtown: From Bowery Saloons to Cocktail Bars in New York City* (Princeton, NJ: Princeton University Press, 2015), chapter 6.

3. Alex Schwartz, "Affordable for Who? New York City's Affordable Housing Plan under Mayor De Blasio and the Limits of Local Initiative in Addressing Shelter," paper presented at the annual meeting of the Urban Affairs Association, Minneapolis, April 1–22, 2017.

4. Mark Schuller, "Jamming the Meatgrinder World: Lessons Learned from Tenants Organizing in St. Paul." In *Homing Devices: The Poor as Targets of Public Housing Policy and Practice*, ed. Marilyn M. Thomas-Houston and Mark Schuller (Lanham, MD: Lexington, 2006), 165–166.

5. Juliet Musso, Christopher Weare, Mark Elliot, Alicia Kitsuse, and Ellen Shiau, *Toward Community Engagement in City Governance: Evaluating Neighborhood Council Reform in Los Angeles* (Los Angeles: USC Civic Engagement Initiative, 2007), 1, www.usc-cei.org/userfiles/file/Toward%20Community.pdf.

6. Hamil Pearsall, "Superfund Me: A Study of Resistance to Gentrification in New York City," *Urban Studies* 50, no. 11 (August 2013): 2293–2310.

to thwart proposed tax hikes, and to fight the construction of new stadium projects and dense housing complexes that they fear will increase traffic congestion and change the character of their communities.

A LADDER OF PARTICIPATION: NOT ALL PARTICIPATORY MECHANISMS ARE CREATED EQUAL

The past half century has seen a virtual explosion in the utilization of processes to enhance citizen participation. Yet, too often, effective citizen engagement has proven be elusive, a noble goal that is difficult to achieve. Entrenched bureaucracies and privileged interests may not even be interested in empowering new voices who may challenge the usual ways of doing things in city. In such cases, "participatory" processes may allow residents to participate, but only in ways that do not give them a meaningful ability to challenge decisions of significance. Even public officials who believe in the importance of citizen participation, when faced with program deadlines and pressures to get things done, have shortcut participatory processes, rationalizing that there is too much debate over "technical questions" where sustained public engagement is not really appropriate. Public officials may exhibit strong commitment to community participation during a program's early stages and years; but that commitment may wane as program administration and implementation drag on.[8]

Which participatory mechanisms truly enhance citizen voices, and which offer only an illusion of power? Sherry Arnstein's eight-rung **ladder of citizen participation**

Figure 8.1 **A Ladder of Citizen Participation**.

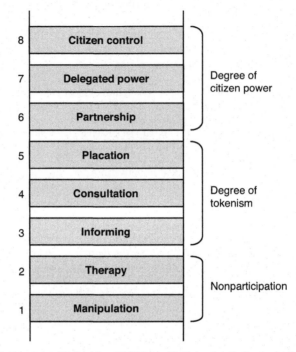

Source: Sherry R. Arnstein, "A Ladder of Citizen Participation," *Journal of the American Institute of Planners* 35 (July 1969): 217. Reprinted with permission from the *Journal of the American Planning Association.* Copyright © July 1969 by the American Planning Association.

(see Figure 8.1), developed a half century ago, still provides a useful tool for helping to sort through the vast maze of participatory arrangements.[9] Using Arnstein's ladder, we can clearly see that all participatory mechanisms are not equal; many participatory vehicles are created with no real intent to share power with ordinary citizens.

On the bottom of the ladder are participatory processes that can be viewed only as *manipulation* and *therapy*, participatory practices that are so rudimentary that they can even be labeled as *nonparticipation*. **Manipulation** occurs when agency officials do not really care to respond to residents's preferences; instead, an agency utilizes a participatory process as a strategy to make citizens more willing to accept a course of action that an agency has already adopted. Such a manipulative process can also be viewed as *cooptation*, where participation is used as part of a strategy to defuse potential community opposition to an agency's plans. **Cooptation** occurs when citizens are brought into the decision-making process and given the illusion that they are being heard when, in reality, they are still denied any ability to influence important outcomes.

What is participation that is only meant as **therapy** and not empowerment? Paternalistic social welfare professionals see participation in house meetings in a homeless shelter, an addiction recovery facility, or a public housing project as a means of helping disadvantaged residents overcome their socio-emotional problems and thereby build the confidence and habits that will allow them to become more successful job applicants and more supportive members of a family. In such cases, the focus of the participatory efforts is on changing the people involved, not on changing the programs that that adversely affect a community.

A little higher up the ladder is **informing**, the various forms of participation that essentially entail a one-way flow of information from public officials to residents. Public officials may make a time-consuming set of presentations at a public meeting (even employing PowerPoint technology) that reviews the history of a community problem and outlines the agency's response. By doing so, the officials dominate a meeting and shape the meeting agenda and ensuing discussion, leaving members of the audience little time to present and discuss concerns of their own.

One-way informational sessions offer participants only the most limited opportunity to affect a course of action that to a great degree has already been set. One-shot meetings offer little opportunity for constructive dialogue. More effective citizen participation requires not a one-shot session but a structured series of meetings where citizens can engage in constructive dialogue with public officials and where citizens have sufficient time to develop project alternatives of their own.

Consultation, in contrast to the lower rungs of participation, does denote the willingness of public officials to solicit and listen to community voices. Under consultation, municipal officials may survey the residents of a neighborhood, distribute a questionnaire to the users of a municipal service, and utilize semi-structured focus groups and a series of neighborhood meetings in an attempt to uncover residents's concerns.

Consultation is admirable. However, mere consultation provides no guarantee of citizen power, as agency officials decide which citizen viewpoints they will incorporate into their action plans and which grassroots insights and perspectives they will simply ignore. Meaningful consultation certainly requires more than a one-time mass public meeting. True citizen empowerment also requires more than the mere administration of a questionnaire or survey. A series of joint meetings with public officials or, better yet, the formation of a residents's steering committee or task force that meets regularly with municipal officials can set in motion a process of dialogue that, over time, allows for mutual education, increased understanding, collaborative action, and compromise—an exercise of citizen influence that goes far beyond the completion of a client questionnaire or a community survey.

Community policing is a noteworthy program built upon public consultation. "Beat meetings" with residents provide an opportunity for the residents of a neighborhood to bring their concerns to the attention of local patrol officers. "Citizen councils" provide a forum for even more extensive discussion between residents and law enforcement officials and thereby help draw the attention of the police to specific problems in a neighborhood.[10] Yet, despite the many achievements of community-oriented policing, the approach offers no shift in power. It is still the police department, not members of the community, who decide just what local actions are and are not undertaken. The more severe critics of a city's police department may also view community policing as little more than an instrument of cooptation, a public relations exercise that police departments use to win the support of neighborhood residents without taking steps to resolve questions regarding police misconduct, racial profiling and the use of deadly force by police officers against inner-city minority youth.[11]

Placation occurs where citizen boards and participatory processes are created with the purpose of muting citizen discontent. Participatory processes created in response to bottom-up pressure can at times provide local residents with real channels of influence. However, such arrangements tend more to cooptation, especially if the number of neighborhood representatives on a joint board or commission can be easily outvoted by other members of the body.

Both consultation and placation entail elements of **tokenism**, where citizens are allowed to influence only minor aspects of an agency's plans. A good example of tokenism is evident in Cincinnati's redesign Washington Park, the green space just across from Music Hall, the city's opera house. Washington Park had become a haven for drug users and the homeless, and civic planners saw the potential to create a cleaned-up, redesigned, and expanded space to serve as the city's "civic green," a place that would host public concerts and festivals. A cleaned-up and modern park would also accelerate the gentrification of the city's Over-the-Rhine neighborhood. The parks department structured meetings where neighborhood residents were given the opportunity to comment on the design of park benches, playground equipment, and the park's water-spray play feature. But the meetings did not offer residents an opportunity to challenge the intentions of planners to repurpose the park so that it would spur the neighborhood's transformation and abet new development in Cincinnati's nearby downtown. No consideration was given to including basketball courts in the park that would attract African-American youth from the surrounding neighborhood.

The highest levels of participation on Arnstein's ladder are *partnership, delegated power*, and *citizen control*, are participatory vehicles that give ordinary citizens some real influence and that entail some limits on the ability of a municipal department to make decisions entirely on its own. **Partnership** denotes mutual power, processes that allow citizens and municipal officials to share in decision making. Municipal agencies understand the advantages that come with partnership—increase community support and the added resources and personnel of community-based organizations that join with the city to remediate community problems.

Partnership is often the highest form of citizen participation that can be achieved, as the two highest rungs on Arnstein's ladder, delegated power and citizen control, are seldom reached. **Delegation** entails a city handing over specific pieces of program authority to a local council, such as giving a locally elected neighborhood board the ability to decide which minor neighborhood improvements will be funded. **Community control** exists when a neighborhood board has the authority to handle a broader range of matters, such as the operation of neighborhood schools, without having to get citywide approval of its decisions. Yet, as critics correctly point out, it would be unwise and often improper for a city to cede authority to community group. Critics also worry that the devolution of authority to communities can lead to NIMBY-ism; the many communities, even poorer communities, will use their new-gained power to keep out new shelters for the homeless or efforts to construct new housing units for exceptionally low-income families and troubled individuals.

Los Angeles's Neighborhood Councils program had only enjoyed limited success in its efforts to have neighborhoods become active partners in making decisions regarding local service delivery. Los Angeles has 80-plus neighborhood councils to develop effective service-delivery partnerships. But the community-oriented process has been undercut by the "disinterest" and "resistance" of administrative officials who see the councils "as annoying distractions from their main work."[12] In Los Angeles and elsewhere, public officials are often reluctant to abdicate program responsibility and to place spending decisions in the hands of neighborhood groups where there is no guaranty that nonelected leaders are truly representative of the larger population they claim to serve.

Sometimes a crisis can lead a municipality to seriously consider new arrangements that will forge a partnership with community groups. In 2014, both St. Louis and the suburb of Ferguson faced a series of protests and civil disturbances as a result of the police shootings of African-American youth. Officials and community activists in both cities discussed the possibility of creating a **police-civilian review board** to allow citizens to help set policing priorities and even review possible instances of police misconduct. But the police-civilian review board that was initially discussed bordered on tokenism and cooptation. The board had no staff and no authority to investigate and review alleged incidents of police misbehavior. It took pressure from the United State Department of Justice during the Obama years to get Ferguson officials to agree to a consent decree that expanded the review board's investigatory power.[13]

THE "NEW" URBAN SERVICE PROFESSIONALS: VALUING PARTICIPATION

Arnstein's ladder of participation reminds us that many public organizations are content with participatory mechanisms that lie on the lower rungs of the ladder. Paternalistic program administrators are reluctant to share power with ordinary citizens whom they see as lacking expert knowledge and sound judgment.

Yet, as we have already noted, many municipal agencies do value partnerships and seek out collaborative working relationships with community groups. A new generation of public service professionals recognizes that more can be accomplished when public officials utilize the insights of, and build trust among, the people being served. Neighborhood residents, too, recognize that sustained **collaboration** enables citizens and public servants to work jointly over time to identify effective remedies for urban problems.[14]

Too often, however, public servants see their attempts to solicit citizen involvement through the limiting lens of consumerism. These public officials rely on surveys, focus groups, and questionnaires to find out what services users want and what program adjustments officials need to make. Yet, surveys and questionnaires, as helpful as they are, fall far short of the ideal of democratic participation. Administrators who rely on surveys and questionnaires to gather program feedback essentially view neighborhood residents as **consumers** of a municipal agency's service offerings. A more democratic-oriented administrator does not view an agency's clients as mere customers to be consulted; instead, the democratic administrator will view clients as **citizens** who possess certain rights, including the right to be part of a process when decisions have a direct impact on their lives. Collaborative public leaders seek to "work with" neighborhood-based and client organizations, **partners** who can help "co-provide" a better level of service.[15] The democratic-oriented public servant is not content with surveys and questionnaires but instead seeks to engage citizen-partners in meetings on a regular basis. Neighborhood watch groups, for instance, help to direct law enforcement officials to neighborhood trouble spots and then work with police officers to find effective responses, scheduling a new pattern of police patrols and organizing groups of parents to accompany children on the walk to and from school.

KEYS TO MAKING CITIZEN ENGAGEMENT WORK

Not all participation efforts successfully engage residents. In neighborhood elections, for instance, neighborhood turnout levels are often extremely poor. Yet, some communities do a lot better job than others in promoting citizen participation. What do successful cities do to enhance citizen engagement?[16]

First, neighborhood residents will be more willing to be a part of local bodies that possess real authority as opposed to community bodies that are only advisory and whose recommendations can easily be ignored by municipal officials. New York City's experiment with participatory budgeting offers participants very real—albeit limited—decision-making authority. City council members in New York can choose to have community residents decide how a certain portion of capital improvement funds will be spent. In 2015–2016, residents in 25 or so districts each decided how more than a million dollars in funds for their district would be allocated to various transportation, education, and parks and recreation projects. Citizen delegates commit to working for several months with the city's budget staff in order to develop a number of alternative projects, which are then presented, discussed, debated, and voted on in community meetings, with the winning proposals sent to the city council for its approval.[17]

In Los Angeles, a system of elected Neighborhood Councils, organized to increase local engagement and the diversity of voices heard in public decision making, have only advisory power. They possess no actual decision-making authority, as noncitizens in a neighborhood may join in the process. As a consequence, elected officials and public program managers often have little interest in the workings of the advisory bodies and show little inclination to implement the recommendations advanced by a Neighborhood Council.[18] As the councils possess so little decision-making power, voter turnout in the neighborhood elections has been quite poor. In the Downtown Los Angeles precinct, an area of 25,000 residents, only 847 people voted in the 2016 Neighborhood Council election. In nearby Pico-Union, a largely Latino district with nearly 24,000 residents, the turnout was even worse: only 150 persons voted.[19] Such dismal turnout levels raise concerns as to the representativeness of the councils, further eroding their potential for influence.[20]

Second, resident commitment to participatory processes is greater in cities that have established a record of working with community groups and building a culture of collaboration. Top managers must communicate to agency personnel the importance of citizen engagement. Top managers can also dispense rewards to incentivize collaborative work with communities. Cities also need to provide budgetary support for participatory efforts.[21]

Third, participatory processes are likely to gain greater public legitimacy if they are instituted throughout a city as opposed to being instituted in only a few low-income or troubled neighborhoods. Participatory arrangements created in only in a handful of targeted neighborhoods do not signify that city hall is fully committed to citizen participation.

Outside assistance is often critical to the success of participatory efforts[22] (see Box 8.2). Governmental grants, corporate philanthropy, and nonprofit sponsorship help provide community groups with the financial resources for newsletters, local surveys, the

Box 8.2
Learning From the Pacific Northwest: How Local Governments Can Support Neighborhood Engagement

In Seattle and other Pacific Northwest cities, grassroots activism is a prominent feature of local politics. Citizen groups seek to protect the Northwest's fabled quality of life and often rise up to question new economic development projects that they see as posing a threat to the natural environment.

Citizen engagement is ingrained in the local political culture and is an expected part of local decision making in the Pacific Northwest. King County (greater Seattle) routinely conducts a series of small-group forums across the county, using volunteers to solicit public feedback on various policy matters. The participants share their opinions, after having first viewed a video and written summary of the key facts and competing perspectives on an issue. The process is structured to reduce the possibility that public officials will be able to manipulate the forums. A citizens's steering committee, not a municipal agency, selects the topics for group discussion.[1]

The City of Seattle offers fairly extensive assistance to help neighborhood groups develop their own plans while respecting the needs of the larger city. A Neighborhood Planning Office and a Neighborhood Matching Fund assist community groups with staffing, financial assistance, and even technological support in such areas as Geographic Information System (GIS) mapping, all "to help neighborhood groups do good planning work." The city seeks long-term collaborative relationships between neighborhood groups and city hall. Seattle also has thirteen district councils. The decentralization of departments further serves to encourage municipal administrators to work with neighborhood groups. The City of Seattle hopes that such collaborative partnerships will offer a constructive alternative to grassroots militancy and oppositional politics in Seattle.[2]

Seattle clearly supports neighborhood participation. Critics, however, worry that that the process often provides a channel of influence for neighborhood groups and NIMBY ("Not In My Backyard") activists opposed to a wide range of growth projects, including proposals to expand the stock of much-needed affordable housing in the city. Such concerns led Seattle Mayor Ed Murray to reduce the city's support for neighborhood councils which had been dominated by homeowners who opposed proposals for denser development and the construction of apartment complexes to ease the city's housing affordability crunch. Murray proposed to set up a new neighborhood engagement process that would be more inclusive of younger residents, renters, and racial and ethnic minorities.[3] The mayor's new citizen engagement plan also included "public engagement and outreach liaisons" experienced in promoting participation among under-represented communities.[4]

1. "King County, WA Initiates Community Forums Program," *PA Times* (April 2008): 8.

2. Carmen Sirianni, "Neighborhood Planning as Collaborative Democratic Design: The Case of Seattle," *Journal of the American Planning Association* 73, no. 4 (Autumn 2007): 373–387; the quotation appears on p. 374.

3. Erica C. Barnett, "How Seattle Is Dismantling a NIMBY Power Structure," *Next City* blog posting, April 3, 2017, *https://nextcity.org/features/view/seattle-nimbys-neighborhood-planning-decisions*; Erica Pandey, "Seattle Mayor, Seeking More Diverse Input, Cuts Ties with District Councils," *The Seattle Times*, July 13, 2016.

4. Seattle Department of Neighborhoods, "Fact Sheet: Equitable Outreach and Engagement—A Key Component of Seattle Department of Neighborhoods," January 20, 2017, http://murray.seattle.gov/wp-content/uploads/2017/01/don_equitableoutreach_factsheet.pdf.

maintenance of community headquarters, and the rental of space for larger community meetings and events. Without outside financial support, neighborhood organizations often are unable to communicate effectively with residents.

The City of Indianapolis created a Neighborhood Resource Center to foster community development and participation. In Indianapolis, nonprofit institutions—including the Lilly Endowment, the Ford Foundation, and the Annie Casey Foundation—played a critical role in funding a Neighborhood Power Initiative that provided staff assistance and training support to community groups.[23]

What do more innovative participatory strategies in look like? A 2006 initiative by Oakland, California, Mayor Ronald Dellums aggressively pursued bottom-up policy development, with 800 residents serving on 41 **citizen task forces**, each charged with formulating specific policy recommendations in a narrowly defined issue area. Ordinary citizens with an interest in an issue area met, without pay, for six sessions. The meetings were facilitated by conveners who, too, were ordinary citizens who had received additional training.[24]

Rochester, New York, established a Neighbors Building Neighborhoods (NBN) program, a **bottom-up visioning process** in which the city invited 37 neighborhood organizations to investigate ten "planning sectors," generating reinvestment and service ideas that would be incorporated into the city budget. The city appointed a liaison to work with each group. The mayor also ordered municipal agencies to respond to the draft plans developed in each committee. The mayor's strong public backing was a key asset in getting other municipal officials to give their commitment to the process.[25]

Planning charrettes are frequently-used techniques in which citizens work with planning officials on a project's design. In a series of structured meetings, participants are asked to specify just what features that they like and dislike in a proposed plan or project. In a typical planning charrette, residents may be asked to paste Post-it notes on photos and maps to indicate just what they liked and did not like and to suggest specific project alterations. In the more far-reaching charrettes, community members work with planning officials over time to develop project alternatives. **Joint steering committees** and citizen review panels are other devices that enable a small group of residents and public officials to meet over time to negotiate a project's direction and details.

A few local governments have even experimented with **citizens juries**, a deliberative-panel technique popularized in Australia and Canada, in which a group of ordinary citizens is asked to decide a course of action after they have first reviewed detailed information regarding the various policy alternatives. The members of the "jury" discuss their preferences and the tradeoffs inherent in each course of action as they attempt to come up with the best solution to a difficult problem. Orono, Minnesota, just outside of Minneapolis, convened a citizens jury that met for five days as members heard from witnesses and toured public schools. The Board of Education assembled the jury as voters had consistently rejected school bonds. The jury drafted a new school bond proposal that ultimately passed.[26]

Deliberative polling differs markedly from a normal poll or survey. A deliberative poll does not seek to uncover what respondents currently think about a project or a controversy. Instead, the deliberative pollster seeks an *informed* opinion, what voters would think and prefer if they knew more about an issue. The deliberative pollster presents detailed and balanced information on the policy issue and only then asks for the respondent's opinion and preferences.[27]

Madison, Wisconsin, is only one of a growing number of cities to utilize technological advances to help gauge citizen preferences. Madison used **Geographic Information System (GIS)** technology to produce computer-generated charts and maps that allow citizen to see spatial patterns of service delivery in a city. More importantly, the GIS maps help citizens to visualize the effects of development alternatives. The maps and related materials, which can easily be shared on the Internet, provide citizens with understandable information, breaking the bureaucracy's monopoly hold on information.[28] Municipalities and advocacy groups use **GIS story maps**[29] to display information to a nontechnical audience. Maps and accompanying photos, video, and audio enable participants to see for themselves such matters as the degree of racial segregation or municipal service inequalities in a city.

POLITICAL PROTEST: UNCONVENTIONAL PARTICIPATION AS A POLITICAL RESOURCE

Community organizing refers to grassroots efforts by which neighborhood organizations mobilize residents and discover a community's power resources and other assets. Community organizing is based on "what people can do for themselves" through neighborhood organizations taking charge of community programs. Community organizing seeks to "change power relations" and get important things done.[30]

When the normal participatory channels fail to gain an acceptable response from the city, community organizers can resort to protest. What are the elements of a protest action? Quite often, protest actions seek to attract the attention of the media, as the media are often indispensable for drawing the attention of the larger public to a problem and in activating sympathetic constituencies to help push for the changes desired by the protestors. Such protest action requires an element of public display. But protest leaders walk a fine line, as they can ill afford to risk losing the sympathies of important third parties.

A much different form of political protest, by contrast, is built around **direct action**, and is especially used when community organizers believe that the media and third parties will prove unreliable. Under direct action, a community organization seeks to discover its own ability to force the target of its action to institute desired changes. The direct-action style of protest was popularized by Saul Alinsky, the renowned and often feared community organizer who worked for the Industrial Areas Foundation (IAF) in the mid-1900s.[31] Alinsky sought tactics that would enable the "have-nots" and "have-little-want-mores"[32] to discover their own political resources and ability to pressure city officials for change. Alinsky believed in democracy and sought to spread power to as many people as possible.[33]

Under the **Alinsky/IAF method of community organizing**, the organizer works in tandem with church and religious leaders, union organizers, and other members of a neighborhood who command local respect.[34] Together, they seek to uncover the most salient grievances in a community. The organizer then **rubs wounds raw**, drawing the attention of residents to a grievous injustice in order to spur community members to action. The organizer **freezes the target** of the protest action, refusing to accept the target's excuses or otherwise allow the target to shift blame and responsibility to other parties.

The protest organizer does not always choose to fight the biggest problems that face a community. Big battles are not easily won, and protest efforts that fizzle may reinforce a community's sense of hopelessness and defeatism. Consequently, the community organizer will start by choosing smaller grievances where community organizing will produce a **quick victory**, a victory that will build the community's spirit and that will draw new participants to future battles. "One LA," an IAF affiliate, focused its attention on improving public schools and set out to build a progressive partnership with school administrators, the teachers's union, and parents in impoverished sections of Los Angeles. One LA, however, did not initially focus its efforts on school reform, as a problem that big is difficult to tackle. Instead, One LA began its organizing effort by focusing on a smaller and more easily winnable issue, combating the expansion of local waste-sorting and landfill facilities in low-income neighborhoods, an expansion likely to worsen the asthma problems suffered by local schoolchildren.[35]

In California, Texas, and throughout the Southwest, community organizers in the Latino neighborhoods have pursued mobilizing efforts that have built on the strong attachments of Latinos to the Catholic Church.[36] In El Paso, a Texas city with a population that is two-thirds Hispanic, EPISO (the El Paso Interreligious Sponsoring Organization) conducts its actions with the assistance of local churches. EPISO fought to build new schools, to restrict payday lending, to deny city licenses to firms that violated wage theft laws, and to increase the minimum wage.[37] In northern California in the Bay Areas, parents, community leaders, and local Catholic clergy in East San Jose and Alum Rock came together to organize PACT (People Acting In Community Together) to push for school reform.

Women often assume key leadership roles in community-based groups, especially in the housing, education, and health-care arena, service areas that relate to family care-giving and are traditionally seen as women's work (see Box 8.3). Women also provide much of the back-office, clerical, and detail work that sustains community organizations.

With women leading community groups, community organizing has become more relational—with people telling their stories and leaders building group cohesion

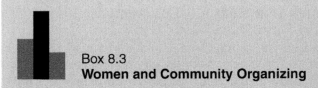

Box 8.3
Women and Community Organizing

As a female community organizer has observed, "community tends to be a woman's realm."[1] It should not be a surprise, then, that a review of community-based groups in Chicago found that "women are important participants in virtually every neighborhood organization. . . . [P]olitical work directed at neighborhood-, housing-, and school-related issues represents a field where women, for generations, have had a conspicuous impact."[2] Community-based organizations are often led by the "invisible tier of community leaders, most frequently women who worked behind the scenes."[3] Black women, in particular, have occupied leadership positions in tenant organizations that have sought to address a variety of the issues faced by poor women and their children who live in public housing.[4]

An examination of immigrant rights marches in Los Angeles points to the pivotal role that Spanish-English bilingual women played in gathering information about the marches and in mobilizing friends and family to participate in the protests.[5] Yet, not all women are willing to participate in community meetings. The engagement of women in community groups varies greatly according to nationality and ethnic customs.

1. Gail Schechter, "Community Organizing: Integrating a Woman's Approach," *Shelterforce*, February 18, 2017, http://shelterforce.org/2017/02/18/community-organizing-integrating-a-womans-approach/.

2. Larry Bennett, *Neighborhood Politics: Chicago and Sheffield* (New York: Garland, 1997), 246.

3. Harry C. Boyte, *Everyday Politics: Reconnecting Citizens and Public Life* (Philadelphia: University of Pennsylvania Press, 2004), 52.

4. Rhonda Y. Williams, *The Politics of Public Housing: Black Women's Struggles Against Urban Inequality* (New York: Oxford University Press, 2004), 174–187, 212–213.

5. Kim Yi Dionne, Darin DeWitt, Michael Stone, and Michael Suk-Young, "The May 1 Marchers in Los Angeles: Overcoming Conflicting Frames, Bilingual Women Connectors, English-Language Radio, and Newly Politicized Spanish Speakers," *Urban Affairs Review* 51, no. 4 (2014): 533–562.

by allowing members to get to know one another.[38] As one member of San Antonio's Communities Organized for Public Services (COPS) described, women are "community sustainers" who are less interested in theatrical political combat and more focused on doing whatever it takes to improve schools and services that families require.[39] As a result, community organizing has shed much of the "conflict orientation" and "macho" posturing that had characterized the leadership style of Saul Alinsky and an earlier generation of community organizers.[40]

THE CHANGED STYLE OF COMMUNITY ORGANIZATIONS: FROM PROTESTS TO PARTNERSHIPS FOR SERVICE DELIVERY

The style of community organizations has also changed markedly over the years. Community organizations in poorer parts of the city no longer emphasize "disruptive protests" and highly combative public confrontations to the degree they did in the 1960s and 1970s, an era when participatory democracy was still gaining acceptance. Instead of protest, community-based organizations devote much of their attention to forming partnerships with public and nonprofit agencies in order to improve neighborhood conditions and service provision.

The evolving approach of San Antonio's Communities Organized for Public Services (usually referred to as COPS, for short) illustrates the changed balance in the activities undertaken by many community-based groups. COPS started out as a model of IAF-style organizing principles. A federation of more than 20 neighborhood groups, COPS fought to correct the underprovision of infrastructure and other services in the Mexican sections of the city. COPS received the largest part of its budget from local parishes. San Antonio's Archbishop also gave his blessing to COPS participation.[41] COPS, like other IAF organizations, relied on direct-action strategies including **mass accountability meetings** crowded with large numbers of neighborhood residents to press public officials to make policy commitments.

COPS today still engages in protest actions when the situation requires. The organization has staged protest actions as well as engaged in more conventional political organizing efforts aimed at securing a local "living wage" higher than the federal minimum wage. Nonetheless, COPS has tended to deemphasize confrontation and public combat in favor of a new approach that stresses the building of more enduring and cooperative relationships with governmental bodies, banks and financial institutions, nonprofit funders, and other entities with the resources critical to neighborhood housing, job training, economic development, health care, and school programs. COPS worked with educators, public health officials, and the city's mayor to help lead the drive for a sales tax to fund pre-K education.[42] For COPS and a great many community organizations, protest has ceded way to a new emphasis on "values-based organizing" and "collaborative leadership."[43] COPS also emphasizes voter registration; by building a formidable electoral base, COPS gained invitations to decision-making councils.

COPS is no longer a political outsider in San Antonio; instead the organization has gained the power advantages that derive from building long-term, collaborative relationships with public officials and private-sector leaders.[44] For younger leaders, collaboration and inclusion are an "embedded" part of "just how we do things" in contemporary San Antonio,[45] a marked contrast to COPS's early days when community organizers and city officials had a more oppositional posture. Civic leaders had once attempted to discredit COPS as a rabble-rousing group. In more recent years, civic leaders have bestowed honors on COPS for its history of public service, including its job training programs and fundraising on behalf of college scholars and school enrichment programs.

"From Protest to Programs" became the slogan that The Woodlawn Organization (TWO), a grassroots organization on the poor African-American South Side of Chicago, adopted to describe the evolution of its neighborhood organizing approach. In the 1960s and 1970s, TWO, reflecting its IAF roots, undertook mobilizing actions in the Alinsky tradition, organizing boycotts of merchants who cheated community members (i.e. merchants who "short-weighed" the meat and other products they sold) or who refused to expand programs to hire local residents. Over the years, TWO refocused its energies, giving less attention to protest actions and more focus and greater devotion to administering a variety of programs that deliver vital services to community residents. The organization runs low-income housing programs, operates day-care centers, and even brings dental services to area families. TWO established working relationships with public, private, and nonprofit organizations to provide the finances for such community-based services.[46] TWO has joined with other local groups and worked with housing developers and city officials to ensure that new residential developments in the neighborhood are mixed-income and do not merely provide housing opportunities only for market-rate buyers.[47]

Baltimoreans United in Leadership Development (BUILD) has similarly sought to balance IAF-style protest actions with the organization's newer responsibilities, as the organization has assumed responsibility for the operation of a number of community service programs. BUILD worked with nearly 50 churches in Baltimore's African-American community to combat redlining and unfair auto insurance rates. BUILD also led the fight to gain the enactment of a "living wage" for workers. But political advocacy alone does not define BUILD's work. BUILD has assumed extensive responsibilities for the daily management of extended-day after-school programs, homework assistance, and the provision of other education and human resource services. BUILD seeks private business partners to offer job training and the promise of jobs to students who stay in school and who graduate with good grades.[48] In El Paso, EPISO has given similar focus to finding partner organizations for improved public education.

The Dudley Street Neighborhood Initiative (DSNI) in Boston similarly seeks to build on the power potential inherent in neighbor-to-neighbor networking and organizing. DSNI initially came into existence in the 1980s to combat illegal trash-dumping and to close harmful trash-transfer sites which posed health hazards to neighboring residents. DSNI also thwarted a Harvard-led technopark plan that threatened to gentrify the area and displace existing residents. Neighborhood protests deepened democracy, strengthening residents's sense of their "right to the city" and their ability to demand action—and to undertake service provision and management—when faced by the seeming detachment of municipal officials. Moving beyond its initial protest style, DSNI has formed partnerships to build quality affordable rental and owner-occupied homes. DSNI has also engaged residents in various neighborhood cleanup, parks reclamation, and agricultural efforts, with numerous community gardens and three urban farms flowering in what was formerly an area of heavy environmental degradation.[49]

Today, few community organizations in the United States rely on an organizing approach that emphasizes disruptive protest. Even those organizations birthed in the Alinsky/IAF tradition have moved to a **hybrid approach to community action**, resorting to protest actions when needed but devoting most of their effort to establishing partnerships with municipal officials and philanthropic organization in order to provide increased levels of job training, health care, affordable housing, and youth and education services in the community.[50]

COMMUNITY DEVELOPMENT CORPORATIONS AND COMMUNITY LAND TRUSTS

COMMUNITY DEVELOPMENT CORPORATIONS (CDCs)

The important work done by partnerships is evident in the accomplishments of community development corporations. A **community development corporation (CDC)** is a nonprofit neighborhood-based organization that works with public- and private-sector actors for new investments to improve conditions in low-income communities.[51] Across the nation, CDCs have gained their greatest success in efforts to build and rehabilitate affordable housing. CDCs have also built local shopping centers and pursued economic development efforts that deliver jobs to impoverished communities. Other CDCs operate health clinics, food pantries, day-care centers, after-school programs, and job training programs. The scope of CDC action is vast, with an estimated 4,600 CDCs operating in the 50 states.[52] The work of community development corporations is clearly one of the pieces of "good news" for cities.

CDCs emphasize pragmatic partnerships to meets a community's needs. To rehabilitate dwelling units and build new affordable homes in a distressed community, a CDC will work cooperatively with government agencies, mortgage lenders, and corporate officials to piece together the financing for the construction of low- and moderate-priced units. CDCs follow a **bridge-building approach**[53] in which they ask banks, private investors, corporate managers, nonprofit and philanthropic organizations, and government agencies each to pick up a piece of the financing necessary for a neighborhood project. A finance institution or other investor is more willing to commit to a neighborhood project when they see that they are not alone, that a CDC has rounded up the participation of other actors to share the load. In post–Hurricane Katrina New Orleans, CDCs formed links with partnering organizations to provide new units of affordable housing that served as a counterforce to the gentrification taking place in the rebuilding city.[54]

In their pursuit of partnerships, CDCs have adopted a "consensus organizing"[55] and "conflict-free"[56] vision of community advancement. According to their critics, CDCs too often exhibit a "disdain"[57] for political advocacy: CDCs have "lost their grassroots mentality."[58] Still, despite the risks that CDC leaders can be coopted by a city's financial and political elites, CDCs have nonetheless demonstrated great success in building affordable housing and bringing improved community services to inner-city areas.[59]

CDCs across the nation vary considerably in terms of their capacity. CDCs require outside support and the sustained commitment of partners. The more effective community development organizations tend to have a full-time director and staff as well as a diversified revenue base. Well-managed and efficient community development corporations have the greatest impact.[60] Still, critics point out that CDC housing tends to be built inside the high-poverty community in which a CDC is located; the new units provide improved housing for residents but do not promote the economic mobility that a family would gain from housing located in more economically vibrant communities.[61]

What role will CDCs play in the future? Much depends on the federal government's willingness to renew programs that help to sustain CDC partnerships. The **Low-Income Housing Tax Credit (LIHTC)** offers tax advantages to private institutions that invest in CDC-style housing projects. LIHTC survived the budget-cutting knife of the early Trump years in office—and even received expanded funding as a result of the efforts of the program's backers in Congress.[62] However, should the LIHTC be substantially reduced or even abandoned in future years, CDCs would likely have great difficulty in finding investment partners to sustain their activities.

The more immediate threat to CDCs comes from the success of Trump and congressional Republicans in lowering the overall tax rates on corporations. Lower tax rates mean a lower tax obligation, giving corporations less incentive to earn LIHTC tax credits by partnering with community groups on affordable housing projects.[63]

COMMUNITY LAND TRUSTS (CLTS)

A **community land trust (CLT)** is another community-led arrangement that provides even stronger neighborhood control over local property uses and revitalization. A CLT seeks to buy up properties in cases where the prospective purchase by a private buyer poses a threat of tenant displacements. Rather than allow market forces, investors, and speculators to determine patterns of land use in a neighborhood, the CLT model has a nonprofit neighborhood-based organization (the "trust") acquire strategic land parcels, assuring that the properties in a neighborhood will be used for affordable housing and community-oriented projects. The CLT retains title to the land underlying a home or development, and seeks to keep rents as affordable as possible. A CLT helps to put homeownership within the reach of low-income families; a new homeowner pays only for the price of the structure, while the CLT retains ownership of the land beneath the home. Restrictions on a home's resale further assure that the dwelling will continue to be affordable in the years to come.[64]

By gaining control over property and assuring the development of affordable housing and other community-oriented facilities, a CLT can help slow the pace of transformation in a low-income community lying in the path of gentrification.[65] The Dudley Street Neighborhood Initiative utilized the CLT approach to assure that the development of new affordable housing would serve as a counter to the new office project and upgrading of the area once envisioned by city planners and Harvard University. In Oakland, California, OakCLT has similarly acquired properties that will be kept permanently affordable. OakCLT also developed a creative financing arrangement to allow a neighborhood coffee shop, a "hub" of the community, to remain in its building.[66]

In Portland, Oregon, the Proud Ground community land trust sought to bring poorer people into the conversation concerning future development and land uses in the city. Portland's Urban Growth Boundary had served to shift new development to the underutilized eastern portions of the city, subjecting the city's low-income northeastern area to transformation pressures. Common Ground was formed to assure that new housing would be built within the price reach of low-income families.[67]

As important as CLTs have been, the land trusts have their critics. Just as we saw with community development corporations, critics worry that CLTs have become too focused on providing affordable housing and meeting the concerns of home financiers, neglecting the emphasis on political activism and the commitment to "community control" that was initially a part of the CLT ideal.[68] CLTs and CDCs alike have become increasingly focused on deal-making and the maintenance of partnerships with city hall and business interests. Decisions in CLTs and CDCs are often made by professionals who understand the business of homeownership and are expert in the technicalities and politics of arranging home finance. As a result, many CLTs and CDCs have deemphasized protest organizing and actions.

E-GOVERNMENT AND E-DEMOCRACY: FROM WEB 1.0 TO WEB 3.0

E-government ("electronic government") provides a number of tools to bring government closer to the people. Municipal agencies set up home pages and use e-mail, social media (including Facebook, Twitter, and YouTube), blog postings, webcasts of public meetings, and other social media tools to inform citizens of local events and changes in service schedule and municipal regulations. Cities across the country allow residents to report service problems and register complaints without having to visit city hall. A resident can go online to request permits and renew licenses; such actions no longer necessitate a trip to city hall and enduring a seemingly endless wait in line.

But democratic participation should entail more than a municipality's posting of announcements and the use of e-technology to facilitate individual service requests. Cities, for the most part, are still in the early stages of tapping the interactive and two-way communications potential of the Internet and social media. A survey of New Jersey municipalities, for instance, found that local governments use the Internet for a variety of purposes, but that "**e-democracy**" (that is, citizen dialogue and empowerment through the Internet) is the "least practiced" element of e-government.[69] Other surveys of cities and suburbs across the nation have largely come to the same conclusion: Few cities use the Internet and social media to offer citizens important new opportunities for interactive democratic participation.[70]

Technology enthusiasts observe that local governments are beginning to move beyond Web 1.0, the early era of local computer usage where municipal agencies did little more than establish home pages and post public announcements—a pattern of one-way information sharing. Numerous cities still do not allow residents to post comments, as city officials do not have the time and staff resources to establish a web commenting policy and to monitor comments to assure that posters participate in a respectful way.[71] Nor do local officials feel comfortable in having to explain to angry citizens why their comments were removed.

Web 2.0 (also called **Government 2.0**) represents a move in the right direction, offering citizens new space for interactive exchanges and two-way dialogue. Web 2.0 seeks to give citizens the opportunity to speak their mind. Web 2.0 also seeks to create forums in hyperspace where citizens can collaborate with public officials in identifying solutions to local problems. A sense of community can be nurtured in neighborhood online forums, where residents report store openings, lost pets, community meetings, crime break-ins, and other hyper-local problems and events. Such online forums are the "fastest-growing networks for participation in land use."[72] Public agencies can take an even more active posture to promote idea sharing, by creating **digital neighborhoods** or online forums where citizens interact with one another and with agency officials.[73]

What do the more innovative local initiatives for e-participation and e-democracy look like? West Hartford, Connecticut, utilized an interactive survey, conducted in real time, that asked residents to choose their desired levels of municipal service provision and taxation. As a respondent chose to increase or decrease the level of a specified service, a computerized program revealed just how the choice would affect the respondent's tax bill.[74] Rather than simply record a respondent's initial program preferences, an interactive survey seeks to discover how respondents change their service preferences when they learn new information about program costs and impacts. Yet, relatively few city agencies engage in such extensive online dialogue and interactive planning.

Seattle is a leader in the e-democracy field, a city where municipal officials seek to promote the interactive capacities of the Web. Seattle established a municipal department, the Office of Electronic Communications, to deepen e-democracy. The city also set up a Web site for e-participation (www.seattlechannel.org) that is separate and distinct from the city's main Web site with its numerous departmental announcements. An Open Data portal organizes city-oriented information and news by issue area in order to provide citizens with easy access to information, a prerequisite for effective local participation.[75] In Seattle, citizens are invited to submit their opinions to public hearings via e-mail.

Public officials often distrust Internet and social media forums as e-participants are not a scientifically representative sample of the larger population. Narrow interests and more extreme voices may dominate online discussions. Municipal administrators also worry that online discussion boards and other forms of e-participation may amplify the most strident anti-government voices in a community, raising the level of controversy.

Yet, in important ways, social media platforms can improve the representativeness of public participation. Social media draws young people into the decision-making process, an important corrective to the age bias often apparent in conventional meetings and in-person public forums where older residents dominate.[76] Younger persons, who face numerous time pressures on their schedule, may prefer the convenience of participating via their cell phone or home computer.

A public agency can use various "metrics" to assess if an agency's message is reaching its desired audience. Metrics entail more than merely counting the number of people who have viewed agency Facebook posting and who clicked "Like" in response to an announced activity. Such indicators of an e-message's "reach" measure participation only at its most basic level. Such tallies tell us virtually nothing about the depth, intensity, and quality of the e-interaction. A good system of assessment will also measure an audience's "engagement" with an agency's posting, as seen in the number of comments that a posting receives and how many times a posting has been forwarded, shared or retweeted.[77]

Only a handful of local governments have taken advantage of digital media tools for **crowdsourcing**,[78] where municipal officials seek the "collective intelligence" of an Internet or social media audience. Crowdsourcing believes in the wisdom of the crowd. The Internet and social media enable local planners and administrators to consult more widely—with experts from beyond the city's borders and with engaged residents and citizens. Crowdsourcing can be used to generate creative citizen-initiated solutions to a problem.

Crowdsourcing is rooted in the notion of partnership, that citizens can be part of service solutions. But crowdsourcing does not represent full bottom-up empowerment or community control, as municipal officials retain the discretion to decide just which e-comments receive serious consideration and which are ignored. Police departments clearly recognize the potential inherent in crowdsourcing when they issue Amber Alerts to have the eyes and ears of the public help find a missing child. A police department may also allow residents to electronically report problems that deserve heightened attention by the police. Yet, municipal law enforcement agencies still retain the authority to decide policing priorities; such final decision making is not jointly shared in e-participation.

As the above discussion reveals, e-government is not the equivalent of e-democracy.[79] Yet, e-platforms contain the potential to expand democratic participation. Web 2.0 seeks to create new avenues for citizen-government dialogue, consultation, and, collaboration. Still, e-participation often provides only a weak substitute for conventional community organizing. E-forums and Web-based comments seldom, by themselves, pose a serious challenge to administrative policies.

Commentators frequently observe that e-participation suffers from a **digital divide** that separates the technologically competent from the less competent, the young from the old, and the well-off from the poor. Yet such gaps in the comfort with digital technology may be diminishing, as digital communication has become so commonplace that even the elderly and the poor have social media accounts and have picked up the habits of social media usage. In low-income inner-city communities, the widespread penetration of cell phones is beginning to mitigate some of the concerns that new forms of e-participation will only replicate the participatory biases—in terms of race and class—of more conventional forms of participation. Mobile phones offer a means by which low-income residents can to some degree increase their online participation in political and economic activities, as data from Latino neighborhoods underscore.[80]

Municipal governments can take additional steps to help bridge the digital divide. The City of Chicago has partnered with community-based organizations in a series of "Smart Communities" outreach and training programs to cultivate a "culture of technology use" in low-income neighborhoods.[81] City agencies also need to develop Web pages and portals that are designed for easy access and navigation by mobile users.

Still, full "digital citizenship" is denied racial minorities and the poor who rely so greatly on cell phones, which do not offer the most convenient means for searching the Internet for important political information. A "smart phone" is a poor substitute for the high-speed and reliable broadband access of a home computer.

Despite the fears that e-government will replicate existing patterns of inequality, a study conducted in Milwaukee underscores the potential of e-technology to help the poor. The Milwaukee study found that online requests to the city's Department of Neighborhood Services were heavily concentrated in poorer areas of the city and neighborhoods with high vacancy rates.[82] E-government in Milwaukee provided a new route for the "voice" of the poor to get to city hall.

The e-world changes very quickly. Even before municipal officials had become fully comfortable with two-way dialogue and collaboration, Web 2.0 was yielding way to a **Web 3.0** world of smart phones, text messages, tablets, and mobile technology where citizens expect immediate updates and announcements as soon as a news event breaks. Citizens demand the opportunity to voice their concerns—and even get a response—in real time. Web 3.0 further denotes an ability of citizens (with the assistance of public officials) to use social media as a platform, an electronic place where citizens can gather information, debate options, and come together to take action on their own. Rather than having to wait for government with its limited resources to solve a community problem, digital platforms can facilitate communal efforts where residents work together to solve problems, a "do-it-ourselves governance" as an alternative to continued dependence on a government agency.[83]

While cities and suburbs have shown a willingness to use social media to improve local service delivery, the new communications technology has yet to galvanize participatory democracy in the ways pictured by urban futurists. Urban police departments, for instance, recognize the advantages of social media when it comes to informing the public and crowd-sourcing (i.e. to solicit tips as to where crimes have taken place and just which parts of a community need greater attention from the police). But scholarly reviews of social media usage by local police departments find virtually no evidence that e-participation leads to deeper collaborations between the police and the communities they serve.[84]

CONCLUSION: CITIZEN PARTICIPATION, DEEP DEMOCRACY, AND THE FACILITATING ROLE OF GOVERNMENT

Over the past half century, urban participation has undergone a virtual revolution, with top-down decision making yielding way to a wide range of processes that give citizens the ability to influence municipal decisions that affect their lives. Federal and state program regulations, too, served to create new forums for citizen engagement. Today, citizen engagement is an expected and routine part of urban governance. E-participation only promises to enhance the opportunities for citizen participation and engagement.

But not all vehicles for citizen participation are created equal. Sherry Arnstein's ladder of participation continues to be of great relevance as it helps to point out just which processes yield deeper participation than others. Even today, in an era where many public service professionals are committed to engaging the public in decision making, many bureaucrats are hesitant to share power with ordinary people; as a result, program officials rely on participatory mechanisms that lie at the bottom rungs of Arnstein's ladder.

Too often public participation is reduced to one-way informing, tokenism, and perfunctory efforts that constitute *thin* participation and fail to provide the opportunities for engagement offered by *thick* participation.[85] **Thin participation** requires very little of the respondent's time and hence enables "citizen empowerment" only in the most limited sense of the phrase. Thin participation often takes the form of polling and user questionnaires that users can quickly complete as they report their degree of satisfaction with a municipal service. Thin-participation is also evident when a citizen hits a "Like" icon or a donation button to make a financial donations online. Such activities take little time and do not allow for give-and-take dialogue and mutual learning.

Thick participation, by contrast, entails face-to-face meetings and other opportunities for interaction, discussion, and idea development. Tools for thick participation include the extensive dialogue of neighborhood assemblies, the interactions entailed by citizen juries and participatory budgeting, and online platforms that enable citizens and public servants to communicate in a process of sustained dialogue.

Not all trends bode well for the future of citizen participation. The increased intrusion of state governments in local affairs means that neighborhood groups may now have to take steps to ensure that their voice is effectively heard inside the state capitol, a daunting task, especially for more under-resourced and impoverished neighborhood groups. Save Our Schools New Jersey (SOSNJ) is an unfunded, all-volunteer organization of parents, grandparents, and other citizens that lobbied state decision makers to protect the funding of public-school programs; SOSNJ fought against the expansion of voucher programs that threatened to drain funds away from public schools. The leaders of SOSNJ recognized that, to be effective, they needed to engage in broad-based coalition building, organizing events across the state and involving suburbs as well as core-city neighborhoods in their state lobbying efforts.[86]

Participatory efforts can make a difference. In Philadelphia a variety of local groups challenged the state takeover of city schools and efforts to reshape local schools according to a corporate model of marketization, efficiency, and technology.[87] The state government's efforts at reform had substantial backing from the charter school industry and national advocacy groups committed to school choice. But the presence of active, mobilized community groups—and their ability to win seats in local elections—meant that the corporate-oriented school reformers did not have the education playing field to themselves.

The contemporary generation of urban professionals has been schooled in the virtues and importance of citizen participation. Public servants have begun to see themselves as citizen-educators and advisers who work in partnership with neighborhood groups.[88] In Boston, city bureaucrats and nonprofit funders work directly with community-based organizations, oftentimes bypassing local elected officials who do not consistently attend meetings where neighborhood concerns are discussed. In such instances, the nonelected leaders of community organizations serve as the effective and legitimate voice of inner-city communities.[89]

While protest will always be an important tactic for relatively powerless groups, contemporary neighborhood organizations are less interested in fighting city hall than in building partnerships with public and private officials to provide vitally needed services. CDCs, CLTs, and other community-based organizations have a track record of success in building affordable housing and other much-needed facilities in impoverished communities. Community organizations today tend to "view development as a way to secure community benefits."[90] Protests can be disruptive, making it difficult for neighborhood groups to reach out to potential partners.[91]

There are limits as to what citizen participation can accomplish. In the urban arena, citizen participation "is rarely transformative." Participatory arrangements cannot by themselves make a city just or "equitable."[92] Ordinary residents also feel excluded when the leaders of more established neighborhood organizations dominate participatory processes.[93]

In an age of limited resources, cities and suburbs have had to do "more with less." Partnering with community organizations offers one such strategy. The next chapter reviews the many other tools in the do-more-with-less municipal toolbox.

KEY TERMS

Alinsky/IAF method of community organizing (*p. 292*)

bottom-up visioning process (*p. 290*)

bridge-building approach of CDCs (*p. 296*)

citizen juries (*p. 291*)

citizen participation (*p. 279*)

citizen task forces (*p. 290*)

citizens as distinct from consumers, treating people as (*p. 279*)

collaboration (*p. 287*)

community control (a level of citizen participation in Sherry Arnstein's ladder) (*p. 286*)

community development corporation (CDC) (*p. 296*)

community land trust (CLT) (*p. 297*)

community organizing (*p. 291*)

community policing (*p. 285*)

consultation (a level of citizen participation in Sherry Arnstein's ladder) (*p. 285*)

cooptation (*p. 284*)

crowdsourcing (*p. 299*)

delegated power (a level of citizen participation in Sherry Arnstein's ladder) (*p. 286*)

deliberative polling (*p. 291*)

digital divide (*p. 300*)

digital neighborhoods (*p. 299*)

direct-action protests (*p. 292*)

e-democracy (*p. 298*)

e-government (*p. 298*)

freeze the target (an Alinksy/IAF organizing principle) (*p. 292*)

geographic information system (GIS) (*p. 291*)

GIS story maps (*p. 291*)

hybrid approach to community action (*p. 295*)

informing (a level of citizen participation in Sherry Arnstein's ladder) (*p. 285*)

joint steering committees (*p. 290*)

ladder of citizen participation, Sherry Arnstein's (*p. 283*)

Low-Income Housing Tax Credit (LIHTC), CDCs and the (*p. 297*)

manipulation (a level of citizen participation in Sherry Arnstein's ladder) (*p. 284*)

mass accountability meetings (an Alinksy/IAF organizing principle) (*p. 294*)

partnership (a level of citizen participation in Sherry Arnstein's ladder) (*p. 286*)

placation (a level of citizen participation in Sherry Arnstein's ladder (*p. 286*)

planning charrettes (*p. 290*)

police-civilian review board (*p. 287*)

quick victory tactics (an Alinksy/IAF organizing principle) (*p. 292*)

rub wounds raw (an Alinksy/IAF organizing principle) (*p. 292*)

therapy, citizen participation as (a level of citizen participation in Sherry Arnstein's ladder (*p. 284*)

thin and thick participation (*p. 301*)

tokenism (a level of citizen participation in Sherry Arnstein's ladder (*p. 286*)

Web 2.0 (also called Government 2.0) (*p. 298*)

Web 3.0 (*p. 301*)

NOTES

1. Harry C. Boyte, *The Citizen Solution: How You Can Make a Difference* (Minneapolis: Minnesota Historical Society, 2008), 152; in particular, see pp. 143–158 on "Citizen Professionals."

2. Archon Fung, "Putting the Public Back into Governance: The Challenges of Citizen Participation and Its Future," *Public Administration Review* 75, no. 4 (July/August 2015), 513–522.

3. Anaid Yerena, "The Impact of Advocacy Organizations on Low-Income Housing Policy in U.S. Cities," *Urban Affairs Review* 51, no. 6 (2015): 843–870.

4. Janet V. Denhardt and Robert B. Denhardt, *The New Public Service: Serving, Not Steering*, exp. ed. (Armonk, NY: M. E. Sharpe, 2007); "The New Public Service Revisited," *Public Administration Review* 75, no. 5 (September/October 2015): 664–672.

5. Eric Avila, *The Folklore of the Freeway: Race and Revolt in the Modernist City* (Minneapolis: University of Minnesota Press, 2014), 12.

6. Avila, *The Folklore of the Freeway*, 1–2, 93–96. Also see 99–100.

7. Alice O'Connor, "Swimming Against the Tide: A Brief History of Federal Policy in Poor Communities," in *The Community Development Reader*, ed. James DeFilippis and Susan Saegert (New York: Routledge, 2008), 9–27.

8. See, for instance, Michael J. Rich and Robert P. Stoker, *Collaborative Governance for Urban Revitalization: Lessons from Empowerment Zones* (Ithaca, NY: Cornell University Press, 2014), especially 81–85.

9. Sherry R. Arnstein, "A Ladder of Citizen Participation," *Journal of the American Institute of Planners* 35 (July 1969): 216–224.

10. Wesley G. Skogan, *Police and Community in Chicago: A Tale of Three Cities* (New York: Oxford University Press, 2006); Michael J. Palmiotto, *Community Policing: A Police-Citizen Partnership* (New York: Routledge, 2011), 210–243.

11. Kristian Williams, *Our Enemies in Blue: Police and Power in America* (Oakland, CA: AK Press, 2004, rev. ed. 2015).

12. Terry L. Cooper, "Citizen-Driven Administration," in *The State of Public Administration*, ed. Donald C. Menzel and Harvey L. White (Armonck, NY: M.E. Sharpe, 2011), 246–247.

13. Alex Stuckey, "Ferguson, St. Louis Contemplate Police Review Boards," *St. Louis Post-Dispatch*, September 22, 2014; Matt Pearce, "Ferguson Plan for Police Oversight Board Is Derided as 'Insulting.'" *Los Angeles Times*, September 11, 2014.

14. Cooper, "Citizen-Driven Administration," 238–256.

15. John Clayton Thomas, *Citizen, Customer, Partner: Engaging the Public in Public Management* (Armonk, NY: M. E. Sharpe, 2012).

16. This section builds on insights provided by Jeffrey Berry, Kent Portney, and Ken Thomson, *The Rebirth of Urban Democracy* (Washington, DC: Brookings Institution Press, 1993), esp. 34–39, 47–51, 61–63, and 295–299.

17. Participatory Budgeting in New York City, "About the Process," http://pbnyc.org/content/about-new-york-city-process, downloaded July 1, 2017. For a description of the participatory budgeting and the key role played by trained facilitators, see: Hollie Russon Gilman, "Transformative Deliberations: Participatory Budgeting in the United States," *Journal of Public Deliberation* 8, no. 2 (2012): Art. 11, www.publicdeliberation.net/cgi/viewcontent.cgi?article=1237&context=jpd. For a brief review of the experience of United States cities with participatory budgeting, see Tina Nabatchi and Matt Leighninger, *Public Participation for 21st Century Democracy* (Hoboken, NJ: Jossey-Bass, 2015), 309–313. Social media strategies can also enhance the public's engagement in a PB process; see Victoria Gordon, *Participatory Budgeting: Ten Actions to Engage Citizens via Social Media* (Washington, DC: IBM Center for the Business of Government, 2014), www.businessofgovernment.org/report/participatory-budgeting-ten-actions-engage-citizens-social-media.

18. Juliet Musso, Christopher Weare, Mark Elliot, Alicia Kitsuse, and Ellen Shiau, "Toward Community Engagement in City Governance: Evaluating Neighborhood Council Reform in Los Angeles," an Urban Policy Brief of the USC Civic Engagement Initiative and USC Neighborhood Participation Project, 2007, 2–8, www.usc-cei.org/userfiles/file/Toward%20Community.pdf; Juliet Musso, Christopher Weare, Thomas Bryer, and Terry L. Cooper, "Toward 'Strong Democracy' in Global Cities? Social Capital Building, Theory-Driven Reform, and the Los Angeles Neighborhood Council Experience," *Public Administration Review* 71, no. 1 (January/February 2011), 102–111, esp. 104–105.

19. Data obtained from "EmpowerLA: Neighborhood Council Election History," https://docs.google.com/spreadsheets/d/1OBnvPvhmSRqGj-9pcD1AMcPehSrZip1uNlYuCw9MYqI/edit#gid=0.

20. The Los Angeles Neighborhood Councils do serve to bring local perspectives and historically disenfranchised voices into the process of governance in Los Angeles. The councils also served as focal points for local political mobilization. See Erwin Chermerinsky and Sam Kleiner, "Federalism from the Neighborhood Up: Los Angeles's Neighborhood Councils, Minority Representation, and Democratic Legitimacy," *Yale Law & Policy Review* 32, no. 2 (2013): 569–581,

21. Robert Mark Silverman, "Sandwiched Between Patronage and Bureaucracy: The Plight of Citizen Participation in Community-Based Housing Organizations in the United States," *Urban Studies* 46, no. 1 (January 2009): 3–25, esp. 20.

22. Carmine Sirianni, *Investing in Democracy: Engaging Citizens in Collaborative Governance* (Washington, DC: Brookings Institution Press, 2009), chap. 3, describes the extensive support provided for neighborhood engagement in Seattle.

23. Stephen Goldsmith, *The Twenty-First Century City: Restructuring Urban America* (Lanham, MD: Rowman and Littlefield, 1999), 159–163.

24. Kitty Kelly Epstein, Kimberly Mayfield Lynch, and J. Douglas Allen-Taylor, *Organizing to Change a City* (New York: Peter Lang, 2012), 27–31, 125–133.

25. Kiran Cunningham, Phyllis Furdell, and Hannah McKinney, *Tapping the Power of City Hall to Build Equitable Communities: 10 City Profiles* (Washington, DC: National League of Cities, 2007), 195–220.

26. John Gastil and William M. Keith, "A Nation That (Sometimes) Likes to Talk: A Brief History of Public Deliberation in the United States," in *The Deliberative Democracy Handbook: Strategies for Effective Citizen Engagement in the Twenty-First Century*, ed. John Gastil and William M. Keith (San Francisco: Jossey-Bass, 2005), 7. In the same volume, the topic is further discussed by Ned Crosby and Doug Nethercut, "Citizens Juries: Creating a Trustworthy Voice of the People," 111–119. Also see Ned Crosby and John C. Hottinger, "The Citizens Jury Process," in *The Book of the States, 2011* (Lexington, KY: Council of State Governments, 2011), 321–325.

27. James S. Fishkin, "Consulting the Public through Deliberative Polling," *Journal of Policy Analysis and Management* 22, no. 1 (2003): 128–133; James S. Fishkin, *When the People Speak: Deliberative Democracy and Public Consultation* (New York: Oxford University Press, 2009).

28. Eleonora Redaelli, "Cultural Planning in the United States: Toward Authentic Participation Using GIS," *Urban Affairs Review* 48, no. 5 (September 2012): 642–669.

29. Institute for Public Administration at the University of Delaware and the Rahall Transportation Institute, *GIS Story Maps: A Tool to Empower and Engage Stakeholders in Planning Sustainable Places* (October 2016), www.ipa.udel.edu/publications/gis-story-maps-2016.pdf.

30. Loretta Pyles, *Progressive Community Organizing: A Progressive Approach for a Globalizing World*, 2nd ed. (New York: Routledge, 2014), 9–10.

31. The election of Barack Obama as president brought renewed interest in work of Saul Alinsky. Obama, after finishing college, moved to the South Side of Chicago where he worked as a local organizer for the IAF-style Calumet Community Religious Conference and its Developing Communities Project. Later, after completing law school, Obama taught classes on community organizing as practiced by Saul Alinsky. Critics from the political Right pointed to Obama's Alinsky-style organizing history in their efforts to tar the president as a "radical." The political Right also attacked the 2016 Democratic presidential nominee, Hillary Clinton for the senior thesis at Wellesley on Alinsky that she wrote over four decades ago. See Peter Dreier, "Hillary Haters' Fixation on Saul Alinsky," *American Prospect, Longform*, July 26, 2016, http://prospect.org/article/hillary-haters%E2%80%99-fixation-saul-alinsky.

32. Saul D. Alinsky gave the clearest description of his principles for organizing in his *Rules for Radicals* (New York: Vintage Books, 1971).

33. Vijay Phulwani, "The Poor Man's Machiavelli: Saul Alinsky and the Morality of Power," *American Political Science Review* 110, no. 4 (2016): 863–875.

34. IAF organizers often work with local churches. Still, advocates of congregation-based organizing argue that the Alinsky approach places too much power in the hands of lay organizers and that the approach fails to take advantage of the power inherent in religious language, prayer, and biblical imagery. See Helene Slessarev-Jamir, *Prophetic Activism: Progressive Religious Justice Movements in Contemporary America* (New York: New York University Press, 2011), 77–80; Loretta Pyles, *Progressive Community Organizing: A Critical Approach for a Globalizing Word* (New York: Routledge, 2009), reviews faith-based and other alternatives to Alinsky-style community organizing.

35. The actions of One LA and San Diego's PACT (discussed in the next paragraph) are reviewed by Mark R. Warren and Karen L. Mapp, *A Match on Dry Grass Community Organizing as a Catalyst for School Reform* (New York: Oxford University Press, 2011), 33–65. Warren and Mapp also present an excellent and concise recounting of the IAF/Alinsky tradition and the evolution of community organizing over the years.

36. Mark R. Warren, *Dry Bones Rattling: Community Building to Revitalize America* (Princeton, NJ: Princeton University Press, 2001), esp. 20–22, 191–210, and 239–247.

37. Kathleen Staudt and Clarence N. Stone, "Division and Fragmentation: The El Paso Experience in Global-Local Perspective," in *Transforming the City: Community Organizing and the Challenge of Political Change*, ed. Marion Orr (Lawrence, KS: University Press of Kansas, 2007), 85–108; Marty Schladen, "On 40th, Group Works to Bring More to the Table," *El Paso Times*, April 29, 2016.

38. Gail Schechter, "Community Organizing: Integrating a Woman's Approach," *Shelterforce*, February 18, 2017, http://shelterforce.org/2017/02/18/community-organizing-integrating-a-womans-approach/.

39. Harry C. Boyte, *Everyday Politics: Reconnecting Citizens and Public Life* (Philadelphia: University of Pennsylvania Press, 2004), esp. 52.

40. Susan Stall and Randy Stoecker, "Community Organizing or Organizing Community: Gender and the Crafts of Empowerment," in *The Community Development Reader*, ed. DeFilippis and Saegert, 245.

41. Warren, *Dry Bones Rattling*, 48–50.

42. Chris Benner and Manuel Pastor, *Equity, Growth, and Community: What the Nation Can Learn from America's Metro Areas* (Oakland, CA: University of California Press, 2015), 152–158.

43. Boyte, *Everyday Politics: Reconnecting Citizens and Public Life*, 51 and 122. See also Robert Fisher, "Neighborhood Organizing: The Importance of Historical Context," in *The Community Development Reader*, ed. DeFilippis and Saegert, 191; and Mark Warren, "A Theory of Organizing: From Alinsky to the Modern IAF," in *The Community Development Reader*, ed. DeFilippis and Saegert, 194–203.

44. J. Rick Altemose and Dawn A. McCarty, "Organizing for Democracy through Faith-Based Institutions: The Industrial Areas Foundation in Action," in *Alliances across Difference: Coalition Politics for the New Millennium*, ed. Jill M. Bystydzienski and Steven P. Schacht (Lanham, MD: Rowman and Littlefield, 2001), 133–145; Warren, *Dry Bones Rattling*, 56–57.

45. Chris Benner and Manuel Pastor, "Whither Resilient Regions? Equity, Growth, and Community," *Journal of Urban Affairs* 38, no. 1 (2016): 13.

46. Richard C. Hula and Cynthia Jackson-Elmoore, "Nonprofit Organizations, Minority Political Incorporation, and Local Governance," in *Nonprofits in Urban America*, ed. Richard C. Hula and Cynthia Jackson-Elmoore (Westport, CT: Quorum Books, 2000), 121–150.

47. Yan Dominic Searcy, "Planning Office and Community Influence on Land-Use Decisions Intended to Benefit the Low-Income: Welcome to Chicago," *Urban Studies Research* (2014): Article ID 146390, 8 pages, 2014. DOI:10.1155/2014/146390.

48. Marion Orr, "BUILD: Governing Nonprofits and Relational Power," *Policy Studies Review* 18, no. 4 (Winter 2001): 71–90; Marion Orr, "Baltimoreans United in Leadership Development: Exploring the Role of Governing Nonprofits," in *Nonprofits in Urban America*, ed. Hula and Jackson-Elmoore, 151–167; and Robert P. Stoker, Clarence N. Stone, and Conn Worgs, "Neighborhood Policy in Baltimore: The Post-Industrial Turn," in *Urban Neighborhoods in a New Era: Revitalization Politics in*

the Postindustrial City, ed. Clarence N. Stone and Robert P. Stoker (Chicago: University of Chicago Press, 2015), 50–80, esp. 67.

49. Isabelle Anguelovski, *Neighborhood as Refuge: Community Reconstruction, Place Remaking, and Environmental Justice in the City* (Cambridge, MA: MIT Press, 2014), 55–69, 177–179, 185–189, and 201–204.

50. Doug McAdam, Robert Sampson, Simon Weffer, and Heather MacIndoe, "There Will Be Fighting in the Streets: The Distorting Lens of Social Movement Theory," *Mobilization: An International Quarterly* 10, no. 1 (2005), 1–18, views "hybrid" organizations as combining protest and civic/service activities.

51. Ross Gittell and Avis Vidal, *Community Organizing: Building Social Capital as a Development Strategy* (Thousand Oaks, CA: Sage Publications, 1998).

52. Census of Industry figures from 2005, cited by Community-Wealth.org, "Overview: Community Development Corporations (CDCs)," www.community-wealth.org/strategies/panel/cdcs/index.html.

53. Barbara Ferman and Patrick Kaylor, "The Role of Institutions in Community Building: The Case of West Mt. Airy, Philadelphia," in *Nonprofits in Urban America*, ed. Hula and Jackson-Elmoore, 93–120. Also see Warren, *Dry Bones Rattling*, 98–123.

54. Myung-Ji Bang, "Understanding Gentrification: The Role and Abilities of Community-Based Organizations in Changing Neighborhoods" (paper presented at the annual meeting of the Urban Affairs Association, New Orleans, March 16–19, 2011).

55. Gittell and Vidal, *Community Organizing*, 51–54.

56. James DeFilippis, "Community Control and Development: The Long View," in *The Community Development Reader*, ed. DeFilippis and Saegert, 34.

57. Larry Lamar Yates, "Housing Organizing for the Long Haul: Building on Experience," in *A Right to Housing: Foundation for a New Social Agenda*, ed. Rachel G. Bratt, Michael E. Stone, and Chester Hartman (Philadelphia: Temple University Press, 2006), 222.

58. Randy Stoecker, "The CDC Model of Urban Development: A Critique and an Alternative," in *The Community Development Reader*, ed. DeFilippis and Saegert, 303. See also Robert Mark Silverman, "Caught in the Middle: Community Development Corporations (CDCs) and the Conflict between Grassroots and Instrumental Forms of Citizen Participation," *Community Development* 36, no. 3 (2005): 35–51; and Robert Mark Silverman, "CBOs and Affordable Housing," *National Civic Review* 97, no. 3 (Fall 2008): 26–31.

59. Rachel G. Bratt, "Community Development Corporations: Challenges in Supporting a Right to Housing," in *A Right to Housing*, ed. Bratt, Stone, and Hartman, 340–359; Norman Krumholz, W. Dennis Keating, Philip D. Star, and Mark C. Chupp, "The Long-Term Impact of CDCs on Urban Neighborhoods: Case Studies of Cleveland's Broadway-Slavic Village and Tremont Neighborhoods," *Community Development* 37, no. 4 (2006): 3–52.

60. Nathaniel S. Wright, "Transforming Neighborhoods: Explaining Effectiveness in Community-Based Development Organizations," *Journal of Urban Affairs* 40, no. 6 (2018): 805–823.

61. For an easy-to-read review of a number of limitations of the CDC approach, see Allan Mallach, *The Divided City: Poverty and Prosperity in Urban America* (Washington, DC: Island Press, 2018), 183–190 and 192–193.

62. National Low-Income Housing Coalition, "Advocates and Congressional Champions Secure Increased Funding for Affordable Housing in 2018," March 22, 2018, http://nlihc.org/article/advocates-and-congressional-champions-secure-increased-funding-affordable-housing-2018.

63. Lancaster Pollard, "Tax Reform Uncertainty Hits LIHTC Market," *Multifamily Executive Blog*, June 19, 2017, www.multifamilyexecutive.com/business-finance/tax-reform-uncertainty-hits-lihtc-market_c.

64. Jeffrey S. Lowe and Emily Thaden, "Deepening Stewardship: Resident Engagement in Community Land Trusts," *Urban Geography* 37, no. 4 (2015): 611–628.

65. Myungshik Choi, Shannon Van Zandt, and David Matarrita-Cascante, "Can Community Land Trusts Slow Gentrification?," *Journal of Urban Affairs* 40, no. 3 (2017): 394–411.

66. Aline Reynolds, "Oakland Land Trust Finds More Ways to Preserve Affordable Housing," *NextCity, Web Posting*, September 10, 2018, https://nextcity.org/daily/entry/oakland-land-trust-finds-more-ways-to-preserve-affordable-housing.

67. Jeffrey Lowe, "Community Land Trusts as a Social Justice Tool" (paper presented at the annual meeting of the Urban Affairs Association, Toronto, April 6, 2018).

68. James DeFilippis, Brian Stromberg, and Olivia R. Williams, "W(h)ither the *Community* in Community Land Trusts," *Journal of Urban Affairs* 40, no. 6 (2018): 755–769.

69. Tony Carrizales, "Functions of E-Government: A Study of Municipal Practices," *State and Local Government Review* 40, no. 1 (2008): 15.

70. Donald F. Norris and Christopher G. Reddick, "Local E-Government in the United States: Transformation or Incremental Change?," *Public Administration Review* 73, no. 1 (January/February 2013): 165–175; Benedict S. Jimenez, Karen Mossberger, and Yonhong Wu, "Municipal Government and the Interactive Web: Trends and Issues for Civic Engagement," in *Digital Democracy: Concepts, Methodologies, Tools and Applications*, vol. 1, ed. Information Resources Management Association (Hershey, PA: IGI Global, 2012), 100–120.

71. The social media policy of a local government can be relatively terse. Alternatively, a more extensive policy can afford local officials even greater direction and protection when taking actions to preserve the civility of e-discussion. For links to sample local government social media policies, including the policies posted by Palo Alto and Marin County (California) and Seattle and King County (Washington), see: Institute for Local Self-Government, *Sample Social Media Policies* (Sacramento, CA, 2015), www.ca-ilg.org/post/sample-social-media-policies.

72. Nabatchi and Leighninger, *Public Participation for 21st Century Democracy*, 171.

73. Ines Mergel, *Social Media in the Public Sector* (San Francisco: Jossey-Bass, 2013), 34 and 146–152; Tina Nabatchi and Ines Mergel, "Participation 2.0: Using Internet and Social Media: Technologies to Promote Distributed Democracy and Create Digital Neighborhoods," in *Connected Communities: Local Government as a Partner in in Citizen Engagement and Community Building*, ed. James H. Svara and Janet Denhardt (Washington, DC: Alliance for Innovation, 2010), 80–87.

74. Mark D. Robbins, Bill Simonsen, and Barry Feldman, "Citizens and Resource Allocation: Improving Decision Making with Interactive Web-Based Citizen Participation," *Public Administration Review* 68, no. 3 (May/June 2008): 564–575.

75. Look at Seattle's Open Data portal to see how the city makes information readily accessible to the people, https://data.seattle.gov/.

76. Daren C. Brabham, *Crowdsourcing in the Public Sector* (Washington, DC: Georgetown University Press, 2015), 15–16.

77. Kate Dunham, "The Beginner's Guide to Social Media Metrics: Engagement," *Hootsuite Blog*, May 27, 2014, https://blog.hootsuite.com/beginners-guide-engagement/; Justin Herman, "Social Media Metrics for Federal Agencies," *DigitalGov Blog*, April 10, 2013, www.digitalgov.gov/2013/04/19/social-media-metrics-for-federal-agencies/.

78. Brabham, *Crowdsourcing in the Public Sector*; Mergel, *Social Media in the Public Sector*, 50–51, 172–174.

79. Marc Brenman and Thomas W. Sanchez, *Planning As If People Matter: Governing for Social Equity* (Washington, DC: Island Press, 2012), 117–118.

80. Karen Mossberger, Caroline J. Tolbert, and Christopher Anderson, "The Mobile Internet and Digital Citizenship in African American and Latino Communities," *Information Communication & Society* 20, no. 10 (2017): 1587–1606.

81. Karen Mossberger, Caroline J. Tolbert, and William W. Franko, *Digital Cities: The Internet and the Geography of Opportunity* (New York: Oxford University Press, 2013), 195–199.

82. Paru Shah and Amber Wichowsky, "The Promise of E-Gov? City Hall's Responsiveness to Neighborhood Interests" (paper presented at the annual meeting of the Urban Affairs Association, Minneapolis, April 20–22, 2017).

83. David Bollier, *The City as Platform: How Digital Networks Are Changing Urban Life and Governance* (Washington, DC: The Aspen Institute, 2016), http://csreports.aspeninstitute.org/documents/CityAsPlatform.pdf. The reference to "DIO: Do It Ourselves!" governance is from Tim O'Reilly, "Government as a Platform," *Innovations: Technology, Governance, Globalization* 6, no. 1 (Winter 2011): 26–27, www.mitpressjournals.org/doi/pdf/10.1162/INOV_a_00056. *Innovations* is an MIT press journal.

84. Lori Brainard and Mariglynn Edlins, "Top 10 U.S. Municipal Police Departments and their Social Media Usage," *American Review of Public Administration* 45, no. 6 (2015): 728–745. For a more positive assessment of the use of social media by the police, see two journalistic articles: James Toscano, "Does Social Media Help the Government-Citizen Relationship? Depends Who You Ask," *Government Technology Magazine, Blog Post*, May 13, 2016, www.govtech.com/social/Does-Social-Media-Help-the-Government-Citizen-Relationship-Depends-Who-You-Ask-.html; and Sara E. Wilson, "Cops Increasingly Use Social Media to Connect, Crowdsource," *Government Technology Magazine, Blog Post*, May 5, 2015, www.govtech.com/social/Cops-Increasingly-Use-Social-Media-to-Connect-Crowdsource.html.

85. Bollier, *The City as Platform: How Digital Networks Are Changing Urban Life and Government* Also see Nabatchi and Leighninger, *Public Participation for 21st Century Democracy*, 14–25.

86. Julia Sass Rubin, "Organizing Goes Statewide: The Case of Save Our Schools NJ," in *The Fight for America's Schools*, ed. Barbara Ferman (Cambridge, MA: Harvard Education Press, 2017), 97–113.

87. Elaine Simon, Rand Quinn, Marissa Martino Golden, and Jody C. Cohen, "With Our Powers Combined," in Ferman, ed., *The Fight for America's Schools*, 55–74.

88. Thomas A. Bryer, "Explaining Responsiveness in Collaboration: Administrator and Citizen Role Perceptions," *Public Administration Review* 69, no. 2 (March/April 2009): 271–283.

89. Jeremy R. Levine, "The Privatization of Representation: Community-Based Organizations as Non-elected Neighborhood Representatives," *American Sociological Review* 8, no. 6 (2016): 1251–1275.

90. Martin Horak, Juliet Musso, Ellen Shiau, Robert P. Stoker, and Clarence N. Stone, "Change Afoot," in *Urban Neighborhoods in a New Era*, ed. Stone and Stokers, 5.

91. Clarence N. Stone, Jeffrey Henig, Bryan Jones, and Carol Pierannunzi, *Building Civic Capacity: The Politics of Reforming Urban Schools* (Lawrence: University Press of Kansas, 2001), 154.

92. Susan S. Fainstein, *The Just City* (Ithaca, NY: Cornell University Press, 2010), 67.

93. Elaine B. Sharp, *Does Local Government Matter? How Urban Policies Shape Civic Engagement* (Minneapolis: University of Minnesota Press, 2012), 53–56.

9 Improving Urban Services

THE BUREAUCRACY PROBLEM

The reform movement rid cities of much of the ills of machine politics. But in doing so, the reformers increased the decision-making authority of civil service careerists, the permanent employees of municipal government, creating new problems of accountability and responsiveness: A tenure-protected bureaucrat cannot easily be fired even in cases where he or she proves irresponsive to the concerns of community residents or slow to respond to the directives given by local elected officials. The reform movement created the bureaucratic city-state.

Over the years, a variety of "cures" have been introduced to correct the "bureaucracy problem." Professionalization, the use of performance measurement systems, and the increased use of public-private partnerships are all efforts to improve public service delivery and responsiveness in the modern city. Anti-government critics who view urban bureaucracies essentially as unredeemable go still further, advocating the *privatization* of municipal services—that is, to have cities and suburbs contract with private firms and nonprofit organizations to do the jobs once performed by municipal workers. Privatization efforts often seek to offer city residents increased *choice*, providing citizens with alternatives to poorly performing public schools and unsatisfactory service in numerous other program areas.

This chapter will discuss the bureaucracy problem and assess various models for improving urban service delivery. This chapter will point to the potential gains, risks, and limitations of alternative service arrangements.

SOURCES OF BUREAUCRATIC POWER: EXPERTISE AND DISCRETION

Bureaucrats derive power from their **expertise**, their possession of a detailed technical body of knowledge gained from having performed specialized tasks. Police officers are expert in the art of law enforcement. Building and housing inspectors are expert in spotting violations of construction and housing codes that pose a threat to health and

310

safety. Teachers are familiar with the wide variety of pedagogical techniques that can be used to reach students who are having difficulty in the classroom.

Yet, expertise has its limits, especially as expert program administrators tend to view problems from the vantage point of their narrow training, without fully considering the needs and opinions of other members of the community. Police officers, for instance, traditionally approached matters of domestic violence from a law enforcement perspective. The 1994 Violence Against Women Act (VAWA) and the continued advocacy of women's groups sought to change that; they wanted to get police officers to intervene in ways that provide a more complete and compassionate response to the victims of domestic violence. The VAWA essentially forced law enforcement agencies across the nation to alter their traditional practices and to enter into working partnerships with women's advocates, health-care providers, the operators of "safe houses" for battered women, and child-welfare workers.[1] The resulting changes represented a vast improvement by the police when responding to instances of domestic violence. Still, a large number of women—especially minority women—remain hesitant to call the police, fearful of the cold, distant, and biased treatment they may receive from law enforcement officials.[2]

Local bureaucrats also have power as a result of the considerable **administrative discretion** they may possess in the performance of their jobs. Administrative officials decide just how the vague provisions of a law and overly broad program rules are applied to the specific situations that service providers confront in their daily work. A patrol officer decides when to issue a traffic citation and when to overlook a traffic violation. Of even greater importance, it is the patrol officer or detective who, in the midst of a heated encounter, decides whether or not to draw a gun and exercise lethal force. Official departmental policy provides overall guidance but cannot totally remove officer discretion.

Each school teacher decides how to allocate his or her time and energies in attempting to meet the needs of a diverse group of children, with each child coming from a different background and having different "issues" at home and in the classroom. A school's written policies can set some parameters but cannot dictate just how a teacher will interact with each student throughout each long class day.

Street-level bureaucrats are the bottom-rung "foot soldiers" of city and suburban government who possess considerable discretion in determining how they perform their jobs.[3] Police officers, school teachers, social welfare case workers, and housing inspectors are just a few of the street-level public servants who do much of their work "in the field," where their actions are not easily reviewed by superiors.

Problems arise when these municipal foot soldiers react to the pressures of their jobs and make decisions that are not in the best interests of their clients or the larger public. A police officer may have to make instant decisions when faced with a challenge to his or her authority in a situation that may pose a danger to physical safety. It was the questionable decision by a New York City police officer to apply a chokehold to Eric Garner, who was being arrested for the minor crime of selling individual untaxed cigarettes, that led to Garner's death. New York Police Department policies governing the use of force could not constrain the discretion that the officer in the field exercised in what proved to be a fatal encounter.[4]

Police departments often respond to such instances by declaring the need to provide officers with more extensive training in the rules regarding the use of force. Such training

can help to minimize abuses of discretion. But even worthwhile training programs cannot eliminate the discretion that officers in the field will continue to possess when they
have to decide on the spot how to response to a situation immediately before them.

PROFESSIONALISM: AN IMPERFECT CURE TO THE BUREAUCRACY PROBLEM

As front-line administrative discretion cannot be totally controlled from above, some
reformers have called for the *professionalization* of the police and other urban service
workers, with the hope that a highly educated workforce will respond appropriately
even in extremely difficult situations. A **professional** has the higher education and an
internalized ethical code of conduct to assure that his or her discretion will be exercised
properly in the interest of the client.[5] A professional is committed to a higher ethic of
service and can be counted on, even in difficult situations, to make decisions for the
good of the public and the client being served.

Better pay certainly can help recruit a higher caliber of worker to the public service.
Advanced education supplemented by in-service classes can help public officials to
make decisions that reflect a respect for the constitutional rights of citizens and an
understanding of the different experiences and perspectives of the diverse groups that
make up the modern American city.

Still, the model of professionalization offers only a partial cure for the street-level
bureaucracy problem. Many cities and suburbs are unwilling to devote the monies necessary to recruit and continually upgrade the skills public servants.

More importantly, many service providers have difficulty in meeting the defining
hallmark of a professional: the adherence to a code of conduct articulated by the profession, a code of ethical conduct that ensures that a public servant will act to benefit the
public and the client even at times when severe job difficulties and peer pressures may
be pushing the public servant to act otherwise. A professional's sense of sense of obligation to the public surpasses any urge to protect coworkers and shield the agency from
critical outside review. This is an obligation of public service that many highly trained
public servants, including police officers, often have difficulty meeting (see Box 9.1).

PERFORMANCE MEASUREMENT: ASSURING EFFECTIVENESS, EFFICIENCY, EQUITY, AND ACCOUNTABILITY IN MUNICIPAL SERVICE DELIVERY

How do public officials know if a program is working well or if changes need to be
made? In cities across the country, public managers are giving new emphasis to systems
of **performance measurement**, especially the use of statistical indicators that provide
insight as to a program's costs and results over time.[6] **Comparative performance
measurement** seeks to rank indicators of a municipality's performance against those
of peer communities. Do local housing inspectors perform fewer or more inspections
per week as compared to cities of similar size? How long does it take for a city to issue
a building permit, and how does that compare to the length of time that homeowners
and builders face when filing such a request in other communities?

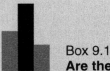

Box 9.1
Are the Police "Professionals"? "Testilying" by the Police

Police officers are highly trained experts who perform difficult jobs, at times in the most trying and dangerous circumstances. But are police officers truly "professionals" deserving of the deference that is accorded to public servants who abide by a higher code of conduct? Video camera recordings have provided disturbing evidence to the contrary, that numerous law enforcement officers in the midst of difficult encounters do not abide by a higher code of conduct.

Advances in technology—patrol-car-mounted video cameras, officer uniform body cams, and even cell phones used by bystanders to record and document incidents—have yielded evidence that officers too often provide a misleading account of events in order to protect fellow and sister officers who have been charged with misconduct: the illegal search and seizure of evidence, the mistreatment of suspects, and even the improper resort to lethal force. The literature in the field uses the term **testilying** to refer to those officer accounts of incidents, in written reports and even in testimony under oath, that turn out to be false or misleading.

Police officers often abide by an unwritten code of silence, where officers are discouraged from reporting the misdeeds of their peers. The culture of peer loyalty serves to protect officers who must make split-second decisions in dangerous settings. However, such unwritten norms of behavior subvert official departmental rules that require truthfulness and transparency. Such unwritten codes do not serve the public interest as they lead police to falsify reports and cover-up abuses of authority.

Patrol officers have even taken actions to undermine official departmental policies that seek to assure the transparency of police actions and that officers will be held accountable for their behavior. Patrol officers turn off body cameras and car-mounted dashcams and, at times, have even disabled recording devices. In extreme cases, officers intentionally mutilated or lost recordings, so there would no video evidence to counter their own reports of what happened during a contested encounter.[1]

In Chicago, patrol officers did not routinely seek to assure that recording equipment was in working order and functioning properly. Officers intentionally damaged the microphones, antennas, and syncing devices so that there could be no high-quality recordings to contradict what officers report in their versions of contested encounters. When 17-year-old Laquan McDonald was shot 16 times by Chicago police, all five dashcam recorders mounted on the patrol cars at the scene failed to function properly. None was able to produce a clear audio tract that could help establish the exact sequence of events and just what officers said to one another during the fatal encounter.[2]

Why is testilying and related abuses tolerated? Many citizens feel that is unfair to the officers involved to second-guess a difficult split-second decision made in very precarious circumstances.[3] Law enforcement supervisory personnel and elected officials are also aware of the importance of maintaining departmental morale, that meting out punishments may lead officers to be less enthusiastic in intervening in future street encounters. As a result, departments seldom vigorously pursue the punishment of officers who file false reports or who have apparently lied under oath. Instead, police departments generously choose to regard false accounts as the product of an officer's faulty memory, a lapse that can be excused.[4]

Labor associations representing police officers resist the adoption of departmental policies to discipline officers who fail to maintain operative recording equipment or who turn off body cams and car-mounted dashcams. Police unions also oppose making such video recordings fully available to the public. The sharing of video footage raises important concerns for the protection of privacy and other constitutional rights.[5]

Unwritten codes of conduct that emphasize officer solidarity contradict the tenets of professionalism. As a consequence, police officers may be regarded as **semiprofessionals** who are clearly expert in their jobs but whose unwritten code of conduct runs contrary to a professional's obligations to be transparent and truthful and to respect the constitutional rights of citizens.

1. Mary D. Fan, "Missing Police Body Camera Videos: Remedies, Evidentiary Fairness, and Automatic Activation," *Georgia Law Review*, 52, no. 1 (2017): 57–108; Matina Kitzmueller, "Are You Recording This? Enforcement of Police Videotaping," *Connecticut Law Review*, 47, no. 1 (2014): 167–196.

2. Dean Reynolds, "Analysis Finds 'Deliberate' Disabling of Some Chicago Dashcams," CBS News, January 2, 2016, www.cbsnews.com/news/analysis-finds-deliberate-disabling-of-some-chicago-police-dashcams/.

3. Jonathan Blanks, "The Police and 'Testilying': Perjury on the Witness Stand?" *The Crime Report*, a news service of the Center on Crime, Media and Justice of John Jay College of Criminal Justice, New York, January 14, 2015, https://thecrimereport.org/2015/01/14/2015-01-reasonable-suspicion-are-police-lying-in-use-of-forc/.

4. Joseph Goldstein, "'Testilying' by Police: A Stubborn Problem." *New York Times*, March 18, 2018; Goldstein, "Promotions, Not Punishments, for Officers Accused of Lying," *New York Times*, March 1, 2018.

5. Howard M. Wasserman, "Recording of and by the Police: The Good, the Bad, and the Ugly," *Journal of Gender, Race, and Justice*, 20, no. 3 (2017): 543–561; and Wasserman, "Police Misconduct, Video Recording, and Procedural Barriers to Rights Enforcement" (December 11, 2017). *North Carolina Law Review* (2018 Forthcoming), 2017, advanced draft available at Florida International University Legal Studies Research Paper No. 17–48, https://ssrn.com/abstract=3086092.

Program implementers pay attention to what is measured and will tend to take steps to boost their performance scores and look good. What gets measured gets done. Hence, public officials must be careful in choosing what exactly they measure. Angry parents criticized No Child Left Behind, the flagship educational initiative of President George W. Bush, for its reliance on performance measures that led local school systems to "teach to the test." School systems and teachers devoted inordinate class time to rote drills in math and English, the areas tested in statewide exams, rather than the teaching of sciences, social studies, history, the dramatic arts, and other valuable aspects of a child's education.

When told that they must produce performance measures, too often municipal agencies simply produce whatever numbers can be easily amassed. Most agencies can easily obtain measures of a programs **inputs** or the resources devoted to a job (an agency's budget or the number of workers—i.e. the number of teachers or patrol officers on the street—that it employs each year). But input measures are really of little value. Input numbers provide no indication if an agency is actually helping people and accomplishing its mission, or if it is using resources well or wasting taxpayer money on actions that have little impact.

Program administrators need to report than more than just inputs. Program evaluations should stress **outcome measures or measures of program effectiveness**, indicators that point to just what difference an agency is making in a community and in the lives of citizens being served. Does a job training program reach the clients most in need of assistance? Does the program help clients to acquire a new skill and result in employment? What percentage of job training clients continue to hold a job one year after the completion of training? What percentage of eligible children in a community do Head Start preschool programs serve? Does Head Start increase children's readiness to learn, as seen in metrics of appropriate social behavior? Does Head Start actually lead children to perform better as they progress through school? These are all questions of program effectiveness.

A police department should not be content to report the number of officers on patrol or the number of patrols that it conducts in a troubled neighborhoods—as these provide only a very elementary understanding of an agency's performance. Instead, departmental reports should emphasize outcome measures that help reveal the extent to which a policing strategy has an impact on the lives of the people or community the police serve. Outcome measures typically track changes in local crime rates. Outcome measures also seek to discover the extent to which residents feel safe, such as their willingness to walk on neighborhood streets after dark. Evaluations of a prenatal outreach program can emphasize such outcomes as the percentage of babies delivered at full term, the birth weights of at-risk babies, and infant mortality rates.

Program officials have an obligation to spend taxpayers's money wisely. Consequently, program evaluators also calculate and report **efficiency measures**, indicators that show if a program is being run at relatively low costs as opposed to higher costs. Efficiency measures reveal how much it costs the sanitation department to collect a ton of garbage or how much the local transit agency spends per trip for each bus rider. A municipal streets department would seek to find out just how much the city is paying for each mile of a city roadway that it resurfaces.

There is the ever-present danger that municipal officials, responding to anti-tax pressure, will pay inordinate attention to efficiency measures to the neglect of other important aspects of public service. It would be foolish for a city to introduce service changes that save money but the provide services so poorly that public education, safety, and a city's infrastructure suffer.

Efficiency measures also fail to reveal the extent to which a city is treating all citizens fairly. As a result, a balanced set of performance metrics must also include **equity measures** that seek to ascertain the extent to which a program is serving all demographic groups and neighborhoods in the city. Do residents on the east side of town enjoy the same level of access to libraries and the same quality of municipal water that residents on the west side of town enjoy?

"Equity" often proves an elusive concept to define and measure. Some citizens argue that all clients and neighborhoods should receive the same level of service. The standard of **strict equity** entails giving all citizens the same level of service. By this definition, inequity exists when some children have new textbooks and access to a wide choice of classes and extracurricular activities that are denied to children attending schools in poorer sections of the city. The standard of strict equity would also require the same frequency of trash collection, say once a week, regardless of the values of the homes and the amount of property taxes paid by homeowners in different neighborhoods.

Yet there are instances where the equal allotment of a public service is not truly equitable. A standard of **social equity** justifies the government's provision of disproportionate assistance to persons who need it the most. Children with greater needs, for instance, require extensive tutoring and support services that are not provided to other children. Police departments typically focus greater resources on high-crime areas.

No single measure or metric by itself can provide a full and valid indication of agency performance. As a result, cities utilize **multiple indicators**, that is, a variety of indicators or metrics to reveal just how well an agency is meeting various aspects of its assigned mission. **Balanced scorecards** utilize a combination of indicators to measure program performance in all three critical dimensions of municipal service delivery: efficiency, effectiveness, and equity. The balanced scorecard utilized by the Oregon Benchmarks Report displays efficiency and effectiveness (program outcome) scores in a number of service areas and gives special attention to social equity indicators that trace the extent to which minority communities are progressing in areas such as education and health care.[7]

Good assessment of service provision almost always entails an attempt to discern to what extent local citizens are satisfied with the quality of services that a municipality provides. Municipal departments utilize a variety of tools, including community surveys, user questionnaires, and program evaluation cards filled out by clients to gauge just how well a local program is meeting the expectations of users and the general public.[8]

Municipal agencies increasingly utilize **focus groups**, where a moderator helps to guide discussion as a select handful of participants talk about their perceptions of an agency's work.[9] Focus groups generally offer a much cheaper alternative to a full-fledged community survey. But as the participants in a focus group are not a scientifically representative sample of the larger community, a focus group does not allow a researcher to present statistics that represent the views of the community as a whole. Despite this shortcoming, focus group methodology has a distinct advantage: It enables citizens to talk in depth about program performance, allowing participants to raise and explore their own concerns. The focus group approach allows for more in-depth discussion than what can be obtained from a survey built around numerous closed-ended (that is, fixed-choice) questions.

Municipal departments also use **trained observers** to rate the levels of trash on streets, the physical condition of roads and school classrooms, and the serviceability of play-ground equipment and ball fields in local parks.[10] The observers are given instructions and practice recording just what condition deserves what exact rating. Such training and the accompanying rubrics that guide the ratings assigned by field observers serve to reduce the arbitrariness of the scores, the chance that different observers will assign different scores to conditions that are essentially the same. Observers also often take

Box 9.2
CompStat, CitiStat, and PerformanceStat: Cities Adopt Advanced Systems of Performance Measurement and Management

New York City Police Chief William Bratton gained national attention for instituting **CompStat**, a weekly reporting system that tracked crime rates precinct by precinct, and sometimes even block by block. District commanders had to explain their unit's performance in departmental meetings conducted before the chief and the mayor or top mayoral assistants. Pushed by "the numbers" and by aggressive questioning, district commanders altered work shifts and reassigned personnel to target high-crime areas. These commanders did not wish to repeatedly defend their unit's poor performance when questioned in regularly scheduled, high-level accountability meetings. CompStat performance data was used to put "relentless pressure" on district commanders, precinct captains and other law enforcement officials to use their discretion to find new ways of achieving better results.

After leaving New York, Bratton was hired by Los Angeles to see if his techniques could bring similar reductions in crime in that city. In 2014 Mayor Bill de Blasio brought the renowned police chief back to New York.

Baltimore Mayor (and later Maryland Governor) Martin O'Malley used a similar data-driven system, **CitiStat**, with detailed maps that revealed patterns of need and service provision throughout the city. As was the case with CompStat, the data became part of a system of "relentless management," where regularly scheduled meetings with the mayor and other top officials put constant pressure on municipal departments to initiate program changes. Baltimore mayors who succeeded O'Malley in office continued to emphasize the use of CitiStat to guide public managers in improving service performance.

San Francisco, King County (Washington), Minneapolis, St. Louis, Columbus (Ohio), Warren (Michigan), Buffalo, Syracuse, Providence, Somerville and Springfield (Massachusetts), New Orleans, Fort Lauderdale, Philadelphia, and Washington, DC, are only a few of the many municipalities across the United States to adopt PerformanceStat systems—variations of the CompStat and CitiStat approaches.[1] Regular and frequent meetings that review the data and set specific performance targets put agency officials under relentless pressure to produce immediate results. The Atlanta Dashboard system similarly tracks departmental indicators in an effort to have local administrators initiate corrective action.

In numerous communities, however, lack the support staff experts has meant that municipal leaders have been unwilling to commit to systems of advanced performance metrics with their heavy data demands. Data collection is time-consuming and expensive. CitiStat requires extensive training to teach managers how to collect, interpret, and utilize data. Even in bigger cities, where CompStat or CitiStat review works with the assistance of a central data-support office, the commitment to such an arduous system of performance review can fade over time.

CompStat and similar PerformanceStat systems get results. Yet, there are also accompanying risks and dangers. Critics charge that CompStat's emphasis on performance measures can lead police officers to aggressively pursue actions so that they can report improved performance numbers. But aggressive action that criminalizes minor infractions, especially in minority neighborhoods, can add to local distrust of the police and heighten police-citizen tensions. Such aggressive enforcement actions also saddle minority youths with criminal records that are an impediment to future employment.[2]

[1] For a partial list of the great many cities that adopted CompStat, CitiStat, and various PerformanceStat systems, see Robert D. Behn, *The PerformanceStat Potential: A Leadership Strategy for Producing Results* Cambridge, Massachusetts: The Ash Center for Democratic Governance and Innovation, Harvard University: and Washington, DC: The Brookings Institution, 2014), esp. Chaps. 1 and 2. The paragraph's "relentless pressure" quotation is also from Behn, although the phrase has been commonly used over the years to describe the workings of CompStat and CitiStat.

[2] Bernard E. Harcourt, *Illusion of Order: The False Promise of Broken Windows Policing* (Chicago: University of Chicago Press, 2001). Patricia J. William, "It's Time to End 'Broken Windows' Policing," *The Nation* magazine, January 27, 2014; John A. Eterno, Christine S. Barrow, and Eli B. Silverman, "Forcible Stops: Police and Citizens Speak Out," *Public Administration Review*, 77, no. 2 (March/April 2017): 181–192.

photographs to document the physical conditions they report. In New York, the Center on Municipal Government Performance even uses state-of-the-art laser technology to provide precise, objective measures ("smoothness scores" and "jolt scores") of the condition of city streets.[11]

The reports by trained observers show that even the collection of relatively simple data can be of great assistance to agencies that seek to improve their performance. Yet systems of data-driven performance management can also be quite sophisticated and complex. The successes of New York's CompStat and Baltimore's CitiStat systems prompted cities across the country to develop their own PerformanceStat systems to collect and analyze data in "real time." Such sophisticated data systems pinpoint where problems persist and prompt agencies to take immediate steps to direct resources to a problem areas and to find new ways to respond to stubborn problems[12] (see Box 9.2). Despite the achievements of such extensive data analysis systems, many cities, especially smaller communities, simply lack the money and even the will to commit to the extensive training and technological support necessary to integrate sophisticated data analysis into agency decision making on a regular (i.e. weekly or biweekly) basis.

COPRODUCTION AND BUSINESS IMPROVEMENT DISTRICTS (BIDS)

Businesses as well as citizens have come to realize that overburdened municipal agencies cannot always provide the full range of much-needed services. As a result, neighborhood and business groups have come to see the importance of working in partnership with governmental agencies in the **coproduction** of improved public services. Community groups help to raise the funds and may even provide the volunteer labor to install new playground equipment. Neighborhood cleanup days entail trash pickup by church parishioners, schoolchildren, and members of environmental clubs and other volunteer groups, with city haulers carting the refuse away. Neighborhood Watch programs enable residents to work in partnership with the police to reduce crime. In Detroit, about 6,000 parents and community activists, armed only with flashlights, walked the streets the night before Halloween, curtailing the reign of "Devil's Night" arson that once plagued the city.[13]

Coproduction can be part of a strategy to "repurpose" vacant neighborhood lots in distressed neighborhoods. In "Green Up Pittsburgh," the city provides soil, grass seed, and even the advice of a landscape architect to community groups that seek to transform vacant properties into play spaces, attractive side lots, and "edible gardens" to provide low-income neighborhoods with healthy food. The city also provides liability insurance for volunteers and helps community groups gain title to the lots.[14] The residents of low-income communities are willing to participate in the coproduction of services that are vital to their neighborhoods, a pattern that was evident in the high levels of citizen engagement in various community projects sponsored by Atlanta's Neighborhood Planning Units.[15]

Businesses, too, have discovered the importance of coproduction and are often willing to contribute financially to actions that supplement the services that a municipality provides. In commercial portions of cities across the country, businesses have banded together to launch a **business improvement district (BID)**, a self-taxing self-help arrangement where the city collects an additional fee from an area's commercial property owners so that is turned over to a local business council to increase levels of sanitation and safety and to bring other improvements that local businesses may desire.

Commercial property owners select the members of a BID's **district management association (DMA)** who then decides on the level of the supplemental charge that is levied on commercial property owners and how exactly the revenue will be used to improve the conditions in, and the business climate of, the area. The municipal government collects the additional charge—just as it collects a city-imposed tax—but then turns the revenues over to the DMA. Cities are happy to have businesses help pay for improved services. Business leaders often are willing to contribute. As one downtown Los Angeles business spokeswoman explained: "These aren't like taxes that get lost in the general fund. . . . The money stays inside the business district . . . where businesses can see results."[16]

BIDs pay for additional street security personnel, improved trash collection, more frequent street cleaning, the installation of new street lamps, and the placement of signs to help direct visitors to local shops and activities. BIDs sponsor local concerts and festivals to entice visitors and potential customers to frequent an area. In Harlem, the historic African-American center of New York City, the 125th Street Business Improvement District directs residents to its "app," "Harlem Happenings," using online technology to encourage residents and visitors to attend local events and patronize the area's restaurants and shops.[17]

A BID is not a purely voluntary or even a democratic organization. Commercial property owners in a district who opposed the creation of a BID must still pay the additional assessment or surtax even if they have not need for a BID's activities. From Hyannis,

Massachusetts, to the "Art District" of Los Angeles, dissident business owners who object to being saddled with additional fees have organized "Rid the BID" campaigns.[18]

BIDs are an increasingly commonplace form of local governance.[19] Not formally a part of the actual local government itself, BIDs nonetheless abet the provision of municipal services. The first BID in the nation was created in the 1970s. By the early 1990s, more than 1,200 BIDs emerged in cities across the United States. Today the figure is even greater.

Nearly all states allow the local formation of BIDs. In some cities, BIDs are especially prominent actors. New York City has 75 BIDs that invest about $150 million annually in local economic development and neighborhood improvement projects.[20] Los Angeles has 40 BIDs; many focus on increasing public safety as part of their efforts to draw new customers to their portion of the city.[21] San Francisco's Union Square BID is the largest of the city's 15 Community Business Districts (the name generally used by California state law to refer to BIDs). In Chicago, BIDs are called Special Service Areas. Atlanta, Baltimore, Boston, Cleveland, Denver, Mesa, Milwaukee, Pasadena, Philadelphia, San Diego, San Francisco, Seattle, and Washington, DC, are only a few of the other cities in which BIDs have been established. Each state determines the exact rules for local BID formation and the exact activities that a BID may undertake.

The rise of BIDs raises questions of democracy, power, and fairness in the city. Typically, a BID does *not* abide by the one-person-one-vote ballot principle that general-purpose local governments are obligated to obey. The courts do not view BIDs as part of the government but only as private associations created for business promotion.[22] There is no equality of representation in a BID's governing arrangements. Instead, the allocation of votes in a BID usually depends on the value of an owner's property: The more property an owner possesses, the greater the vote that he or she can cast at BID meetings. Even the vote to create a BID is weighted according to the value of the commercial property that a person owns. Mere residents of a neighborhood who do not own commercial property are denied a vote on BID formation and its activities, even though a BID's activities can have considerable impact on the quality of life in a neighborhood. Private-led BIDs are "shadow" governments that do not have to meet the levels of transparency, citizen participation, and voting rights required of municipal government.[23]

BIDs of different sizes tend to serve different purposes.[24] The largest are **corporate BIDs** dominated by major national and international businesses and with annual budgets of more than $1 million—sometimes way more. In New York City, the Grand Central Partnership undertook a "Clean and Safe" effort to help revitalize the larger area surrounding the famed midtown Manhattan train station. The Partnership in 2016 alone spent over $12.6 million on activities in a 70-block section of midtown Manhattan.[25] In Philadelphia, the Center City District employs 138 uniformed sidewalk cleaners and another 42 community service representatives who serve as "eyes on the street" as the BID seeks to improve sanitation and reduce crime in a 120-city-block section of Philadelphia's downtown.[26]

A **Main Street BID**, by comparison, is a smaller organization that seeks to revitalize declining shopping areas (often sections outside a city's downtown) that have lost retail customers. Main Street BIDs typically have budgets in the $200,000 to $1 million range and cover 5 to 20 square blocks.

Box 9.3
The Continuing Debate Over BID Activity

In New York City, the Times Square BID undertook a series of actions that helped to transform the image of the Big Apple's famed but gritty entertainment and theater district. The BID helped to pay for increased trash pickup, graffiti removal, and new street guides and safety patrols to make tourists feel safe. The Times Square BID succeeded in helping to revive one of city's most fabled destinations. The rejuvenation of Times Square led to new residential developments and rising property values both in the district and in nearby neighborhoods. The continued upscaling of mid-Manhattan, which has its roots in numerous actions first precipitated by the Times Square BID, raises an important question: Just whom do BIDS serve and whom do they tend to ignore?

The actions of another giant New York City BID, the Grand Central Partnership, similarly raised questions of equity and fairness, especially when the business association paid workers to remove the homeless from the train station and the surrounding area.[1] In San Francisco, the red-and-blue uniformed street "ambassadors" of the Union Square BID have harassed the homeless and attempted to oust them from the city's upscale downtown shopping district.

Even a BID decision to raise money to support law enforcement can raise questions of democracy and equality. The Alliance for Downtown New York, a BID financed primarily by the multinational corporate giants who occupy Lower Manhattan, helped secure a new police substation for the city's financial district, despite crime statistics that revealed that the area had one of the lowest rates of street crime in the city. The Alliance offered the city $5 million to help set up a new substation with 200 officers, with 40 or more officers assigned to the financial district. Neighborhood activists argued that the Wall Street substation site served to divert officer presence away from low-income and higher-crime residential portions of the city. Queens Councilmember Sheldon Leffler decried that affluent Wall Street had bought a level of police protection denied to poorer neighborhoods: "It raises very disturbing questions about whether city resources are going to be allocated where they're needed or auctioned off to the highest bidder."[2]

Questions of power and social class were even apparent in the Queens when the owners of small businesses fought against a proposal to extend a business improvement district along a 20-block portion of Roosevelt Road. The city's growth coalition backed the BID, arguing that its creation would bring new commercial activity to a working-class portion of the city. But grassroots organizations such as Queens Neighborhood United opposed the move, fearing that BID activities would make the area increasingly attractive to national chain stores, resulting in an inflation in commercial rents that would force out the area's small immigrant-owned businesses.[3]

1. Heather Barr, "More Like Disneyland: State Action, 42 U.S.C. 1 1983, and Business Improvement Districts in New York," *Columbia Human Rights Law Review* 28 (Winter 1997).

2. David Kocieniewski, "Wall St. to Pay to Add a Base for the Police," *New York Times*, February 17, 1998.

3. Arturo I. Sánchez, "The Roosevelt Avenue BID and the Politics of Exclusion," *QueensLatino, Blog Posting*, March 26. 2015, http://queenslatino.com/the-roosevelt-avenue-bid-and-the-politics-of-exclusion/.

A **community BID** is the smallest type of BID and is usually found in declining neighborhoods. Working with budgets of only $200,000 or so, the activities of a Community BID may cover only a few city blocks. Community BIDs lack the ability to finance extensive capital improvements and major neighborhood promotional campaigns.

The proliferation of BIDs raises serious equity concerns. The formation of a BID enables commercial districts with well-organized businesses to receive a higher level of service provision that is denied to poorer and more disorganized sections of the city that cannot afford a BID (see Box 9.3).

Corporate BIDs tend to reflect the agendas of some of the city's most powerful commercial interests. But questions of democracy emerge even in the operation of smaller BIDs where, as a result of their undemocratic voting arrangements, a BID can decide on an area's development strategy without the full participation of an area's small business owners and apartment dwellers.[27]

SERVICE CONTRACTING AND PRIVATIZATION

Cities and suburbs look to the private sector for ways to increase efficiency and improve service delivery. Loosely used, the term "privatization" refers to any application of private-sector techniques that can improve public management. More strictly defined, **privatization** denotes a series of strategies intended to restructure local government; privatization represents an effort to have private-sector and nonprofit providers replace municipal bureaucrats in urban service delivery. Under privatization, services once provided by governmental agencies are turned over to private-sector firms and nonprofit organizations.

The privatization movement is driven by the belief that private businesses can provide services better and less expensively than does government. The advocates of privatization argue for the inherent superiority of **market mechanisms**: In a free market, private providers must be efficient and responsive as they compete for a city's business and for customers. Market mechanisms also give citizens greater choice, ending their dependence on irresponsive public bureaucracies.

Cities across the country utilize **service contracting**, where a municipal government signs a legally binding agreement for a private firm or nonprofit agency to provide a specified service. Contemporary cities and suburbs "contract out" the provision of a vast array of municipal services: private haulers pick up trash; community-based organizations assist in drug-abuse counseling and operate shelters for the homeless; private janitorial firms clean governmental offices; and private information technology companies are hired to update a city's data processing system and to train municipal workers in new technology. New York City turned over the daily management of Central

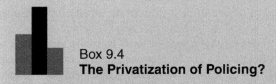

Box 9.4
The Privatization of Policing?

Even a service as seemingly "public" as law enforcement can be privatized or at least partially privatized. There is no reason why protective services must be delivered solely by officers who work directly for the government. Private security firms can be contracted to perform a number of law enforcement functions: monitoring parking meters and issuing parking tickets; walking the streets to maintain the safety of downtown entertainment districts; watching over the entrances to large public housing projects; and performing some aspects of an investigation of crime scenes. Oakland, California, hired a private firm to conduct extra patrols in high-crime areas. A number of communities contract for-profit corrections firms to operate local detention centers.

The turn to privatized law enforcement arrangements is largely driven by the search for efficiency. In an age where public dollars are stretched thin, cities have to look for ways to carry out important tasks without making expensive long-term commitments. Fiscally strapped Fresno, California, sought cost savings by turning to private security firms to monitor shopping malls, sporting events, and even the city zoo rather than hire higher-salaried city police officers for such activities. Cities also seek flexible hires instead of new officers who may earn tenure rights under civil service. Fresno (California), Mesa (Arizona), and Charlotte (North Carolina) have even recruited volunteers to respond to low-level service calls and interview witnesses, taking some of the pressure off fiscally strapped municipal police departments.

Critics, however, worry about the loss of public control when private companies and volunteers are used to help provide for public safety and run prisons. Private firms may not give their personnel the same extensive training that public law enforcement officers receive. Private security and prison guards and neighborhood volunteers may also lack the respect for civil liberties and civil rights that is expected of public law enforcement officials. An unfortunate municipality may only too late discover that it is fiscally liable for the wrongful actions of contracted private security officers.

Sources: Brian Forst and Peter K. Manning, *The Privatization of Policing: Two Views* (Washington, DC: Georgetown University Press, 1999); Jesse McKinley, "Police Departments Turn to Volunteers," *New York Times*, March 1, 2011; Pace William Rawlins and Sung-Wook Kwon, "Walking the Line on Police Privatization: Efficiency, Accountability, and Court Decisions," *International Review of Administrative Sciences*, 82, no. 3 (September 2016), 580–57

Park to the Central Park Conservancy, a not-for-profit private group that was able to tap the donations of major corporations to help finance park improvements.[28] Even certain law enforcement and correctional activities do not need to be run by the government as they can be operated by private and nonprofit organizations in the field. (See Box 9.4.)

Privatization is based on the distinction between the decision to *provide* a service to the public, and the decision as to who can best deliver or *produce* the desired service:

> [T]o provide a service is to decide that a service shall be made available and to arrange for its delivery. This is an integral part of a local government's policy-making process. To deliver a service is to actually produce the service. Although a local government may decide to provide a service, it does not necessarily have to be directly involved in its delivery.[29]

Municipal governments do not necessarily need to use government workers to produce and deliver every service that citizens require. Instead, cities can arrange for private firms and nonprofit agencies to deliver public services, especially when such alternative service arrangements prove to be cheaper and more effective than having the service produced by the municipal bureaucracy.

THE ADVANTAGES OF PRIVATIZATION

When it comes to physical services and administrative tasks—including trash collection, fire protection, automotive fleet maintenance, the upkeep of local parks, the performance of housing inspections, and the computerization of record keeping—private firms often offer similar or better service at lower cost than do municipal agencies.[30] Why is this so?

Service contracting encourages a **competition** among potential service providers that can reduce the costs that a city must pay. A private firm must update the skills of its workers and adopt newer and more innovative practices, or else find that it has little chance to submit the winning bid on a contract to perform work for the city. A municipal agency, by contrast, is a **public monopoly** that faces no real competition; its workers do not have to update their skills and perform well and efficiently in order to keep their civil-service-protected jobs.

Former Indianapolis mayor Stephen Goldsmith argues that competition is the key to better performance and cost savings, that privatization without competition will seldom generate any real advantages. Only when a number of qualified firms bid on a municipal contract does each hopeful feel compelled to submit bids without excess "fat." Privatization is not likely to save a city money when only one private firm has the capacity to perform requested services. When no competition exists among the potential suppliers of a service, privatization only winds up replacing an inefficient public monopoly with an inefficient private monopoly.[31]

As competition is the key to efficiency, a city can receive the benefits of competition without actually turning over a service to a private firm. Under a process known as **managed competition**, public agencies are permitted to bid on a contract: the city can then choose to award the contract to either the municipal agency or to a private contractor. In order to win the contract and keep their jobs, workers in a municipal agency will have to "shape up," redesigning work processes and adopting innovative and more efficiency-oriented practices.

In Phoenix, a reenergized public sanitation department won back many of the contracts that had previously been awarded to private haulers. Phoenix rebids its solid waste removal contracts every six years to assure that competitive pressures persist. In

Indianapolis, public agencies bid against private contractors for the right to perform specific service activities. City officials estimated that managed competition saved the city $100 million in just the program's first three years! In San Diego, city employees have succeeded in winning a number of competitive bids, often by reducing staffing levels. In a number of cities, managed competition is resisted by municipal labor unions who warn that their members may lose jobs.[32]

Service contracting enables the "hired" agency a new level of managerial flexibility that is not normally found in public agencies. Compared to public agencies and their civil service rules, private firms have a greater ability to transfer workers as needed from one division to another. The managers in a private firm also possess greater authority to penalize and even dismiss a worker whose work performance is unsatisfactory. Private firms can also dispense large bonuses to top managers for outstanding performance; in public agencies, civil service rules severely constrain such awards in order to limit the risks of partisan manipulation. Private firms also have the greater flexibility to pay lower salaries and benefits and even to make greater use of part-time workers.

Cash-starved cities can even turn to privatization, selling or auctioning off municipal facilities and the right to provide a service, as a means of gaining a much-needed short-term infusion of revenues. Facing over $300 million in debt and teetering on the edge of bankruptcy, Harrisburg, Pennsylvania, in 2011 sought to sell the city incinerator. Harrisburg also had private companies bid for the privilege of operating the city's parking meters and garages. The city received an immediate cash windfall that it used to repay creditors and help cover shortfalls in the city budget. Private bidders saw the potential for long-term profit in offering services that were once provided by government.

Private companies pay substantial sums for city assets that have profit-making potential. Chicago in 2005 received $1.8 billion for a lease that gave an Australian-Spanish entity a 99-year right to operate and collect the tolls on the Chicago Skyway, a major toll road connecting the city to neighboring Indiana. The private company was obligated to make improvements in the important but physically deteriorating roadway. Two years later, Chicago received $1.15 billion from a different private contractor in return for a 75-year lease for the firm to operate the city's parking meters.

Service contracting can be a strategy for upgrading or modernizing a municipal service. A fiscally strapped city may lack the ability to buy new equipment, but a for-profit firm may be quite willing to make the substantial investments necessary to replace a city's aging coin-operated meters with a new generation of "smart" meters that accept credit cards and allow parking rates to be adjusted by the hour of the day. The city gets a modernized parking system and rakes in immediate revenues from the sale of its parking operations. The private operator, in turn, sees the profit potential inherent in a business that was previously operated by municipal government.

THE DISADVANTAGES AND RISKS OF PRIVATIZATION

Privatization does not always save a city money. Nor does it always improve service delivery. Advocates of privatization often present an exaggerated picture of what privatization can accomplish, contrasting an idealized portrait private-sector operations with stereotypes of public-sector waste and indifference. The performance of private firms, too, can suffer from extensive waste, favoritism, payoffs, and corruption. In Chicago, service contracting did not simply provide a route to improve service efficiency. As observed in Chapter 7, privatization also provided Chicago politicians a means to dispense service contracts as *pinstripe patronage*, a reward to political friends and campaign contributors.

The savings that a city actually achieves depends on the service area and how well the privatization arrangement is managed. An auditor's report reveals that the City of Denver gained savings when it contracted out janitorial work, but the city lost money when it contracted out sewer replacement work instead of having the work done by municipal workers.[33]

Contracting entails **hidden costs**, including the costs that a municipality incurs in preparing a contract for bid and overseeing the work performed by the contractor.[34] Not all costs to a city go away when a municipality privatizes a service. Even when a city no longer directly provides a service itself, the municipality still faces the costs of having to maintain buildings that are no longer in use. The municipality will also bear the costs of salary and pension obligations that must be paid to former municipal workers who are no longer needed. A city also confronts still additional costs if it needs to dismiss and replace a contractor whose work has been disappointing.

Unscrupulous contractors maximize profits by "cutting corners" and lowering service quality. To win the city's business, a private firm may submit a **lowball contract bid**, that is, an unrealistically low bid that does not represent the full cost of service provision over the life of the contract. A city or suburb that is dependent on a contractor may find that it has no real alternative but to pay the cost overruns that a contractor later bills the city.

Bid-rigging, too, can diminish the competitive nature of a process based on the submission of "blind bids." In New York City and in suburban communities on nearby Long Island, trash haulers met to "fix" bids, to "collusively decide the low bid and low bidder"[35] and thereby gain extra profits. In Connecticut, James Galante, the head of a trash-hauling empire, was imprisoned for racketeering, for having engaged in bid-rigging to win contracts and also in inflating the prices his firms charged its customers.[36]

Service contracting is also **anti-union**. Privatization enables a municipality to replace unionized municipal workers with lower-wage workers who enjoy much less in the way of benefits and job security. Faced with competition from low-cost nonunion bidders, unionized municipal and private workforces will often find it necessary to restrain salary and workplace demands. In Fresno in 2013, a public ballot measure pushed by local labor unions reversed an earlier decision of the city council to privatize residential trash removal.

When contracts are awarded for periods as long as 75 and 99 years, competitive pressures—a private firm's fear of losing a contract that is about to come up for possible renewal—that lead to cost savings are minimized. Cities need to make sure they "get it right" before they commit to such long-term arrangements.[37] In Chicago, residents felt "ripped off" when private operators continued to hike parking prices and extend the hours and days of parking meter operations, even requiring payment on the Fourth of July national holiday. Public outrage further mounted when the city's Inspector General reported that Chicago had received nearly a billion dollars less than its parking assets were worth, despite having offered the contract through competitive bidding.

Chicago officials discovered that the contract burdened them with unanticipated and hidden costs. The city was obligated to pay millions of dollars each year to the private operator as compensation for parking spaces lost due to parades, block festivals, and the necessity of making street repairs. The city sought arbitration to reduce the amount that the private company billed the city parking spaces used by city police, by other municipal workers, and by disabled citizens.[38]

Chicago residents were not alone in their displeasure with the higher rates charged by private service providers.[39] In small cities like Bayonne (New Jersey) and Rialto and Santa Paula (California), privatization led to a dramatic jump in customer utility bills to cover the costs of infrastructure improvement and the profits earned by private investors.[40] When the privately operated water company in Dillon Beach (California) had difficulty covering its costs and generating profits, the company raised its rates, charging rates that were four to six times the rates charged by municipal water systems in neighboring jurisdictions. When contract terms barred the privatized Nassau County–New York express bus system from raising fares during the contract's first year, the private operator responded by reducing service on 30 routes—and then increased fares when the time limit expired.[41]

Even when service operations are placed in the hands of nonprofit providers, equity concerns can arise. In New York, the Prospect Park Alliance raised tens of millions of dollars to help restore a major park located in the midst of a gentrifying Brooklyn—but equivalent monies were not provided for neighborhood parks in poorer sections of the city.[42] The Central Park Conservancy invested more than 100 million dollars to upgrade and maintain New York's Central Park, the city's green space popular with both tourists and many of New York's more affluent residents who live nearby. The upgraded park served to reinforce gentrification pressures in Manhattan.[43]

THE PRIVATE MANAGEMENT OF PUBLIC SCHOOLS

A number of states and cities have turned to private management firms to run troubled local schools. Private managers are charged with a clear mission: to shake up school operations and instill a new culture of achievement in failing schools. The private educational management firms are given relief from a number of state regulations governing the operations of schools, an effort designed to give innovative managers greater freedom to hire classroom teachers committed to the school's mission and to introduce cutting-edge teaching practices. The private-school operators utilize various cost-saving approaches, such as individualized computer-assisted instruction, deployed by private businesses.

Yet the record shows that privately managed public schools do not consistently produce the results that enthusiasts of private management promise. Miami contracted with a private firm, Educational Alternatives, Inc. (EAI), to take over the operations of a failing public school. EAI promised to create a "dream school" with the latest in computers and innovative instructional programs in math and reading. EAI developed an individualized learning plan for each student. EAI subcontracted maintenance and building repair tasks to partner firms, allowing principals and teachers to devote greater attention to their core mission. Baltimore and Hartford also turned to EAI to run a number of their troubled schools.

In each city, the teachers's union complained of EAI's all-out assault on tenure, as the company hired low-cost instructional personnel instead of certified teachers to fill classroom support positions. Teachers further complained that EAI managers forced educators to work a longer school day with no extra pay. In Baltimore, African-American activists decried that the shift to private management placed control over instruction in the hands of outside white managers, overriding the authority of black elected officials.

Baltimore, Miami, and Hartford eventually decided not to renew their contracts with EAI. In each city, the introduction of private management proved to be a tumultuous affair that failed to produce a dramatic increase in student test scores.

The State of Pennsylvania in 2001 turned over 45 Philadelphia elementary and middle schools to three for-profit private firms that specialized in school operations. Edison Schools, the nation's largest private **education management organization** (EMO) at the time, was one of the private providers chosen by the State. The Philadelphia arrangement constituted the nation's most extensive experiment with the private management of public schools. Privatized management would allow the city's schools to draw on the expertise of managerial talent who did not reside in the city. The private management teams introduced a new curriculum. The schools were also received an infusion of additional resources.

But the results were disappointing. Even with the advantage of added state assistance, the private management of Philadelphia's schools did not lead to a statistically significant improvement in student math and reading scores.[44] In some cases, the gains in student achievement in the Edison schools lagged behind those seen in the city's regular public schools.[45] In 2008, Philadelphia, tired of continuing controversy and disappointed with the results, terminated its experiment with private-school management; the city did not renew its contracts with the EMOs.

Despite the mixed record of private-school management in Philadelphia and other cities, advocacy groups, including the Bill and Melinda Gates Foundation, have sought to give parents the ability to turn over the operations of a local school to an EMO. California is one of seven states where Parent Revolution and other Gates-inspired groups have gained the enactment of **parent trigger laws** under which the signatures of 51 percent of the parents in a failing public school can force the school district to hand over operations to a private management organization.[46] Such laws have effectively enabled the creation of *charter schools*, a popular school reform which is discussed in further detail in later sections.

THE LOGIC AND VARIETY OF PROGRAMS FOR SCHOOL CHOICE

A variety of **school choice programs** seek to give parents greater ability to decide just which school their child will attend, empowering them to find a school with a curriculum and approach that match their child's interests and needs. School choice programs seek to liberate parents and students from dependence on local public schools.

There are a variety of ways by which governments can seek to promote parental and student school choice. Three stand out: (1) *Vouchers* offer eligible families a certificate or scholarship that can be used to help a family pay for a child's education. (2) *Tax credits and other tax advantages* seek to subsidize the choice of private schooling by using the tax code to repay parents for some of the costs of private schooling. (3) A system of *charter schools* offers parents a greater choice of specialized schools organized within the public-school system.

The three approaches to school choice will be discussed below in further detail. All three share the same fundamental assumptions: that the public schools are essentially public-sector monopolies that are often wasteful, unaccountable, irresponsive to the concerns of parents and students, and, slow to change and adopt new technology and innovative pedagogical practices. The school choice movement seeks to shatter the public sector's near-monopoly hold over K–12 schooling. Choice advocates seek to create a market for education, where parents and guardians can choose a school that embodies the family's values. Choice advocates further seek to give parents a route to escape public schools where teacher tenure and teacher unions make it difficult to fire incompetent teachers.[47]

DOES SCHOOL CHOICE WORK? A LOOK AT THE EVIDENCE

The evidence on whether or not school choice improves education is not at all clear. School choice programs in certain communities produce positive results; choice programs in other communities do not. As the evidence is quite confusing, it is worth reviewing the overall findings in key areas before delving into the details regarding the degree of success of each school choice mechanism.

SCHOOL CHOICE AND TEST SCORES

School choice programs are not a "cure-all" for the ills of urban education. The great bulk of the studies indicate that school choice programs have only the most marginal impact on student performance. Although there are cases where choice schools have produced impressive results, overall, students who participate in school choice programs do not learn more as compared to similar students who continue to attend a city's regular public schools.

The disappointing results of early choice programs led the prestigious Carnegie Foundation to conclude that the movement for school choice was guided more by ideology than by evidence: "many of the claims for school choice have been based more on speculation than experience."[48] The Carnegie Foundation warned that school choice programs could exacerbate **urban dualism**, widening the class and racial gulfs that divide American society. Choice programs often enable more capable students and the children of more active parents to escape troubled schools. Lesser advantaged children risk being left behind in **dumping-ground schools** that have even less funding and fewer engaged students and parents than before.

The evidence provided by recent studies is more mixed, but overall the conclusions are the same. While there are some noteworthy school choice programs that do work, the overall gain in terms of the achievement scores of students in choice programs remains underwhelming.

The evidence is not unidirectional. Data from Milwaukee, for instance, indicates that voucher students enjoy higher graduation rates than do comparable students who attend a city's public schools.[49] School choice advocates further contend that standardized state test scores do not reveal everything of importance. The students and parents who take advantage of choice programs are often quite enthusiastic in their support of the programs. In Milwaukee, African-American parents expressed their profound gratitude for a program of school vouchers that enabled their children to escape problem-ridden schools. As the parent of a seventh-grade voucher student explained, "As soon as I came here it was a big change. Here teachers care about you. . . . [In public schools] the teachers were too busy to help."[50]

SCHOOL CHOICE AND RACIAL INTEGRATION

The evidence in one other part of the school choice controversy however does seem quite clear: School choice plans do *not* generally increase the racial integration of schools. In some instances, choice programs do enable minority students to attend church-related schools that are less racially stratified than the public schools the students left behind.[51] But such pro-integration student moves are exceptions to the general rule.

The Milwaukee and Cleveland voucher programs did not lead to new levels or racial integration; vouchers merely reinforced the segregation of the region's schools. Why was this so? Simply put, public schools in the suburbs do not participate in the program and do not admit voucher recipients.

In some metropolitan areas, school choice programs have even facilitated "white flight" from schools undergoing racial change. Yet, while choice programs do not generally increase racial integration, they do not lead to massive white flight and extensive school resegregation. High levels of school segregation continue to exist with and without school choice programs. In cases where the provision of choice is highly targeted, as is the case in Milwaukee and Cleveland where vouchers that are given only to students in failing inner-city schools, school choice programs do not further aggravate patterns of segregation that already mar public-school enrollments.

While the major school choice approaches have common philosophical underpinnings, the three major school choice programs are not equivalent. Each choice mechanism has its unique impacts, as we shall now discuss.

SCHOOL VOUCHERS

A system of **school vouchers** awards students (or, to be more precise, their parents or guardians) a certificate or scholarship to help pay tuition at a participating school of their choice. School vouchers have been offered in Milwaukee and Cleveland for a quarter of a century. A number of states offer scholarships that are variations of the voucher approach. The Trump administration proposed to shift federal school assistance to provide support for the expanded use of educational vouchers. Betsy DeVos, Trump's Secretary of Education, came to her position with a record of vocal advocacy of vouchers and other school choice programs.

Yet vouchers do not automatically provide a student the ability to enroll in a school of his or her choice. The **monetary size of the voucher** determines just how much choice parents and students truly possess. A large monetary voucher enables a child to pay tuition at a wide range of private schools. But as choice advocates often look to vouchers as a way to contain government spending, school vouchers are seldom so generous.

States typically offer vouchers and scholarships that are only about half the cost of a private education. North Carolina's "opportunity scholarship" provides a student with a maximum of $4,200 per year, an amount that does not come close to paying the tuition and fees at a high-end private academy. Families that lack the funds to supplement the vouchers do not possess a great range of choice but have only more limited options. Over 90 percent of the voucher children in North Carolina enroll in Christian academies and other low-tuition religious schools.[52]

A **voucher program's accompanying regulations** also help to determine how much choice a student actually possesses. In the absence regulations barring such actions, a private school may discriminate against voucher applicants with learning disabilities and students who are more difficult and costly to teach.[53] A school with total freedom to set its admissions criteria may also engage in an admissions process characterized by **creaming** (or **cream-skimming**), admitting only the most capable voucher applicants (the "cream of the crop"), denying entry to less outstanding and more troubled students.

Eligibility provisions also determine just who is and is not empowered by a voucher or scholarship program. As we have already observed, Cleveland and Milwaukee utilized **targeted voucher programs** where assistance was dispensed to low-income children seeking to escape failing schools. In contrast, more **universal voucher plans** offer assistance to a broader range of working- and middle-class families. A universal voucher plan would have vastly different impacts than the Cleveland and Milwaukee programs that targeted aid to the poor. More universal voucher programs could even facilitate white flight from racially-mixed city schools.[54]

The universal approach to vouchers is illustrated by Indiana, which issues a larger number of school vouchers (or "scholarships," as they are called in Indiana) than any other state in the nation. In 2013, under then-governor Mike Pence, Indiana broadened eligibility for school vouchers, increasing the percentage of white, suburban, and middle-class students who received voucher assistance. The program even gave tuition assistance to students who are already attending private and parochial students. Such widespread issuance of vouchers has quite different effects as compared to a targeted program that focuses its assistance in helping lower-income students trapped in schools that fail to meet their needs.[55]

In Georgia, the award of scholarships has done relatively little to aid students with the greatest need. Instead, Georgia's scholarship program channels financial assistance primarily to parents whose children are already attending private academies and to families who seek schools that provide a strong values and religious education.[56]

DO SCHOOL VOUCHERS IMPROVE EDUCATION? WHAT THE EVIDENCE INDICATES

A wave of current analytical studies underscores the inability of vouchers to produce consistent and positive education results. In Indiana, Ohio, Louisiana, and the District of Columbia, voucher and choice scholarship recipients did not outperform comparable students who remained in the public schools. In some cases, the performance of voucher recipients even lagged behind those of comparable public-school students.[57] A study by the Stanford University School of Education and the Economic Policy Research Institute reviewed the research on voucher programs over a 25-year period and concluded that there is, at best, only very weak evidence that vouchers produce strong gains in student learning.[58]

Extensive data analysis from Milwaukee further underscores the rather mild and largely disappointing educational impacts of school vouchers. Students who used voucher assistance to attend parochial and private schools showed only minimal and inconsistent gains on standardized tests; voucher students generally did not outperform comparable students in the city's public schools. A fairly large number of students chose not to reenroll in the city's voucher program, indicating some disenchantment with a program that failed to produce dramatic educational improvements.[59]

In one important area, school vouchers did have a mild, but important, positive impact. Voucher recipients were more likely to continue on to college, a result that is likely explained by the emphasis that many charter schools place on communicating to their students that college can be part of their career path. But the gains achieved in college enrollment rates were rather small. Tracking their performance throughout college further revealed that voucher students did not enjoy higher graduation rates from college: Voucher students did not outperform matched public-school students when it came to completing a college degree.[60]

A leading Stanford University researcher summarized the evidence on school choice from Milwaukee as disappointing. In Milwaukee, only a quarter of the students attend traditional public schools: "If choice were the answer, Milwaukee would be one of the highest-scoring cities in the country."[61] It was not.

Despite the lack of evidence that vouchers increase student learning, Wisconsin Governor Scott Walker and a Republican-dominated state legislature in 2011 expanded the state's voucher program. School vouchers were no longer limited to Milwaukee but would also be offered in nearby Racine. The new law also relaxed eligibility provisions, making a number of middle-class families eligible for assistance. A Milwaukee family of four with an income of $71,000 could qualify for school vouchers.[62] The changes in state law led to a surge in voucher-supported enrollments at parochial and private schools in greater Milwaukee.

DO SCHOOL VOUCHERS VIOLATE THE SEPARATION OF CHURCH AND STATE? WHAT THE SUPREME COURT RULED

In Cleveland and Milwaukee, large numbers of students use government-funded vouchers to enroll in **parochial schools**, that is, Catholic-run schools in the inner city that teach religion during parts of the school day. In the South, vouchers have supported increased enrollments at Baptist schools and Christian academies. The state's provision of vouchers have helped to keep a number of church-affiliated schools from closing. In Fort Wayne, Indiana, $1.1 million in state voucher assistance wound up going to a single school, St. Jude Catholic School. State-subsidized tuition payments provided the school a means to escape its fiscal travails.[63]

Critics argue that voucher spending so heavily subsidizes religious-oriented schools that it violates the constitutional requirement for the separation of church and state. That argument, however, was rejected by a sharply divided U.S. Supreme Court in

Zelman v. Simmons-Harris (2002).[64] The Court ruled that the Cleveland voucher program's inclusion of parochial schools is constitutionally permissible, that the voucher program does *not* violate the Constitution's First Amendment prohibition against the state establishment of religion. Even though a large number of voucher families enroll their children in religious-based schools, the Court did not view the program as one of state support of religious instruction. Instead, the Court viewed the Cleveland voucher program as "neutral" in terms of its respect toward religion. As a majority of justices on the Court reasoned, vouchers do not provide state aid directly to church schools; instead, parents and guardians freely choose the schools their children would attend. The voucher program has a clearly permissible non-religious or **secular purpose**—to provide opportunities for children to escape failing public schools. The program was not enacted with the stated intent of advancing religious instruction.

TAX DEDUCTIONS AND TAX CREDITS FOR SCHOOL CHOICE

About fourth of the states offer **tax deductions and tax credits** to spur school choice. The tax incentives vary from state to state, but tend to take one of two forms: (1) Eligible families who send their children to private schools may receive tax deductions or credits that lower their tax bill. In effect, the government uses the tax system to help reimburse families for the costs of private schooling. (2) Alternatively, a state may offer tax incentives that encourage potential donors to help fund scholarships that students can use to attend a private schools.

Florida's system of tax incentives helps to generate approximately 100,000 private scholarships a year that lower-income students use at private and religious-based schools.[65] The Florida Tax Credit Scholarship Program, the largest such program in the nation, is fairly well targeted, as scholarships are offered only to lower-income families. The scholarships also appear to have a positive impact on putting an increased number of students on a path to enter—if not always to complete—college.[66]

But not all state tax incentives are highly targeted to assist low-income students. Where the eligibility for scholarships is quite loose, tax-supported programs scholarship program can suffer a pernicious **class bias**, as the programs wind up subsidizing the school decisions of middle- and upper-class families while providing only the most minimal assistance to the poor. The offer of a tax credit does little to aid low-income families who owe little in the way of taxes or who lack the savings to pay up front for private-school tuition.

The State of Georgia has a very controversial system that offers a dollar-for-dollar tax credit for every contribution that is made to a scholarship fund. Georgians can reduce their state income tax by one dollar for each dollar they give to a private-school scholarship fund—up to a maximum of $2,500 for a couple filing jointly, and up to $10,000 for a business owner. In essence, the dollar-for-dollar tax credit makes a contribution to a private-school scholarship cost-free to the donor. The state loses revenues that it would have otherwise collected and could have used to support public education. Alabama, Arizona, Florida, Montana, Nevada, and South Carolina are other states that, through the offer of tax advantages, similarly allow taxpayers to redirect a portion of their taxes to support private schools.

In Georgia, state-supported private-school scholarships are not targeted to assist poor children seeking to leave underperforming public schools. Instead, contributors channel the bulk of the funds into school-designated scholarships that can even help pay for scholarships that are awarded to the children of the families that helped raise the money. Georgia tax-supported scholarships also serve to promote enrollments in religious-based schools, including schools with policies that require the expulsion of gay and lesbian students. Georgia's tax-supported scholarships can even be spent at schools that refuse to admit children with learning disabilities.[67]

CHARTER SCHOOLS: A MIDDLE WAY?

One particular choice program is especially popular and has spread across the United States. A **charter school** is authorized (that is, "chartered") and funded by the state but is operated by an independent group. Compared to regular public schools, the state allows the management team that runs a charter school greater flexibility in the choice of curriculum, disciplinary and attendance policies, requirements for parental participation, and other matters pertaining to school philosophy and operation. A charter school may have a unique specialization—with special attention devoted to sciences and technology, the arts, military-style discipline, or an ethnic group's heritage and history

Charter schools are popular (see Figure 9.1) because of their smaller-size classes, their emphasis on academics, and innovative teaching approaches. Some charter academies

Figure 9.1 **Charter Schools Receive Political Support From Prominent Figures in Both the Democratic and Republican Parties.**

(On left): President Barack Obama and First Lady Michelle Obama pose with students at a charter school in Washington, DC.
(On right): First Lady Melania Trump visits Excel Academy, an all-girls charter school in the low-income Anacostia section of Washington, DC. However, not all charter schools perform well. Just a year after Melania Trump's visit, the Washington, DC, school board voted unanimously to close Excel Academy as a result of the negative trend in the performance scores of its students.

Source: Obama photo by Joyce N. Boghosian, February 3, 2009, from Wikimedia Commons, http://commons. wikimedia.org/wiki/File: Barack_%26_Michelle_Obama_at_Washington_DC_public_charter_school_2-3-09_1.jpg. Melania Trump photo from The White House via Flickr and Wikimedia Commons, April 17, 2017, and https://commons. wikimedia.org/wiki/File: Melania_Trump_visits_Excel_Academy_Public_Charter_School,_April_2017.jpg.

have "no excuses" policies when it comes to student behavior and expectations of parental engagement. Charter schools make a concerted effort to involve parents, grandparents, and guardians in the educational process. Charter schools also typically emphasize the use of computers and technology-assisted instruction.

The growth of charter schools has been explosive. In 1995 only 250 charter schools existed in the United States. By 2016, the number mushroomed to more than 6,900 charter schools in more than 40 states that enrolled over 3 million children. The largest number of charter schools are found in California (1,253), Texas (761), Florida (656), Arizona (547), Ohio (362), Michigan (301), New York (267), Colorado (238), Wisconsin (234), Pennsylvania (183), North Carolina (168), Minnesota (167), and Louisiana (146).[68] As part of its post-Hurricane revival efforts, New Orleans became an all-charter-school system; nearly every public school in the city is a charter school.

Charter schools are *not* private schools. Charter schools are still public schools largely funded by public taxes. Consequently, while charter academies are accorded new flexibility, they do not possess the full range of freedoms enjoyed by private schools and academies that receive assistance provided through the attendance of voucher students. State rules may limit the ability of charter school operators to abridge teacher tenure and dismiss teachers who are unwilling to commit fully to a charter school's mission. Each charter academy also operates under the general supervision of a state-designated body, typically a state university, community college, or even the local public-school district.

As a public school, a charter school (quite unlike a private school) cannot charge tuition. Each charter school receives state aid according to a formula, with the total aid provided largely based on the number of pupils enrolled. States and private foundations award grants to assist the start-up and operation of charter schools. As a public school, a charter school is also nonsectarian (that is, nonreligious).

Many parents and educators view charter schools as a middle ground between voucher schools and traditional public education. The creation of charter schools is a less revolutionary and more pragmatic "choice" program than the extension of vouchers. Each state also tends to "cap" or limit the number of new schools that can be chartered each year, thereby limiting the threat that charter schools pose to more conventional public schools.

The funding losses that traditional public schools suffer as the result of competition from charter schools can be quite substantial. In a single school year, the Albany (New York) city school district lost between $23 million and $26 million, and Buffalo's traditional schools lost between $57 million and $77 million, as a result of a shift in enrollment to charter schools. How does such diminished funding affect classroom performance? Albany wound up with about $1,000 less per pupil to spend, even after adjusting for a reduced school enrollment.[69] In Durham, North Carolina, competition from charter academies meant a net annual loss of more than $500 for each pupil who remained in traditional public schools.[70] In Chicago, in just a single year (2013), the city shuttered 49 public schools, closings that were concentrated in African-American areas of the city where the opening of a charter academy undermined the stability of neighborhood public schools.[71]

Public-school teachers recognize the financial threat that charter schools pose to a city's regular public schools. Nonetheless, teacher unions have come to recognize that a reform initiative as popular as charter schools cannot be stopped. Teachers view charter schools as less threatening than a system of school vouchers or K–12 tax credits.[72]

In New York, Mayor Bill de Blasio promised to rein in charter schools that had a "destructive impact" on regular schools. De Blasio proposed charging rents to the charter academies for the space they occupied in regular city schools. But de Blasio's efforts were blunted by New York Governor Andrew Cuomo who declared that he would "save" charter schools.[73]

Despite their dynamic growth, charter schools must be kept in perspective: Charter schools educate only about 6 percent of all students in America's public schools. True school reform will have to maintain a focus on improving conditions and outcomes in regular public schools, the schools that provide most children their education.

CHARTER SCHOOLS AND QUESTIONS OF RACE

Do charter schools serve poor and minority children? Do charter schools offer the prospect of voluntary school integration? Or do charter academies provide yet one more route for "white flight" that will hasten the resegregation of school systems?

The answer to these questions is rather complex, especially as charter schools vary greatly from one to another. Also, when it comes to race, charter schools in big cities tend to have different impacts than do charter schools in less populous areas.[74]

Two overall answers emerge. First, charter schools do admit and serve minority children. Second, charter schools do not provide a viable path toward school integration.

National data clearly reveals that urban charter schools enroll and serve low-income and racial minority children. Compared to regular public schools, urban charter schools have a higher percentage of African-American students—although the charter academies do not always enroll the most disadvantaged black students in the region.[75] Urban charter academies offer minority and low-income students the opportunity to pursue college-prep programs and specialized instruction in data technology and the industrial and the creative arts.

In a number of communities, however, charter schools bow to political pressure and are not models of inclusion. In North Carolina newer charter academies enrolled very few minorities. Instead, charter schools in North Carolina largely served more advantaged white students, children whose parents had gone to college.[76]

The impact of charter schools on racial segregation and isolation is even more nettling. In a number of states, student (and parent) decisions to attend charter academies have reinforced patterns of racial segregation. In Pennsylvania, white students chose to enroll in urban charter schools with a student population that was whiter than the public school they left. African-American and Latino students wound up attending urban charter schools with large and isolated minority student bodies.[77] In Minnesota's Twin Cities, 70 percent of students of color who attended charter schools were in "completely segregated environments."[78] In 2014–2015, more than 1,000 charter schools across the nation were all-white, that is, the schools had student bodies that were over 99 percent minority.[79] New York City has a number of single-race charter schools.[80] Charter schools tend to exhibit higher levels of racial imbalance than do conventional public schools.[81]

The advocates of charter schools respond that the charter schools do not add greatly to segregation as much as they reproduce racial patterns that already exist in big cities and their public schools.[82] Both conventional public schools and charter schools are not well integrated.

Particularly troubling are the cases where the creation of charter academies serves to facilitate white flight, exacerbating levels of school segregation. In Michigan, charter schools in Pontiac and the inner-ring suburb of Ferndale (located just outside Detroit) allowed white parents a non-tuition escape from school districts that were implementing court-ordered school desegregation plans.[83] In New Castle County (Wilmington), Delaware, the establishment of charter academies diminished the levels of racial balance achieved by earlier school integration efforts.[84] In Charlotte-Mecklenburg, North Carolina, charter schools were "drivers" of resegregation, pulling white, Asian, and middle-class students out of traditional public schools.[85] In Holland, a small city in western Michigan, the city's public schools served a population that became increasingly poor and more Hispanic, as white students chose to leave the city's traditional public schools to enroll in charter academies located outside the city's borders.[86]

THE IMPACT OF CHARTER SCHOOLS ON STUDENTS: DO CHARTER SCHOOLS IMPROVE STUDENT LEARNING?

It is difficult to assess the educational impact of charter schools, as there exists a variety of charter schools, each with its own educational philosophy and student selection and disciplinary policies. KIPP (Knowledge Is Power Program) academies, for instance, usually require a longer school day and emphasize a college preparatory pedagogy coupled with a "no excuses" policy that enforces clear standards of behavior and student responsibility. The KIPP academies have generally demonstrated a record of success.[87]

Charter schools are especially likely to achieve educational gains when the school sets a longer day of instruction and a longer school year, insists on classroom discipline, requires parental involvement in their child's education, and utilizes student assessment data to create individualized student learning plans. Tracking students over the long term indicates that "no excuses" charter schools have a positive impact, increasing the number of students who attend college and increasing a participant's annual earnings.[88]

But critics observe that no-excuses charter schools achieve such gains by relying on policies that disproportionately suspend black students and students with disabilities, including students who exhibit hyperactivity associated with attention deficit disorders. A study of the disciplinary records of more than 5,250 charters schools reveals that charter schools have suspended over a quarter of their student body one time or more. Students with educational disabilities were especially likely to suffer suspension. An amazing 235 of charter schools had suspended over half of their students with disabilities.[89]

Some urban charter schools require the completion of long and detailed applications, discouraging all but the most motivated parents to apply. In admissions and disciplinary consultations, charter academy officials can give the parents of a hyper-active or difficult child not-so-subtle cues that it would be in the best interests of the child to enroll elsewhere rather than risk carrying an expulsion on the student's official school record.[90]

Other charter schools that operate according to a different philosophy fail to exhibit student growth similar to that reported by the no-excuses charters. Numerous assessments of reading and math scores have been disappointing, with students in charter schools at times even failing to exhibit the gains made by comparable students who attend conventional public schools. An important RAND Corporation analysis of charter schools in eight states found little positive impact on student performance, with a mild improvement in graduation rates as the most noteworthy exception.[91]

A 2009 Stanford University Center for Research on Educational Outcomes (CREDO) study of charter schools presented similarly disappointing results. CREDO discovered that about a fifth of charter schools performed well. The plurality of charter schools, however, appeared to have no impact on student learning. In a third of the charter schools observed, student performance even trailed behind that of students who remained in traditional public schools.[92]

More recent studies by CREDO, however, have reported more positive findings. A 2013 CREDO report observed that charter schools continued to make strides each year, with student gains in math and reading scores being the equivalent of having received eight extra days of classroom instruction. African-American children and low-income students were especially likely to benefit from attendance at a charter school.[93] Two years later, CREDO was even more effusive in its praise for charters schools: "Our findings show urban charter schools in the aggregate provide significantly higher levels of annual growth in both math and reading compared to their TPS [traditional public-school] peers." Black, Hispanic, low-income, and special education students all enjoyed gains in their math and reading scores. Still, the gains made by charter schools were rather small. Disappointingly, in a number of urban regions—including Las Vegas, Fort Worth, Las Vegas, Memphis, Mesa, Phoenix, St. Petersburg, San Antonio, and West Palm Beach—the performance of charter school students lagged behind that of their public-school peers.[94]

Parents generally report that they are quite satisfied with charter schools. In Milwaukee, parents expressed their fondness for charter academies that gave specialized attention to at-risk students.[95] But parental satisfaction diminished over time in cases where a charter school failed to produce a dramatic turnaround in a student's performance.[96]

Charter school advocates often cite results from New Orleans where a citywide switch to charter schools appears to have increased student standardized test scores, high school graduation rates, and college entry and graduation rates.[97] Critics, however, observe that the actual gains are rather small and that the city's schools continue to receive unsatisfactory ratings from the state. Critics further question whether the operation of charter schools should even be credited with achieving the apparent gains. New Orleans's switch to charter schools was accompanied by a substantial increase in the levels of funding for the city's schools, an increase of $1,400 per pupil per school year. In New Orleans, as in other school districts, money counts. The rise in scores and graduation rates may simply be the outcome of increased spending, rather than clear evidence of the superiority of charter schools. The loss of the city's public housing stock as a result of Hurricane Katrina flooding may also have something to do with the increases in test scores; with fewer students living in concentrated poverty, average test scores and graduation rates in the city were bound to rise.[98]

THE NATIONALIZATION OF SCHOOL POLITICS: THE BATTLE OVER CHARTER SCHOOLS

Traditionally, schooling in the United States has been viewed as the most "local" of local politics, where decisions are best made by the members of a local community. Today, however, school board elections are no longer purely a local affair. Instead, outside interests and big-money lobbying groups—ideological groups committed to school choice, nonprofit educational reform organizations, teacher unions, and even wealthy philanthropists—pay for extensive political advertising when a particular ballot initiative or an important local school board election revolves around questions of school choice.[99]

Los Angeles, New Orleans, Denver, Atlanta, and Bridgeport are among the cities where wealthy national donors have become embroiled in local school campaigns. The Los Angeles case is especially instructive. In Los Angeles in 2017, charter school supporters and teacher unions and their allies spend nearly $15 billion in what at the time was the most expensive school board election in American history. Charter school advocates outspent their opponents ($10 million to $5 million) to win control of the city's seven-member board of education and oust the union-backed board president. Pro-charter group forces spent an estimated $144 for each vote cast for one of its candidates![100]

CONCLUSION: IMPROVING PUBLIC SCHOOLS AND PUBLIC SERVICES

Performance measurement, coproduction, business improvement districts, neighborhood-based delivery systems, contracting out, vouchers, tax credits, and school choice are all strategies that seek to improve municipal service provision or, failing that, allow citizens to make an "end run" around irresponsive and ineffective local bureaucracies. The anti-bureaucracy reformers hope that the borrowing of private-sector managerial techniques and the introduction of competition will improve service delivery while also allowing for new cost efficiencies. Too often, however, the emphasis on cost reduction overshadows concerns for the effective and equitable provision of municipal services.

In the field of education, reform is clearly necessary. Yet, the advocates of markets and choice have clearly oversold what privatization can accomplish. The more extensive school restructuring efforts have often been driven by ideological groups hostile to public-sector unions and what they see as the public-sector monopoly in education.

The utilization of vouchers is not restricted solely to policy area of education. **Housing choice vouchers (HCV)** are now the backbone of federal housing assistance, having superseded the older national strategy of having the government construct and operate public housing. Housing vouchers are meant to enable low-income families to flee dilapidated dwellings and find better housing in better neighborhoods. The recipients of choice vouchers do not have to reside in public housing but can choose more satisfactory housing units in the private rental market.

But in cities with "tight" housing markets with few vacant units, vouchers are seldom large enough to allow tenants to find suitable housing in nondistressed neighborhoods.[101] In Broward County (greater Fort Lauderdale), Florida, the offer of housing vouchers did not lead tenants to pick up and move to lower-poverty and more racially integrated neighborhoods. Instead, Broward's HCV recipients, an overwhelmingly black population, wound up clustered in the impoverished "low opportunity" neighborhoods in the central core of the county.[102] Vouchers did not produce the positive outcomes that choice enthusiasts had promised.

In the modern city, the effective, efficient, and equitable provision of service also has a metropolitan dimension. As the next chapter describes, improving public services often requires local officials to work across political border lines in joint actions with neighboring communities.

KEY TERMS

administrative discretion as a source of bureaucratic power (*p. 311*)

anti-union, municipal contracting as (*p. 326*)

balanced scorecard, performance measurement's use of a (*p. 316*)

bid-rigging (*p. 326*)

broken windows policing (*p. 318*)

business improvement district (BID) (*p. 319*)

charter school (*p. 334*)

CitiStat (*p. 317*)

class bias of tax deductions and tax credits for school choice (*p. 333*)

community BID (*p. 322*)

comparative performance measurement (*p. 312*)

competition as a key to the success of municipal service contracting (*p. 324*)

CompStat (*p. 317*)

coproduction (*p. 318*)

corporate BIDs (*p. 320*)

creaming (also called cream-skimming) (*p. 331*)

district management association, a BID's (*p. 319*)

dumping-ground schools, the charge that school choice programs will result in (*p. 329*)

education management organizations (EMOs) (*p. 328*)

efficiency measures (*p. 315*)

equity measures (*p. 315*)

expertise (*p. 310*)

focus groups (*p. 316*)

hidden costs of a service contract (*p. 326*)

housing choice vouchers (HCV) (*p. 339*)

input measures (*p. 315*)

lowball contract bid (*p. 326*)

Main Street BID (*p. 320*)

managed competition (*p. 324*)

market mechanisms, privatization's reliance on (*p. 324*)

monetary size of the voucher, the critical importance of the (*p. 330*)

multiple indicators, performance measurement's use of (*p. 316*)

NOTES

1. Sandra J. Clark, Martha R. Burt, Margaret M. Schulte, and Karen Maguire, *Coordinated Community Responses to Domestic Violence in Six Communities: Beyond the Justice System* (Washington, DC: Urban Institute, October 1996), www.urban.org/publications/406727.html; American Civil Liberties Union, *Responses from the Field: Sexual Assault, Domestic Violence, and Policing* (New York: ACLU, 2015), www.aclu.org/sites/default/files/field_document/2015.10.20_report_-_responses_from_the_field.pdf.

2. Madiba Dennie, "Black and Blue: The Inadequacy of Police Responses to Domestic Violence in the African-American Community," *USA Today*, July 12, 2016.

3. The classic work on this subject is Michael Lipsky, *Street-Level Bureaucracy: Dilemmas of the Individual in Public Services*, 30th anniv. ed. (New York: Russell Sage Foundation, 2010).

4. Marcus Bright, "The Plight of Eric Garner and Undocumented Immigrants Highlight the Impact of Street-Level Bureaucrats," *The Blog, Web Posting, HuffPost*, October 6, 2014, www.huffingtonpost.com/marcus-bright/the-plight-of-eric-garner_b_5651290.html.

5. Tony Evans, "Professionals and Discretion in Street-Level Bureaucracy," in *Understanding Street-Level Bureaucracy*, ed. Peter Hupe, Michael Hill, and Aurélien Buffat (Chicago: University of Chicago Press, 2016), 279–295.

6. David N. Ammons, "Signs of Performance Measurement Progress among Prominent City Governments," *Public Performance and Management Review* 36, no. 4 (June 2013): 507–528; Ammons, *Municipal Benchmarks: Assessing Local Performance and Establishing Community Standards*, 3rd ed. (New York: Routledge, 2015); Theodore H. Poister, Maria P. Aristigueta, and Jeremy L. Hall, *Managing and Measuring Performance in Public and Nonprofit Organizations: An Integrated Approach* (San Francisco: Jossey-Bass, 2015).

7. Beryl A. Radin, *Challenging the Performance Movement* (Washington, DC: Georgetown University Press, 2006), 100–102. Charlotte, North Carolina, is another community that gained national renown for use of a balanced scorecard approach.

8. Kathryn E. Newcomer and Timothy Triplett, "Using Surveys," in *Handbook of Practical Program Evaluation*, 4th ed., ed. Kathryn E. Newcomer, Harry Hatry, and Joseph Wholey (Hoboken, NJ: Jossey-Bass, 2015), 344–382.

9. Richard A. Krueger and Mary Anne Casey, "Focus Group Interviewing," in *Handbook of Practical Program Evaluation*, 4th ed., ed. Kathryn E. Newcomer, Harry, Hatry, and Joseph Wholey (Hobo-

ken, NJ: Jossey-Bass, 2015), 506–534; Richard A. Krueger and Mary Anne Casey, *Focus Groups: A Practical Guide for Applied Research*, 5th ed. (Thousand Oaks, CA: Sage Publications, 2014).

10. Barbara J. Cohn Berman and Verner Vasquez, "Using Ratings by Trained Observers," in *Handbook of Practical Program Evaluation*, 4th ed., ed. Kathryn E. Newcomer, Harry Hatry, and Joseph Wholey (Hoboken, NJ: Jossey-Bass, 2015), 412–443.

11. The Fund for the City of New York, Center on Municipal Government Performance, *How Smooth Are New York City's Streets?*, 2008, http://venus.fcny.org/cmgp/streets/pages/indexb.htm.

12. Robert D. Behn, *The PerformanceStat Potential: A Leadership Strategy for Producing Results* (Cambridge, MA: The Ash Center for Democratic Governance and Innovation, Harvard University and Washington, DC: The Brookings Institution, 2014).

13. James David Dickson, "Detroit: 21 Fires Fought on Halloween Eve," *Detroit News*, October 31, 2017.

14. Kim Graziani, director of neighborhood initiatives, City of Pittsburgh and Daniel Kildee, former treasurer of Genesee County (Flint), Michigan, remarks delivered at the Conference on Reclaiming Vacant Properties, Cleveland, Ohio, October 14, 2010.

15. Kelechi Uzochukwu and John Clayton Thomas, "Who Engages in the Coproduction of Local Public Services and Why? The Case of Atlanta, Georgia," *Public Administration Review*, forthcoming, online advance publication, December 2017, https://doi-org.ezproxy.libraries.wright.edu/10.1111/puar.12893.

16. Maria Dickerson, "Improvement Districts Spur Revival: And Division," *Los Angeles Times*, January 20, 1999.

17. Winnie Hu, "Property Owners Spend on Quality of Life (But Is That Fair?)," *New York Times*, March 13, 2017.

18. Tina Carey, "Dissolution of the Hyannis Main Street Improvement District (Commonly Called the BID)," *RidtheBid.org*, March 7, 2013, http://ridthebid.org/?q=node/1.

19. Göktuğ Morçöl and James F. Wolf, "Understanding Business Improvement Districts: A New Governance Framework," *Public Administration Review* 70, no. 6 (November/December 2012): 906–913.

20. Department of Small Business Services, The City of New York, "Business Improvement Districts," *Web Posting*, www1.nyc.gov/site/sbs/neighborhoods/bids.page, downloaded May 2, 2018.

21. Los Angeles City Clerk, "A Quick Guide to Business Improvement Districts: BIDs 101," http://clerk.lacity.org/sites/g/files/wph606/f/LACITYP_025722.pdf, downloaded May 2, 2018.

22. Carol J. Becker, "Democratic Accountability and Business Improvement Districts," *Public Performance and Management Review* 36, no. 2 (December 2012): 187–202.

23. Abraham Unger, *Business Improvement Districts in the United States: Private Government and Public Consequences* (New York: Palgrave Macmillan, 2016).

24. Jill Simone Gross, "Business Improvement Districts in New York City's Low-Income and High-Income Neighborhoods," *Economic Development Quarterly* 19, no. 2 (2005): 174–189. The typology of BIDs presented here relies on the work of Jill Gross.

25. Grand Central Partnership, *Annual Report 2016* (New York: GCP, 2016), www.grandcentralpartnership.nyc/wp-content/uploads/2010/07/GCP_AR16_final4web.pdf.

26. Center City District, Philadelphia, "State of Center City: 2018 Report," https://centercityphila.org/research-reports/state-of-center-city-2018#center-city-district.

27. Jill Simone Gross, "Business Improvement Districts in New York: The Private Sector in Public Service or the Public Sector Privatized?," *Journal of Urban Research Practice* 6, no. 3 (2013): 346–364.

28. Critics charge that the Central Park Conservancy's reliance on private fundraising activities has "commodified" a precious public resource and the park no longer serves as a peaceful green haven. See Oliver D. Cooke, *Rethinking Municipal Privatization* (New York: Routledge, 2008), chap. 4.

29. Carl F. Valente and Lydia D. Manchester, *Rethinking Local Services: Examining Alternative Delivery Approaches* (Washington, DC: International City Management Association, 1984), xi.

30. E.S. Savas, *Privatization in the City: Success, Failures, Lessons* (Washington, DC: CQ Press, 2005), esp. chap. 6.

31. Stephen Goldsmith, *The Twenty-First Century City: Resurrecting Urban America* (Lanham, MD: Rowman and Littlefield, 1999), esp. 18–19.

32. Kimberly L. Nelson, "Managed Competition," in *Alternate Service Delivery: Readiness Check*, ed. Kurt Thurmaier (Washington, DC: ICMA Press, 2014), Chap. 3; Goldsmith, *The Twenty-First Century City*, 96–99.

33. Office of the Auditor, City of Denver, *Privatization Practices: Performance Audit*, June 2015, www.denvergov.org/content/dam/denvergov/Portals/741/documents/Audits_2015/Privatization_Practices_Audit_Report_6-18-2015.pdf.

34. Kelly LeRoux, *Service Contracting: A Local Government Guide* (Washington, DC: ICMA Press, 2007), details the various tasks and costs that a government still incurs even when it contracts out a service.

35. James B. Jacobs, Coleen Friel, and Robert Radick, *Gotham Unbound: How New York City Was Liberated from the Grip of Organized Crime* (New York: New York University Press, 1999), 91.

36. Mark Langlois, "State Collects $600,000 in Galante Trash Suit," *Danbury Patch*, April 15, 2011.

37. Aaron M. Renn, "The Lessons of Long-Term Privatizations: Why Chicago Got It Wrong and Indiana Got It Right," The Manhattan Institute, Report #17 July 2016, www.manhattan-institute.org/sites/default/files/R-AR-0716.pdf.

38. Dan Mihalopoulos and Chris Fusco, "Chicago Parking Meter Company Wants More Money: Mayor Balks," *Chicago Sun-Times*, May 4, 2012.

39. Molly Ball, "The Privatization Backlash," *The Atlantic*, April 23, 2014, www.theatlantic.com/politics/archive/2014/04/city-state-governments-privatization-contracting-backlash/361016/.

40. Danielle Ivory, Ben Protess, and Griff Palmer, "In American Towns, Private Profits from Public Works," *New York Times*, December 24, 2016.

41. In the Public Interest, *How Privatization Increases Inequality* (Washington, DC, September 2016), 15–18, www.inthepublicinterest.org/wp-content/uploads/InthePublicInterest_InequalityReport_Sept2016.pdf.

42. *Public-Private Partnerships for Green Space in NYC*, section on "Cracks in the Model," a case study of the School of International and Public Affairs, 2014, Columbia University, New York, http://ccnmtl.columbia.edu/projects/caseconsortium/casestudies/128/casestudy/www/layout/case_id_128_id_904.html.

43. Lisa W. Foderaro, "New York Parks in Less Affluent Areas Lack Big Gifts," *New York Times*, February 17, 2013; Jacob Hodes, "Law to Expose City Parks' Inequalities Is Neglected," *New York Times*, August 26, 2012; Joshua K. Leon, "Who Really Benefits from Central Park?" *Metropolis Magazine*, December 6, 2013, www.metropolismag.com/cities/landscape/who-really-benefits-from-central-park/.

44. Brian Gill, Ron Zimmer, Jolley Christman, and Suzanne Blanc, *School Restructuring, Private Management, and Student Achievement in Philadelphia* (Santa Monica, CA: RAND Corporation, 2007), www.rand.org/pubs/monographs/MG533.html. Despite the RAND study's conclusion, the advocates of private management argue that the evidence on achievement scores, while mixed, is on the whole still supportive of private management of troubled public schools. See Paul E. Peterson and Matthew M. Chingos, "For-Profit and Nonprofit: Management in Philadelphia Schools," *Education Next* (Spring 2009): 64–70, http://educationnext.org/for-profitand-nonprofit-management-in-philadelphia-schools/educationnext.org/files/ednext_20092_64.pdf.

45. Vaughan Byrnes, "Getting a Feel for the Market: The Use of Privatized School Management in Philadelphia," *American Journal of Education* 115 (May 2009): 437–455. Also see Brian Gill, Laura S. Hamilton, and Ron Zimmer, "Perspectives on Education Management Organizations," in *Handbook of Research on School Choice*, ed. Mark Berends, Matthew G. Springer, Dale Ballou, and Herbert J. Walberg (New York: Routledge, 2009), 555–568.

46. Philip E. Kovacs, ed., *The Gates Foundation and the Future of U.S. "Public" Schools* (New York: Routledge, 2011); Diane Ravitch, "Another Battle in the War against Public Schools," *New York Times*, March 20, 2012, www.nytimes.com/roomfordebate/2012/03/18/hopes-and-feard-for-parent-

trigger-laws/another-battle-in-the-war-against-public-schools; Center for Education Organizing, *Parent Trigger: No Silver Bullet* (Providence, RI: Annenberg Institute for School Reform at Brown University, 2012).

47. Terry M. Moe, *Special Interest: Teachers Unions and America's Public Schools* (Washington, DC: Brookings Institution Press, 2011); Terry M. Moe, "Teachers Unions in the United States: The Politics of Blocking," in *The Comparative Politics of Education: Teachers Unions and Education Systems around the World*, ed. Terry Moe and Susanne Wiborg (Cambridge, UK: Cambridge University Press, 2017), 24–55.

48. Ernest L. Boyer, "Foreword," in *The Carnegie Foundation for the Advancement of Teaching, School Choice: A Special Report* (Princeton, NJ: Carnegie Foundation, 1992), xv. A dozen years later, Diane Ravitch, *Reign of Error: The Hoax of the Privatization Movement and the Danger to America's Public Schools* (New York: Alfred A., 2013), 206–213, would likewise point to the triumph of ideology over evidence as she attempted to explain why Republican governors continued to push for extensive voucher programs despite the evidence of the paucity of positive educational impacts of school vouchers.

49. Paul J. Wolf, John J. Witte, and Brian Kisida, "Do Voucher Students Attain Higher Levels of Education? Extended Evidence from the Milwaukee Parental Choice Program," a report of The Urban Institute, Washington, DC, February 2018, www.urban.org/sites/default/files/publication/96721/do_voucher_students_attain_higher_levels_of_education_0.pdf.

50. Paul Peterson, "School Choice: A Report Card," *Virginia Journal of Social Policy and the Law* 6, no. 1 (1998): 47–80. Also see John F. Witte, *The Market Approach to Education: An Analysis of America's First Voucher Program* (Princeton, NJ: Princeton University Press, 2000), 117–118.

51. Brian P. Gill, P. Michael Timpane, Karen E. Ross, and Dominic J. Brewer, *Rhetoric versus Reality: What We Know and What We Need to Know about Vouchers and Charter Schools* (New York: RAND Education, 2001).

52. "School Vouchers in North Carolina: The First Three Years," a report issued by the Children's Law Clinic, Duke University Law School, Durham, NC, March 2017, https://law.duke.edu/childedlaw/docs/School_Vouchers_NC.pdf.

53. American Civil Liberties Union, "Justice Department Says State Voucher Programs May Not Discriminate against Students with Disabilities," *Press Release*, May 2, 2013, www.aclu.org/racialjustice/justice-department-says-state-voucher-programs-may-not-discriminate-against-students.

54. Witte, *The Market Approach to Education*, 205.

55. Turner, "The Promise and Peril of School Vouchers."

56. Stephanie Saul, "Public Money Finds Back Door to Private Schools," *New York Times*, May 21, 2012; Claire Suggs, "Push to Expand Private School Tax Scholarships Disregards Lack of Evidence, Accountability," *Georgia Budget and Policy Institute*, February 8, 2018, https://gbpi.org/2018/georgia-private-school-scholarships-lack-evidence-accountability/.

57. Mark Dynarski and Austin Nichols, "More Findings about School Vouchers and Test Scores, and They Are Still Negative," *Brookings Institution Evidence Speaks Report* 2, no. 18 (July 13, 2017), www.brookings.edu/wp-content/uploads/2017/07/ccf_20170713_mdynarski_evidence_speaks1.pdf; Mark Dynarski, "On Negative Effects of Vouchers," *Brookings Institution Evidence Speaks Report* 1, no. 18 (May 26, 2016), www.brookings.edu/wp-content/uploads/2016/07/vouchers-and-test-scores.pdf.

58. Martin Carnoy, "School Vouchers Are Not a Proven Strategy for Improving Student Achievement," a report of the Economic Policy Institute, February 28, 2017.

59. Witte, *The Market Approach to Education*, 119–143; Tawnell D. Hobbs, "Do School Vouchers Work? Milwaukee's Experiment Suggests an Answer," *Wall Street Journal*, January 28, 2018.

60. Paul J. Wolf, John J. Witte, and Brian Kisida, "Do Voucher Students Attain Higher Levels of Education? Extended Evidence from the Milwaukee Parental Choice Program," a report of The Urban Institute, Washington, DC, February 2018, www.urban.org/sites/default/files/publication/96721/do_voucher_students_attain_higher_levels_of_education_0.pdf; Joshua M. Cowen, David J. Fleming,

John F. Witte, Patrick J. Wolf, and Brian Kisida, "School Vouchers and Student Attainment: Evidence from a State-Mandated Study of Milwaukee's Parental Choice Program," *Policy Studies Journal* 41, no. 1 (2013): 147–168.

61. Stanford University Education Professor Martin Carnoy, quoted by Carrie Spector, "Vouchers Do Not Improve Student Achievement, Stanford Researcher Finds," *Stanford News*, February 2, 2017, https://news.stanford.edu/2017/02/28/vouchers-not-improve-student-achievement-stanford-researcher-finds/.

62. Wisconsin Department of Public Instruction, "2013–14 Income Limits for New Students: Milwaukee Parental Choice Program and Parental Private School Choice Program," http://sms.dpi.wi.gov/files/sms/pdf/pcp_income_limits_2013-14.pdf.

63. Cory Turner, "The Promise and Peril of School Vouchers," *Morning Edition Report, National Public Radio, NprEd*, May 12, 2017, www.npr.org/sections/ed/2017/05/12/520111511/the-promise-and-peril-of-school-vouchers.

64. *Zelman v. Simmons-Harris*, 536 U.S. 639 (2002).

65. Florida Department of Education, Office of Independent Education and Parental Choice, "Fact Sheet: Florida Tax Credit Scholarship Program," 2017, www.fldoe.org/core/fileparse.php/15230/urlt/FTC_Sept_2017_1.pdf.

66. Matthew M. Chingos and Daniel Kuehn, *The Effects of Statewide Private School Choice on College Enrollment and Graduation: Evidence from the Florida Tax Credit Scholarship Program* (Washington, DC: The Urban Institute, 2017), www.urban.org/sites/default/files/publication/93471/2017_12_05_the_effects_of_statewide_private_school_choice_on_college_enrollment_and_graduation_finalized.pdf.

67. Saul, "Private Money Finds Back Door to Private Schools"; Ty Tagami, "School Superintendents Say Georgia's Tax Credit Program Is Profitable for the Rich," *Atlanta Journal-Constitution*, May 1, 2017; Sasha Pudelski and Carl Davis, "Public Loss, Private Gain: How School Voucher Tax Shelters Undermine Public Education," a report of the AASA: The School Superintendents Association, 2017, www.aasa.org/uploadedFiles/Policy_and_Advocacy/Resources/AASA_ITEP_Voucher_Tax_Shelter.pdf.

68. National Alliance for Public Charter Schools, *Estimated Charter Public School Enrollment, 2016–2017*, 2017, www.publiccharters.org/sites/default/files/migrated/wp-content/uploads/2017/01/EER_Report_V5.pdf.

69. Robert Bifulco and Randall Reback, "Fiscal Impacts of Charter Schools: Lessons from New York," *Education Finance and Policy* 9, no. 1 (Winter 2014): 86–107. Figures are for the 2009–2010 school year.

70. Helen F. Ladd and John D. Singleton, "The Fiscal Externalities of Charter Schools: Evidence from North Carolina," Economic Research Initiatives at Duke (ERID) Working Paper No. 261, April 2018, https://ssrn.com/abstract=3082968 or http://dx.doi.org/10.2139/ssrn.3082968.

71. Rachel Weber, Stephanie Farmer, and Mary Donoghue, "Why These Schools? Explaining School Closures in Chicago, 2000–2013," a report of the Great Cities Institute, University of Illinois, Chicago, November 2016, https://greatcities.uic.edu/wp-content/uploads/2017/01/School-Closure.pdf; Stephanie Farmer, Ashley Baber, and Chris Poulos, "Closed by Choice: The Spatial Relationship between Charter School Expansion, School Closures, and Fiscal Stress in Chicago Public Schools," a report of the Project for Middle-Class Renewal, School of Labor and Employment Relations, University of Illinois, Urbana-Champaign, March 2017, https://ler.illinois.edu/wp-content/uploads/2017/03/Closed-By-Choice.pdf. The count of charter schools in Chicago and Illinois is provided by the Illinois Network of Charter Schools, "Get the Facts about Charter Schools in Illinois," 2000–2014, www.incschools.org/about-charters/get-the-facts/. Also see Ashley Barber, Chris Poulos, and Stephanie Farmer, "The Logic of School Choice: A Spatial Analysis of Charter Schools in Chicago" (paper presented at the annual meeting of the Urban Affairs Association, Minneapolis, April 2017).

72. Robert Maranto and Evan Rhinesmith, "Losing the War of Ideas? Why Teachers Unions Oppose School Choice," in *The Wiley Handbook of School Choice*, ed. Robert A. Fox (Chichester, West Sussex, UK: John Wiley & Sons, 2017), 450–464.

73. Al Baker and Javier C. Hernandez, "De Blasio and Builder of Charter School Empire Do Battle," *New York Times*, March 5, 2014.

74. Erling E. Boe, Shaun R. Harper, and Katherine M. Barghaus, "Segregated by Choice? Urban Charter Schools and Education Choices for Black Students and Disadvantaged Families in the United States," in *The Charter School Solution: Distinguishing Fact from Rhetoric*, ed. Tara L. Affolter and Jamel K. Donnor (New York: Routledge, 2016), 131.

75. Boe, Harper, and Barghaus, "Segregated by Choice?" 132.

76. Helen F. Ladd, Charles T. Clotfelter, and John B. Holbein, "The Growing Segmentation of the Charter School Sector in North Carolina," *Education Finance and Policy* 12, no. 4 (2017): 536–563.

77. Stephen Kotok, Erica Frankenberg, Kai A. Schafft, Bryan A. Mann, and Edward J. Fuller, "School Choice, Racial Segregation, and Poverty Concentration: Evidence from Pennsylvania Charter School Transfers," *Educational Policy* 31, no. 4 (2017): 415–447.

78. The figures are for the 2014–2015 school year. Will Stancil, researcher for the Institute on Metropolitan Opportunity at the University of Minnesota, quoted in George Joseph, "What Betsy DeVos Didn't Say about School Choice," *CityLab*, January 19, 2017, blog posting, www.citylab.com/equity/2017/01/what-betsy-devos-didnt-say-about-school-choice/513269/.

79. Ivan Moreno, "US Charter Schools Put Growing Numbers in Racial Isolation," *Associated Press New Story*, December 3, 2017, https://apnews.com/e9c25534dfd44851a5e56bd57454b4f5. The AP had surveyed charter schools in 42 states and the District of Columbia.

80. N.R. Kleinfield, "Why Don't We Have Any White Kids?," *New York Times*, May 11, 2012.

81. Grover J. "Russ" Whitehurst, Nathan Joo, Richard V. Reeves, and Edward Rodrigue, "Balancing Act: Schools, Neighborhoods and Racial Imbalance," a report of the Center on Children and Families, The Brookings Institution, Washington, DC, November 2017, 20–21, www.brookings.edu/wp-content/uploads/2017/11/es_20171120_schoolsegregation.pdf.

82. Ron Zimmer, Brian Gill, Kevin Booker, Stephanie Lavertu, Tim R. Sass, and John Witte, *Charter Schools in Eight States: Effects on Achievement, Attainment, Integration, and Competition* (Washington, DC: RAND Corporation, 2009), 12–19, www.rand.org/pubs/monographs/2009/RAND_MG869.pdf; Jeffrey R. Henig, *Spin Cycle: How Research Is Used in Public Policy Debates: The Case of Charter Schools* (New York: Russell Sage Foundation, 2008), 6–7. Also see Matthew M. Chingos, "Does Expanding School Choice Increase Segregation?," *The Brown Center Chalkboard Report*, May 15, 2013, www.brookings.edu/blogs/brown-center-chalkboard/posts/2013/05/15-school-choice-segregation-chingos.

83. Tamara Audie, "Desegregation an Issue in Charter School Plan," *Detroit Free Press*, September 3, 1998.

84. Doug Archbald, Andrew Hurwitz, and Felicia Hurwitz, "Charter Schools, Parent Choice, and Segregation: A Longitudinal Study of the Growth of Charters and Changing Enrollment Patterns in Five School Districts over 26 Years," *Education Policy Analysis Archives* 26, no. 22 (2018), http://dx.doi.org/10.14507/epaa.26.2921.

85. Jenn Ayscue, Amy Hawn Nelson, Roslyn Arlin Mickelson, Jason Giersch, and Martha Cecilia Bottia, "Charters as Drivers of Resegregation," a report of The Civil Rights Project/Projecto Derechos Civiles, UCLA, Los Angeles, January 2018, www.civilrightsproject.ucla.edu/research/k-12-education/integration-and-diversity/charters-as-a-driver-of-resegregation.

86. Mike Wilkinson, "School Choice Producing Segregation in Districts Across the State," *Bridge Magazine, The Center for Michigan*, September 20, 2016, www.bridgemi.com/talent-education/school-choice-producing-segregation-districts-across-state.

87. Christina Clark Tuttle, Brian Gill, Philip Gleason, Virginia Knechtel, Ira Nichols-Barrer, and Alexandra Resch, *KIPP Middle Schools: Impacts on Achievement and Other Outcome* (Washington, DC:

Mathematica Policy Research, 2013), www.mathematica-mpr.com/our-publications-and-findings/publications/kipp-middle-schools-impacts-on-achievement-and-other-outcomes-full-report.

88. Sarah Cohodes, "Charter Schools and the Achievement Gap," a report of The Future of Children, a joint publication of Princeton University and The Brookings Institution, Winter 2018, https://future-ofchildren.princeton.edu/news/charter-schools-and-achievement-gap.

89. Daniel J. Losen, Michael A. Keith, II, Cheri L. Hodson, and Tia E. Martinez, *Charter Schools, Civil Rights and School Discipline: A Comprehensive Review* (Los Angeles: The Center for Civil Rights Remedies at UCLA, 2016), https://civilrightsproject.ucla.edu/resources/projects/center-for-civil-rights-remedies/school-to-prison-folder/federal-reports/charter-schools-civil-rights-and-school-discipline-a-comprehensive-review/losen-et-al-charter-school-discipline-review-2016.pdf. Also see A. Chris Torres and Joanne W. Golann, *NEPC Review: Charter Schools and the Achievement Gap* (Boulder, CO: National Education Policy Center, 2018), http://nepc.colorado.edu/thinktank/review-no-excuses.

90. Barbara Ferman, "Lessons from the Grass Roots," chap. 6 in *The Fight for America's Schools: Grassroots Organizing in Education*, ed. B. Ferman (Cambridge, MA: Harvard Education Press, 2017), esp. 133–134. Also see: Stephanie Simon, "Special Report: Class Struggle: How Charter Schools Get Students They Want," *Reuters*, February 15, 2013; Valerie Strauss, "Why Charter Schools Get Public Education Advocates So Angry," *Washington Post*, July 24, 2016; and Mark Stern, Sheila Clonan, Laura Jaffee, and Anna Lee, "The Normative Limits of Choice: Charter Schools, Disability Studies, and Questions of Inclusion," *Educational Policy* 29, no. 3 (2015): 448–477.

91. Zimmer et al., *Charter Schools in Eight States*, esp. 35–39.

92. Center for Research on Education Outcomes (CREDO), *Multiple Choice: Charter School Performance in 16 States* (Stanford, CA: CREDO, 2009), https://credo.stanford.edu/reports/MULTIPLE_CHOICE_CREDO.pdf.

93. Center for Research on Education Outcomes, *National Charter School Study, 2013* (Stanford, CA: CREDO, 2013), http://credo.stanford.edu/documents/NCSS%202013%20Final%20Draft.pdf.

94. Center for Research on Education Outcomes, *Urban Charter School Study Report on 41 Regions* (Stanford, CA: CREDO, 2015), https://urbancharters.stanford.edu/download/Urban%20Charter%20School%20Study%20Report%20on%2041%20Regions.pdf. The quotation appears on p. v.

95. John F. Witte, David L. Weimer, Paul A. Schlomer, and Arnold F. Shober, "The Performance of Charter Schools in Wisconsin," in *University of Wisconsin-Madison La Follette School of Public Affairs* (2004), www.lafollette.wisc.edu/wcss/docs/persum.doc.

96. Buckley and Schneider, *Charter Schools: Hope or Hype?* chap. 10.

97. Douglas N. Harris and Matthew F. Larsen, "What Effect Did the New Orleans School Reforms Have on Student Achievement, High School Graduation, and College Outcomes?" a policy brief of the Education Research Alliance for New Orleans, an initiative of Tulane University, July 15, 2018, https://educationresearchalliancenola.org/publications/what-effect-did-the-new-orleans-school-reforms-have-on-student-achievement-high-school-graduation-and-college-outcomes.

98. Valerie Strauss, "The Real Story of New Orleans and Its Charter Schools," *Washington Post, Answer Sheet posting* by Carol Burris, September 4, 2018, www.washingtonpost.com/education/2018/09/04/real-story-new-orleans-its-charter-schools/?utm_term=.ddfebe1d0c29; Bruce D. Baker, "What We Should Really Learn from New Orleans after *The Storm?*," a report prepared for the Network for Public Education, New York City, 2018, https://networkforpubliceducation.org/wp-content/uploads/2018/08/BBaker.NPE_.NOLA_.pdf.

99. Sarah Reckhow, Jeffrey R. Henig, Rebecca Jacobsen, and Jamie Alter Litt, "'Outsiders with Deep Pockets': The Nationalization of Local School Board Elections," *Urban Affairs Review* 53, no. 5 (2017): 783–811.

100. Howard Blume and Ben Poston, "How L.A.'s School Board Election Became the Most Expensive in U.S. History," *Los Angeles Times*, May 21, 2017. Also see Elizabeth DeBray, Johanna Hanley, Janelle Scott, and Christopher Lubienski, "Local Politics Turns National: The Influence of Philanthropic and

Intermediary Organizations in School Board Elections in Los Angeles and Atlanta" (presented at the annual meeting of the Urban Affairs Association, Toronto, April 6, 2018).

101. Martha M. Galvez, *What Do We Know about Housing Choice Voucher Program Location Outcomes? A Review of Recent Literature,* a report of the What Works Collaborative (Washington, DC: The Urban Institute, August 2010), www.urban.org/uploadedpdf/412218-housing-choice-voucher.pdf.

102. Rebecca J. Walter, Yanmei Li, Serge Atherwood, and Auntaria Brown-Davis, "Moving to Opportunity? An Examination of the Impact of the Housing Choice Voucher Program on Reducing Urban Inequality" (paper presented at the annual meeting of the Urban Affairs Association, San Antonio, Texas, March 22, 2014).

10 Regional Cooperation and Governance in a Global Age

The governing authority in metropolitan regions is highly fragmented, that is, splintered into numerous small pieces. In virtually all regions in the United States, no single governmental body has the authority to rule over the entire metropolis and undertake effective region-wide action. Even when dealing with such important policy areas as economic growth and environmental protection, it often proves nearly impossible to get the region's large number of local governments and independent commissions, special districts, and agencies to work together.

In large metropolitan areas, the number of local decision-making bodies can reach into the hundreds and sometimes even the thousands. Each metropolitan area, of course, has numerous multipurpose governments such as municipalities, counties, villages, towns, and townships. These are the entities that Americans commonly recognize as local government. Less visible, however, are the great many narrow special-purpose governments (including school districts, community college districts, library districts, park districts, fire districts, and water and sewer districts) and broad multipurpose districts, and planning authorities whose members possess their own authority and whose independence pose a severe obstacle to coordinated region-wide action. Each autonomous municipality and independent agency has the ability to pursue its own objectives and interests, often with little regard for how its actions will affect neighboring communities and the region as a whole.

As this chapter will describe, there are a number of possible remedies for the problem of metropolitan fragmentation. For many years, structural reformers advocated the seemingly simplest and most far-reaching solution: the creation of a new level of government with metropolitan-wide reach, a governmental body with the authority to act in response to a region's needs. But, as this chapter describes, any effort to create a strong metropolitan government almost always runs into the determined opposition of suburbanites (and often local office holders as well) intent on defending the autonomy of their home communities. As a result, even in areas where some variant of metropolitan government exists—greater Jacksonville, Nashville, Baton Rouge, Lexington,

Louisville, Indianapolis, Miami, Portland (Oregon), Seattle, and the Minneapolis-St. Paul Twin Cities—metropolitan governing bodies seldom possess a full and extensive set of governing powers.

Is it really necessary to create a new metropolitan or regional government to address problems that spill beyond the borders of a single community? Suburban residents and other critics of metropolitan reform say "No!" that the cure is worse than the disease. Voters, especially in the suburbs, object to the loss of local autonomy and to the costs and irresponsiveness that "big government" in a region would bring. As a result, the movement toward strong metropolitan governments has waned in recent years. More pragmatic metropolitan reformers have turned their attention to a more incremental and politically realistic alternative strategy: pursue the more limited forms of interlocal cooperation and the informal and often business-led efforts of the *New Regionalism*. The advocates of New Regionalism do not wish to engage in a laborious and likely politically unwinnable struggle to reshape the government of metropolitan areas. Instead, the advocates of the New Regionalism seek ways that will increase opportunities for businesses and local governments in a region to collaborate on economic development and other matters, oftentimes outside the formal processes of government.

REGIONAL FRAGMENTATION: THE PROLONGED DEVELOPMENT OF REGIONAL RAIL IN THE SAN FRANCISCO BAY AREA

The fragmentation of public decision making impedes the development of effective solutions to regional problems, a fact that is evident in the unduly long time that it took the greater San Francisco area to develop BART (Bay Area Rapid Transit), a regional rail system to serve commuters over a five-county area. A quick look at a transit map reveals the strange shape of the BART system that was created: BART does not serve all parts of the region! (See Figure 10.1.) BART primarily connects San Francisco to communities in the East Bay. The rail system does not extend north into Marin County or south into the populous communities and major job centers of the high-tech Peninsula and much of the South Bay.

Why does BART fail to fulfill its regional service mission? Simply put, for decades, numerous localities refused to join BART, impeding a more rational layout of rail lines that would effectively serve the entire region. Affluent Marin County objected to the financial obligations expected of its communities; as a result, Marin (indicated as "North Bay" in Figure 10.1) is not served by BART rail. Similarly, San Mateo County, to the south of San Francisco, persisted for many years in its refused to levy the sales tax that other counties had adopted to pay for BART service. San Mateo saw no great need to join and help build BART as a separate commuter rail line (Caltrain) already existed and enabled riders from the Peninsula to travel into San Francisco. For many years BART's tracks stopped at the county line, and BART trains failed to provide service to the region's airport (located in San Mateo County) and to major job and population centers south of the city. Prolonged and quite difficult negotiations among San Mateo County officials and the officers of the various local transit agencies at long last produced an agreement for a limited five-station extension into San Mateo in order to serve San Francisco International Airport and provide a new transfer point with Caltrain.

Figure 10.1 **The Strange and Incomplete Shape of BART.** The map of BART rail service in 2012 reveals the impact of metropolitan fragmentation. Marin County (the North Bay) and much of the Peninsula and the South Bay are not served by a rail system that was originally intended to improve commuting over the entire region. Even the relatively short five-stop extension to San Francisco International Airport and into San Mateo County was built late. Riders on Caltrain (not shown on the map) must transfer to a BART train in order to reach the airport. Today, riders still cannot easily ride from the South Bay to the East Bay but must switch trains.

In more recent years, BART has extended rail service east to Antioch and south into the North San Jose area. BART still does not serve important population and job centers in Marin County and much of the Peninsula.

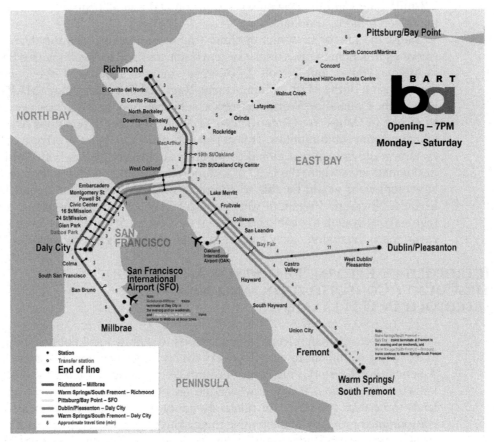

Source: BART developer map. Derivative work uploaded to Wikimedia Commons by Train2104, https://commons.wikimedia.org/wiki/File:BARTMapDay.svg.

It was not only certain counties that refused to cooperate that impeded the development of effective transit in the region. Each autonomous local transit agency in the Bay Area showed no great urgency to coordinate bus routes and schedules with transit systems that served other jurisdictions. As a consequence, travelers in the Bay Area still do not enjoy the ease of "seamless" travel throughout the region provided by a single system.

Instead, travelers, are confronted by a disjointed, chaotic, and highly inefficient system of public transit.[1] There is no easy ride from much of the Peninsula (the populous area south of San Francisco) to much of San Francisco or to the cities of the East Bay, as Caltrain tracks from the Peninsula terminates short of the San Francisco's downtown at King Street (near the Giants's ballpark). After arriving in San Francisco on Caltrain, a commuter must walk more than a mile to access the nearest BART station and continue a journey to other parts of San Francisco or to Oakland and other East Bay communities. Only after decades of outcries by frustrated travelers did the various transportation authorities in the region at long last join together in a very expensive effort to correct the problem of the mismatched routes of a regional train system. The construction of 1.3-mile-long Caltrain Downtown Extension and a new Transbay Transit Center cost the region billions of dollars.[2]

Sadly, the tale of how metropolitan fragmentation impedes the development of a smoothly functioning mass transit system is not confined to San Francisco but is repeated in Atlanta, Dallas, and Detroit. In Georgia, voters in suburban Cobb County objected the extension of the Metropolitan Atlanta Regional Transit Agency (MARTA) rail service. In the Dallas-Fort Worth metroplex, suburban opposition to new taxes delayed the extension of Dallas Area Rapid Transit (DART) light rail to populous Arlington and to other up-county communities. Transit planners had argued that an effective public transit system would help attract global corporations to greater Dallas-Fort Worth, especially to suburban sites where the CEO of a corporation would no longer have to worry about how employees would be able to commute to their jobs. In the greater Detroit area, Livonia, Novi, and Plymouth were among 50 suburbs that refused to participate in a regional bus system to enable riders from the central city and close-in suburbs to more easily reach the region's new centers of employment in growing suburbs.[3]

METROPOLITAN REFORM, OLD STYLE: ANNEXATION, CITY-COUNTY CONSOLIDATION, AND NEW METROPOLITAN GOVERNMENTS

Old-style metropolitan reform entailed efforts to redraw local political borders in order to allow a government to act effectively over a larger geographical area. For much of American urban history, cities grew outwards by capturing new territory through a process known as *annexation*. Today, however, the age of annexation is largely over; annexation tends to be used primarily for relatively minor local border adjustments. *City-county consolidation* provides an alternative route to creating a local government with a greater geographical reach: Under a consolidation, a county and its municipalities merge to form a single government capable of taking effective action over a county-wide area. Yet, as we shall see, the prospect of city-county mergers, too, has waned in more recent years, with the 2001 merger of Louisville and Jefferson County standing as the lone semi-contemporary exception. Minnesota's Twin Cities (Minneapolis and St. Paul) and Portland (Oregon) followed an even more aggressive path of regional reform, creating a new and strong multipurpose government with the ability to act beyond the borders of a single county. Yet, the resistance of local residents and public officials makes it very unlikely that such strong metropolitan governments will be created in other areas of the country.

ANNEXATION

Annexation gives a city the ability to capture a piece of neighboring territory, making it part of the extended city. Where a state allows, annexation enables a municipality to expand its boundaries outwards.

Through the nineteenth century and much of the twentieth century, annexation was a tool for dynamic city growth and expansion. Chicago achieved its present-day size through major annexations that captured important communities like Hyde Park and industrial Pullman to the south and Rogers Park and other growing bungalow neighborhoods to the north. Los Angeles aggressively pursued annexation to expand its geographic size by a factor of four, growing from 108 to 415 square miles in just ten years (from 1915 to 1925). Los Angeles pursed a policy of **water imperialism**: The city refused to supply water to outlying communities in the near-desert southern California region, unless the communities agreed to accept incorporation with the city (see Box 10.1). By contrast, cities in the Northeast and the Midwest have not been able to force already established suburbs to unify with the city. Jersey City and Newark, for instance, had no control the region's water supply and hence could not coerce growing suburban areas to agree to annexation.[4]

Each state determines just what annexation powers a locality possesses and under what conditions an annexation may proceed. State laws have been relatively permissive in allowing a city to annex **unincorporated areas** where residents have not established their own units of municipal government to provide municipal services as outlined in a state's constitution and laws.[5] The states also tend to look favorably on a city's effort to annex and develop small parcels of adjoining land for a new factory or for some other economic growth project, Such expansions are especially likely to gain approval when the request for annexation is initiated by a commercial property owner who discovers that the expansion of his or her business requires greater water provision, fire protection, or some other municipal service that only a larger neighboring government has the capacity to provide. In about a dozen states, a state-appointed boundary commission has the authority to approve (or disapprove) relatively small annexations.

Local elites have often pushed major annexations to assist their business ambitions. The City of Albuquerque in the 1950s and early 1960s acquired a large volume of sparsely populated acreage in response to the demands of property developers who needed the provision of water and other municipal services in order to build new residential subdivisions.[6] In Houston and Denver, political leaders responded to the demands of the region's business elite by annexing the vast acreage needed to construct a new international airport capable of advancing global connections and trade.

But the age of massive annexation has clearly ended. As the suburbs grew and gained political power, state legislatures altered their statutes to protect suburban areas from unilateral central-city expansion. As a result, cities no longer possess the ability to annex large tracts of land and areas that have a sizable number of residents.[7]

When a city seeks to annex a parcel of land situated in an already-incorporated neighbor, state law typically requires **dual approval**: For the annexation to proceed, *both* the larger municipality and the smaller area being annexed must consent to the

Box 10.1
Urban Film Classics: *Chinatown* and the Story of Los Angeles Water Imperialism

In the arid West, water is a scarce and vital resource. Consequently, Los Angeles in the early twentieth century was able to wield its municipal water system as a weapon of territorial expansion. The city forced other communities to consent to annexation in exchange for much-needed water.

The power-play of municipal water politics provides the backdrop for Roman Polanski's 1974 *cinema noir* classic, *Chinatown*, a film that received 11 Academy Award nominations. Despite its name, the film does not focus on the city's Chinese immigrant enclave. Instead, the movie presents a fictionalized version of the efforts undertaken by Los Angeles water chief William Mulholland to construct the Owens Valley aqueduct, a project that, in 1913, brought water from over 200 miles away to a thirsty Los Angeles. Situated in a desert region, Los Angeles needed an assured supply of water for the city to grow. Control over water enabled L.A. to annex communities in the water-starved San Fernando Valley. The region's orchard growers and ranchers, however, were unhappy with the changes being forced upon them; they charged that Los Angeles had stolen the water from the Owens River and was using it for political extortion. In the 1920s, angry protestors dynamited sections of the new aqueduct.

In the fictionalized account presented in the movie, private detective Jake Gittes (played by Jack Nicholson) explores the mystery of why Los Angeles is secretly dumping water at a time when fruit growers and urban dwellers are suffering from drought conditions. Gittes is shot at by resentful Valley farmers. He uncovers a cesspool of corruption: The city's growth machine, including its leading newspaper, has whipped up a frenzy over water in order to win approval for the city's efforts to gain control over the Owens River water supply, thereby making possible the dynamic growth of Los Angeles—and their own power and wealth.

The film is only loosely based on the story of L.A.'s water wars. The film distorts the timeline of events, moving them from the early 1900s to the 1930s and the New Deal era. It also exaggerates the sinister motives underlying the acquisition of water, using cinematic license to "amp up" the drama of a screen detective story.

Sources: For comparisons of the film *Chinatown* with the actual history of L.A.'s water imperialism and events surrounding the Owens Valley water controversy, see: John Walton, "Film Mystery as Urban History: The Case of *Chinatown*," in *Cinema and the City: Film and Urban Society in a Global Context*, ed. Mark Shiel and Tony Fitzmaurice (Oxford, UK: Blackwell, 2001), 46–58; Gary D. Libecap, *Owens Valley Revisited: A Reassessment of the West's First Great Water Transfer* (Stanford, CA: Stanford University Press, 2007); and Les Standiford, *Water to the Angels: William Mullholland, His Monumental Aqueduct, and the Rise of Los Angeles* (New York: HarperCollins, 2015).

boundary change. Of course, voters and officials in the area being annexed are unlikely to consent to the change! The requirement for dual approval means that major cities like Los Angeles, San Francisco, Chicago, Detroit, St. Louis, Milwaukee, Pittsburgh, Cleveland, New York, Baltimore, and Boston can no longer expand via annexation. These are **landlocked cities** completely surrounded by already-incorporated suburban municipalities unwilling to cede land to the central city.[8]

For much of the twentieth century, however, a number of important Sunbelt cities expanded rapidly, in terms of both geography and population, as permissive state laws gave cities the ability to unilaterally annex rather large pieces of territory even without the consent of the residents or the areas being absorbed. Houston in the 1970s gained over 200,000 new residents as a result of various annexations! San Antonio, Charlotte, Phoenix, and (outside the Sunbelt) Portland (Oregon) were other national annexation leaders.[9]

In more recent decades, however, even in the Sunbelt, the tide of annexations ebbed. Charlotte and Oklahoma City no longer abut vast acreage that can be easily annexed. In Fort Worth, Amarillo, Denver, Wilmington, Asheville, and other cities, antigovernment "Tea Party" activists rose up to resist annexation efforts.[10]

Even more important, as the voting power of the suburbs increased, state governments enacted new curbs on unilateral expansion. Virginia renewed its moratorium on local annexations. The Republican-controlled legislature in Ohio in 2013 placed new obstacles in the path of even relatively small annexations. Two years later, the Tennessee legislature effectively banned unilateral annexation. For an annexation to proceed in Tennessee, state law requires the written consent of the owners of the properties being annexed or voter approval gained through a referendum held in the area targeted for annexation. The new Tennessee law also curbed **non-contiguous annexations**, where cities had acquired sites for development that were not located immediately next to the city; cities simply skipped over the properties of owners opposed to being absorbed into the city.[11]

The State of Texas enacted procedures to make large-scale annexations more time-consuming and difficult. The changes were prompted by the anger of suburbanites when the residents of Kingwood, an upscale suburb with a population of 50,000, failed in their desperate attempts to stop Houston from swallowing up their community. Yet, Texas statutes do not ban all annexations; nor do they require homeowner consent or dual approval in all cases. In Texas, a city can unilaterally annex an adjoining area with fewer than 5,000 residents if the city is already providing water and sewer service to the targeted area. State lawmakers in Texas sought to balance their concerns for property rights with the need for economic development. They did not wish to impose excessively rigid hurdles to the dynamic economic growth of cities like Houston and San Antonio.[12]

Why do cities pursue annexation? Annexation enables a city to acquire taxable properties and space for new development that will contribute to a municipality's long-term fiscal health. David Rusk, the former mayor of Albuquerque, observes how **elastic cities** such as Albuquerque, Phoenix, Charlotte, Houston, and San Antonio were able to maintain their fiscal health over the years by using annexation to capture new tax revenues generated by economic activity occurring on the city's rim. Phoenix reaped substantial sales tax revenues by absorbing areas where retail development was occurring.

In contrast, Hartford, Cleveland, and Detroit and other landlocked or **inelastic cities** suffered continued fiscal distress as they had no ability to annex surrounding land parcels and thereby reap revenues from the economic growth taking place in suburban areas.[13]

Columbus, Ohio, is the rare elastic Frostbelt city that was able to use its control over water and sewer hookups to force growing rim areas to agree to annexation. Columbus grew from 39 square miles (in 1950) to 210 square miles (in 2000). By absorbing new areas of economic activity in the region, Columbus was able to maintain an enviable fiscal position, especially when compared to that of inelastic Cleveland and Cincinnati.[14]

The politics of race can affect annexation. Voters in the central city are more likely to approve the annexation of white communities as opposed to black areas located on the city's suburban rim.[15]

CITY-COUNTY CONSOLIDATION (MERGER): FOCUS ON INDIANAPOLIS AND LOUISVILLE

City-county consolidation denotes the merger of municipalities with their surrounding county to form a single government. After consolidation, a city and the county are no longer separate entities; no longer does each have its own legislative body, elected officeholders, and administrative departments.

At one time, consolidations of cities and counties allowed for the emergence of dynamic, powerful cities such as Greater New York and San Francisco. Yet, as Table 10.1 reveals, the movement toward city-county consolidation has clearly greatly slowed. The consolidation of Louisville with Jefferson County is the only merger of great significance to have occurred in the last 40 years.

Back in the 1950s and 1960s, when the suburbs of a number of cities were still developing, the residents of growing areas around Nashville and Jacksonville may have welcomed merger with the city as a means of gaining paved streets, curbs, gutters, and other municipal improvements. Today, however, the residents of established suburbs view merger not as a help but as a threat. Central-city officials, too, often resist the loss of local control that may result from merger.

Why has the consolidation movement abated? The answer is three-fold: (1) Contemporary voters value local control and resist the loss of local autonomy that city-county consolidation entails. (2) Important interests, including local officeholders, oppose consolidation. (3) City-county mergers seldom deliver the full range of benefits that the early advocates of consolidation had promised.

By merging governments together, consolidation was supposed to reduce the number of local governments and municipal officials in a region. Mergers would produce cost savings by allowing the merged government to eliminate duplicative municipal agencies and close facilities that were no longer needed.

In reality, however, consolidations seldom produce the extensive cost savings that merger enthusiasts promised, in part because city-county mergers are almost always partial, and are never total or complete. Voters resist complete consolidation efforts that threaten to remove their community from the map. Voters want to preserve their community's identity. They also value small-scale government. In response to these

Table 10.1
City–County Consolidations, 1805–2012

Year	City–County	State
1805	New Orleans–Orleans Parish	Louisiana
1821	Boston–Suffolk County	Massachusetts
1821	Nantucket–Nantucket County	Massachusetts
1854	Philadelphia–Philadelphia County	Pennsylvania
1856	San Francisco—San Francisco County	California
1874	New York (Manhattan)–New York County	New York
1984	New York–Bronx and Staten Island	New York
1898	New York–Brooklyn, Queens, and Richmond County	New York
1904	Denver–Arapahoe County	Colorado
1907	Honolulu–Honolulu County	Hawaii
1947	Baton Rouge–East Baton Rouge Parish	Louisiana
1952	Hamilton and Phoebus–Elizabeth City County	Virginia
1957	Newport News–Warwick City County	Virginia
1962	Nashville–Davidson County	Tennessee
1962	Chesapeake–South Norfolk–Norfolk County	Virginia
1962	Virginia Beach–Princess Anne County	Virginia
1967	Jacksonville–Duval County	Florida
1969	Indianapolis–Marion County	Indiana
1969	Carson City–Ormsby County	Nevada
1969	Juneau and Douglas–Greater Juneau Borough	Alaska
1970	Columbus–Muscogee County	Georgia
1971	Holland and Whaleyville–Nansemond County	Virginia
1971	Sitka–Greater Sitka Borough	Alaska
1972	Lexington–Fayette County	Kentucky
1972	Suffolk–Nansemond County	Virginia
1975	Anchorage, Glen Alps, and Girdwood–Greater Anchorage	Alaska
1976	Anaconda–Deer Lodge County	Montana
1976	Butte–Silver Bow County	Montana
1984	Houma–Terrebonne County	Louisiana
1988	Lynchburg–Moore County	Tennessee
1992	Athens–Clarke County	Georgia
1992	Lafayette–Lafayette Parish	Louisiana
1995	Augusta–Richmond County	Georgia
1997	Kansas City (KS)–Wyandotte County	Kansas
2001	Hartsville–Trousdale County	Tennessee
2001	Louisville–Jefferson County	Kentucky
2002	Haines City–Haines Borough	Alaska
2003	Cusseta City–Chattahoochee County	Georgia
2006	Georgetown–Quitman County	Georgia
2007	Tribune–Greeley County	Kansas
2008	Statenville–Echols County	Georgia

Sources: National Association of Counties, Research Division, "Research Brief," no date, NACO, Washington, DC, 1999; National Association of Counties, "City-County Consolidation Proposals, 1921-Present," 2011, www.naco.org/Counties/learn/Documents/City%20County%20Consolidations.01.01.2011.pdf; Kathryn Murphy, *Reshaping County Government: A Look at City-County Consolidation* (Washington, DC: National Association of Counties, February 2012).

Box 10.2
**Political Motives and Consolidation in Indianapolis:
Unigov or Unigrab?**

The creation of Unigov in Indianapolis–Marion County was not simply a good-government reform intended to save money and strengthen municipal operations in Indiana's capital region. The merger was also prompted by the partisan concerns of state Republican leaders who feared that they were losing the ability to win elections in the state's capital city. Democrats charge that the Indiana's Republican governor and GOP-controlled state legislature engineered a partisan power grab so brazen that the reform should be referred to as **Unigrab** not Unigov.

Population trends at the time of the merger clearly indicated that the Democrats would soon gain control of city hall as a result of the city's growing numbers of low-income voters and racial minorities. But the creation of Unigov changed the boundaries of the city and just who could vote in city elections. By expanding the city's political borders (making them the same as the county's borders), Unigov added thousands of suburban residents—a largely Republican voting bloc—to the electorate that would choose the Unigov mayor and council.

The results of the elections that immediately followed the merger attest to the success of the Republican strategy. In 1975, Republican votes from the suburbs provided their party's mayoral candidate, William Hudnut, with his margin of victory, despite the Democrats having won the "old city" by 17,500 votes. In 1991, Republican Stephen Goldsmith similarly won Unigov's mayoralty, despite his Democratic opponent having won the old city by 15,000 votes. It was not until 1999, 30 years after the creation of Unigov, that a Democrat, Bart Peterson, was at long last elected mayor. Even the creation of Unigov could not forever hold back the demographic tide that was changing Indianapolis politics.

Source: The vote tallies are from William Blomquist, "Metropolitan Organization and Local Politics: The Indianapolis-Marion County Experience," paper presented at the annual meeting of the Midwest Political Science Association, Chicago, April 9–11, 1992.

concerns, smaller municipalities and towns—and in some cases even fairly big suburbs as well—are often permitted to opt out of a proposed consolidation. As a result, numerous municipalities and more specialized districts, local boards, and commissions continue to remain in existence even after a so-called consolidation of local governments in a county has taken place. As a consequence of such opt outs, the number of elected positions is seldom reduced as a result of annexation.[16] City-county mergers that eliminate few duplicative positions seldom save real money.

City-county merger enthusiasts promise that consolidation will provide strong regional leadership by creating a central executive who serves as the voice of the region when negotiating with the heads of national and global corporations over the location of a new facility. But the promise of future economic development tends to fall on the deaf ears of suburbanites who are more interested in maintaining their community's identity and autonomy.

Local business leaders have often played a significant role in pushing city-county consolidation as a means to alter power arrangements in a community. In Nashville and Jacksonville at mid-century, business leaders saw consolidation as a way to oust parochial city officials who were unwilling to finance expensive downtown renewal projects. In Indiana, business leaders worked with Republican Party officeholders to create **Unigov**, the "unified" or merged government of the City of Indianapolis and Marion County. Republican-oriented business leaders and politicians sought to preserve their control over Indianapolis and its downtown in the face of demographic trends that showed that, if the city's political borders were left unaltered, a new Democratic majority would soon control the city (see Box 10.2).

Consolidation's Unmet Promises? Efficiency and Equity

City-county consolidations seldom increase efficiency and cost savings in municipal operations.[17] The incomplete nature of mergers serves to reduce the savings that can be obtained from consolidation, especially as relatively few municipal offices are closed and few positions eliminated.

Some mergers have produced minor savings by restraining the growth of administrative costs. Yet, studies have not found extensive cost savings and gains in efficiency. In Athens–Clarke County (Georgia), Carson City–Ormsby County (Nevada), and Kansas City–Wyandotte County (Kansas), city-county consolidation produced no substantial savings.[18] Another review of contemporary consolidations similarly reveals that mergers seldom wind up reducing local spending. Modest cost savings are achieved in very narrow service areas and are rarely sustained over time.[19] More typically, the cost savings that appear to accompany a consolidation soon vanish as citizens demand improved services and municipal workers seek increased wages.

City-county consolidation has not led to increased service equality and fairness in local government. Despite its promise, all residents of a county are not treated alike. The incomplete nature of city-county mergers means that, post-consolidation, people who reside in different communities continue to pay different tax rates and receive different levels of municipal services; there is no equality or uniformity. In general, poorer communities continue to receive lower levels of public services even after consolidation has nominally occurred. City-county consolidation also do little to promote equal schooling funding and increased levels of racial integration in a region's K–12 schools. The reasons for this is simple: As suburbanites bitterly oppose any consolidation effort that would abridge the local control of schools, a region's public schools are rarely, if ever, included in the merger of city and county governments. The inclusion of schools in a proposed merger would doom the plan to certain political defeat.

City-county mergers also dilute African-American voting power, as consolidation effectively adds white suburban voters to the city's electorate, diminishing the prospects that African Americans will gain control of city hall. The adoption of a district voting system can help to ensure that a spatially concentrated minority community will be able to elect one of their won to the new city/county council.

Yet, the impact of consolidation on racial minorities is not purely negative. Data from Nashville and Jacksonville provides preliminary evidence that city-county consolidation may help facilitate a region's economic growth, increasing job opportunities for racial minorities. In Nashville and Jacksonville, city-county consolidation led business leaders to take a regional perspective on problems, a perspective that embraced a more inclusive orientation toward citizen participation.[20]

A brief review of the two most recent major city-county consolidations—Indianapolis/Marion County and Louisville/Jefferson County—will help to provide greater insight as to just what contemporary mergers can and cannot accomplish.

Indianapolis's Unigov: Economic Concerns Drive Consolidation

As Indiana lacks a strong home rule tradition, the state legislature in 1969 was able to order the unification of Indianapolis and Marion County without having to gain the approval of the affected local jurisdictions. Business leaders pushed for the creation of Unigov to change the city's "Indiana-no-place" reputation. Overnight, Indianapolis gained stature and appeared to become a "major league" city; the boundary change made Indianapolis/Unigov the twelfth most populous city in the nation (1990 figures).

Extending the city's boundaries increased the total assessed value of property within the city's limits, thereby increasing the amount of money that the city could borrow, under state law, to finance downtown redevelopment and other growth projects.[21] This provided the merged city with an important means to finance new sports facilities, a key part of the city's strategy for economic revival. Indianapolis built an indoor football stadium, an NBA basketball arena, and various facilities for amateur tennis, swimming, bicycle racing, and track and field. Indianapolis became the self-proclaimed amateur sports capital of the United States and home to the National Collegiate Athletic Association.[22]

By unifying governments in the region, the merger created a county government with the capacity to promote major downtown revitalization projects and other economic development projects throughout the county. Unigov's mayor presides over one of the strongest regional planning and economic development departments in the country.[23] The city's economic team steered new investment to Indianapolis's center, something that likely could not have been achieved in the older fragmented political system where suburban officials competed with the central city for new businesses. Unigov planners succeeded in persuading the developers of Market Square Arena to locate their new sports facility in the center of the city rather than along an interstate highway. Unigov officials similarly convinced American United Life to abandon plans for a suburban headquarters and instead build a 38-story downtown office tower, the tallest building in the state, to bring an estimated 1,500 employees into the heart of the city. Unigov's ability to speak with one voice also helped the region win the 93-city competition for an $800 million United Airlines maintenance facility.[24]

Despite its noteworthy achievements, Unigov also suffers a number of important limitations. A consolidated county government cannot control development beyond the borders of the county. Unigov could not curb the rapid growth of Carmel and Fishers, affluent communities lying just outside the Marion County boundary line.

Unigov's achievements in planning and economic development are not matched by equivalent success in social policy. Unigov's expensive infrastructure projects helped spark the revival of Indianapolis's once-failing downtown. But the unified government has not been able to stem the decline of the city's poorer residential neighborhoods.

Nor did a "unified" countywide equalize service provision and tax rates throughout the county. In fact, the name "Unigov" is a misnomer, as post-consolidation Marion County has 6 municipalities, 9 townships, and more than 100 separate taxing units and school districts.

Louisville: Was the Merger Necessary?

The 2003 merger of Louisville with surrounding Jefferson County made Louisville the sixteenth most populous city in the nation, an overnight gain in prestige as the old city ranked only as 64th largest. Civic pride helped drive the consolidation effort. Louisville residents feared that, without a merger to stretch their borders, consolidated Lexington-Fayette would soon surpass Louisville to become Kentucky's most populous city. Advocates further argued that the merger would help generate a regional vision that would prove important in rejuvenating the area's economic fortunes.

As was the case in Indianapolis's Unigov, the consolidation of governments in Louisville-Jefferson County was very incomplete. The old City of Louisville lost its independent status; yet 84 smaller suburban municipalities remained in existence post-consolidation.[25]

Consolidation improved the fiscal solvency of the city, with the new enlarged city having a lower debt ratio than unconsolidated Louisville.[26] The merger also provided the leadership to promote new development both in the old downtown and in attractive suburban areas in the county. However, as was the case in Unigov, Metro brought little new investment to inner-city residential neighborhoods.[27] The residents of Louisville's troubled neighborhoods are "just as poor after consolidation as before."[28] The merger also diluted black electoral power. African Americans were a third of the population of Louisville prior to the merger; in the election held immediately after consolidation, African Americans won less than a fourth (6 of 26) of the seats on the new Metro Louisville council.

Was the Louisville consolidation really necessary? As public choice theorists observe, consolidation is not the only way to produce cost savings; interlocal arrangements enable communities to cooperate to save money even in the absence of merger. In the greater Louisville area, a limited form of regional tax sharing even helped address equity concerns in the region *before* the merger took place! Louisville and Jefferson County had agreed in 1986 to a formal "compact" that reduced the interlocal competition for new economic development and that redistributed $5 million a year in fiscal assistance to the city.[29] Why would Louisville's suburbs extend such help to the city? Simple! Suburban officials hoped that the compact would be sufficient to deter threats by the city to annex surrounding areas.[30]

Overall, the creation of Louisville's Metro was not the "breakthrough" event that jump-started the local economy. The years immediately following consolidation saw no sharp growth in employment, payrolls, or other measures of regional economic health.[31] Yet the merger did have positive impacts on downtown renewal and tourist-related development. Consolidation also improved the fiscal position of the city, a factor that led private financial houses to upgrade the city's bond rating, reducing the costs of city borrowing.[32]

MIAMI-DADE'S TWO-TIERED SYSTEM

Miami's **two-tiered system** of metropolitan government was created in 1957. Unlike city-county consolidation, the two-tier system does not eliminate any local governments from the map, Instead, the two-level arrangement simply assigns a number of important planning and service responsibilities to a strengthened Dade County government while normal daily municipal service delivery remains in the hands of the cities.

The creation of Miami-Dade (originally called Metro-Dade) brought a new professionalization to municipal government, an upgrade that posed quite a contrast to the episodes of corruption, maladministration, and patronage abuses that, over the years, had plagued the City of Miami (the City of Miami is a separate government from Metro-Dade, the strengthened Dade County), Hialeah, and other municipalities in the region. The creation of Miami-Dade led to the construction of expanded highway and mass transit systems as well as improvements in county-administered land-use planning, social service provision, voter registration, and tax assessment and administration.

Like Unigov, however, Miami-Dade is a governing arrangement that is limited to a single county. At best, it provides improved subregional government in a metropolitan area that extends over multiple counties. Miami-Dade cannot control continued development by, and competition from, its dynamic neighbors: Broward (Fort Lauderdale), Palm Beach, and Monroe counties.

In the more than half century or so since Miami-Dade's creation, no U.S. region has copied the two-tiered model, a hint as to the intensity of political forces opposed to surrendering land-use planning and related service powers to a strengthened county. Were it not already in existence, it is doubtful that the two-tiered system could be adopted in greater Miami. Over the years, wealthier communities in the county—including Miami Beach, Surfside, Golden Beach, Bal Harbour, Key Biscayne, and North Bay Village—have attempted, albeit without success, to secede from the governing arrangement. Hundreds of lawsuits have also been filed in an attempt to diminish the authority of the Miami-Dade government.[33]

STRONG METROPOLITAN GOVERNMENT: PORTLAND (OREGON) AND MINNESOTA'S TWIN CITIES

The nation's two prime examples of strong metropolitan government are found in Portland (Oregon) and Minneapolis-St. Paul. Both the Greater Portland Metropolitan Service District and the Twin Cities Metropolitan Council entail the creation of a new metropolitan level of general-purpose government, what can be viewed as a third tier of local government atop the municipal and county levels of government.

Portland

The Portland Metropolitan Service District (commonly called "Metro") is unique, as it is the only directly elected multi-county regional government in the United States. Metro's jurisdiction cuts across three counties and 24 cities.

The State of Oregon created Metro to deal with issues of growth and to protect farmland, forests, and green spaces from the encroachment of urbanization. Oregon state law gives Metro real authority in areas such as land use, environmental protection, and transportation planning. Oregon law mandates that local land-use and zoning regulations comply with the overall framework set by Metro. As described in Chapter 3, Metro also sets the region's urban growth boundary. Downtown revitalization and neighborhood infill projects provide an alternative to sprawled development.

Metro has achieved notable successes in development planning and the expansion of public transit. Portland planners channel new development to growth nodes located along light-rail lines.

Over the years, Oregon state law broadened Metro's powers, giving Metro the responsibility to formulate a regional affordable housing plan that details how each of the district's 24 cities will accept its share of low- and moderate-income housing units. Metro's actions led to an increase in the production of apartments and small-lot housing in Portland's suburbs. Metro has advanced an Equity Housing strategy to develop and preserve affordable housing throughout the region.[34]

Paradoxically, while Portland's Metro is arguably the most powerful regional general-purpose government in the nation, in important ways Metro's authority is still quite limited: Metro "is at once pathbreaking as a mode of regional governance yet benign in its functions."[35] Metro's "budget is piddling by comparison to many other governmental units" in the region.[36] Existing municipalities, not Metro, retain responsibility for most service provision.

Over the years, suburban jurisdictions have gone to court to challenge Metro's plans for fair share affordable housing.[37] Conservative political forces also led repeated political assaults on Metro's land-use planning actions that seek to constrain development in order to protect green spaces. Property-rights activists used the ballot box in 2004 to pass Measure 37, an initiative requiring that the government pay compensation to owners for planning decisions that diminish the economic value of a piece of property. The measure seemed likely to cripple regional land-use planning. Environmentalists, however, quickly countermobilized, and only three years later gained voter approval for Measure 49 that reduced the threat of lawsuits and ensured that Metro and other local governments would continue to be able to enact land-use measures to protect farmland, forests, and groundwater from the threat of new development.

Regional planners and eco-activists across the country often hold up Portland as a model for other cities to follow. Yet, even Portland's strong system of government does not operate by fiat. Despite its extensive state-given authority, Metro does not rule by command; the Metro government tries to avoid situations where it issues controversial land-use decisions in top-down fashion. Instead, Metro officials build support by negotiating, compromising, and collaborating with local officials.[38] Metro seeks to win the support of local officials for regional action by documenting the consequences of unabated growth and by educating local officials as to the requirements that accompany federal and state assistance.

The Twin Cities Met Council

The Minnesota state legislature in 1969 created the Twin Cities Metropolitan Council (the Met Council) to help cope with the rapid growth taking place in the state's seven-county capital region. Over the years, the state gave the Met Council additional powers in such areas as sewers, wastewater management, maintaining the region's water supply, open space protection, airport and light-rail construction, transportation-oriented development (TOD), and the development of affordable housing, parks, stadiums, and sports facilities. Quite significantly, the Met Council can levy property taxes and issue bonds, important financial powers that give the Met Council a real ability to undertake projects. Such a formidable array of planning, program, taxing, and borrowing powers effectively distinguishes the Met Council from a mere COG (council of governments) or RPC (regional planning council), the much weaker and more commonplace regional organization found in other metropolitan areas across the nation (a vehicle for cooperation that will receive greater discussion later in this chapter).

The Met Council formulates a **metropolitan development guide**, a "blueprint" or "binding plan" that designates certain areas of the region for concentrated development while safeguarding farmland and more rural areas from development encroachment and sprawl. A visitor to the Twin Cities region can look out an airplane window and see the difference that the Met Council has made: Despite the region's immense population growth, large green and natural areas are preserved, and sprawl is largely contained.

Unlike Portland's Metro and Indianapolis's Unigov, the Twin Cities Met Council is not an elected governmental body; rather, its members are appointed by Minnesota's governor. The absence of election imposes a serious limit on the Met Council's power to get things done. The Met Council lacks the visibility, sense of legitimacy, and leadership potential that derive from popular election. The state legislature and the governor have also intruded at times to limit the ability of the Met Council to review specific projects such as airport relocation and new stadium construction, projects clearly of regional significance and projects that seemingly merit review by the region's governing body.[39]

The Met Council also serves as the region's housing authority. The Council assigns housing goals to local communities and then encourages local governments to work with developers in order to reach their goal for new affordable housing units.[40] Especially when compared to the other metropolitan areas, the Met Council has enjoyed a fair degree of success in spreading affordable housing throughout the region. Yet, even here, the Met Council is cognizant of the limits of its power.

The Metropolitan Council's early achievements in promoting fair share housing in communities across the region have not been matched by similar success in more recent years. The Met Council has been subdued in its efforts to convince the region's better-off suburbs to allow construction of affordable housing. The Met Council sets affordable housing goals, but it is still the prerogative of each local community to approve specific projects and to build the actual housing units. More affluent suburbs in the region still resort to exclusionary zoning to keep out low-income rental housing. The more recalcitrant suburban communities have responded to regional fair housing efforts with never-ending foot-dragging; at times, the local authorities even fail to solicit proposals to build new affordable housing units, arguing that the affordable housing goals are unrealistic, especially as state and federal subsidies for such housing have dried up.[41]

Faced with intense opposition, from both suburban residents and their representatives in the state legislators, the Met Council essentially turned to a policy of noninterference: The Council largely pursues the construction of low-income housing only in communities willing to accept new units.[42] One review of the Met Council's housing efforts observed that, even as early as "the end of the 1980s," the Metropolitan Council's system of fair share housing was "all but dismantled, and what remained was largely ignored by local and regional officials."

The Council's power to promote fair share housing is, paradoxically, both impressive and limited. The Met Council initiated actions that increased the racial diversity of the suburbs, reducing the degree of residential segregation in the metropolis.[43] The Council's more recent policy of noninterference, by contrast, serves to reinforce the spatial concentration of minorities: "Low-cost housing supply expands where such housing is already concentrated, and racial inclusion gains are marginal at best."[44] Myron Orfield, the former state legislator who was one of the prime movers behind the creation of the Council expressed his disappointment: "The Met Council did a pretty good job the first 20 years of its existence meeting its goals. . . . And then it kind of came apart."[45]

The Twin Cities area is also renowned for another innovative regional approach authorized by state law: **regional tax-base sharing**. Under Minnesota's **fiscal disparities law**, a local government in the Twin Cities region does not receive all of the increase in property tax revenues generated by new commercial development that takes place within its borders. Instead, 40 percent of the gain in revenues is placed in a pool for distribution to localities throughout the region, with each jurisdiction's share determined by its population and need. The program effectively redistributes revenues from booming communities to more stagnant localities. Not surprisingly, the region's better-off suburbs bitterly criticize the plan, although, perversely, some wealthier bedroom communities that bar new development actually receive financial assistance under the program's distribution formula.[46]

To a great degree, regional tax-base sharing in the Twin Cities has worked as intended, and has provided needed assistance to poorer communities, especially to blue-collar suburbs bypassed by the growth of more dynamic suburbs. Interestingly, the region's two major cities do not always receive additional monies as a result of regional tax-base sharing. St. Paul has a long record of receiving assistance from the program. But beginning in 2011, Minneapolis, the site of substantial downtown development, has been a net "loser" that contributes to the pool of money that is redistributed to other communities.[47]

The creation of a strong regional governing body evokes strident opposition. In Minnesota, suburban activists bitterly criticize how the appointive Met Council has pursed regional growth plans, affordable housing, and the expensive construction of light rail over local opposition: "The Met Council has been a five-decade experiment in something other than democracy."[48] As was also evident in Portland, developers complain of the delays and costs of regional actions intended to protect the natural environment. Minnesota Republican legislators continue to propose measures to roll back the Met Council's powers, not just its authority in planning and housing development, but also its ability to extend the region's light-rail system:

> "Today the Minnesota State Senate took the first step in preventing a $2 billion taxpayer boondoggle from being rammed down the throats of Minnesota by an unelected, unaccountable group of Metro liberals," said Sen. David Osmek R-Mound.[49]

Despite its impressive accomplishments, were it not already in existence, it is highly questionable whether Minnesota's state government would have the political will today to vote for the creation of the Met Council.

POLYCENTRISM AND THE DEBATE OVER METROPOLITAN GOVERNMENT

VIEWPOINT #1: THE METROPOLITANIST PERSPECTIVE

As we have already seen, the creation of strong metropolitan governments is exceedingly difficult. But is strong metropolitan government truly a goal worth pursuing? *Metropolitanists* and *polycentrists* (also called *public choice theorists*) offer two sharply contrasting answers to this question.

Metropolitanists argue for a centralized regional government to provide more efficient, uniform, and equitable service provision across the metropolis. The "monocentrists"[50] argue that a single power center—a metropolitan-scale government—will help counter some of the vast inequalities that characterize communities in a metropolitan region. Environmentalists, too, often argue for a strong regional authority to constrain the revenue-seeking actions of individual local governments that encourage sprawled development.

Metropolitanists emphasize the savings to the taxpayer that result from **economies of scale**: When a government serves a large service area it can save money. A government that serves a broad region can secure price discounts by making purchases in bulk volume. A government can also avoid waste by rationally planning the provision of services over a broader geographic area, something that cannot be done when each small local community must have its own facility. A regional police or fire force, for instance, can set up a single communications center to serve the entire region, replacing the many smaller centers run by individual municipalities. Regional planning could allow for the closing of a number of redundant police and fire stations maintained by each individual local department in the fragmented metropolis. Health planning done on a regional basis can also save money by concentrating expensive and specialized health services in a few key hospitals, rather than incur the high cost of replicating such specialized care in every local hospital.

Metropolitanists also argue that services provided on a metropolitan or regional basis can promote greater equality. When school systems are region-wide, no student is trapped in a poor school hindered by the lack of property wealth in the immediate community. Larger school districts can also promote integration as opposed to the racial stratification that tends to characterize the student bodies in a region of smaller school districts.

VIEWPOINT #2: IN DEFENSE OF THE POLYCENTRIC METROPOLIS

Polycentrists, by contrast, deny the virtues that metropolitanists see in centralized regional government. Polycentrists see great virtue in having a multitude of local governments in a region. Polycentrists prefer the choice of residence offer by a multiplicity of communities with different tax rates and levels of service. Polycentrists also argue for the greater responsiveness of smaller governments as opposed to centralized and bureaucratized regional government.

Polycentrism is rooted in **public choice theory**, which observes that individuals have different tastes and want different things. No single government can possibly meet the great variety of service and taxing preferences of the many citizens who reside in a metropolitan area. A number of smaller governments, by comparison, can more easily meet the heterogeneity of citizen expectations in a region.

The existence of numerous local communities offers citizens variety and choice. Citizens who desire quality parks and recreational services and public schools with expensive curricular and co-curricular offerings can choose a home in a community that offers high-level amenities at a high rate of taxation. Citizens who do not wish to pay high local taxes can choose to reside in a community that keeps taxes low by providing a more modest level of public services.

Polycentrists reject the metropolitanist contention that bigger government is better and that a metropolitan government will save taxpayer money. Public choice theorists doubt that economies of scale exist in most service areas. Instead, public choice theorists observe that there are **diseconomies of scale**: as the scale of service provision gets larger, production suffers from new bottlenecks and other inefficiencies that drive up service costs! In larger political jurisdictions, bureaucrats may slough off work where the scale of production does not allow for effective administrative oversight. In larger settings, labor unions may also fight for increases in salaries for their members that can add to the cost of service provision. Public choice theorists argue that a metropolitan-wide government will be bloated, bureaucratized, irresponsive, and wasteful.

Our earlier review of the fiscal impact of city-county mergers would seem to confirm at least some of the insights offered by public choice theory: major city-county consolidations seldom yielded great savings.[51] Whatever costs did emerge were concentrated in only a few administrative areas. The initial savings gained from consolidation also fade over time, as service providers "level up" the wages and benefits paid municipal workers across the region to the highest levels found in the metropolis.[52] In a consolidated or metropolitan government, officials cannot justify giving lower remuneration to a firefighter or bus driver in one part of the region while offering better pay and benefits to workers performing the same job in another part of a merged or unified system.

Public choice theory applies the perspective of market economics to defend the fragmented or polycentric metropolis.[53] Public choice theorists contend that **interlocal competition** for businesses and better-off residents spurs communities to place greater emphasis on the high quality and efficient delivery of municipal services.

Polycentrists also observe that there is no need to create a strong, centralized metropolitan government to capture those economies of scale that do exist. Instead, where the efficiency gains of larger scale service provision are obvious, local communities can voluntarily enter into joint purchasing agreements and other cooperative arrangements with neighboring jurisdictions to save money.

BLIND SPOTS IN PUBLIC CHOICE THEORY?

Polycentricism and public choice theory provide a highly articulate critique of metropolitan governments. Polycentrism emphasize the virtues of the grassroots ideal and the severe shortcomings of big government. Yet there are a number of shortcomings of the public choice perspective.

At times, service consolidation—the turn to bigger government—does in fact yield important new efficiencies and service improvements. The consolidation movement achieved its most noteworthy success in the area of K–12 education, where mergers dramatically slashed the number of school districts in the United States from a whopping 117,000 (in 1940) to just 14,200 (in 2005).[54] Consolidation eliminated thousands of tiny school districts that were too small to take advantage of economies of scale. The mergers saved money by eliminating duplicative administrative positions. The consolidations also improved the quality of the schools by giving students a variety of courses and services that no tiny school district could offer.[55]

The critics of public choice theory also ask an important question: In the fragmented metropolis, just who does, and who does not, get to exercise a true choice of communities? Poorer persons do not really have the option of choosing to buy a house in a high amenity community. Just as important, the choices exercised by more privileged residents in the metropolis serve to reduce the residential choices available to the working class and the poor! The exclusionary zoning ordinances and land-use regulations of more affluent communities impede the construction of apartments and other affordable dwelling units that an unobstructed free market would otherwise provide. Exclusionary ordinances serve to limit the ability of working- and middle-class families to choose housing in a community with high-performing schools and quality community services. Poorer residents, especially in the suburbs, have no real choice but to live in poorer communities that seek to protect the community's financial well-being by limiting the services provided to the poor.[56]

Polycentrists point to the extensive intergovernmental cooperation that exists in metropolitan areas. Cooperative arrangements enable governments to take advantage of economies of scale and jointly work to improve local service delivery. Yet jurisdictions cooperate only when they find it in their mutual interest to do so. There is less interlocal cooperation to combat such serious social problems as the isolation of the poor or the racial imbalance of local school systems. Similarly, localities do not always willingly enter into agreements that constrain local development in order to preserve green space and limit sprawl in a region. Instead, the leaders of many suburban and exurban communities continue to pursue the tax gains that accompany new development within their borders

INTERLOCAL COOPERATION, OLD STYLE: THE VARIETY OF WAYS THAT CITIES AND SUBURBS WORK TOGETHER

A fairly large array of interlocal arrangements offer local communities a variety of ways to work with one another to save money and to address problems that transcend local borders. Communities cooperate no only to save money. Yet, as we shall see, local communities rarely cooperate with one another to combat major social ills or to achieve greater equity in local development and service provision.

INFORMAL COOPERATION AND JOINT POWERS AGREEMENTS

Informal cooperation occurs when two or more localities share equipment or work together without having an agreement spelled out in writing. Smaller municipalities, in particular, often work with one another on the basis of informal understandings.

A casual arrangement can evolve into a formalized **joint powers agreement**, with a legally binding document that spells out each community's contribution, say, to support a shared training center for firefighters. A joint powers agreement can be quite simple; alternatively, it can be complex and detailed. A fairly short and straightforward joint powers agreement may be all that is necessary to enable residents to patronize the libraries of neighboring communities. In contrast, the agreement between Dallas and Fort Worth that set the terms for the financing and operations of the region's international airport runs well over 100 pages.[57]

Mutual aid agreements commit localities to helping one another in times of emergency, Thornton and Westminster, Colorado, for instance, have an agreement to back up each other's computer system in the event of a disaster.[58]

The flawed response of police and fire departments in the New York region to the 9/11 terrorist attacks on the World Trade Center underscores the importance of interlocal agreement in disaster preparedness. Prior to 9/11, neighboring jurisdictions were leery about entering into agreements with an agency as huge as the Fire Department of New York (FDNY). As a result, when the 9/11 attacks struck the city, there were no clear procedures or practiced routines in place to allow the FDNY or another agency to direct the actions of first responders who came from other communities; the initial response to the emergency was poorly coordinated.[59] Interlocal agreements can establish a clear chain of command for action amid the chaos of a crisis.

Informal cooperation is especially important for communities that lie on different sides of an international border. As the intricacies of constitutional and international law often preclude a city from signing formal agreements with governments in another country, cities in a cross-border metropolis often have little alternative but to expand informal understandings.[60] (See Box 10.3).

Box 10.3
San Diego and Tijuana: Informal and Formal Cooperation in a Cross-Border Metropolis

Over the years, cooperation between San Diego, California, and its giant neighbor, Tijuana, Mexico, has become increasingly commonplace. Officials from the two cities meet to regulate traffic, to coordinate disaster response plans, to share intelligence on street gangs, to arrange ride-along exchanges for police officers, and to promote tourism and the economic development of the region. The two cities even have a joint effort to promote recycling.

Local law enforcement officials often work informally with their counterparts across the border. Under Mexico's centralized political system, municipalities generally lack the authority to enter into formal joint efforts that would help combat drug trafficking and to maintain homeland security.[1] The United States Constitution similarly bars state and local governments from negotiating their own agreements with foreign nations. As a result, even the cooperative efforts of law enforcement agencies in Tijuana and San Diego are to a great extent based on informal understandings.

The interdependence of the two cities, however, does at times necessitate joint action that extends well beyond informal understandings. The commitments of huge sums of money to construct a light-rail system to connect the two downtowns required a binding international arrangement. The Agreement on Binational Cooperation formalized a number of joint cross-border actions. San Diego residents pressed for the construction of new sewage facilities to lessen the untreated effluent from Tijuana that washes up on California beaches. Local officials have also discussed plans for the possible construction of an international airport that would straddle the border.

In the interim, San Diego has come up with an innovative solution, working with Tijuana to relieve congestion at San Diego's antiquated one-runway airport by making it easier for U.S. residents to fly out of neighboring Tijuana airport, located just five minutes across the international border. A public-private partnership came up with a novel solution that took into consideration the concerns of travelers leery of driving into Mexico and who worried about long lines at the border. New parking lots were built on the U.S. side of the border. Passengers would then pay a $16 or so fee to pass through immigration control and security as they traversed a 390-foot enclosed walkway (a "sky bridge" above the border fence!) to directly enter the terminal at Tijuana International Airport. People who do not have a scheduled flight are prohibited from using the sky bridge.[2]

In a global era, more frequent and extensive cross-border cooperation can be expected. San Diego mayor Bob Filner called on the two cities to join together to submit a bid to host the 2024 Summer Olympic Games. Filner also set up a municipal office located in Tijuana, testifying to the new geographic reality: the two cities were interdependent parts of a single region.

1. José María Ramos, "Security: The Tijuana-San Diego Region," paper presented at the Public Research Seminar on Mexico and U.S.-Mexican Relations, The Center for U.S.-Mexican Studies, University of California, San Diego, La Jolla, California, October 15, 2003, http://repositories.cdlib.org/usmex/ramos/.

2. Sandra Dibble, "Cross-Border Airport Bridge to Open in December," *San Diego Union-Tribune*, August 8, 2015; Ethan Epstein, "How San Diego Built a Bridge Over the Wall," *Politico Magazine*, February 16, 2017, www.politico.com/magazine/story/2017/02/san-diego-bridge-border-wall-airport-tijuana-214788.

INTERGOVERNMENTAL SERVICE CONTRACTING

A municipality does not always have to use its own municipal workers to provide a public service. Where state law allows, a locality can sign an **intergovernmental service contract**, purchasing the performance of a service from another city or a county. Smaller communities, for instance, contract for the provision of drinking water, a service that they cannot afford to provide on their own. Service contracting enables local governments of all sizes to save money by sharing with neighboring jurisdictions the costs of expensive equipment and facilities. Service contracting also enables localities to join together to buy products from vendors at a discounted price.

Cities turn to intergovernmental service contracting in times of fiscal distress. Cities also look to private provision in instances where municipal service provision has been severely deficient. In 2013, financially strapped Camden, New Jersey, a city suffering a high murder rate and extreme fiscal distress, disbanded its local police department and signed a shared-services agreement that gave the county law enforcement agencies new responsibilities in policing the city.

The new contract (coupled with increased financial assistance from the state) improved police service in a city that in the past had been forced to lay off a number of municipal police officers. Camden's short-staffed police department had even stopped responding to calls reporting property crime. Preliminary data shows that the new contracting arrangements helped to turn things around. Just a year after the intergovernmental service contract was put into effect, the murder rate in the city fell sharply. Police response times to calls for help fell from an outrageous 60 minutes to just 4.4 minutes. The reorganization undercut unionized city officers by turning service responsibilities over to lower-paid, nonunionized county personnel.[61]

Southern California's **Lakewood Plan** is perhaps the most expansive variant of intergovernmental service contracting in the United States. The Lakewood Plan offers communities in Los Angeles County an extremely large "menu" of services (from dead animal pickup to police patrols, ambulance service, and fire protection) that can be purchased from the county. A municipality in Los Angeles County does not even have to maintain its own police force! The municipality can choose to have the county provide protective services, with a legally binding contract specifying such details as the frequency of patrols, the number of officers in each patrol car, and the price that the city will pay. The plan takes its name from the City of Lakewood, which incorporated

Box 10.4
The Lakewood Plan: Cure or Contributor to Metropolitan Fragmentation?

Under the Lakewood Plan, a municipality in Los Angeles County may choose to have the county provide local police patrols, fire protection, road construction, building inspections, and any of a large number of other municipal services. The arrangement allows communities—especially smaller communities—to save money. A community can secure high-quality and professionalized services without having to incur the expense of setting up its own municipal departments and hiring and training its own personnel.

The Lakewood Plan emphasizes economies of scale (cost savings!) and quality improvements that can be gained from the countywide provision of services. But in an important way, the plan also exacerbated metropolitan fragmentation by catalyzing the formation of new and autonomous suburban governments. The years following the initial creation of the Lakewood Plan saw a rash of municipal incorporations: Previously unincorporated areas became formal general-purpose governments, gaining the protections of home rule while relying on the county for the provision of important local services. The City of Lakewood itself was formed as residents saw municipal incorporation as a means to avert possible annexation by the neighboring Long Beach.

The Lakewood Plan led to the creation of a number of **minimal cities**—small, independent suburban jurisdictions that purchase a large portion of municipal services from the county. The newly incorporated suburbs often were centers of "white flight," where more affluent residents sought refuge away from the region's troubled core cities. The newly created communities then used their zoning and land-use powers to price out low-income and renter populations. Rancho Palos Verdes restricted new development, preserving the community's exclusive, estate-like character. The racial bias embedded in the plan was substantial: 28 of the 32 communities created as a result of the Lakewood Plan had a population that was less than 1 percent African-American.

Business interests engineered a number of the early incorporations, creating small municipalities that contracted with the county for service provision. Business interests did not wish to pay the high taxes—especially school taxes—that were almost certain to be levied if their commercial properties were annexed by a populous neighboring community.

The strange names of some of the newly created Lakewood communities reflect their industrial and commercial roots. The City of Industry was created as a tax shelter for local railroad yards, factories, and warehouses. In order to meet the minimum population of 500 required by state law for incorporation, the community even had to include the 169 patients and 31 employees of a local psychiatric sanatorium in its population count. By the year 2000, the City of Industry, with a population of only 777, was still not really all that much of a city: The city levied no taxes on industrial and residential property. The City of Commerce likewise was formed by industrial leaders as a tax haven for railroad and industrial property. The City of Dairy Valley was similarly created as a **tax island** to protect large agricultural land holdings from the higher rates of taxation that would likely accompany annexation. As Dairy Valley grew over the years and agricultural interests sold off their acreage to residential developers, the city changed its name to Cerritos.

As these case studies illustrate, service contracting under the Lakewood Plan has been more than just a vehicle for communities to realize service improvements and cost savings. The Lakewood Plan has also been part of an exercise of power that exacerbated inequality in the Los Angeles region, shielding wealthy home-owners and large industrialists and commercial landowners from the higher taxes that annexation would lead them to pay in support of low-income and minority-dominated school systems.

Sources: Gary J. Miller, *Cities by Contract: The Politics of Municipal Incorporation* (Cambridge, MA: MIT Press, 1981); Michan Andrew Connor, "'Public Benefits from Public Choice': Producing Decentralization in Metropolitan Los Angeles, 1954–1973," *Journal of Urban History* 39, no. 1 (January 2013): 79–100. The figures on the African-American population of Lakewood communities are provide by Connor, p. 81

in 1954 and became the first community in the region to contract with L.A. County for law enforcement and other services.

The Lakewood Plan enables municipalities to provide upgraded services while sharing in cost savings. Municipalities, nonetheless, complain about a loss of local control as the Lakewood Plan cedes substantial service-delivery authority to county administrators. The Lakewood Plan also prompted communities in the county to incorporate and thereby shield themselves from annexation. By promoting the incorporation of new "minimal cities,'" the Lakewood Plan served the interests of corporate heads who did not wish to have their factories and rail yards taxed at higher rates in order to support local schools and other public services (see Box 10.4).

COUNCILS OF GOVERNMENTS (COGS) AND REGIONAL PLANNING COUNCILS (RPCS)

A **council of governments (COG)** is a voluntary association of the top elected local officials in a region. A COG functions much like a metropolitan version of the United Nations: Top city and suburban officials meet to discuss matters of mutual interest. The COG's staff highlights regional trends, federal funding opportunities, and helps identify possible solutions to regional problems. Again, much like the United Nations, the COG possesses little authority or ability to enforce action on unwilling members.

COGs are found in metropolitan areas across the nation. Some of the more noteworthy COGs include: Boston's Metropolitan Planning Area Council (MAPC), the Baltimore Metropolitan Council (BMC), the Metropolitan Washington Council of Governments, the Southeast Michigan Council of Governments (SEMCOG) in greater Detroit, the Houston-Galveston Area Council, the Denver Regional Council of Governments (DRCOG), the Association of Bay Area Governments (ABAG) in greater San Francisco, the San Diego Association of Governments (SANDAG), and the Southern California Association of Governments (SCAG) which serves 6 counties, 91 cities, and 18 million residents.

A **regional planning council (RPC)** is a staff-dominated variation of a COG. An RPC lacks the assembly of a region's mayors and city managers at its top. Instead, an appointed executive director determines RPC research and planning activities.

COGs and RPCs tend to be rather weak organizations. The councils are advisory only: They possess no legislative authority, no ability to force local governments to comply with regional plans, and no ability to levy taxes to raise funds for regional projects. Although it rarely happens, a member local government can even withdraw from the COG or RPC rather than comply with council-developed plans. Orange County in 1989 stopped paying its dues and withdrew from SCAG. In the San Francisco Bay Area, Corte Madera in 2013 voted to withdraw from ABAG, a protest against the regional council's efforts to build new housing in the scenic Marin County community.

As the leading officials of a COG or RPC are not directly chosen by the voters, the organization lacks the sense of legitimacy and the leadership potential that derive from popular election. As a COG or RPC is an unelected planning council and not an elected government, deicision making in the organization does not have abide by the one-person-one-vote principle. Typically, each member city and suburb in a COG receives that exact same vote—a single vote—regardless of the size of the local population. Such malapportionment serves to underrepresent a region's more populous cities and suburbs.[62]

The inherent weakness of the COG approach is evident in greater Detroit where SEMCOG (the Southeast Michigan Council of Governments) has been historically unable to get local governments to collaborate in creating a system of mass transit to better serve the region. Even federally assisted transit projects fell apart as the region's suburbs battled with Detroit over how federal funds would be divided. The suburbs generally oppose any initiative they fear will saddle them with new taxes or the liability for past projects undertaken outside their local communities. The suburbs favor improved bus transit projects rather than rail centered on Detroit. As a consequence, the Detroit region does not have a viable commuter rail system.[63]

In California, a number of suburban jurisdictions have refused to comply with the fair share housing plans developed by regional planning agencies such as SCAG and ABAG. Recalcitrant municipalities simply would not take the actions necessary to meet the construction targets outlined for them in the region's affordable housing plan. In the Bay Area, a number of suburban residents opposed plans for density development as envisioned by ABAG's Smart Growth plan, a plan that sought to build 188,000 new homes in "stack and pack" developments in "transit villages" centered on commuter rail stations.[64]

COGs tend to shy away from controversial housing and social policy initiatives that may estrange dues-paying cities. As a result, many COGs and RPCs simply devote staff efforts to conducting studies and providing the technical assistance that member communities require to secure federal and state grants. The Baltimore Metropolitan Council (BMC) has a history of avoiding hard choices when recommending local transportation projects for funding. Instead, the BMC simply aids local communities in their efforts to win federal funding even for more parochial transportation projects.[65] Boston's Metropolitan Area Planning Council (MPAC) similarly avoids hard issues and instead has relied on presenting demographic and economic trends, data to help convince local officials of the need for transportation-oriented development. MPAC also lobbies the state to fund sustainable development projects.[66]

Over the years, COGs and RPCs have ramped up their policy efforts in one prominent policy area: transportation. The federal **Intermodal Surface Transportation and Efficiency Act (ISTEA** or "Ice Tea" as it is commonly pronounced) requires that a region designate a **metropolitan planning organization (MPO)** to serve as "a voice for metropolitan areas"[67] in promoting more balanced transportation systems and protecting the natural environment. In most regions, the COG or RPC serves as the MPO, thereby gaining the authority under federal law to establish project priorities and coordinate transit spending in a region.

In succeeding years, ISTEA has been renewed, modified, and given a variety of new names: **TEA-21** (the Transportation Equity Act for the 21st Century), **SAFETEA-LU** (Safe, Accountable, Flexible, Efficient Transportation Act: A Legacy for Users), and **MAP-21** (Moving Ahead for Progress in the 21st Century). But the role played by the designated MPO remains essentially the same. In numerous regions across the nation, MPOs have succeeded in taking some of the monies that would normally be spent on highways and shifting the funds to improvements in commuter rail and bus service. In Salt Lake City, Denver, Dallas, Charlotte, Las Vegas, San Jose, and San Diego, regional planners targeted funds to the development of light-rail systems.[68] But in other metropolitan areas, weak and understaffed COGs have been no match for state highway departments, construction unions, and other interests committed to highway spending.[69]

MPO authority is often critical to COG influence. DRCOG, the Denver Regional Council of Governments, serves as the Denver region's MPO. Local elected officials in the Denver area feel the need to attend and participate in COG work sessions or else worry that their constituencies may lose out when the MPO doles out its federal transit improvement monies (see Box 10.5). By contrast, the greater Boston MAPC does not serve as the Boston region's MPO, with the consequence that busy local officials often fail to attend MAPC sessions.[70]

What is the overall assessment of COGs and RPCs? A COG or RPC can be effective, but it depends on the organization's powers (most importantly, whether or not the council possesses MPO authority) and on the quality of its leadership. But even regional organizations that possess quite limited formal powers have value. In the ten-county greater Pittsburgh region continued dialogue among the members of the Southwestern Pennsylvania Commission (SPC) resulted in a shift away from the "parochial protection" of local interests to a "more enlightened discussion of the needs of the region."[71] Regional associations bring officials from different communities into face-to-face contact with one another, leading to the development of personal relationships and a sense of trust essential to collegial action.[72]

Regional association toe a fine line when they attempt more far-reaching actions. The Southern California Association of Governments (SCAG) strategically sought to side-step possible controversy in formulating a *2012–2035 Regional Transit Plan and Sustainable Communities Strategy*. The plan proposed to increase the number of affordable housing units in the region. The plan also emphasized transit-oriented development to lessen automobile reliance and to reduce greenhouse gas emissions. But SCAG did not force unwilling suburbs to increase development densities. Instead, SCAG offered priority funding to communities that concentrated new housing and job sites around rail stations and bus stops.[73]

Box 10.5
**Calling "Doctor COG" (DRCOG): The Denver Regional Council
of Governments**

Denver provides a prime example of a region where collaborative action has produced a number of noteworthy successes, especially in terms of projects devoted
to economic development. The Denver Metro Chamber of Commerce formed a
new regional leadership group, which evolved into the Metro Denver Economic
Development Corporation, in order to increase the pressure for a new international
airport. Adams County allowed the City of Denver to annex land to build the Denver International Airport, providing direct air service to Tokyo and Mexico City and
opening the Denver region to new global investment and markets.,

Residents of Denver's suburbs approved ballot measures that provided funds
for mass transit and various cultural facilities and sports stadiums situated in
downtown Denver. The votes indicated that the people of Aurora, Littleton, and
other communities in the region "were starting to understand that they were united
for better or worse."

The Denver area's ethos of regionalism is the result of the leadership provided
by "Doctor COG" or DRCOG (the Denver Regional Council of Governments).
DRCOG did not attempt to force local officials to comply with regional plans.
Instead, DRCOG turned to a strategy of extensive consultation, participation, and
collaboration that succeeded in getting member governments to buy into MetroVision 2020. Member governments even signed the "Mile High Compact" that sought
to steer new development to growth centers located along the stations of a new
light-rail system. The DRCOG relies on member education. The COG provides
local officials with information that points to key economic and demographic trends
in the region, underscoring the mounting costs of continued sprawl and inaction.
DRCOG then clarifies the possible options for dealing with emerging problems.

The largely voluntary system of collaboration evident in greater Denver, of
course, has its limitations. DRCOG lacks the power to ensure that local governments actually abide by MetroVision principles when they approve specific new
local developments. Member governments have ignored the region's "voluntary"
growth boundary when new development promises a locality significant new
tax receipts. DRCOG has enjoyed its greatest successes in assisting economic
development. The council has given less attention to social policies and efforts to
improve the racial balance of the region, policy areas where there is little prospect
of gaining consensual action.

The "voluntary regionalism" evident in greater Denver actually is not entirely
voluntary. Serving as the region's designated MPO, DRCOG controls the dis-
bursement of federal transit project monies. Local governments believe that they
must proclaim their fealty to the principles outlined in MetroVision 2020 and other
regional planning documents, or else risk seeing their transit projects fall to the
bottom of the list when DRCOG determines the priorities for federal transit funds.

Sources: Bruce Katz and Jennifer Bradley, *The Metropolitan Revolution: How Cities and Metros Are Fixing Our Broken Politics and Fragile Economy* (Washington, DC: Brookings Institution, 2013), chap. 3; the "united for better or worse" quotation appears on p. 43; and Christina D. Rosan, *Governing the Fragmented Metropolis: Planning for Regional Stability* (Philadelphia: University of Pennsylvania Press, 2016), 59–98.

SPECIAL DISTRICTS

There are nearly 90,000 units of local government in the United States (see Table 10.2), but most are *not* **general-purpose governments**, the cities, counties, villages, and townships, the sort of local governments that provide a wide range of municipal services. Instead, many local governments have much more narrow responsibilities, so narrow, in fact, that many Americans do not even recognize that these entities are, in fact, independent bodies or local governments. More than 38,000 **special districts** provide a single specific service (such as drainage and flood control, solid waste management, fire protection, water supply, mosquito control, community college classes, or assisted housing) or a small set of related services. Another 13,000 **independent school districts** provide K–12 education and do not take orders from the local mayor or city council. While the number of school districts in the United States has shrunk considerably over the years due to consolidation, as Table 10.2 reveals, nonschool special districts are the fastest-growing form of government in the United States!

A special district may be small or large; its size depends on the service (or services) the district provides. Special districts for libraries, fire protection, and local recreation often serve relatively small geographic areas. By contrast, the Metropolitan Sanitary District of Greater Chicago and the Forest Preserve District of Cook County both serve an area that is greater in size than the city of Chicago. The Barton Springs Edwards Aquifer Conservation District covers an eight-county region in central Texas in its efforts to protect and recharge local sources of groundwater.

The prominence of special districts varies considerably by state; each state determines the service responsibilities, taxing powers, and geographical boundaries of special

Table 10.2
Number of Local Governmental Units in the United States

Type of government	1952	1962	1972	1982	1992	2002	2012
County	3,052	3,043	3,044	3,041	3,043	3,034	3,031
Municipal	16,807	18,000	18,517	19,076	19,279	19,429	19,519
Town/Township	17,202	17,142	16,991	16,734	16,656	16,504	16,360
School district	67,355	34,678	15,781	14,851	14,422	13,506	12,880
Special district	12,340	18,323	23,885	28,078	31,555	35,052	38,266

Source: U.S. Census Bureau, 2002 and 2012 Census of Governments. The figures for 2012 based on updates reported by the Bureau in 2016 in "Local Governments by Type and State, 2012," *American FactFinder*, https://factfinder.census.gov/faces/tableservices/jsf/pages/productview.xhtml?src=bkmk.

districts. In Florida, some 600 Community Development Districts issue billions of dollars in municipal bonds to finance water and sewage projects, new parks, and other local infrastructure improvements. By contrast, Maryland, North Carolina, and Virginia make virtually no use of special districts.[74]

The boundaries of a special district can cross established local political borders, enabling more effective service delivery and the cost savings that can be gained from economies of scale. Where a special district's boundaries encompass both poorer and richer communities, its actions can even begin to address equity concerns. Suburban taxpayers, for instance, help to fund the Milwaukee Technical College, a special-district institution that disproportionately serves central-city residents.[75] Similarly, while the Five Rivers MetroParks provides programming in parks throughout Montgomery County, Ohio, the taxes collected by MetroParks District over the county in effect help to sustain the numerous ethnic festivals and community celebrations that take place in Riverfront Park in downtown Dayton.

The majority of special districts and independent school districts have the authority to levy taxes. Other districts rely on user fees and charges; a parks or recreation district, for instance, may charge group for reserving a picnic shelter or a baseball diamond. The ability of special districts to raise revenues helps to explain the increasingly prominent role that special districts are playing in local government. In states where voters or the legislature have imposed strict limits on the taxing and borrowing authority of cities and counties, civic leaders have turned to special districts to raise revenues and to "get things done."

Special service districts represent a flexible approach in an attempt to deal with problems that spill over the usual local political borders. In Ohio, port districts have at times acted as hidden regional governments, borrowing money and providing the funding for affordable housing, neighborhood revitalization, commercial redevelopment, brownfields reclamation, and even museum modernization and the construction of a new sports arena—projects not always directly related to port activities. The port districts, quite importantly, offer project financing tools that may not be readily available to other local governments, powers that are often denied smaller communities.

Special districts are relatively **invisible and unaccountable governments**. Most citizens cannot name any of the officials in charge of community college districts, sewer and water districts, parks districts, and the various other special-purpose local government that affect their lives. Newspapers and television devote little coverage to the actions of narrow-purpose district boards. As a result, the general public has difficulty in holding these bodies accountable.

The absence of public scrutiny creates a vacuum into which highly motivated special interests can enter and seize control. In Texas and numerous other states, private developers and real-estate interests have dominated the boards of **urban fringe districts**, using these public bodies to issue the bonds and borrow the money to help pay for the infrastructure to support the construction of new subdivisions.[76] When building Disney World in Florida, the Disney Corporation turned to the creation of a special district to shield its development plans from political scrutiny, thereby ensuring that the corporation would not have to respond to the concerns of local officials and voters in the region (see Box 10.6).

Box 10.6
Was Walt Disney World Given Its Own Government?

When the Disney Corporation sought to build Walt Disney World, one of the corporation's first actions was to have the Florida legislature create the Reedy Creek Improvement District. The state in 1967 established a 40-square-mile tourism-related special district, effectively ensuring the Disney Corporation that it would not have to ask the elected officials of Orlando, Kissimmee, or any other municipality for approval of its development plans. Within the 40-square-mile district, Disney effectively assumed the powers of local government, with the ability to make decisions concerning land use, building codes, police and fire services, drainage, sewer line extensions, and other infrastructure investment. As the district is a unit of local government, Disney was even able to use Reedy Creek to issue public bonds, borrowing money at low interest rates to finance theme park development. Having gained control of its own special local government, the Disney Corporation did not have to worry that outside local political actors, not loyal to the Disney vision, could intrude and impose unwanted taxes, impact fees, environmental safeguards, and requirements for subsidized housing.

Disney officials adopted rules that effectively limited the voting power of residents in the district. Reedy Creek is a special district and not a general-purpose local government, even though the district possesses a fairly broad range of municipal powers, including the ability to operate an airport and a heliport. Not comprising a "government," Reedy Creek was not obliged to follow the one-person-one vote principle of representation. Instead, votes in the district were allocated according to property acreage. The Disney Corporation, as the most sizable property owner, possessed effective control of the district.

The Disney Corporation also initially sought to limit the construction of housing; as the few houses in the district were largely occupied by Disney executives and employees, assuring that there would be no residents in a position to challenge Disney's plans. When the Disney Corporation built the new residential town of Celebration, Florida, the property was de-annexed (that is, detached) from the Reedy Creek District, so that the new residents of Celebration would have no vote or say over Disney's actions and plans for expansion.

Sources: Richard Foglesong, "When Disney Comes to Town," in *The Politics of Urban America: A Reader*, ed. Dennis R. Judd and Paul P. Kantor (Boston: Allyn and Bacon, 1998), 238–241; Richard E. Foglesong, *Married to the Mouse: Walt Disney World and Orlando* (New Haven, CT: Yale University Press, 2003); Chad D. Emerson, "Merging Public and Private Governance: How Disney's Reedy Creek Improvement District 'Re-imagined' the Traditional Division of Local Regulatory Powers," *Florida State University Law Review* 36 (2009): 177–213.

In Texas, political conservatives complain that special districts with their "ghost-like governments" and the power to tax have grown "like weeds."[77] In Ohio, anti-tax groups similarly criticize local port districts for helping to fund sports arenas, arts museum renovation, and various economic projects that are not even located in close proximity to a lake or river.[78]

REGIONAL DISTRICTS AND AUTHORITIES

States also establish **regional districts and authorities** that are broader and more powerful variants of the special district. The Bay Area Rapid Transit District, the Southern California Metropolitan Water District, the Massachusetts Bay Transit Authority, the Chicago Metropolitan Sanitary District, and the Seattle Port District are all quite important regional entities. Quite often, regional authorities derive much of their power from their ability to issue bonds and borrow the extensive amounts of money needed for important infrastructure projects.

The Port Authority of New York and New Jersey possesses broad powers in a number of service areas that go well beyond the maintenance of the region's freight terminals and shipping facilities. The Port Authority runs the region's major airports, highways, and bridges. The Port Authority also helps maintains commuter rail and bus systems, including a giant bus terminal in midtown Manhattan. The Port Authority also pursues commercial office development, and takes the lead in spatial and economic planning in the bi-state region.

The Port Authority built the original "Twin Towers" World Trade Center skyscraper in Lower Manhattan; 37 Port Authority police officers died when the gigantic structure collapsed in the 9/11 terrorist attacks. The Port Authority is also a major real-estate holder and developer; the PA was a major player in the negotiations and infighting over just what would be built in the post-9/11 reconstruction effort at Ground Zero.[79]

To whom do such powerful regional districts and authorities answer? Regional authorities "are frequently as accountable to bond buyers as to the localities and the citizen consumers."[80] In the 1970s, the directors of the Port Authority of New York and New Jersey neglected the region's ailing commuter rail system, which they viewed as a never-ending "bad" investment; instead, the PA's directors continued to promote highway construction.[81] A shift in the balance of political forces at the state level eventually forced the PA to forego its conservative business sensibilities and finally agree to divert some of its funds to the revitalization of the PATH commuter rail tubes that run under the Hudson River.

While the Port Authority has a number of impressive powers and is assigned responsibility for regional planning in the bi-state region, the Authority, truth be told, is only a weak vehicle for regional cooperation. The Port Authority could not get state and local governments in New York and New Jersey to abide by the "nonaggression pact" to which they had earlier agreed. State and local leaders had promised not to engage in economic poaching; they promised not to offer tax incentives and other subsidies to lure businesses away from neighboring communities. The agreement, however, lacked teeth and was repeatedly broken. New York leaders were especially outraged when state and local officials in New Jersey helped pay for the cross-river relocation of over 1,000 First Chicago Trust jobs from the corporation's offices in Lower Manhattan.[82]

STRENGTHENED COUNTY GOVERNMENT

Counties have the potential to act regionally, as a county generally governs a greater expanse of territory than does a single municipality.[83] Yet, for much of the country's history, this potential was not utilized as the counties were America's "forgotten governments,"[84] units of government that could meet the limited needs of rural areas but were underfunded, understaffed, and generally ill-disposed to tackle the varied problems of urban communities.

Today, America's counties are quite different. Urban and suburban counties have assumed new service responsibilities in law enforcement, social services, housing assistance, workforce training, and economic development. To be able to do so, counties had to reform their operations in order to build a greater capacity for actions. Counties tapped new sources of revenue to finance their expanded activities. Numerous counties modernized their administrative systems and gave an elected executive new powers and capacity to lead the county. In Florida, modernized county governments led by an elected executive or a professional county manager are more likely to abide by sustainable growth policies; counties operating under the older commissioner form of government, by comparison, are more likely to approve "leap frog" development that exacerbates sprawl.[85]

Yet, even the strengthened urban county faces an important limitation when it comes to regional action: No county can govern beyond its borders. In the more than 150 metropolitan areas that spill over two or more counties, a county's initiatives can, at best, provide only for subregional—not true regional—action.

TOWARD A NEW REGIONALISM BUILT ON PUBLIC-PRIVATE PARTNERSHIPS

Neighboring municipalities voluntarily cooperate when there are mutual cost savings and the promise of other "win-win" benefits. Local officials are hesitant to cooperate when regional agreements involve numerous partners and provide no guarantees that other communities will deliver on their promises of future action. Local officials are also reluctant to commit local monies to regional actions that entail tax increases or that in other ways may incur the ire of local voters.[86]

The more commonplace forms of interlocal cooperation described in the preceding section of this chapter do not always provide for the more sustained or "deeper" collaborations that are necessary to reposition a troubled regional economy and attract new industries to a metropolitan region. As Theodore Hershberg has observed, "The most important lesson that the global economy teaches is that regions—not cities or counties—will be the units of economic competition."[87]

When deciding where to locate a major facility, a global corporation does not look only at an individual community; instead, corporate officials assess a region's capacity to provide the trained labor, transportation access (whether roads and mass transit will permit workers to easily reach the corporation's facility), and other public infrastructure (i.e. quality of water) and services (i.e. firefighting capabilities) that have an impact on business operations. Major corporations also look at a region's schools, parks, and cultural facilities to see if an area will be able to attract executives and talented workers. A shortage of housing at a reasonable price will work to a region's detriment, as a corporation may have difficulty in attracting key personnel who must commute long distances from homes they can afford.

No city or suburb, acting on its own, can provide the expanded airport facilities, roadways, university-provided technological assistance, workforce training, and entrepreneurial supports that are valued by technology-based businesses.[88] A region improves its chances of winning a major new investment if it can present an interested business with a clear plan for "holistic economic development,"[89] a multifaceted strategy that details how various communities in a region will work together to provide the trained labor, infrastructure improvements, transportation, and workforce housing that meet a firm's needs. Communities that work together enjoy a distinct advantage in the competition for new businesses.

How does the new generation of regional collaborations differ from the older forms of interlocal cooperation? Quite often, the collaborative efforts of the **New Regionalism** are business-led and take place outside the formal hallways of government. The New Regionalism seeks long-range goals, such as the economic repositioning of a region, that venture far beyond many of the narrower and more limited voluntary interlocal arrangements reviewed earlier in this chapter. Advocates of the New Regionalism do not waste time on the seemingly futile task of creating strong new institutions of metropolitan govern*ment*. Instead, the New Regionalism emphasizes **govern*ance***, creating a process for existing governments, private officials, and other civic leader to work hand in hand.

In the 16-county Cleveland region, private foundations and philanthropic organizations formed the Fund for Our Economic Future, committing $30 million to bring municipal leaders together to redefine and reposition postindustrial Northeast Ohio. The Fund financed research that clearly reported long-term trends, thereby helping local leaders see just which industrial sectors offered the best opportunities for job growth in Northeast Ohio. The Fund also assisted local governments as they applied for public- and foundation-funded grants that helped provide the initial financial incentives for collaborative actions. Quite significantly, in a region marked by racial cleavages, the Fund stressed equity goals as well as economic growth. The Fund promoted minority-owned businesses and urged other businesses to have an "inclusion officer" or the assistance of an outside inclusion adviser to assure that poorer residents in the Cleveland region would share in the jobs and benefits provided by the region's economic revival.[90]

As the greater Cleveland example illustrates, New Regionalism efforts tend to focus on collaborations for economic development. The collaborations are often initiated by business and philanthropic leaders and not just by public officials. The regional undertakings of collaborations such as the Fund for Our Economic Future in Northeast Ohio blur the lines that normally separate government, businesses, and nonprofit organizations.

Public-private partnerships lie at the core of the New Regionalism. The Allegheny Conference similarly brought together a wide range of corporate, nonprofit, and governmental leaders to "re-vision" the Pittsburgh region: The regional partners decided to recast greater Pittsburgh, then a dying center of steel manufacturing, as a high-tech and office-headquarters city. The private-led planning process was crucial to overcoming the seemingly debilitating hindrances posed by the region's severe political fragmentation: There are over 300 units of government in Allegheny County alone.[91]

In southern California, BIOCOM (an industry association) and the San Diego Regional Economic Development Corporation joined with local municipalities, the San Diego Association of Governments, and area universities to transform the region's economic base. When the Cold War came to an end, the greater San Diego area suffered extensive job losses in defense-related industries. The new public-private discussions focused on how to replace the jobs lost in defense-related industries with new opportunities that could be created in the growing biotechnology and biomedical sectors.[92]

New Regional collaborations typically seek to avoid the bitter controversies that flare up whenever reformers attempt to redraw local political boundaries. Rather than restructure local governments, the New Regionalism seeks a more politically pragmatic path to overcoming metropolitan fragmentation. The New Regionalism creates ad hoc public-private partnerships that are less rigid and rule-bound than are the more traditional and bureaucratized means of cooperation. The New Regionalism seeks govern*ance* that comes through ad hoc arrangements that gets things done. The New Regionalism is also largely focused on economic development, a sharp contrast to the earlier generations of metropolitan reform that sought cooperative efforts to save money and upgrade municipal service provision.

Whose interests are enshrined in the New Regionalism? Business-led partnerships can emerge and become **shadow governments** that make important developmental decisions with no clear lines of accountability to voters or to the general public.[93] Business-led collaborations often fall short of the standards of openness ("transparency") and public participation expected of democratic governments.

The New Regionalism has been most successful in the economic development arena. When it comes to housing and social policy, the New Regionalism often fails to produce results beyond what was already being obtained by more traditional forms of interlocal cooperation. Communities tend to cooperate with neighboring communities that have similar populations and political leanings.[94]

CAN THE NEW REGIONALISM MOVE BEYOND ECONOMIC DEVELOPMENT? THE POLITICS OF BUILDING REGIONAL COALITIONS

Can the New Regionalism move beyond its emphasis on economic development? The greater Cleveland collaboration was noteworthy for the attention it gave to equity concerns and social inclusion. On the whole, however, the New Regionalism has had only the most limited success in pursuing equity and social justice.

Former Minnesota state legislator and metropolitanist Myron Orfield argues that creative regional alliances can be mobilized even on such contentious policy matters as taxation, environmental protection, and social policy. Metropolitan politics does not have to be marked by a clear and rigid cleavage that divides a central city and its suburbs. Numerous suburbs have begun to discover that they have much to gain by working with a central city.

According to Orfield, only a region's more affluent or **favored-quarter communities** are the true beneficiaries of the unfettered interlocal competition for new development. Declining inner-ring and working-class suburbs are not often chosen as the site of upscale commercial and residential projects, as developers prefer to locate such development in a region's favored-quarter communities. Rapidly growing working- and middle-class suburbs too often discover that they lack the resources to provide the quality schools and services that residents expect. Inner-ring communities, working-class suburbs, and the central city can all benefit from an alliance that redirects state economic assistance away from a region's favored-quarter communities.[95]

Smart Growth policies for infill development, green space protection, and farmland preservation (discussed in Chapter 3) offer the possibilities of building a broad coalition of central cities, inner-ring suburbs, environmentalists, and agriculture interests. In Ohio, the First Suburbs Consortium joined with farmers and environmentalists in support of the state's Agricultural Preservation Act, a measure that preserved farmland and thereby helped to steer new investment to central cities and already built-up suburban areas. In greater Portland, Oregon, environmentalists and farmers joined downtown business interests to fight for growth management measures to preserve agricultural acreage and green space, and, in doing so, to steer new growth to already developed city and suburban communities.

A program of regional tax sharing (such as Minnesota's fiscal disparities law) can work to the mutual advantage of central cities and declining inner-ring suburbs. GIS (geographic information system) data and computer-generated maps provide clear visuals that can illustrate how revised programs can enable a wider range of communities to share in the benefits from new investment in a region.[96]

In Arizona, tax sharing helped provide a solution to the territorial infighting that stalled a major commercial project. Tempe, rapidly growing suburban Chandler, and the Town of Guadalupe all fought aggressively to win the location of a major new shopping plaza. The infighting finally came to an end when the developer signed an agreement to share the sales tax revenues generated from the 200-plus store development with all three communities. Typical of New Regionalism, the solution was business-led. Elsewhere in Arizona, Phoenix and suburban Glendale agreed to share both the construction costs and the gains in sales tax revenues from a new 15,000-seat ballpark and spring training complex. The ballpark was built on land that Glendale owned, even though the acreage was situated inside the city limits of Phoenix.[97]

The experience of Salt Lake City reveals that the New Regionalism can address equity and environmental as well as economic concerns. Civic leaders in Utah came together to discuss how the region could pursue growth while also preserving the area's scenic beauty. The visioning process involved the state's Mormon community. Faith-based groups and business groups came to a consensus: Utah should reject unbridled sprawl in favor of compact development, with new growth concentrated around the region's light-rail system. Faith-based communities also directed discussions to poverty reduction and the incorporation of immigrants.[98]

Church groups and nonprofit associations add a "justice" dimension to regional action. In Minnesota, church congregations were advocates of regional fair-share-housing and other social justice measures.[99] In Chicago, Bethel New Life, active in the city's low-income African-American community, joined with nearby suburbs in the fight to save a rail line that served both poorer and better-off communities on Chicago's west side.[100]

CONCLUSION: GOVERNING REGIONS IN A GLOBAL AGE

In the vast majority of metropolitan areas, measures to implement strong metropolitan government are not politically feasible. Even city-county mergers are no longer viable options, except in relatively small communities. Annexation remains the most commonly used tool of boundary adjustment but operates within a system of rather severe state-imposed restrictions. The major annexations that fundamentally changed the shape of local governments are a thing of the past.

Americans as a whole, and suburbanites in particular, remain opposed to the creation of strong metropolitan governments. In some cases, racial minorities, too, are suspicious that metropolitan reform plans will dilute their voting strength and undermine their chances of winning control of city hall. Abstract arguments that emphasize the virtues of regionalism for efficiency and economic growth are insufficient to offset the American insistence on preserving local autonomy.[101] Americans allow the creation of regional institutions to handle specific regional problems—as long as local autonomy in general is respected.

Regional action rarely addresses the fundamental inequalities of the metropolis. City-county consolidation does not lead to school integration, as the public schools are universally left out of such consolidation plans. The continued post-consolidation existence of numerous cities, and taxing and service districts further undermines the ability of city-county mergers to increase equity in service provision. The governments of consolidated areas continue to support infrastructure investment and development projects in already-prospering portions of the metropolis.[102]

Still, despite its obvious limitations, regionalism is a strategy worth pursuing. Metropolitan reform and collaborative actions can yield significant cost savings and enhance regional economic development. The creation of Unigov did help spur the rebirth of downtown Indianapolis. The merger of Kansas City (Kansas) with surrounding Wyandotte County similarly enabled civic leaders to win the location of a new NASCAR track and the tourism-related development that accompanied it.[103]

In most metropolitan areas, the key to a more prosperous economic future lies not in city-county consolidation or the creation of a strong metropolitan government but in launching creative partnerships for regional govern*ance*. As this chapter has detailed, there exists a fairly large array of cooperative arrangements that enable local governments to work together. The business-led strategies of the New Regionalism offer the prospect of deeper collaborations for a region's economic growth.

The New Regionalism emphasizes potential of informal, flexible, and extra-governmental partnerships that enable public, private, and nonprofit officials to collaborate outside the formal channels of government. The business-led nature of much of the New Regionalism, however, raises important questions of democracy and accountability, questions that are also raised when decision-making power is exercised by "invisible" special districts and powerful metropolitan authorities. Oftentimes, major corporations and private developers enjoy privileged access to special districts, regional planning commissions, and business-led regional summits and visioning processes. By contrast, neighborhood groups face great difficulty in mobilizing to pressure seemingly distant regional bodies and to participate in the discussions of relatively obscure quasi-governmental associations. Latino and African-American activists have been hesitant to embrace regional environmental measures and other regional efforts that seemingly offer very little to improve the lives of the inner-city poor.[104]

The processes of governance have also enabled suburban residents to use their seats on the boards of nonprofit organizations and public-private partnership councils to influence the direction of activities located in central cities, including economic development initiatives, the operation of museums, and even the emphasis on school choice programs.[105] As Detroit teetered on the edge of bankruptcy, good-government civic groups argued for the benefits of regionalism, that nonprofit associations could run key institutions with members who reside outside of Detroit helping to sustain the Detroit Institute of Arts, the Cobo Convention Center, and the Detroit Zoo. Members of Detroit's city council, however, objected that the black-dominant city was being shown no respect, that outsiders were urging the city to deliver its crown jewels to outsiders.[106]

Requirements for transparency, public election, and citizen participation can help increase the democratic nature of regional decision making. In the intergovernmental city, community-based organizations have been able to use the opportunities offered by federal transportation legislation to press a number of MPOs (metropolitan planning organizations) to include, as part of their regional transportation plan, job training and hiring measures targeted to disadvantaged citizens of the region.[107] Grants from the states have provided important incentives spurring regional collaborations.[108]

The next chapter describes more fully how federal and state actions continue to exert a powerful influence on cities and suburbs.

KEY TERMS

annexation (p. 353)
city-county consolidation (p. 356)
council of governments (COG) (p. 373)
diseconomies of scale (p. 367)
dual approval requirement for an annexation (p. 353)

economies of scale (p. 366)
elastic cities (p. 355)
favored-quarter communities, a region's (p. 384)
fiscal disparities law. Minnesota's (p. 365)
general-purpose governments (p. 377)

NOTES

1. Patricia Leigh Brown, "Bay Area's Disjointed Public Transit Network Inspires a Call for Harmony," *New York Times*, August 1, 2015; Michael Cabanatuan, "Milbrae BART Station Ridership Isn't Near Original Expectations," *San Francisco Chronicle*, July 4, 2017.
2. The 2016 estimated price tag also includes the costs of a possible light-rail station.
3. Stephen Henderson and Kristi Tanner, "Region's Transit System Can't Get Many to Job Centers," *Detroit Free Press*, February 22, 2015.
4. Richardson Dilworth, *The Urban Origins of Suburban Autonomy* (Cambridge, MA: Harvard University Press, 2005), 108–193.
5. Seven states do not allow local annexations: Connecticut, Hawaii, Maine, Massachusetts, New Hampshire, New Jersey, Pennsylvania, Rhode Island, and Vermont. See Tennessee Advisory Commission on Intergovernmental Relations, "Annexation Methods in the 50 States," www.tn.gov/tacir/topic/annexation-methods, accessed August 17, 2016.

6. Howard N. Rabinowitz, "Albuquerque: City at a Crossroads," in *Sunbelt Cities: Politics and Growth Since World War II*, ed. Richard M. Bernard and Bradley R. Rice (Austin: University of Texas Press, 1983), 258–259.

7. San Antonio is a major exception, a city that continues to pursue aggressive annexation, even targeting the absorption of 66 additional square miles with a population of 200,000 in order to expand its tax base. See Nathan Koppel, "San Antonio Weighs Annexation Plan," *Wall Street Journal*, December 21, 2014.

8. Christopher J. Tyson, "Annexation and the Mid-Size Metropolis: New Insights in the Age of Mobile Capital," *University of Pittsburgh Law Review* 73 (2012): 505–561, reviews the various state restrictions placed on municipal annexations. Tyson also reviews various court rulings as mid-size cities like Memphis, Raleigh, and Ashville continued to pursue annexation.

9. Rodger Johnson, Marc Perry, and Lisa Lollock, "Annexation and Population Growth in American Cities, 1990–2000," in *Municipal Year Book 2004* (Washington, DC: International City/County Management Association 2004).

10. Monte Whaley, "'Tea Party' to Fight City's Annexation," *Denver Post*, February 7, 2008.

11. Tennessee Advisory Commission on Intergovernmental Relations, *Municipal Boundaries in Tennessee: Annexation and Growth Planning Policies after Public Chapter 707* (January 2015); the report can be downloaded at www.tn.gov/tacir/section/annexation.

12. Nicole Cobler and Brian M. Rosenthal, "Lawmakers Kill Bill to Put Annexation Plans to Vote," *San Antonio Express-News*, May 14, 2015.

13. David Rusk, *Inside Game/Outside Game: Winning Strategies for Saving Urban America* (Washington, DC: Brookings Institution Press, 1999), 3–10 and 126–145; David Rusk, *Annexation and the Fiscal Fate of Cities* (Washington, DC: Brookings Institution, August 2006), www.brookings. edu/reports/2006/08metropolitanpolicy_rusk.aspx; Carol E. Heim, "Border Wars: Tax Revenues, Annexation, and Urban Growth in Phoenix," *International Journal of Urban and Regional Research* 36, no. 4 (July 2012): 831–859.

14. The importance of annexation in Columbus is detailed by Chris Benner and Manuel Pastor, *Just Growth; Inclusion and Prosperity in America's Metropolitan Regions* (New York: Routledge, 2012), 96–109.

15. Noah J. Durst, "Racial Gerrymandering of Municipal Borders: Direct Democracy, Participatory Democracy, and Voting Rights in the United States," *Annals of the American Association of Geographers* (2018), DOI: 10.1080/24694452.2017.1403880.

16. Suzanne Leland and Kurt Thurmaier, "Political and Functional Local Government Consolidation: The Challenges for Core Public Administration Values and Regional Reform," *American Review of Public Administration* 44, no. 4S (2014), 31S.

17. Lawrence L. Martin and Jeannie Hock. Schiff, "City-County Consolidations: Promise versus Performance," *State and Local Government Review* 43, no. 2 (2011): 167–177.

18. Suzanne Leland and Kurt Thurmaier, "When Efficiency Is Unbelievable: Normative Lessons from 30 Years of City-County Consolidations," *Public Administration Review* 65, no. 4 (July–August 2005): 475–489; Suzanne M. Leland and Kurt Thurmaier, eds., *City-County Consolidation: Promises Made, Promises Kept?* (Washington, DC: Georgetown University Press, 2010). A summative review of the studies in the field concluded that city-county consolidations generally produced no real gains in terms of efficiency, equity, and economic development; see Martin and Schiff, "City-County Consolidations: Promise versus Performance," 162–177.

19. Charles D. Taylor, Dagney Faulk, and Pamela Schaal, "Where Are the Cost Savings in City-County Consolidation?," *Journal of Urban Affairs* 39, no. 2 (2017): 185–204.

20. Chris Benner and Manuel Pastor, *Just Growth: Inclusion and Prosperity in America's Metropolitan Regions* (New York: Routledge, 2012), 77–96.

21. Mark Rosentraub, "City-County Consolidation and the Rebuilding of Image: The Fiscal Lessons from Indianapolis's UniGov Program," *State and Local Government Review* 32, no. 3 (Fall 2000): 180–191.

22. Suzanne M. Leland and Mark S. Rosentraub, "Consolidated and Fragmented Governments and Regional Cooperation: Surprising Lessons from Charlotte, Cleveland, Indianapolis, and Wyandotte/Kansas City, Kansas," in *Governing Metropolitan Regions in the 21st Century*, ed. Donald Phares (Armonk, NY: M.E. Sharpe, 2009), 143–163.

23. C. James Owen and York Willbern, *Governing Metropolitan Indianapolis: The Politics of Unigov* (Berkeley: University of California Press, 1985), 1–2.

24. Owen and Willbern, *Governing Metropolitan Indianapolis*. Former Indianapolis Mayor Stephen Goldsmith, *The Twenty-First Century City: Resurrecting Urban America* (Lanham, MD: Rowman & Littlefield, 1999), 75–94, describes his success in shepherding regional cooperation for economic development. The gains that he reports for the airport can be found on p. 36.

25. Hank V. Savitch, Ronald K. Vogel, and Lin Ye, "Beyond the Rhetoric: Lessons from Louisville's Consolidation," *American Review of Public Administration* 40, no. 1 (2010): 3–28.

26. Janet M. Kelly and Sarin Adhikari, "Indicators of Financial Condition in Pre-and Post-Merger Louisville," *Journal of Urban Affairs* 35, no. 5 (2013): 560.

27. Joseph Gerth, "Merger: One Year Later," *Courier-Journal (Louisville)*, December 22, 2003 H.V. Savitch and Ronald K. Vogel, "Suburbs Without a City: Power and City-County Consolidation," *Urban Affairs Review* 39, no. 6 (2004): 758–790.

28. H.V. Savitch and Ronald K. Vogel, "Metropolitan Consolidation versus Metropolitan Governance in Louisville," *State and Local Government Review* 32, no. 3 (Fall 2000): 210.

29. Savitch and Vogel, "Metropolitan Consolidation versus Metropolitan Governance in Louisville," 201. This paragraph relies greatly on the authors's extended argument, pp. 198–212.

30. Savitch and Vogel, "Suburbs Without a City"; H.V. Savitch, Takashi Tsukamoto, and Ronald K. Vogel, "Civic Culture and Corporate Regime in Louisville," *Journal of Urban Affairs* 30, no. 4 (2008): 437–460, esp. 441.

31. Savitch, Vogel, and Ye, "Beyond the Rhetoric: Lessons from Louisville's Consolidation," 3–28.

32. Kelly and Adhikari, "Indicators of Financial Condition in Pre- and Post-Merger Louisville," 553–567; Patricia Atkins, Pamela Blumenthal, Adrienne Edisis, Alec Friedhoff, Leah Curran, Lisa Lowry, Travis St. Clair, Howard Wial, and Harold Wolman, *Responding to Manufacturing Loss: What Can Economic Development Policy Do?* (Washington, DC: The Brookings Institution, June 2011), 28–33; and Barry Kornstein, Prakitsha Bhattarai, Sarah Ehresman, and Janet M. Kelly, *Destination Tourism: Economic and Community Impacts of Tourism* (Louisville: University of Louisville Urban Studies Institute, 2012), http://usi.louisville.edu/images/Publications/Destination%20Louisville.pdf.

33. Raymond A. Mohl, "Miami: The Ethnic Cauldron," in *Sunbelt Cities*, ed. Bernard and Rice, 82–83.

34. See Metro's Report, *Opportunities and Challenges for Equitable Housing*, January 2016, www.oregonmetro.gov/tools-partners/guides-and-tools/guide-equitable-housing.

35. Arthur C. Nelson, "Portland: The Metropolitan Umbrella," in *Regional Politics: America in a Post-City Age*, ed. H.V. Savitch and Ronald K. Vogel (Beverly Hills, CA: Sage Publications, 1996), 253.

36. Nelson, "Portland: The Metropolitan Umbrella," 263–220, presents more detailed discussion of Metro's limitations.

37. John Provo, "Risk-Averse Regionalism: The Cautionary Tale of Portland, Oregon, and Affordable Housing," *Journal of Planning Education and Research Urban Affairs* 28, no. 3 (March 2009): 369–381.

38. Christina D. Rosan, *Governing the Fragmented Metropolis: Planning for Regional Stability* (Philadelphia: University of Pennsylvania Press, 2016), 17, 117–146.

39. Citizens League Metropolitan Council Task Force 2015–2016, *The Metropolitan Council: Recalibrating for the Future*, 23, https://citizensleague.org/wp-content/uploads/2016/06/FinalReportv2.pdf.

40. Frederick Melo, "Metropolitan Council Adopts New Regional Housing Policy," *Twin Cities Pioneer-Press*, December 10, 2014.

41. Bob Shaw, "Twin Cities Low-Cost Housing Is Drying Up: Especially in Suburbs," *Twin Cities Pioneer-Press*, June 6, 2015; Edward G. Goetz, Karen Chapple, and Barbara Lukermann, "The Rise and Fall of Fair Share Housing: Lessons from the Twin Cities," in *The Geography of Opportunity: Race and Housing Choice in Metropolitan America*, ed. Xavier de Souza Briggs (Washington, DC: Brookings Institution Press, 2005), p. 259, report that only one-third of the communities in the region regularly solicit proposals for affordable housing.

42. Goetz, Chapple, and Lukermann, "The Rise and Fall of Fair Share Housing: Lessons from the Twin Cities," 247–265; Myron Orfield, Nick Wallace, Eric Myott, and Geneva Finn, "Governing the Twin Cities," in *Region: Planning the Future of the Twin Cities*, ed. Myron Orfield and Thomas F. Luce, Jr. (Minneapolis: University of Minnesota Press, 2010), 57–59.

43. Myron Orfield and Baris Dawes, "Metropolitan Governance Reform," *Chapman University Local Government Reconsidered Series, Paper 8* (February 2016), 8, http://digitalcommons.chapman.edu/cgi/viewcontent.cgi?article=1220&context=localgovernmentreconsidered.

44. The quotations are from Goetz, Chapple, and Lukermann, "The Rise and Fall of Fair Share Housing," 247 and 248 respectively.

45. Eric Roper, "As the Met Council Turns 50, the Regional Government Agency Faces Challenges," *(Minneapolis) Star-Tribune*, May 25, 2017.

46. David Peterson, Katie Humphrey, and Laurie Blake, "Twin Cities Tax-Share Program Receives Scrutiny," *(Minneapolis) Star-Tribune*, January 31, 2012; Steven Dornfeld, "Affluent Suburbs Challenge Twin Cities' Unique Tax-Base Sharing Law," *Minnesota Post*, September 22, 2011.

47. The possibility that this would occur was even foreseen by the state legislator most responsible for the creation of the Twin Cities fiscal disparities law. See Myron Orfield, *Metropolitics: A Regional Approach for Community and Stability* (Washington, DC: Brookings Institution Press, 1997), 109–111.

48. Kim Crockett, the Center for the American Experiment, in "The Met Council Problem: Regionalism," the Community Voices column she authored for the *Minnesota Post*, October 30, 2014.

49. Peter Callaghan, "Republican Legislators Take Aim, Once Again, at the Met Council," *Minnesota Post*, February 21, 2017.

50. H.V. Savitch and Sarin Adhikari, "Fragmented Regionalism: Why Metropolitan America Continues to Splinter," *Urban Affairs Review* 52, no. 2 (2017): 382.

51. Also see Dagney Faulk and Georg Grassmueck, "City-County Consolidation and Local Government Expenditures," *State and Local Government Review* 44, no. 3 (Fall 2012): 196–205.

52. Dagney Faulk and Michael Hicks, *Local Government Reform in Indiana* (Muncie, IN: Ball State University, Miller College of Business, January 2009), https://cms.bsu.edu/-/media/WWW/DepartmentalContent/MillerCollegeofBusiness/BBR/Publications/LocalGovReform.pdf; and Leland and Thurmaier, *City-County Consolidation: Promises Made, Promises Kept?*

53. For classic statements of public choice theory applied to metropolitan areas, see: Robert L. Bish, *The Public Economy of Metropolitan Areas* (Chicago: Markham, 1971); Robert L. Bish and Vincent Ostrom, *Understanding Urban Government: Metropolitan Reform Reconsidered* (Washington, DC: American Enterprise Institute, 1973); and Vincent Ostrom and Elinor Ostrom, "Public Choice: A Different Approach to the Study of Public Administration," *Public Administration Review* 31 (March/April 1971): 203–216. For a readable overview of the debate over public choice, see Kathryn A. Foster, *The Political Economy of Special-Purpose Governments* (Washington, DC: Georgetown University Press, 1997), 35–41.

54. William Duncombe, "Strategies to Improve Efficiency: School District Consolidation and Alternative Cost-Sharing Strategies" (presented at the Conference on School Finance and Governance in Providence Rhode Island, November 13, 2007).

55. All of these successes were gained in school consolidation in Pennsylvania. See Standard & Poor's, *Study of the Cost-Effectiveness of Consolidating Pennsylvania Districts* (New York: Standard & Poor's School Evaluation Services, 2007).

56. Benedict S. Jimenez, "Separate, Unequal, and Ignored? Interjurisdictional Competition and the Budgetary Choices of Poor and Affluent Municipalities," *Public Administration Review* 24, no. 2 (March/April 2014): 246–257.

57. Patricia S. Atkins, "Local Intergovernmental Agreements: Strategies for Cooperation," MIS Report, Washington, DC: International City/County Management Association, 1997, 2–3.

58. Atkins, "Local Intergovernmental Agreements," 5.

59. Donald F. Kettl, *System under Stress: Homeland Security and American Politics* (Washington, DC: CQ Press, 2003), 30–31 and 63–66.

60. Mauricio Covarrubias, "The Challenges of Interdependence and Coordination in the Bilateral Agenda: Mexico and the United States," in *Networked Governance: The Future of Intergovernmental Management*, ed. Jack W. Meek and Kurt Thurmaier (Los Angeles: Sage Publications/CQ Press, 2012), 250–257.

61. Darran Simon and Claudia Vargas, "Financial Details Outlined for Camden Regional Police Force," *Philadelphia Inquirer*, August 30, 2012; Charlie Ban, "Regional Police Force in Camden County, N.J. Nears Launch Date," *County News, a Publication of the National Association of Counties*, March 11, 2013, www.naco.org/newsroom/countynews/Current%20Issue/3-11-2013/Pages/Regional-police-force-in-Camden-County,-N-J—nears-launch-date.aspx; and Kate Zernike, "Camden Turns Around with New Police Force," *New York Times*, September 1, 2014. The dramatic decrease in response times is reported by Zernike.

62. Thomas W. Sanchez and James F. Wolf, "Environmental Justice and Transportation Equity: A Review of MPOs," in *Growing Smarter: Achieving Livable Communities, Environmental Justice, and Regional Equity*, ed. Robert D. Bullard (Cambridge, MA: MIT Press, 2007), 249–271.

63. Jen Nelles, "Regionalism Redux: Exploring the Impact of Federal Grants on Mass Public Transit Governance and Political Capacity in Metropolitan Detroit," *Urban Affairs Review* 49, no. 2 (March 2013): 220–253.

64. Tony Barboza, "Irvine Is Told to Accommodate 35,000 Homes in 7 Years," *Los Angeles Times*, July 25, 2007; Eric Young, "New Housing Targets Spur a Bay Area Backlash," *San Francisco Business Times*, May 30, 2013, www.bizjournals.com/sanfrancisco/print-edition/2013/05/31/newhousing-targets-spur-a-bay-area.html?page=all.

65. Donald F. Norris and Carl W. Stenberg, "Governmental Fragmentation and Metropolitan Government: Does Less Mean More? The Case of the Baltimore Region," in *Governing Metropolitan Regions in the 21st Century*, ed. Phares, 132–133.

66. Rosan, *Governing the Fragmented Metropolis*, 26–58.

67. Bruce Katz, Robert Puentes, and Scott Bernstein, *TEA-21 Reauthorization: Getting Transportation Right for Metropolitan America* (Washington, DC: Brookings Institution, March 2003), 4, www.brookings.edu/research/reports/2003/03/transportation-katz. According to the National Association of Regional Councils, COGs and RPCs make up more than half of the 420 or so MPOS that operate across the country, http://narc.org/about-narc/cogs-mpos/.

68. Katz, Puentes, and Bernstein, *TEA-21 Reauthorization*, 4.

69. Bruce Katz, Robert Puentes, and Scott Bernstein, "Getting Transportation Right for Metropolitan America," in *Taking the High Road: A Metropolitan Agenda for Transportation Reform*, ed. Bruce Katz and Robert Puentes (Washington, DC: Brookings Institution Press, 2005), 21–25; Kate Lowe, "Bypassing Equity? Transit Investment and Regional Transportation Planning," *Building Resistant Regions Working Paper No. 210–07*, Institute of Governmental Studies, University of California, Berkeley, December 10, 2010, http://brr.berkeley.edu/brr_workingpapers/2010-07-lowe_bypassing_equity.pdf.

70. Rosan, *Governing the Fragmented Metropolis*.

71. David Y. Miller and Raymond W. Cox, III, "Reframing the Political and Legal Relationships between Local Governments and Regional Institutions," in *Network Governance: The Future of Intergovernmental Management*, ed. Jack W. Meek and Kurt Thurmaier (Los Angeles: Sage Publications/CQ Press, 2012), 112–114. The quotation appears on p. 113.

72. Kelly LeRoux, Paul W. Brandenburger, and Sanjay K. Pandey, "Interlocal Service Cooperation in U.S. Cities: A Social Network Explanation," *Public Administration Review* 70, no. 2 (March/April 2010): 268–278.

73. Josh Stephens, "Southern California Adopts $524 Billion Regional Housing Plan," *California Planning & Development Report*, April 4, 2011.

74 U.S. Census Bureau, 2012 Census of Governments, "Local Governments by Type and State, 2012" and "Special Purpose Local Governments by State: Census Years 1942 to 2012" (ORG005), www.census.gov/govs/go/special_district_governments.html.

75. Brett W. Hawkins and Rebecca M. Hendrick, "Do Metropolitan Special Districts Reinforce Socio-spatial Inequalities? A Study of Sewerage and Technical Education in Milwaukee County," *Publius: Journal of Federalism* 27, no. 1 (Winter 1997): 135–143.

76. Martin V. Melosi, *Precious Commodity: Providing Water for America's Cities* (Pittsburgh: University of Pittsburgh Press, 2011), 144–145 and 165–166; Joe B. Allen and David M. Oliver, Jr., "Texas Municipal Utility Districts: An Infrastructure Financing System," *Allen Boone Humphries Robinson, LLP Attorneys at Law*, 2014, http://westten.com/sites/default/files/texas-municipal-utility-districts-an-infrastructure-financing-system.pdf.

77. Deena Winter, "Special Districts with Power to Tax: Grow Like Weeds in Texas," *Fox News Issues Brief*, December 25, 2015, www.foxnews.com/politics/2015/12/25/special-districts-with-power-to-tax-grow-like-weeds-in-texas.html.

78. Darin Painter, "Hoop Dreams," *IBmag.com*, June 2008, http://ibmag.com/Main/Archive/Hoop_Dreams_9776.aspx; Steven Litt, "Cleveland Cuyahoga Port Authority Approves $75 Million Bond Issue for Cleveland Museum of Art Expansion," *The Plain Dealer (Cleveland)*, June 8, 2010; James F. McCarty, "Should the Port Authority Be Saved or Dismantled? Critics Say Other Public Entities Could Do the Job Better," *The Plain Dealer (Cleveland)*, January 11, 2010; Nancy Bowen-Ellzey, "Community Development Fact Sheet: Port Authorities as an Economic Development Tool for Local Government," *Fact Sheet CDFS-1567-10, The Ohio State University Extension*, 2010, http://ohioline.osu.edu/cd-fact/pdf/1567.pdf; Jason Williams, "Port Authority Tests New Muscle with Development," *Cincinnati Enquirer*, May 30, 2012.

79. Lynne B. Sagalyn, *Power at Ground Zero: Politics, Money, and the Remaking of Lower Manhattan* (New York: Oxford University Press, 2016).

80. David Walker, "Snow White and the 17 Dwarfs: From Metro Cooperation to Governance," *National Civil Review* 76 (January/February 1987). See also Dennis R. Judd and James M. Smith, "The New Ecology of Urban Governance: Special-Purpose Authorities and Urban Development," in *Governing Cities in a Global Era: Urban Innovation, Competition, and Democratic Reform*, ed. Robin Hambleton and Jill Simone Gross (New York: Palgrave Macmillan, 2007), 151–160.

81. Jamieson Doig, *Empire on the Hudson: Entrepreneurial Vision and Political Power at the Port of New York Authority* (New York: Columbia University Press, 2002), 379–386 and 397–402; Gerald Benjamin and Richard P. Nathan, *Regionalism and Realism: A Study of Governments in the New York Metropolitan Area* (Washington, DC: Brookings Institution Press, 2001), 126–134.

82. Bruce Berg and Paul Kantor, "New York: The Politics of Conflict and Avoidance," in *Regional Politics: America in a Post-City Age*, ed. Savitch and Vogel, 39–50.

83. New York City, of course, is a peculiar exception, as consolidated New York City was formed as a result of the merger of five counties (or boroughs): New York County (Manhattan), King's County (Brooklyn), Queens, the Bronx, and Richmond (Staten Island).

84. Vincent L. Marando and Robert D. Thomas, *The Forgotten Governments: County Commissioners as Policy Makers* (Gainesville: Florida Atlantic University/University Presses of Florida, 1977).

85. Aaron Deslatte, "Boundaries and Speed Bumps: The Role of Modernized Counties Managing Growth in the Fragmented Metropolis," *Urban Affairs Review* 53, no. 4 (2017): 658–688, esp. 678.

86. This paragraph is based on Christopher V. Hawkins and Jered B. Carr, "The Costs of Services Cooperation: A Review of the Literature," in *Municipal Shared Services and Consolidation: A Public Solutions Handbook* (New York: Routledge, 2015), 17–35.
87. Theodore Hershberg, "Regional Imperatives of Global Competition," in *Planning for a New Century*, ed. Jonathan Barnett (Washington, DC: Island Press, 2001), 13.
88. Savitch and Vogel, eds., *Regional Politics*.
89. Beverly A. Cigler, "Economic Development in Metropolitan Areas," in *Urban and Regional Policies for Metropolitan Livability*, ed. David K. Hamilton and Patricia S. Atkins (Armonk, NY: M.E. Sharpe, 2008), 296–323, here 311.
90. Fund for Our Economic Future, "Catalyzing Regional Economic Transformation: Lessons from Funder Collaboration in Northeast Ohio," a report of The Knight Foundation, Akron, Ohio, October 2013, www.knightfoundation.org/publications/catalyzing-regional-economic-transformation.
91. Louise Jezierski, "Pittsburgh: Partnerships in a Regional City," in *Regional Politics: America in a Post-City Age*, ed. Savitch and Vogel, 159–181; H.V. Savitch and Ronald K. Vogel, "Perspectives for the Present and Lessons for the Future," in *Regional Politics: America in a Post-City Age*, ed. Savitch and Vogel, 292.
92. Joan Fitzgerald, David Perry, and Martin Jaffe, *The New Metropolitan Alliances: Regional Collaboration for Economic Development*, Kitty and Michael Dukakis Center for Urban and Regional Policy, Paper 22, Northeastern University, Boston, 2002, http://hdl.handle.net/2047/d20003672.
93. Judd and Smith, "The New Ecology of Urban Governance," 151–161; Jonathan S. Davies, "Against 'Partnership': Toward a Local Challenge to Global Neoliberalism," raises many of the same concerns as he reviews public-private development bodies in England and Scotland; his work can be found in *Governing Cities in a Global Era*, ed. Hambleton and Gross, 199–210.
94. Elisabeth R. Gerber, Adam Douglas Henry, and Mark Lubell, "Political Homophily and Collaboration in Regional Planning Networks," *American Journal of Political Science* 57, no. 3 (July 2013): 598–610.
95. Myron Orfield, *Metropolitics: A Regional Agenda for Community and Stability* (Washington, DC: Brookings Institution, 1997, 1998), 104–172.
96. Myron Orfield, *American Metropolitics: The New Suburban Reality* (Washington, DC: Brookings Institution, 2001); Myron Orfield and Thomas F. Luce, Jr., *Region: Planning the Future of the Twin Cities* (Minneapolis: University of Minnesota Press, 2010).
97. Heim, "Border Wars," 831–859.
98. Chris Benner and Manuel Pastor, "Whither Resilient Regions? Equity, Growth, and Community," *Journal of Urban Affairs* 38, no. 1 (2015): 5–24, esp. 9–12.
99. Orfield, *Metropolitics*, 129–131, 140–141, and 169–170.
100. Manuel Pastor, Jr., Chris Benner, and Martha Matsuoka, *This Could Be the Start of Something Big: How Social Movements for Regional Equity Are Reshaping Metropolitan America* (Ithaca, NY: Cornell University Press, 2009), 9–10.
101. Donald F. Norris, "Prospects for Regional Governance Under the New Regionalism: Economic Imperatives Versus Political Impediments," *Journal of Urban Affairs* 23, no. 5 (2001): 557–571. Also see Donald F. Norris, *Metropolitan Governance in America* (New York: Routledge, 2016).
102. Savitch and Adhikari, "Fragmented Regionalism: Why Metropolitan America Continues to Splinter," 381–402.
103. Suzanne M. Leland, "Kansas City/Wyandotte County, Kansas," in *Case Studies of City-County Consolidation*, ed. Leland and Thurmaier, 266; Susan M. Leland and Curtis Wood, "Improving the Efficiency and Effectiveness of Service Delivery in Local Government: The Case of Wyandotte County and Kansas City, Kansas," in *City-County Consolidation: Promises Made, Promises Kept?*, ed. Leland and Thurmaier, 251 and 255.
104. Joel Rast, "Environmental Justice and the New Regionalism," *Journal of Planning Education and Research* 25, no. 3 (2006): 249–263.

105. Carolyn Adams, *From the Outside In: Suburban Elites, Third-Sector Organizations, and the Reshaping of Philadelphia* (Ithaca, NY: Cornell University Press, 2014).

106. George Galster, *Driving Detroit: The Quest for Respect in the Motor City* (Philadelphia: University of Pennsylvania Press, 2012), 263–266.

107. Todd Swanstrom and Brian Banks, "Community-Based Regionalism, Transportation, and Local Hiring Agreements," *Journal of Planning Education and Research* 28, no. 3 (March 2009): 355–367; Pastor, Benner, and Matsuoka, *This Could Be the Start of Something Big.*

108. Ssuh-Hsien Chen, Richard C. Feiock, and Jun Yi Hsieh, "Regional Partnerships and Metropolitan Economic Development," *Journal of Urban Affairs* 38, no. 2 (2016): 196–213; John Hoornbeek, Tegan Beechey, and Thomas Pascarella, "Fostering Local Government Collaboration: An Empirical Analysis of Case Studies in Ohio," *Journal of Urban Affairs* 38, no. 2 (2016): 2252–2270, esp. 270 and 273. Also see Michael Leo Owens, "Public Support for the 'Regional Perspective': A Consideration of Religion," *Urban Affair Reviews* 45, no. 6 (July 2010): 745–774.

11 | The Intergovernmental City

National and State Urban Policy

Cities and suburbs in the United States exist in an **intergovernmental system** where the actions of the national and state governments exert a powerful influence on the well-being of local communities. To a great degree, local communities, especially communities suffering fiscal distress and long-term decline, are dependent on policy actions taken by the national government and the states.

President Donald Trump came to office having promised to "drain the swamp" in Washington and disrupt the cozy political arrangements of what Trump advisers labeled the "administrative state" and the "deep state." The Trump administration sought to upset program relationships between the central government and local communities that had existed for decades. Trump proposed to terminate the Community Development Block Grant Program, the nation's largest aid program to cities. He sought to relax the requirements of the Community Reinvestment Act, a regulatory program that over the decades led banks to make hundreds of billions of dollars in loans to projects in overlooked portions of the inner city. Trump moved to liberate banking and housing finance institutions from the rules that had been put in place to protect homebuyers from deceptive lending practices and to safeguard communities against a new wave of home loan foreclosures and property abandonment. Trump's Department of Housing and Urban Development even moved to drop the enforcement of housing antidiscrimination laws from the department's mission statement.

The Trump administration effected numerous policy changes via new legislation, administrative rules changes, and executive fiat. Still, Trump could not simply impose his will on local communities. At times, even Republicans in Congress were unwilling to make the extensive program cuts that Trump had proposed, fearing the impact that the cutbacks would have on their home constituencies. The 2018 midterm elections also brought a Democratic majority to the House of Representatives, further limiting Trump's ability to effect major program changes via new legislation. Just as important, in the American federal system, local governments have their own authority and are not mere puppets who jump when their strings are pulled from above by the national government.

The constitutional structure of federalism establishes state and local governments with constitutional prerogatives of their own. In the American intergovernmental system, power is not easily asserted in a hierarchical and "coercive" manner. As Trump, much like presidents before him, discovered, state and local political leaders have the ability to pursue their own policy initiatives and protect the interests of their communities. Municipal leaders resist federal program initiatives that they see as harmful to local residents.

For more than a half century, Democrats viewed national government action quite favorably, seeing it as a tool to promote economic growth, protect the public against harmful economic downturns, safeguard the natural environment, assist people and communities in need, and combat discrimination. Republicans, in contrast, point to the undue costs and waste of federal programs and regulation. Republicans also viewed federal power as an intrusive threat to individual liberty.

In more recent years, members of both political parties began to rethink their traditional positions regarding the desirability of national government power relative to subnational power. President Barack Obama, frustrated by the ability of an obstructionist Congress to block major legislative change, began to forge more collaborative relationships with those states and communities that were willing to extend health-care benefits and initiate innovative social policy, housing, and urban policy solutions. Republicans, when in control of Washington, sought to limit the discretion allowed local officials.

The debate over the role that the federal government should play in urban affairs is rooted in competing readings of key provisions of the United States Constitution. Critics argue that the central government has overstepped its constitutional authority, exercising numerous domestic and urban policy powers that properly belong to the states. But, as this chapter will soon discuss, such a strong anti-Washington perspective is based on a quite selective reading of the Constitution, an interpretation that emphasizes certain provisions and words while neglecting other provisions and phrases that do enable the central government to play a more expansive role in domestic and urban affairs. The chapter then turns to a review of the evolving Democratic and Republican perspectives as to just what constitutes "good" national urban policy. The chapter concludes by examining the key role that the states play in urban affairs.

THE U.S. CONSTITUTION: WHAT ROLE CAN THE NATIONAL GOVERNMENT PLAY IN DOMESTIC AND URBAN AFFAIRS?

The U.S. Constitution establishes a **federal system** of government, which means that more than one level of government has the right to exist and can exercise substantial powers. The Constitution explicitly mentions the national government and the states— but not cities. As noted in Chapter 6, constitutionally speaking, local governments are the administrative subdivisions of each state.

Over the years, the **federal government** (the popular phrase used to refer to the "central government," that is, the national government of the United States) has acted across a very broad range of domestic and urban policy matters. The federal government has provided billions of dollars to help localities upgrade roads, airports, hospitals, and sewage processing plants. Federal assistance has also enabled localities to stem the decline of troubled neighborhoods, expand community health services, improve child nutrition, increase the availability of child care and early child education, extend subsidized housing to the needy, and provide housing and supportive services to the homeless, with special priority given to homeless veterans. Federal assistance supports numerous other urban activities, including a variety of policing initiatives as well as local actions that provide for the protection of critical facilities and homeland security. Federal statutes require that local governments prevent discrimination in housing, ensure that public transit systems and other facilities are accessible to disabled persons, and that federally assisted local development projects minimize environmental harm.

Anti-government activists contend that a great many of the above-mentioned federal programs are improper as they go beyond the powers explicitly listed for the national government under the United States Constitution. These critics argue that the Constitution sets up a system of **dual federalism** that clearly demarks those program responsibilities given to the national government as opposed to the states. Dual federalists contend that the Constitution gives the central government only a select few powers—the **expressed powers** (also called **delegated powers** or **enumerated powers**) explicitly listed in Article I, Section 8 of the Constitution (where the powers to borrow and coin money, regulate interstate commerce, raise an army, declare war, enter into treaties with other nations, and establish post offices and roads can all be found). All other powers, dual federalists argue, are **reserved powers** given to the states by the **Tenth Amendment**, which reads:

> The powers not delegated to the United States by the Constitution, nor prohibited by it to the States, are reserved to the States respectively, or to the people.

As urban responsibilities are not explicitly listed under the federal government's enumerated powers, the Tea Party (the grassroots anti-government movement that foreshadowed the election of Donald Trump) and other anti-Washington activists see no constitutional basis for a great many national urban actions. The right to decide on urban assistance, they argue, properly belongs to the states.

The simplicity of the dual federalist perspective is attractive. Unfortunately, its view of a national government that has sharply limited domestic policy powers is highly deceptive as it rests on only a very partial reading of the Constitution. Dual federalists stress the wording of the Tenth Amendment, which is indeed the basis of the "states's rights" argument. But they neglect other provisions of the Constitution that serve to expand the domestic program authority of the central government and, in doing so, narrow the powers reserved exclusively for the states. Supreme Court decisions, especially those in the 80 or more years since the Great Depression, clearly denote that the language of the Constitution does indeed permit the national government to take action in a wide range of domestic policy areas.

The United States does *not* operate under a system of dual federalism, even though the dual federalism model fairly well describes the rather limited scope of central government actions when the United States was an agrarian nation. Instead, *cooperative federalism* provides a more accurate picture of the contemporary American system. In the American system of **cooperative federalism**, the state governments do not have exclusive authority over most areas of domestic policy; instead, the central government also possesses widespread domestic powers. Cooperative federalism gets its name as the different levels of government often share program responsibilities and work together (although not always smoothly or easily) to combat domestic ills.

The national government's possession of broad authority in the domestic arena is supported by Supreme Court rulings that go back over three-quarters of a century to the 1930s (the era of Franklin Roosevelt's New Deal); some Court rulings were handed down nearly two centuries ago![1] Just what exact language of the United States Constitution permits the extended domestic policy reach of the national government? The Constitution's **interstate commerce clause** gives the central government the ability "to regulate commerce . . . among the several states." As the Supreme Court has recognized, this wording gives the national government the authority to take action in a broad range of policy areas that have an impact on economic activity that spills beyond the borders of a single state. Such policy areas include public education, job training, local economic development, the protection of air and water quality, and even programs that maintain the health of citizens and workers.

Equally important, the Constitution's **necessary and proper clause** expands the range of policy areas in which the central government may undertake action. At the very end of the list of enumerated powers in the Constitution, Article I, Section 8 clearly declares that the national government has the right "to make *all* laws which shall be *necessary and proper* for carrying into execution the foregoing powers" (emphasis added). This wording indicates that the federal government possesses a whole host of unstated but **implied powers** that are only hinted at in the Constitution's list of enumerated powers.[2] In essence, the necessary and proper clause is an **elastic clause** that stretches the list of policy areas in which the central government may act. The clause is a counterweight to the Tenth Amendment. By elasticizing the powers of the national government, the necessary and proper clause narrows the policy areas reserved for the states by the Tenth Amendment.[3]

It was not until the twentieth century that the central government began to exercise much of the authority that it possessed in domestic affairs. In the 1930s, the national government expanded as it launched various programs to manage the economy and battle the miseries brought by the Great Depression.

A second surge in the central government's domestic program actions began in the 1960s with President Lyndon Johnson's War on Poverty and Great Society programs. At the same time, in what has been called the **Fourteenth Amendment Revolution**, the federal government began to take strong actions to stop racial discrimination and to protect civil rights, ensuring that all citizens receive the "equal protection of the laws" guaranteed by the Fourteenth Amendment of the U.S. Constitution.

Only on rare occasions has the United States Supreme Court struck down an action of the national government for overstepping the rather nebulous boundaries imposed by the very existence of a federal system of government. In *United States v. Lopez* (1995),[4] the Court invalidated the Gun Free School Zones Act, because Congress had made no attempt whatsoever to show how the prohibition of firearms in school zones was related to interstate commerce. Two years later, in *Printz v. United States*,[5] the Supreme Court again referred to the doctrine of federalism in striking down a provision of the Brady Handgun Prevention Act that required local law enforcement officials to conduct background checks on handgun buyers. The Court ruled that subnational governments have the freedom to act as they see fit within their own spheres of authority.

In a federal system, state and local officials cannot be "commandeered" or "dragooned" by the central government into administering federal law. Decades later, the logic of the Court's ruling in *Printz* would serve to limit the ability of the Trump administration to command unwilling state and local law enforcement departments to cooperate with federal agencies in detaining and ousting undocumented immigrants.

The Supreme Court's momentous "Obamacare" decision, ***National Federation of Independent Business v. Sebelius*** (2012), poses a bit of a puzzle for political observers who seek to discern if the Constitution imposes serious limits on the national government's domestic policy powers. In *Sebelius*, the Court approved a broad exercise of central government authority; the Court recognized that the national government does indeed possess the power to enact a health-care program as far-reaching as Obamacare (the popular label for the Affordable Care Act or ACA). The Court even affirmed the constitutionality of the federal government's offer of subsidies to incentivize health insurance exchanges to expand the coverage of their plans. The Court went still further, upholding as constitutional the federal program requirement that Americans purchase health insurance. All of this was a clear recognition that the central government possesses broad domestic program authority.

Yet, the Court in *NFIB v. Sebelius* also ruled that the existence of a federal system does impose some limits on the central government's powers. The Court struck down the portion of the ACA that the justices saw as an attempt by the national government to "coerce" the states to expand their Medicaid programs for the poor.[6] As it had earlier ruled in *Printz*, the Court in its Obamacare decision continued to enunciate a principle that would later prove troubling to President Trump in his efforts to cut off federal assistance to "sanctuary cities" that refused to cooperate in efforts to detain and deport undocumented immigrants. In a federal system, the national government cannot simply coerce or dragoon local governments and local law enforcement officials to administer the national government's programs.

In sum, the Supreme Court has recognized the system of cooperative federalism and has not attempted to resurrect an antiquated doctrine of dual federalism with sharp limitations on the domestic program authority of the national government.[7] The Constitution does not pose a severe impediment to the national government's engagement in a very broad range of domestic program areas. Even a Supreme Court dominated by Republican appointees has not to any significant degree rolled back the reach of the central government in domestic and urban affairs. Still, since the early 2000s, a small but important set of decisions by the Roberts Court (the Supreme Court led by Chief Justice John Roberts, a Republican appointee) has ruled that a respect for federalism does impose some limits on efforts by the national government to coerce the actions of unwilling state and local officials.[8]

THE BASIC ELEMENTS OF INTERGOVERNMENTAL ASSISTANCE: CATEGORICAL GRANTS AND BLOCK GRANTS

The intergovernmental system in the United States centers around money, or, to be more precise, the transfer of federal money to help states and localities achieve desirable program objectives. A **grant-in-aid** (or **grant**, for short) is a transfer of money from one level of government to another to accomplish specified purposes. The amount of money that the federal government gives states and localities each year is quite substantial. In 2017, federal grants to states and localities totaled nearly $675 billion.[9]

The intergovernmental grant system, with its various forms of intergovernmental assistance and program rules, is quite complex. Yet, one simple classification can abet understanding: Federal fiscal assistance to cities and localities generally takes one of two forms—assistance can be in the form of a *categorical grant* or a *block grant*.

When President Richard Nixon assumed office in the late 1960s, virtually every federal intergovernmental aid program came in the form of a **categorical grant**. In a categorical grant, the federal government defines program objectives rather precisely and dispenses aid that is accompanied by numerous program "strings" or rules that seek to constrain just how the states and localities spend program funds. Narrowly defined purposes and accompanying program rules and reporting requirements seek to limit recipient discretion in the use of federal assistance, ensuring that states and local governments do not shift the grant money to unintended purposes. A municipality that receives a categorical grant to upgrade its police communications equipment, for instance, must use federal funds only for that purpose; it cannot shift the grant money to any other police or non-police action, even if a more pressing law enforcement need arises.

An intergovernmental system that relies on categorical grants is excessively rigid, as state and local officials have only limited flexibility to spend federal assistance in ways that they feel will best respond to local needs. State and local officials further complain that they spend excessive amounts of time filling out grant paperwork and responding to the concerns of federal monitoring bureaucrats.

Nixon's attempt to give state and local officials greater program flexibility is known as the **New Federalism**. The most enduring New Federalism reform gave states and localities increased program latitude through a relatively new form of federal assistance, the *block grant*.[10] As contrasted to narrow-purpose categorical grants, a **block grant** covers a much wider set of program goals and allows the recipient jurisdiction much greater freedom to decide how to spend federal aid dollars within a rather broad program area (see Box 11.1).

Republicans and Democrats tend to differ when it comes to the use of categorical grants as opposed to block grants. Republicans prefer block grants that keep the regulations accompanying federal assistance to a minimum. Republicans want federal administrators to be deferential to the spending decisions made by state officials and local officials. Democrats, by contrast, see the importance of program rules to ensure that states and localities use federal funds to accomplish the purposes specified in an aid program. Accompanying program rules often require local elected officials to use a portion of federal assistance to help low- and moderate-income communities (see Box 11.2). Democrats also insist on program regulations that require citizen participation, that protect civil rights and advance equal opportunity goals, and that ensure

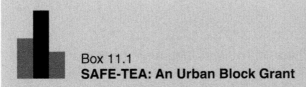

Box 11.1
SAFE-TEA: An Urban Block Grant

SAFE-TEA (the Transportation Equity Act) provides a relatively contemporary illustration of an urban-related block grant. SAFE-TEA replaced a number of small categorical grants that helped to maintain **program silos**: different federal agencies administered and oversaw their own grants, each with its own application processes and specific program priorities. As a consequence, there was little coordination of a region's transportation projects. Program officials that focused on advancing commuter rail, for instance, did not always seek the cooperation of public officials who were in charge of programs aimed at promoting bus transit or even commuting to work by bicycle.

In an effort to break the narrow focus of categorical grants administered in separate program silos, a new block grant, SAFE-TEA, was created. SAFE-TEA merged several smaller categorical programs into a single larger block of money for transportation. The block grant gave communities in a region greater say in choosing the exact transportation-related projects that would be funded with federal assistance. Broad discussion over SAFE-TEA priorities and projects served to bring local road officials, mass transit administrators, bicycle advocates, and the representatives of various local communities to the same table, allowing for a new degree of joint planning and coordination of transit-related projects.

For more detailed description and analysis of ISTEA, SAFE-TEA, and similar transportation efforts, see Robert J. Dilger, *Federalism Issues in Surface Transportation Policy: Past and Present*, Congressional Research Service Report R40431 (Washington, DC: CRS, July 27, 2012), www.fas.org/sgp/crs/misc/R40431.pdf.

that federal funds will not be used to support local projects that harm the natural environment.

The introduction of block grants added a much-needed dose of flexibility to intergovernmental assistance; but block grants did not truly revolutionize the intergovernmental aid system. As Table 11.1 documents, block grants do not dominate intergovernmental assistance; instead, their introduction and growth have been rather tepid. Most federal aid to states and cities continues to come in the form of categorical grants. Congress—especially when the Democrats are in control—views categorical grants as a means to ensure program accountability, that recipient governments will spend federal assistance for the purposes stated in a program's authorizing legislation.

Box 11.2
Can the Cities Be Trusted? Debating the Rules That Accompany Community Development Block Grants

Over the years, Democrats and Republicans have disagreed as to the program rules that should accompany **Community Development Block Grant (CDBG)** assistance. Created by Republican President Richard Nixon and signed into law in 1974 by his successor Gerald Ford, the CDBG program gave localities considerable flexibility in program spending. The CDBG program folded a number of categorical grants—including urban renewal, urban parks, and the social services monies of the Model Cities program—into a single block of monies that allowed local officials to decide just what precise local projects they would pursue.

The new block grant, however, did not allow cities and counties total freedom. From CDBG's very beginning, Democrats opposed unbridled program decentralization out of fear that officials in numerous communities would reduce social services and shift community development spending away from poor inner-city communities. The Democratic-controlled Congress succeeded in adding provisions that listed community development priorities, including the elimination of slums and blight, and targeting projects to aid low- and moderate-income neighborhoods—all quite suitable objectives for a program that had its origins in the older urban renewal and Model Cities programs. The Democrats added program regulations or "strings" to increase public participation in the process that a city uses to decide just how to spend its community development monies. Municipal officials could not simply ignore the needs of low-income neighborhoods.

Bridgeport, Connecticut, provides an all-too-commonplace example of a city where municipal officials made little attempt to fund low- and moderate-income housing or to target community development spending to low-income communities. Instead, Bridgeport officials devoted a sizable chunk of CDBG funds for parks development and improved recreational facilities in the better-off parts of town, including new tennis courts on the city's affluent north side. Bridgeport officials also voted to spend CDBG funds for a pier and marina project. The federal Department of Housing and Urban Development overrode this latter decision, ruling that the construction of an upscale marina was not an eligible project under CDBG regulations.

While many localities spend their CDBG funds fairly and wisely, municipal officials in other communities tended to slight the needs of poorer citizens and low-income neighborhoods. From 2005 to 2009, for instance, Hamilton County, a largely affluent community outside of Indianapolis, spent over half of its community development program funds on sidewalks and infrastructure improvements that provided little benefit to low-income residents.

Local officials and private developers chafed at the constraining nature and paperwork requirements of CDBG rules. As a result, federal regulations and oversight of local CDBG spending has been greatly reduced over the years. By George W. Bush's final years in office, the U.S. Department of Housing and Urban Development (HUD) no longer even provided a serious review of local plans for community development spending. HUD no longer required a recipient city to spell out its plan for targeting community development spending to low-income communities. Federal on-site monitoring of local community development programs virtually disappeared.

When Democrats occupy the White House, federal monitoring of CDBG spending increases. Toward the end of his tenure in office, President Obama sought to enforce long-ignored grant provisions that mandated nondiscrimination in housing. Obama sought to condition the continued award of CDBG assistance upon a municipality's willingness to modify zoning and land-use policies that posed an obstacle to racial and class integration. Republicans in Congress saw the move as an unwise assault on the nation's suburbs. When Donald Trump and the Republicans regained the White House, the nondiscrimination rules were immediately repealed. Federal CDBG spending would no longer be used as a lever to get recipient governments to give greater respect to fair-housing concerns.

Trump saw CDBG spending as wasteful and unnecessary. In his 2018 and 2019 budgets Trump proposed the elimination of the CDBG program. The contemporary Republican interest in defunding social spending superseded the vision of the Republicans who had created the CDBG program and who saw the importance of using block grants to increase the flexibility allowed local governments in their problem-solving efforts.

Sources: Charles J. Orlebeke and John C. Weicher, "How CDBG Came to Pass," *Housing Policy Debate* 24, no. 1 (2014): 14–45; Maureen Groppe, "Critics: Block Grants Designed for Needy End Up in Wealthier Communities," *Indianapolis Star*, August 17, 2011; and Michael J. Rich, "Community Development Block Grants at 40: Time for a Makeover," *Housing Policy Debate* 24, no. 1 (2014): 46–90, Donald F. Kettl, *Government By Proxy: (Mis?)Managing Federal Programs* (Washington, DC: CQ Press, 1988), 54–66, details the evolution of the CDBG program in Bridgeport; Brett Theodos, Christina Plerhoples Stacy, and Helen Ho, "Taking Stock of the Community Development Block Grant," a policy brief of The Urban Institute, Washington, DC, April 2017, www.urban.org/sites/default/files/publication/89551/cdbg_brief.pdf.

Table 11.1

Federal Grants to State and Local Governments, by Type (Selected Years, FY1968-FY2017)

Fiscal Year	# of Grants	# of Categorical Grants	# of Block Grants
1968	387	385	2
1978	498	492	5
1981	541	534	6
1989	492	478	14
1993	593	578	15
1998	664	640	24
2013	1.052	1,030	22
2017	1,319	1,299	20

Note: The total number of grants for 1978 and 1981 also includes the general revenue sharing program, a program that was terminated during the Reagan administration.

Adapted from Robert Jay Dilger, *Federal Grants to State and Local Governments: A Historical Perspective on Contemporary Issues*, Congressional Research Service, Report 7-5700, Washington, DC, 2018, pp. 10–11, https://fas.org/sgp/crs/misc/R40638.pdf.

THE EVOLVING REPUBLICAN APPROACH: FROM PROGRAM DECENTRALIZATION TO DEFUNDING URBAN PROGRAMS

During the Nixon and Reagan years, Republicans pushed for block grants as part of their policy of *New Federalism*. The New Federalism was an effort to restructure intergovernmental assistance programs in order to take power out of the hands of Washington officials and thereby place increased program authority in the hands of state and local officials. The New Federalism extols policy **decentralization**, that is, having program decisions made by non-Washington officials who are closer to the people.

In more recent years, however, the use of block grants has taken a new twist. Republican "budget hawks" no longer seek to merge categorical grants into block grants simply to increase state and local program authority. Instead, Republicans have created **new-style block grants**, where increases in subnational program discretion are accompanied by significant reductions in federal program funding. The reduced levels of program assistance serve to force states and localities to cut back their programs. As a new-style block grant sets a fixed program spending level, the program's assistance provided to states and localities does not even expand during troubled economic times when local need rises. In contrast to the original Nixon-era block grants, the new-style Republican block grants do not seek to increase state and local decision making in intergovernmental programs as much as they seek to shrink the size of the public sector by reducing government spending at the subnational as well as the national level.

The budget hawks argue that new program flexibility enables subnational officials to find new ways to save money, justifying the reduction in federal program assistance. State and local officials object, however, that the federal aid cutbacks go far beyond the amounts of money that can be recovered through administrative reform. The new-style block grants "cap" federal aid at reduced levels while saddling cities and suburbs with costly program responsibilities in uncertain times.

The evolution of the Community Development Block Grant (CDBG) program illustrates the transformation of the Republican bock grant ideal. President Nixon created the CDBG program by merging Model Cities assistance and other urban-oriented categorical grants into a new block grant that gave municipalities enhanced freedom to choose their own priorities. In more recent years, however, Republicans in Washington have slashed CDBG funding, undermining CDBG's ability to support decentralized decision making. CDBG funding, which stood at $12.7 million in 1978 fell to a mere $3 billion in 2012; more than three-quarters of the money for community development had been eliminated.[11] The cutbacks forced municipalities to delay scheduled infrastructure replacement and to reduce the assistance given to day care, substance abuse treatment, housing inspections, and affordable housing efforts.[12]

While President Trump proposed the elimination of the CDBG program, local Republican elected officials joined their Democratic peers in protesting that elimination would curtail the ability of cities and suburbs to aid poor neighborhoods, prepare for natural disasters and emergencies, and provide shelter to lower-income families. Still, the national Republican budget hawks in Congress continued in their efforts to defund not only the CDBG program but also other block grants that support local housing and community actions. The Republican Party had clearly moved away from its earlier ideals that celebrated block grants as a means to respect and liberate the decision-making authority of grassroots officials.[13]

THE EVOLVING DEMOCRATIC PARTY APPROACH: FROM THE GREAT SOCIETY TO "STEALTH" URBAN POLICY

LEARNING FROM THE FAILED ATTEMPT AT NATIONAL URBAN POLICY

The United States has never had an explicit "national urban policy" to guide the development of cities and suburbs. While federal programs have provided considerable assistance to local communities, such programs represent only a piecemeal approach to urban problems rather than a coherent and coordinated strategy to ameliorate urban ills. The United States, for instance, has never had a strong policy to guide patterns of development in metropolitan areas in order to assure the protection of green space and catalyze the growth of already-built-up communities.

A suburban nation has little interest in fashioning a strong policy to steer economic investment to central cities, problem neighborhoods, and aging suburbs. The geography of representation makes such a strong urban policy impossible. Many members of the House of Representatives serve middle-class and more affluent suburban districts. Still other representatives come from rural areas and growing communities in the Sunbelt. As a result, the Congress has little will to develop a policy that would use federal action to promote the revitalization of troubled communities, especially the declining former industrial centers of the Northeast and Midwest. The equal apportionment of the states in the United States Senate—where each state gets two senators irrespective of the state's population—further serves to thwart strong pro-urban policies. Senators from the least populous states, for instance, have exercised the power to strike down proposed changes in highway spending that would target assistance to the more traveled highways of the nation, roadways typically found in the nation's more populous states and urban areas.[14]

The reticence of Congress to target assistance to needy urban areas is not new. Even in the 1960s, an era of program expansion, House members and Senators were concerned with protecting their constituencies and were reluctant to approve President Lyndon Johnson's **Model Cities** program, a major part of Johnson's vision of a "Great Society." Johnson had responded to the wave of urban riots that rocked the nation in the 1960s by proposing to create a select few Model Cities that could demonstrate what could be accomplished by a well-funded and coordinated multiagency attack on the complex problem of urban poverty. But members of Congress would not approve the Johnson administration's initial proposal, as it focused spending on a select few cities, denying benefits to the districts of most congressional members.

In the face of continuing congressional parochialism, President Johnson had little choice but to significantly alter the program. Instead of creating a few showplace or "model" cities, Johnson sought to gain increased congressional support by spreading program benefits to communities across the nation. Congress, however, was not satiated and went still further, changing to program to dispense Model Cities monies to 140 communities, including communities in nonurban states and in the home districts of powerful congressional committee and subcommittee chairs.[15] Congress undermined the original Model Cities concept; no single city or set of cities received the critical mass of monies necessary to demonstrate just what could be accomplished by a well-financed multipronged attack on ghetto conditions.

A decade later, a Democratic-controlled Congress would thwart the National Urban Policy effort of another Democratic president, Jimmy Carter. The idealistic Carter was the first president ever to propose an explicit policy focused on the revitalization of troubled communities. But Congress would not approve. Members of Congress from suburban districts, rural areas and the Sunbelt killed the major pieces of the Carter urban program. Congress rejected the policy's centerpiece, an urban development bank that would help to provide financing for important urban projects overlooked by private lenders. Congress also refused to enact the president's proposed programs to create public works jobs and to give immediate fiscal assistance to the nation's most distressed communities.

In the wake of the crushing legislative defeat of his urban policy, Carter turned to a more limited initiative, proposing that the Department of Commerce's Economic Development Administration (EDA) target its job-creation funds to local areas with the greatest need. But a constituency-oriented Congress would not even accept the mild targeting that Carter suggested. Instead, Congress spread EDA benefits (or, to be more accurate, the eligibility for program benefits) quite widely: Congress absurdly defined "distress" so broadly that 90 percent of the nation's population lived in areas eligible to apply for economic development assistance! This was not an urban policy by any stretch of the concept.

Democratic presidents have learned the political lessons inherent in the dramatic defeat of the Carter urban policy. No president since Carter has highlighted a strong national policy intended to counter urban decline. Instead, presidents Bill Clinton and Barack Obama pursued a more politically pragmatic strategy, focusing on more narrow and politically acceptable program initiatives in such areas as crime control, energy conservation, environmental protection, homeland security, the provision of day care, and public education.

BILL CLINTON: THE "REFRIGERATOR LIST" AND "STEALTH" URBAN POLICY

Bill Clinton was a self-styled **New Democrat** who declared that the "era of big government is over." The defeat of his national health-care bill during his first year in office only served to heighten his concern for pragmatism in advancing domestic policy initiatives. Republicans won control of Congress midway during Clinton's first term, a stinging electoral event that reminded Clinton of the political costs that result from pushing broad policies beyond what voters are willing to tolerate.

Clinton, in contrast to Carter, did not announce an explicit national urban policy. Instead, he pursued a **refrigerator list approach**[16] to urban assistance, a "to-do" list of a number of relatively small programs that appealed to middle-class voters and that still delivered substantial benefits to urban communities. Clinton called for the federal government to fund 100,000 local police officers. He increased the funding of after-school and summer activities aimed at reducing youth crime. He proposed brownfields reclamation programs that won the support of environmentalists. Clinton emphasized relatively small and "do-able" **urban policy pieces**, not an explicit, comprehensive, and coordinated national urban strategy.

Clinton's efforts can also be viewed as a **stealth urban policy**, as he often sought to pursue urban goals through "nonurban" programs.[17] The phrase is an allusion to the Stealth Bomber, a cutting-edge weapon of the time that had a profile that was so well-engineered that the plane could not be detected by enemy radar. Clinton sought domestic aid programs that similarly would not mobilize the shoot-down systems of urban policy opponents. He did not stress in public speeches how his programs would help cities; instead, he rallied people around the banners of heightened law enforcement, the reform of public schooling, brownfields reclamation, and "ending welfare as we know it"— policy visions that had a broad appeal to people who lived outside of troubled cities. Clinton secured new levels of assistance for job training, housing vouchers, and day care, all framed in terms of the popular goal of moving people from welfare to work. Clinton pursued targets of opportunity, taking advantage of Congress's willingness to expand such highly popular programs as Head Start, child nutrition, and efforts to reduce violence against women. Even his Empowerment Zone proposal, a Clinton program that was targeted to troubled communities, was framed not solely as an urban program but as a measure to promote corporate expansion and the nation's economic growth.

Clinton's expansion of the **Earned Income Tax Credit (EITC)** provides an important illustration of the potential inherent in the stealth urban approach. The EITC provides millions of dollars in income assistance to the working poor. (EITC benefits go only to low-income people who have a job, not to nonworkers.) The EITC gives low-income workers a refundable tax credit, that is, money that supplements what they have earned on their jobs. Clinton expanded EITC eligibility and increased EITC benefits. A working mother with two children could receive as much as $3,370 a year in income assistance; families earning as much as $27,000 would receive smaller income supplements. In cities and suburbs that have large concentrations of poor workers, EITC spending helps boost the local economy.[18] In 2006, the EITC provided an estimated $40 billion in assistance to the working poor, an investment that is greater than all traditional urban spending programs combined.[19]

As EITC provides assistance only to people who work, opponents cannot easily attack EITC as a welfare program that rewards indolence. As the EITC program is embedded as a provision in the nation's tax code, the program enjoys yet another political advantage as compared to more conventional social spending programs: Tax provisions are not easily understood by the public and are not as politically salient as "welfare" programs that provide cash assistance to the poor.

BARACK OBAMA: RESPONDING TO WASHINGTON GRIDLOCK THROUGH THE OPPORTUNITIES PROVIDED BY FEDERALISM

President Barack Obama's sympathies clearly were with troubled communities. The Obama White House instructed federal departments and agencies to develop "effective place-based policies" when submitting their annual budget requests.[20] Yet Obama, like Clinton, did not call for an explicit national urban policy. Nor did he propose an overhaul of the federal grant system.[21]

For much of his two terms in office, Obama's legislative agenda was stuck amid partisan gridlock, with the Republicans controlling one or both houses of Congress. Obama essentially continued the stealth urban policy approach of Clinton, relying on a series of relatively small-scale efforts that provided disproportionate assistance to big cities and troubled urban communities. The **Choice Neighborhoods Program** sought to strengthen areas in close proximity to public housing projects. The Department of

Education's **Promise Neighborhoods Program** sought to help poverty-impacted urban and rural communities create programs similar to those of the **Harlem Children's Zone**, the famed program in New York's City that offered "cradle-to-career" support for children, a comprehensive approach to the education, health, safety, and nurturing of children.[22]

The assistance that Obama provided was *not* always highly targeted, as his programs spread benefits over a wide geography. Confronting a dire economic recession in his initial year in office, Obama responded with what was arguably the most important economic initiative of his presidency, the **American Recovery and Revitalization Act of 2009 (ARRA)**, a whopping $780 billion package for job creation. By offering generous anti-recessionary assistance to a vast number of communities across the nation for "shovel ready" road and infrastructure projects, Obama sought to generate jobs and put an end to the economic recession, while improving local infrastructure.

ARRA, as important as it was, did not challenge existing urban and anti-urban patterns. ARRA, for instance, "did not fundamentally alter highway funding and implementation."[23] Instead, the government continued to support roadway and infrastructure improvements that abetted suburban development. ARRA provided communities, especially hard-hit cities, with much-needed relief; but the program did not constitute an *urban* policy. ARRA, like much of Obama's initiatives, represented the "subordination of urban and social policy to economic policy."[24]

Obama's program of foreclosure assistance, too, spread benefits widely. The program gave relief to overextended homeowners, including persons who had overinvested in upscale condominiums and vacation villas in Florida and in the Las Vegas and Phoenix areas. Relief was not targeted solely to lower-income owners facing the prospect of eviction or to hard-hit inner-city neighborhoods in the Northeast and Midwest. Obama's **Neighborhood Stabilization Program (NSP2)** similarly provided disproportionate assistance to distressed communities in shrinking cities such as Cleveland and Detroit but still dispensed considerable aid to growing Sunbelt communities, including Phoenix, Las Vegas, Miami, and Sacramento and Riverside (California).[25]

Progressives criticized that Obama was too politically timid and too deferential to major financial institutions. Obama helped bail out failing banks and a home finance system on the verge of collapse, without first taking the necessary steps to ensure that the lending institutions would actually deliver on their promises to protect lower-income and working-class citizens at risk of losing their homes.[26] In some cities, the Neighborhood Stabilization Program perversely even wound up destabilizing poorer neighborhoods as the program led to new property investment that catalyzed the gentrification and upscaling of neighborhoods.[27]

Obama retreated from the HOPE VI program, a program of the Bush and Clinton years that gave cities assistance to tear down distressed public housing projects. HOPE VI was meant to pave the way for higher-quality replacement housing. But replacement housing was not always built on site. By tearing down public housing, HOPE VI, too, helped to open new areas of the inner city to new private investment and gentrification (see Box 11.3). Obama promised better management of the nation's remaining stock of public housing. He also strengthened neighborhoods surrounding public housing. But he could not build extensive numbers of new public housing units.

Box 11.3
The Debate Over HOPE VI and Chicago's Demolition of Cabrini-Green Public Housing

The **HOPE VI**, program, first introduced by President George H. W. Bush and implemented in earnest under Bill Clinton, provided federal assistance to enable local housing authorities to raze their most dilapidated and dysfunctional public housing projects and construct more attractive lower-rise and mixed-income developments in their place. In some cases, public housing authorities tore down buildings that were beyond repair and built new and more habitable units for the poor. But numerous cities used HOPE VI monies for another purpose: to remove the poor from near-downtown areas where public housing towers posed a barrier to new commercial development and to the construction of more upscale market-rate housing. Some cities constructed replacement housing that allotted relatively few units to former public housing tenants.

The HOPE VI program proved quite controversial. In many cities, mixed-income projects offered very few units to the public housing poor. Tenants, ousted from their public housing units as a result of demolition and construction, had no right of return.

When the Chicago Housing Authority razed Cabrini-Green, a large and troubled public housing complex that had gained a notorious reputation in the news media, only a small portion of the new mixed-income replacement units were given to the former Cabrini residents. By demolishing the Cabrini-Green high-rises, the city effectively opened nearby areas, located in close proximity to city's central business district, to a new wave of residential development and gentrification.

Today, the Cabrini-Green site and neighboring area look quite different compared to the days when high-rise public housing towers dominated the landscape (Figure 11.1). Upper-income condominiums, a big-box retail outlet, and new shops and cafes have all been built not too far from where the Cabrini-Green towers once stood. A few lucky former residents gained units in the low-rise replacement housing built on site. Other tenants were relocated elsewhere. The demolition of Cabrini-Green was a key part of a city economic strategy aimed at the transformation and upscaling of Chicago's near-north side, a site that was situated close to the city's booming global business core.

As one housing advocate, familiar with HOPE VI's history, summarized: "Predicated on the claim that mixed-income housing could benefit poor people, the HOPE VI program was the real end of public housing as we knew it."[1]

1 Janet L. Smith, "Between a Rock and a Hard Place: Public Housing Policy," *Journal of Urban Affairs*, 37, 1 (February 2015): 42–46; the quotation appears on p. 43. Also see Amy T. Khare and Janet L. Smith, "Putting the 'Public' Back into Public Housing: A Justice-oriented Agenda," *Rooflines: The Shelterforce Blog*, October 21, 2016, www.rooflines.org/4665/putting_the_public_back_into_public_housing_a_justice-oriented_agenda/.

Figure 11.1 **HOPE VI: The Demolition of Chicago's Cabrini-Green Public Housing Towers and the Rise of Replacement Housing.** A limited number of new housing units were built on the Cabrini-Green site. Most of the units in the attractive mixed-income development did not go to the former public housing tenants. Instead, many of the new units were sold at market rates to new homebuyers interested in living near the city's thriving downtown. The demolition of the hulking public housing towers thinned out the number of poor people who resided in the area, opening neighboring areas to a wave of upscale condominium and rental housing construction and gentrification.

Source: Photo by Payton Chung, February 2006, Flickr/Wikimedia Commons, https://commons. wikimedia.org/wiki/File:Cabrini%E2%80%93Green_Tear_Down.jpg.

Blocked by a Republican Congress unreceptive to his urban initiatives, Obama pursued an alternative route to action, seizing the opportunities for policy change afforded by the federal structure of American political system. Unable to get his changes through Congress, the Obama administration resorted to a fallback policy strategy: working cooperatively with those states and localities willing to implement parts of his domestic agenda.[28]

In an approach that can be characterized **variable speed federalism**, the Obama administration gave **waivers** that relaxed regulations for states and communities willing to undertake program changes that the administration desired. The Obama administration offered NSP2 project monies, "Race to the Top" educational funds, and other grants to localities on a competitive basis, in effect allowing resistant states and cities to opt out while other communities worked to pursue the president's more far-reaching domestic program changes.[29] The support that Obama gave the expansion of charter schools helped lead to a shift in school enrollments which, in some neighborhoods, led to the closing of schools that had served as the "anchors" of lower-income African-American and Latino neighborhoods.[30]

In pursuing changes in K–12 education, the Obama administration forged still additional partnerships with willing subnational governments. Obama sought to work collaboratively with those states and cities willing to implement the policy changes he desired, including an expansion of charter schools and the introduction of efforts to provide a more meaningful evaluation of school teachers.[31] The Obama administration issued **conditional waivers** to districts willing to adopt Common Core standards, exempting those jurisdictions from a number of burdensome **No Child Left Behind (NLCB)** regulations. Obama's "hybrid" approach to education mixed central government direction with a respect for state and local creativity in problem solving.[32]

DONALD TRUMP AND AMERICA'S CITIES: THE ANTI-GOVERNMENT ORTHODOXY OF AN UNORTHODOX PRESIDENT

Donald Trump proved to be a very unorthodox presidential candidate and president who invited controversy and conflict. But when it came to cutting urban spending and to reducing the burden that taxes and governmental regulation impose on economic growth, however, the Trump administration largely mirrored contemporary Republican anti-government orthodoxy.

THE TRUMP CABINET: A REFLECTION THE PRESIDENT'S ANTI-URBAN POLICY VIEWS

Trump viewed numerous government programs as posing an unnecessary and intrusive interference with the workings of business and wealth creation. His hostility toward government regulations and spending to counter urban ills was reflected in the people he chose for key Cabinet and other top administrative posts.

Housing and Urban Development (HUD): A Disdain for Dependency and "Social Engineering"

Dr. Ben Carson, Trump's Secretary for Housing and Urban Development, was a medical surgeon who had no prior history of involvement in, or commitment to, housing and urban programs. As a candidate for the 2016 Republican presidential nomination, Carson criticized federal programs for encouraging welfare dependency. In his Senate confirmation hearings, Carson argued that the provision of housing assistance to the poor led to "generation after generation living in dependent situations." As HUD Secretary, Carson deprioritized HUD's efforts to fight housing discrimination: He placed a hold on fair-housing investigations and even dropped the words "inclusive" and "free from discrimination" from the department's mission statement.[33]

Carson terminated the HUD effort announced by Obama to withhold community development assistance from localities with land-use laws that effectively barred low-income housing. Carson saw Obama's Affirmatively Further Fair Housing effort as just one more instance of ill-conceived federal "social engineering."[34]

Carson argued that HUD's focus should be less on the provision of housing and more on nurturing residents's attitudes of self-reliance and independence. He proposed the creation of a series of "EnVision Centers," located near public housing projects, where public housing residents could develop greater self-reliance through character and leadership development. But as the past history of similar programs reveals, an emphasis on character development by itself was unlikely to enable many residents to attain good-paying jobs and exit public housing. Trump's early budgets provided only the most modest level of funding support for Carson's unproven EnVision Centers approach.[35]

Department of Justice: Turning Away From Fair Housing, Voting Rights, and Matters of Racial Justice

Jeff Sessions, Trump's first Attorney General, assumed office after having served in the United States Senate where he opposed efforts for metropolitan fair housing. In the Senate, Session co-sponsored the Local Zoning Decisions Protection Act, a move to block the Obama administration's effort to have more affluent communities modify their exclusionary land-use practices as a condition of for receiving federal community development assistance.

Sessions did not have the Justice Department intervene in instances where citizens believed that their voting rights were unfairly denied. Sessions criticized the Department of Justice (DOJ) under Obama for what he saw as efforts to use the Voting Rights Act to advance the registration of likely-to-vote-Democratic minority voters. As Attorney General, Sessions deferred to the states, supporting their right to enact tougher Voter ID laws and other measures to strengthen voting requirements. According to Session, Texas and other states were not engaged in voter suppression but were properly motivated by a concern to minimize voter fraud.

In further contrast to the Obama years, the DOJ under Sessions had little interest in documenting just where local law enforcement agencies had violated federal civil rights guarantees in their use of deadly force. In Chicago, a police officer was found guilty of second-degree murder and 16 counts of aggravated assault in the killing of Laquan McDonald, a black youth who was shot 16 times, Sessions had the United States Justice Department object to the terms of a proposed consent decree in which the City of Chicago agreed to institute a number of policing reforms in order to reduce the chances of future lethal encounters.[36] In matters pertaining immigration, as we shall soon discuss in greater detail, the Department of Justice under Trump threatened to punish states and localities that refused to cooperate with federal efforts to oust undocumented immigrants.

Department of Treasury: Favoring Deregulation, Disregarding Community Reinvestment

Trump argued that the increased availability of new investment capital was a key growing the economy. He argued that deregulation—relaxing the rules that credit institutions were obligated to follow—would give lenders new opportunities to invest in all communities.

Trump and a Republican Congress eased the restrictions placed on lending practices, restrictions that had been instituted by the 2010 Dodd-Frank Wall Street Reform Act. The Trump administration exempted numerous banks from having to comply with Dodd-Frank's safeguards, including rules intended to minimize home foreclosure rates, to prevent bank failures, and to protect borrowers against deceptive and predatory lending practices.

Steve Mnuchin, Trump's Secretary of the Treasury, reflected the president's commitment to roll back Dodd-Frank and other regulations that had been imposed on banking and mortgage-finance institutions. Before joining the Trump cabinet, Mnuchin had profited handsomely from the 2008 financial crisis; he was the head of a bank that aggressively pursued property foreclosures in minority-dominated inner-city neighborhoods. Community activists charged that Mnuchin's OneWest Bank engaged in redlining, that the bank failed to make business loans in inner-city neighborhoods as required by the Community Reinvestment Act (CRA). The California Reinvestment Coalition and the Fair Housing Advocates of Northern California filed a redlining complaint with HUD, documenting the virtual absence of OneWest activity in inner-city communities in California. Only two of OneWest's 73 branches were located in low-income areas. OneWest issued very few loans to people and communities of color.[37]

As Treasury Secretary, Mnuchin led efforts to "modernize" the 40-year-old CRA, to update it for a digital age. A 2018 legislative proposal sought to redefine the service obligations of federally insured lenders in a digital age where financial institutions have the ability to make loans beyond the borders of a specific neighborhood or geographi-cally defined service area.[38] The 2018 proposal emphasized a reliance on "incentives" to promote banks to extend credit in low- and moderate-income neighborhoods, a retreat from the long-stablished CRA approach that threatened to impose penalties on finan-cial institutions that discriminated against low-income and minority communities. The Republican legislation also relaxed institutional reporting requirements, lessening the ability of community groups to gain access to the data that would allow them to uncover discriminatory patterns in an institution's lending.

Department of Education: The Turn to School Choice

Trump called school choice "the civil rights issue of our time." His Secretary of Educa-tion, Betsy DeVos, fervently backed school choice programs (as we reviewed in Chap-ter 9) to break the public-sector "monopoly" on education. DeVos had earlier declared that efforts to expand school choice were a means to "advance God's kingdom," as the public schools had displaced religion from the center of America's communities.[39] Before coming to Washington, she had used her family fortune to push her home state of Michi-gan to expand school choice programs, pressing state legislators to remove the "cap" limiting charter school enrollments in the state. She even lobbied Michigan legislators to defeat a measure that would have prevented the organizers of failing charter schools from sponsoring still additional charter academies. DeVos argued that such restrictions posed too great an impediment to the growth of charter schools.[40]

As Secretary of Education, DeVos sought to steer federal support to private and paro-chial schools as well as to charter academies, even at the costs of diminishing the level of assistance provided more traditional public schools. Trump's budget proposed expanded funding for school choice, including new funding to help charter schools to construct or acquire facilities.[41] In what advocates claimed was an important new incentive to spur school choice, the Republican rewrite of the nation's tax laws included a provision to give tax advantages to parents who set up **Section 529 Educational Savings Accounts** to help pay tuition at K–12 schools.[42]

DeVos scaled back staff in the Education Department office charged with responding to complaints that a local school system had violated civil rights, including the rights of disabled students. The Department of Education instituted new procedures that allowed the department to dismiss hundreds of civil rights concerns that were too "burdensome" for the office to pursue.[43]

The Department of Energy and the Environmental Protection Agency (EPA); Turning Away From Concerns for Global Warming and Green Cities

Trump revoked executive orders issued by President Obama to curb greenhouse gas (GHG) emissions. Announcing that he would end "the war on coal," Trump rolled back the restrictions on carbon emissions from coal-fired power plants. The Trump administration would not assist municipalities in their efforts to curb GHG emissions, to promote "green" building design, and to develop local plans to counter such climate-induced problems as rising sea levels. Nor did the Trump administration prioritize energy conservation and compact urban development. Trump even withdrew the United States from international efforts to have communities abide by the 2015 United Nations Paris accords to reduce climate change,

Even before Trump took the oath of office, his presidential transition team signaled the administration's hostility to scientific studies that pointed to the dangers of global warming policy. The transition team circulated a questionnaire in an effort to discover just which Department of Energy employees and contractors had attended conferences on global warming and who worked on matters of climate science and clean energy.[44]

The Environmental Protection Agency (EPA) technically is not part of the president's Cabinet. Nonetheless, the EPA is a cabinet-level agency of great policy significance. Scott Pruitt, Trump's initial head of the EPA, was a denier who did not believe studies that pointed to global climate change. As the head of EPA, Pruitt took steps to limit the contact of EPA careerists with outsiders. Pruitt also limited the research that agency officials would be allowed to present in support of proposed climate-related regulations. Pruitt scorned much of the agency's past work as faulty "secret science," where administrators obtained data on pollution through confidentiality agreements with a firm's insiders and otherwise drew conclusions from data that was not fully available to the larger public.

Trump's budgets proposed steep slashes in EPA spending, including sharp reductions in the funds allocated to states and localities for air quality monitoring, the Superfund program to clean up polluted brownfields sites, water system improvements along the U.S.-Mexico border, and the restoration of the Chesapeake Bay.[45] Trump announced his intention to roll back the tailpipe emissions and mileage standards that California imposed on automobiles and light trucks, standards that he said were "too high" and that were based on assumptions "that didn't comport with reality."[46]

The American Institute of Architects and nearly 800 design and construction firms warned of the long-term impacts on neighborhoods that would result from cuts in programs intended to incentivize green-building construction and energy conservation.[47] A number of states and cities took the lead on climate remediation by introducing green policies even in the absence of federal support.[48] Chapter 12 of this book details the variety of actions that "green cities" have initiated.

THE TRUMP BUDGETS: DEFUNDING URBAN PROGRAMS

The EPA's programs were not the only urban-related programs that suffered under Trump's budget axe. The president increased military spending and enacted one of the largest tax cuts in the nation's history. The result was a soaring increase in the federal budget deficit that, in turn, put a squeeze on urban and social programs.

Trump proposed to terminate funding for a number of urban-related programs, including:

- 21st Century Community Learning Centers that fund before- and after-school programs and summer programs;
- Low-Income Home Energy Assistance to help poor people pay their winter heating and summer air conditioning bills;
- Community Development Block Grants;
- Community Services Block Grants administered by the Department of Health and Human Services (HHS);
- The Department of Commerce's Economic Development Administration;
- The HOME program to assist low-income families in home buying;
- The Choice Neighborhoods Program to upgrade the areas surrounding public housing developments;
- The Legal Services Corporation; and
- The Neighborhood Reinvestment Corporation.[49]

Trump's budgets also proposed steep cuts in a number of other urban-related programs that were not targeted for elimination: the Striving Readers Program; the Teacher Quality Partnership, programs to combat homelessness; grants to assist local housing authorities repair and operate public housing; grants for capital investment in new public transit projects; and even a reduction in "basic aid" provided to school systems located near military bases to help compensate them for the costs of educating the children of military personnel. Trump proposed large reductions in Section 8, the nation's major program of housing assistance provided low-income renters. Trump proposed reductions in food stamps (also known as SNAP or the Supplemental Nutritional Assistance Program); he even mentioned the possibility providing some of the assistance in the form of high-nutritional food packages instead of stamps. Such a proposal would represent a return to the commodity distribution approach that had proved so inadequate when it was utilized a half century earlier.

The president's budgets even proposed cuts in the grant money awarded to cities for their activities in support of homeland security! His initial budgets proposed to cut by half the federal funds provided to support assist local training and disaster preparedness exercises.[50]

Congress did not approve all of the spending reductions that Trump requested. Important urban projects such as Community Development Block Grants, low-income housing assistance, the HOME program, funds to combat homelessness, and grants for the upkeep of public housing structures all survived Trump's initial efforts at program termination. But the programs were given funding levels well below what they had received during the Obama years.

THE TAX CUTS AND JOBS ACT (TCJA) OF 2017: TAX POLICY AS URBAN POLICY

Budgets, spending levels, and regulation do not constitute the entirety of public policy. As Chapter 2 has already identified, tax policy is an extremely important, albeit often unrecognized or "hidden," urban policy tool.

Trump and the Republican Congress enacted a major overhaul of the nation's tax code, the Tax Cuts and Jobs Act (TCJA) of 2017. The changes in taxes contained in the TCJA are likely to have major impacts on cities and communities. In Chapter 9, we already observed how the TCJA extended the use of Education Savings Accounts to K–12 schooling, offering tax advantages that will go primarily to upper-middle and upper-income families who enroll their children in private schools. Other provisions of the TCJA are likely to have still greater (although not always easily seen) impact on cities.

The TCJA raised the standard deduction allowed taxpayers, a move that may adversely affect the ability of urban nonprofits to raise money to support their work in inner-city neighborhoods.[51] The increase in the standard deduction means that fewer taxpayers will choose to list or itemize deductions. The change threatens charitable giving, as donations to a charity do not result in a tax savings if a person chooses not to itemize deductions. Such a change is likely to weaken the funding base of a number of urban nonprofits, although the extent to which nonprofit organization are actually affected remains to be seen.

The TCJA's deep cut in corporate tax rates (lowering the top rate from 35 to 21 percent) is likely to diminish the interest of many corporations in investing in LIHTC housing projects. As Chapter 8 has already observed, business partners invest in the projects sponsored by community development corporations partly to gain credits that offset a corporation's tax obligation. Decreased corporate tax rates reduce the urgency of a corporation to find a community partner and invest in affordable housing projects.

OPPORTUNITY ZONES: USING TAX POLICY TO SHIFT POWER TO THE PRIVATE SECTOR TO SPUR INNER-CITY INVESTMENT

The TCJA of 2017 also contained a new program, **Opportunity Zones**, to spur new investment in high-poverty census districts in both rural and urban areas. The program offers investors substantial tax incentives for building projects in designated low-income census districts. Profits made from Opportunity Funds that help finance projects in the designated census districts are not subjected the federal capital gains tax. The TCJA places no cap as to how much private investors can claim in Opportunity Zone tax incentives.

Local governments were enthusiastic in their support for the new tax tool that its backers declared had the potential to bring over one trillion dollars in new economic activity to distressed communities in just ten years[52] The federal government initially identified 8,700 census districts across the United States and five U.S. territories that met the criteria for Opportunity Zones. Each state's governor then narrowed the list, to help select those communities in a state that would receive Opportunity Zone designation.

The Opportunity Zone tax provisions gained the backing of both Democrats and Republicans in Congress. But, make no mistake about it, despite the program's bipartisan support, Opportunity Zones are a Republican free-market approach that is quite different from more traditional Democratic urban programs. Private investors maintain complete freedom to decide where they will make investments and in just what activities they will and will not invest. There is no requirement for local government approval or neighborhood participation for projects located in an Opportunity Zone community. Mayors and city councils were reduced to the role of mere lobbyists in their attempts to influence the privately managed investment decisions that the TCJA provision encouraged.

There is no requirement for local job training or that firms in the zone hire zone residents. New residential developments in Opportunity Zones earn tax advantages even if they do not include affordable dwelling units. Rather than incentivize the construction of affordable housing, the Opportunity Zone program is more likely to catalyze the construction of hotels and condominiums and upper-end housing. Specific provisions of the law actually discourage investment in low-income housing. The law requires that a project earn a substantial return on investment in order to qualify for the tax advantages awarded an Opportunity Zone investment. Such a requirement will likely lead investors to turn away from projects that include a substantial number of dwelling units for low-income families, as low-income housing does not promise a substantial return on investment.[53]

Opportunity Zones also held out the prospect of spurring gentrification and neighborhood transformation, especially in communities where gentrifying pressures are already apparent.[54] The legislation even offered tax incentives for investment in areas located adjacent to low-income census districts. In some cities, these areas were hardly distressed and were likely to suffer new gentrification pressures as a result of the investments fueled by the promise of Opportunity Zone tax advantages.

There was also no guarantee that Opportunity Zones would provide great assistance to the nation's most distressed communities. When choosing among the thousands of designated Opportunity Zones, investors can easily overlook the nation's most troubled communities.

THE TRUMP INFRASTRUCTURE PLAN: PROPOSING ANOTHER POWER SHIFT

During his 2016 presidential campaign, Donald Trump promised to invest over $1 trillion in new and modernized infrastructure, a program that seemed to offer cities the prospect of extensive assistance to make much-delayed bridge repairs, modernize their transportation infrastructure, and invest in the technology that would meet the needs of tech-oriented entrepreneurs and corporations.

But Trump's promise, as the president later admitted, did not mean that federal government's assistance for infrastructure would increase by a trillion dollars. Rather, as Trump told Congress, his intention was to call for generous tax "incentives" to "stimulate" private actors to invest $1.5 trillion (an amount that was even higher than the figure that Trump had mentioned during the campaign) in infrastructure modernization. Federal tax incentives, as Trump explained, would spur private investment in a broad range of infrastructure undertakings, including the modernization of the nation's electrical grid, an upgrade of airport facilities, and the construction and rehabilitation of highways and bridges. The great bulk of the huge increase in funding, as Trump continued, was to come from the private sector and from state and local governments, not from the national government.

Similar to the Opportunity Zones program, Trump sought to increase the investment opportunities afforded private capital. The details of the infrastructure program were not clearly spelled out during Trump's early years in office. But it did not appear that he was intending to provide an infusion of federal funds to assist cash-strapped local governments to chip away at the backlog of infrastructure projects.[55] Similar to his Opportunity Zone approach, Trump's infrastructure policy sought to give private investors—not local officials—the power to decide just what projects would be undertaken.

Critics argued that Trump's infrastructure agenda offered only the false hope of improved mass transit, as private investors were not likely to earn substantial profits in public transit. Despite his public speeches that called for heightened investment in the nation's antiquated infrastructure, President Trump did not prioritize investment in public transit. His administration even delayed the release of grant money to cities that Congress had previously appropriated for bus and rail projects.[56]

Freight rail improvements hold out the promise of profits to investors. Similarly, the modernization of airport facilities, the addition of toll lanes to highways, and the rehabilitation of bridges that impose a toll for vehicular access all promise a fair return on investment. In contrast, the Trump infrastructure approach holds out little promise of spurring new investment in non-tolled roads and bridges or in municipal water facilities sorely in need of modernization. Why? Such projects promise little or no profit.

Promoting infrastructure improvement and other urban actions through the use of tax incentives places decision-making power squarely in the hands of private actors and raises an important question of accountability: "[W]ho controls it—private investors or public interests?"[57] The decision to undertake a specific project is made by a private investor or developer who then claims the allowable tax advantages. No public forums or approval from a government agency is required. There is no guarantee that a particular investment will produce jobs for neighborhood residents or otherwise serve the neighborhood's needs or the public's interest.

SANCTUARY CITIES: TRUMP CONFRONTS THE NEW "IMMIGRATION FEDERALISM"

President Trump sought to deport immigrants who lacked the legal status to stay in the United States. But not all cities were willing to pursue a policy of expulsion. Consequently, in one of his first actions as president, Trump issued an executive order threatening to bar federal aid to *sanctuary cities* that "willfully violate Federal law in an attempt to shield aliens from removal from the United States." His Attorney General, Jeff Sessions, sought to reduce the flow of law assistance grant funds to cities that refused to cooperate with federal detention and expulsion efforts. Despite these threats, Trump continued to face resistance from cities and, in some cases, even from a number of states.

There is no agreement as to just what exactly constitutes a **sanctuary city** as few cities adopt a resolution formally declaring that they are a sanctuary city. Generally speaking, in a sanctuary city local law enforcement officers and other local public servants do not routinely inform federal immigration authorities of undocumented residents who have committed no crime other than their residency status. Estimates of the number of sanctuary cities in the United States range from 40 to 300, depending on the exact definition used. The higher count includes communities that have declared themselves "welcoming cities" (a more positive appellation than "sanctuary cities") and municipalities where officials have stated their disinclination to cooperate with federal deportation actions.[58]

Sanctuary cities and welcoming cities seek to protect otherwise law-abiding undocumented immigrants and their families from the threats of detainment and deportation. As reviewed in Chapter 4, local leaders may also view the new arrivals as assets—a source of economic entrepreneurship and a critical resource in repopulating abandoned neighborhoods.[59]

Trump's threats did not produce the actions that the president wanted. Some cities complied. Fearing the loss of federal aid money, Miami-Dade commissioners voted to back the order handed down by Cuban-born mayor Carlos Giminez that municipal officials cooperate with federal immigration officials. Officials in other cities, by contrast, swiftly reacted against the Trump's deportation efforts. Los Angeles Police Chief Charlie Beck stated that the LAPD would continue its decades-long policy of not seeking out undocumented immigrants or handing undocumented persons arrested for low-level offenses over to federal immigration officials. Los Angeles Mayor Eric Garcetti declared the city's law enforcement officials would not act as immigration police who "go around asking people for their papers."[60]

Philadelphia Mayor Jim Kenney reiterated his order that municipal officials not cooperate with the expulsion efforts of federal immigration officials. New York Mayor Bill de Blasio met Trump and reminded the president that New York is a "city of immigrants" and that strict enforcement of immigration laws would create a rift between the police and the communities they serve, impeding the cooperation the police need to battle more serious crime. The police chiefs of Seattle and Denver similarly noted the importance of maintaining good police-community relations, relations that would be severed by local action for deportation. Other mayors, including Chicago's Rahm Emanuel, Seattle's Ed Murray, Portland's Ted Wheeler, San Francisco's Ed Lee, Oakland's Libby Schaff, Minneapolis's Betsy Hodges, Nashville's Megan Barry, Santa Fe's Javier Gonzales, and Washington, DC's Muriel Bowser, declared that their cities would remain sanctuary or welcoming communities.[61]

Trump's attempts to force compliance did not enjoy equal success across cities. A preliminary look at the data indicates that local resistance to Trump's detention and expulsion efforts were able to constrain some of the increase in arrests for immigration violations that was apparent in other communities.[62]

In the American federal system, the national government and national officials cannot simply command the action of states and localities. Studies of program implementation in other policy areas point to the **"illusion of federal control"**.[63] The federal system is not hierarchical; instead, subnational officials retain considerable leeway even in the face of a threat by the national government to cut off grant funds in cases of noncompliance.

A president lacks the authority to simply order the termination of program assistance to a city that refuses to cooperate with federal immigration law enforcement efforts. Pragmatic and political concerns constrain federal actions. A reduction in federal anticrime funds, for instance, would likely hurt innocent citizens and businesses. A reduction in homeland security assistance would increase the vulnerability of important facilities. Members of Congress also seek to protect communities in their district that are faced with the prospect of losing federal funds.

The federal government lacks the legal authority to cut off aid in unrelated service areas in an attempt to punish cities for their failure to cooperate on immigrant expulsion efforts. Supreme Court rulings in other policy areas disapproved of the punitive cutoff of program assistance for activities that are not germane or tied to the purposes of the federal program in question. As one legal scholar explained, "Congress likely could not, for example, condition the receipt of a grant for economic development on cooperation with immigration enforcement."[64]

Basic principles of federalism meant that Trump could not simply command cities to do his bidding. As discussed earlier in this chapter, the Supreme Court in *Printz v. United States* ruled that the federal government cannot "dragoon" or coerce local law enforcement officers into administering federal law. As one constitutional law expert elaborated: "Under the anti-commandeering principle, the federal government can no more require state and local governments to help it carry out mass deportations than it can require local officers to investigate and enforce federal gun laws."[65] The Supreme Court in *NFIB v Sebelius* in 2012 similarly struck down as unduly "coercive" that portion of the American Care Act ("Obamacare") that forced states to expand their Medicaid programs. Judicial authorities were not likely to look favorably upon Trump's efforts to cut federal funds to penalize to communities that did not comply with the president's wishes on immigration matters. Such a penalty would be an unwarranted "gun to the head" of states and localities.[66]

Considerations of due process further limited Trump's ability to penalize sanctuary cities. The federal government cannot impose sanctions unless the immigration-enforcement requirement was "unambiguously" stated in the law that authorized the aid program. When a community agrees to federal assistance it must know the exact terms and the aid conditions to which it has agreed. If the assistance program does not contain language that makes the award of a federal grant contingent upon a local government's compliance with federal immigration directives, the government cannot reduce the monies under the program that are provided to sanctuary cities.[67]

The concerns discussed above led a number of federal judges to strike down Trump administration efforts to penalize sanctuary cities. A federal Court of Appeals in 2018, for instance, placed an injunction on the Attorney General prohibiting him from withholding law enforcement funds from cities that would not cooperate in deportation efforts; the judge would not permit "the sword of federal funding to conscript state and local authorities to aid in federal civil immigration enforcement." The appellate court further observed that Congress had refused to make immigration-related restrictions part of the law assistance program. Nor did the Congress give the Attorney General the authority to add such conditions. The authority to change a program enacted by the U.S. Congress requires action by the U.S. Congress and does not belong to the Attorney General.[68]

A Federal District Court in Philadelphia similarly ruled that Attorney General Sessions could not withhold Byrne Justice Assistance Grant monies from a city that refused to report the scheduled release of "aliens" to federal immigration officials and that refused to give immigration officers access to interrogate "aliens" while held in local jails. The federal judge ruled that the Trump administration had impermissibly attempted to dragoon local officials into federal service. As the judge further explained, the Attorney General's threat to impose aid penalties violated the constitutional principle of separation of powers, as such aid conditions were not part of the law written by Congress.[69]

Continued local government and judicial resistance to Trump's attempt to penalize sanctuary cities represents what can be called the rise of **immigration federalism**.[70] States and cities have become increasingly active in asserting their constitutional prerogatives to act on matters concerning the plight of undocumented members of their communities, irrespective of the president's policy preferences.

Despite the new actions by local governments in the face of the federal government's immigration actions, the extent to which subnational activism can constrain the actions of the national government should not be overstated. Trump increased border screening to reduce the entry of undocumented arrivals. The Trump administration even succeeded in reducing levels of *legal* immigration to the United States.[71] Border officials even turned back refugees who had a right under the law to seek asylum in the United States. The Trump administration further clogged up the asylum system by reducing the number of U.S. officials overseas who could process the applications of persons applying for refugee status.[72] To further deter both asylum seekers and undocumented arrivals, Trump even pursued a policy of family separation: Immigration officials separated parents and children who lacked proper documentation at the border, holding the children in separate detention centers, and then sending parents back to their home countries without knowing if they would see their children again.

THE IMPORTANCE OF THE STATES

THE STATES: A NEW URBAN ORIENTATION

As discussed throughout this book, the states play a critical role in urban affairs. State laws determine what revenue sources a municipality is permitted, including how much a city may tax or borrow. State laws can be permissive or restrictive when it comes to annexations, city-county mergers, service contracting, and the formation of interlocal cooperative arrangements. State-enacted Smart Growth and growth management plans can serve to contain sprawl development and promote infill development in core urban areas—a matter than was reviewed in Chapter 3.

The states play a particularly important role in K–12 education—a matter than was also underscored in Chapter 3. Each state establishes a formula that determines the basic assistance that a school district receives from the state. The aid formula determines the degree to which local education will be marked by inequalities in school finance. A state also has the power to alter school district lines, force the consolidation of smaller school districts, award scholarships or tax credits to promote school choice, and facilitate the creation of charter schools—or, alternatively, put a "cap" on the number of charter schools that can be created in the state.

More than thirty states have **educational bankruptcy laws** under which the state can take control of failing individual schools and problem-filled school districts. The states have become increasingly assertive in using this power, with state-appointed managers making decisions on matters of school operations that were traditionally the domain of local school officials. The list of cities where the states have abridged local autonomy by taking control of an individual problem school or an entire school district is actually rather long and includes: New York; Los Angeles, Inglewood, Compton, and Oakland (California); Chicago; Philadelphia and Harrisburg (Pennsylvania); Baltimore and Prince George's County (Maryland); Boston and Lawrence[73] (Massachusetts); Detroit and Pontiac (Michigan); Hartford and New Haven (Connecticut); Newark, Jersey City, Paterson, Camden, and Trenton (New Jersey); Cleveland; Providence (Rhode Island), and Birmingham and Montgomery (Alabama). Typically, the state appoints an emergency manager or receiver to take charge of failing public schools or a troubled school district.

As we saw in Chapter 9, in what was arguably the most far-reaching state takeover in U.S. history, the State of Pennsylvania's governor in 2002 appointed a School Reform Board which, in turn, placed responsibility for the operation of the city's elementary and middle schools in the hands of nonprofit management companies.[74]

Other states have followed a somewhat different path of school reform, giving the mayor increased authority over the schools, abrogating the power of local elected school boards.[75] New York City Mayor Michael Bloomberg used his state-granted authority to abolish the local school board and take direct control of a public-school system with more than one million students. A decade later, city Mayor Bill de Blasio and state Governor Andrew Cuomo dueled over just who—the city's or the state's top executive—had the greater responsibility for school operations. In Chicago, mayors Richard M. Daley and Rahm Emanuel used their expanded school powers to close underperforming public schools (located disproportionately in minority neighborhoods) and to expand the number of charter schools in the city.[76] The new "education mayors" have helped secure new resources for public education, reduce the average class size, and increase student scores on standardized achievement exams (although the evidence is mixed).[77]

The states have enabled cities to expand their problem-solving efforts in numerous policy arenas. The states have allowed municipalities to adopt innovative approaches to the problem of vacant properties. State statutes set forth the steps for a city or county to establish a **land bank** with the power to strategically acquire tax-delinquent properties. Land banks give municipalities an alternative to allowing distressed properties fall into the hands of speculators who buy the properties at rock-bottom prices and skim off whatever profits they can make by collecting rents while ignoring maintenance, running a property—and its surrounding environs—into the ground. Land banking can also be part of a local strategy to repurpose vacant properties so that they will be used in ways that add to a community's livability and marketability (see Box 11.4). Supportive state laws are necessary to remove past-due tax obligations and liens on problem properties, so that a city or county can offer the properties to community developers clear of legal and financial entanglements.

Box 11.4
Land Banks: The States Give Cities a Tool to Repurpose Vacant Properties

Can cities "repurpose" or find new uses for abandoned and tax-foreclosed properties? A growing number of states have given cities and counties the authority to create a land bank as a means to "gain control" over the disposition of vacant lots and distressed properties that, if left untended, are likely to accelerate a neighborhood's decline. Land-banking statutes enable a municipality to acquire, hold, and develop properties in instances where property owners owe substantial back taxes or have failed to meet their legal obligations for the care and maintenance of their properties.

When there is no local land bank, a city or county typically puts tax-delinquent properties up for auction in an attempt to recoup even a small amount of money for the public treasury. Such auctions, where distressed properties are sold for absurdly low prices, too often put the future of a troubled neighborhood at the mercy of some of the more scurrilous actors operating in the housing market. The buyers of a house at auction seldom seek to refurbish or repair the "distressed" property they have acquired. Instead, the speculators seek to make a quick profit by collecting rents without spending money on upkeep and repairs. A speculator may even try to "flip" or resell a property to a new buyer for a price far above what the speculator paid at auction. If a property no longer generates profits and cannot be sold, the speculator will board up the structure (if he or she decides to meet that minimal requirement for maintaining a property), producing an eyesore and a vacant building that often becomes a haven for drug abuse and other lawlessness, decreasing the attractiveness of the surrounding neighborhood.

Land banking gives a city or county a tool that a city can use to avoid having distressed properties cause a chain of community decline. A city or a county land bank can acquire and set a property aside (virtually putting the property into a "bank") for possible future development. Until a proper buyer is found, the local authority mows the grass and maintains the property, steps that help to assure that blight does not spread to neighboring properties.

Land banking allows a city to repurpose distressed properties for more positive uses. Land banking can be part of a **greening strategy** that a city uses in order to increase a neighborhood's residential attractiveness. A government can offer **side lots** at virtually no cost to the owners of abutting properties, so that disused land is converted into attractive side yards and gardens. The city can even provide assistance in landscaping and reseeding. Such lots can also be used for urban farming. Neighborhood groups can be offered vacant properties at a near-zero price, allowing them to repurpose the properties as community gardens and playgrounds. Detroit offered lots for only $100 apiece to community groups, part of the city's efforts boost to urban farming and fresh food access. A city, if it can put together the funding, can even assemble a string of vacant properties to create an expanded inner-city park or bicycle path. Cleveland acquires properties in neighborhoods that have market potential, where new gardens and green spaces can help make an area attractive to potential homebuyers.

Land banking first gained popularity in Genesee County, Michigan, where, under Michigan Public Act 123, county treasurer Dan Kildee took control over every new piece of land entering Flint's foreclosure system, preventing, as Kildee phrased it, the "late-night infomercial speculators" from taking title and spreading further ruin in the city's neighborhoods. In a relatively short period of time, from 2003 through the beginning of 2009, Genesee County took charge of some 7,400 properties—12 percent of all land in Flint—and demolished over 1,000 abandoned homes.

State law is critical to land banking. State statutes determine whether and under what conditions a locality can acquire and hold a nuisance property. State law also determines the extent to which a city will be permitted to use eminent domain authority to acquire a land parcel that is essential to the redevelopment of a commercial strip or the renewal of a troubled neighborhood.

Changes in state statutes can also streamline what otherwise would be an excessively lengthy and intricate tax foreclosure process. In Michigan, tax foreclosure on a property once took from four to seven years! Public Act 123 fast-tracked the process and shortened the typical foreclosure proceedings to a year or two. In Ohio, House Bill 294 similarly cut the foreclosure process from two years to only four months.

More than a dozen states authorize land banking activities. The list includes Georgia, Illinois, Indiana, Kentucky, Maryland, Michigan, Missouri, Nebraska, New York, Ohio, Pennsylvania, and Texas. In 2016, municipalities operated about 140 land banks across the United States.

Sources: "State Policy Toolkit: State Land Bank Enabling Legislation," Restoring Prosperity Initiative, 2008, www.restoringprosperity.org/wp-content/uploads/2008/09/land-bankpolicy-package-pdf.pdf. Kameshwari Pothukuchi, "'To Allow Farming Is to Give Up on the City': Political Anxieties Related to the Disposition of Vacant Land for Urban Agriculture in Detroit," *Journal of Urban Affairs* 39, no. 8 (2017: 1169–1189), describes the continuing hassles and obstructions that gardeners in Detroit encountered when trying to gain control of side lots and other city-owned land that would be devoted to urban agriculture. The 2016 figures on the number of land banks in operation across the United States are reported by The Center for Community Progress, www.communityprogress.net/land-banking-faq-pages-449.php.

The states also employ various tax policy tools to encourage local economic growth and revitalization. The Pennsylvania Tax Increment Financing (TIF) Guarantee Program encourages lenders to invest in projects on brownfield sties, repurposing former industrial sites that often have toxic soil. By doing so, the state takes some of the risk out of the financing of such reclamation projects: The state reimburses creditors if a strategic reclamation project fails to produce sufficient revenues to repay bondholders.[78]

Why are the states so supportive of local action for local economic growth and revitalization? The answer is actually quite simple. Over the years, state leaders have become increasingly aware that a state's economic future is often intertwined with the fate of its major cities. A blighted city can drag down the image and economic competitiveness of an entire state. The State of New Jersey recognized the economic drag that the state would suffer if it sat by and did nothing to reverse the steep decline of much-troubled Newark, the state's largest city. New Jersey responded with a number of efforts, including the provision of over \$100 million in funds and loans to build a world-class performing arts center in Newark.[79] New Jersey's arts-based strategy was aimed at jump-starting Newark's rebirth and raising the state's international profile.

STATE-LOCAL TENSIONS

In areas outside economic development, state officials have not always supported local policy making. Numerous states continue to be unreceptive to the pleas of local officials for expanded taxing and bonding authority. Local managers further complain that, in an era of tight public resources, the states have reduced program assistance. Some states have even raided local revenue sources to help fund state programs. Such actions reveal a continuing distrust and disregard of municipal officials by state officials.[80]

Local officials also complain of the costs of state-imposed **unfunded mandates** where a state government requires a locality to provide a specific service without providing the financial assistance to pay for the required action. Such service mandates shift the burden of paying for service provision from a state to its local governments. State and local official commonly have both voiced their criticisms of unfunded mandates by the national government that have burdened subnational governments with billions of dollars of service responsibilities.[81] Yet, the states, themselves, have been quite willing to impose their own service mandates on local communities. The Connecticut Conference of Municipalities complains that cities in Connecticut have to absorb the tremendous costs of complying with an estimated 1,250 state-imposed mandates.[82]

Mayors further complain of state preemption and regulations, especially as more politically conservative states have attempted to restrict local efforts that regulate fracking, protect the natural environment, and adopt sanctuary city or welcoming city policies. The states have also overruled local actions in such policy areas as gun control, the protection of LGBT rights, efforts to raise the local minimum wage, and even attempts to levy additional local taxes on the sale of soda and sugared beverages in an effort both to raise funds and to curb childhood obesity.[83] This record of state preemption underscores the continuing anti-urban attitude of a sizeable number of states.[84]

The heightened Democratic versus Republican polarizations of more recent years have served to exacerbate state-local tensions.[85] State legislatures represent communities that are quite different economically, demographically, and politically from central cities with their large minority and immigrant populations and Democratic voting proclivities. The result is an anti-urban bias that is evident in such policy areas as transportation funding: The states provide disproportionate funding to less-traveled roadways in suburban and rural areas while failing to provide equivalent levels of assistance to more heavily utilized urban roadways and transportation projects.[86]

CONCLUSION: THE EVOLVING POSITION OF CITIES IN THE AMERICAN INTERGOVERNMENTAL SYSTEM

Census data reveals that the growth of the suburbs has once again picked up steam.[87] The long-term shift of population and political power to the suburbs continues. The growing representation of suburban constituencies in Congress means that that national legislature is likely less inclined than ever to target substantial assistance to big cities and communities in need.

Presidential politics, too, reflects the shifts in population and power. Population density was clearly related to the presidential vote in 2016, and the suburban vote proved decisive. Hillary Clinton ran best in big cities, especially among racial minorities. Donald Trump's "white identity politics," by contrast, played best in small town and rural areas but also appealed to a large swath of the nation's suburbs.[88] In 2016, rural and suburban whites, propelled by a sense of racial resentment (a sense that government programs unfairly favored racial minorities) and an animosity to immigration, provided the vote margins that allowed Trump to win the White House.[89] Trump carried suburban counties,[90] and with their support he won an Electoral College (not a popular vote) victory.

Bill Clinton and Barack Obama governed with an eye on the constraints that suburban political power imposes on urban policy. Bill Clinton put suburban "soccer moms" at the center of his politics, recognizing the importance of suburban middle-class constituencies both to his reelection and to his domestic policy efforts. Presidents Clinton and Obama governed with an eye on the political realities imposed by suburban power. Clinton and Obama recognized that they could not gain the enactment of strong and explicit national urban policies, especially programs that were strictly targeted to communities with the greatest need. As a consequence, these Democratic presidents chose to pursue more limited but "do-able" urban policy pieces. These presidents also pursued change with programs that were not framed as "urban." Clinton and Obama supported programs that provided assistance to middle-class Americans and to suburban communities; they did not emphasize a more "radical" alternative that would target benefits more heavily to inner cities and the poor. Faced with divided government and partisan obstructionism, President Obama turned to the states and localities, where he found intergovernmental partners who welcomed his domestic and urban policy changes.

Under the Trump administration, the role played by cities in the intergovernmental system continued to evolve with a number of cities emerging as "nodes of resistance"[91] to salient Trump policies. In the Trump years, cities sought a more vigorous presence on the world political stage. Trump disavowed the Paris Accords, and cities responded by continuing their own engagement in international forums and their own efforts to reduce energy consumption and the prospects of global warming. After Trump withdrew the United States from the United Nations effort to develop a Global Compact on Migration, the mayors of New York, Los Angeles, Chicago, Philadelphia, Dallas, Atlanta, and Washington, DC, requested that U.S. cities be given a formal seat at international talks devoted to arranging joint actions in the face of global migration pressures.[92] The cities were helping to fill the void created by Trump's withdrawal of the national government from the world stage.

The American federal system is not hierarchical, and states and cities have the constitutionally protected ability to pursue courses of action contrary to a president's wishes. The balance of national and subnational power evolves over time. Dual federalism gave way to cooperative federalism. The excesses of Washington power sparked the New Federalism reaction. Clinton and Obama sought creative partnerships with willing states in health care and a number of other policy areas.

Trump's arrival in Washington "prompted a reversal of partisan perspectives" on the proper role of states and cities in the American federal system.[93] Republican leaders no longer pleaded the virtues of New Federalism devolution and decentralization; instead, they demanded that state and local governments toe the policy line as set by the Republican government in Washington. Trump proffered a highly centralized and "coercive" form of federalism that did not recognize the authority of states and cities as autonomous actors.[94]

Democrats, too, reversed their more traditional views and came to see newfound virtues in subnational action. Democrats had once viewed the call for states's rights and subnational discretion as little more than a thinly veiled excuse to allow continuing racial segregation and other local inequities. With Trump in office, however, Democrats emerged as full-throated defenders of subnational action, celebrating when cities and states such as California exercised their constitutionally given powers to defend progressive policies and sustainable development.

Local governments have proven to be increasingly important agents of policy changes. Localities pushed the policy envelop, acting in advance of the federal government, in such areas as the legalization of same-sex marriage and providing safe havens for undocumented immigrants and their families.[95]

KEY TERMS

American Recovery and
  Revitalization Act of 2009
  (ARRA) (*p. 408*)
block grants (*p. 400*)
categorical grants (*p. 400*)
Choice Neighborhoods Program,
  Obama's (*p. 407*)
Community Development Block
  Grant (CDBG) program (*p. 402*)
conditional waivers (*p. 411*)
cooperative federalism (*p. 397*)
decentralization, New Federalism's
  emphasis on (*p. 404*)
dual federalism (*p. 397*)
Earned Income Tax Credit (EITC)
  (*p. 407*)
educational bankruptcy laws (*p. 422*)
elastic clause, the U.S.
  Constitution's (*p. 398*)
expressed powers (also called
  delegated powers or enumerated
  powers) (*p. 397*)
federal government, the (*p. 396*)
federal system (*p. 396*)

Fourteenth Amendment Revolution
  (*p. 398*)
grant-in-aid (or, more simply, a
  grant) (*p. 399*)
greening strategies (*p. 423*)
Harlem Children's Zone (*p. 408*)
HOPE VI program (*p. 409*)
illusion of federal control, the
  federal system's (*p. 419*)
immigration federalism (*p. 421*)
implied powers, the doctrine
  of (*p. 398*)
intergovernmental system of the
  United States (*p. 395*)
interstate commerce clause, the U.S.
  Constitution's (*p. 398*)
land bank (*p. 422*)
Model Cities program (*p. 405*)
*National Federation of Independent
  Business v. Sebelius* (*p. 399*)
necessary and proper clause, the
  U.S. Constitution's (*p. 398*)
Neighborhood Stabilization
  Program (NSP) (*p. 408*)

NOTES

1. In 1819, the U.S. Supreme Court recognized that the national government's power to regulate interstate commerce gives it the constitutional authority to establish a national bank, even though the constitution contains no explicit listing or enumeration of the national government's power to build such a bank. See *McCulloch v Maryland*, 17 U.S. 316 (1819).
2. The doctrine of implied powers was first enunciated 200 years ago in the classic U.S. Supreme Court decision *McCulloch v Maryland*, 17 U.S. 316 (1819).
3. At the height of the New Deal, the U.S. Supreme Court ruled in *United States v. Darby*, 312 U.S. 100 (1941), that the Tenth Amendment's "reserved" powers language states is only a "truism" that states the obvious, that "all is retained which has not yet been surrendered." Such a statement is a tautology, a statement this is true by definition: Of course, what is not given to the national government is reserved for the states. But a truism does not have great meaning; it does not necessarily denote that there are many powers reserved for the states and denied to the national government. As the Supreme Court further added, the Tenth Amendment does little to confine the powers of the national government; the central government is entitled to the full exercise of its powers found elsewhere in the Constitution.
4. *United States v. Lopez*, 514 U.S. 549 (1995).
5. *Printz v. United States* 117 S. Ct. 2365 (1997).
6. *National Federation of Independent Business v Sebelius,* 567 U.S. 519 (2012); *King v Burwell*, 576 U.S. ____ (2015); Ilya Somin, "Federalism and the Roberts Court," *Publius: The Journal of Federalism* 46, no. 3 (Summer 2012): 441–462.
7. Christopher C. Banks and John C. Blakeman, *The U.S. Supreme Court and New Federalism: From the Rehnquist to the Roberts Court* (Lanham, MD: Rowman & Littlefield, 2012); Christopher Shortell, "The End of the Federalism Five? Statutory Interpretation and the Roberts Court," *Publius: The Journal of Federalism* 42, no. 3 (Summer 2012): 516–537.
8. Somin, "Federalism and the Roberts Court," 445, observes that, over the past decade, the Supreme Court has taken "some major steps forward" in the "judicial enforcement of federalism" (p. 445).
9. Robert Jay Dilger, "Federal Grants to State and Local Governments: A Historical Perspective on Contemporary Issues," Congressional Research Service, Report 7-5700, Washington, DC, 2018, p. 5.
10. Nixon introduced a second innovation in the grant system to allow even greater state and local flexibility. *General revenue sharing* gave communities no-strings-attached money, federal assistance

that could be used on almost any program the recipient government wished. But revenue sharing proved short-lived. In the face of budgetary pressures, Congress deleted shared revenues with the states. Ronald Reagan brought the program to an end by eliminating general revenue sharing for cities. Reagan was not simply committed to program decentralization. He had a larger goal: to reduce the size of the government at all levels in the domestic economy.

11. William M. Rohe and George C. Galster, "The Community Development Block Grant Program Turns 40: Proposals for Program Expansion and Reform," *Housing Policy Debate* 24, no. 1 (2014): 3–13, esp. 6. The figures are in 2012 constant dollars to control for the impact of inflation.

12. Michael Cooper, "Cities Face Tough Choices as U.S. Slashes Block Grants Program," *New York Times*, December 11, 2011; National Association of Development Organizations, "HUD CDBG: FY2013 Appropriations Update," July 13, 2012, www.nado.org/hud-cdbg-fy13-appropriations-update. For further evidence documenting the shrinking significance of a diminished CDBG program, see Eugene Boyd, "Community Development Block Grants: Recent Funding History," Congressional Research Service Report R43390, Washington, DC: CRS, February 6, 2014, 8, http://digital.library.unt.edu/ark:/67531/metadc282304/m1/1/high_res_d/R43394_2014Feb06.pdf.

13. David Reich, Isaac Shapiro, and Chloe Cho, "Trump Budget's Deep Cuts to Block Grants Underscore Danger of Block Grant Funding," a report of the Center on Budget and Policy Priorities, Washington, DC, June 20, 2017, www.cbpp.org/research/federal-budget/trump-budgets-deep-cuts-to-block-grants-underscore-danger-of-block-granting, details how Trump proposed the elimination of six major block grant programs and sharp spending reductions in five additional block grants.

14. Emily Badger, "As American as Apple Pie? The Rural Vote's Disproportionate Slice of Power," *New York Times*, "Urban Upshot" column, November 20, 2016.

15. Benjamin Kleinberg, *Urban America in Transformation: Perspectives on Urban Policy and Development* (Thousand Oaks, CA: Sage Publications, 1995), 175–184.

16. Robert J. Waste, *Independent Cities: Rethinking U.S. Urban Policy* (New York: Oxford University Press, 1998), 90.

17. Myron A. Levine, "Urban Policy in America: The Clinton Approach," *Local Economy* 9 (November 1994): 278–281.

18. Alan Berube and Natalie Holmes, *The Earned Income Tax Credit and Community Economic Stability* (Washington, DC: Brookings Institution, November 2015), www.brookings.edu/articles/the-earned-income-tax-credit-and-community-economic-stability/.

19. Alan Berube, "Using the Earned Income Tax Credit to Stimulate Local Economies, a paper of the Living Cities Policy Series, The National Community Development Initiative Uploaded 2016," www.brookings.edu/wp-content/uploads/2016/06/Berube20061101eitc.pdf.

20. The White House, "Memorandum for the Heads of Executive Departments; Subject: Developing Effective Place-Based Policies for the FY 2012 Budget," June 21, 2010.

21. Robert Jay Dilger and Eugene Boyd, *Block Grants: Perspectives and Controversies*, CRS Report to Congress R40486 (Washington, DC: Congressional Research Service, 2013), 15.

22. Lara Hulsey, Andrea Mraz Esposito, Kimberly Boller, and Sarah Osborne, *Promise Neighborhoods Case Studies: Final Report* (Princeton, NJ: Mathematica Policy Research, 2015), report prepared for the Promise Neighborhoods Institute, www.mathematica-mpr.com/our-publications-and-findings/publications/promise-neighborhoods-case-studies-issue-brief.

23. Sheldon N. Edner and Matthew J. Critchfield, "The Rush to Pave: Adapting the Federally Aided Highway Network to ARRA," in *Governing Under Stress: The Implementation of Obama's Economic Stimulus Program*, ed. Timothy J. Conlan, Paul L Posner, and Priscilla M. Regan (Washington, DC: Georgetown University Press, 2017), 65.

24. Robert W. Lake, "The Financialization of Urban Policy in the Age of Obama," *Journal of Urban Affairs* 37, no. 1 (February 2015): 75–78; the quotation appears on p. 75.

25. Dan Immergluck, "The Foreclosure Crisis, Foreclosed Properties, and Federal Policy: Some Implications for Housing and Community Development Planning," *Journal of the American Planning Association* 75, no. 4 (2009): 406–423, esp. 408.

26. See, for instance, Dan Immergluck, "Too Little, Too Late, and Too Timid: The Federal Response to the Foreclosure Crisis at the Five-Year Mark," *Housing Policy Debate* 23, no. 1 (2013): 199–232.

27. James C. Fraser and Deirdre Oakley, "The Neighborhood Stabilization Program: Stable for Whom?," *Journal of Urban Affairs* 37, no. 1 (February 2015): 38–41.

28. Garrettt M. Graf, "The Urban Inheritance That Trump Stands to Squander," *Next City Blog Article*, December 12, 2016, https://nextcity.org/features/view/obama-urban-policy-donald-trump-inherits, describes a number of the partnerships that Obama formed with willing cities and suburbs.

29. Timothy J. Conlan and Paul L. Posner, "American Federalism in an Era of Partisan Polarization: The Intergovernmental Paradox of Obama's 'New Nationalism,'" *Publius: The Journal of Federalism* 46, no. 3 (2016): 281–307. The reference to "variable speed federalism" appears on p. 283. Jessica Bulman-Pozen and Gillian E. Metzger, "The President and the States: Patterns of Contestation and Collaboration under Obama," *Publius: The Journal of Federalism* 46, no. 3 (2016): 308–336, further details how the Obama administration built new partnerships with willing states through the award of program waivers, the dispensation of competitive grants, and other actions that that drew on the perspectives of the states in the implementation of intergovernmental programs.

    Variable-speed federalism was also evident in health care reform as the nation's states varied widely in their willingness to implement the Affordable Care Act. Some expanded Medicaid and took the necessary steps to help create a new marketplace to offer expanded health insurance coverage to the working poor. Yet other states engaged in active "dissent," seeking to undermine the nation's new health law. See Daniel Béland, Philip Rocco, and Alex Waddan, *Obamacare Wars: Federalism, State Politics and the Affordable Care Act* (Lawrence, KS: University Press of Kansas, 2016).

30. Pauline Lipman, "Urban Education Policy under Obama," *Journal of Urban Affairs* 37, no. 1 (February 2015): 57–61; the reference to community anchors appears on p. 59.

31. The discussion of Obama's strategy for K–12 school reform draws heavily on Patrick McGuinn, "From No Child Left Behind to the Every Child Succeeds Act: Federalism and the Educational Legacy of the Obama Administration," *Publius: The Journal of Federalism* 46, no. 3 (2016): 392–415.

32. Timothy Conlan and Paul Posner, "Inflection Point? Federalism and the Obama Administration," *Publius: The Journal of Federalism* 41, no. 3 (2011): 421–446.

33. Glenn Thrush, "Under Ben Carson, HUD Scales Back Fair Housing Enforcement," *New York Times*, March 28, 2018. Also see: *New York Times* (editorial), "Ben Carson's Warped View of Housing," December 19, 2016; and Peter Dreier, "Why Trump Picked Ben Carson as HUD Secretary," *The American Prospect*, December 6, 2016.

34. Ben Carson, "Experimenting with Failed Socialism Again: Obama's New Housing Rules Try to Accomplish What Busing Could Not," *The Washington Times*, July 23, 1015, http://prospect.org/article/why-trump-picked-ben-carson-hud-secretary. Also see NAACP Legal Defense Fund, "Civil Rights Groups Sue HUD over Suspended Implementation of Affirmatively Furthering Fair Housing Rule," *Press Release*, May 8, 2018, www.naacpldf.org/press-release/civil-rights-groups-sue-hud-over-suspended-implementation-affirmatively-furthering-f-0.

35. Robert Abare, "Ben Carson's Plan for 'EnVision Centers' Looks Familiar and Needs Realistic Expectations," *An Urban Wire Posting of the Urban Institute*, March 1, 2018, www.urban.org/urban-wire/ben-carsons-plan-envision-centers-looks-familiar-and-needs-realistic-expectations. Abare interviews public housing expert and Urban Institute fellow Susan Popkin who observes that the focus on character development in past programs produced only modest results. Public housing residents need child care assistance, transportation, and other supports in order to get jobs that pay a sufficient wage that will allow them to escape poverty and leave public housing.

36. Dan Hinkel, "Attorney General Jeff Sessions Plans to Weigh In against Chicago Police Consent Decree," *Chicago Tribune*, October 10, 2018.

37. Peter Dreier, "Steve Mnuchin: Evictor, Forecloser, and Our New Treasury Secretary," *The American Prospect*, November 30, 2016, http://prospect.org/article/steve-mnuchin-evictor-forecloser-and-our-new-treasury-secretary; Ben Lane, "Steve Mnuchin's OneBank West Accused of Redlining,"

HousingWire, November 17, 2016, www.housingwire.com/articles/38551-steven-mnuchins-onewest-bank-accused-of-redlining; and Paulina Gonzales, executive director of the California Reinvestment Coalition, "California Reinvestment Group Responds to Steve Mnuchin's Likely Nomination for Treasury Secretary," *Press Release*, November 29, 2016, www.calreinvest.org/news/california-reinvestment-coalition-responds-to-steve-mnuchins-likely-nomination-for-treasury-secretary.

38. The Trump administration declared that its efforts were intended to modernize the CRA. See U.S. Department of Treasury, "Treasury Releases Community Reinvestment Act Modernization Recommendations," *Press Release*, April 3, 2018, https://home.treasury.gov/news/press-releases/sm0336.

39. Benjamin Wermund, "Trump's Education Pick Says Reform Can 'Advance God's Kingdom,'" *Politico*, December 2, 2016, www.politico.com/story/2016/12/betsy-devos-education-trump-religion-232150.

40. Stephen Henderson, "Betsy DeVos and the Twilight of American Public Education," *Detroit Free Press*, December 6, 2016.

41. Brian Charles, "Trump Proposes Unprecedented Expansion in School Choice," *Governing Magazine*, February 12, 2018.

42. Nat Malkus, Richard V. Reeves, and Nathan Joo, "The Costs, Opportunities, and Limitations of the Expansion of 529 Education Savings Accounts," *The Brookings Institution Evidence Speaks Reports* 2, no. 47 (April 12, 2018), www.brookings.edu/research/the-costs-opportunities-and-limitations-of-the-expansion-of-529-education-savings-accounts/

43. Erica L. Green, "DeVos Education Dept. Begins Dismissing Civil Rights Cases in the Name of Efficiency," *New York Times*, April 20, 2018.

44. Coral Davenport, "Climate Change Conversations Are Targeted in Questionnaire to Energy Department," *New York Times*, December 9, 2016, www.brookings.edu/wp-content/uploads/2018/04/529-reports_njproofed.pdf.

45. Elgie Holstein, "Trump's EPA Budget: 5 Critical Public Health Programs on the Chopping Block," *Environmental Defense Fund Blog*, May 22, 2017, www.edf.org/blog/2017/05/22/trumps-epa-budget-5-critical-public-health-programs-chopping-block; Brady Dennis, "Trump Budget Seeks 23 Percent Cut at EPA, Eliminating Dozens of Programs," *Washington Post*, February 12, 2018.

46. EPA Administrator Scott Pruitt, quoted by Hiroko Tabuchi, "Calling Car Pollution Standards 'Too High.' E.P.A. Sets Up Fight with California," *New York Times*, April 2, 2018.

47. "The AIA and Nearly 800 Firms Rebuke the Trump Administration's Budget Cuts," *Architect*, March 17, 2017, www.architectmagazine.com/practice/the-aia-and-nearly-800-firms-rebuke-the-trump-administrations-budget-cuts_o.

48. Mark Muro, "Climate, Energy, and Trump: Progress Is Still Possible," blog of the Metropolitan Policy Program, The Brookings Institution, Washington, DC, November 15, 2016, www.brookings.edu/blog/the-avenue/2016/11/15/climate-energy-and-trump-progress-is-still-possible/?utm_campaign=Metropolitan+Policy+Program&utm_source=hs_email&utm_medium=email&utm_content=37831843.

49. The analysis presented in this section focuses on the urban program changes that the Trump administration outlined in its proposed budgets for 2018 and 2019.

50. Jacob Terrell, "DHS Secretary Testifies on FY 2019 Budget Request; Proposal Contains Wins and Concerns for Counties," *NACo (National Association of Counties) Blog*, May 8, 2018, www.naco.org/blog/dhs-secretary-testifies-fy-2019-budget-request-proposal-contains-wins-and-concerns-counties.

51. The TCJA nearly doubled the standard deduction to $12,000 for an individual taxpayer and to $24,000 for a married couple filing jointly

52. U.S. Department of Treasury estimate cited by Sam Alcorn, "Now Is the Time to Look at Opportunity Zones," *MRSC: Local Government Success*, a web posting of the Municipal Research and Service Center, Seattle, Washington, March 6, 2019, http://mrsc.org/Home/Stay-Informed/MRSC-Insight/March-2019/Now-Is-the-Time-to-Look-at-Opportunity-Zones.aspx#.

53. Remarks at the "Opportunity Zones: Understanding the Potential of the New Community Development Tax Incentives" webinar; Ruth Simon and Richard Rubin, "New Hotel or Affordable Housing? Race Is On to Define 'Opportunity Zones,'" *Wall Street Journal*, July 13, 2018.

54. Adam Looney, "Will Opportunity Zones Help Distressed Residents or Be a Tax Cut for Gentrification?," *The Brookings Institution "Upfront" Blog*, February 16, 2018, www.brookings.edu/blog/upfront/2018/02/26/will-opportunity-zones-help-distressed-residents-or-be-a-tax-cut-for-gentrification/; Scott Eastman and Nicole Kaeding, "Opportunity Zones: What We Know and What We Don't," a report of the Tax Foundation, Washington, DC, January 8, 2019, https://taxfoundation.org/opportunity-zones-what-we-know-and-what-we-dont/.

55. Patricia Cohen and Alan Rappeport, "Trump's Infrastructure Plan Puts Burden on State and Private Money," *New York Times*, February 12, 2018.

56. Laura Bliss, "The $1.4 Billion Transit Fund the U.S. Government Won't Release," *CityLab Blog Posting*, August 15, 2018, www.citylab.com/transportation/2018/08/the-14-billion-transit-fund-the-government-wont-release/567467/?utm_source=citylab-daily&silverid=MzEwMTkwMTE1MjE2S0.

57. Donald Cohen, "Public Infrastructure as Stealth Privatization," *The American Prospect*, December 21, 2016, http://prospect.org/article/public-infrastructure-stealth-privatization. Also see former Obama Economic Adviser Ronald A. Klain, "Trump's Big Infrastructure Plan? It's a Trap," *Washington Post*, November 18, 2016.

58. Conor Swanberg, "Map Shows How Many 'Sanctuary Cities' Are Sheltering Illegal Immigrants in the US: And Where They Are," *Independent Journal Review*, 2015 http://ijr.com/2015/07/364099-tragic-murder-kate-steinle-americans-rethinking-sanctuary-cities-across-country/. The 300 estimate is cited by Barbara E. Armacost, "'Sanctuary' Laws: The New Immigration Federalism," *Michigan State Law Review* no. 5 (2016): 1197–1265.

59. John Austin, Akaash Kolluri, and Steve Tobocman, "Michigan: We Are All Migrants Here—Immigrants and Newcomers Built Michigan's Economy; Immigrant Engine of Economic Growth Threatened by Trump Administration Policy," a joint report of the Michigan Economic Center and Global Detroit, 2017.

60. Kate Mather, "LAPD Will Not Help Deport Immigrants Under Trump, Chief Says," *Los Angeles Times*, November 15, 2016.

61. Geneva Sands, "Cities Across the US Push Back against President-Elect Donald Trump's Proposed Immigration Policies," *ABC News*, November 17, 2016; Sara Rathod, "Here Are the Sanctuary Cities Ready to Resist Trump's Deportation Threats," *Mother Jones*, www.motherjones.com/politics/2016/11/sanctuary-city-immigration-federal-deportation-trump-threats-budget.

62. Tanvi Misra, "The Effect of Trump's Immigration Crackdown, in 3 Maps," *CityLab Blog*, February 15, 2018, www.citylab.com/equity/2018/02/mapping-trumps-immigration-crackdownand-the-local-response-to-it/552881/; George Joseph, "Where Trump's Immigration Crackdown Is Failing," *Slate*, June 20, 2018, www.slate.com/culture/2018/06/pixars-new-short-bao-captures-the-asian-immigrant-experience.html.

63. Charles J. Orlebeke, "The Evolution of Low-Income Housing Policy, 1949 to 1989," *Housing Policy Debate* 11, no. 2 (2000): 505–506.

64. Ilya Somin, "Federalism, the Constitution, and Sanctuary Cities," *Washington Post*, November 26, 2016.

65. Erwin Chemerinsky, Anne Lai, and Seth Davis, "Trump Can't Force 'Sanctuary Cities' to Enforce His Deportation Plans," *Washington Post*, December 22, 2016.

66. Somin, "Federalism, the Constitution, and Sanctuary Cities."

67. Somin, "Federalism, the Constitution, and Sanctuary Cities."

68. *City of Chicago v Sessions*, United States Court of Appeals for the 7th District, 17-2991 (April 1, 2018).

69. *City of Philadelphia v. Sessions*, United States District Court for the Eastern District of Pennsylvania, 17-3894 (2018).

70. Gary Reich, "Hitting a Wall? The Trump Administration Meets Immigration Federalism," *Publius: The Journal of Federalism*, special issue, forthcoming (2018), advanced copy published online, May 25, 2018, doi:10.1093/publius/pjy013. Also see Armacost, "'Sanctuary' Laws: The New Immigration Federalism."

71. Abigail Hauslohner and Andrew Ba Tran, "How Trump Is Changing the Face of Legal Immigration," *Washington Post*, July 2, 2018.

72. Liz Robbins and Miriam Jordan, "Apartments Are Stocked, Toys Donated: Only the Refugees Are Missing," *New York Times*, May 16, 2018.

73. Lawrence, Massachusetts, represents a largely successful instance of a state takeover of local public education. See Beth E. Schueler, Joshua Goodman, and David J. Deming, "Can States Take Over and Turn Around School Districts? Evidence from Lawrence, Massachusetts," *Education Evaluation and Policy Analysis* 39, no. 2 (2017): 311–332.

74. For a discussion of the impact that the takeover had on children's education, see Brian Gill, Ron Zimmer, Jolley Christman, and Suzanne Blanc, *State Takeover, School Restructuring, Private Management, and Student Achievement in Philadelphia* (Santa Monica, CA: RAND Education, 2007), www.rand.org/pubs/monographs/2007/RAND_MG533.pdf.

75. Kenneth K. Wong, Francis X. Shen, Dorothea Anagnostopoulos, and Stacey Rutledge, *The Education Mayor: Improving America's Schools* (Washington, DC: Georgetown University Press, 2007). Also see Frederick M. Hess, "Assessing the Case for Mayoral Control of Urban Schools," *American Enterprise Institute* 4 (August 2008), www.aei.org/outlook/28511. For an early review of mayoral takeover efforts, see Joseph P. Viteritti, ed., *When Mayors Take Charge: School Governance in the City* (Washington, DC: Brookings Institution Press, 2009).

76. For a critical analysis of mayor-centered school reform in Chicago, see Pauline Lipman, "Economic Crisis, Charter School Expansion, and Coercive Neoliberal Urbanism in the United States," in *Privatization and the Educations of Marginalized Children*, ed. Bekisizwe S. Ndimande and Christopher Lubienski (New York: Routledge, 2017), 17–40.

77. Kenneth K. Wong and Francis X. Shen, "Mayoral Governance and Student Achievement: How Mayor-Led Districts Are Improving School and Student Performance," a report of the Center for American Progress, Washington, DC, 2013, www.americanprogress.org/issues/education/reports/2013/03/22/56934/mayoral-governance-and-student-achievement/. Wong and Shen's interpretation of the evidence, of course, remains highly contentious. For a competing perspective that reports no substantial gains from mayoral control of schools in New York, Chicago, and Washington, DC, see Elaine Weiss and Don Long, "Market-Oriented Education's Reforms' Rhetoric Trumps Reality," a report of A Broader, BOLDER Approach to Education and the Economic Policy Institute, 2013, https://cdn.americanprogress.org/wp-content/uploads/2013/03/MayoralControl-6.pdf.

78. Evans Paull, "Vacant Properties, TIFs, and What's Working Now," (presentation to the Reclaiming Vacant Properties Conference, Cleveland, Ohio, October 14, 2010).

79. Elizabeth Strom, "Let's Put on a Show! Performing Arts and Urban Revitalization in Newark, New Jersey," *Journal of Urban Affairs* 21, no. 4 (1999): 423–435.

80. Gerald E. Frug and David J. Barron, *City Bound: How States Stifle Urban Innovation* (Ithaca, NY: Cornell University Press, 2008).

81. For a review of the costs that federal mandates impose on state and local governments and the inability of the federal Unfunded Mandates Reform Act of 1995 to effectively correct the problem, see Robert J. Dilger, "Federal Grants to State and Local Governments: A Historical Perspective on Contemporary Issues," CRS Report to Congress R40638, Washington, DC: Congressional Research Service, 2015, https://fas.org/sgp/crs/misc/R40638.pdf.

82. Connecticut Conference of Municipalities, "Unfunded State Mandates: The Corrosive Impact on Property Taxes," *Candidate Bulletin*, 2016, www.ccmct.org/sites/default/files/files/2016Bulletins_Mandates_web.pdf.

83. Katherine Levine Einstein and David M. Glick, "Cities in American Federalism: Evidence on State-Local Government Conflict from a Survey of Mayors," *Publius: The Journal of Federalism* 47, no. 4 (October 2017): 599–621.

84. Richard C. Schragger, *City Power: Urban Governance in a Global Age* (New York: Oxford University Press, 2016); Richard C. Schragger, "The Attack on American Cities," *Texas Law Review* 96 (2018): 1163–1233.

85. Einstein and Glick, "Cities in American Federalism."

86. Edward Hill, Billie Geyer, Robert Puentes, Kevin O'Brien, Claudette Robey, and John Brennan, "Slanted Pavement: How Ohio's Highway Spending Shortchanges Cities and Suburbs," in *Taking the High Road: A Metropolitan Agenda for Transit Reform*, ed. Bruce Katz and Robert Puentes (Washington, DC: Brookings Institution Press, 2005), 101–135.

87. William H. Frey, "City Growth Dips Below Suburban Growth, Census Shows," *The Avenue Newsletter of the Brookings Institution*, May 30, 2017, www.brookings.edu/blog/the-avenue/2017/05/30/city-growth-dips-below-suburban-growth-census-shows/; William H. Frey, "US Population Disperses to Suburbs, Exurbs, Rural Areas, and 'Middle of the Country' Metros," *The Avenue Newsletter of the Brookings Institution*, March 26, 2018; www.brookings.edu/blog/the-avenue/2018/03/26/us-population-disperses-to-suburbs-exurbs-rural-areas-and-middle-of-the-country-metros/?utm_campaign=Metropolitan%20Policy%20Program&utm_source=hs_email&utm_medium=email&utm_content=61738659.

88. Robert E. Lang and David F. Damore, "The End of the Democratic Blue Wall?," *A Brookings Mountain West Digital Publication* (December 2016): 7–8, http://digitalscholarship.unlv.edu/brookings_pubs/45.

89. Marc Hooghe and Ruth Dassonneville, "Explaining the Trump Vote: The Effects of Racist Resentment and Anti-Immigrant Sentiments," *PS: Political Science and Politics*, April 2018, "first view" version published online, doi.org/10.1017/S1049096518000367; and Alan J. Abramowitz, "It Wasn't the Economy, Stupid: Racial Polarization, White Racial Resentment, and the Rise of Trump," in *Trumped: The 2016 Election That Broke All the Rules*, ed. Larry J. Sabato, Kyle Kondik, and Geoffrey Skelley (London, UK: Rowman and Littlefield, 2017), 202–210. Gary C. Jacobson, "The Triumph of Polarized Partisanship in 2016: Donald Trump's Improbable Victory," *Political Science Quarterly*, 132, no. 1 (2017): 9–41, similarly cities poll data that underscores the sentiment of Trump supporters that "government has gone too far in assisting minority groups" (p. 20).

90. Lazaro Gamio and Dan Keating, "How Trump Redrew the Electoral Map, from Sea to Shining Sea," *Washington Post*, November 9, 2016; Joel Kotkin and Wendell Cox, "It Wasn't Rural 'Hicks' Who Elected Trump: The Suburbs Were—and Will Remain—the Real Battleground," *Forbes*, November 22, 2016, report that Trump won "suburbia" by a decisive five percentage-point margin (based on *New York Times* data published after the election), up from Mitt Romney's two-point edge four years previously.

91. Peter Eisinger, "Cities as Nodes of Resistance to the Trump Agenda," *Urban Affairs Forum, an Online Scholars' Series Presented by the Urban Affairs Review*, February 22, 2017, https://urbanaffairsreview.com/2017/02/22/cities-as-nodes-of-resistance-to-the-trump-agenda/.

92. Rachel Dovey, "World's Mayors Demand a Say in UN Immigration Discussions," *Next City Blog*, December 7, 2017, https://nextcity.org/daily/entry/mayors-demand-say-un-immigration-discussions.

93. Greg Goelzhauser and Shanna Rose, "The State of American Federalism 2016–2017: Policy Reversals and Partisan Perspectives on Intergovernmental Relations," *Publius: The Journal of Federalism* 47, no. 3 (Summer 2017): 285–313. The quotation appears on 285.

94. John Kincaid, "Introduction: The Trump Interlude and the Status of American Federalism," *State and Local Government Review* 4, no. 3 (2017): 156–169.

95. Lori Riverstone-Newell, *Renegade Cities, Public Police, and the Dilemmas of Federalism* (Boulder, CO: First Forum Press, 2014) observes that the rise in local activism predates Trump's arrival in the White House.

12 The Future of Urban America

What is the future of urban politics and policy in the United States? Two trends seem certain to continue. First, in an age of capital mobility and global competition, cities and suburbs will devote considerable effort and resources to the pursuit of jobs and local economic development. Second, in age where intergovernmental assistance is tenuous and where voters are hesitant to approve tax increases, municipal leaders will continue to give attention to the tools of urban management, including the expanded use of program systems of performance management and innovations that allow cities to "do more with less."

Yet urban politics is not solely about the search for economic development and managerial efficiency. Urban politics encompasses much, much more. Matters related to social class, race, and ethnicity, and concerns for "equity" and "fairness," will continue to define urban politics. Issues of housing affordability, the incorporation of immigrants into American society, equality in education, and racial justice will continue to occupy important positions on the urban agenda.

Cities will also be increasingly preoccupied with questions regarding their ecological vulnerability. As a result of global warming, municipal leaders have to confront the mounting threat and costs that accompany rising sea levels and increased coastal flooding. With increasingly dry forest areas and grasslands providing the tinder, wildfires have also become more virulent and lethal. The Camp Fire of 2018 in northern California was the deadliest wildfire in U.S. history, leaving 88 persons dead and nearly 200 still missing three weeks after the fire. The fire completely destroyed the town of Paradise, a 27,000-person Sacramento Valley community just east of Chico.

How will government respond to the threat posed by natural disaster as well as that posed by more traditional urban problems? As this book has detailed, local governments have become increasingly active problem solvers. But their power is still limited. Effective local action often requires both intergovernmental and popular support, and that support is not guaranteed. Urban leaders and advocates will have to engage in courses of action that are capable of building such support.

POLITICS COUNTS! THE PIVOTAL IMPORTANCE OF SUBURBAN POWER

Donald Trump rode to the White House on an anti-government message that found its greatest appeal among white voters in rural areas and in more thinly populated suburban and exurban communities.[1] Population density was clearly related to the 2016 presidential vote. The residents of less-densely populated communities rejected big cities and their political leaders for not sharing their values.[2] These voters were deeply skeptical of affirmative action and other urban and social programs that they viewed as elitist and a rejection of heartland values. They resented governmental elites who embraced welfarism, racial favoritism, globalization, and immigration. These voters saw Donald Trump as a fighter who would not conform to "political correctness."

As president, Trump had little interest in helping those constituencies—including big cities—that did not vote for him. Trump's taxing, spending, and regulatory programs represented an assault on the entire concept of "urban policy."

However, Trump's 2016 victory does *not* necessarily indicate a future politics that will be so severely anti-urban. Trump in 2016 won an Electoral College victory, but he lost the popular vote. Although the nation's suburbs provided Trump with the vote margins he needed to take the White House, "suburbia" was not firmly in the Trump camp.

America's suburbs are the swing communities that will decide future national and state elections and just how receptive the national and state governments will be to urban policy. The United States is in a suburban age, but suburban communities are not all alike and are not solid Trump country. Contemporary suburbia is comprised of a heterogeneity of communities that defy the stereotype of suburbia as a string of universally white, affluent, and Republican bastions. The most populous suburban communities even tend to resemble cities in terms of population density, greater ethnic diversity, more tolerant cultural attitudes, and more mixed land uses (including multifamily dwellings). In numerous ways, the residents of more populated suburbs have more in common with city residents than they have with the residents of rural areas.

Voting patterns in the 2018 midterm congressional elections, just two years into the Trump presidency, reveal the existence of large portions of suburbia that had little fondness for Trump's more severe policies, including the president's harsh approach to immigration. In 2018 Democrats won a clear majority of the suburban vote and regained control of the House of Representatives. The Democrats in 2018 picked up a net gain of 40 congressional seats, the greatest gain by any political party in a midterm election in more than four decades, since the 1974 landslide when Democrats picked up 49 House seats in the wake of the Watergate scandal.[3]

President Trump sought to whip up an anti-immigration frenzy that he hoped would enable the Republicans to maintain control of Congress. In the weeks and days immediately preceding the midterm elections, the president tried to keep the public's attention focused on illegal immigration. He even took the extraordinary step of sending thousands of U.S. Army troops to the nation's southern border, in what he claimed was a response to a national "emergency." The troops, according to Trump, would defend the nation against an "invasion" by a caravan of immigrants from Central America who walked through Mexico to reach the U.S. border. Trump further charged, without substantiation, that the caravan had been infiltrated by "unknown Middle Easterners" and terrorists. The ploy appealed to Trump's political base, but it did not resonate throughout suburbia.

A spatial analysis of the vote in 2018 midterms documents the extent of the support that Democrats gained in the suburbs. As expected, Democrats won the nation's cities ("pure urban" census districts) and the Republicans carried "pure rural" districts. The most interesting voting patterns were in the suburbs where, overall, the Democrats did quite well. The Democrats won over 90 percent of the congressional races in "urban-suburban" districts; the Democrats also won over 80 percent of House seats in "dense suburban districts" (congressional districts dominated by inner-ring suburbs). Democratic candidates even won a majority of the congressional contests in the political "swing" portions of suburbia, the more sprawling and exurban (or "sparse suburban") congressional districts. Trump's actions had dominated the headlines and essentially served to nationalize the 2018 congressional contests. But the results were not what Trump expected. Overall, the Republicans fared poorly in suburbia in 2018, winning only the nation's least densely populated (or "rural-suburban") districts that had no dense urban-like neighborhoods.[4]

Polling data further reveals that suburban voters in the Northeast, Midwest, and the West in 2018 "supported Democratic House candidates by a healthy margin over Republican candidates."[5] Only in the South did the Republicans fare better; but even here, in this more conservative region of the country, Democratic and Republican candidates ran just about even in the suburbs. In just two short years, from Trump's victory in 2016 to 2018, the nation's suburbs had flipped politically.

The political evolution of suburbia and the gains made by Democrats can be further illustrated by a quick look at election outcomes in both greater Philadelphia and southern California. The 2018 results in the Philadelphia region confirm a political transformation that has been under way for two decades: rising education levels and a new population diversity have served to make Philadelphia's suburbs a bastion of Democratic support.[6] Even more startling were the results in southern California, where the Democrats in 2018 swept all seven congressional seats in Orange County, an area that was once renowned as the heart of political conservatism, a part of suburbia that in previous decades had been characterized as "Nixon country" and "Reagan country." Changes in demography had transformed Orange County's suburbs from a Republican to a Democratic stronghold.

The policy choices and fate of urban America are not foreordained. Politics counts. The suburbs hold one of the keys.

THE CONTINUING EMPHASIS ON LOCAL ECONOMIC DEVELOPMENT

Concerns for economic development enjoy a near hegemonic position in the contemporary city. The primacy that civic leaders give to the chase for economic development and jobs tends to crowd out the attention that municipal officials give to competing issues

To a fair degree, cities have always paid a considerable degree of attention to projects to enhance local economic growth. In the preindustrial city, civic leaders in New York, Buffalo, Chicago, Dayton, and numerous other communities pushed for the construction of canals to abet commercial expansion. In the age of the big-city political machine, party bosses pursued street construction, the extension of tram lines, and other growth projects that had the side-benefits of enriching machine leaders and providing the party organization with a supply of job patronage to dispense to the machine's supporters. Throughout the twentieth century, Sunbelt cities such as Houston, Los Angeles, and Long Beach made considerable investments to expand port facilities, deepen shipping channels, and build new airports, providing the infrastructure necessary for continued economic growth.[7] In Denver, Dallas-Fort Worth, Atlanta, and other Sunbelt cities, local business leaders argued that the construction of a new international airport was critical to the region's economic future.

Still, economic matters were not always on the front burner of urban politics. In the decades after the Great Depression and World War II, cities and the federal government worked together to construct public housing as the nation made a commitment to ensure that all Americans would have habitable shelter. In the 1960s, social policy and issues of race—antipoverty and community action programs, community control, school busing, and the demand for "law and order"—dominated the agendas of both the national and local governments. The wave of riots that tore across big- and medium-sized cities in the 1960s raised the profile of the "urban crisis," and governments experimented with a vast array of social policy, antipoverty, and community action programs. By the mid-1970s, a quite different set of issues gained preeminence in the urban arena. As New York City and Cleveland flirted with municipal bankruptcy, the urban agenda shifted, yielding a new emphasis on managerialism and "cutback management" as opposed to the social policy and community development efforts of the Great Society era of the1960s. Rising voter anti-tax sentiment soon reinforced the pressures for municipal belt-tightening. All of this was urban politics. None of these urban eras had local economic development at the forefront.

But as postindustrial restructuring and globalization continued to degrade local economies, municipal leaders gave new urgency to pursuing economic growth and jobs. Only the most affluent cities and suburbs could afford to be selective and allow economic vitality pass to other communities. Each city began to replicate the approaches that it saw other communities use in the battle for businesses and jobs. In contemporary urban America, local economic initiatives have become a normal municipal function, a local government activity as commonplace as repaving local streets and ensuring that trash is hauled away.

In their attempts to lure and retain businesses, cities provide the infrastructure improvements that business firms require. Municipalities also promise major firms a variety of tax concessions and other subsidies. Numerous cities have turned to a creative development finance tool known as **tax increment financing (TIF)** to help pay for the infrastructure improvements demanded by business (see Box 12.1).

Box 12.1
Tax Increment Financing: How Cities Find the Monies for New Economic Development

Big- and medium-size communities often create a **TIF district** in order to help pay for the infrastructure improvements that are needed to support business expansion. Dallas, for instance, created the 9.5-mile-long Skillman Corridor TIF District in the northeast part of the city to provide the funding for the site work and public improvements needed for the construction of a new commercial town center and nearby residential developments surrounding a soon-to-be-opened DART light-rail stations.

A TIF district is created with clearly delineated boundaries. The TIF arrangement guarantees that increases in property tax yields that result from new business investment and property improvements inside the district will be plowed back into the district. TIF revenues are often used to repay much of the debt that the district had incurred in order to provide the strengthened streets, improvements in water quality and sewage capacity, and other infrastructure upgrades that new businesses demanded.

Politicians see a TIF as a relatively costless means to "self-finance" new development. Increased yields in property tax revenues resulting from new investments are used to repay the funds that the city or district had borrowed to begin work on the project. Businesses located in the district are often quite supportive of the TIF arrangement, as the property taxes they pay are not simply handed over to the city to spend anywhere it wishes. Instead, the tax gains from the investments made in a TIF district are dedicated to paying for further improvements within the district and cannot be spent on services and infrastructure improvements elsewhere in the city beyond the borders of the TIF district.

TIFs are one of the most widely used local economic strategies, a tool that virtually every state allows.[1] But the tool is also subject to serious criticisms, especially as a TIF prioritizes business needs and precludes a city from using new revenue gains to help pay for programs in response to other city problems. Business expansion in a TIF does little to help a city's schools; the public schools gain little when the revenues generated by the new development are, by law, dedicated for a set number of years to repaying a TIF's debt and to financing future upgrades in a TIF district.[2] Chicago's public schools lose $500 million yearly as TIF arrangements divert property tax revenues away from the schools and instead spend the monies on improvements inside the designated commercial districts.[3]

The money lost as a result of TIF revenue diversion is increasingly a problem for the suburbs and not just cities, as increasing numbers of suburban governments have turned to TIFs to finance infrastructure improvements as part of their local economic strategies. Just outside Chicago, Oak Park faced a lawsuit brought by the area's local school district. The district was upset by the amount of money that its schools would lose as a result of the city's creation of a TIF district. Oak Park eventually decided to discontinue its downtown TIF. But questions as to the impact of TIFs on local schools soon emerged in other Chicago suburbs. In 2018, the Northwest Suburban High School District succeeded in pressuring the city of Mount Prospect to narrow the boundaries of its proposed TIF district in order to leave a bank tower and other pieces of commercial property outside the district's boundaries, so that tax revenues gained from these developments would go to the local schools.[4]

Many economists charge TIFs as being inefficient and wasteful. A city loses extensive revenues even when it creates a TIF, especially when the TIF arrangement winds up having only a very minor influence on a business siting decision. One statistical analysis concluded that the growth in property value in TIF districts was "unremarkable," and that, even where it occurred, it often represented business activity that was drawn away from other parts of the city.[5] Chicago's extensive utilization of TIFs has cost the city treasury billions of dollars in foregone revenues. Despite the claims of the city's business community, much of the corporate expansion that has taken place in Chicago over the past decades would have occurred anyway, even in the absence of favorable TIF arrangements.[6] Suburban and exurban governments have created TIFs that grant sizable tax concessions to already profitable big-box retailers like Cabela's, the outdoors hunting and fishing retailer.[7]

Critics charge that big cities like Chicago often tolerate the waste and inefficiency inherent in TIFs as local politicians gain other political advantages from the award of a TIF. A mayor, for instance, can reward major campaign contributors by arranging a TIF district that will pay for the infrastructure improvements sought by the mayor's developer friends.

Yet despite these critiques, local officials across the nation continue to offer prospective businesses modernized infrastructure paid via a TIF district. Local officials feel that they are in a competitive race to attract business and that they have no choice but to match whatever other communities are offering.

1 Richard Briffault, "The Most Popular Tool: Tax Increment Financing and the Political Economy of Local Government," *University of Chicago Law Review* 77, no. 1 (2010): 65–95, reports that 9 states allow TIF financing.

2 Robert G. Lehnen and Carlyn E. Johnson, "The Impact of Tax Increment Financing on School Districts: An Indiana Case Study," in *Tax Increment Financing and Economic Development: Uses, Structures, and Impact*, ed. Craig L. Johnson and Joyce Y. Man (Albany: State University of New York Press, 2001), 137–154. For a review of various problems inherent in the TIF approach and possible ways to ameliorate them, see David Merriman, "Tax Increment Financing (TIF) for Economic Development," a report of the Lincoln Institute of Land Policy, Cambridge, Massachusetts, September, 2018; a free copy can be downloaded by clicking on the link at www.lincolninst.edu/publications/policy-focus-reports/improving-tax-increment-financing-tif-economic-development.

3 Ted Dabrowski and John Klingner, "Chicago TIFs Take Nearly $500M in Yearly Tax Revenues Away from Other Local Governments," a report of Illinois Policy, August 22, 2017, www.illinoispolicy.org/chicago-tifs-take-nearly-500m-in-yearly-tax-revenues-away-from-other-local-governments/.

4 Steve Zalusky, "Mount Prospect, District 214 Settle TIF District Lawsuit," *Daily Herald: Suburban Chicago's Information Source*, April 20, 2018; Marty Stempniak, "Oak Park, Schools Settle TIF Lawsuit," *Wednesday Journal of Oak Park and River Park*, December 20, 2011, www.oakpark.com/News/Articles/12-13-2011/Oak-Park,-schools-settle-TIF-lawsuit/.

5 Richard Dye and David Merriman, "Tax Increment Financing: A Tool for Local Economic Development," *Land Lines*, a publication of the Lincoln Institute of Land Policy 18, no. 1 (January 2006), www.lincolninst.edu/pubs/1078_Tax-Increment-Financing.

6 T. William Lester, "Does Chicago's Tax Increment Financing (TIF) Program Pass the 'But-for' Test? Job Creation and Economic Development Impacts Using Time-Series Data," *Urban Studies* 51, no. 4 (March 2014): 655–674.

7 Daniel McGraw, "Giving Away the Store to Get a Store: Tax Increment Financing Is No Bargain for Taxpayers," *Reason* (January 2006), https://reason.com/archives/2006/01/01/giving-awaythe-store-to-get-a.

Figure 12.1   **The Atlanta BeltLine and Nearby Development**. The Atlanta BeltLine is a major development, a recreational area built largely on abandoned railway land. The BeltLine has contributed to city livability and has helped change Atlanta's image. The BeltLine is also an economic tool that helps to attract new development to Atlanta. However, as a Tax Increment Financing (TIF) district was created as a means to finance the project, much of the growth in revenues gained from new activity in the immediate vicinity of the BeltLine can only be use to repay bondholders and to make still further physical improvements in the district. Such revenue gains cannot be used to support local schools or to meet the service needs of residents throughout the city.

Source: Photo by Agable / Shutterstock.com.

Even the funding for Atlanta's BeltLine (Figure 12.1), a major park-like project circling the city, was provided partially through the creation of a TIF district. The borders set for the BeltLine Tax Allocation District (the formal name of the Atlanta TIF district) ensure that property tax revenues received as a result of new development will be used to repay the bonds that the TIF district issued (that is, the funds that the TIF district had borrowed) to finance the BeltLine's construction. The new development did not produce a surge in general revenues that Atlanta could use to support area schools or improve service provision to residents living outside the TIF district's boundary lines.

Numerous cities have begun to worry about the costs of the tax abatements and other expensive concessions offered to businesses. The extensive subsidies that cities and states give to major projects do not always represent "good value" for a city. Louisville's massive investment in the KFC Yum Center is often hailed as a success, as the riverfront basketball arena and concert venue has been a centerpiece of the city's downtown revival. But a closer look at the funds that state and local authorities provided the project raises questions. Including the fees associated with debt repayment, the cost to the public of building the sports arena totaled nearly a billion dollars, a whopping diversion of taxpayer money that could have been used to improve living conditions in the city's neighborhoods.[8]

Cities have also begun to worry that even the generous provision of tax concessions provides no guaranty that a community will emerge as a winner in the intercity "job wars." The tax concessions that a city offers to a prospective firm can easily be matched or even surpassed by other communities.

As a result, cities have begun to look beyond tax abatements in a search for alternative economic development strategies that build upon a city's unique advantages. Numerous cities have chosen to provide the *hard factors* that promote local economic growth. Other cities have sought to manipulate the *soft factors* that can make a city (and a region) attractive to a major corporation.

A city can take steps to improve the local transportation infrastructure, strengthen streets to allow greater truck access, increase the quality of municipal water provision, expand sewage treatment capacity, and modernize the area's telecommunications system—all efforts to meet the **hard factors** that provide what a corporation needs and that are not easily replicated in other communities. Many cities create a TIF district to help pay for such physical improvements.

Alternatively, however, a city can pursue a much different development strategy, in an attempt to affect the **soft factors** that help to attract private investment. Not all businesses search for low-tax sites. Corporations are also drawn to communities with good schools, capable and educated workers, plentiful parks and recreational facilities, interesting arts and cultural activities, and a pleasant living environment. As the long-term growth of the Seattle, Portland, and other Pacific Northwest communities attests, an excellent **quality of life** also helps to make a city and a region attractive to the **creative class**, the skilled and knowledge-based workers whose local presence in turn serves to attract tech-related firms and other high-end corporations.[9]

Yet, the interlocal economic chase continues. The exaggerated lengths to which cities and states go to "win" a major employer was most clearly evident in the bidding war to win the location of Amazon HQ2, the giant Internet retailer's second national headquarters. Amazon asked for bids on its new headquarters, seeking to find out just what each city would provide in terms of subsidies and the hard and soft factors that support investment. In the amazing economic race that ensued, cities and states made Amazon exceedingly generous offers, sometimes totaling billions of dollars in subsidies—although the exact costs of most of the proposals was not made known to the public at the time as the bidding process and the submission of the proposals were shrouded in secrecy. When the process concluded, a number of cities released details of their bid. Philadelphia and the State of Pennsylvania combined in an offer of $5.7 billion in subsidies in an unsuccessful attempt to win the Amazon HQ2 location.[10] Pittsburgh and the State of Pennsylvania jointly offered Amazon even more, an awe inspiring

$9.7 billion package.[11] The State of New Jersey and the City of Newark offered between $7 billion to $8 billion in public subsidies and favors.[12] Other cities across offered Amazon valuable sites, free of charge, and promised to exempt Amazon from various state and local taxes and regulations.

Amazon ultimately decided to split its second headquarters between two cities, New York City (to be exact, the Long Island City section of Queens, just across the East River from Manhattan) and northern Virginia (in Crystal City, just outside of Washington, DC). Amazon also announced that Nashville would be the site of the firm's new Center of Excellence overseeing customer service and supply chain operations.

While the winning applications contained billions of dollars in subsidies, they were not the most generous offers made to Amazon.[13] Amazon gladly reaped the subsidies that cities and states offered. But the extent of the concessions was not the only factor in Amazon's choice of sites. In selecting New York City and suburban Washington, DC, Amazon clearly considered the position of the city in the global economy and the quality and talents of the local workforce, that is the degree to which a region had a "deep tech talent pool" with the scientific, mathematical, creative, and technological skills that Amazon required.[14]

Can the local economic chase be reduced? Maybe not in instances when a giant corporation such as Amazon sets in motion a bidding war. Yet, certain public policies, if enacted, have the potential to ease the stranglehold that corporations have enjoyed on the local arena. Federal (and state) revenue sharing with cities, metropolitan tax-base sharing, and a greater state assumption of school expenditures can ease the fiscal pressures that lead localities to uncritically woo new development. Strict land-use regulations, statutes that limit condominium conversion and tenant displacement, and laws that require a factory to give workers and a municipality advance notice before closing, too, can temper some of the dislocation that accompanies unfettered free-market growth.[15] But none of these "solutions" are easy to enact.

In the privatist United States, there is little general interest in such strong-government solutions. Instead of strong urban programs, more oblique market-led strategies prevail. National policy, too, reflects such a privatist orientation. The generous tax provisions of the Trump-era Opportunity Zones program cater to private investors interested in finding the most profitable sites for investments, sites that will yield favorable tax treatment and maximum profits. Opportunity Zones were likely to produce a great upswing in investment in designated low-income communities, but with no processes for community participation and no guarantees that new developments will include affordable housing units, provide jobs for zone residents, or even focus on investments that would improve the lives of the inner-city poor rather than accelerate gentrification and displacement. Investors were clearly interested the program as a result of the increased profits that would be derived from the generous tax treatment of investments made in the zones. Cities were interested in attracting new investment, especially to low-income communities. Despite the huge cost of the program in terms of foregone public revenues, there is no guarantee that the program will actually do much to provide public, as opposed to private, benefits.

The first round of local Opportunity Zone designations made by the states exhibited "minimal targeting" as governors demonstrated only a slight tendency to name the more needy eligible communities as Opportunity Zones. Instead, the states awarded Opportunity Zone designation to low-income areas that were already witnessing a surge in new investment.[16] An investor could bypass the most hard-hit areas of a city and choose to site new projects in low-income neighborhoods where economic dynamism and the potential for profit were already being demonstrated. In areas of the city already experiencing gentrification, the generous tax advantages provided by Opportunity Zone designation were almost certain to spur further residential displacement. The Act even awarded favorable tax treatment to investments made in less destressed areas that were contiguous to low-income census districts, a provision that, too, was likely to spur gentrification and exacerbate urban inequality.[17]

The love affair of local governments with economic development is certain to continue. Laws for greater transparency, public participation, the inclusion of affordable housing units in residential developments, safeguards for environmental protection, rewards for "green" construction, and even campaign finance reform can all add a degree of balance to an important area of urban politics that is too often dominated by developers, corporate interests, and the members of a city's and a region's growth coalition.

THE FUTURE OF MINORITY EMPOWERMENT

THE NEW STYLE OF LATINO AND AFRICAN-AMERICAN POLITICS

Half of the 15 largest cities in the United States are "majority minority" with Hispanics, African Americans, and Asians combining for over 50 percent of the local population.[18] The growth of the Hispanic population has been quite dynamic: 2010 Census data shows that Latinos comprised 22 percent of the population of the 100 largest metropolitan areas, a figure that surpasses the African-American population.[19] In the Southwest, especially in California, Texas, and Florida, the Latino "sleeping giant" is beginning to awaken to its potential voting and political power.

Low rates of voter turnout, however, continue to diminish Latino power.[20] In the 2016 election, the voting turnout rates for Hispanics lagged behind those for whites and African Americans.

However, low Latino voter turnout "is not predestined," nor is it universal. The rising numbers of Latino candidates on the ballot, especially for visible public offices like a city's mayoralty, can help draw increased numbers of Latinos to the polls.[21] Continuing immigration, too, is likely to swell the overall importance of the Hispanic vote, if not turnout rates.[22]

But Latinos are a heterogeneous group. In 2016, one-third of Latinos voted for Donald Trump despite the candidate's racialized rhetoric and repeated assaults on immigration. The Latino vote did not provide a "firewall" capable of assuring Hillary Clinton an electoral victory. The Latino community is more diverse and varied in its preferences than political commentators had assumed.

Restrictive state voter identification laws and other hostile voting rules also lessen Latino ballot-box power. Latino influence on presidential elections is further diminished as a large portion of the Latino population resides in California and Texas, one-party states where the outcome of the contest for the state's Electoral College vote is not likely to be affected by increases in the rate of Latino voter turnout.[23]

As Latinos and African Americans have gained representation in city hall, the more militant or race-conscious rhetoric of earlier leaders has ceded way to a new generation of African-American and Latino elected officials interested in the pragmatic concerns of managing and improving municipal services. Black and Latino mayors have demonstrated their interest in forging public-private partnerships to bring new investment and job and educational opportunities to the city.

The new generation of "post-racial" minority mayors works comfortably across class and racial lines to build the coalitions that can get things done (a trend reviewed in Chapter 6). These mayors are at ease in working with corporate leaders and in using Twitter and other forms of social media to reach a broad spectrum of citizens. Political observers called San Antonio Mayor Julián Castro a "Post-Hispanic Politician,"[24] a reflection of his success in coalition building.

Progressive activists, however, often criticize the degree of deference that the new breed of black and Latino mayors accords the business community. One critic further contends that the success of the new-style Latino mayors is "more an achievement of the conservative middle class than of the masses."[25] Nikuyah Walker, who in 2017 became the first black woman to be elected mayor of Charlottesville, Virginia, explains that her election had its seeds in the tepid response of liberal reformers to the hate and divisions resulting from a series of white supremacist rallies held in the city, "What changed was that people were faced with the fact that we're not a post-racial nation." Pragmatic, liberal policies and civil dialogue, according to Walker, have done little to counter the systematic racism, poverty and racial inequality that shape the daily lives of African Americans, Hispanics, and low-income whites in Charlottesville.[26]

New Jersey's Cory Booker, first as mayor of Newark and then as U.S. Senator, typifies a number of the aspects of the leadership approach of the new-generation post-racial politician. Booker's more deracialized approach allowed him to address issues of inequality while reaching out to corporate executives and the directors of national foundations and other nonprofit organizations to support activities in Newark.[27] At the national level, Barack Obama's election and terms a president provide still further evidence as to the possibilities—and limitations—of the pragmatic post-racial approach to leadership.

Despite the criticisms, the new generation of African-American and Hispanic mayors see cooperation with business leaders as essential to bringing jobs and other benefits to a city's poorer residents. Post-racial mayors "view economic growth and neighborhood improvement as complimentary goals,"[28] not as either-or propositions.

LIMITS ON USING RACIAL PREFERENCES AS A TOOL TO PROMOTE MINORITY ECONOMIC ADVANCEMENT

In the contemporary era, can African-Americans and Latino leaders use municipal purchasing and the issuance of city contracts as a means to promote minority-owned enterprises and to create good jobs for minorities? There are important limits as to what a city can do in its efforts to spur the development of minority-owned firms. The courts have not tended to look kindly on programs that entail race-based preferences in the award of municipal contracts.

In a very important decision, the U.S. Supreme Court placed sharp restrictions on municipal **contract compliance** programs, the affirmative-action-style preferences that municipal governments have used in an effort to steer city contracts to minority-owned firms. To do work for a city, a business must agree to meet specified program conditions, including diversity hiring targets, which are part of the language written into the contract. In *Richmond v. Croson* (1989), the Court struck down the City of Richmond's contract compliance program as a noxious racial classification.

What were the facts of the Richmond case? African Americans were more than half of the population of Richmond, Virginia, the former capital of the Confederacy. In past times when whites controlled city hall, less than 1 percent of the city-issued contracts was awarded to black-owned firms. The city's economic muscle was used to spur white-owned, not black-owned, enterprises. When the minority population of the city grew. African Americans gained electoral control of city hall and sought to correct the vast imbalance. The City of Richmond established a **minority set-aside program**, specifying that at least 30 percent of the total dollar amount of municipal contracts be awarded to minority firms.

The city's business community was divided in its reaction to the program. More pragmatic white business leaders recognized how the contract compliance program could help build a political coalition behind economic growth projects; black elected officials could show their supporters how new development projects would deliver jobs to the black community. Contract compliance set asides, in essence, were the "glue" that allowed African Americans and whites to work together on economic development initiatives.[29] But the white owners of other businesses, especially in the construction trades, objected that the program amounted to reverse discrimination. They argued that the city should simply award a contract to whichever qualified firm submitted the lowest bid, with no added preferences for firms owned by racial minorities or firms that promised to deliver a specified percentage of jobs to racial minorities.

In its *Croson* decision, the Supreme Court ruled that a city cannot simply refer to the past history of societal discrimination to justify a system of racial preferences in the award of municipal contracts. According to the Court, a municipality can only use a system of racial preferences if it first presents clear evidence that the municipal government itself had engaged in unconstitutional discriminatory practices in the particular service area in question. **Disparity studies**—statistical analyses that documents the failure of minority businesses to receive a fair percentage of city contracts in a specified service field—are an important first step in documenting that a pattern of discrimination *may* have occurred. New York Mayor Bill de Blasio turned to a disparity study to help justify city efforts to promote minority- and women-owned business enterprises.[30] But Richmond, at the time, had presented no such convincing evidence.

Even a well-done disparity study is often insufficient to justify a far-reaching program of racial preferences and hiring targets in the award of municipal contracts. The Supreme Court ruled that an acceptable minority set-aside program must be **narrowly tailored**: The program cannot offer preferences to all minority groups but only to individuals and to the members of groups proven to have suffered actual discrimination at the hands of the city.

Croson poses a difficult set of requirements for a city to meet if it wishes to use contracting to further minority economic empowerment. In the wake of the *Croson* decision, a number of cities simply decided to reduce or terminate their contract compliance programs. Relatively few cities were willing to assume the burden and costs of preparing the detailed racial disparity studies necessary to justify minority preferences.[31] Many cities lack the data to defend in court the use of contract compliance preferences. Cities are hesitant to establish preference programs that could drag the city into protracted and costly court proceedings resulting from the legal challenges brought by aggrieved white-owned firms and activist groups.

The logic of the Supreme Court's rulings in a related policy area—education—also do not bode well for expansive contract compliance programs. In 2014 the Supreme Court upheld a voter ballot initiative in Michigan that banned the state's public universities from considering a college applicant's race in admissions decisions.[32] Two years later, in *Fisher v. University of Texas*, a four-to-three Supreme Court vote ruled otherwise, that universities may indeed consider race as one element in their admission decisions, as campus diversity is an important element of education.[33] But the dissenting justices fervently argued against such a system of preferences. Given the sharp division of the Court on the subject and the retirement of Justice Anthony Kennedy, a swing vote on affirmative action, President Trump's appointments of new Supreme Court justices (beginning with Neil Gorsuch, Kennedy's replacement, and soon followed by Brett Kavanaugh) is likely to yield a Supreme Court majority that is less inclined to approve systems of racial preferences, whether in municipal contracting or in university admissions.

Resegregation and America's Schools

In the 1950s, the Supreme Court was a potent force for desegregation. The Court struck down as unconstitutional the *de jure* **segregation** of public schools, where states and localities by law mandated segregation classrooms. The Court, however, did not take similar aggressive action against *de facto* **segregation**, the racial imbalances in school enrollments that are not explicitly ordered by state and local law but are a reflection of residential patterns; blacks and whites tend to live in different areas of the city and the metropolis, resulting in great variation in the racial composition of each local school's population.

Of great significance, the Court's 1975 *Milliken v. Bradley* decision effectively brought metropolitan school desegregation efforts to a halt. In striking down a school busing program that encompassed Detroit and its nearby suburbs, the Court ruled that no suburb has to participate in a plan to correct the *de facto* segregation of schools in a metropolitan area. The *Milliken* decision "sent the unmistakable message—urban apartheid would not be overcome through judicial decree."[34]

In the decades that followed, the Supreme Court weakened a number of school desegregation efforts that the Court had earlier approved during its pro-integration era. A new generation of Supreme Court rulings permitted DeKalb County (Georgia), Kansas City (Missouri), Charlotte-Mecklenburg (North Carolina), and a whole host of other cities across the nation, in the North as well as in the South, to call a halt to their school desegregation efforts. The Court's rulings allowed school systems to relax integration plans that had been tried for a substantial period of time, even if the plans had not yet produced integrated schools and otherwise overcome the legacy created by a locality's history of segregationist policies. The Court relaxed its oversight, and city after city terminated major local desegregation efforts. As a consequence, the percentage of students in the United States who attend racially integrated schools began to fall.

In the wake of the Court's rulings, school officials turned to other techniques in an effort to achieve some degree of classroom integration. School authorities established **magnet schools** with their enriched curriculums and promise of a safe school environment in an effort to persuade willing parents voluntarily to send their children to quality schools that would have a racially diverse student population. But the Supreme Court again intervened and placed limits on the ability of local school districts to use magnet schools to promote racial integration. The Court ruled that a school district may indeed establish a specialized program in a magnet school. But the school district, according to the Court, cannot consider a student's race in admissions decisions, a process that is necessary to assure that student enrollments in a magnet school are racially balanced.[35] The Supreme Court had struck down the use of magnet schools, a relatively mild and voluntary racial integration approach that, in contrast to school busing, did not force families to send their children to more racially integrated schools.

As the population of suburbia continues to grow, suburban schools have exhibited heightened patterns of resegregation. State and national leaders have shown little interest in countering the new patterns of segregation that are emerging. Each suburban district is essentially left "on its own," without backing from the federal government and the states, when it comes to initiating efforts to assure that school enrollments are racially and ethnically diverse.[36]

The demographic changes evident in the schools in cities like Boston are especially troubling. During the 2017–2018 school year, nearly 60% of the Boston's public schools were "intensely segregated" with "students of color" comprising over 90% of a school's enrollment. Just 20 years previous, only 42% of the city's schoolchildren attended such intensely segregated schools. **Resegregation** is a word that clearly describes the trend occurring in Boston's schools. Of course, minorities continue to arrive in the city while white families have moved to the suburbs. In the city of Boston, whites comprise only 8% of city public-school enrollments! Large gaps in performance continue to distinguish the city's few majority-white schools from the city's minority-dominated schools.[37]

The proliferation of charter schools, too, has served to compound problems of racial isolation in public education. Whatever the many merits of charter academies, on the whole they have not aided school integration. Of course, there is no stereotypical charter school, and not all charter schools reinforce segregation. There are numerous instances where the leaders of charter academies value and promote racially mixed classrooms. However, in other cases, the existence of charter schools serves to reinforce racial isolation. An Associated Press study of the nation's 6,747 charter schools (2014–2015) found that more than 1,000 suffer extreme racial isolation, having a minority enrollment of 99% or more![38]

Charter schools are not the cause of racial segregation; nonetheless, in numerous communities, the opening of charter academies has added to the school segregation problem. In Charlotte-Mecklenburg, a North Carolina city that was hailed during the nation's pro-integration era as a model of school integration efforts, the rise of charter schools gives white parents yet one more tool they can use to oppose integration efforts in the public schools. In the region's suburbs, aggrieved parents threaten to enroll their children in charter academies should public-school leaders follow through on stated plans to redraw school attendance zones in order to promote school integration.[39]

Polling data reveal that African Americans continue to value racially integrated schools but have recognized the limited prospects for integration. They have had to recognize the apparent permanence of *de facto* segregation. Rather than continue the seemingly fruitless struggle to increase school integration, parents and activists in the African-American community have shifted their agenda to focusing on efforts to improve neighborhood schools and reduce the disparities in funding and technology that oftentimes serves to diminish the quality of schooling in African-American neighborhoods.[40]

RACIAL INTEGRATION AND COMMUNITY DEVELOPMENT: CAN WE PURSUE BOTH?

Over the past half century, the United States has made extensive progress in dismantling the more extreme forms of residential segregation. Very, very few communities in the United States are exclusively white. The all-white suburb has virtually disappeared from the metropolitan landscape. Still, discrimination—barriers to residential mobility—remain, and the members of different racial and ethnic groups tend to reside in different portions of the metropolis, producing demographic patterns that are not simply a reflection of differences in income and buying power.

As this book has discussed (especially in Chapter 3), local control of zoning and land uses plays a major role in maintaining residential exclusion. Local governments use their control over land use to restrict the production of multifamily and more affordable housing. Especially in the suburbs, such actions deny minority families the opportunity to reside in communities with high-quality schools, public safety, and reasonable accessibility to the growing number of jobs found on the suburban rim.

A suburban nation, however, is unlikely to surrender the advantages that suburban residents derive from their control over zoning and land uses. In both residential patterns and school enrollments, continuing racial imbalances underscore the "hollow prospect"[41] of integration.

However, as urban scholar Edward Goetz observes, racial integration is not the only policy objective that serves the interests of the urban poor. Goetz argues for the importance of neighborhood development, of empowering poor people and strengthening the neighborhoods in which poor people and racial minorities reside. Goetz gives great respect to minority self-determination and culture; he does not favor policy efforts that force minority families to leave their homes in the inner-city and move to more racially integrated communities. Programs such as HOPE VI sought to reduce ghettoization and deconcentrate poverty. But by razing public housing, HOPE VI disrupted the lives of poor people, ousting low-income and minority families from their homes and from familiar neighborhoods where they had received the support of extended family and friends and even the assistance of social services.

Racial integration remains a core American value, and government still has an important role to play in the battle against discrimination that keeps minorities out of better and safer communities. Government action is needed to fight the reemergence of discriminatory practices by lenders, real-estate firms, and insurance companies. Government programs can also increase the supply of affordable homes in tight housing markets and provide assistance to low-income and minority families who seek to move to communities of greater opportunity.

But many low-income and minority residents do not wish to leave their home communities and move elsewhere. Consequently, Goetz calls for a renewed commitment to community development programs, bottom-up and community-based partnerships to increase the supply of affordable housing and improve living conditions in low-income and minority neighborhoods. A renewed emphasis on community development is also a strategy that is consonant with the power realities of the contemporary United States, where the residents of better-off communities are unwilling to relax exclusionary barriers to bring about significant increases in residential integration.

Minneapolis provides a glimmer of hope. In 2018, the city, in its *Minneapolis 2040 Plan*, abolished single-family zoning throughout the city. The new plan sought to open the city's better neighborhoods to the construction of triplexes, that is, multifamily structures with three housing units. But will Minneapolis be able to follow through on its intentions? How many other cities and suburbs will be as progressive as Minneapolis? In most cities and metropolitan areas, the residents of low-income minority neighborhoods will continue to cope with the political fact, that the undoing of racial integration is no longer a "realistic outcome."[42]

URBAN POLICY IN A SUBURBAN AGE: NINE KEYS TO BUILDING A REALISTIC URBAN POLICY

Over the years, urban advocates have called for a strong and coordinated set of policy measures to alleviate urban ills: "Only a total rethinking of the nation's priorities and a reinvestment in social and human capital can transform urban life."[43] When Barack Obama became president, one urban scholar observed that "The need for a strong urban policy has been abundantly clear." But more progressive urbanists, such as community development advocate James DeFilippis, would ultimately express their disappointment, observing that Obama's initiatives were often "small and incremental" and incapable of providing solutions to urban problems: "There has been nothing in the Obama administration's urban policies that stirs anyone's blood."[44]

The political realities of a suburban nation pose strong obstacles to the enactment and implementation of a strong and sweeping, national urban policy. In Chapter 11, we related how Presidents Lyndon Johnson and Jimmy Carter could not even convince a majority-Democratic Congress to approve strong programs targeted on the needs of distressed communities. Since that earlier time period, the continued outflow of population and power to the suburbs has diminished still further the prospects for a strong and comprehensive urban policy.

Even a moderately progressive urban policy requires that Democrats regain the White House and control of Congress. The swing suburban vote provides the key. Bill

Clinton won the presidency twice running as a self-styled "New Democrat" who sought programs that could appeal to "soccer moms" and America's middle-class suburbia.

But even a Democratic president must cope with the realities of political power that impose limits when it comes to urban policy. If the past is any guide to the future, far-ranging proposals that fail to meet the program needs and concerns of suburban residents will wind up failing in Congress, as Democrats from the suburbs join with Republicans to defeat or water down strong urban programs.

Allan Mallach points to the "fallacy" of calling for a federal Marshall Plan to aid cities. Of course, the federal government with its resources can be either a powerful "ally" or "adversary" of cities as they confront pressing problems. But the federal government over the past few decades has reduced its profile in urban affairs. Mallach further questions whether the federal government even truly possesses the capacity to enact and implement programs capable of bringing an end to the urban crisis.[45]

Mallach and other politically pragmatic urban advocates see little to be gained by waiting for the impossible-to-achieve dream of a strong and comprehensive national urban policy. Mallach has little patience with "utopian" idealists who decry the inadequacy of limited urban policy steps and who continue to insist on "radical" change to fight racism and bring about a fundamental urban and social restructuring. Mallach counters:

> We need a way of thinking that is pragmatic, focused on concrete results, rather than driven by symbolism and self-expression, however powerful and deeply felt; one that accepts the reality of the existing American political and economic framework, while working to bring about change within that system, rather than pining for a socialist or anarchist utopia.[46]

Mallach, much like Presidents Bill Clinton and Barack Obama, sees great virtue in focusing on "incremental" and "pragmatic" steps, especially those seemingly limited local actions that can deliver concrete results.[47] In a suburban age, at a time when the call for a "national urban policy" lacks the ability to rally public support, urban advocates will do well to remember that politics is the art of the possible. They will discover the possibilities inherent in "non-urban programs"[48] that provide substantial assistance to cities and the needy communities. Programs aimed at such non-urban goals as improving public education and increasing America's ability to compete economically can often deliver substantial assistance to distressed communities. A series of discrete and even "isolated" programs may prove effective in commanding broad political support and in delivering much-needed assistance to troubled communities.[49]

The nine suggestions listed below provide tactical advice for developing a pragmatic urban policy, for finding do-able and meaningful urban programs in an American age that is not conducive to strong, comprehensive, and coordinated urban policy.

EMPHASIZE A PROGRAM'S BENEFITS FOR MIDDLE-CLASS AMERICANS

In a middle-class nation, urban advocates need to stress how a program will provide benefits to a majority of Americans—to the middle-class and to the residents of suburbs and the Sunbelt—and that program initiatives are not targeted only to troubled central cities and the poor. Educational reforms, for instance, not only empower the inner-city poor; reforms can also strengthen the voice of middle-class parents concerned about their children and the quality of the public schools. Programs aimed at repurposing vacant properties do not provide assistance only to inner-city communities in Frostbelt cities such as Cleveland, Detroit, and Baltimore. Vacant properties relief also provides extensive assistance to communities in California, Florida, Nevada, Arizona, and other Sunbelt states that suffered some of the highest foreclosure rates in the nation when the buyers of condominiums and suburban homes could not meet their monthly mortgage obligations. Efforts to reduce diesel emissions, groundwater pollution, and other toxins can be sold as policies intended to protect the health of everybody's children, not just the children of inner-city neighborhoods.

EMPHASIZE PROGRAMS THAT REWARD PARTICIPATION IN THE WORKPLACE

Pointing to the larger systematic causes of inequality and joblessness by itself is insufficient to produce policy change. Americans as a whole are committed to work norms and are hostile to "welfare" programs that they view as unearned giveaways to recipients who fail to show a proper work ethic. Yet, despite this expressed opposition to "welfare," the American public over the years has demonstrated a willingness to support governmental assistance for skills training, adult education, and job placements programs that abet workforce participation.[50] The provision of day care, too, garners widespread support when tied to the workplace; the provision of day care enables poor women to attend school and obtain job and skills training, providing a path to exit welfare and return to work.

Urban programs that reinforce workforce participation can garner political support. Such an approach is quite different from "workfare," the imposition of work requirements and sanctions that do little more than provide reasons to cut benefits to families in need. The Trump administration sought to toughen the work requirements imposed on able-bodied SNAP ("food stamps") beneficiaries. Such a punitive approach can in no way be viewed as part of a pro-urban strategy that emphasizes workforce participation. Such harsh program rules only serve to diminish the provision of benefits to families in need, families who often reside in central cities and in older working-class suburbs.

Closer scrutiny reveals that the Trump SNAP initiative was even more explicitly anti-urban than it initially appeared. The rules promulgated by the Trump administration allowed states like Michigan to exempt counties—most often rural counties or counties on the suburban/rural interface—with high unemployment rates, as jobs were not presumed to be easily accessible to SNAP residents who reside in less dense and more remote areas. No such exemption was given to inner-city residents whom, it was presumed, could somehow reach jobs in the more remote suburban portions of their home county.[51] The Trump SNAP measure was an attempt to cut "welfare" in urban areas while insulating the residents of rural areas—Trump's political base of support—from bearing the burdens of the cutbacks. The Trump rules were anti-urban.

PURSUE RACE-NEUTRAL AND UNIVERSAL PROGRAMS

Americans as a whole disapprove of programs that they believe embody racial favoritism. Americans, especially white American, oppose actions that provide benefits to the members of a specific racial or ethnic group while denying benefits to members of other racial and ethnic groups.

By contrast, Americans give much greater support to **race-neutral programs** that promise assistance to people in need irrespective of their race or ethnicity. Affirmative action and contract compliance programs that emphasize race are highly controversial. Programs that provide opportunity to economically disadvantaged persons and communities, irrespective of skin color and ethnic heritage, are less controversial. The American public approves of *universal* education and job training programs that offer help to all citizens in need, as opposed to programs open only to the members of designated racial and ethnic minority groups.[52] **Universal programs** promise benefits to all persons who meet basic program eligibility requirements, without defining participation on the basis of race, ethnicity, and, at times, even gender.

Programs that promote local economic growth and job creation provide benefits that cross lines of race and ethnicity. Programs aimed at entrepreneurship and expanding job creation have the potential to win backing from business leaders. Workforce development and job creation programs can serve as the race-neutral center of a pragmatic urban policy. A politically viable urban policy starts with a simple guiding rule: "Jobs Are Job Number One."[53]

SPREAD BENEFITS! TARGET WHEN POSSIBLE! TARGET WITHIN UNIVERSALISM!

Programs that **spread benefits** to a larger population have the potential to garner broad public support. Of course, such programs suffer a major drawback: high cost! The wide spread of program benefits also dilutes the assistance provided to recipients and communities most in need. As a consequence, many urban advocates argue for the opposite approach; they favor programs that **target benefits**, that is, programs that concentrate their limited resources on residents and areas with the greatest need. But, the problem with such an approach is simple: Major targeted programs will often fail to build the support necessary to sustain urban policy initiatives.

A mixed approach of **targeting within universalism** actually provides the most satisfactory overall urban strategy. An aid program can define program eligibility quite broadly, allowing participation by a great many communities and a large percentage of the population, while allocating a higher level of benefits (or supplemental services) to people and communities with the greatest need.[54] The Community Development Block Grant (CDBG) program provides a textbook example of targeting within universalism. The CDBG program delivers assistance annually to nearly 1,200 communities. Yet the CDBG aid formula ensures that financial assistance is disproportionately given to the nation's larger cities and to smaller jurisdictions that have evidence of need. The Low Income Housing Tax Credit likewise gains broad political support as it provides assistance to construct much-need affordable housing in rural communities, not just in low-income city neighborhoods.[55]

Federal programs to combat homelessness have proven to be politically sustainable and have enjoyed increased funding levels over the years[56] as federal homelessness grants are not dispensed only to cities. *Home, Together*, the federal government's strategic plan to end homelessness, commits to tailoring strategies to the needs of less populous suburbs and rural communities "where housing and services are scarce."[57] Federal homelessness programs do not only help big cities; the programs also seek to enhance the capacity of smaller and suburban communities to identify and serve persons and families at risk of homelessness

Housing policies seek to provide an answer to "the Goldilocks dilemma," that is, to finding the "just right" balance of housing subsidies that will satisfy the expectations of a larger and political powerful constituencies while targeting disproportionate assistance to low-income families. A politically "just right" housing policy does *not* focus exclusively on the poor, The nation's housing policy also seeks to address the needs of the "missing middle" in housing markets, middle-class families that, despite their seemingly good incomes, continue to face substantial difficulty in finding a suitable home at a price they can afford.[58]

Head Start enjoys overwhelming popularity as the program provides education and support services to children and families in need irrespective of geography. Despite its popular image, Head Start does not focus exclusively on big cities and inner-city neighborhoods. Head Start also provides much-needed child care and early childhood education in rural communities. Head Start serves nearly every rural county in the United States.[59]

Economic development programs that promise jobs and benefits to a wide range of communities have a great potential to attract support. The massive economic stimulus spending of ARRA, Barack Obama's multibillion-dollar American Recovery and Revitalization Act (reviewed in Chapter 11), was made politically possible as the program provided assistance to road construction and other shovel-ready projects in rural and suburban communities as well as in the nation's cities. Federal transportation programs also survived the early Trump budget axe as they commanded considerable political support in Congress, having spread program benefits widely as opposed to targeting transit assistance exclusively to big cities and major metropolitan areas.

A classic debate in urban affairs concerns whether urban policy should emphasize **place-based strategies** that target resources to distressed communities or **people-based strategies** that provide assistance to persons in need no matter where they live. The advocates of strong spatial-based urban policy argue against the people-based strategies that deliver substantial assistance to growing suburbs and Sunbelt communities with lesser needs. Assistance given to already growing and prosperous communities reinforces their competitive advantage, undercutting efforts to revitalize more troubled communities.

Today, however, the place-based-versus-people-based debate no longer seems as relevant as it once was. The simple answer for urban advocates is this: Do both! Do whatever works and can gain political support! In an age that is hostile to urban policy, urban strategists need to pursue whatever place-based and people-based programs have the best chances of gaining enactment and producing positive outcomes.

Barack Obama, a president with strong urban sympathies, pursued both approaches. Obama endorsed place-based strategies that sought the revitalization of poorer inner-city neighborhoods, including troubled neighborhoods surrounding public housing projects. He sought to foster public-private partnerships to bring more innovative school offerings to inner-city communities. But other important programs such as ARRA were not targeted so heavily to troubled communities. Obama also pursued people-based programs, emphasizing the enforcement of fair housing practices and attacking exclusionary practices, actions that would allow poor people to move to safer communities and to suburban areas where job growth was occurring.[60]

TAX POLICY IS URBAN POLICY! LOOK TO THE TAX CODE!

Bill Clinton expanded the **Earned Income Tax Credit (EITC)**, a program of wage supplements to the working poor. In doing so, he faced virtually none of the harsh debate that almost always accompanies proposals to expand more direct urban and "welfare" programs. As EITC benefits are given only to low-income persons who work—and nonworkers do not receive the program's benefits—the changes could not easily be assailed as an expansion of welfare to the undeserving. Clinton understood that Americans will support the extension of assistance to persons who hold jobs but who still face difficulties in "getting by." Just as important, Clinton recognized the political advantages of using the tax code to provide expanded assistance to families in need. Embedded in a complex and difficult-to-understand tax code, EITC expansion enjoyed a certain degree of political insulation and was able to fly "under the political radar" of many potential opponents.

Another program embedded in the tax code, the **Low Income Housing Tax Credit (LIHTC)**, has arguably become the federal government's most important policy tool in constructing housing for families in need. When the program's cost is measured in terms of **tax expenditures,** the revenues lost to the public treasury as a result of the program's incentives, LIHTC is clearly a formidable venture. LIHTC cost the government $45 billion in foregone revenues in just five years (2016–2020).[61] Yet, embedded in an immense tax code, LIHTC does not suffer the political salience and vulnerability of a program that directly spends $45 billion to build "public housing" for the poor. Embedded in the tax code, LIHTC has repeatedly gained renewal, even if, on occasion, the residents of a working-class or middle-class neighborhood in a city may rise up to oppose a city's siting decision for a specific LIHTC-funded project.[62]

The LIHTC and the New Markets Tax Credit (another federal program that offers tax advantages to investors in inner-city revitalization projects) both eluded President Trump's early budget-cutting knife. A Republican-controlled Congress renewed the New Markets Tax Credit. The Congress also provided a 12.5% increase in LIHTC funding for four years![63] As we have also seen, the Tax Cuts and Jobs Act of 2017 also created Opportunity Zones, a major new program of tax incentives to spur private investment in projects in high-poverty census districts. The political viability of the Earned Income Tax Credit, LIHTC, the New Markets Tax Credit, and Opportunity Zones serves to underscore the privileged position that tax policy enjoys as an urban policy tool.

BUILD CITIES AND COMMUNITIES BOTTOM UP! COMMUNITY DEVELOPMENT CORPORATIONS, COMMUNITY LAND TRUSTS, AND COMMUNITY BENEFITS AGREEMENTS

Urban affairs journalist Neal Peirce once observed that the hope for the urban future lies largely with Community Development Corporations (CDCs), mutual housing associations, land trusts, reinvestment corporations, and a myriad of civic, neighborhood, and citizen-volunteer organizations.[64] State and federal policy can nurture and extend the problem-solving capacities of the tens of thousands of nonprofit and community organizations that "do the public's work" in urban and suburban America. Nonprofit and community organizations also possess expertise and accumulated knowledge; these organizations know a neighborhood's needs and unique circumstances, having worked in a community for many years. An urban problem-solving approach that works through community-based, faith-based, and other nonprofit organizations can garner greater legitimacy and public support.

CDCs have demonstrated impressive success in leveraging the money and other resources necessary to construct and rehabilitate low-income housing. CDCs also have an enviable record in providing job training for low-income residents, in building neighborhood health-care centers, and, in general, in enhancing a community's "social capital."[65] The Youngstown (Ohio) Neighborhood Development Corporation, for instance, was instrumental in assuring that the city's poorer neighborhoods would be partners in rehabilitating properties. YNDC acted to have low-income residents and the city's poorer neighborhoods share in the small business opportunities and the benefits of other transformative projects that civic leaders and the state university campus were helping to create.[66]

As good as they are, however, CDCs cannot do their work in isolation. Their work requires the financial support of corporate philanthropy, nonprofit foundations, and government agencies. Three key federal programs—the LIHTC program, the Community Development Block Grant (CDBG) program, and the HOME Investment Partnership—have helped to catalyze much of the bottom-up revitalization work that has taken place in lower-income neighborhoods across the nation. The LIHTC program, in particular, provides a financial incentive for corporations to invest as partners with CDCs in low-income housing.

The actions of CDCs and other community-based organizations build equitable communities. Such community-based organizations help to ensure that city decisions that affect a neighborhood's residents are not driven solely by the concerns of a city's growth coalition. In San Francisco, The Mission Economic Development Agency (MEDA) has helped preserve affordable housing and restrain gentrification and displacement pressures in the city's most important Latino neighborhood. MEDA actions helped Mission Street to retain its character as a shopping district with discount grocers and small clothing stores that serve the area's large immigrant population, a sharp contrast to the upscale dining and art galleries that have sprouted only a few blocks to the west on Valencia Street.[67]

Community-based organizations are essential parties in the negotiation of a community benefits agreement (CBA) to assure that the developers of a new stadium or other major facility provide jobs, skills training, apprenticeship opportunities, and procurement set-asides for minority- and women-owned firms that will benefit neighborhoods and their residents. A CBA may even include a pledge by a firm to provide financial support for parks development or the provision of new community day-care facilities. A city can insist that the developers of a major project sit down, negotiate, and sign an agreement with a community before development permissions are granted. A city can adopt a model CBA that sets the general parameters for the services and linkages that the city normally expects to be spelled out in the agreement. A model agreement aids the "learning curve" of grassroots organizations, enabling them to insist upon corporate-provided benefits that can be readily delivered and monitored.[68]

A Community Land Trust (CLT) removes key properties, especially abandoned properties, from the speculative market. In doing so, CLTs help to slow the pace of change in gentrifying neighborhoods, preserving elements of housing affordability and racial diversity in neighborhoods facing transformative pressures.[69]

CLTs have proven to be especially effective in preserving and adding to a community's stock of affordable housing. The Oakland Community Land Trust (OakCLT) acquires properties that it then preserves in perpetuity for community-oriented uses.[70] Acquisition by OakCLT assures that affordable residential units are not demolished and converted to office and commercial uses. CLT ownership further provides an alternative to the sort of rent hikes that often result in displacement when a private buyer acquires a piece of property as an investment. Yet, some CLT enthusiasts lament the moderate pragmatism of such efforts, the "expulsion of radical politics" that occurs when a CLT becomes intricately involved in the details of housing acquisition and finance.[71]

FOCUS ON POWERFUL EMOTIONAL SYMBOLS AND "DESERVING" CONSTITUENCIES: EDUCATION, CHILDREN, THE ELDERLY, WOMEN, VETERANS, AND THE NATURAL ENVIRONMENT

The American public supports programs focused on children and education. Children are a particularly sympathetic constituency. Head Start and the Supplemental Food Program for Women, Infants, and Children (WIC) continued to grow even during years when the government scaled back other "welfare" programs. Few people can justify withholding vital nutrition from babies who are likely to be born at risk and from infants. Education programs, too, can further be justified as they provide aid and opportunity to innocent children. Educational programs also can tap another reservoir of political support, as they provide the United States with future workers who have the skills necessary for the nation's continued economic growth.

Spending in support of programs such as WIC and public education can also be justified as a cost-efficient alternative to "welfare." If schools do their jobs and children are born healthy with the greatest potential for brain development, governments will have less need in the future for expensive social welfare and correctional programs. New York City's early childhood education initiatives, San Antonio's "Pre-K for SA," and the Chicago Promise program are all among the more noteworthy programs to follow the multifaceted nurturing approach modeled by the Harlem Children's Zone in New York City.

THE FUTURE OF URBAN AMERICA

Programs that aid the elderly, veterans, families on the street, and battered women also enjoy considerable public support. Communities, for instance, build subsidized housing for the elderly and for veterans in need even during times when local decision makers are unwilling to provide new housing opportunities for nonveterans and the nonelderly poor.

The federal government declared a goal of ending veteran homelessness. The prioritized attention accorded veterans produced remarkable results. Point-in-time counts of veterans living on the streets reveal that public spending on transitional housing, case management and support services, and housing vouchers served to greatly reduce, if not quite entirely eliminate, homelessness among veterans.[72]

The elderly are another sympathetic constituency. Programs that serve the elderly also enjoy a second political advantage: the elderly turn out and vote! The political clout of the elderly gives policy makers an extra incentive to provide housing, community centers, and other programs that respond to the needs of seniors.

Powerful symbols are important in rallying political support. President Trump sought to deter illegal immigration by cruelly separating undocumented parents from their children as they crossed the international border into the United States. Trump's program went too far and provoked great public outrage, as it transgressed on the respect that Americans accord the preservation of "family" and the protection of "children" from undue harm.

"Environmentalism" provides yet another powerful symbol or rallying cry that can mobilize support for a range of urban-related programs. Brownfield reclamation projects in fading industrial sections of the city can be framed as good environmental policy, not as urban policy. Similarly, infill development and various regional land management and Smart Growth initiatives gain broad public support by emphasizing the importance of a program in preserving green space, farmland, and natural habitats. Younger persons not otherwise interested in city affairs are nonetheless likely to approve of programs for sustainable growth, the cleanup of brownfields, the diversion of waste from landfills, the "greening" of abandoned properties, construction regulations that reduce the runoff of storm water that carries contaminants into rivers and streams, the protection of farmland against development intrusions, and the expansion of urban agriculture.[73]

TAKE ADVANTAGE OF THE WIN-WIN BENEFITS OF REGIONAL ACTION, ESPECIALLY FOR JOB CREATION AND ECONOMIC DEVELOPMENT

As we saw in Chapter 10, effective metropolitan or regional action is extremely difficult to organize. In the great majority of metropolitan areas, the creation of new and strong metropolitan governments is not a viable political option. Interlocal cooperation and more creative and in-depth collaboration are the only possible alternatives.

As Chapter 10 observed, cities and suburbs cooperate with one another when mutual cost savings and other win-win advantages are obvious. A region's economic development presents an important policy arena that holds the promise of win-win benefits—in particular, shared job growth and revenue gains that no locality can bring about acting solely on its own. A region enjoys its best chances of attracting a major corporation when local governments work together to provide the roads, sewers, water, transportation, housing, and job training programs that a corporation requires.

When a national or global corporation examines possible sites for a major development, its officers look beyond any single local community as they assess what the broader region offers. Corporate officials seek to determine the degree to which the larger metropolitan region can meet the corporation's specific needs. Does the region provide a well-trained and capable labor force with the skills that the firm requires? Does the region have both an adequate highway infrastructure and sufficient public transit to allow a firm's workers to commute easily from home to work? Does the region's transportation infrastructure allow the firm easy access to the raw materials it requires and to ship its finished products to market? Does a region have a nearby airport with the connections that allow corporate executives easy travel?

Modern corporations seek the advantages of locating in an **industrial cluster**, of being in a region where a firm enjoys relatively close geographical proximity to similar businesses. Clustering enables a firm to tap a ready pool of specialized talent—the computer programmers, financial experts, and other skilled technocrats—as well as the ability to call on support firms that provide legal advice and specialized support services that firms in a particular industry require.

An industrial cluster by its very nature is regional in scope; a cluster transcends the political borders of a single municipality. The city of Milwaukee and its suburbs comprise the heart of an eight-county southeastern Wisconsin region that has emerged as a center for firms in the water-technology industry. In greater Milwaukee, the Water Council, a 501(c)(3) nonprofit entity, led a private-public effort that also included active participation by the area's universities and by various public and quasi-public bodies, including the TIF-funded city water district. The collaboration was given a specific mission: to build the infrastructure and develop the necessary support services required to attract new firms to the area's already existing collection of firms offering various water-related technologies.[74] The collaboration was regional in scope. No single community could provide the wide range of services and sites that a water-related business required.

Yet, despite the promise of shared gains, local officials are often hesitant to enter into regional commitments. A locality's officials often fear that regional action will wind up working to the benefit of neighboring communities and not to their own residents. Consequently, federal and state governments have an important role to play, providing the incentives that can lead communities to overcome their initial suspicions of joint action. The ISTEA/NEXTEA/TEA-21 programs provide an example of how a higher level of government can promote regional conversation and cooperation. ISTEA and its successor programs offered a clear financial incentive for regional cooperation: Governments in a region must establish a metropolitan planning organization (MPO) to coordinate transit spending or else suffer the loss of a portion of various federal transit monies. State-provided incentives, too, can promote regionalism. New Jersey, New York, and Ohio are among the states that offer grants, to pay for the research that documents just how much the various partnering municipalities can expect to gain from a new collaborative undertaking.

CLAIM POWERS! THE IMPORTANCE OF ACTIVE CITIES

Cities in recent years have emerged as increasingly active urban problem solvers, even venturing into nontraditional municipal areas in order to assure the well-being of local residents. Cities and suburbs have initiated measures to advance gay and lesbian rights, protect vulnerable immigrant populations, raise the local minimum wage, nurture "start-ups" by local business entrepreneurs, and pursue sustainable development that respects environmental values. To effectively lead their cities, big-city mayors and other local officials have found that they must begin to challenge some of the limits that have traditionally confined a city's powers.[75]

What are cities to do when a state seeks to limit and preempt local action? Simply put, cities can keep pushing the envelope; cities do not have to be self-denying in the actions they undertake. Home rule laws and traditions can serve as a springboard for more expansive municipal power. Cities, especially home-rule cities, can choose to more fully exercise powers that are not clearly denied to them. The persistent actions of municipalities can lead to more expansive local authority. City power is not fixed but "contested,"[76] the balance of power between states and cities continue to shift over time:

> [C]ities need not accept the existing structure of Home Rule, or how it is currently implemented. Cities can take control of the Home Rule authority that they have been given, through law and politics. Cities should decide for themselves what kind of city they would like to be, and work collectively to realize a Home Rule structure that will get them there. It may be too early to conclude that cities have abandoned Home Rule. Yet it is not too late for cities to reclaim it.[77]

THE FUTURE: TOWARD SUSTAINABLE CITIES AND SUBURBS

The concluding pages of this book describe the range of local initiatives that cities and suburbs have taken in an increasingly important policy area: sustainable development and the protection of the natural environment.

The advocate "let 'er rip" economic growth often misportray *sustainable development* as the work of "no growth" environmental extremists who seek to enact tough regulations that will cripple the national and local economies. The truth, however, is quite different: **sustainable development** *does* seek population and economic growth; but it emphasizes development patterns and practices that minimize the harm that new development imposes on the natural environment. Sustainable cities emphasize construction and development practices that preserve energy, clean air and water, and green space, and that otherwise help to maintain a healthy living and work habitat for future generations.[78] "Reduced to its most basic tenets, sustainable urbanism is *walkable and transit-served urbanism integrated with high-performance buildings and high-performance infrastructure*."[79]

Sustainable development serves to preserve green and natural areas to and make communities more walkable, cycling-oriented, and aesthetically pleasing. Smart Growth strategies, Urban Growth Boundaries (UGBs), and transit-oriented development (TOD) promote mass transit and cycling, lessen reliance on the automobile, reduce air and water pollution, and minimize the loss of the natural environment and farm acreage. In making communities more livable and attractive, sustainable development also increases local property values.[80]

Cities and suburbs, in the United States and around the world, are giving increased attention to matters of sustainability. As more affluent California communities have discovered, local wealth provides no respite from such climate-induced disasters as wildfires

Figure 12.2 **Destroyed Home and Washer/Dryer: The 2018 Thomas Fire in the Via Arroyo and Via Pasito Neighborhoods of Ventura, California.** The fire was the largest in southern California history.

Source: Photo by Joseph Sohm / Shutterstock.com.

and mudslides. Unsustainable patterns of development compound the costs of fires. From Malibu and Ventura County (Figure 12.2) in southern California to Santa Rosa, the Mendocino Complex, and Butte County in the northern part of the state, land-use policies that allowed new construction in fire-prone areas and in the suburban-wildland interface contributed to the property destruction and lethality of wildfires. In southern California, fire contagion is further whipped up by the Santa Ana winds.[81] Development around mountain communities, such as Gatlinburg, Tennessee, is especially vulnerable to wildfires. The National Climate Assessment has demonstrated how climate change has contributed to the frequency and severity of extreme weather events, including wildfires and urban flooding.[82] Warmer and drier conditions at higher elevations reduce snowpack formation, resulting in less water runoff to areas down below, making forest areas drier and susceptible to burning. Compact development policies can reduce residential construction in the suburban-wildland interface where risks of wildfire contagion are especially high.

Various international organizations have spurred local communities to pay heightened attention to sustainability goals and practices. The International Olympic Committee, not exactly the world's most prominent environmentalist advocacy group, requires applicant cities to spell out their sustainability plans when submitting a bid to host the Olympic Games. New York City, as part of its unsuccessful bid for the 2012 games, detailed plans to have visitors rely on mass transit. New York also detailed the steps the city would take to promote the natural filtration of water runoff and thereby minimize pollution originating from the Olympics event site. New York further proposed to construct a sustainable "urban village" for the Olympics athletes that, after the games, would be converted to housing. The city also proposed, after the games, to convert much of the Olympics site into parkland. London's winning bid for the 2012 games emphasized the reliance on low-carbon-emission mass transit and how the event organizers would achieve a 25 percent gain in the energy efficiency at the Olympic Village through the use of renewable resources and recycled materials in construction. London also promised to reduce water consumption and the dedication of new bicycling and walking paths.

Los Angeles submitted multiple bids to host the Olympics and ultimately landed the 2028 games. Casey Wasserman, the chair of L.A.'s bid committee, highlighted the city's commitment to sustainability, that the city in its bid was "offering a lasting definition of Olympics sustainability."[83] Los Angeles proposed to use existing venues rather than build new stadiums and arenas for the various competitions. Plans for the Olympics also built on the commitment to renewable energy sources that the city had already made as part of Mayor Eric Garcetti's "Sustainable City pLAn."[84] Los Angeles, seeking to escape its image as an automobile-reliant city, submitted a bid that embraced public transit, including plans to construct a rail connector to the airport and to extend the Purple Line tracks out to UCLA, the location of numerous sports arenas.

THE SUSTAINABILITY TRIANGLE

Concern for the natural environment is only one of three legs of the **sustainable development triangle**. Policies that protect the natural environment will *not* be politically sustainable—that is, have the political support to endure of the years—if they fail to provide for the economic and social needs of urban populations, the other two legs of the sustainability triangle. Voters will not approve of local environmental measures that constrict job growth and economic opportunity. Disadvantaged groups will rise in protest to policies that, in the name of protecting the environment, decrease the job and housing opportunities available to racial and ethnic minorities, working-class families, the poor, younger persons just entering the job market, and newcomers to the city. The sustainability triangle has clearly been the basis for action in cities like Kansas City, Missouri, where a "KC Green" policy declares the city's commitment to a "broader triple bottom line" of environmental quality, economic vitality, and social equity.

Portland's Urban Growth Boundary (UGB) illustrates the balanced or triangular set of policy objectives at the heart of sustainable development. The UGB seeks to avert destructive sprawled development. Portland officials also undertook additional policy actions to counter criticisms that a UGB is inequitable, that it constricts the supply of affordable housing in the region. Portland provides extensive funding for affordable housing and has enacted inclusionary ordinances to require developers to include affordable units in new residential developments.[85] Portland officials have also over the years expanded the borders of the growth boundary to increase the number of sites in the region for new economic development as well as for housing construction.

GREEN CONSTRUCTION AND DEVELOPMENT PRACTICES

More than 138 U.S. communities with a population greater than 50,000 have "green" building ordinances that promote sustainable practices in construction.[86] Green cities often condition the issuance of a building permit on a developer's willingness to meet or surpass the federal government's **Energy Star standards** or the U.S. Green Building Council's **Leadership in Energy and Environmental Design (LEED) standards** for energy efficiency, reduced water consumption, and the use of recycled building materials in construction.

Municipal green building efforts typically rely on the offer of incentives. A municipality awards a private builder **tax incentives, expedited permit approvals, density bonuses** (that is, city permission to build at greater floor-to-area ratios than local regulations normally allow) and various other advantages in return for a developer's willingness to adhere to design features that reduce a structure's energy consumption, preserve green space, and otherwise embody sustainability.[87] A city may permit a developer to build an increased number of residential units in return for a for a tight building "envelope" that reduces the "footprint"[88] or square footage that a structure will occupy, a planning feature that helps to preserve an area's green space. Cities reward developers, architects, and builders for passive solar heating (i.e. the use of skylights and windows that take advantage of sunlight; Figure 12.3)

Figure 12.3   **Solar Panels on Car Parking Lot, Arizona State University**. Green building construction codes can encourage the utilization of renewable energy, such as the construction of photovoltaic cells over a parking lot.

Source: From Wikimedia Commons via Flickr; © Kevin Dooley, http://commons.wikimedia.org/wiki/ File:Solar_panels_on_car_parking.jpg.

and the installation of energy-efficient heating and cooling systems. Some cities even incentivize the construction of European-style **passive houses** that are thoroughly insulated, lose very little heat through windows, and have ventilation systems that recycle heat—all features that act to greatly reduce energy consumption and a home-owner's winter heating bill.

In an increasingly number of cities, green building practices are the norm, a regularized and expected part of the local development and permit-approval processes. San Diego, Sacramento, Denver, El Paso, Kansas City, St. Louis, Nashville, and Tampa generally require LEED silver-level certification for building projects over 5,000 square feet;[89] smaller projects are exempted so their developers are not burdened with the costs of a LEED review. Municipal administrators seek to work through "education," that is help developers understand the various features they can use to meet local expectations for sustainable construction.[90]

Developers complain of the substantial costs entailed by submitting a project for LEED certification, a process which quite often necessitates the hiring LEED consultants and can saddle a commercial home builder with expenditures in excess of $50,000.[91] As a consequence, relatively few cities actually require that a new building or project go through the formal LEED certification process. Instead, cities ask developers to meet alternative energy and environmental construction guidelines that are similar to LEED without requiring formal certification by the LEED council. In some cases, however, developers are quite willing to apply for LEED certification, having discovered that LEED certification can enhance a new structure's marketability by underscoring the substantial savings in the costs of energy that a commercial or residential tenant can expect over the life of a building.

LEED standards have reshaped building construction, as architects and developers have begun to pay heightened attention to energy efficiency and various other aspects of sustainability. Yet, there are limits to LEED's success. A large number of cities do not actively pursue LEED-type building standards as they fear that such regulations could interfere with new growth and development. Other cities only require LEED standards to be applied to new government buildings[92] or to new high-end office buildings and other commercial structures and residential edifices. Local officials fear the political backlash that could result if growth advocates organize a public relations campaign that convinces voters that public officials have added thousands of dollars to the costs of buying a home.

LEED is important; but the extent to which LEED-like standards have been adopted in a city should not be exaggerated. Cities seldom impose LEED energy efficiency standards on existing structures unless a building is undergoing substantial rehabilita-tion. As a consequence, over 99 percent of the buildings in the United States are *not* LEED-certified![93]

Still, LEED has already helped to shape a more sustainable urban future. San Francisco, Washington, DC, Seattle, Portland, and Denver are leaders in terms of LEED certification; in each city more than a thousand buildings are LEED-certified or in the pipeline for certification.[94] Other municipalities, as we have seen, have used LEED standards as a guide to their own municipal construction regulations.

Some environmentalists, however, object that LEED standards were formulated by the construction industry, and, as a consequence, are relatively easy for builders to meet.

A project can even earn LEED certification on the basis of design features that produce only very modest energy savings.

Environmental activists were outraged when the "gold" level of LEED certification was awarded to the Mettawa suburban Chicago headquarters of HSBC, the giant banking and financial services firm, a facility built in in a location that was not readily accessible to mass transit. Workers at the new facility could not rely on mass transit! The controversy over the award led the LEED council to elaborate a more holistic set of LEED certification standards called **LEED Neighborhood Design (LEED-ND)**. LEED-ND designation is awarded only when a project shows evidence of connectivity to public transit as well as having adopted various other energy efficiency and green-construction standards required for LEED certification.[95]

GREEN PROMOTION AT CITY HALL

By its own action, a municipal government can model sustainability practices for private employers and developers to adopt. The City of Chicago placed a *green roof* atop its 100-year-old city hall (Figure 12.4), a demonstration project to show builders just how such an investment can lead to a long-term reduction in energy usage and costs.

Figure 12.4 **Green Roof Atop Chicago City Hall**.

Source: Photo by DWaterson, March 2007 / Wikimedia Commons, https://commons.wikimedia.org/w/index.php?curid=3075027.

Portland (Oregon) and Dayton (Ohio) are among other cities with a green roof on city hall. Milwaukee also has a green roof on its library.

A **green roof** is a layer of grass or vegetation that covers the top of a building and provides the structure with natural insulation, helping to minimize energy consumption. Green roofs reduce the urban **heat island effect**, where, especially during summer months, a city's downtown becomes warmer than the surrounding area as a result of the heat attracted by a city's black and gray surfaces (including normal rooftops). Green roofs also serve to retain rainwater, reducing storm water runoff and the flow of pollutants downstream.[96] A properly designed green rooftop can even offer space for gardens and urban farming (Figures 12.5 and 12.6).

Chicago, Portland, and Seattle offer density bonuses, allowing developers to build at higher densities, when a project includes green rooftops.[97] San Francisco adopted a more aggressive regulatory approach, mandating that 15 to 20 percent of the roof space of a new building over a certain size be covered with either vegetation or solar panels.[98] The city has even placed a green roof—that is, a swath of vegetation—atop the shelters at municipal bus stops.[99]

The municipal promotion of greening extends beyond green roofs. The Chicago Trees Initiative seeks to persuade developers to plant shade trees that will expand the

Figure 12.5 **Rooftop Urban Farm Atop Boston Medical Center.**

Source: Photo & Farm Installation by Recover Green Roofs, LLC. Used by permission. Recover Green Roofs is devoted to the development of urban rooftop green spaces, including rooftop farms.

Figure 12.6   **Urban Farm Atop Whole Foods. Brooklyn, New York City**. In Brooklyn, Whole
Foods supermarkets has partnered with Gotham Greens, an agribusiness that
specializes in urban farming, to construct a 20,000-square-foot climate-controlled
urban farm atop the Whole Foods Superstore in Gowanus, Brooklyn. The rooftop
farm provides fresh vegetables to Whole Food outlets throughout New York City.
The greenhouse enables a long growing season despite wintry weather. The
urban farm is energy-efficient and sustainable. City farming lessens the energy
that is consumed when vegetable have to be shipped long distances to the city
from the countryside. As Gotham Greens observes, the rooftop farm uses a
technologically advanced drip method of irrigation that can use up to 20 times
less water as compared to conventional agriculture.

Source: Ana Iacob Photography / Shutterstock.com.

city's tree canopy or "urban forest." Davis, California, an affluent and bicycle-oriented
university community, requires that a minimum of 15 percent of any new development
be set aside for greenways.[100]

Green cities can also reduce storm water runoff by narrowing the widths of new streets
and by using **porous surfaces** (or "permeable pavers") instead of impervious concrete
and asphalt in parking lots and public plazas. Porous paving allows rainwater to seep into
the underlying ground where layers of rock and soil help to filter contaminants naturally,
minimizing the pollution that results when impermeable surfaces necessitate the piping
of storm water through sewers into nearby rivers and streams. Cities also place **green
dividers**, strips of trees and low-lying grassy areas, between the aisles of a parking lot,
in order to minimize storm water runoff and the downstream flow of pollutants.

Even small steps by a city can serve as a statement of a city's commitment to sustainability and provide a model for others to emulate. Miller Park, the domed home field of
the baseball Milwaukee Brewers, has three 1,500-gallon rain barrels to collect rainwater

runoff from the stadium's 8.5-acre roof. The water collected by the barrels is then used to irrigate the ball diamond. Rain collection in the barrels serves to reduce the volume of water that is discharged into the Menomonee River.[101]

Municipal governments can promote mass transit ridership by distributing reduced-cost transit passes to city workers and by ending the provision of free parking for employees. Cities also make fuel efficiency an important consideration when purchasing new municipal vehicles.

Cities have begun to convert municipal vehicle fleets from diesel to **"cleaner" fuels**—natural gas, hybrid electric, biodiesel, and even hydrogen fuel cells. The conversion does more than reduce air pollution. The switch of fuels reduces the incidence of asthma suffered by inner-city children who reside in neighborhoods choked by diesel exhaust fumes.[102] San Diego, San Francisco, Berkeley, Portland, Honolulu, Las Vegas, South Bend (Indiana), Chicago, and the Forest Preserve District of DuPage County (Illinois) are among the large number of municipalities that have switched much of their municipal fleets from diesel to cleaner-burning **biodiesel** (a fuel that is essentially made from vegetable oil) and compressed natural gas. New York City announced plans to have an all-electric bus system by 2040.

Portland and Seattle, as we shall soon discuss, are among the national leaders in the use of **performance indicators** to measure local environmental progress and the extent to which the city is achieving important local economic growth and equity objectives. The data that the city collects is integrated into a system of **performance management** that provides agency heads and grassroots groups the information that they can use to demand further action in cases where city departments have failed to meet sustainable growth goals.

SUSTAINABLE DEVELOPMENT: FIVE CITIES

What do sustainable cities look like? A brief look at Chattanooga, Austin, Boulder, Portland (Oregon), and Seattle[103] yields insight as to how cities can simultaneously promote economic growth while decreasing their "ecological footprint" and advancing equity concerns.

Chattanooga

Chattanooga, Tennessee, was once a center of coke foundries and textile manufacturing. Industries were attracted to the region's natural resources and the availability of low-wage labor. By the 1960s, Chattanooga was reputed to be the most polluted city in the United States. Today, Chattanooga is a vastly different community. The city cleaned up pollution and cast its future with sustainable development.

Businesses and nongovernmental organizations took the lead in a New-Regional-style public-private partnership that envisioned a modern, clean, and revitalized Chattanooga. The Chamber of Commerce provided much of the impetus behind the Vision 2000 effort that pinpointed sustainable development as the key to developing a new image and future for the former industrial center. Chattanooga employs a sustainability officer to oversee and coordinate the city's various initiatives. The city even has an urban forester devoted to efforts to green the city. Chattanooga turned to a system of electric buses to provide a visible statement of the city's reorientation and commitment to pollution reduction and livability. Regional nonprofit organizations helped piece together the Chattanooga Greenways, a 75-mile network of parks and open space, that made greater Chattanooga a more livable and recreation-oriented community.[104]

Local leaders reconnected the city's central business to its riverfront and also developed new parks and trails along the river. Chattanooga resorted to a **road diet**, shrinking the number of automobile lanes and slowing traffic speeds on a highway section that had effectively blocked pedestrians from walking over to the riverfront. Chattanooga transformed the limited-access five-lane Riverfront Parkway into a much different thoroughfare: a two-lane, low-speed street bordered by trees and a riverfront promenade, an area that became suddenly popular with pedestrians, joggers, and cyclists. The riverfront conversion helped attract new office and residential development to the downtown and nearby neighborhoods.[105] In Chattanooga, "livability" became a local "economic development issue."[106] Chattanooga's civic leaders advertise the area's air quality and the quality of local life.

Still, not everyone is satisfied with this tale of Chattanooga's renaissance. Critics charge that Chattanooga's "Cinderella story" is largely a "mirage," a "rebranding" pursued by local elites that has coopted the public to support an effort largely focused on the rejuvenation of the city's downtown business district.[107]

Austin

Austin, Texas, utilizes a system of "Sustainable Community" performance indicators to measure progress in areas such as air quality, energy and water conservation, and the reduced use of hazardous materials. The Austin city council emphasizes efforts to reduce greenhouse gas emissions; the city set a goal of zero GHG emissions by 2050.

The Austin city council also set targets to increase the purchase of energy from renewable resources, including wind and solar power. Austin Energy responded with a promise that by 2020 over half its energy would come from renewable sources. The local utility offers customers a **Green Choice option**: utility customers can direct that the electricity used in their homes be generated by wind, solar, and other renewable sources. The city library and municipal buildings are 100-percent powered by renewables.[108]

Austin gives priority to capital improvement projects that contribute to sustainability. City planners channel new development toward "smart growth zones" as opposed to sites lying above the local aquifer.[109]

Austin waives fees and provides other incentives to contractors who meet sustainability goals. The city's **Green Building Program** provides technical assistance to aid developers in energy-efficient construction. The program also rates new homes and commercial buildings according to the sustainability of their construction practices. New homes are awarded one to five stars based on such factors as water and energy conservation, indoor air quality, and the use of recycled materials. Austin does more than just offer incentives; local ordinances require energy efficiency in new construction.

The Green Building Program has achieved results! The program lowered the demand for energy during peak months and hours, reducing emissions from Austin Energy power plants and thereby lessening the need to construct new power-generating facilities. By 2018, 29 buildings in Austin received LEED certification, with another 21 in the pipeline toward certification. The municipality serves as an exemplar to the private sector, having built ten LEED-certified municipal buildings, including city hall.[110] A municipal Office of Sustainability oversees the achievement of various elements in the city's comprehensive plan, which emphasizes transit-oriented development and green space protection.

Boulder

Boulder (Colorado) gained international attention as a result of its program of regulations and incentives for green practices in new home construction. The city awards **Green Points** to builders and contractors for a wide variety of sustainable construction practices, including: permeable paving; water efficiency; roof overhangs that provide natural shade; passive solar heating; enhanced insulation; heat recovery in ventilation systems; the use of engineered lumber in a floor or roof; the use of local-sourced materials; and even contracting the services of a green building consultant.[111] The city issues a building permit only *after* a project has earned a specified number of Green Points.

Similar to Austin, Boulder has a municipal department devoted to Community Planning and Sustainability. Also like Austin, Boulder utilizes a system of statistical performance indicators to monitor environmental quality. Boulder tracks such factors as municipal energy and water consumption, the number of miles driven by city employees, the reliance on renewable energy sources, and the extent to which recycled materials are used in home construction.

Boulder looks to public-private partnerships as a route to sustainability. The Partners for a Clean Environment (PACE) program utilizes a nonintrusive, nonregulatory approach in its efforts to educate business owners as to the variety of actions they can take to achieve environmental goals. A cooperating business can gain certification as a "PACE partner" for actions that curb energy consumption, solid waste, and the use of hazardous materials. A region-wide Boulder Valley Comprehensive Plan entails partnerships to manage land uses beyond the city's borders.

Boulder has also expressed its commitment to meet the goals set by international accords to reduce global warming. As early as 2006, Boulder voters approved a **local carbon tax** that is added to homeowner and business electric bills. The tax was part of a local strategy to reduce energy consumption and greenhouse gas emissions. Boulder uses the proceeds from the tax to fund residential energy audits and to assist landlords in making improvements that increase the energy efficiency of rental properties.

In 2012, 60 percent of voters in Boulder, an environmentally conscious Rocky Mountains community, chose to extend the carbon tax an additional five years. In 2015, Boulder citizens voted to renew the Climate Action Plan tax yet again, until the year 2023.

Portland

Portland, Oregon, as we have already seen, has gained international attention for its Urban Growth Boundary and associated efforts at infill and transit-oriented development (TOD). Portland planners recognize that TOD is not an appropriate fit, and should not be attempted in, all communities. TOD is most likely to succeed when implemented in areas that have the potential to draw new development. As a consequence, Portland planners focused TOD efforts on the downtown, the revival of the Pearl District with its streetcars (an area that had once been dominated by aging warehouses), and areas of the region that have the potential to support fairly dense and walkable patterns of development, usually sites within a half mile of a light-rail station.[112] Portland designates fragile areas as **environmental zones** where development is approved "only in rare and unusual circumstances."[113]

In 1993 Portland became the first city in the United States to adopt a plan to reduce carbon emissions. In the ensuing years, the city council mandated stronger actions, including a reduction in greenhouse gas emissions by 80 percent. Portland's Comprehensive Plan sets the targets in various areas for reduced energy consumption as well as the increased use of recycled materials. The plan also seeks more sustainable patterns of development through the construction of multifamily housing.

A municipal Office of Sustainable Development oversees and coordinates various energy savings and sustainability strategies. Like Austin and Boulder, Portland utilizes **sustainability benchmarks** to track just how well the city is meeting economic and environmental goals and in providing residents with a high quality of life. Portland publicizes **comparative performance measurement** data that enables residents to see just how Portland's performance stacks up to that of other cities. The data, which is also available on the city's Web portal, even includes clear indicators regarding the implementation status of program actions, enabling citizens to quickly discern which actions have been completed, which are on track, and which actions have run into serious obstacles and have made little progress. Such information enables Portland's very active citizenry to keep the pressure on the government.[114] Portland also assembled the representative of various local organizations into an Equity Working Group to assure that all communities in the city share in the benefits of sustainable growth.[115]

Seattle

Seattle was one of the nation's early leaders in green construction.[116] Like the other cities reviewed in this section, Seattle in its construction codes and development regulations stresses sustainability practices. The **Street Edge Alternatives (SEA Street) program** seeks to promote natural storm water drainage by narrowing the width of paved streets, by adding trees and bordering **green swales** along the edges of streets, and by eliminating curbs and gutters that impede the flow of water into surrounding green areas (Figure 12.7). On-site storm water retention reduces the pollution that accompanies water runoff that is piped downstream.

Seattle has adopted a number of other sustainability initiatives, including policy of environmentally friendly purchasing. Seattle's Sustainable Indicators Project, the King County Benchmark Program, and the extensive performance measures initiated by the Puget Sound Regional Council all provide indicators that help the city to assess the progress being made. Seattle monitors the degree to which municipal agencies reduce the generation of solid waste, conserve energy and water, and prepare plans of action

Figure 12.7   **Green Streetside Swale, Seattle.** By allowing for the capture of water runoff from abutting sidewalks and roadways, this low-lying green swale allows for natural on-site filtration of rainwater, minimizing the pollution of streams and rivers that result from underground piping and drainage of storm water that contains roadway contaminants.

Source: U.S. Environmental Protection Agency, Document No. EPA-833-F-08-009, https://commons. wikimedia.org/wiki/File:Streetside_swale_Seattle.jpg.

for the safe handling of hazardous wastes. As in other cities, publicly available performance data enables community activists to keep the pressure on municipal officials to achieve sustainability goals.[117]

From its very beginnings, Seattle's sustainability program has been shaped by the culture of grassroots participations. Active citizen organizations, neighborhood dialogue, and nonprofit groups all play an integral role in deciding just what efforts the city ultimately undertakes in the pursuit of sustainability. A nonprofit organization, Sustainable Seattle, serves as the public's watchdog, criticizing public agencies when the performance indicators show that environmental goals are not being met. Seattle's *Equitable Development Implementation Plan* elaborates specific race and social equity goals and policies, including efforts to reduce racial disparities and to minimize displacement.[118]

Seattle has largely succeeded in making the transition from fossil fuel reliance to renewable energy sources. The city gets only 7% of its energy from coal, gas, and nuclear power. Even more than other cities in the Pacific Northwest, Seattle relies on hydropower, a low-carbon source of energy. Over 80% of Seattle's energy comes from hydropower.[119]

The city's comprehensive plan, *Toward a Sustainable Seattle*, promotes compact development by setting forth the vision of a growing population that is housed in a number of mixed-use residential-commercial **urban villages**. Each urban village has the population density needed to support mass transit as well as commercial facilities around a transit center.

THE IMPORTANCE OF LOCAL ACTION: BUILDING THE SUSTAINABLE CITY

Cities across the United States are turning to sustainable development. Four-fifths of the nation's 55 largest cities have municipal offices to promote sustainable practices. The nation's five largest cities adopted explicit policies to protect the natural environment while also promoting a high quality of local life that will help attract world-class businesses.[120]

Sustainable development efforts have taken root in heartland cities. The Minneapolis Sustainability Office prioritizes social equity goals as well as the preservation of the region's natural environment. Neighboring St. Paul strengthened its Sustainable Building Policy. In Tennessee, Nashville created a Livable Cities Committee, where municipal officials work with private-sector and nonprofit partners to identify specific strategies to improve air quality, reduce GHG emissions and pollution, and enhance local livability while promoting economic growth and social equity.[121] Even pro-business Houston, once noted as a bastion of anti-government sentiment, established the Green Houston initiative to reduce both energy consumption and pollution (see Box 12.2).

Across the United States, cities have increased their efforts to promote the use of bicycles as a form of transportation. Cities have removed automobile lanes along major street routes in order to create green-painted and protected bicycle lanes (Figure 12.8).[122] Green-painted boxes at the front of traffic intersections, and, in some cases, a separate system of traffic signals for cyclists, enable bicycle commuters who have stopped at a red light to start up quickly and safely in advance of cars. Numerous cities have also created a system of "Divvy bikes" (as the program is called in Chicago) where residents and workers have the opportunity to sign up annually or use a credit card to rent a bicycle at bicycle-rack kiosks scattered throughout the city.

Still, when it comes to cycling, policy actions in the United States still lag behind those found in Europe. Cities in the United States do *not* provide the degree of governmental investment and commitment to separate bicycle roadways and cyclist safety found in countries like the Netherlands:

> [T]he Dutch cycle because they built a dense, 35,000 kilometer (22,000-mile) network of fully separated bike infrastructure, equal to a quarter of their 140,000 kilometer (87,000-mile) road network. The Dutch cycle because they've tamed the motor vehicle, with over 75 percent of their urban streets traffic-calmed to a speed of 30 km/h (about 19 mph) or less. The Dutch cycle because their government spends an astonishing €30 ($35 USD) per person per year on bike infrastructure—fifteen times the amount invested in nearby England.[123]

Box 12.2
Anti-Government Houston Turns to Sustainability

Houston is known as the free-enterprise city of the American South, a city that does not look fondly on zoning and other governmental regulations that intrude on business freedom and individual self-reliance. Hence, Houston's turn to sustainability in more recent years is quite noteworthy. As early as 2004 Houston adopted a Green Building Resolution which set a target of Silver LEED certification for new construction. Since then, the city has also turned to benchmarking energy utilization and conservation.

"Free market" Houston, a city where growth was based on "Big Oil," now gives heightened attention to measures to improve the local quality of life in order to maintain the city's economic competitiveness. Houston's burgeoning interest in sustainable development is also rooted in the considerable savings that the city hopes to achieve by reducing energy consumption.

In 2012, the U.S. Conference of Mayors honored Mayor Annise Parker for Houston's decision to use federal stimulus money for a variety of green building and energy reduction initiatives: the retrofitting of city buildings; the provision of weatherization assistance to homeowners; incentives given commercial owners to reduce energy usage; the procurement of hybrid vehicles for the municipal fleet; and even the introduction of wind turbines as an alternative source of energy. The city switched its lighting to LEDs, cutting its streetlight energy usage by half. Houston also teamed up with Blue Cross and Blue Shield and a local nonprofit, Houston Bike Share, to place 200 gray-and-red bikes at 24 self-service kiosks located throughout the city, providing residents and workers with a health-oriented transportation alternative. Under Mayor Sylvester Turner, Parker's successor, Houston formulated the city's first-ever Climate Action and Adaptation Plan, which included measures to track the success of city's efforts to mitigate GHG emissions and climate change.

Despite these noteworthy initiatives, free-market Houston still lags behind other big cities when it comes to local sustainability. Commuter patterns in Houston, as in other Texas cities, reveal relatively little reliance on mass transit. In Houston, nearly 70% of residents are seen as having "abysmal" access to mass transit, with residents in lower-density portions of the region continuing to oppose spending for public transit. Houston also ranks extremely low when it comes to the recycling of trash, partly a reflection of the reluctance of Houstonians to impose a garbage collection fee to pay for recycling efforts.

But even such areas are beginning to change. In 2018, Houston officials announced a MetroNEXT plan to increase public transit. MetroNEXT embraced the construction of 34 miles of Bus Rapid Transit (BRT) routes (where train-like buses run largely on bus-access-only lanes of highways) and the addition of 12 miles of track so that light rail could serve the region's airports. The preference for high-seed buses over light rail was a matter of costs: BRT systems, especially when high-speed buses use existing roadways, are cheaper than rail.

Sources: Chris Moran, "Houston's Green Efforts Win Accolades," *Houston Chronicle*, April 25, 2012; Kent E. Portney, *Taking Sustainable Cities Seriously: Economic Development, the Environment, and Quality of Life in American Cities*, 2nd ed. (Cambridge, MA: MIT Press, 2013), 131–141, 198–203, 256–271, and 283–297; Kent E. Portney, *Sustainability* (Cambridge, MA: MIT Press, 2015), 174–175, Table 6.2 and Dug Begley, "Houston's Public Transit Challenges Highlighted in U.S. Analysis of Bus, Rail Networks," *Houston Chronicle*, June 10, 2016; and Dug Begley, "Metro Gets Rolling on Long-range Plan, Favoring Buses," *Houston Chronicle*, September 14, 2018. Also see the City of Houston's "Green City Project Links" and its "Climate Action and Adaptation Plan" at its "Green Houston" web portal, www.greenhoustontx.gov/climate-action-adaptation-plan.html.

Figure 12.8   **Bicycle Lane Along Market Street, San Francisco**. To encourage commuting by bicycle, San Francisco has lanes along Market Street, a major city thoroughfare, dedicated to cyclists. Even though the cyclists and cars share a roadway, the bicycle lanes are clearly separated from other lanes, with the green paint and a bicycle icon clearly indicating that these are reserved for cyclists. Plastic barriers or bollards placed along the bike way further help to keep automobile drivers out of the bike lanes, enhancing cyclist safety.

Source: David Tran photo / Shutterstock.com.

However, automobile users in the United States are not the only interests who often oppose the introduction of bicycle lanes. Shop owners object when the construction of a bicycle lane results in the loss of parking spaces in front of their stores. The residents of lower-income minority neighborhoods may also view the appearance of bicycle lanes as indicators that the city intends to transform their neighborhoods, an omen of future gentrification and displacement.[124]

The United States also lags behind Europe when it comes to modernizing and extending commuter rail lines, providing faster, more frequent, and comfortable rail service. Again, when compared to Europe, governments in the United State have considerable difficulty in imposing the sort of strong land-use regulations to assure the population densities necessary to support public transit and promote walkability.[125]

But even here, the picture in the United States is beginning to change, even if future progress remains uncertain. State officials in California and regional planners in the Los Angeles and San Francisco areas have embraced *upzoning*, the promotion of patterns of dense develop that will enable transit-oriented development. **Upzoning** typically entails the construction of mid-rise offices and residences, townhouse with small backyards and side yards (or no yards at all), and multilevel mixed-use structures all sited within walkable distances of a transit stop. But as seen Austin, Texas, as well as in California, planning efforts that embrace upzoning and transit-oriented development often encounter intense resistance from area residents who object to the crowding and congestion that denser development will bring to its immediate environs. Local residents fight to defend the "livability" of low-rise communities dominated by single-family homes.[126]

Portland, Cincinnati, Boston, and Rochester are only a few of the growing number of cities to reduce the number of off-street parking places that developers must include in a new residential or commercial project, a move that may lead some people to use mass transit. By relaxing parking requirements, a city can improve housing affordability, as the provision of a parking space can add thousands of dollars to the price of a new apartment or condominium. Buffalo in 2017 in its Green Code initiative became the first city in the United States to completely eliminate minimum parking requirements for new construction throughout the city (at least for projects larger than 5,000 square feet).[127] The next year, Minneapolis followed suit, approving a Minneapolis 2040 plan provision to abolish parking minimums for all new construction.

American cities are also beginning to show renewed interest in the creation pedestrian zones to promote the sidewalk cafés and a more congenial and active street life. Such projects seek to emulate the vital pedestrian shopping streets and plazas found in Britain, Germany, the Netherlands, Scandinavia, and other parts of Europe.[128]

Bus Rapid Transit (BRT) is another innovation, popular in other countries, that is just beginning to gain a prominent presence in metropolitan areas in the United States. BRT vehicles (which oftentimes resemble connected buses) run along exclusive or dedicated roadways where automobiles are denied entrance. Running on their separate paths, BRT vehicles do not get stuck amid automobiles traffic. BRT buses run at relatively high speeds as they are not slowed by the necessity of crossing numerous intersections. BRT stations are spaced much further apart than are the stops along ordinary bus routes; such spacing allows BRT vehicles to run at greater speeds between stops. Regional planners can provide park-and-ride lots at BRT stops, climate-controlled waiting rooms, and raised station platforms that enable quick all-door boarding—all amenities that enhance BRT usage. Rubber-tired BRT systems are generally seen to be a cheaper alternative to the construction of light- and heavy-rail systems.

The BRT buses of Cleveland's nine-mile long "HealthLine" system travel an exclusive roadway in the city's Euclid Corridor, connecting the city's dominant economic centers: the downtown, the Cleveland Clinic medical district, and University Circle with its research-oriented firms. The HealthLine also reaches into the inner-ring suburb of East Cleveland.

The South Miami-Dade Busway is a 20-mile BRT system with a two-lane roadway that is used only by buses. Civic leaders, however, faced great difficulty in their efforts to expand BRT routes and upgrade stations in South Miami. Mayor Carlos Gimenez's plans to modernize the BRT system even faced opposition from mass transit advocates who worried that an improved busway would preclude a future extension of light rail in South Miami-Dade.[129]

Los Angeles's Metro Busway is arguably the nation's most successful BRT system. The Orange Line bus stations are spaced approximately a mile apart, allowing buses to pick up speed as they travel an exclusive 18-mile road right-of-way in the San Fernando Valley. Travel speeds however, slow where road intersections cannot be avoided. L.A.'s Silver Line BRT runs south to San Pedro, providing an additional 38 miles of fast bus service along dedicated and semi-dedicated roadways. The system is widely used, and buses often run at or above passenger capacity. Still, a number of mass transit advocates in L.A. are opposed to the expansion of BRT service, as they want Los Angeles to convert its BRT routes to light rail. Citizen and business groups opposed to new taxes, however, helped kill a ballot measure to provide the more extensive funding that a light rail system requires.[130]

U.S. cities in more recent years have undertaken a vast range of public transit and green programs. The once-large "sustainability gap" that separates cities in the United States from the rest of the world has "certainly been greatly narrowed."[131] The processes of globalization, too, have helped to narrow the gap. Municipal managers attend international conferences where they gain familiarity with the innovative transit approaches and green practices being used in other nations.[132] Supranational organizations from the International Olympic Committee to various working groups of the United Nations have also put the spotlight on the need for cities to support sustainable development. President Trump withdrew the U.S. national government from the Paris accords on global warming. But he could not stop the information exchanges that occur where municipal officials around the globe meet and work collaboratively in response to such problems as climate change.

President Trump sought to rein in federal clean air efforts and the development of alternative vehicles. Trump also sought to relax the federal standards for automobile emissions.

Cities countermobilized; 246 U.S. communities in 2017 pledged to honor the goals and commitments of the Paris Agreement despite President Trump's withdrawal.[133] At the 2018 Global Climate Conference in San Francisco, New York Mayor Bill de Blasio and the managers of the city's pension fund announced that they were doubling to $4 billion the amount that the city's pension funds were investing in clean energy and other climate solutions.

By 2018, more than 400 mayors of American cities had joined Climate Mayors, a peer-to-peer organization that enables cities to work with one another to uphold the Paris agreement and share best practices to reduce GHG emissions.[134] Co-founded and chaired by Los Angeles Mayor Eric Garcetti (and co-chaired in 2018 by Houston's Sylvester Turner, Boston's Martin Walsh, and Knoxville's Madeline Rogero), the organization's efforts receive support from the City of Los Angeles sustainability office.[135] The inter-actions of Climate Mayors have helped cities, especially smaller and medium-sized communities, to undertake ameliorative actions. The City of Knoxville, for instance, switched it streetlights from high-pressure sodium to energy-efficient LED systems, a retrofit that reduced GHG emissions and saved city taxpayers $2 million a year.[136] The association also helped 30 cities to form a joint purchasing collaborative for vehicle purchases. By aggregating municipal demand, the cities increased their leverage to spur manufacturers to develop zero-emission trucks and medium- and heavy-duty vehicles.[137]

It is unclear to what extent U.S. cities will be able to meet their green-city goals and pick up the slack of a federal government that has lessened its own environmental commitments and that has withdrawn from international forums. What can be said for sure is that contemporary cities will continue to act when the federal government fails in its obligations to protect urban citizens and their communities. More than a thousand city and county officials joined state officials, CEOs, and other community leaders to declare "We Are Still In," affirming their commitment to lowering emissions and achiev-ing other sustainability targets in the wake of President Trump's withdrawal from the Paris Climate Agreement.[138]

Urban diplomacy, where mayors act on a global stage, is now a regular and expected part of a mayor's job. Mayors enter the international arena to find new investors in a city's economy, to find new markets for a city's products, to protect undocumented city residents and immigrant entrepreneurs, and to minimize the adverse impacts that accom-pany climate change. In 2017, the Trump administration refused to secure pavilion space for public officials, NGOs, and business leaders at the United Nations Climate Change Conference in Bonn, Germany. In response, New York Mayor Michael Bloomberg joined with California Governor Jerry Brown to establish an unofficial American pavilion for U.S. cities, states, and corporate leaders to learn about what steps they can initiate and how they can track the progress of local efforts to curb GHG emissions. The pavilion was larger than those set up by other countries.[139]

POSTSCRIPT: ACTIVE CITIES AND THE URBAN FUTURE

In 2018, Baltimore Mayor Catherine Pugh sued the federal government as a result of a rules change initiated by the State Department under the Trump administration. The State Department had changed its Foreign Affairs Manual, instructing its officers to look at a family's history of public support (including noncash support) as the officers sought to assess if a visa applicant was likely to become a "public charge" if allowed to enter the United States. Baltimore residents who had family members living abroad were hesitant to participate in public assistance programs and claim needed benefits for themselves and their children, fearing that the State Department could use such a benefit history as a reason to deny a visa to a relative who wished to enter the United States.[140]

Mayor Pugh objected that the rules change would harm Baltimore residents, deterring their willingness to participate in public job training programs and even have their children participate in school lunch programs or take advantage of vaccinations and health services provided children at public health clinics, Baltimore would not sit idly by. Instead, the city acted in accordance to its own Welcome City policies.

A few months later, Baltimore would sue the Trump administration yet again, this time over the federal administration's changes in assistance rules in order to steer low-income people away from abortion providers. In era of polarized politics, Baltimore and other cities have become increasingly active and assertive.

KEY TERMS

biodiesel and other "clean" fuels
(*p. 468*)

Bus Rapid Transit (BRT) (*p. 476*)

comparative performance
measurement (*p. 471*)

contract compliance programs
(*p. 446*)

creative class as a factor in economic
development, the (*p. 442*)

de facto segregation (*p. 447*)

de jure segregation (*p. 447*)

density bonuses (*p. 463*)

disparity studies (*p. 446*)

Earned Income Tax Credit (EITC)
(*p. 455*)

Energy Star standards (*p. 463*)

environmental zones, Portland's
designation of (*p. 471*)

expedited permit approvals as a
reward for green development
practicvs (*p. 479*)

Green Building Program, Austin's
(*p. 469*)

Green Choice option to utility
customers, Austin Energy's offer
of a (*p. 469*)

green dividers to contain storm
water runoff (*p. 467*)

Green Points program, Boulder's
(*p. 470*)

green roof (*p. 466*)

green swales (also known as green
streetside swales) (*p. 471*)

hard factors in local economic
development (*p. 442*)

heat island effect, a city's (*p. 466*)

industrial cluster (*p. 459*)

LEED (Leadership in Energy and
Environmental Design) standards
(*p. 463*)

LEED-Neighborhood Design
(LEED-ND) standards (*p. 465*)

local carbon tax (*p. 470*)

Low Income Housing Tax Credit
(LIHTC) (*p. 455*)

magnet schools (*p. 448*)

Milliken v. Bradley (*p. 447*)

minority set-aside program (*p. 446*)

narrowly tailored, The Supreme
Court's view that remedies
for discrimination must be
(*p. 446*)

passive houses. European-style
(*p. 464*)

people-based strategies, urban
policy bases on (*p. 454*)

performance indicators (*p. 468*)

performance management (*p. 468*)

placed-based strategies versus
people-based strategies, the
debate over (*p. 454*)

porous surfaces as a green-city tool
(*p. 467*)

quality of life factors in local
economic development (*p. 442*)

race-neutral programs (*p. 453*)

NOTES

1. Chad Shearer, "The Small Town-Big City Split That Elected Donald Trump," *The Avenue, a Web Posting of the Brookings Institution*, November 11, 2016, www.brookings.edu/blog/the-avenue/2016/11/11/the-small-town-big-city-split-that-elected-donald-trump/; Dante J. Scala and Kenneth M. Johnson, "Political Polarization along the Urban-Rural Continuum? The Geography of the Presidential Vote, 2000–2016," *ANNALS of the American Academy of Political and Social Science* 672, no. 1 (2017): 162–184.

2. Kim Parker et al., "What Unites and Divides Urban, Suburban, and Rural Communities," a report of the Pew Research Center, May 22, 2018, http://assets.pewresearch.org/wp-content/uploads/sites/3/2018/05/02094832/Pew-Research-Center-Community-Type-Full-Report-FINAL.pdf.

3. Democrats picked up 40 seats in the House in 2018, yet Republicans maintained control of the Senate, even picking up two Senate seats to yield a 53–47 Republican Senate majority. In part, the failure of the Democrats to win the Senate was a matter of bad luck in election scheduling. Only one-third of the seats in the Senate are on the ballot every two years. Of the 35 Senate seats that were up for a vote in 2018, 25 were already occupied by Democrats and the two Independents who aligned with the Democrats in the Senate. In 2016, it was primarily Democratic Senate seats, not Republican seats, that were on the ballot and at risk.

4. David Montgomery, "Suburban Voters Gave the Democrats Their House Majority," *CityLab Web Posting*, November 7, 2018, www.citylab.com/equity/2018/11/house-races-election-results-democrats-suburbs-blue-wave/575287/.

5. Brian F. Schaffner, "These 5 Charts Explain Who Voted How in the 2018 Midterm Election," *Washington Post*, "Monkey Cage Analysis," November 10, 2018, www.washingtonpost.com/news/monkey-cage/wp/2018/11/10/these-5-charts-explain-who-voted-how-in-the-2018-midterm-election/?utm_term=.16efad671c34. *The Washington Post* analysis is based on the interviews and data from the Cooperative Congressional Election Study, a large-scale academic survey.

6. Holly Otterbein, Andrew Seidman, and Jonathan Lai, "Think GOP Losses in Philly Suburbs Are Trump's Fault? It's More Complicated," *The (Philadelphia) Enquirer*, November 18, 2018.

7. Steven P. Erie, *Globalizing L.A.: Trade, Infrastructure, and Regional Development* (Stanford, CA: Stanford University Press, 2004), details the history of spending decisions and actions taken by L.A officials that subsidized growth in the city and the region.

8. Allison Ross, "How KFC Yum Center Became Louisville's Billion-Dollar Baby," *Louisville Courier Journal*, July 12, 2018.

9. Richard Florida, *The Rise of the Creative Class* (New York: Basic Books, 2002); Richard Florida, *Who's Your City: How the Creative Economy Is Making Where to Live the Most Important Decision of Your Life* (New York: Basic Books, 2008). For a critique of the strategies that cities often use to attract the "creative class," see Allen J. Scott, "Creative Cities: Conceptual Issues and Policy Questions," *Journal of Urban Affairs* 28, no. 1 (2006): 1–17.

10. Mark Belko, "Pennsylvania Offered Up to $4.6 Billion to Amazon for HQ2," *Pittsburgh Post-Gazette*, November 13, 2018; Max Marin, "What Amazon Rejected: $5.7 Billion HQ2 Package from Philly and PA," *Billy Penn, an Independent Media Organization*, November 13, 2018, https://billypenn.com/2018/11/13/what-amazon-rejected-5-7-billion-hq2-package-from-philly-and-pa/.

11. Mark Belko, "Region's Bid for Amazon's HQ2 May Have Been the Biggest of Them All," *Pittsburgh Post-Gazette*, November 21, 2018.

12. Sarah Holder, "What Did Cities Actually Offer Amazon?," *CityLab, Web Posting*, May 2, 2018, www.citylab.com/life/2018/05/what-did-cities-actually-offer-amazon/559220/?utm_source=nl__lin k1_052918&silverid=%%RECIPIENT_ID%%; Sarah Holder, "The Extreme Amazon Bidder Just Got Real," *CityLab, Web Posting*, November 28, 2017, www.citylab.com/life/2017/11/the-extreme-amazon-bidder-just-got-real/546857/.

13. Under the terms of New York's agreement with Amazon, the giant retailer was to pay over $1 billion in Payments in Lieu of Taxes (PILOTs) over 40 years, with over half going to fund transportation and other infrastructure improvements. But those funds are dedicated to projects in the vicinity of Amazon's Long Island City location and cannot be used to improve transportation or help programs in other neighborhoods. See Gersh Kuntzman, "Sweetheart Deal for Amazon Includes Tiny 'Infrastructure Fund' for City," *StreetsBlog NYC Web Posting*, November 13, 2018, https://nyc.streetsblog.org/2018/11/13/breaking-sweet-deal-for-amazon-includes-large-infrastructure-fund-for-city/. Amid continuing protests from groups critical of the extensive subsidies awarded Amazon and fearful that new development would further strain the city's already overcrowded subway system, Amazon reversed its earlier decision and announced that it would no longer open a New York/Long Island City headquarters.

14. Alan Berube, "For Amazon HQ2 Location Decision Was about Talent, Talent, Talent," *The Avenue, a Web Posting of the Brookings Institution*, November 13, 2018, www.brookings.edu/blog/the-avenue/2018/11/13/for-amazon-hq2-location-decision-was-about-talent-talent-talent/.

15. Thad Williamson, David Imbroscio, and Gar Alperowitz, *Making a Place for Community: Local Democracy in a Global Era* (New York: Routledge, 2003).

16. Brett Theodos, Brady Meixell, and Carl Hedman, "Did States Maximize Their Opportunity Zone Designations?," a report of the Urban Institute, Washington, DC, May 2018 (revised July 2018), www.urban.org/sites/default/files/publication/98445/did_states_maximize_their_opportunity_zone_selections_6.pdf. The "minimal targeting" reference appears on p. 3.

17. Noah Smith, "How to Get Growth in the Places That Need It the Most," *Bloomberg Opinion*, December 3, 2018, www.bloomberg.com/opinion/articles/2018-12-03/how-to-get-growth-in-the-places-that-need-it-most.

18. Stephanie Czeckalinski and Doris Dhan, "7 of 15 Most Populous U.S. Cities Are Majority-Minority," *National Journal*, July 2, 2012, www.nationaljournal.com/thenextamerica/demographics/7-of-15-most-populous-u-s-cities-are-majority-minority-20120702.

19. William H. Frey, "The New Metro Minority Map: Regional Shifts in Hispanics, Asians, and Blacks from Census 2010," State of Metropolitan American Report No. 37, Brookings Institution, August 31, 2011, www.brookings.edu/research/papers/2011/08/31-census-race-frey.

20. According to a U.S. Census analysis, the turnout rate for eligible Hispanics in the 2016 presidential election was 47.6 percent, well below the 59.6% turnout for African Americans and 65.3% voting rate of non-Hispanic whites. See Thom File, "Voting in America: A Look at the 2016 Presidential Election," May 10, 2017, a Census Blog of the U.S. Census Bureau, Washington, DC, May 10, 2017, www.census.gov/newsroom/blogs/random-samplings/2017/05/voting_in_america.html. Also see William H. Frey, "Census Shows Pervasive Decline in 2016 Minority Voter Turnout," *The*

Avenue, a Web Posting of the Brookings Institution, May 18, 2017, www.brookings.edu/blog/the-avenue/2017/05/18/census-shows-pervasive-decline-in-2016-minority-voter-turnout/.

21. Matt A. Barreto, "¡Sí Se Puede! Latino Candidates and the Mobilization of Latino Voters," *American Political Science Review* 101, no. 3 (August 2007), 425–441; the quotation appears on p. 439. Of course, a Latino candidate on the ballot who has little chance of victory also has little ability to draw Latinos to the polls. Latino turnout, for instance, fell in the 2013 first-round election for mayor of Los Angeles, as all of the Latino candidates were "long shots" with little chance to succeed term-limited Mayor Antonio Villaraigosa. Latino voters did have some affinity for City Councilmember Eric Garcetti. Garcetti, who would become the first Jewish Angeleno to be elected mayor, stressed his Mexican roots: His mother was Jewish, and his father was of Mexican and Italian heritage.

22. Paul Taylor, Ana Gonzales-Barrera, Jeffrey Passel, and Mark Hugo-Lopez, "An Awakened Giant: The Hispanic Electorate Is Likely to Double by 2030," *Pew Research Hispanic Trends Project*, November 14, 2012, www.pewhispanic.org/2012/11/14/an-awakened-giant-the-hispanic-electorateis-likely-to-double-by-2030/.

23. Atiya Stokes-Brown, "The Latino Vote in the 2016 Election: Myths and Realities about the 'Trump Effect'," in *Conventional Wisdom, Parties, and Broken Barriers in the 2016 Election*, ed. Jennifer C. Lucas, Christopher J. Galdieri, and Tauna S. Sisco (Lanham, MD: Lexington Books, 2018), 61–80; the quotation appears on p. 61.

24. Zev Chafets, "The Post-Hispanic Politician," *New York Times Magazine*, May 6, 2010; Andrew Romano, "Can Castro Turn Texas Blue?," *Newsweek*, April 15, 2013. Also see the portraits of three San Antonio mayors—Henry Cisneros, Ed Garza, and Julián Castro—provided by Heywood T. Sanders, "Mayoral Politics and Policies in a Divided City: Latino Mayors in San Antonio," in *Latino Mayors: Political Change in the Postindustrial City*, ed. Marion Orr and Domingo Morel (Philadelphia: Temple University Press, 2018), 71–97.

25. Roberto E. Villarreal and Howard D. Neighbor, "Conclusion: An Overview of Mexican-American Political Empowerment," in *Latino Empowerment: Progress, Problems, and Prospects*, ed. Roberto E. Villarreal, Norma G. Hernandez, and Howard D. Neighbor (New York: Greenwood Press, 1988), 128.

26. Lois Beckett, "Charlottesville's First Black, Female Mayor: 'We're Not a Post-Racial Nation'," *The Guardian*, August 7, 2018, www.theguardian.com/us-news/2018/aug/07/charlottesville-virginia-nikuyah-walker-interview.

27. Andra Gillespie, *The New Black Politician: Cory Booker, Newark, and Post-Racial America* (New York: New York University Press, 2012); Andra Gillespie, "Losing and Winning: Cory Booker's Ascent to Newark's Mayoralty," in *Whose Black Politics? Cases in Post-Racial Black Leadership*, ed. Andra Gillespie (New York: Routledge, 2010), 67–83.

28. Marion Orr and Domingo Morrell, "Latino Mayors and the Evolution of Urban Politics," in *Latino Mayors: Political Change in the Postindustrial City*, 3–22, esp. 15–16; the quotation appears on p. 16.

29. W. Avon Drake and Robert D. Holsworth, *Affirmative Action and the Stalled Quest for Black Progress* (Urbana and Chicago: University of Illinois Press, 1996), 71–79 and 120–125.

30. MGT Consulting Group, *City of New York Disparity Study*, May 2018, www1.nyc.gov/assets/mwbe/business/pdf/NYC-Disparity-Study-Report-final-published-May-2018.pdf.

31. D. Wilson Consulting Group, *Disparity Study for the City of Milwaukee: Final Report* (Jacksonville, FL: December 20, 2010), http://city.milwaukee.gov/ImageLibrary/Groups/doaEBEP/Events/Disparity_Study_-_Full_Report.pdf, discusses whether the statistical evidence presented by the study is sufficient to meet the threshold that *Croson* requires to justify a city's use of race- and gender-conscious preferences in municipal contracting:

32. *Schuette v. Coalition to Defend Affirmative Action*, 572 U.S. 291 (2014).

33. *Fisher v. University of Texas at Austin*, 136 S.Ct. 2198 (2016).

34. David L. Kirp, "Retreat into Legalism: The Little Rock School Desegregation Case in Historical Perspective," *PS: Political Science and Politics* 30, no. 3 (September 1997): 443–447; quotation on p. 446.

35. *Parents Involved in Community Schools v. Seattle School District No. 1* and *Meredith v. Jefferson County Board of Education*, 551 U.S. 701 (2007).

36. Erica Frankenberg and Gary Orfield, eds., *The Resegregation of Suburban Schools: A Hidden Crisis in American Education* (Cambridge, MA: Harvard Education Press, 2012); the quotation can be found on p. 2.

37. James Vaznis, "Boston's Schools Are Becoming Resegregated," *Boston Globe*, August 4, 2018.

38. Ivan Moreno, "US Charter Schools Put Growing Numbers in Racial Isolation," *AP News*, December 3, 2017, https://apnews.com/e9c25534dfd44851a5e56bd57454b4f5.

39. Jenn Ayscue et al., "Charters as a Driver of Resegregation," a joint report of the Civil Rights Project/Proyecto Derechos Civiles (UCLA) and the University of North Carolina-Charlotte, January 2018, www.civilrightsproject.ucla.edu/research/k-12-education/integration-and-diversity/charters-as-a-driver-of-resegregation/Charters-as-a-Driver-of-Resegregation-012518.pdf.

40. Larry Gordon, "Black and Latino Parents Worried about Funding Disparities in Schools, Poll Finds," *EdSource Web Posting*, May 3, 2017, https://edsource.org/2017/poll-finds-black-and-latino-parents-worried-about-funding-disparities-in-schools/581236.

41. Edward G. Goetz, *The One-Way Street of Integration: Fair Housing and the Pursuit of Racial Justice in American Cities* (Ithaca, NY: Cornell University Press, 2018), 63. As Goetz (p. 71) acknowledges, the "hollow prospect" of integration refers to a quotation from Malcolm X.

42. Goetz, *The One-Way Street of Integration*, 28.

43. Edward J. Blakely and David L. Ames, "Changing Places: American Urban Planning Policy for the 1990s," *Journal of Urban Affairs* 14, no. 3–4 (1992): 423–446; quotation on p. 423.

44. James DeFilippis, ed., *Urban Policy in the Time of Obama* (Minneapolis: University of Minnesota Press, 2016); the quotations are from DeFilippis's "Introduction."

45. Allan Mallach, *The Divided City: Poverty and Prosperity in Urban America* (Washington, DC: Island Press, 2018), 247.

46. Mallach, *The Divided City*, 257.

47. Mallach, *The Divided City*, 255–257.

48. Marshall Kaplan and Franklin James, eds., *The Future of National Urban Policy* (Durham, NC: Duke University Press, 1990).

49. Joshua Sapotichne, "The Evolution of National Urban Policy: Congressional Agendas, Presidential Power, and Public Opinion" (paper prepared for the Woodrow Wilson International Center for Scholars project "National Urban Policy: Is a New Day Dawning?" Washington, DC, January 25, 2010), www.wilsoncenter.org/sites/default/files/Sapotichne.pdf.

50. Robert Greenstein, "Universal and Targeted Programs to Relieving Poverty," in *The Urban Underclass*, ed. Christopher Jencks and Paul E. Peterson (Washington, DC: Brookings Institution Press, 1991), 437–459.

51. Kriston Capps, "Few Will Be Spared from Michigan's Medicaid Work Requirements," *CityLab Web Posting*, May16, 2018, www.citylab.com/equity/2018/05/few-will-be-spared-from-michigans-medicaid-work-requirements/560135/; Jeff Stein and Andrew Van Dam, "Michigan's GOP Has a Plan to Shield Some People from Medicaid Work Requirements: They're Overwhelmingly White," *Washington Post "Wonkblog" Post*, May 11, 2018, www.washingtonpost.com/news/wonk/wp/2018/05/11/michigans-gop-has-a-plan-to-shield-some-people-from-medicaid-work-requirements-theyre-overwhelmingly-white/?utm_term=.7760ededc758. For an analysis that is sharply critical of the Republican effort to strengthen the work requirements of the SNAP program, see Stacy Dean, Ed Bolen, and Brynne Keith-Jennings, "Making SNAP Work Requirements Harsher Will Not Improve Outcomes for Low-Income People," a research report of the Center on Budget and Policy Priorities, March 1, 2018, www.cbpp.org/research/food-assistance/making-snap-work-requirements-harsher-will-not-improve-outcomes-for-low.

52. William Julius Wilson, *The Truly Disadvantaged* (Chicago: University of Chicago Press, 1981); William Julius Wilson, "Public-Policy Research and the Truly Disadvantaged," in *The Urban Underclass*, 460–481. See also Greenstein, "Universal and Targeted Programs to Relieving Poverty," 437–459.

53. Mallach, *The Divided City*, 260.

54. Theda Skocpol, "Targeting Within Universalism: Politically Viable Policies to Combat Poverty in the United States," in *The Urban Underclass*, ed. Jencks and Peterson, 411–436, esp. 414.

55. Corianne Payton Scally, Amanda Gold, Carl Hedman, Matt Gerken, and Nicole DuBois, *The Low-Income Housing Tax Credit: Past Achievements, Future Challenges* (Washington, DC: The Urban Institute, 2018), www.urban.org/sites/default/files/publication/98761/lithc_past_achievements_future_challenges_final_0.pdf.

56. Congressional Research Service, "Homelessness: Target Federal Programs," CRS Report RL303442, October 18, 2018, https://fas.org/sgp/crs/misc/RL30442.pdf.

57. United States Interagency Council on Homelessness, *Home, Together: The Federal Strategic Plan to Prevent and End Homelessness* (Washington, DC: Interagency Council on Homelessness, 2018), especially pp. 5 and 16, www.usich.gov/resources/uploads/asset_library/Home-Together-Federal-Strategic-Plan-to-Prevent-and-End-Homelessness.pdf. The quotation appears on p. 16.

58. Kurt Paulsen, "The Goldilocks Dilemma of Moderate-Income Housing Subsidies: Finding the 'Just Right' Amount for the Missing Middle," *Cityscape: A Journal of Policy Development and Research* 19, no. 1 (2017): 245–251, www.huduser.gov/portal/periodicals/cityscpe/vol19num1/ch13.pdf.

59. Rasheed Malik and Leila Schochet, "A Compass for Families: Head Start in Rural America," *Center for American Progress*, April 10, 2018, www.americanprogress.org/issues/early-childhood/reports/2018/04/10/448741/a-compass-for-families/.

60. Kelly L. Patterson, Robert Mark Silverman, Li Yin, and Laiyun Wu, "Neighborhoods of Opportunity: Developing an Operational Definition for Planning and Policy Implementation," *Journal of Public Management & Social Policy* 22, no. 3, Article 2: 143–158, esp. 143–150, http://digitalscholarship.tsu.edu/jpmsp/vol22/iss3/2.

61. Joint Committee on Taxation, U.S. Congress, "*Estimates of Federal Tax Expenditures for Fiscal years 2016–2020*," JCX-3-17 (January 30, 2017), Table 1.

62. John Henneberger, "Houston, It's Time to Stop Accommodating Segregation," *Shelterforce: The Voice of Community Development*, February 7, 2017, https://shelterforce.org/2017/02/07/houston-its-time-to-stop-accommodating-segregation/.

63. National Low Income Housing Coalition, "Advocates and Congressional Champions Secure Increased Funding for Affordable Housing in 2018," March 22, 2018, http://nlihc.org/article/advocates-and-congressional-champions-secure-increased-funding-affordable-housing-2018.

64. Neal Peirce, "An Urban Agenda for the President," *Journal of Urban Affairs* 15 (1993): 457–467.

65. Ross Gittell and Avis Vidal, *Community Organizing: Building Social Capital as a Development Strategy* (Thousand Oaks, CA: Sage Publications, 1998), esp. 33–56. Williamson, Imbroscio, and Alperovitz, *Making a Place for Community: Local Democracy in a Global Era*, observe both the potential and the limitations of CDCs.

66. Mallach, *The Divided City*, 156–157 and 275–276.

67. Oscar Perry Abello, "How the Mission District Took Equitable Development into Its Own Hands," *Next City Blog Posting*, January 23, 2018, https://nextcity.org/daily/entry/the-mission-district-takes-equitable-development-into-its-own-hands.

68. Nicholas Belongie and Robert Mark Silverman, "Model CBAs and Community Benefits Ordinances as Tools for Negotiating Equitable Development: Three Critical Cases," *Journal of Community Practice* 26, no. 3 (2018): 308–327.

69. Myungshik Choi, Shannon Van Zandt, and David Matarrita-Cascante, "Can Community Land Trusts Slow Gentrification?," *Journal of Urban Affairs* 40, no. 3 (2018): 439–411.

70. Aline Reynolds, "Oakland Land Trust Finds More Ways to Preserve Affordable Housing," *NextCity*, September 10, 2018, https://nextcity.org/daily/entry/oakland-land-trust-finds-more-ways-to-preserve-affordable-housing.

71. James DeFilippis, Brian Stromberg, and Olivia R. Williams, "W(h)ither the *Community* in Community Land Trusts?," *Journal of Urban Affairs* 40, no. 6 (2018): 755–769.

72. In just seven years, the number of homeless veterans was cut nearly in half, from 73,367 in 2009 to 39,471 in 2016. The January 2017 point-in-time count revealed a small uptick, with the number of homeless veterans rising to 40,056. See the Department of Housing and Urban Development (HUD), *The 2017 Annual Homelessness Assessment Report (AHAR) to Congress* (Washington, DC: DHUD, 2017), 52–52, esp. Exhibit 5.1 "PIT Estimates of Homeless Veterans," www.hudexchange.info/resources/documents/2017-AHAR-Part-1.pdf.

73. Christina D. Rosan and Hamil Pearsall, *Growing a Sustainable City? The Question of Urban Agriculture* (Toronto: University of Toronto Press, 2017) observe the political conflicts that inhibited the growth of urban farming in Philadelphia. The advocates of urban agriculture—environmentalists, millennials interested in food systems, economic development practitioners, and even newly arrived farmers who are experienced in agriculture—are largely white. Their views on urban farming differed markedly from those of younger farmers of color and neighborhood leaders who view urban farming as a tool for youth education, individual empowerment, and community development.

74. Brad McDearman, "Rethinking Cluster Initiatives: Case Study: Milwaukee Water Technology," a report of the Metropolitan Studies Program at The Brookings Institution, Washington, DC, July 2018, www.brookings.edu/wp-content/uploads/2018/07/201807_Brookings-Metro_Rethinking-Clusters-Initiatives_Milwaukee-Water-Technology.pdf.

75. Alaina Harkness, Bruce Katz, Caroline Conroy, and Ross Tilchin, "Leading Beyond Limits: Mayoral Powers in the Age of New Localism," a report of the Brookings Institution, Washington, DC, 2017, www.brookings.edu/wp-content/uploads/2017/10/bro17006_0091.pdf.

76. Richard C. Schragger, *City Power: Urban Governance in a Global Age* (New York: Oxford University Press, 2016), 57.

77. Rick Su, "Have Cities Abandoned Home Rule?," *Fordham Urban Law Journal* 44, no. 1 (2017), article 6, 181–217, https://digitalcommons.law.buffalo.edu/cgi/viewcontent.cgi?article=1137&context=articles. The quotation appears on p. 216.

78. Steven Cohen, *The Sustainable City* (New York: Columbia University Press, 2018), 3–6 and 13–28 defines sustainable cities and discusses various dimensions of sustainable urban systems, including: reliance on renewable energy sources; solid waste minimization; the reduction of toxins and emissions; the availability of clean water and ample food supplies; open spaces and parks; and transportation.

79. Douglas Farr, *Sustainable Urbanism: Urban Design with Nature* (Hoboken, NJ: Wiley, 2007), emphasis in the original.

80. Two books describe the advantages, including economic advantages, of green development and urban place-making strategies. See Timothy Beatley, *Green Urbanism: Learning from European Cities* (Washington, DC: Island Press, 2000), especially 29–106; and Robert Cervero, Erick Guerra, and Stefan Al, *Beyond Mobility: Planning Cities for People and Places* (Washington, DC: Island Press, 2017), especially 47–63.

81. Richard Halsey, "Why Are California's Homes Burning? It Isn't Natural Disaster It's Bad Planning," *Los Angeles Times*, December 7, 2017; Mike Davis, "Southern California's Uncanny, Inevitable Yule Time Fires," *The New Yorker*, December 11, 2017; Kelly Shannon and Donielle Kaufman, "California Is Burning: Rethinking the Wildland/(Sub)urban Interface," *Landezine*, January 9, 2018, www.landezine.com/index.php/2018/01/california-is-burning-rethinking-the-wildland-suburban-interface/.

82. For a voluminous summary of the evidence on climate change and its impact on the United States, see the U.S. Global Change Research Program, *Impacts, Risks, and Adaptation in the United States: Fourth National Climate Change Assessment* (Washington, DC: USGCRP, 2018), https://nca2018.globalchange.gov/downloads/. President Trump and his administration attempted to bury the *Climate Change Assessment* and its findings by making the mandated 2018 report public on the Friday after Thanksgiving, when few people would be paying attention to such matters.

83. Erick Trickey, "5 Ways L.A. Could Change the Olympic Games Model for the Better," *NextCity Blog Posting*, July 12, 2017, https://nextcity.org/daily/entry/los-angeles-win-olympics-2024-summer-olympics.

84. Los Angeles's Sustainable City pLAn, with its stated commitment to a cleaner environment, a strong economy, and equity concerns, can be found at http://plan.lamayor.org/. The site also contains a progress report which documents the extent to which L.A. is attaining its sustainability goals.

85. Portland has considered relaxing a city-enacted inclusionary requirements in the face of criticism that such regulations have been a disincentive to new construction, exacerbating the city's housing problems. See Dirk VanderHart, "Portland's Bet on Forcing Developers to Build Affordable Housing Is Getting Lackluster Results," *Portland Mercury*, January 31, 2018, www.portlandmercury.com/news/2018/01/31/19643709/portlands-bet-on-forcing-developers-to-build-affordable-housing-is-getting-lackluster-results.

86. Figures from 2009 provided by American Institute of Architects, *Local Leaders in Sustainability: Green Building Policy in a Changing Economic Environment* (Washington, DC: AIA, 2009), 13, www.aia.org/aiaucmp/groups/aia/documents/document/aiab081617.pdf. For a more recent analysis and a more complex breakdown of cities and counties according to their green construction ordinances, see Daniel C. Matisoff, Douglas S. Noonan, and Mallory E. Flowers, "Policy Monitor–Green Buildings: Economics and Policies," *Review of Environmental Economics and Policy* 10, no. 2 (Summer 2016): 329–346, esp. Table 1.

87. The American Institute of Architects and the National Association of Counties, *Local Leaders in Sustainability: Green Building Incentive Trends* (Washington, DC: AIA, 2012), www.aia.org/aiaucmp/groups/aia/documents/pdf/aiab093472.pdf, reviews the variety of green building requirements and incentives offered by U.S. municipalities.

88. For a brief review of the concept of a city's "ecological footprint," see Peter Newman and Isabella Jennings, *Cities as Sustainable Ecosystems: Principles and Practices* (Washington, DC: Island Press, 2008), 80–91.

89. "Cities Requiring or Supporting LEED," *Everblue*, update October 17, 2018, www.everbluetraining.com/blog/cities-requiring-or-supporting-leed-2015-edition.

90. American Institute of Architects and the National Association of Counties, *Local Leaders in Sustainability: Green Building Incentive Trends*, 47.

91. Jerry Yudelson, *Reinventing Green Building: Why Certification Systems Aren't Working and What We Can Do about Them* (Gabriola Island, BC, Canada: New Society Publishers, 2016), 89.

92. Matisoff, Noonan, and Flowers, "Policy Monitor–Green Buildings: Economics and Policies," Table 1.

93. Yudelson, *Reinventing Green Building*, 87–88.

94. "The 40 Most Sustainably Powered US Cities, Ranked," *CommercialCafé Blog Posting*, August 1, 2018, www.commercialcafe.com/blog/2018/08/01/top-40-sustainably-powered-us-cities-2018/.

95. Austin Troy, *The Very Hungry City: Urban Energy Efficiency and the Economic Fate of Cities* (New Haven, CT: Yale University Press, 2012), 169–171, 225–230.

96. For a discussion of rainwater catchment systems, green roofs, rain gardens, the value of natural and artificially constructed wetlands, and pervious alternatives to more solid pavement, see: Raquel Pinderhughes, *Alternative Urban Futures: Planning for Sustainable Development in Cities throughout the World* (Lanham, MD: Rowman and Littlefield, 2004), 38–46; and Christopher G. Boone and Ali Modarres, *City and Environment* (Philadelphia: Temple University Press, 2006), 101–106 and 124–126.

97. Timothy Beatley, *Biophilic Cities: Integrating Nature into Urban Design and Planning* (Washington, DC: Island Press, 2011), 133.

98. Peter Newman, Timothy Beatley, and Heather Boyer, *Resilient Cities: Overcoming Fossil Fuel Dependence*, 2nd ed. (Washington, DC: Island Press, 2017), 43; San Francisco Planning Department, "San Francisco Better Roofs," *Web Posting*, January 2017, http://sf-planning.org/san-francisco-better-roofs.

99. Jackie Snow, "Green Roofs Take Root around the World," *National Geographic*, October 27, 2016, https://news.nationalgeographic.com/2016/10/san-francisco-green-roof-law/.

100. Beatley, *Biophilic Cities*, 131.

101. Don Behm, "Brewers Plan Rain Barrel Rollout," *Milwaukee Journal Sentinel*, December 24, 2013.

102. Swati R. Prakash, "Beyond Dirty Diesels: Clean and Just Transportation in Northern Manhattan," in *Growing Smarter: Achieving Livable Communities, Environmental Justice, and Regional Equity*, ed. Robert D. Bullard (Cambridge, MA: MIT Press, 2007), 273–298; Pinderhughes, *Alternative Urban Futures*, 176–179; New York University Medical Center and School of Medicine, "Asthma Linked to Soot from Diesel Trucks in Bronx," *ScienceDaily*, October 30, 2006, www.sciencedaily.com/releases/2006/10/061017084420.htm; Boone and Modarres, *City and Environment*, 106–114, review the advantages that biodiesel and other alternative fuels offer urban communities.

103. Except where otherwise noted, the description of the sustainability efforts of the five cities draws heavily on Kent E. Portney, *Taking Sustainable Cities Seriously: Economic Development, the Environment, and Quality of Life in American Cities*, 2nd ed. (Cambridge, MA: MIT Press, 2013), 131–141, 198–203, 256–271, and 283–297.

104. For a discussion of the importance of greenways to urban populations and to ecological systems, see: Boone and Modarres, *City and Environment*, 170–175.

105. Cervero, Guerra, and Al, *Beyond Mobility*, 148–150.

106. Portney, *Taking Sustainable Cities Seriously*, 289.

107. Ernest Y. Yaranella and Richard S. Levine, *The City as Fulcrum of Global Sustainability* (New York: Anthem Press, 2011), esp. 123–126.

108. "Austin Energy Resource, Generation and Climate Protection Plan to 2027," October 2, 2017, https://austinenergy.com/wcm/connect/6dd1c1c7-77e4-43e4-8789-838eb9f0790d/2027+Austin+Energy+Resource+Plan+20171002.pdf?MOD=AJPERES&CVID=lXv4zHS; Austin Energy, "Our Energy Roadmap," n.d., downloaded August 10, 2018, https://austinenergy.com/wcm/connect/b08ba414-ce2f-43f8-a78b-676c5583ed73/ourEnergyRoadmap.pdf?MOD=AJPERES&CVID=meJrOPE.

109. Beatley, *Green Urbanism*, 70–72.

110. Office of the Architect, City of Austin, "Welcome to Austin's Municipal Green Buildings," *Web Page*, www.leedatx.com, downloaded August 13, 2018. Also see Eric Mackres, Kate Johnson, Annie Downs, Rachel Cluett, Shruti Vaidyanathan, and Kaye Schultz, *The 2013 Energy Efficiency Scorecard* (Washington, DC: American Council for an Energy Efficient Economy, 2013), www.lawandenvironment.com/wp-content/uploads/sites/5/2013/09/energy-scorecard.pdf, for details as to the various steps taken by Austin and other leading "green building" communities.

111. Beatley, *Green Urbanism*, 320–321; Portney, *Taking Sustainable Cities Seriously*, 284–285.

112. Cervero, Guerra, and Al, *Beyond Mobility*, 115–118 and 125–129.

113. Portland zoning ordinances, as cited by Portney, *Taking Sustainable Cities Seriously*, 133.

114. City of Portland and Multnomah County, "Climate Plan Action Report," April 2017, www.portlandoregon.gov/bps/article/636700.

115. City of Portland and Multnomah County, "Climate Action through Equity; The Integration of Equity in the Portland/Multnomah County 2015 Climate Action Plan," July 12, 2016, www.portlandoregon.gov/bps/article/583501.

116. Lucia Athens, *Building an Emerald City: A Guide to Creating Green Building Policies and Programs* (Washington DC: Island Press, 2010).

117. Donald Miller, "Developing and Employing Sustainability Indicators As a Principal Strategy in Planning: Experiences in the Puget Sound Urban Region of Washington State," in *Towards Sustainable Cities: East Asian, North American and European Perspectives on Managing Urban Regions*, ed. André Sorensen, Peter J. Marcotullio, and Jill Grant (Hampshire: Ashgate, 2003), 112–131.

118. Seattle Office of Planning and Community Development, "Equitable Development Implementation Plan," April 2016, www.seattle.gov/Documents/Departments/OPCD/OngoingInitiatives/SeattlesComprehensivePlan/EDIImpPlan042916final.pdf.

119. 2016 figures, as reported by CommercialCafé, "The 40 Most Sustainably Powered US Cities, Ranked," August 1, 2018, www.commercialcafe.com/blog/2018/08/01/top-40-sustainably-powered-us-cities-2018/.

120. Portney, *Taking Sustainable Cities Seriously*, 23 and 234–244.

121. See "Livable Nashville Draft Recommendations," 2017, for a summary of Nashville's strategy and links to the committee's action recommendations, www.nashville.gov/Mayors-Office/Transportation-and-Sustainability/Livable-Nashville-Recommendations.aspx.

122. There are actually a great many steps that public officials and city planners can follow to create protected bike lanes and promote the safety of cyclists. See: Federal Highway Administration, *Separated Bike Lane Planning and Design Guide* (Washington, DC: FHWA-HEP-15-025, 2015), www.fhwa.dot.gov/environment/bicycle_pedestrian/publications/separated_bikelane_pdg/page00.cfm; and Massachusetts Department of Transportation, *Separated Bike Lane: Planning & Design Guide, 2015* (Boston: MassDOT, 2015), www.mass.gov/lists/separated-bike-lane-planning-design-guide.

123. Melissa Bruntlett and Chris Bruntlett, *Building the Cycling City: The Dutch Blueprint for Urban Vitality* (Washington DC: Island Press, 2018), 2.

124. Melody L. Hoffman, *Bike Lanes Are White Lanes: Bicycle Advocacy and Urban Planning* (Lincoln, NE: University of Nebraska Press, 2016).

125. John Norquist, president of the Council on New Urbanism, as cited in Troy, *The Very Hungry City*, 8.

126. Elizabeth J. Mueller, "Struggling toward Livability in Austin, Texas," in *Livable Cities from a Global Perspective*, ed. Roger W. Caves and Fritz Wagner (New York: Routledge, 2018), 61–78; Catherine Marfin, "CodeNext Draft Proposes Major Changes for Anxious Allandale Community," *Austin American-Statesman*, July 16, 2017; Jenna Chandler, "Proposal to Add Density Near Transit Stations Quickly Rejected in California Senate," *Curbed Los Angeles Blog Posting*, April 17, 2018, https://la.curbed.com/2018/4/17/17249654/california-senate-bill-827-housing-transit-vote.

127. Linda Poon, "Buffalo Becomes First City to Bid Minimum Parking Goodbye," *CityLab Blog Posting*, January 9, 2017, www.citylab.com/equity/2017/01/buffalo-is-first-to-remove-minimum-parking-requirements-citywide/512177/.

128. See Donald Shoup, ed., *Parking and the City* (New York: Routledge, 2018) for an analysis of the many ways that cities mismanage parking requirements, underprice parking, and otherwise promote commuting by car.

129. Jason Hellendrung, "HealthLine Drives Growth in Cleveland," *Urban Land* (May/June 2012): 61–64; Douglas Hanks, "Miami-Dade Has a $300 Million Plan for Modern Buses in South Dade: Next Up. A Fight," *Miami Herald*, July 5, 2018; Douglas Hanks, "A Miami-Dade Rarity: A Speedy Bus Route That's Actually Attracting Passengers," *Miami Herald*, July 30, 2017.

130. Patrick Sisson, "Can the Valley's Orange Line—the Nation's Most Successful BRT—Get Any Respect?," *Curbed Los Angeles Web Posting*, August 8, 2017, https://la.curbed.com/2017/8/8/16115274/orange-line-valley-bus-light-rail.

131. Portney, *Taking Sustainable Cities Seriously*, 23.

132. Sofie Bouteligier, *Cities, Networks, and Global Environmental Governance: Spaces of Innovation, Places of Leadership* (New York: Routledge, 2013).

133. Laura Bliss, "Can Cities Actually Meet the Paris Commitments on Their Own?," *CityLab Blog Posting*, June 6, 2017, www.citylab.com/equity/2017/06/can-us-cities-meet-the-paris-commitments-on-their-own/528996/.

134. Climate Mayors, "Paris Climate Agreement," June 1, 2018, http://climatemayors.org/actions/paris-climate-agreement/.

135. Patrick Sisson, "Climate Mayors: The Impact a Year After the U.S. Left the Paris Agreement," *Curbed, Web Posting*, www.curbed.com/2018/5/30/17411024/paris-accord-climate-change-climate-mayors.

136. City of Knoxville, "Knoxville Streetlight Retrofit," *Web Posting*, May 30, 2018, www.knoxvilletn.gov/government/city_departments_offices/sustainability/led, downloaded December 6, 2018.

137. Climate Mayors, "Initiatives," 2017, http://climatemayors.org/actions/initiatives/.

138. "'We Are Still In' Declaration," www.wearestillin.com/we-are-still-declaration, downloaded December 17, 2018.

139. Ian Klaus, "When Mayors Spoke Up," *CityLab Web Posting*, December 29, 2017, www.citylab.com/equity/2017/12/when-mayors-spoke-up/549356/.

140. Sarah Meehan, "Baltimore Sues Trump Administration over Immigration Policy City Says Keeps Residents from Seeking Benefits," *Baltimore Sun*, November 29, 2018.

Index

Note: Page numbers in italics indicate figures and page numbers in bold indicate tables on the corresponding pages.